D1415696

SIXTH EDITION

Check-In
Check-Out

Gary K. Vallen
Northern Arizona University

• • •

Jerome J. Vallen
University of Nevada, Las Vegas, Emeritus

PRENTICE HALL
Upper Saddle River, New Jersey 07458

Library of Congress Cataloging-in-Publication Data

Vallen, Gary K.
  Check-in check-out / Gary K. Vallen, Jerome J. Vallen. — 6th ed.
     p. cm.
  Includes bibliographical references and index.
  ISBN 0-13-082916-1
  1. Hotel management. 2. Motel management. I. Vallen, Jerome J.
II. Title.
TX911.3.M27V32 2000
647.94'068—dc21   99–12878
                                                        CIP

Acquisitions editor: *Neil Marquardt*
Editorial / production supervision: *Barbara Marttine Cappuccio*
Director of manufacturing and production: *Bruce Johnson*
Managing editor: *Mary Carnis*
Manufacturing buyer: *Ed O'Dougherty*
Creative director: *Marianne Frasco*
Interior design: *Jill Little*
Cover design: *Bruce Kenselaar*
Cover photo: *Jeffrey Aaronson/Network Aspen*
Formatting / page make-up: *Pine Tree Composition*
Printer/Binder: *R. R. Donnelley & Sons*

Printed in the United States of America

10 9 8 7 6 5 4 3 2 1

ISBN 0-13-082916-1

Prentice-Hall International (UK) Limited, *London*
Prentice-Hall of Australia Pty. Limited, *Sydney*
Prentice-Hall Canada Inc., *Toronto*
Prentice-Hall Hispanoamericana, S.A., *Mexico*
Prentice-Hall of India Private Limited, *New Delhi*
Prentice-Hall of Japan, Inc., *Tokyo*
Pearson Education Asia Pte. Ltd., *Singapore*
Editora Prentice-Hall do Brasil, Ltda., *Rio de Janeiro*

● ● ●

To fathers and sons who work together

Brief Contents

• • •

Contents

• • •

List of Exhibits

• • •

➤ PART II   The Reservations Process   109

CHAPTER 4 ➤ *Changing Methods for Making Today's Reservations   111*

CHAPTER 5 ➤ *Individual and Group Reservations   139*

CHAPTER 6 ➤ *Forecasting Availability and Overbooking   171*

Preface

• • •

Change, a dynamic force in all of American business, is the very essence of the lodging industry. It certainly accounts for the frequent and thorough revisions that have marked this book throughout its 25 years. New ownership structures, new marketing approaches, new computer applications, new telecommunications media, even new means of managing the human resource have altered the field just since the last edition, a brief four years ago! *Check-In Check-Out* treats these critical topics within the framework of the hotel's front desk and its rooms department.

Even as the industry's pace accelerates, the direction of change twists and turns. Unexpected shifts have taken place even within the brief period between the start of this revision and the date we go to press. Companies have consolidated: Promus' takeover of Doubletree; companies have disengaged: Hilton's split into two parts; companies have diversified: Marriott's acquisition of health care housing. Segments—the casino hotels—have waned; segments—the all suites—have flourished. The high-flying REITs of a year ago have plummeted, their stock prices in free fall. Hotel keeping, an ancient industry, continues the restructuring that keeps it dynamic and exciting.

It is with such a recognition—and anticipation of change—that we offer this sixth edition. Like the previous ones, this revision weighs each topic anew, matching it against the relevancy, accuracy, and importance of the times. Occasionally, as has happened here, materials from earlier editions—RevPar, for example—have been returned as the industry reworks old ideas and offers them again as a best practice. As we trim and edit the old, the speed of technological and conceptual change is reinforced. Updated statistics and figures and exhibits demonstrate the equally amazing growth that lodging has experienced in these past several years.

Each edition of the book blends the old and the new. While looking ahead to the latest technologies, we have remained grounded in the history and logic that led to the innovation. That strategy remains the focus of our work. It is good pedagogy to examine what has been done and why, even as we step forward toward the innovations promised by the new millennium.

Changes in the Sixth Edition

The preceding edition (in 1996) included one very major change among several. Topics were reexamined, reorganized, restructured, and combined. The result was a book of 14 chapters in place of the 17 chapters of previous editions. This was welcomed with positive feedback from faculty members, who found the fewer chapters more adaptable to the length of the traditional term. That basic structure remains in place with this latest revision.

In keeping with the high standards of past publications, an extensive rewrite has been completed once again. Regular users of *Check-In, Check-Out* will recognize the differences as they read the text; among them are some very apparent improvements:

➤ Operational changes have been updated and future innovations explored.

➤ Figures and photos have been revised, replaced, and improved.

➤ Chapters have been reorganized in part or in whole to increase clarity.

➤ Revisions in the accounting discussions simplify this difficult topic for nonaccountants.

➤ New questions have been added at the ends of chapters.

➤ The comprehensive glossary offers the faculty member an important supplemental tool.

➤ Night-audit procedures have been reworked and revised.

➤ Readability has been improved with new sentence structure and vocabulary.

➤ A variety of topics have been added or enhanced, including:

- *Cycle of the industry*
- *RevPar*
- *Break-even points*
- *REITs*
- *Property leases*
- *Financial history of the industry since 1980*
- *Spas*
- *Timeshares*
- *Hotel security*
- *Floor plans and room sizes*
- *Global distribution systems*
- *On-line reservations bookings*
- *Inventory nesting and hurdle pricing*
- *Training*
- *Guest history databases at the property and corporate levels*
- *Convention and visitor bureaus*
- *Overbooking*
- *Americans with Disabilities Act*
- *Empowerment*
- *Environmental awareness*
- *Early-check-in policies*
- *Self-check-in kiosks*
- *Group luggage handling*
- *Rate inflation and elasticity of demand for hotel rooms*
- *The effect of bed taxes on demand*
- *Repeal of the 1990 Fire Safety Act*
- *Cost to the hotel of employee tips on credit cards*
- *ATMs*

- *Euro currency*
- *New U.S. currency*
- *Debit cards*
- *Smart cards*
- *Standardization of interfaced computer systems*
- *Hospitality Industry Technology Integrated Standards (HITIS)*

More Than a Front-Office Text

Although *Check-In, Check-Out* is written at the undergraduate level, it serves a number of other uses as well. The book is regularly found on the desks and bookshelves of industry executives, where it functions as a reference on a range of hotel topics. In fact, since its introduction, *Check-In, Check-Out* has been the premier rooms management text for both two- and four-year educational institutions. They have used it as a front-office text, an introductory text, a general resource, and a supplemental enrichment for courses in hotel accounting. Such versatility is possible because the book remains current, accurate, thorough, and professionally based.

Supplements to the Textbook

An Instructor's Manual is available to faculty who adopt the book. The Instructor's Manual offers a range of helpful materials for both new and experienced teachers. Chapter summaries, help in lecture preparation, overheads, vocabulary, alternative calendars, and guidelines for classroom discussion are part of the Manual. Sample examination questions are provided for each chapter and for each of the five units that structure the text. Also included is a final examination with objective-type questions, short-answer questions, and brief subjective-style essay questions, all with answers. There are answers to the chapter-end questions, too. These questions, which follow each of the 14 chapters, are open-ended. They are designed for classroom discussion and homework assignments, but some faculty members use them to supplement the examination questions.

The glossary, the bibliography, and the very detailed cross-referenced index provide additional aid. Although these three resources are not truly supplemental materials (they are part of the bound book), they are well appreciated by students and faculty members alike.

With this latest edition comes an exciting new enhancement, the Moreo/Sammons night-audit workbook. Theirs is a new edition designed to complement the new edition of this book. The workbook moves the student through a series of paper-and-pencil exercises, augmenting the textbook's discussion with practical, hands-on materials specific to front-office procedures and record keeping. In concert with the text's dual approach, a customized software package provides a similar course of study using a computerized format.

Acknowledgments

The authors note with appreciation the contribution of the professional community in making available some of the exhibits used throughout the book.

The authors would also like to thank the following reviewers for their help in making a great book even better: Charles Boswell, University of South Carolina; Pat Moreo, New Mexico State University; Victor L. Bagan, Truckee Meadows Community College; Leland Nicholls, University of Wisconsin-Stout.

About the Authors

• • •

*I*t is not unusual for a professional text to be coauthored. However, it is rare that the two authors are father and son. Jerry Vallen, the father, launched the book in 1974. Gary Vallen, the son, pursued several degrees and a dozen years in hotel management before becoming a joint author of the fourth edition. He has been the lead author for both the fifth and sixth editions.

➤ *Dr. Gary K. Vallen* Gary Vallen is Associate Professor in Hotel and Restaurant Management at Northern Arizona University. He became one of the founding faculty members when the program was initiated in 1988, joining the team after more than a dozen years of industry management. He has worked a variety of positions, including vice-president and assistant general manager of a hotel casino operation in Reno, Nevada; sales manager, financial analyst, and casino dealer. He has been a field representative for a ski magazine, and an associate manager for a variety of private clubs.

Dr. Vallen received his undergraduate degree in Hotel Administration at the University of Nevada, Las Vegas. Despite the long hours of industry, he simultaneously worked and earned an MBA degree at the University of Nevada, Reno. Later, after entering the field of education, he was awarded the EdD degree with an emphasis in hospitality management from Northern Arizona University.

The author has a consulting business with several specialties, including visitor analyses for festivals, fairs, rodeos, and ski slopes. He has developed criteria and carried out numerous secret shopper evaluations for hotels and restaurants. His location in the Southwest has enabled Dr. Vallen to consult with many Native American groups, including the Hopi and Navajo. He is also well known for his work in rural tourism and casino gaming education.

➤ *Dr. Jerome J. Vallen* Jerome J. Vallen was the founding Dean of the College of Hotel Administration, University of Nevada, Las Vegas, and served in that capacity for 22 years. He is now professor emeritus and dean emeritus at UNLV. Following retirement from administration, he spent several terms at two universities in Australia and then became the Founding Dean of the Australian International Hotel School, Canberra, an affiliate of the School of Hotel Administration, Cornell University.

After earning a baccalaureate degree at Cornell University, Jerome Vallen entered the hotel industry, carrying with him the food experience gained from the family's small chain of four restaurants. For a period of several years, Vallen taught and worked in industry. Dr. Vallen also earned a master's degree in Educational Adminis-tration (St. Lawrence University) and a doctoral degree from Cornell's Hotel School.

Dr. Vallen has authored and edited several texts, including a text in hotel man-agement and a work on the legal basis for obtaining gaming licenses in the state of Nevada. He has served as a consulting editor for textbook publishers, a consultant to the U.S. Department of Commerce, an outside examiner for the University of the West Indies, president of a consulting company, and a member of the board of several pub-lic and private companies.

Dr. Vallen has been the recipient of awards from such diverse groups as the Uni-versity Alumni Association, the National Restaurant Association, and the Educational Institute of the American Hotel & Motel Association. Dean Vallen has served as Presi-dent and Chairman of the Council on Hotel, Restaurant, and Institutional Education and was awarded that organization's prestigious H. B. Meek Award. He is listed in the American biography, *Who's Who in the West,* and has been cited in the *Congres-sional Record.*

PART I
The Hotel Industry

Chapter 1
The Traditional Hotel Industry

Chapter 2
The Modern Hotel Industry

Chapter 3
The Structure of the Hotel Industry

Business and industry experienced three periods of major consolidation during the 20th Century. The era opened with the consolidation of heavy industry, motivated by the economies of scale that were the most evident advantage of mass production. So it was the giant manufacturers, railroads, and oil producers that expanded during this first stage.

The middle of the century witnessed a second period of consolidation, but it was driven by a different need. This time U.S. business found its economy of size not in the unification of production, but in the consolidation of administrative and financial processes. Through consolidation, the conglomerates of this period were able to span industries and products to build larger and larger enterprises. One of the best known conglomerates was ITT, which eventually merged its Sheraton Hotels' brand with a later consolidator, Starwood Lodging Trust, as the third wave of consolidation got under way.

The 20th Century closed, as the 21st Century opened, on still another theme, globalization. As business and industry crisscross the oceans and enter foreign territories, consumers become more important than producers. Brand names and recognizable logos (McDonald's and Coca-Cola) drive company profits and sales as did the production and financial issues of previous consolidations 50 or 100 years earlier.

In Part I we review this need for identification. Since the move toward consolidation is just emerging, contradictions abound. On the one hand, the industry stresses choice and variety. It offers a range of facilities, accommodations, prices, and locations that have spawned an uncountable and confusing number of brands, subbrands, and allied brands. There is a simultaneous recognition among hotelkeepers (and among the heads of other consumer-product industries) that consumers bypass the unknown in favor of brands that they recognize and respect. So even as new concepts and products are announced, a wave of consolidation sweeps over the hotel business. Company 1 merges with company 2 and eventually the weaker brand disappears. Stouffers, a well-known hotel name, was gobbled up by Renaissance and disappeared from the scene. Let's watch and see what happens to such brands as Sheraton, Westin, and Caesars, which are now under one ownership umbrella.

In the first two chapters we identify changes in the industry, trace some of its history, and set the foundation for the operational issues that are treated in the balance of the book. Chapter 3 continues by illustrating the products more specifically and explaining how the industry organizes itself to deliver them. Throughout is the theme of restructuring, by which the hotel industry remains dynamic and competitive.

CHAPTER 1
The Traditional Hotel Industry

Outline

Hotel keeping is one of humankind's oldest professions, tracing its simple beginnings back thousands of years to the prehistoric cave. Tourism, of which hotel keeping is a part, is one of humankind's newest endeavors. So hotel keeping is an old industry with a young future. It builds on ages of tradition even as it changes with dynamic and often unexpected twists.

Hotel keeping, or innkeeping, has flourished through centuries of change, adapting its form and type of service to changing customer demands. The present-day hotel evolved from the relay houses of China, from the khans (roadside stopping places) of the Middle East, from the tabernas (taverns) of ancient Rome, from the roadhouses of Europe, and from the inns of stagecoach America. The lodging industry has emerged from this rich cultural background with a special place in society. Today, hotel keeping is an integral part of tourism's worldwide boom, a major player in the global outreach of business, and a continuing presence in the social, political, and cultural life of every community.

➤ SCOPE OF THE INDUSTRY

At first, travel was an individual thing: a solitary traveler on foot or horseback, a loose band of pilgrims, or a small coach full of strangers. Travel was a rare experience because traveling by foot or horse was slow and difficult. Besides, most persons were neither politically nor economically free to move about. All three factors have changed dramatically during the past 100 years. Rapid means of transportation have emerged from the industrial and electronic ages, and political and economic freedoms have appeared to help shape the modern travel industry.

A Look Back

For many, many centuries hotels remained small, rarely exceeding a handful of rooms. Early guests shared their accommodations with strangers and often decided themselves how much to pay their hosts. Small establishments were adequate for the times because the number of travelers were few, and they were housed and fed as part of the innkeeper's own family. All that changed with the Industrial Revolution, which provided the structural steel to build upward. With it came the invention of the corporation, which financed the skyscrapers that housed the new hotels. Creative marketing and amazing developments in transportation enticed the world's travelers, completing the circle of forces that created the tourism phenomenon.

The modern hotel with its exciting architecture (see Exhibit 1–1) has become a destination in itself, but that wasn't always the case. The historical role of innkeeping has been one of response, of providing services along a traveler's predetermined route. As long as the traveler's course, method of transportation, and travel time were restricted, as long as there were no options, there was no need to differentiate the inn. For nearly two millennia, even the ultimate destination was predetermined. Innkeepers merely located their accommodations along the traveler's known path and waited for the call to service. That was true even as recently as 50 years ago, when roadside motels dominated the U.S. highway segment of the market. The range and quality of accommodations reflected the innkeeper's inclination, not the needs of the guests. Shelter from the elements and an opportunity to rest from bone-wearying travel were the major services that the early inns provided. Food and lodging were basic products then; both were essential since the guest had no alternatives. Lodging is still a basic commodity, but many hotels no longer offer food. Tomorrow may be another story

Exhibit 1–1 Entrance to the Luxor Hotel, an Egyptian-themed resort. The exciting designs of many hotels, including the atrium hotels (see Exhibit 3–8), have become attractions in and of themselves. *Courtesy of The Luxor, Las Vegas, Nevada.*

altogether. There may come a time in which neither rooms nor food is the industry's basic good or service. Accommodations may have an extirely different meaning in two or three generations.

> ➤ *Palaces of the People.* Many magnificent hotels were built in the United States between the Civil War and World War I. Serving guests from all walks of life, these hotels reflected the uniqueness of American democracy. The hotel of this era served as home and office, meeting site, and social gathering place. Calling these inns *palaces of the people*[1] was a play on the size and splendor of the structures—like a palace—and a reaffirmation of the American way of life—open to all the people. In contrast, only the aristocracy used European hotels during the 19th Century.

The word *hotel* appeared in London about 1760 but wasn't used in the United States until some three decades later. It was then Anglicized from the French *hôtel garni,* "large, furnished mansion." The name change from *inn* and *tavern* to *hotel* signaled a worldwide shift from an industry based on roadside accommodations to one located within cities. The third building to be erected in the new U.S. capital, following the White House and the Capitol Building, was a hotel. Its physical structure resembled that of a palace, but its name, the Union *Public* Hotel, guaranteed it to be a palace of the people. The theme was repeated when the City Hotel opened in New York City in the same year, 1793. It was financed by a public stock offering, actually permitting the public to own that palace of the people.

After World War II, when the U.S. currency was strong and American business was dominant, U.S. hotel companies expanded around the globe. They carried with them both the American approach to business and the American culture. The situation reversed in the 1980s when the dollar weakened. Foreign hotel companies, chiefly British and Japanese, found many hotel bargains within the United States, especially in those properties that were poorly financed and dependent on their real estate rather than on their operations. The situation reversed once again as the 20th Century closed. The strong U.S. dollar made foreign investors less inclined to pit their currencies against the greenback. U.S. chains were profitable again and looked anew for overseas opportunities. Through these back-and-forth investments, hotels bind the world's cultures. Management and management philosophies are one of the links, hotel guests another. Tourism plays a role; business guests, who use the hotels as company offices, meeting places, and temporary residences, have a different role. Local residents play still another role.

▶ *The Service Culture.*   The latter half of the 20th Century has been dubbed the "age of service" or the "service society." This contrasts with the agricultural age of the 18th Century and the industrial age of the 19th Century. The hotel industry, along with many other businesses (medicine, banking, retailing) carries this service label. As with many labels, there is sometimes confusion. All hotels do not offer the same level of service, and consequently, do not charge the same rates. Although we speak of one industry, lodging has many, many parts with but a single commonality: courtesy. The hotel industry has responded rapidly, vigorously, and innovatively to a growing demand for choice. In so doing, it leaves unclear exactly what the hotel business is.

What Is the Hotel Business?

The lodging industry is so broad an endeavor worldwide, divided into so many pieces, that a single definition is not practical. A single theme is not apparent, and an accurate measurement cannot be made. Nevertheless, many declare lodging to be among the world's largest industries, bigger than _____ (just fill in the blank). It is certainly a major segment of international business, but how much so remains an elusive measure. As part of tourism, hotel keeping helps drive the economic engines of developing countries. Because tourism development goes hand-in-hand with construction, hotels and other elements of tourism (roads, airports, etc.) account for huge investments even in diversified economies. One example is the 5,000-room MGM Grand Hotel and Entertainment Park in Las Vegas, which spent $1 billion in construction costs alone! Together, tourism and construction accelerate both the economic rise and the economic downturn of a tourist area.

▶ *How Hotels Count and Measure.*   Once every 10 years, the Bureau of the Census issues statistical studies (SC series) about the lodging industry. Among other information, this *Census of Hotels* reports the number of lodging establishments and the number of guest rooms in the United States. According to the last rounded count, there are 48,600 properties with 3,100,000 rooms in the country. Other agencies and organizations also count. As one would expect from the dynamics of the industry, they don't all agree. But they are amazingly close for an industry as diverse as lodging.

Smith Travel Research estimated the number of hotels to be about 47,600 and the number of rooms to be some 3,588,000 at the start of 1998. A year earlier, the American Hotel & Motel Association offered figures of 47,000 properties and 3,600,00 rooms.[2] Other estimates come from such public organizations as the WTO (World Tourism Organization; 3,740,000 rooms) and such private companies as PricewaterhouseCoopers 3,712,000, an accounting firm with a large practice in the lodging and gaming industries. Estimates by the International Hotel Association (IHA) put the number of hotel rooms at approximately 11,300,000 worldwide, with about one-third, or 3,750,000, in the United States. The actual figure will never be known since the industry is in constant flux. A U.S. figure of between 3,500,000 and 3,750,000 rooms is a good round number that leaves the hotelier with a realization that the hotel industry cannot possible be one easily defined business.

A Cyclical Industry.   The hotel industry is cyclical. It goes through wide swings, from periods of very good times to periods of very bad times. Consequently, the number of hotels and the number of hotel rooms vary over time, shifting up and down as the cycle moves through its loops. That's what happened beginning in the early 1980s. Revisions in federal tax law and the collapse of the real estate market (remember, hotel buildings are pieces of real estate) brought the cycle to a devastating low—a low that lasted for well over a decade. Then came a slow reversal in the cycle. By the mid-1990s, hotel construction began to reappear. That upward momentum accelerated as the 1990 decade was closing. About three years are needed between planning and opening a hotel, longer if there are special zoning, financing, or environmental issues. Therefore, the building boom that followed the upward cycle of the late 1990s was not readily evident until the close of the century and the beginning of the new millennium.

An improved business environment encourages construction of new hotels, adding more rooms to the marketplace. On the other hand, declining business accelerates the removal of antiquated and worn-out hotel rooms. These old hotels are kept in place during the preceding boom when there aren't enough rooms, but fall to the wrecker's ball as the lack of guests (customers) makes such properties less competitive. At any given time, the room count reflects the mathematics of the new and the old (see Exhibit 1–2).

Occupancy.   During declining cycles, more rooms are available for sale, but fewer guests are buying. During upward cycles, more guests are buying, but fewer rooms are available. Demand by customers is measured by the number of rooms that guests buy. This is called the *number of rooms occupied* or *the number of rooms sold.* As explained later, this information is counted every night by every hotel. Although the total number of rooms in the world is an estimate at best, hotel managers know accurately the number of rooms in their particular hotels. That number is called the *number of rooms available for sale.*

The relationship between the number of rooms actually sold (demand) and the number of rooms available for sale (supply) is a barometer of the industry's health. It is a closely watched value. This relationship (or ratio) between the two values asks: How well did the hotel sell rooms in relation to the number of rooms that it could have sold? That's a big mouthful to say all the time, so the industry uses a shortcut, calling the relationship the *percentage of occupancy,* or just *occupancy,* or sometimes, *occupancy percent.*

Guest Room Supply Calculation[a]					
	1994	1995	1996	1997	1998
Room supply at the start of the year (last year's close)	3,271	3,306	3,355	3,455	3,588
Plus:					
rooms completed[b]	155	186	125	150	140
Total	3,426	3,492	3,480	3,605	3,728
Minus:					
rooms removed[b]	120	137	25	17	10
Room supply at the end of the year (next year's start)	3,306	3,355	3,455	3,588	3,718

[a]In thousands: add 000 to each figure.
[b]Figures so indicated are hypothetical, approximates at best, designed to produce the year-end totals, which are rounded from values furnished by *Smith Travel Research, Hendersonville, Tennessee.*

Exhibit 1–2   The number of rooms available each year is a net of last year's count, plus new construction, minus uneconomical rooms lost to demolition or to nonhotel uses. The closing balance is the denominator of the ratio used to determine the national percentage of occupancy, rooms sold ÷ number of rooms available for sale. *Courtesy of Smith Travel Research, Hendersonville, Tennessee.*

The occupancy calculation is a simple division represented by a fraction in which the number of rooms sold is divided by the number of rooms available for sale and expressed as a percentage (see Exhibit 1–3):

$$\frac{\text{number of rooms sold}}{\text{number of rooms available for sale}}$$

Occupancy can be computed by one hotel for one night, one month, or one year. Citywide occupancy, regional occupancy (the Northeast, for example), or national occupancy (see Exhibit 1–4) can be, and are, tracked by hotels, consulting companies, convention bureaus, and state tourism offices. Of course, the figures become less accurate as the breadth of the count broadens from the individual property to a worldwide count. We saw earlier that there is no agreement even in counting the number of rooms available for sale. Nevertheless, everyone becomes engrossed in occupancy figures when companies such as Sheraton announce that a 1% rise in occupancy represents a $25 million improvement in profits. Andrew Young, mayor of Atlanta for eight years, phrased it from a different perspective, telling a group of hotel professionals that each 1% rise in hotel occupancy resulted in 400 new jobs for his city![3]

Sales per Occupied Room.   Occupancy measures the hotel's "share of the market," so it measures *quantity.* The *quality* of the business being done is measured by the amount received for each room sold, *sales per occupied room.* Sales per occupied room goes by another, more commonly used name, *average daily rate* (ADR). ADR is

Given		
	Number of rooms in the hotel available for sale	800
	Number of rooms in the hotel	820
	Number of rooms sold to guests	600
	Number of dollars received from guests for rooms	$48,000
	Number of employees on staff	500

Computations

Percentage of occupancy is 75%.

$$\frac{\text{number of rooms sold (to guests)}}{\text{number of rooms (in the hotel) available for sale}} = \frac{600}{800} = \frac{3}{4} = 75\%$$

Sales per occupied room (average daily rate, ADR) is $80.00.

$$\frac{\text{room sales (as measured in dollars)}}{\text{number of rooms sold (to guests)}} = \frac{\$48,000}{600} = \$80.00$$

Sales per available room (RevPar) is $60.00.

$$\frac{\text{room sales (as measured in dollars)}}{\text{number of rooms (in the hotel) available for sale}} = \frac{\$48,000}{800} = \$60.00$$

Mathematical check:

$$\text{ADR} \times \text{occupancy} = \text{RevPar} \qquad \$80 \times 0.75 = \$60.00$$

Number of employees per guest room is 0.625.

$$\frac{\text{number of employees (on staff)}}{\text{number of rooms (in the hotel) available for sale}} = \frac{500}{800} = 0.625$$

Exhibit 1–3 Computation of standard measures used throughout the U.S. hotel industry. Non-U.S. companies and international agencies usually use bed occupancy rather than room occupancy as the critical measure. (70% room occupancy approximates 50% bed occupancy.)

the second of several ways that hotels count and measure. It, too, is computed with a ratio or fraction:

$$\frac{\text{room sales (measured in dollars)}}{\text{number of rooms sold}}$$

Note that the number of rooms sold (or occupied) appears in both formulas (see Exhibit 1–3).

The health of the hotel business depends on a combination of occupancy and price. Normally, price (ADR) increases as occupancy percentage increases. That is, the more the customers want rooms, the higher the rate they'll pay. As the industry goes through a declining cycle, it is sometimes possible to keep the ADR climbing for a short time, sometimes even faster than the consumer price index, even as occupancy is falling. That's true for both an individual property and the industry as a whole. As more vacancies occur, prices (ADR) begin to level off because front-office managers reduce rates to maintain higher occupancies. How well they do their job of filling rooms without cutting prices is what the next measure measures.

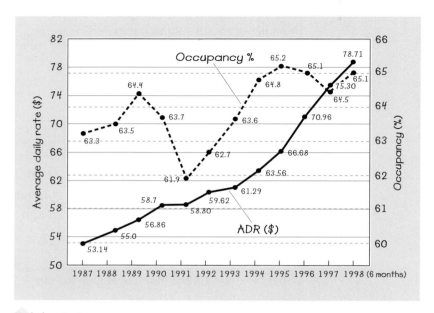

Exhibit 1–4   The industry tracks average daily rate and the percentage of occupancy in order to evaluate the economic health of the lodging industry. The close of the millennium has been one of the most profitable periods in U.S. history. Note the rapid rise in ADR as the century draws to a close. *Courtesy of Smith Travel Research, Hendersonville, Tennessee.*

RevPar (Revenue per Available Room).   RevPar is an old industry standby that has reemerged recently as a far more important value than it was 25 years ago when it had a different name, *average rate per available room*.[4] Yield management has come onto the scene during that time. Yield management balances demand and price. Normally, as guest demand (occupancy) falls, price (room rate) declines. One hears that old standby, "hotels fill from the bottom up," meaning that guests elect lower rates when an empty house allows it. The superior manager strives to stabilize or even increase both price and occupancy, especially during dips in the cycle. RevPar (sometimes written as REVPAR) measures that performance. It measures revenue (or sales) per room relative to the total room inventory available. In contrast, ADR measures revenue per room relative to the number of rooms actually sold.

Exhibit 1–3 illustrates the computation. Keep in mind that room revenue and room sales are two different terms for the same value! So the fraction is

$$\frac{\text{room revenue}}{\text{number of rooms available for sale}}$$

Since RevPar involves both price and occupancy, the mathematics of the three ratios is interlocked. Multiplying the ADR by occupancy results in RevPar (see Exhibit 1–3). If nothing else, it is a good means of checking the arithmetic. Under debate is what figure to use as the denominator of the RevPar fraction. The illustration uses number of rooms *available* for sale. However, some rooms may not be *available*. Rooms may be out of order, out of inventory, in use for hotel purposes, rented as office space, and so on. To measure management's ability to use all its rooms, some argue that the denominator should be the absolute number of rooms (the total in the house), not merely those available for sale. Using the larger denominator, (total) number of rooms, results in a smaller RevPar and that reflects less well on the management team.

Break-even Point. A hotel's break-even point is that level of volume in which there are neither profits nor losses. Break-even points are expressed in occupancy percent. So the break-even point is said to be, for example, 67% occupancy.[5] Two factors are built into the break-even point: the amount of sales and the amount of costs. When the two are equal, the hotel is said to be at the break-even point.

A large portion of a hotel's costs are fixed expenses: the payment of debt on the funds borrowed to erect the building, for example. Reducing fixed costs such as interest rates drops the amount of occupancy needed to break even. Similarly, raising the ADR, or doing more food and beverage sales, increases the flow of income. More income per room sold, a higher RevPar, means that a smaller percentage of occupancy is needed to pay off the costs, to break even.

Break-even points are important, because there are no profits until that point is reached. Until the business pays its fixed expenses (interest, for example), its semifixed expenses (power, for example), and its variable expenses (wages, for example), there are no profits. But once that point is reached, profits accumulate quickly. Each dollar before the break-even point has a mission: pay off the debt, pay the electricity, pay the employee. Each dollar after the break-even point has a lesser mission because fixed expenses no longer need to be paid! Even some of the semifixed expenses have been met. Therefore, each dollar beyond the break-even point has a very large portion earmarked as profit.

► *Special Characteristics of the Hotel Business.* The room manager's ability to maximize the number of rooms sold or to increase the average daily rate obtained is limited by several characteristics special to the lodging business. Some of these peculiarities are also found in other industries, chiefly among the airlines.

Perishability. Even the industry's newest recruit knows that a room left unsold tonight cannot be sold again. Empty hotel rooms, like empty airline seats or unsold television commercials, cannot be shelved, cannot be stored, cannot be saved, and cannot be used again.

Location. Ellsworth Statler coined the expression "Location, location, location" to emphasize its importance to the hotel. Good economic locations are difficult to find in urban America. Changing neighborhoods and shifting markets sometimes doom a hotel whose original location was good. Unlike the airline seat, there is no way to change a hotel's location. So management has learned to depend less on desirable real estate and more on marketing and sales; less on drive-by or walk-in traffic and more on central reservation systems.

Fixed Supply. Not only is the location of the hotel fixed but so is its supply of (the number of) rooms. Airlines can adjust the number of seats by adding or removing planes from the route. With hotels, what you see is what you get.

High Operating Costs. Unlike manufacturing industries, which offset labor with large capital investments, hotels are both capital- and labor-intensive. The result is high fixed costs (a *large nut* in the jargon of the industry), which continue whether or not the hotel has business. Thus, a high percentage of occupancy is needed just to break even.

Seasonality. Throwing away the key is a traditional practice when a new hotel is opened. The act signifies that the hotel never closes. Yet hotel keeping, even for commercial hotels, is a very seasonal business. The cyclical dip strikes the commercial hotel every seven days as it struggles to offset poor weekend business. The federal holiday law, which assigned long weekends to national holidays, reinforces the negative pattern of the commercial hotel.

Occupancy computations must account for this weekend phenomenon. Especially so since the business traveler—the one who is not in the hotel during the weekends—still accounts for the majority of the lodging industry's business. Given the usual profile of the commercial, urban hotel (see Exhibit 1–5), national occupancy percentages in the high 70s and 80s remain an elusive goal.

Annual cycles compound the problem. Commercial business is down even in midweek between Thanksgiving and New Year's Day and from May through Labor Day.

The ultimate solution is difficult to comprehend. Hotels in urban areas may someday operate on the same five-day week that their customers, their employees, and their suppliers do. They will respond to corporate demand cycles by closing the hotel on weekends and holidays. Managers will no longer symbolically "throw away the key."

The resort pattern is the opposite of the commercial pattern. Weekends are busy and midweek less so. The slack period of the commercial hotel is the very season of the resort. At one time, resorts opened Memorial Day and closed Labor Day. This 100-day pattern made the hotel's success dependent on the weather. Two weeks of rain are devastating when the break-even point is 80 days of near-full occupancy.

Although the dates of the winter season differ, there are still only 100 days between December 17 and March 15.

Both winter and summer resorts have extended their seasons with groups, conferences, and special activities. Hotels that operate on the four-day season may be worse off now than those on the four-season year. At least the latter have a higher double occupancy (two persons to a room).

Monday	100%
Tuesday	100
Wednesday	90
Thursday	90
Friday	40
Saturday	20
Sunday	20
Total	460%
Average per 7 days	66%

Exhibit 1–5 The typical occupancy pattern of a downtown hotel, with its weekend slump, makes an annual occupancy of 80% or more difficult to achieve. Airline pricing, which reduces flight costs for Saturday overnights, may work to the advantage of convention hotels if groups are willing to schedule weekend activities in order to save transportation costs. In 1998, Smith Travel Research began tracking weekend occupancies.

➤ *TRADITIONAL CLASSIFICATIONS*

The inns of old evolved from private homes. Today's hotel, even the mom-and-pop variety, is not represented as anyone's home. It is either a point of destination or an accommodation for those in transit. Yesterday's tavern offered the family meal to all who came. Dining today is a created experience in design, decor, and menu. The old inn was almost indistinguishable from its neighbors. Today's edifice is a sharp contrast in style and packaging.

Although the basic concepts of food, shelter, and hospitality remain, their means of delivery have changed. These changes have been marked by shifting terminology: hostel, tavern, public house, inn, guest house, hotel, resort, motel, motor lodge, motor inn, bed and breakfast, airtel, boatel, hometel, skytel, and condotel.

Despite the speed of change, several traditional classifications have withstood the test of time. Some have more objective measures than others. None are self-excluding: Hotels can fall into every category or into only some. Moreover, there are degrees of belonging. One property may be well within a classification, whereas another may exhibit only some of the characteristics. Each category has an impact on the scope and function of the front office.

Size

Many yardsticks could be used to measure the size of a hotel, but the number of available rooms (the very figure used for occupancy computations; see Exhibit 1–3) is the traditional standard. Other possible measures of size (number of floors, acres of land, number of employees, gross dollar sales, or net profits) are just not used. Of course, an obvious relationship exists between the number of rooms and these other values.

Although size is the most objective of the several classifications, there is uncertainty even here. Often, more rooms are advertised than are actually available for sale. Old hotels have many rooms that are just not salable. Even newer properties may have rooms converted for other uses, such as offices leased to businesses and associations. Still others are converted for storage or other operational facilities as unanticipated needs become evident. Generally, the older the hotel, the fewer the available rooms in relation to total rooms.

Hotels are grouped by size for purposes of study, for financial reporting, and for membership dues. The Bureau of the Census groups them this way as well. Although the Bureau uses several categories, a quick and easy classification considers 100 rooms or less to be a small hotel, between 100 and 300 rooms one of average size, and over 300 rooms a large property.

The recent boom in hotel construction offers an interesting footnote. New hotels are small; 80 rooms is the average size of recent hotel construction, hardly surprising when the AH&MA reports the average size of its membership at approximately 125 rooms. Visualizing such small properties as *the* lodging industry is difficult when one thinks of the Waldorf-Astoria in New York City (1,852 rooms) or the New Otani in Tokyo (2,057 rooms) (see Exhibit 1–6). More typical are cities like Atlanta. With some 450 hotel properties and about 67,000 hotel rooms, it averages 150 rooms per hotel. In contrast, hotels in the European Economic Area, where family ownership still prevails, average fewer than 50 rooms per property, Japanese hotels about 70 rooms per property. The Small Business Administration (SBA) has defined "small" for hotels seeking government loans as properties doing $3.5 million or less in annual receipts.

Hotel	Location	Room Size[a]
MGM Grand	Las Vegas	5,000
Luxor	Las Vegas	4,475
Excalibur	Las Vegas	4,025
Circus Circus	Las Vegas	3,750
Flamingo Hilton	Las Vegas	3,650
Las Vegas Hilton	Las Vegas	3,175
Mirage	Las Vegas	3,050
Monte Carlo	Las Vegas	3,025
Treasure Island	Las Vegas	3,000
Opryland Hotel	Nashville	2,900
Bally's	Las Vegas	2,825
Imperial Palace	Las Vegas	2,600
Hilton Hawaiian Village	Honolulu	2,550
Stardust	Las Vegas	2,475
New York, New York	Las Vegas	2,200
Caribbean Beach	Orlando	2,100
New York Hilton	New York	2,050

[a]Figures rounded to 25 rooms.

Exhibit 1–6   The largest hotels in the United States (over 2,000 rooms) are megaresorts, evidence of the importance of casino gaming in the American resort business. Construction in progress will eclipse even some of these giants.

➤*Motels.*   Attempts to distinguish hotels, motels, and motor inns (motor hotels, motor lodges) by size were abandoned long ago. Many motor hotels have in excess of 300 rooms and many hotels less than 25. Even the Census Bureau allows each property to assign its own classification rather than attempting a nationwide definition. Still, people usually assume that motels are smaller than hotels.

At one time, the American Hotel & Motel Association excluded motels and clung to the term *American Hotel Association*. The city of Palm Springs, California, still insists there is a difference and has a law to prove it. City ordinances prohibit any of the 200-plus resort properties from using *motel* in advertising and display signs. *Hotel*, *lodge*, and *inn* are the only terms acceptable to the city fathers.

An opposite viewpoint is taken by the Canadian Provincial Conference on Tourism. It has developed three working definitions: A hotel is a commercial establishment in which the units (rooms) are accessible from the interior; motels have units that are accessible from the exterior; and motor hotels (or motor inns) have units that are accessible from both the interior and exterior.

Many years ago, the Florida tourism department offered a cash prize for a workable definition of *hotel* and *motel*.[6] The money is still waiting. A more recent tempest was averted when AT&T agreed with an AH&MA recommendation to list hotels, motels, and resorts separately in the Yellow Pages of the directory. The telephone company had planned to consolidate the three because a survey showed that nearly three-fourths of AT&T's customers looked under "Motels" when in need of accommodations.

➤*Mom-and-Pops.* There are certain economics of size that account for the decline of the small hotel. They start with financing and construction and involve every aspect of the operation from marketing to purchasing. Size determines the quality of management that the property can afford. A motel with less than 100 rooms cannot budget management talent at the same level as a competitor with 300 rooms or a chain controlling several 100-room properties in the same area.

How then does the mom-and-pop establishment (the small, family-owned and family-operated motel) continue to survive? It does, in the same way that small grocery stores and tailor shops do. It offers individual attention by the owners and their families. Guests receive the personal attention that is impossible with any other kind of organization. Labor costs are almost nonexistent, because the proprietor and the family babysit the establishment 24 hours per day, 365 days per year.

As the mom-and-pops become less able to compete for location and financing and less willing to serve the unremitting demands on their time, their numbers decline.

Class

Hotels are ranked or graded into distinct classes. There are two objective methods of making the divisions, but properties are also classified subjectively. One often says or hears that a particular hotel is a "first-class" (or "fourth-class") property. Nothing measurable is used to arrive at the conclusion—it's just sensed. Fortunately, more objective measures are available, but even these are far from perfect. One approach uses the average daily room rate; the other, a worldwide rating system.

➤*Average Daily Rate (ADR).* In large measure, the price that the guest pays for the room is the best criterion of class. Delivering elegance and service costs money. Large rooms, costly construction, and expensive furnishings mean larger finance costs, depreciation, taxes, power usage, and so on. All of these are recovered by higher room rates. If towels are elegantly large and thick, the higher costs of purchase and laundering (by weight) are recovered by higher room rates. Similarly, a high level of maintenance, 24-hour room service, sauna baths, and other extra services represent both a better class of hotel and higher room rates.

Average daily rate has been increasing (see Exhibit 1–4). But the increase does not necessarily measure greater service or elegance (that is, class) across the industry, or even at an individual property. A higher ADR is needed to recover increased operating costs (labor, energy, interest, etc.). Furthermore, properties in small towns have a different measure than their big-city cousins. A $50 rate in Los Angeles conjures up a totally different class of hotel than does the same $50 rate in a small rural town. However, at a given time and with a judicious concern for size, type, and location of the hotel, the ADR seems to be a fair measure of class, so much so that published rates allow us to classify the nation's hotels (see Exhibit 1–7).

Full Service to Limited Service. Hotel/motel facilities are as diverse as the traveling public. Handling this enormous range of guests has created a heterogeneous industry, from the plush, full-service high rise to the squat, limited-service motel. On the one hand is a group of operator–investors who maintain that guests want nothing more than a room with a good mattress and a clean bath. Guests get along nicely without swimming pools, lobbies, or closets, according to this viewpoint. This hotelier offers limited service at a limited charge. There is such a market, of course, served by the $40 to $50 room rate of the budget motel.

Exhibit 1–7
Average daily rate
(ADR) can be used
to categorize hotels
since rate is one
measure of class.

Luxury Hotels (typical room rate at $150±)
  Four Seasons
  Hyatt
  Renaissance
  Ritz-Carlton
  Westin
  Wyndham

First Class (typical room rate at $125±)
  Crowne Plaza
  Doubletree
  Hilton
  Marriott
  Radisson
  Sheraton

Midrange (typical room rate at $75±)
  AmeriSuites
  Clarion
  Four Points
  Hampton Inns
  Holiday Inn
  Quality Inns

Upscale Budget (typical room rate at $60±)
  Best Western
  Comfort Inns
  Fairfield Inns
  Howard Johnson
  La Quinta

Economy (typical room rate at $45±)
  EconoLodge
  Knights Inn
  Microtel
  Motel 6
  Red Roof Inns
  Super 8

One hundred and eighty degrees away is the full-service upscale hotel. Not only does this hotel include superior facilities, it also offers a full complement of services. Limited service means guest rooms only, with some vending machines or perhaps a nearby restaurant to service several competing properties. Full service adds a menu of dining options and a range of extras, including lounges, in-room newspapers, and specialties such as swimming pools, exercise facilities, and a wide range of telecommunications. Expense-account business executives patronize the full-service hotels, although something less costly may do nicely when they travel as family members.

Between the two extremes lies the bulk of the industry, adding services where competition requires and costs allow, paring them as market shifts and acceptable self-service equipment appear. In Chapters 2 and 3 we introduce these newer innovations to hotel keeping. Among them is the all-suite hotel. Commercial and leisure guests alike have been attracted to all-suite accommodations such as Marriott's Residence Inns or Promus's Embassy Suites. By locating on less costly real estate and reducing the amount of public space, all-suites offer more guest room space at lower prices than at the luxury hotels. All-suites are closer to the limited-service hotel than to the full-service hotel.

Number of Employees. Almost by definition, *full service* and *limited service* refer to the size of the hotel's staff: the number of employees. Thus, the

$$\text{number of employees per guest rom} = \frac{\text{number of employees on staff}}{\text{number of rooms available for sale}}$$

becomes another measure of class (see Exhibit 1–3). As it does with room rates, the industry provides a wide range of offerings.

Budget properties, which have no restaurants, no bars, no room service, and no convention space, score as low as 0.25 employees per guest room. An 80-room hotel might have as few as 20 persons on staff. There's a limit to how small the staff can shrink. Regardless of the number of rooms, the desk must be staffed every hour of the day and night. Workers need days off. Housekeeping staff, maybe laundry workers, a night watch, a manager, and someone for repairs and maintenance must be among the count. The size of the hotel matters only after that basic staffing guide is met. A hotel of 60 rooms may have almost as many workers as one twice its size. Housekeeping would be the big difference. If a housekeeper can clean 15 rooms per shift, three or four additional employees are needed to do the extra 60 rooms if occupancy is around, say, 80%. Other staff members at the desk, the manager, the housekeeper, maintenance and grounds, the accountant, and so on, might number almost the same for each property.

The in-between class of hotel uses an in-between number of employees. That ratio ranges from 0.5 (one-half) an employee per room to as much as a 1:1 ratio. Depending on the services offered, a 300-room hotel could have as few as 150 employees and as many as 250 or so. The number is most likely to be about 200 to 225 if there's food service and a bar that need staffing.

Full-service hotels staff a full complement of departments, including bell service, restaurants, turn-down bed service, and telecommunications persons, among others. Hotels with theater shows, acres of grounds to be maintained, casinos, and 24-hour services require extra personnel and have still higher ratios, perhaps 1.5 employees per guest room. A 1,000-room hotel/casino operating fully over 24 hours could easily have 1,250 to 1,500 employees.

Asian properties offer the best in service. Labor is less costly, so the number of employees per room is the world's highest. At the Bangkok Shangri-La, for example, 1073 staff members handle 697 rooms, a ratio of 1.5:1. Hong Kong's Peninsula Hotel ranks better still with a staff of 655 for its 300 rooms, better than 2:1.

►*Rating Systems.* Formal and informal, government-run and privately developed rating systems are another means of identifying the class of hotel. Using formal rating systems, the approach has been standardized, certainly more so within each country than across boundaries. Most members of the World Tourism Organization have adopted the WTO's five recommended classifications. Top is deluxe (or luxury) class, then first class, which is not top-of-the-line despite its name, followed by tourist class, sometimes called economy or second class. Third and fourth classes, which usually have no private baths, centralized heat, or even carpeting, are not for international tourists.

Each country implements its own categories. Local inspectors tend to be quite subjective in their ratings. If there is a pool on the premises, it will meet standards whether or not it is clean. An elevator adds to the ratings whether or not it works. Government rating systems also fall prey to bribery, politics and bickering within the trade association.

International travelers soon learn to limit stays in Africa or the Middle East to deluxe properties and to discount the deluxe category that many Caribbean properties give themselves. However, in Europe, first class is a perfectly acceptable level.

Worldwide.   Worldwide there are almost 100 rating systems. They range from the self-evaluation plan of Switzerland to the mandatory grading plan of South Africa, where tax incentives encourage properties to upgrade. Sometimes, however, rating systems work in the opposite way. Some deluxe Parisian hotels closed their dining rooms because that allowed them to pay taxes at the lower rates of first-class hotels. Many Italian hotels are underrated for the same reason.

Europe's four- and five-star hotels always have restaurants and bars; those with three stars may or may not. Two-star properties almost never do. *Garni* means that no restaurant is available, but a continental breakfast is usually served. In England, *hotel garni* is the U.S. version of bed and breakfast.

The French have broadened the WTO's five categories. Two-star N (French for *nouveau,* "new") has been inserted to represent hotels under renovation, on their move up. Four-star L (*luxe,* for luxury) is now at the top of the scale. Australia and Israel go one better by using a six-star category.

The Swiss Hotel Association now uses five criteria instead of the single measure (price), which was its original category for classification. The Swiss system is unique because it is a private organization evaluating itself. Mexican hotels are also trade-association graded using the WTO's five classes, plus a luxury class, Gran Turismo.

Spain has standardized the rating system of its *paradors* ("stopping places") despite the great differences in physical facilities and furnishings. The government-operated chain of nearly 100 inns maintains approximately one-third at the four-star level. All but a few of the remaining group are two- or three-star properties. Just recently, Spain introduced a new rating system for a single destination, Puerto de la Cruz, an older resort area in the Canary Islands. There are very few international chains there, so tourism has been slipping. Whereas their other rating systems are based on facilities, the new Q (for quality) system evaluates quality standards as a means of competing with newer resort destinations.

Japanese *ryokans,* which are traditional inns, are rated according to the excellence of their guest rooms, kitchens, baths, and—of all things to Western values—gardens. These very traditional hotels serve two meals, which are often taken in the uncluttered guest room that opens onto those gardens. There are an estimated 75,000 ryokans, of which about 1,000 have been registered by the Japanese Travel Bureau as appropriate for international guests.

Like Japan, Korea has fine, Western-style hotels at top international standards. It also has budget-priced lodgings called *yogwans* (or inns). Unlike the ryokans, most yogwans have Western-style accommodations, including private baths. Upscale yogwans can be identified because their names end in *jang* or *chang.*

The People's Republic of China (PRC) also adheres to the WTO guidelines, but it recently added a star-rating system. Ratings are carried out by the National Hotel

Evaluation Committee, which operates under the authority of the China National Tourism Administration.

Stars are not used universally. Britain uses "ticks" for grading Holiday Parks (upscale caravan parks), and before the recent war, Yugoslavia had an alphabetical system. L, luxury, denoted a deluxe property. The expectations ranked downward from A, first class, to D, which promised no more than hot and cold water.

The United Kingdom probably has the largest number of rating systems by the greatest range of organizations. Among them are the National Tourist Board (NTB), the Automobile Association (AA), the Royal Automobile Club (RAC), and commercial enterprises such as Egon Ronay and the better known Michelin. The ratings are by crowns (NTB) and stars (both the AA and the RAC) and pavilions or small buildings (Michelin). Each classification is then subdivided by grades or percentage marks. Thus the AA might rate a property as Four Star, 65%.

The alphabetical grading system once used by the Irish Tourist Board, Bord Failte, has been replaced by a star system of classification. The new system indicates the presence of particular facilities rather than a subjective ranking of their quality. This brings Ireland into agreement with the position of the European Community, which is to list, not rank, accommodations. European directories identify which hotels have elevators, laundries, air conditioning, and so on. They also classify facilities according to location: seaside/countryside; small town/large city. European auto associations add a little extra by classifying properties as privately owned or government run.

The U.S. Experience. In a uniquely American way, government is not involved in the ratings, which are done by private enterprise. Mobil and the American Automobile Association (AAA) are the major competitors. Individual hotel chains have informal self-rating systems that emerge as a by-product of their efforts at market segmentation. For example, Choice Hotels International has (top to bottom) Clarion Hotels, Resorts and Suites; Quality Inns, Hotels and Suites; Comfort Inns and Suites; Rodeway Inns; Sleep Inns; Econo Lodges; and Friendship Inns.

Membership in Preferred Hotels, a loosely knit affiliation of independent hotels, requires ratings of superior or above from one of the recognized services. So just belonging to Preferred gives the property a superior-plus rating.

Mobil and AAA distribute the two most popular consumer publications. Michelin's hotel red guides, which are very popular in Europe, have not yet reached the United States, although Michelin has U.S. guidebooks. Zagat, which uses consumer input, as does Michelin, focuses on restaurant guides, not hotel classifications. J.D. Powers and Associates, famous for its rating of other consumer experiences, has recently put its toes into the rating game. Even the Web is participating. Netline has introduced a Web site rating that relies on the well-tested five-star grouping. There are many other publications, such as bed-and-breakfast guides or geographic-sector guides, but their coverage is narrower. *Mobil Travel Guide* covers all of North America, but North America only. The *AAA Tour Book* has expanded to include Mexico and the Caribbean.

Mobil's ratings are done with stars; AAA uses diamonds. Both organizations are stingy with their five-level ratings, awarding only two or three dozen nationally although each looks at some 20,000 properties annually. In most cases, Mobil gives lower overall scores. Both companies field inspectors, who make on-site visits, often at the request of the particular establishment. Evaluations are based on written standards (see Exhibit 1–8); consumer voting is not their technique. The AAA and the AH&MA

★ ★ ★ ★ ★

The key criteria for every rating are cleanliness, maintenance, quality of furnishings and physical appointments, service, and the degree of luxury offered. There will be some regional differences, as customers have different expectations for a historic inn in northern New England, a dude ranch in the Southwest, and a hotel in the center of a major city.

★

One-star establishments should be clean and comfortable and worth the prices charged when compared to other accommodations in the area. If they are below average in price, they may receive a checkmark for good value in addition to the one star. They offer a minimum of services. There may not be 24-hour front desk or phone service; there may be no restaurant; the furniture will not be luxurious. Housekeeping and maintenance should be good; service should be courteous; but luxury will not be part of the package.

★ ★

Two-star accommodations have more to offer than one-star and will include some, but not necessarily all, of the following: better-quality furniture, larger bedrooms, restaurant on the premises, color TV in all rooms, direct dial phones, room service, swimming pool. Luxury will usually be lacking, but cleanliness and comfort are essential.

★ ★ ★

Three-star motels and hotels include all of the facilities and services mentioned in the preceding paragraph. If some are lacking, and the place receives three stars, it means that some other amenities are truly outstanding. A three-star establishment should offer a very pleasant travel experience to every customer.

★ ★ ★ ★

Four-star and five-star hotels and motels make up a very small percentage (less than 2%) of the total number of places listed; therefore they all deserve the description of "oustanding." Bedrooms should be larger than average; furniture should be of high quality; all of the essential extra services should be offered; personnel should be well trained, courteous, and anxious to please. Because the standards of quality are high, prices will often be higher than average. A stay in a four-star hotel or motel should be memorable. No place will be awarded four or five stars if there is a pattern of complaints from customers, regardless of the luxury offered.

★ ★ ★ ★ ★

The few five-star awards go to those places which go beyond comfort and service to deserve the description "one of the best in the country." A superior restaurant is required, although it may not be rated as highly as the accommodations. Twice-daily maid service is standard in these establishments. Lobbies will be places of beauty, often furnished in antiques. If there are grounds surrounding the building, they will be meticulously groomed and landscaped. Each guest will be made to feel that he or she is a Very Important Person to the employees.

have been holding focus meetings recently to provide industry feedback and develop fairness in the implementation of these standards.

Not all guides are consumer oriented. Several list conference and meeting facilities, an American specialty. Others are important to travel agents and meeting planners. Among the publications that focus on the trade are the *Official Meeting Facilities Guide* and the *Hotel & Travel Index*. The *Official Hotel Guide (OHG)*, whose ratings are favored by the cruise lines, uses subjective assessments of service as well as objecting listings of actual accommodations.

We may eventually see a new environmental rating. Research from the United States Travel Data Center indicates a willingness of guests to pay more for environmentally friendly lodgings (EFLs). EFL could be another criterion for, or a completely separate rating from, the usual standards.

Type

Size, class, type, and plan (discussed next) are the four traditional classifications describing the lodging industry. Type is subdivided into three parts: commercial hotels, resort hotels, and residential hotels. Like the distinctions between hotel and motel, all definitions within the lodging industry have begun to blur. Traditional designations do not always provide the best descriptions for a changing industry. They make no provision for such new concepts as conference centers or condotels, the condominium hotel. A host of other new concepts has appeared in recent times, and they are classified in the emerging patterns of Chapter 2.

➤*Commercial Hotels.*   The commercial hotel, the largest category of American hotels, is also called the transient hotel (see Exhibit 1–9). It is a hotel for short-stay guests, guests who are transient, temporary, coming for many reasons but chiefly for business. The corporate business traveler, the conventioneer, the company executive, the consultant, the engineer, and the small businessperson form the core of the customer base. By consensus, the commercial guest is viewed as the backbone of the lodging industry. The business traveler is equally critical to the large urban property and to the small roadside motel. Increasing leisure travel is quickly promoting the importance of the tourist within the mix.

A true commercial hotel is located close to its market—the business community, which means an urban area. As the population center has left the downtown area, so has the commercial hotel. Arterial highways, research parks, business parks, airports, and even suburban shopping centers have become favorite locations. This helps explain the poor weekend occupancy (businesspersons are not working) of the urban hotel (see Exhibit 1–5). Attempts to offset this weekend decline with tourists, conventions, and special promotions have been only moderately successful.

Transient hotels are usually full-service hotels. Until recently, businesspersons have been expense-account travelers who wanted (and could afford) four- and five-star accommodations. Lately, the travel offices of many businesses have begun to monitor travel costs more closely. Travel costs do affect a business's bottom line! Furthermore, Congress has enacted several restrictions on the amount that may be taken as tax-deductible meal costs (currently 50%).

From suite hotels to upgraded budgets, everyone is after business travelers, even though they are value shopping more diligently than ever before. Still, the commercial hotel remains the business center, catering to the various groups that have been enu-

Exhibit 1–9   The urban hotel is a transient hotel serving several markets, chiefly business and convention guests, and is usually located in the center of commercial activity: if not "downtown," then in a business park or research center. The Marriott Marquis on 45th and Broadway, New York is a fine example of the type. It offers 1,919 rooms and over 90,000 square feet of meeting space, a 37-story atrium, and a very central location. *Courtesy of the New York Marriott Marquis, New York.*

merated, hosting trade shows, and serving as company training centers and meeting places.

➤*Residential Hotels.*   In contrast to the transient commercial guest, the residential guest takes up permanent quarters. This creates a different legal relationship between the guest and the landlord and may be formalized with a lease. In some locales, the room occupancy tax is not payable for a residential guest in a transient hotel.

Some residential hotels accommodate transient guests, and many transient hotels have permanent guests, with and without leases. The Waldorf-Astoria (New York City) is a good example of this combination: its Towers house permanent, often famous guests. About two-thirds of all U.S. hotels reported both transient and permanent guests in the last census.

Apartment hotels are another type of residential hotel. They offer very few services, so kitchens are provided in the apartments. Front desks are limited or nonexistent in residential and apartment hotels.

Extended-Stay Hotels.   Extended-stay facilities offer more than a mere hotel room but are not the same genre as residential hotels, which connote permanency. Extended stay merely means long term.

Extensive travel and suitcase living quickly lose their glamour. Something different is needed for those persons moving locations or having extended business assignments away from homes and home offices. Keeping workers comfortable and productive takes more than a traditional hotel room. Extended-stay hotels provide kitchens, grocery outlets, office space—even secretarial support and office equipment, fireplaces, exercise rooms, laundry facilities, and more, but all with maid service.

The extended-stay hotel goes all out to make the stay-away as comfortable as possible. The all-suite hotel had its origin in this segment of the travel market. The all-suite/extended-stay distinction is blurred today because the same building caters to the long-term business traveler and to the other market segments (families, in-room meetings, interviews) to which the all-suite appeals.

➤ **Resort Hotels.**   Transient hotels cater to commercial guests, residential hotels to permanent guests, and resort hotels to social guests—at least traditionally they do (see Exhibit 1–10).

Economics has forced resorts to lengthen their operating period from the traditional summer or winter season to year-round operations. Resorts have marketed to the group and convention delegate at the expense of their social guest. As this began happening, the commercial hotel shifted its design and markets toward the resort concept, dulling once again the distinctions between types. What emerged is a mixed-use resort. Sometimes these resorts are found in residential areas as part of a master-planned community.

Many believe that the modified resort is the hotel of the future. It is in keeping with the nation's move toward increased recreation and compatible with the casual air that characterizes the vacationer. Unlike the formality of the vacationer of an earlier time, today's guest is a participant. Skiing, golfing, boating, and a host of other activities are at the core of the successful resort.

The Megaresort.   The megaresort, one of the lodging industry's newest segments, contains such a large variety of entertainment and recreational facilities that it is a self-contained unit. Guests need not leave the property during their entire stay. Size distinguishes the megaresort from similar self-contained properties, such as the Club Meds.

Although the megaresort is a feature of Las Vegas (see Exhibit 1–6), it is not special to that location alone. Hilton's Hawaiian Village in Honolulu and the 640-acre Ko'Olina (Oahu's west coast), which contains rooms, condos, and retail and office space, as well as a marina, also represent this genre. So does the 900-room Marriott Desert Springs and Spa near Palm Springs in California.

On the other hand, single-feature specialty resorts have also proven quite successful. They appeared earlier than the hotel industry's general move toward segmentation. Tennis clubs (all types of sports clubs), spas, and health (diet) resorts opened and flourished. Club Meditérranée became the prototype of a new style of resort—one that featured an all-inclusive price, tips included.

Exhibit 1–10   The venerable Grand Hotel, a *grande dame*, represents perfectly the traditional destination resort. Guests and supplies come to the island by boat, restricting operations to the summer and to the modified American plan. *Courtesy of the Grand Hotel, Mackinac Island, Michigan.*

Weather plays a key role in every type of resort. Geographic location is to the resort hotel what commercial location is to the transient hotel and population location is to the residential hotel.

Plan

The rates that hotels charge for their rooms are based, in part, on the plan under which they operate. By quoting the plan, the hotel identifies which meals, if any, are part of the basic charge. Rates will be higher if meals are included with the room charge, less if they are excluded. With very few exceptions, every hotel in the United States operates on the European plan. Classification by plan offers much more certainty than the other three classifications: size, class, or type. Either the meal is included or it's not.

➤*European Plan.*   When rates are quoted as European plan (EP) only the room accommodations are included. Extra charges at prevailing menu prices are made for each meal taken. Evidence of the widespread use of the European plan is its lack of designation. Guests are not told, "This is the European plan." Rate quotes always assume EP unless otherwise stated. The European plan is sometimes substituted as an alternative if guests object to another plan being offered by the hotel.

European hotels usually include some form of breakfast, although not as hearty as an American bacon-and-egg spread, as part of the room charge. This makes the pure European plan, which is no meals, less common in Europe than it is in the United States. Providing breakfast of sorts has gained support in the United States during the past decade or so as the all-suite hotel has grown in popularity. More than any other meal, travelers eat breakfast in the hotel.

➤*American Plan.*   Rates quoted under the American plan (AP) include room and all three meals: breakfast, luncheon, and dinner. The AP, which is occasionally called *bed and board,* had its origin in colonial America, when all guests ate at a common table with the host's family. The plan was still in use when the affluent resorts of the Northeast began operating a century later. They adopted and held onto the plan for almost another half-century. The American plan is offered by the cruise lines, but they don't use AP terminology.

New England's resorts held on to the American plan for the same reason that the colonial innkeeper offered it in the first place. Both were isolated, so there was no place else to eat. Better roads and better cars gave guests the mobility that spelled the end of the plan. Conference centers and even some resorts still use it, but give it a more modern term, "an all-inclusive plan."

Europe's full *pension* (pen'-si-own) is almost equivalent to the American plan. Breakfast is the big difference. Full *pension* includes an abbreviated continental breakfast, not the complete breakfast of the American plan. To market the American plan to international guests, European hotels rely on the more descriptive "inclusive terms." The *pension* of Europe is the guest house or boardinghouse of Britain and the United States, with residential hotels in Europe using the term *en pension. Pensiones* are usually longer-stay facilities with limited services, so guests become members of an extended family.

➤*Modified American Plan.*   The modified American plan (MAP) is an astute compromise by which the hotel retains some of the AP advantages, and the guest feels less restricted. Guests get breakfast and dinner as part of the room rate quote, but not luncheon. This opens the middle of the day for a flexible schedule of activities. Guests need not return for an inconveniently scheduled luncheon nor suffer the cost of a missed meal. The hotel retains the obvious benefits of a captive market for the dinner hour. In an effort to make the difference clear, some APs are now called FAP—full American plan.

Half-pension or *demi-pension* (DP) is the European equivalent of the MAP. It includes breakfast and one other meal along with the lodgings. Granting either luncheon or dinner gives the foreign guest the same flexibility of scheduling offered in the United States with the modified American plan.

➤*Continental Plan.*   Under the Continental plan (CP)—mainland Europe being the Continent—breakfast is included with the room rate. This continental breakfast, consisting of coffee or chocolate, roll, and a bit of cheese (cold meat or fish in Holland and Norway), is on the wane even in Europe. (A hearty English breakfast is served in Ireland and the United Kingdom. It usually includes cereal, eggs with a choice of meat, toast with butter and jam, and tea or coffee, but no juice. However, it is rarely included in the room rate.)

In some parts of the world, this abbreviated breakfast goes under the name of bed–breakfast. With the same line of reasoning, the modified American plan becomes half-board. Neither should be confused with the Bermuda plan, which includes a full breakfast in the rate.

Café complet, a midmorning or afternoon coffee snack, is mistakenly called a continental breakfast. The distinction is neither the time of day nor the menu items, but the manner of payment. *Café complet* is not included in the room rate.

The appearance of late afternoon tea as a pleasant supplement to the overworked happy hour is certain to bring further confusion in terminology. Many top U.S. hotels have latched onto that quintessential British ritual, afternoon tea. Delicate sandwiches and small sweets served with tea, or even sherry, comprise this light snack. It is not to be confused with high tea, which is a supper, a substantial meal almost always served with meat. High tea is a rarity today, even in British hotels.

Continental Breakfast. Continental breakfast has many meanings. A coffee urn with sweet rolls and juice left in the lobby when the dining room closes is often called a continental breakfast. A similar setup at a group registration desk or at the rear of a meeting room during a speaker's talk appears on the program as continental breakfast. Juice is included in the United States or when the delegates are Americans, but it is not usually served elsewhere.

All-suite hotels have eliminated full-service dining rooms because they are expensive to operate. To accommodate overnight guests, who almost always want breakfast before departing, all-suites provide a full breakfast without charge as part of their marketing strategy. It is a revival of America's view of the Continental plan, which took form in the 1950s with the opening of the no-dining-room motel. In-room coffee makers, coffee in the lobby, or coffee and sweet rolls in the small proprietor's kitchen were all touted as continental breakfast.

Bed and Breakfast (B&B). Bed and breakfast surged onto the American scene so strongly that one might think it to be a whole new concept in hotel keeping. It's hardly that. Bed and breakfast in the United States takes its cue from the British B&B, the Italian *pensiones,* and the German *zimmer frei* (room available)—lodging and breakfast offered by families in their own homes. The Japanese version of the U.S. B&B is *minshuku.*

B&B is a modern version of the 1930s roominghouse, once called the tourist home. The bed and breakfast was reborn for much the same reasons as its Depression-era predecessor—the landlord's need to supplement income and the lodger's hunt for less costly accommodations. Of course, for some innkeepers, it is an adventure, and for others, a hobby. The acceptability of the B&B gets a boost from the experience of a generation of owner–renters sharing living accommodations and time-share facilities.

Under the plan, guests take rooms with private families, who often furnish camaraderie along with the mandatory breakfast. The lack of privacy—shared bath, conversation at breakfast—forces the host and guest into a level of intimacy that brings new friendships along with the business relationship.

Like the rest of the industry, change is part of the B&B's vocabulary and no one definition fits all the parts. There are many subcategories because the business is very individualized and localized. The B&B changes identity as it moves across the country. The B&B Inn, for example, is a product of California. It is a large version (over half the B&Bs in the United States are 8 rooms or less) and is usually the owner's primary occupation. Some observers see another subcategory, the Country B&B, as an upscale boardinghouse because it serves all meals, not just breakfast. Country B&Bs have their origin in New England. In between the coasts are a variety of facilities serving their local markets (see Exhibit 1–11). Like other small businesses, B&Bs often lack staying power. Results can be ruinous where zoning laws prohibit even a "rooms-for-let" notice in the window. One positive sign is the new Yellow Pages listing of B&B referral organizations under "B&B" rather than under their previous category of "hotels, motels, and tourist homes."

In one way, B&Bs are no different from other American hotels. They fight for business and rely on themselves for referrals. In Europe and Japan, government tourist agencies make B&B referrals and even rate them by price and accommodations. The French call them *café-couette* (coffee and quilt), and their rating system uses three to six coffee pots instead of stars. Since the U.S. government has never entered the tourist-rating business, several private rating and referral systems have emerged. Like the B&Bs themselves, these rating/referral systems come and go quickly, for they, too, lack staying power.

Boutique and Trophy Hotels.   Boutique hotels are a unique species. They are very small inns, 10 to 30 room perhaps, with all the amenities of a fine hotel but without the size and bustle. The phrase *European-style hotel* is sometimes used in reference to boutiques. Boutique hotels are fashionable, meaning that they are found in very good urban locations. Therefore, they are also called *urban inns,* or in Britain, *baby grand hotels.*

A good definition of a boutique hotel has yet to be coined. The term has been attributed to Steve Rubell, one of the founders of a New York City club, Studio 54.

Exhibit 1–11   Bed and breakfast (B&B) facilities operate under a variety of names, such as B&B Inns (chiefly California) or Country B&Bs (chiefly New England). In between the coasts are a range of wonderful stopping places like this one close to the Grand Canyon. Suites with private baths, fireplaces, and homemade chocolate-chip cookies make strong competitors to the standard, traditional guest room. *Courtesy of The Inn at 410, Flagstaff, Arizona.*

When asked for a description of his new hotel, the Morgans, he said that other hotels were large department stores, but Morgans was a small boutique. However described, boutique hotels are full-time businesses requiring substantial capital investment. Traditional financing for so risky an adventure is difficult to find. Moreover, earning a fair return on this unconventional investment pushes rates upward toward the level of other four-and five-star hotels. Since the volume on which costs are prorated is small, boutique hotels are unlikely to be profitable. They are, therefore, often designated *trophy hotels*. Their owners have the property as a personal achievement (a trophy) rather than as a viable business enterprise.

Any hotel can be a trophy hotel; it need not be a boutique hotel. Many *grande dames*[7] of the hotel business have such wonderful reputations and historical lineage that hoteliers acquire them just to say they are mine. Some are profitable ongoing properties. Denver's Brown Palace would be one such. But many trophy hotels struggle during economic dips, although they may be profitable during up-cycles. Listing these unique buildings in the National Register of Historic Places provides some helpful tax relief if the hotel is a historical site or if the boutique hotel results from a historical conversion, as it sometimes does.

➤ SUMMARY

The lodging industry has played an important role in the historical development of commerce, culture, and politics. Its ability to adapt to changes in these environments has assured its place in modern business. By providing over 10 million rooms worldwide, it serves today as an integral part of global business, including the leisure industry.

Even though the industry is changing at a furious pace, it retains some of its traditional measures and methods of identification. Among those measures are the percentage of room occupancy and the average daily rate (ADR); the first measures the quantity of the business and the second its value. Another long-time measure, revenue per available room (RevPar), has been rediscovered as an important statistic since yield management (Chapter 4) has found its way into the toolbox of the rooms manager.

To maximize the values of these measures, management must overcome several limitations that are inherent in the hotel business. These include a highly perishable product, an unmovable location, a fixed supply of inventory, a high break-even point, and seasonal operating periods. In addition, hotel keeping is a cyclical industry, with long up and down waves that sometimes last a decade: tough hurdles all.

Understanding the industry's traditional identifications (size, class, type, and plan) helps in identifying the new permutations (all-suite, B&B, budget) that keep the industry economically sound and exciting as a career. Competition sharpens the new direction, and rating systems keep the individual hotel attuned. As the changes continue, new classifications and new categories are needed. Those identities are provided in Chapter 2.

➤ QUESTIONS AND PROBLEMS

1. Using appropriate guides (*OAG Travel Planner, Hotel & Motel Red Book, The Official Hotel & Resort Guide*, and others) identify two or three U.S. hotels that quote rates on the full or modified American plans. Identify the source(s) used. Is there any commonality among the hotels? If so, what?

2. Create a checklist with two dozen objective listings that could be used by an evaluator inspecting guest rooms for a national rating system.

3. Explain where the hotel industry is in its economic cycle. Be specific. Is it at the bottom of the trough? The highest point of its rise? Somewhere in between? If so, moving in what direction? Submit evidence to support your position.

4. Give three to five examples of each type of expense that is used to determine the cost portion of a hotel's break-even point: fixed expenses; semifixed expenses; variable expenses.

5. How many rooms does the MGM Grand Hotel need to sell annually if it budgets operations on an annual occupancy of 82%? (*Hint:* See Exhibit 1–6.)

6. Using information contained in Chapter 1, justify or challenge the statement of Andrew Young, the former mayor of Atlanta, who said that a 1% rise in room occupancy creates 400 new jobs for that city. (*Hint:* You will need to know the approximate number of rooms in the city and an estimate of the staff-to-room ratio.)

➤ *NOTES*

1. Daniel Boorstin, *The American National Experience,* Chapter 18, "Palaces of the People" (New York: Random House, 1967); and Arthur White, *Palaces of the People* (Marlboro, NJ: Taplinger Publishing Co., Inc., 1970).

2. Smith Travel Research, Hendersonville, Tennessee, and *Lodging Industry Profile* (New York: American Hotel & Motel Association, 1996).

3. *Hotels & Restaurants International,* June 1989, p. 40, quoting John Kapioltas, then Sheraton's Chief Executive Officer; and Andrew Young, keynote speech, CHRIE, Washington, DC, August 12, 1996.

4. Average rate per available room was the terminology that appeared in the first four editions of this book. The concept and the name fell into disuse only to reemerge as RevPar. Similarly, the average daily rate was originally called average room rate, a name that was gradually replaced beginning about 1980 because some thought it to mean the rate the hotel was charging. [*Lodging Hospitality* (August 1998) reported that the Lowell Hotel in New York City had a whopping RevPar of $256,459!]

5. A recent estimate placed the industry at a break-even point of 55% occupancy, a very, very low figure and one that will serve the industry well during the next cyclical decline.

6. An early definition was offered by Howard E. Morgan, *The Motel Industry in the United States: Small Business in Transition* (Tucson, AZ: Bureau of Business and Public Research, University of Arizona, 1964).

7. *Grande dames* is French for ladies of aristocratic bearing—hence elegant, grand hotels.

CHAPTER 2
The Modern Hotel Industry

Outline

New Product Patterns
Segmentation of the Product Line

New Market Patterns
Marketing to the Individual Guest
Marketing to the Group

New Ownership Patterns
The State of the Industry
Ownership and Financing Alternatives

New Management Patterns
Chains
Management Companies and
Management Contracts
Franchises

The introductory material of Chapter 1 provides a strong foundation from which the hotel industry can be viewed. It is to the credit of this industry that the traditional structures discussed there are insufficient for today's tasks. Present-day lodging has evolved and restructured itself—and continues to do so almost daily it seems—to meet the demands of rapid and continuous change. The lodging industry has recast itself more in the previous several decades than it did in the previous several centuries. Those changes involve every facet of innkeeping. The list is long: guests, staff, finances, raw materials, business concepts, communications, politics, social expectations, travel patterns, and transportation. Every aspect of hotelkeeping is in change!

Throughout the centuries, innkeepers have reacted to the demands of the traveler. Seldom—until now—have they created the product or generated that demand. Until as recently as the 1950s, hotels served primarily as the storage arm of transportation, carefully locating along the traveler's route, waiting for the traveler to rest. Today, there is an array of routes. No longer is there just one from which to choose as the traveler wings around the globe at the speed of sound.

Rather than a fixed destination along a predetermined route, the 21st-Century hotel will be a fixed destination along no one's route and along everyone's potential route. To meet its altered role, the industry has undergone major shifts and reconstructed itself into new arrays. In this chapter we look at four of those new patterns: product, market, ownership, and management.

➤ NEW PRODUCT PATTERNS

Chapter 2 is really all about choice. Modern times and modern businesses offer a range and a variety of alternatives in every aspect of life. Guests, owners, and managers have taken advantage of this multiplicity by shaping and molding the business of lodging into interesting new patterns.

Segmentation, which started in the 1980s as a "brand stretching" movement, continues changing the face of the hotel business and the business's guests. Segmentation cuts up the identifications of the operation and of the guest into smaller and smaller pieces. It makes the industry vibrant and competitive, but it makes identification of the whole more and more difficult (see Exhibit 2–1).

Segmentation of the Product Line[1]

Segmentation had its source, as did so many other recent industry changes, in decades of turmoil. As business conditions worsened, hotel chains sought methods of broadening their markets—of finding new customers. Upscale chains moved into more moderately priced operations. Marriott introduced its Fairfield Inns, for example. Hotels in the middle range had the advantage of going both ways. Choice Hotels stepped upward with Clarion properties and downward with Sleep Inns (see Exhibit 2–2).

Other chains shifted horizontally as well as vertically in a desperate attempt to reverse the erosion of occupancy. Holiday Corporation went upscale with its Crowne Plaza properties, which meant shifting from traditional highway locations to compete against the Hyatts and Hiltons in urban markets. Similarly, most of the commercial chains stretched into the resort business. Some of these changes put new products onto the market; others merely put new faces onto older properties whose logos were no longer an asset.

If nothing else, the range and rate of new product introduction proved how dynamic the lodging industry is. New products have taken hold and outstripped the ex-

Exhibit 2–1 A segmenting industry increases the number of divisions and subdivisions by which it is identified. A single property may well fall into several categories.

A Segmented Industry

Segmented by Activity
Casino hotel
Convention hotel
Dude ranch

Segmented by Financing
Public corporation
Private individual
REIT

Segmented by Location
Airport
Highway
Seaside

Segmented by Management
Chain
Management company
Self-managed

Segmented by Markets
Business
Groups
Leisure

Segmented Miscellaneously
Collar
Hostel
Mixed use

Segmented by Ownership
Chain
Condominium
Mom-and-pop

Segmented by Plan
American plan
Continental plan
European plan

Segmented by Price (ADR)
Deluxe (Above $100)
Midrange ($50–$90)
Budget ($35–50)

Segmented by Ratings
Five-star
Four-star
Three-star

Segmented by Service
Full service
Moderate service
Self-service

Segmented by Structure
High rise
Low rise
Outside corridor

Segmented by Type
Commercial
Residential
Resort

Segmented by Use
Bed and breakfast
Extended-stay
Health spa

pectations of even their most ardent supporters. Chief among these are the economy (budget) properties, the all-suite hotels, and the casino hotels.

➤ *Economy Hotels.* The history of the motor court, the original economy hotel, is a story of *amenity creep*. An amenity is a special extra that the hotel provides in an effort to distinguish itself from competitors. After a time, guests expect the amenity. No longer do they view the extra product or service as anything special. Other hotel chains are then forced to provide as standard service what the industry previously viewed as something special. So the old amenity creeps into standard service and a new round of amenities is forced upon the industry.

The first motor courts (1930s) were very limited roadside facilities with almost no services (see Exhibit 2–3). Along came Kemmons Wilson's Holiday Inn. He founded these inns as clean, no-frill accommodations. However, existing motor court operators saw the inns as amenity creep. Since the process is ongoing, Holiday Inn itself eventually faced the creep of competition. How else could it respond? Creep further!

| | Brand Names[a] | | | |
Company Name	Low End	Mid-scale	Upscale	Suites
Bass Hotels and Resorts (Holiday Inn)	Holiday Inn Express	Holiday Inn Holiday Inn Select Forum Hotels	Crowne Plaza Inter-Continental	Holiday Inn Suites
Choice Hotels International	Comfort Inn EconoLodge Friendship Inn Rodeway Inn Sleep Inn	Quality Inn	Clarion	Clarion Suites Comfort Suites MainStay Suites Quality Suites
Howard Johnson International	Howard Johnson Express Inn Howard Johnson Inn	Howard Johnson Hotel	Howard Johnson Plaza Hotel Howard Johnson Resort Hotel	Howard Johnson Hotels and Suites
Marriott International	Fairfield Inn	Courtyard Residence Inn	Marriott Hotel and Resort Ritz-Carlton Hotels Renaissance Hotels	Fairfield Suites TownePlace Suites

[a]Each listing refers only to other hotels in the same chain. The chart is not intended for comparisons between hotel companies. Bass's mid-scale hotel is not being compared to Choice's mid-scale hotel. Read horizontally, not vertically. Some of the company brands are incomplete.

Exhibit 2–2 Segmentation of selected companies. A company's search for additional market segments can lead to confusion among the buying public, which faces a long list of brand names and logos, including those of frequent-guest programs. See also Exhibits 2–6, 2–11, and 2–14.

Little by little, small rooms grew larger. Direct-dial telephones were installed where there had been none. Free television replaced coin-operated sets; then remote controls were added. Expensive but infrequently used swimming pools were everywhere. Airconditioning, in-room coffee makers, and two wash basins to the room became standard. Guest rooms supplies such as three varieties of soap, combs, and lotions joined the rush of extras. Estimates place the cost of these toiletries at $2 per room per night when the amenity was introduced. A decade later, the figure had vaulted to between $6 and $7. Then the trimming started, and no wonder (see Exhibit 2–4).

Each upgrade pushed room rates higher. Hotel companies that started in the economy segment (Holiday Inn, Ramada, Days Inns) found themselves in the midrange. Undoubtedly, personal egos played a role in upgrading the chains. So did the introduction of franchising. Franchise fees are based on room revenues. As amenity creep pushes up room revenues, franchise fees to the parent company also increase.

As room rates inch upward, new chains fill the void at the lower end. (Some date the start of this rotation from 1964, when Motel 6 entered the market.) The new companies forgo new amenities but most include accommodations that are by now basic requirements. Telephone, remote television, acceptance of credit cards—even breakfasts and frequent-stay programs—are seen as fundamentals today. How is it being

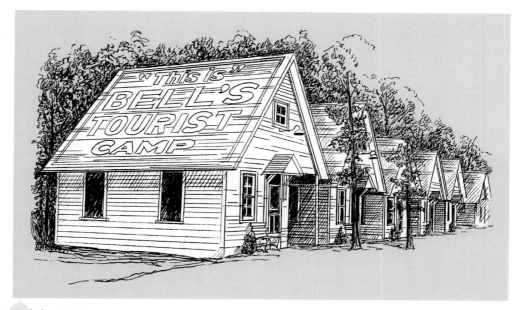

Exhibit 2–3 Tourist courts predated the highway hotel/motel that originated with Kemmons Wilson's Holiday Inn Chain, now owned by Bass PLC of the United Kingdom. Bass, which also owns Inter-Continental Hotels, renamed the chain the Holiday Hospitality Corporation in 1998, and within the same year, changed it again to Bass Hotels and Resorts. Individual hotels are still called Holiday Inn.

done? There are three techniques: fewer bathroom amenities, better value in construction, and attention to operations.

Newer and newer rounds of economy chains employ newer and newer techniques. Rooms smaller than the standard 300 to 325 square feet are being offered now. (Microtel rooms are 178 square feet.) The chains are selecting less costly land, and they are building on smaller sites, 1.5 acres or less for 100 rooms. Nonbasic amenities such as pools, lobbies, meeting space, and restaurants have been eliminated

Exhibit 2–4
Amenity creep in the bathroom has been halted with substantial savings in costs, but new ideas such as night-lights and bathrobes threaten to accelerate the pace again.

Savings from Managing Amenity Costs	
Assume:	Number of rooms available 400
	Percent occupancy 75%
	Per room cost of amenities $3.50
Required:	Compute the annual savings that results from reducing amenity costs to $2.50/room.
Solution:	400 rooms available × 0.75 occupancy = 300 rooms sold per night.
	300 rooms sold per night × 365 nights per year = 109,500 rooms sold per year.
	109,500 rooms sold per year × $1.00 ($3.50 − $2.50) savings per room = $109,500 annual savings from amenity management.

once again. (Providing free continental breakfasts is actually less costly than operating a restaurant that loses money. Besides, budget hotels/motels are almost always located near outlets of national restaurant chains, with one restaurant often serving several competitors.)

The latest round of budget hotel/motels has focused on savings in design and construction. Economy is coming from standardized architectural plans and from using a limited number of qualified builders. Structures have low ceilings and improved insulation. Costs of initial construction have been reduced, and so have later operating expenses.

Some budgets employ fewer than 20 employees per 100 rooms, almost 60% less than the traditional figures suggested in Chapter 1. Eliminating the dining room is just one technique for reducing labor. Hanging the guest room furniture and providing a shower but not a tub increase the productivity of the housekeeping department. Automating telephone calls and assigning extra duties (including laundry operations to the night clerk) improve productivity on that side of the house.

Planned savings like these require new, well-designed facilities. And these were built—and succeeded—during and despite the 1981–1991 decline in hotel construction. Because it takes about 250 properties to ensure market identification, some emerging chains acquired old mom-and-pop operations at fire sale prices in order to establish themselves as viable budget operators. Days Inns was one such company.

Hard Budgets.   The economy (or budget) segment reigned as the most profitable segment of the lodging industry throughout the falling cycle of the 1980s and 1990s. In fact, the economy sector outpaced the luxury group even during the recovery period. But like the industry of which it is part, the economy segment has no one identity. It is itself divided.

The entire low-end segment is called economy, budget, limited service, or simply low-end. All are euphemisms for inexpensive. Adding confusion is a jumble of names and affiliations. There are upscale budgets—what an oxymoronic term—(La Quinta, for example), intermediate budgets (Red Roof Inns, for example), and low-end budgets (Super 8 Motels, for example). At one time it was thought that Microtel, a chain of low-end budget hotels, might become the generic name for all budgets. The term would be used in lowercase letters, *microtel.*

Hard budget, including capsule rooms and truck-stop accommodations, is a fourth category of economy hotels. Hard budgets are located at airports and at the hundreds of truck stops that dot the interstate highways. Airports in Los Angeles and Honolulu offer rooms of 75 square feet (25 to 30% of a normal-sized room) for rest, showers, and stopovers between flights. Interestingly, France has a large number of hard budgets, reflecting perhaps its high payroll taxes and the need to minimize labor use.

Capsule rooms, which are somewhat like railroad sleeping berths, are smaller still, some as small as 5 feet by 5 feet, with headroom only to sit. Capsule rooms were an innovation of the Japanese. Although larger in dimension, self-service hotels—get your own linens and make your own beds—also fall into the hard budget category. Rooms are cleaned only between guests, and no other services are offered.

▶*All-Suite Hotels.*   The all-suite hotel has undergone a change from its original concept. With that change have come new names and identities. All-suite hotels started out as extended-stay hotels or suite hotels. The three terms have blurred, so now they are used interchangeably. By whatever term, all-suites appeal to investors because of their strong weekend occupancy.

Suite hotels were the brainchild of Robert Wooley, who created the first chain, Granada Royale Hometel. The idea was born in Phoenix in 1969, but it grew up in the years of the Texas oil boom. Extended-stay facilities were an important service to the transient oil economy. The idea was innovative—some say the best in a generation—but it borrowed from the traditional: the apartment hotel and the residential hotel.

Holiday Inn acquired Granada Royale Hometel, renamed it, and became the largest all-suite chain in the nation. It tested this segment of the market with two logos. Embassy Suites, which was spun off to Promus (1990) when the Holiday Corporation broke up, was and is a top-of-the-line, all-suite facility. Residence Inn was Holiday's other all-suite logo. In need of cash, Holiday sold the chain to Marriott in 1987.

Many new players entered the market as the all-suite became the darling of hotel developers. The lure has been good occupancies and good rates, both made possible by the high value that the customer perceives. So once again, the pattern of proliferation prevailed with new names, new operators, and new products (see Exhibit 2–2). Economy, midmarket, and upscale units emerged as they have done within other segments. Even the original concept of extended stay (*Home*tel) is no longer a determinant.

Some all-suite brands franchise, some do not, and some only franchise. Several have two or three brands: Clarion, Quality, and Comfort Suites are all by Choice, and Marriott has added Marriott Suites to its Residence Inn. By so doing, Marriott distinguishes between the extended stay of its Residence brand, which Marriott defines as five consecutive nights or more, and the transient accommodations of its Marriott Suites.

Extended stay was the original concept, and corporate users the target. The extended-stay hotel was designed for executives and their families who were being relocated. It was for training and educational sessions and for employees on long-term but not permanent field assignments. Private entrance, kitchenette, and separate living–sleeping facilities are the attractive features.

Separate living–sleeping accommodations (see Exhibit 3–17) are attractive to personnel conducting interviews, to women executives, and to others who require private space outside the intimacy of a bedroom. That's why the market shifted away from just extended-stay use. The living space contains a sofa bed and sometimes a second bath. That opened still another market: traveling couples and families seeking economical accommodations.

The kitchenette is to the all-suite as the swimming pool is to the motel. Everyone looks for the amenity, but few use it. So we might get still another variation. That is the most exciting part of the hotel business. New patterns continue to emerge as new market niches are identified and new entrepreneurs shake up the establishment.

➤*Casino Hotels.*   The casino hotel has shaken up the established industry as nothing before in this generation. As legalized gaming (gambling) spreads, this unique destination resort shows signs of becoming the most important player of the lodging industry. That comes as no surprise when profits are counted up. Over one-half of Hilton's profits are said to be from its domestic gaming division.

The operating profile of hotel casinos differs from that of the traditional hotel. Gaming revenues, called *win*, not room sales, become the major income producer. Therefore, having rooms occupied (potential casino players) is more important than the price for which those rooms sell. To generate casino volume, room rates are lower at casino hotels; single and double occupancy are the same rate—more players; and food and beverage are often viewed as loss leaders—means of attracting traffic into the casino.

Hotels with casinos are nothing new to the United States. Gaming has gone in and out of favor since the first raffle to raise money for the Continental Army. It has swept across the land again because of recent changes in the national psyche. Gaming is viewed now as another type of entertainment rather than as a vice. Tax revenues earned directly from gaming and indirectly from the tourism spurred by the presence of casinos have become essential to the economies of many states. That dollar flow has shut out opponents arguing against the casino industry. The biggest surprise, perhaps, has been the location of these new resort destinations. Biloxi, Mississippi, the heart of the Bible Belt; South Dakota's worn-out mining area, Deadwood City; and the Mashantucket Pequot Nation, Connecticut's Indian tribe, have become major tourist draws and boom centers.

►*Other Hotel Segments.*   The dynamic nature of the hotel business—out with the old and in with the new—has kept it viable and changing. New segments and new adaptations of older ideas are taking shape continuously.

Some hotels have joined up with Elderhostel, a program designed to fill vacant dormitory beds during the summers. In this program, retired persons stay in hotels near a campus, where they choose from a variety of courses offered by distinguished professors.

On the other side of the age spectrum is Camp Hyatt, a children's camp operating within the Hyatt hotels. The camp caters to the children while the parents are at work or play. Hyatt even offers a frequent-stay program for the kids.

Because of the manner in which they ring the city, suburban hotels have been dubbed *collar hotels.* These hotels have followed industry from high-rent downtown districts to the open spaces of the suburbs. Beltway roads, which collar the city, have made the transition possible. Suburban hotels are narrowly segmented with few opportunities to add to the customer pool other than from the industries that they followed to the suburbs.

Conference Centers.   Conference centers are specialized "hotels" that cater to meetings, training sessions, and conferences of all types. Unlike the typical convention hotels, conference centers usually take no transient guests. Food service is also restricted to the in-house groups. Catering to this special market, conference centers provide a complete line of audiovisual materials, special seminar rooms and theaters, closed-circuit television with interactive teleconferencing, and simultaneous translation capabilities.

The special design of the meeting facilities distinguishes conference centers from other meeting places (see Exhibit 2–5). That distinction is not always understood by conference planners. Conference centers are not necessarily separate facilities, but they do have permanent and dedicated meeting space. Hotel meeting space is temporary as the function room changes from meetings to banquets, from trade shows to dances.

Other operational differences distinguish the conference center from the hotel. Double occupancy is higher. Even top-level senior managers are doubled up. Two to a room encourages greater familiarity, which is one goal of conference planners. Lower management and upper management get to know one another.

Rates at conference centers are bundled. Room, food, and beverage are quoted as one figure. Conference centers call this quote a *corporate meeting package* (CMP), but the reader will recognize it as a variation of the American plan. CMP is a modern ver-

Exhibit 2–5 Conference centers blend pleasant surroundings with high-tech meeting facilities. Some hotels have started to compete in this segment of the lodging industry, but building specialized facilities negates the multiuse space that most convention hotels offer. *Courtesy of The Northland Inn and Executive Conference Center, Minneapolis, Minnesota.*

sion of the AP because the conference center is a modern marriage of the convention hotel and the traditional resort. When physically combined, a five-day workweek in the conference facility can be followed by a two-day weekend in the resort complex. Like convention hotels, conference centers are plagued by low weekend occupancy. Some have been forced to look at social guests to fill the hole. Growth in conference centers is apt to be in university conference centers; in nonresidential conference centers, perhaps in city centers or Silicon Valleys; and in special conference facilities built within convention hotels.

Spas. Spas are mineral springs or curative waters. As the resorts of New England developed around these waters, the resorts themselves became known as spas. Spas were known and used as far back as the Romans, who "took the waters" in the city of Spa, Belgium. Obviously, that is the source of the present-day term.

Today's spas are far different from those of the Romans or of even such famous spas as Saratoga (Springs) in New York State.[2] White Sulphur Springs, West Virginia, and its bubbling fountains were widely known even in the Colonial period. These spas and others, like the Broadmoor in Colorado Springs, were sought initially for their restorative properties and their promises as fountains-of-youth. It wasn't long before the spas became playgrounds for the rich and socially well placed. Horse racing, cricket matches, casinos (Morrissey's Club House at Saratoga was a famous casino), cycling, water sports, and other entertainment gradually replaced the water as the main attraction at these still well-known landmarks.

Early American spas were chiefly health focused, whether or not there was any truth to the curative claims for the waters. The modern spa had its origin more in hedonism (self-indulgence and pleasure being the highest good) for the wealthy. Its intent, too, has shifted. The spa has become more democratic. An almost religious mixture of health and exercise, massage, and supervised diets dominates the 21st-Century spa. If there are any "waters" to be taken, they are humanmade: swimming pools and mud packs.

Spas can stand alone as complete facilities with food, housing, and therapy, or they are found in more limited editions within a variety of hotels. There they are seen to be an upscale amenity for both men and women.

➤ NEW MARKET PATTERNS

Hotels zero in on particular market segments (niches) as their chief sources of business. Similarly, guests go to a particular hotel because they find there the kind of accommodations and services that they seek. So the guest's very presence at a hotel tells us much about both the hotel and the guest.

Guests take lodging for many different reasons, but actually for only one of two purposes. Either the hotel is their ultimate destination, or it offers them accommodations in transit. Although there are similarities, this transient-destination category is not the same as the commercial-resort grouping discussed in Chapter 1.

A transient hotel is a passing-through facility. Guests are en route to somewhere else: tourists en route to a national shrine, business executives to a corporate meeting, families to weddings, or ball teams to the destination of a big game. Rarely does the transient hotel hold the guest beyond one night.

In contrast, the destination hotel is the objective, the very purpose of the trip. It is the hotel that houses the convention or corporate meeting. It is the family's temporary residence while it seeks housing in the new locality. It is the best location near the medical center for persons visiting the sick. More and more, the destination hotel is part of the destination resort complex, often a megaresort, which is typified by the Disney properties.

Location helps fix the classification. The hotels of Acapulco and Miami Beach are unquestionably destination points. Equally certain is the transient nature of many a motor inn. There, on the outskirts of town near the freeway, it awaits the traveler en route to the megalopolis still a day's ride away. Most hotels are not so clearly one type or another—those of New York City, for example.

The role of any hotel changes from guest to guest. In this context, the transient hotel is obviously not the commercial property of Chapter 1. Nor is the destination hotel necessarily a resort. So certain destination guests coming to a commercial hotel might be more interested in an American plan than would be a transient guest coming to a resort. For example, an international traveler, who is a first-time visitor to an unfamiliar land, might like hotel meals included in the rate, even at a commercial hotel. Not so for a transient guest who stops for a single night at a resort that operates on the American plan. From the historical view covered in Chapter 1, the destination hotel is obviously the new kid on the block.

Marketing to the Individual Guest

Whereas yesterday's travelers were happy enough to find shelter and food, today's tourists need to be wooed and won. Whereas the guests of old stopped automatically at the only designated hostel, their modern counterparts select from competitive offerings with many attractive inducements. An explosion of choice has taken place around the globe in all the goods and services that customers buy. Consumers are offered a rich selection of products, from bottled water to investment options. Such is also the case for lodging, which has joined the movement by introducing the new array of products that were just discussed. Now the problem is to entice the guest in.

➤ *The Guest Profile.* Guests stay at hotels under different circumstances. Consequently, what appeals to one guest may be of indifference to another. Indeed, the same guest displays different responses during separate stays. The guest has a different profile as a businessperson than as a tourist. The single traveler has different expectations when returning as part of a business group or as part of a family unit. Looking at the guest under various circumstances enables the hotelier to build and manage for a variety of market segments.

Guest profiles have been developed by trade associations, governmental agencies, rating firms, purveyors, external consultants, magazines, and the hotel companies themselves.[3] The typical study focuses on demographic profiles. Age, income and job, gender, residence, education, and the number of travelers in the party are all determinable with a good degree of accuracy. Knowing the guests is the starting point for servicing them.

Some patterns take their lead from profiles less measurable than demographics. Developers differentiate between what have been called upstairs/downstairs buyers. *Upstairs buyers* are more oriented toward the room. These guests want large sleeping and bathing facilities and comfortable work space. For this, they will sacrifice theme restaurants, bars, banquet facilities, and exercise rooms. Not so the *downstairs guests,* who want public space above all else.

Extended-stay guests, those who remain five or more days, attempt to recreate a little of their home in the guest room. They bring personal items such as pillows, photos, stuffed animals, and personal toiletries. The kitchenette is used, but mostly for breakfast or for snacks, less often for dinner preparation. The extended-stay guest wants working space and good lighting. So does the business traveler.

Business/Leisure Travelers. Businesspersons need to be at a given place at a given time. Therefore, price is less important—not unimportant, but less important—to the business guest than to the leisure traveler. Businessmen and women are not apt to cancel a trip because of high rates, and they are not apt to make a trip because of low rates. Theirs is an *inelastic* market—there is very little change in demand from a change in price. The response from leisure guests is more dramatic: High rates repel them and low rates attract them. By responding to price changes, leisure guests represent a more *elastic* market.

All guests demonstrate some degree of elasticity. Even leisure guests may be inelastic, they just have to be there—a wedding, a funeral, and so on. Business guests may be elastic, rescheduling or postponing their meetings. Companies with travel desks, which schedule and buy travel (air, hotels, and car rentals) for their personnel, are more price sensitive. With someone other than the traveler doing the planning, businesses have shifted toward the elastic side. This shift helps explain the buyer's focus on value. Thus, all-suite hotels have grown in popularity, and expensive five-star properties suffered during the decade-long downturn in business.

Business guests are mostly men; tourists are mostly couples. Almost everyone watches television from the bed. Some 20% actually rearrange furniture, more often at extended-stay properties. Business travelers use the telephone, the shower, and the TV movie channel more than leisure travelers do. Tourists hold the edge on the pool and other recreational facilities. Leisure tourists tend to be 5 to 10 years older than businesspersons. They make reservations less often and pay less for their rooms than business travelers do.

Businesswomen present still another profile pattern. They are among the fastest-growing segment of the commercial hotel market, numbering about one-third of all business travelers. The latter description is a demographic measure. How best to please that market is uncertain. That's a psychographic factor. Psychographic profiles detail personality traits, desires, and inner motivations. Every demographic or psychographic profile is necessarily flawed because no individual guest is ever 100% of the composite study. Besides, as we explain in the next section, the guest who stays at the hotel (the one whose profile the industry develops) is often not the person who bought the room initially.

Business travelers, be they male or female, use the room as an office. No surprise, then, that surveys indicate that a comfortable desk and desk chair are a high priority to this group. Business guests may need other special services such as in-room computers, private telephone lines for messages and faxes, and business centers with secretarial support. Specific requirements like these reduce the businesspersons' options, and this means still less elasticity. Meanwhile, the hotel industry struggles to decide how worthwhile are expensive, business-oriented investments in attracting this single segment of the market.

Whether business or leisure, guests are opting for smoke-free rooms. The no-smoking room is a not a surprising outcome from studies of guest preferences. Bad odors are among the top complaints voiced by the traveling public. Smoke is one source of that bad smell. The perfumed sprays used by housekeeping to mask smoke and other odors merely contribute to the problem.

Some leisure guests are out for a change of experience rather than the leisure of lie-in-the-sun beach and ocean. This niche searches for a change of pace, not for idle leisure. Hiking, mountain climbing, planting trees, rafting, and archeological digs are the sort of leisure activities that many resorts are offering and many vacationers are buying. Guests are willing to pay handsomely for these out-of-the-ordinary experiences.

The economy market is just the opposite. Price-sensitive guests form the core of the budget customers. Who are they? Governmental employees on a fixed per diem (per day) allowance make up one segment. Retirees, whose time is more flexible than their budgets, will go to the less convenient and less costly locations that economy properties require. Family vacationers and small-business persons sensitive to travel costs help round out this segment. International guests, who have different expectations than domestic travelers, are also part of the budget market.

The International Guest.   Globalization requires special attention to the profile of the international guest. Foreign visitors are big business. The World Tourism Organization (WTO) forecasts 102 million visitors to the United States by 2020. Since they spend more time and more money reaching their destinations, international guests stay longer than do domestic guests. Typically, theirs is a six-day visit, more than half again the usual domestic hotel stay. International visitors to the United States help the nation's balance of trade, representing some $50 billion in export equivalence.

Japanese visitors to Hawaii spend three times that of the U.S. tourist to Hawaii. Japanese visitors almost always tour in groups, even when they are honeymooning. Office groups (women), ski groups (men), business groups (rarely women), and silver groups (retired couples) are the profiles of the Japanese traveler. Hotels seeking foreign guests need to provide accommodations (Japanese, for example, want bedroom slippers provided), and meals, especially breakfasts, that cater to the tastes of their international patrons.

▶*Frequent-Guest Programs.* No one is really certain whether or not frequent-guest programs (FGPs) or their model, frequent-flier programs (FFPs), actually increase market share. It is a difficult determination to make when all competitors use the same marketing technique. FFPs and FGPs are so alike that hotels and airlines have merged their awards (see Exhibit 2–6). Points earned with the one can be used with the other. Auto rentals and selected gifts are also packaged in.

FGPs are offered by hotels in all rate ranges. Hyatt (*Gold Passport*), Marriott (*Honored Guest Award*), and Hilton (*HHonors Club*) are examples on the high end. Companies such as La Quinta (*Returns*) are on the low end. In between are Holiday Hospitality Corporation's *Priority Club* and Best Western's *Gold Crown Club.*[4] All of this adds to the garble of new trademark names that segmentation has already muddled.

These are costly programs, estimated as high as $10 per room per night. They saddle the hotel chains with unused travel-credit liabilities. FGPs also irritate franchise holders, who must pay their share of program costs, creating another sensitive issue in the franchisor–franchisee relationship. But they have their positive sides, too.

Guest profiles are one positive aspect. Vast amounts of information can be gathered about guests who must report in and signal their travel patterns in order to get posted for the prizes. Frequent-guest prizes are what entice guest loyalty, and it is the direct-mail contact to interested participants that entices the chains into the program. Having the demographic and preferential profiles of their guests is the trade-off to the hotels. Several boast membership rosters of 2 million names.

Gifts range from the simple to the expensive. Many are services that are available even to nonmembers under certain circumstances. Among them are check cashing, room upgrade, daily newspaper, late check out, express check in and check out, toll-free reservation number, and guaranteed rates. Other gifts are specials: room

Typical Frequent Guest Programs (FGPs) Used by American Hotel Chains

Hotel Company	FGP Name	Date FPG Launched	Approximate Number of Hotels/Rooms[a]	Airline Partnerships
Bass (Holiday)	Priority Club	1993	2,500/350,000[b]	Yes
Best Western	Gold Crown Club	1988	3,750/300,000	No
Hyatt	Gold Passport	1987	100/25,000	Yes
La Quinta	Returns	1989	250/32,000	No
Marriott	Honored Guests[c]	1983	1,500/325,000[d]	Yes
Sheraton	Sheraton Club	1986	500/175,000[e]	Yes
Super 8	V.I.P.	1986	1,750/102,000	No

[a]The dynamics of acqustions, consolidations, and sales limit names and numbers to best estimates at the time of publication.
[b]Without Inter-Continental's FGP figures.
[c]Changing to Marriott Rewards, which was started in 1993.
[d]Without Ritz-Carlton's FGP figures.
[e]Without Starwood's (Sheraton's parent company) FGP figures.

Exhibit 2–6 Frequent-guest programs (FGPs) are popular marketing tools with almost every hotel chain, because they provide important demographic information about their member/customers. Brand names for FGPs add further confusion to the babble of new hotel names and logos.

discounts, discounts with travel partners such as airlines, auto-rental companies, or local tourist companies; health club membership; and free accommodations in exotic destinations. Tie-ins with credit-card companies often mean double or triple points earned.

Some hotels give travel-related awards like those just discussed. Others, sensing the guest's travel fatigue, offer premiums instead. U.S. savings bonds, upscale gifts from special catalogs, and memberships in national organizations have all been tried. Travelers really get motivated to rack up points when a Jaguar is on the gift list! Below the surface is an ethical issue. Should the hotel issue bonds, gifts, and awards to the guest when the room rate is paid by a third party, the traveler's company?

FGPs can be seen as win–win situations. Guests win with prizes and discounts. Hotels win with improved marketing capabilities. FGPs can also be seen as win–lose propositions, just another form of giveaway. It is more likely, however, that hard-core FGP participants are actually paying premiums to participate in the programs. FGPs are favored by executives on expense accounts. So the companies paying the bills may look less favorably at the premiums paid to participate.

Some critics suggest that FGPs are like hotel swimming pools. They need to be visible but are used by relatively few customers. Despite the costs and the problems, no one is daring enough to close a program. The hotel chain that first cancels its FGP will have some brave, and some say foolish, executives. Airlines with their FFPs are caught in the same dilemma. In fact, it was the chairman of American Airlines, Robert Crandall, who invented FFPs. The solution remains elusive for both industries. Amenity creep has crept in.

▶***The New Amenities.*** Except in five-star properties, opulent bathroom amenities have lost favor with both guests and innkeepers. As discussed earlier, products such as toothbrushes, combs, cotton balls, and deodorant soaps were deemphasized during the last down-cycle. Most hotels still make these extras available through the housekeeper, but only on request. Even the biggies like the Waldorf-Astoria have eliminated in-room shoehorns and sewing kits, historical amenities. The downward shift in toiletries carried over to the contents of in-room bars and refrigerators. After expensive candies, nuts, and drinks, including nonalcoholic beverages, were ignored by cost-conscious travelers, hotels shifted to more popular-priced brands.

Traditional amenities have been replaced with newer amenities that correspond more closely to the market niche of individual properties and chains. More practical amenities such as hair dryers and in-room coffee makers, a favorite among women guests, have returned to hotel rooms regardless of the market segment.

To the business traveler especially, electronic support is the best amenity of all. High-tech in-room electronics range from the almost frivolous to the absolutely essential. Special bedside panels fall into the first category. From the bed, guests control lighting and temperature, radio and television, electric-powered draperies, and do-not-disturb signals on the corridor door. It's fun, but not essential. Viewed as far more important are in-room faxes with dual telephone lines, in-room computers or at least data ports, electronic check in and check out, in-room films on call at any hour, electronic keys, and private in-room telephone voice mail messages.

After studying its guest profile, Hyatt began installing those very amenities. Business travelers are provided with in-room fax, telephone access without fees, printers and copiers, an express breakfast, and workstations. By no means is Hyatt the exception. Electronic amenities are on the march everywhere there is the slightest chance of attracting businesspersons.

Each hotel has its own version of an amenity. One offers a pet for company overnight; another a free shoeshine; a third, a jogging map. Alarm clocks promote a good night's sleep (the guest needs confidence they'll go off). To aid cocooning, the restless guest has new pillow styles and mattresses types, better black-out drapes, and equipment that masks noise or provides soothing, lullaby sounds. What about a free telephone call home to reassure the family?

Environmentally friendly amenities help the hotel even as they appeal to the "green" guest. Refillable soap or shampoo dispensers reduce waste from soap bars and plastic bottles. Water, cleaning products, and energy can be saved, and hotel expenses reduced, by reusing sheets and towels for an extra day (see Exhibit 2–7).

Exhibit 2–7 Conservation makes good sense: good ecological sense and good economic sense because of savings in water and energy consumption and linen wear, among others.

A New Look at an Old Amenity.   Food service is the oldest amenity of innkeeping. Yet hotel dining rooms are not favored by the traveling public today and they certainly are not profitable for the host hotel. Nevertheless, industry watchers were amazed when first the motels and economy hotels and then the all-suites eliminated restaurants. Many felt it to be a poor business decision. After all, travelers had to eat. The decision proved to be just the opposite, because alternatives were offered.

All-suite hotels provided free breakfasts, the Continental plan of Chapter 1, and the one meal that almost all travelers take in the hotel. Indeed, several surveys indicate that breakfast is one amenity for which guests are willing to pay extra. Those hotels without foodservice, chiefly economy properties, solved the problem by locating near freestanding restaurants.

Hotels have entered into partnerships, some with formal and some with informal agreements, with either national restaurant chains or well-reputed local operators. Often the result is a cluster. Three, four, or five brand-name hotels are built around the brand-name restaurant. (Howard Johnson tried this idea without success as early as the 1950s.) Working with these neighboring restaurants to accommodate their guests, even with room service in some cases, hotels are able to close nonprofitable food outlets and improve their earnings picture.

The next move, one that is going on right now, was to invite these independent restaurants into the hotel building. Larger hotels have done that. Hamburger, chicken, and pizza franchises have opened in the lobbies—usually with street access also—of some very major hotels. Not only do they offer the type of foodservice that today's traveler prefers, but they pay rent as well!

Even hoteliers who have not given up their dining facilities have borrowed a page from the successful restauranteurs. Pizza and other fast foods are being offered by hotels. Some are using catchy new names, while others are holding onto corporate logos.

►*Nonguest Buyers.*   The price paid for many hotel rooms is negotiated by persons (usually legal persons, companies and corporations) who are not guests and have no intention of becoming guests. Similarly, many rooms are sold to persons who never occupy them! These "nonguest" buyers act as intermediaries for the actual occupants. In later chapters, which deal with reservations and room rates, we sharpen the distinctions. Nonguest buyers are part of the modern marketing structure that has developed as a means of selling hotel rooms. Of course, each layer adds costs that must be recovered in the room rate. Nonguest buyers add an additional layer of organization between the hotel and the guest/occupant. As a result, hotels are not selling hotel rooms as much as they are trying to buy guests from these new marketing channels.

Because of their negotiating strength, nonguest buyers pay less for their rooms than do regular guests. Groups such as the American Automobile Association (AAA) and the American Association of Retired Persons (AARP) haggle with hotel chains over price. They obtain special rates for their members, although the hotel doesn't know who those members are until they arrive and claim the room. So widespread is the practice that almost every hotel entertains the request for discount, whether negotiated or not, in order to stay competitive.

Special travel clubs—Amoco Traveler and Encore Travel Club are among the best known—have arranged similar discounts for their members. The clubs specialize in second-night-free deals.

Another side of the reservation picture paints the third party as a buyer, not merely a rate negotiator. Business travel arrangements are often made by company travel desks, which may or may not be part of the traveler's business. Either way, paring travel costs is the mission of these tough negotiators. The range of third-party buyers is broadened further by the list that is detailed in the next section of the chapter. Group tours, incentive firms, and wholesalers are making huge space commitments, but someone else actually uses the room.

Similarly, travel agents commit the hotel to room bookings—but the travel agents don't come; their clients do. Franchisees rely heavily on the franchise reservation system, but the system is just another third party, which may not be owned even by the franchisor! In every instance, the guest who actually arrives is different from the third party who made the reservation.

Airlines and auto-rental companies are also in the business of booking reservations. New companies are springing up locally, nationally, and internationally to reserve, buy, and resell hotel rooms. Each of these interposes a third party between the guest and the hotel. Allied with the broader picture of third-party buyers are the numerous frequent-guest programs that were reviewed earlier.

Marketing to the Group

Seeking out and servicing group business is one of the major distinctions between modern hotelkeeping and the historic wayside inn. Selling hotel space, which is a post–World War II activity, concentrates on attracting group business. One group sale secures dozens, hundreds, or even thousands of room nights. With group business, the hotel is a destination site, rather than a transient accommodation. As with individual travelers, groups come both as tourists (leisure guests) and as businesspersons (commercial guests).

▶ *Tourist/Leisure Guests.*   Rising disposable income and broader travel horizons have made travel appealing to every level of society. As the relative cost of travel and accommodations decline, the market potential grows ever larger. The travel and hotel industries have finally embarked on the same kind of mass production that has brought increased efficiency to the manufacturing industries. The delay was unavoidable because the large hotel is of recent origin, and only the large hotel is interested in and able to service large groups.

The Tour Package.   A new entrepreneur, the wholesaler—another party, another nonguest buyer—has emerged in the past 25 years to handle the mass movement of leisure guests. Entrepreneurs are risk takers, and wholesalers are certainly that! Wholesalers buy blocks of rooms (commitments to take so many rooms for so many nights) from the hotel, blocks of seats from the airlines, and blocks of seats from the bus company. Then the wholesalers try to sell their packages, which now include transportation, ground handling, and baggage along with whatever else they are able to get without cost from the hotel (see Exhibit 2–8).

Quantity buying gives the wholesaler a good airline price. Special room and meal rates are negotiated with the hotel under the same umbrella—quantity discounts. With the promise of year-round, back-to-back charters, the hotel sales manager and accountant sharpen their pencils. One sale books hundreds of rooms. One correspondence confirms all the reservations. One billing closes the books. There is no commission to credit-card companies, and there is a minimum loss from bad debts. It is a bargain buy for the traveler, a profitable venture for the wholesaler, and a basic occupancy for the hotel, which also gets free advertising.

Exhibit 2–8 Sample of print advertising used by tour operators to sell packaged vacations, priced at less than the sum of the individual parts because of quantity purchases and guarantees that put the wholesaler at risk. *Courtesy of MLT Vacations, Minnetonka, Minnesota.*

Mass marketing has introduced many new customers to travel. Some have come despite the lack of individual service and attention. Others might have come because of it: Inexperienced travelers find comfort in the safety and security of the group; experienced travelers find irrefutable savings.

Group tours are packaged in a variety of wrappings, some reminiscent of the old American plan. Transportation, room, food, beverage, entertainment, tips, and baggage handling are offered for one fixed price. Sometimes, the wholesaler can sell the "package" for less than the guest could buy the airfare alone. That's because the wholesaler has bought seats and rooms at sharp discounts.

The wholesaler also benefits from *breakage*. Every guest does not use every part of the package. Some may not play golf. Others may not use the drink coupon in the lounge. Others may skip the buffet that is included in the package in preference for a specialty meal that they pay for separately. If the guest does not use the service, the hotel is not paid. Still, the item was computed in setting the package price. That small gain per guest, multiplied by many guests, accrues to the wholesaler as breakage.

Mass packaging enables the customer to buy the services at a fraction of their separate, individual costs. But there is a loss of guest identity. Even the hotel feels a reduced responsibility when guests deal through third parties.

Almost any destination hotel can host a tourist group if it can attract the group to the site. It must meet the price of a very competitive market to appeal to the wholesaler. And it must be large enough to accommodate the group and still handle its other guests. Hotels in out-of-the-way places cater to bus groups. They're a broader market because the number of guests is smaller and almost any hotel can handle them. With bus tours, hotels provide a mix of destination and transient service.

The Inclusive Tour (IT) Package.   First, an explanatory note. This IT package is marketed to individual guests. Therefore, it should have been discussed under that topic, "Marketing to the Individual Guest." It has been repositioned here as part of "Marketing to the Group" because it is best understood as a modification of the wholesaler's IT package, the tour package just discussed. Unlike the wholesaler's IT package, which requires numerous buyers to make it profitable, the hotel's IT package is directed toward the individual couple or small group of friends.

The popularity of the wholesaler's IT package did not escape the notice of hoteliers. "Why give all the profits to the wholesaler?" hotel managers asked. Because wholesale tour packages are very risky, involving air and land transportation costs outside the hotel's control, hotel ITs eliminate the transportation, and with it the risk. What is left is exactly what the hotel normally packages for the wholesaler. Hotels now sell hotel tour packages, no transportation, which they sweeten with free extras not normally made available to the wholesaler. The basics remain in the hotel's package: room, meals, drinks. Hotel packages add "free" use of the tennis court (or putting green, swimming pool, playground, shuffleboard, or table tennis, etc.) and free admission to the theater (or formal garden, exhibit, animal habitat, spas, or exhibition matches, etc.). The products that the hotel includes look even better if small fees are normally paid for such services or admissions. Casino hotels often include one free play on the tables.

With ITs of its own, breakage accrues to the hotel, not to the wholesaler, who is no longer in the picture. Both wholesalers and hotels market directly to the public through the media (see Exhibit 2–9). At other times they sell through travel agents. Then, of course, the travel agency collects its standard 10% commission. Since packages do not separate room charges from other charges, the commission is paid on the

Exhibit 2–9   Hotels offer packaged vacations, similar to the wholesalers' but without transportation. Hotel packages compete with individual room sales, so they are offered and withdrawn as occupancy dictates under yield-management systems.

full value of the package, whereas normally, the commission is paid on the room rate only.

One hotel may offer several packages. Each package (a weekend package, a winter package, a golf package, and so on) is aimed toward a different market niche and includes different items at various prices. Hotel ITs must be marketed carefully because the hotel competes with itself. IT packages are discounted rooms with extra services at lower prices than the room alone sells for. Later chapters dealing with yield management and room rates raise again this issue of self-competition.

➤*Business/Commercial Guests.*   Our fondness for forming into groups has produced an astonishing number of organizations. People come together under many umbrellas: business, union, fraternal, social, historical, veteran, health and medical, educational, religious, scientific, political, service, athletic, and on without end. For short, the industry uses the acronym SMURF: societies, medical, university, religious, fraternal. Each classification translates into numerous organizations, societies, clubs, and associations. Each of them meets, holds shows, and stages conventions. Functioning at local, state, regional, national, and international levels, these groups offer business to a variety of destination facilities.

Conventions.   Conventioneers assemble to promote their common purposes. These aims are as diverse as the list of associations that hold conventions (see Exhibit 5–12). During the gathering of two, three, or four days, papers, meetings, speeches, and talks are given on a range of topics. Some are professional and some merely entertaining. The members also interact individually, discussing common goals and problems. Professional conventions may serve as formal or informal job-placement forums.

Both urban and resort properties vie for convention business as the growth of mixed-use facilities spreads. To be competitive, the convention hotel must provide a range of self-contained facilities. Meeting space with appropriate furnishings and equipment and food facilities large enough to accommodate the groups at banquets are the minimum facilities needed. Conventioneers are a captive audience for the program and the planned activities. The more complete the property, the more appealing the site.

Sports activities, a change of scenery, and isolation from the hubbub of busy cities are touted by a resort's sales department. Urban properties respond with theaters, museums, and historical locations. Urban areas may have the advantage of publicly financed convention halls.

Hotels sometimes combine facilities with those of nearby competitors when the convention size is too large for one property. Although not the rule, conventions of 50,000 to 100,000 delegates have been recorded, usually when combined with trade shows.

Trade Shows.   Trade shows are exhibits of product lines shown by purveyors to potential buyers. Conventions and trade shows are often held together. Shows require a great deal of space, particularly if the displays are large pieces of machinery or equipment (see Exhibit 2–10). Space requirements and the difficulty of handling such products limit shows to a small number of hotels. The city convention bureau has a role here. It builds halls to accommodate the exhibits, leaving the housing and guest service to the local hotels.

Exhibits of small goods (a perfume show or a jewelry show are two examples) can be housed almost anywhere. They do not need public convention halls of 1,000,000 and more square feet. Hotels with limited exhibit space can still accommodate trade shows by carefully choosing what market segments to pursue. Although less common, assigning several sleeping floors to such a trade show and converting guest rooms into individual exhibit spaces is still done by hotels with no dedicated meeting areas. Then the exhibitor occupies the exhibit room as a registered guest.

The Single Entity.   The single entity group is neither a tour package nor a convention/trade show. As its name implies, *single entity* has an adhesive that binds its members together. Attendees already belong to "the" group (a company, an orchestra, a college football team) before they come to the hotel. The unit (the company, the or-

Exhibit 2–10   Hotels and convention centers accommodate trade shows that sometimes number tens of thousands of delegates. Consider the economic impact on a community if each delegate spends approximately $700 daily for three or four days! *Courtesy of the Albuquerque Convention and Visitor's Bureau, Albuquerque, New Mexico.*

chestra, the college football team) makes the reservation, and the unit pays the bill. The single entity stays together during the engagement: They hold meetings; they perform; they play ball.

The tour group offers a contrast. Tour group members have no previous relationships; they come together only for the trip. Each member pays the wholesaler a share of the cost; by contrast, with an entity, the single entity pays costs, not the individual members/players. The tour group dissolves after the trip; not so, the single entity. The hotel negotiates with the (team) manager of the single entity, himself a team member, whereas the tour group negotiator is a businessperson out for profit. Both commit to a block (group) of rooms, and both pay for that block.

Similar differences exist with convention/trade shows. Convention attendees represent a wide range of companies or associations. Their only likeness is their common interest in the subject matter. There is no single entity. Each conventioneer comes and goes without concern for the schedule of other delegates, whom he or she probably doesn't even know. The room block has been made by an organizer, often a trade show manager or association president, but each attendee makes his or her own individual reservation, and each pays the hotel his or her own bill.

Although the visiting athletic team is the best example of a single entity, hotels cater to a wide range of other groups. There are company sales and technical meetings, new product line showings, traveling concert groups, annual high-school graduation trips, and others. Hotel/casinos have their own form of the single entity, the gambling junket. High-rollers are brought in to the hotel for several days of entertainment and play.

Incentive Tours.   Incentive tours are special kinds of single entities. Many businesses run incentive programs to encourage sales and production workers to improve output. A cash bonus, a prize, or an incentive trip—for example, a free vacation for two to a destination resort—is the reward for those who meet the announced goals.

Hotels like to book incentive tours because all the participants are winners and only the best accommodations are chosen. Unfortunately, the deals for these facilities are frequently negotiated through intermediaries—incentive (tour) companies, which have emerged as still another nonguest buyer in the sale and distribution of hotel rooms. Incentive companies negotiate for hotel rooms and deliver them to clients, the companies holding the incentive programs. Often, the incentive companies are also the consultants handling the clients' incentive programs.

Incentive companies represent many client–enterprises. This gives the incentive companies a great deal of leverage when they negotiate with the hotel. Everyone bargains tough when accommodations for several groups are at stake. It is the very same pressure that hotels experience when dealing with the quantity purchases of the tour-package companies. Price and quality are the differences: Cost is critical for the wholesaler, quality for the incentive buyer.

Tours, be they single entity, incentive, or as yet unnamed, are the group markets of tomorrow. One can foresee a growth of vertical integration with one large holding company owning the means of transportation, reservation system, tour wholesaler, incentive company, and hotel/resort. U.S. airlines might move in that direction again if the airline recovery continues. (At one time, U.S. railroads and later the nation's airlines owned numerous hotels. These destination hotels hosted the guests that the transportation companies were trying to promote as passengers.) JAL and ANA, both Japanese carriers, have owned destination hotels for some time. The incentive is simply profits. One hotel room sold as part of an integrated sale that includes travel agent, airline, hotel, and entertainment fees is worth many times more than a single room sale made by a stand-alone hotel.

➤ NEW OWNERSHIP PATTERNS

The changes in guests and markets that have been reviewed in the first half of this chapter have taken place at the same time that the industry has undergone major shifts in ownership structures and methods of raising money. New management patterns, discussed in the final section of the chapter, have appeared as well, adding to the dynamics of the industry.

The State of the Industry

Historically, the inn was a family affair with the host–guest relationship paramount. That circumstance began to change after World War II (early 1950s) when ownership and management became separate activities. Those who owned the hotel did not operate it. Those who operated the hotel did not own it! As the separation widened, the famous hotel chains concentrated on managing both their own hotels and those belonging to others. Those others, who actually owned the buildings and the lands on which the hotels stood, were concerned more with the hotels as properties, pieces of real estate. Income taxes, depreciation, rent, and financing are more important to owners than are day-to-day operational problems. That difference brought huge changes in the lodging industry.

➤*From Turmoil to Health.*   In Chapter 1 we highlighted the poor economic period (1981–1991) that hurt the industry for a dozen years. Actually, the hotel real estate business has been in turmoil for more like 25 years, beginning in the early 1970s when real estate speculators set sights on the hotel industry.

The experience was worldwide. It was caused by a unhappy combination of low customer demand and high interest rates. Hotel owners were unable to pay off their huge debts, which included high interest rates, because revenues were falling. The industry had entered one of the down cycles outlined in Chapter 1. The situation was fostered in the United States by special income-tax benefits, which Congress then eliminated. Good room sales were needed to pay off the loans from expensive real estate transactions. But as occupancy fell (too many rooms and too few customers), so did rates. Hotel buyers were unable to meet the interest and loan repayments demanded by the banks. Estimates approximate that two-thirds of all hotel properties were in some level of financial distress.

As one real estate deal after another collapsed, so did the banking industry, which provided the loans. (All real estate, not just the hotel industry, suffered during this period of overbuilding and overspeculation.) With no payment flow, the banks were as badly off as the real estate investors. America's savings and loan associations (banks) obtained the money to make these bad loans from their depositors. These depositors were insured by the Federal Deposit Insurance Corporation (FDIC), an agency of the federal government. As a result of the credit emergency, hotels (and other real estate, too) that were unable to meet their bank obligations ended up in the hands of a new federal agency established to bail out the sick banks. This Resolution Trust Corporation (RTC) assumed control of the banks and began selling off the sick hotels, which were security for the loans. It was a fire sale—hotels were sold at substantial discounts from the original loan values. Although it hurt a great many hotel owners, it helped speed the recovery!

The recovery brought optimism to hoteliers for the first time in better than a decade. Business travel was increasing and occupancy improving. Low inflation kept borrowing costs and operating expenses steady. Most important of all, distressed hotels had either gone out of business (reducing supply) or had been repurchased during bankruptcy sales at low per-room costs. This meant lower debt and easier repayment of the mortgage loan even if sales were flat—which they weren't; demand actually increased. Since repentant lenders and disappointed speculators had not yet rushed back in to build, room supply was restricted. With increased demand and restricted supply, room rates as well as room occupancy began rising. The industry was healthy again.

The turnaround from the early 1990s until today is startling. Lodging staged a comeback to heady profits from near disaster (see Exhibit 1–4). Lower operating costs reduced the industry's break-even point from the low 60s to the mid-50 range (55 to 58% annual occupancy). Profits have soared, so the industry is getting ready to recycle upward again. New construction is accelerating and new financing money is pouring in. Hotels have come to the attention of investors once again.

Estimates suggest that 100,000 or so rooms are being added each year. Economy hotels and extended-stay properties felt the first wave of new construction. Rising demand soon focused construction on high-cost upscale hotels with higher ADRs. Warnings about overbuilding have begun to sound, if not in general at least for specific locations.

This time there is one new element that was not present before: aggressive trading on the stock market. Once considered the worst form of investment, the lodging industry had become a publicly traded darling. With high-priced stocks and eager investors, hotel companies finally had the means to consolidate.

➤*A Consolidating Industry.*   Even as hotel chains expand their market lines, they consolidate their ownership interests (see Exhibit 2–11). The big guys get bigger, all made possible because of low borrowing costs and high-priced share values on the stock market. The stock market's evaluation of the hotel industry increased 500% during the latter part of the 1990s. As more hotel shares are traded, investors become more knowledgeable about the lodging industry and participation increases, pushing prices still higher. With share values high, hotel companies are positioned to buy other hotel companies with shares, instead of cash, as their currency. Little of the financing needed for this wave of consolidations comes from debt, and where it is used, the cost of borrowing is small.

Buyer	Companies Acquired	
Cendant (by merger of Hospitality Franchise Systems and CUC International, Inc.)	Days Inn Knights Inn Ramada Inns Super 8 Villager Lodges	Howard Johnson PHH Corporation Resort Condominiums Travelodge Wingate Inns
Hilton Hotels	Bally Entertainment Corporation Grand Casinos	
Marriott	New World Hotels Ramada International Renaissance Hotel Group Ritz-Carlton Hotel Company	
Patriot America[a]	Arcadian CalJockey ClubHouse Inns Grand Heritage Hotels Registry WHG Resorts and Casinos	Carefree Resorts Carnival Hotels and Resorts Glencom American Interstate Hotels Summerfield Suites Hotels Wyndham Hotel Corp.
Promus	Club Hotels Doubletree Hotels and Suites Harrison Conference Associates Red Lion Hotels and Inns	
Starwood REIT	HEI Hotels ITT Corporation (Sheraton, CIGA, and Caesars World) W Hotels Westin	

[a]Paired-shared REIT.

Exhibit 2–11   Small sample of the numerous mergers, takeovers, and consolidations that have altered the lodging industry since 1997. The situation is very dynamic; all brands may not be listed and some listings may no longer be accurate.

As we shall see a few topics ahead, real estate investment trusts (REITs) have been major players in the consolidation movement. The REIT emerged as a new concept in hotel real estate and contributed measurably to the rising price of hotel company stocks.

Acquiring other hotel chains is important to stock market evaluations, but consolidation is more than a stock market game. Consolidation promises economies of scale and larger marketing and distribution networks for the chains. Growth comes faster and flashier from acquisitions than from internal growth. Buying instead of building produces immediate increases in revenues. It also makes good business sense. Acquiring hotels from an existing company costs less than building new ones. To purchase that amount of real estate means amassing the large amounts of capital that consolidation and REITs provide.

Although many good reasons exist for consolidation, there is also a less rational one. Corporate executives are afraid to stand still lest they be taken over. "Acquire or be acquired!" Consolidation has dislocated many executives, so there is plenty of good talent around. Whether that talent can integrate the culture of a large hotel company into the culture of an acquiring hotel company is still unclear. Yet that may be essential for operational success, and hence for the long-range financial stability that consolidation supporters anticipate. Maybe the vertical integration just discussed under the topic of "Incentive Tours" will be an unexpected result of the consolidation movement.

Hotel companies, even consolidated ones, look tiny when compared to international giants such as Coca-Cola. Still, the larger scale of a consolidated company makes it easier to compete internationally. International operations are of great importance these days, especially when selling to group buyers who are themselves scattered across the globe. Some consolidation took place during the 1980s, but it was chiefly by international buyers coming to the United States in order to gain broader geographic diversification.

► *The Global Village.*   The appearance of the global village (shorthand for "shrinking political differences and interlocking economic activity worldwide") has encouraged business interests to cross national borders and major oceans. Innkeeping has participated along with almost every other type of business. Consolidation is caused, in part, by the realities of the global marketplace.

The direction of business flow often depends on the value of international currencies. Foreign investors who want to buy U.S. hotels need to have U.S. dollars. Before they can buy the hotels, they must buy the dollars. When the dollar is weak, fewer units of the strong foreign currency are needed to buy the necessary greenbacks. This makes the purchase price an attractive bargain to international buyers with strong currencies.

What goes around, comes around. After World War II (1950s), the U.S. dollar was the world's premium currency. That made foreign hotels inexpensive to American buyers, so U.S. chains went overseas. Twenty-five years later (late-1970s) the situation reversed. The dollar had weakened, so foreign chains saw great bargains and entered the U.S. hotel market. Twenty years later (late-1990s), the situation reversed again and U.S. hotelkeepers were active internationally once more.

There is more to global participation than currencies. Companies go international to acquire a foothold on another continent, to acquire assets (management talent or reservation systems) that they do not yet have, and to open new markets for their brands. Political stability is still another factor. Foreign investors may face serious financial loss from political uncertainty and upheaval in their own lands. Better to invest in the United States even if the purchase price is high or the chance of loss significant. At least, there is no political risk—the U.S. government is not likely to confiscate or nationalize the hotel. Furthermore, international investors differentiate, even more than U.S. developers, between the hotel as an operating company and the hotel as a piece of real estate. Buying the hotel to get the real estate is a long-run view, and international companies have a longer business horizon than do domestic companies.

Global Village Examples. Hotel companies compete in a vast arena that stretches in every direction across the globe. European hotel companies are in North America, North American companies in Asia, and Asian companies are in Europe. There are many examples of this global outreach. Here are three at which to marvel.

Four Seasons Hotels is a premium brand of North America, based in Toronto, Canada. Twenty-five percent of the company is owned by a prince of Saudi Arabia. (The prince also owns controlling interests in other hotel chains, including Fairmont Hotels.) Four Seasons took control of the Regent Chain, an Asia operation whose quality brand equals or exceeds that of Four Seasons. Four years later, Radisson (Hotels) Hospitality Worldwide (Minneapolis) acquired use of the Regent name through a joint venture with Four Seasons. Both Four Seasons and Radisson will continue to develop the Regent brand. North America, the Middle East, and Asia were wrapped into one deal over a very brief period.

Stouffer Hotels, which was based in Ohio, owned and operated upscale hotels across North America. Stouffer was acquired by Nestlé, a Swiss company. The 15,000-room chain was later sold by Nestlé to the Hong Kong–based Cheng Yu-Tung family, which also owned a controlling interest in New World Development Company. New World, a large hotel conglomerate, based in Hong Kong, was the parent company of a one-time U.S. chain, Ramada Inns. Ramada had an upscale brand, Renaissance Hotels. The upscale Renaissance properties fit Stouffer's image, but Renaissance was better known outside the United States. New World folded Stouffer into Renaissance and the Stouffer brand disappeared. More recently, Marriott International (Washington, DC) outbid Doubletree Inns (Phoenix) and purchased the Renaissance Group. Over several years, the deals involved North America, Europe, and Asia.

Case 3 involves two very well–known brands, Holiday Inn and Inter-Continental. Holiday Inn acquired Harrah's, a gaming company, in the 1980s. It then created a gaming division named Promus, which also took control of Holiday Inn's Homewood Suites, Embassy Suites, and Hampton Inns. At that time, 1990, Holiday Inn (later called Holiday Hospitality) sold the Holiday name and the remaining hotels to Bass PLC. Bass is Great Britain's largest brewer and the owner/operator of numerous hotels. Recently, Holiday Inn (Bass) acquired Inter-Continental Hotels, adding the upscale brand that Bass sorely needed to round out the chain, which it renamed Bass Hotels and Resorts. Inter-Continental has its own story.

Inter-Continental was owned originally by Pan American Airlines. In need of cash, Pan Am sold the chain to Grand Metropolitan of Great Britain, a Bass competitor. Soon thereafter it went to Scandinavian Airline System (SAS) and to the Japanese retail and leisure conglomerate Seibu Saison Group, who sold it to Bass some time later. Undoubtedly, the strength of the British currency and the weakness of the Japanese currency contributed to the timing (1998) of the Bass/Saison deal. Parents to Inter-Continental have been the Americans, the English, the Japanese, and the Scandinavians. Talking global, Inter-Continental, with nearly 200 hotels including its Forum Hotels division, operates in 60 countries!

By no means is globalization limited to the hotel segment of the leisure industry. Many airlines and travel agencies have intraglobal connections. The marketplace demands it. Over 100,000 U.S. corporate groups (about one-half of which are involved in incentive travel) meet overseas annually! Still unclear is the impact of the new European currency, the euro, on overseas travel and global investment.

Name changes have kept pace with the growth of the overseas movement. Best Western became Best Western International, and Quality Inns became Quality International and then Choice Hotels International. Even without the global terminology, hotels operate easily across national borders, and the flow goes both ways. For example, two Paris-based companies have spread internationally—Accor and Club Med into some three dozen countries each. Spain's Occidental Hotels are in a dozen lands, and Brussels-based SAS International Hotels are in about the same number.

Ownership and Financing Alternatives

Management of the hotel has not always been separate from ownership of the hotel building. Early inns were family homesteads, and the buildings were under the control of the innkeepers. They ran things in a rather dictatorial way. Building larger hotels required larger sums of money, far beyond the means of most families. So there was a gradual separation of the hotel asset from traditional individual ownership. The initial step was the creation of the modern corporation. Of recent times, financing hotels has become a very creative undertaking.

▶*Individual Ownership.*   There are still plenty of individually owned hotels. Best Western International is an affiliation of individual hotel owners. Owning a single hotel or even several hotels is not the same as maintaining a family homestead. Physically, of course, the family doesn't live there, but more to the point, the financing rarely comes from within the family. There are instances still when loans to build or buy come from the extended family: uncles and aunts; cousins and grandparents. More often, the money is borrowed from public sources.

The small, local hotel may get equity (ownership) money from prominent professional and businesspersons, who want to invest both for profit and community pride. Investment groups, entrepreneurs, hotel companies, and franchise companies are examples of the more likely investors. In all cases, investors seek borrowed money to complete the deal. Small business loans can be financed through local and regional banks. Under the federal government's Small Business Administration and the Department of Agriculture's Business and Industry Loan Guarantee Program, a federal guarantee is possible for some portion of the loan. Small borrowers can find loan money more easily when 80% or so is guaranteed to the lending bank.

As projects grow larger, more equity money is needed and the effort shifts from Main Street to Wall Street. The public corporation becomes the likely source of invested capital and the means by which borrowed capital is obtained. Large amounts of borrowed money rely on bigger, money-center banks or on insurance companies or pension funds. Some pension funds invest directly, others do so through mutual funds. As reviewed earlier, foreign investors are always a possibility. The 1980s–1990s downturn in hotel prices saw companies that normally only franchise begin to buy and own—Choice Hotels, for example. Within a few brief years, a new financing vehicle emerged to take hold of the real estate market, the real estate investment trust.

▶*Real Estate Investment Trusts.*   Real estate investment trusts (REITs) raise the funds with which to acquire hotel (or apartment, office building, health care, etc.) real estate as much from the stock market as from borrowed money. REITs do not pay federal income tax, so they must pay out 95% of taxable income to their shareholders. That's appealing to individual investors, who bid up the stock market price of REIT shares as they scramble to buy. Using the high-priced shares, REITs can go into the real estate market and buy real estate. Essentially, they trade their shares for the (hotel) real estate. Selling shares raises cash, which is also used to buy hotel properties.

There is another restriction on REITs. No less than 95% of gross income must come from certain sources, including rent. Room, food, and beverage sales are business revenues, not rents. Therefore, REITs cannot operate hotels; instead, REITs rent the property to the hotel managing company. But then the REIT doesn't control the hotel's operation. So the REIT forms its own hotel management company, which is a traditional corporation (referred to as a C-Corporation), that does pay income tax. The two work hand in glove, because the REIT owns the building and the management company owns and directs the operations.

There are four unusual REITs that were grandfathered in under the 1984 tax law. These REITs, called *pair-shared REITs,* are permitted to mix rents with room, food, and beverage sales, and still not pay federal income tax. What an advantage! It was that edge which enabled the pair-shared REIT Starwood to outbid Hilton Hotels Corporation in 1997 for the purchase of Sheraton Hotels. There were two such REITs in the hotel field, but Starwood Lodging elected to give up its advantage after Congress passed unfavorable legislation in 1998 (see Exhibit 2–11). Shareholders of pair-shared REITs have one set of shares since there is but one company to own.

Pair-shared REITs have a close cousin in *paper-clip REITs.* Paper-clip REITs must keep separate the real estate and managing arms of the company. But they establish intercompany agreements that have managers, and board-of-director members serve in both companies. This enables the two separate companies to make decisions as if they were one. Equally important is the savings in management fees since the REIT pays its partner, not an outside management company. Still, one company is taxed as a REIT and the other as a C-Corporation. In total, there are about 15 hotel REITs, including regular REITs, paired-REITs, and paper-clip REITs.

►*Condominiums and Timeshares.* Both condominiums and timeshares have their origins in destination resorts. Condos, which predate timeshare intervals by some 20 years, are an American invention. Timeshares originated in Europe, but North America is a far larger market now. Ski resorts such as Aspen and Tahoe were the birthplaces of condo developments. U.S. timeshares began in the sunshine coasts of Florida and Hawaii. Both segments are in a pattern of consolidation similar to the pattern driving the hotel industry. Moreover, there's a shift taking place in consumer preferences. Buyers are investing more heavily in interval ownerships now that the unethical practices of timesharing have been addressed. They are switching from permanent condo owners to part-time interval owners. As that shift takes place, the interests of the hotel industry change from occasional managers to active developers.

Condominium Ownership. Despite some surface similarities, there are differences in the two options. The confusion comes from their physical appearance. They look alike. Condominium units were first offered as real estate purchases, and they are that still. As real estate, condos were nurtured in an income-tax environment that no longer exists. Today's owner buys for rental income, perhaps for hopes of real estate appreciation, most likely for personal and family use, only somewhat for tax advantages. Guests own condominiums as they own any home. Common space and common grounds are also owned, but as part of the group association. Each unit is complete with all the amenities, kitchen and general family space included. Owners furnish their units and maintain them according to personal preferences.

Since the owners are not always on-property, units are placed in a common rental pool. This requires on-site management to rent and service the units. Profits, if any, are paid to the owners on a pro rata basis. The complex might be part of a large resort facility that is operated by a well-known hotel chain or management company. Or, the condo owners might employ their own staff to operate and manage the units.

There are endless permutations to the basic plan. In its simplest form, the guest owns the condominium, reserves so many days per year for personal use, and—if the guest wishes—places the unit into the rental pool for the balance of the time.

Actually, condos are an unusual mix of functions. The owners finance the facility for the developer; then they occupy the units as guests, sometimes guests of themselves, since they also hire the management company that services their stay. Mixed use may prove to be the resort of the future. On the one property would be transient hotel rooms, all-suite extended-stay facilities, condos, and timesharing units.

Timeshare Membership.   Unlike condominium ownership, the original timeshares were not real estate purchases! One did not buy the unit and did not get a deed. One bought only *the right to use* the unit for so many days each year over some fixed period of years. Hence the term *interval ownership*. Contracts ranged from 10 to 40 years of use. At the end of the contract, the developer—not the guest who had paid and paid for many years—owned the property. In contrast, the condo buyer had title from the start. "Nondeeded" plans are still around.

Timesharing started out with a sleazy reputation. Because nondeeded sales were not considered real estate sales, the industry was not regulated in any of the 50 states. After numerous consumer complaints about misrepresentation and unethical selling methods, the real estate commissioners of the most heavily affected states began enforcing standards. That brought credibility to the industry and encouraged the entry of Disney, Hilton, Hyatt, Promus, Westin, Inter-Continental, and Four Seasons. Marriott lead the way and now even has timesharing in urban areas as well as at resorts. Despite the arrival of the big names, the vast majority of timeshares are owned by independents. As with hotels and condos, timeshare consolidation is under way.

The poor reputation of timesharing has been overcome in part by changing the name. Timeshares have become *interval ownerships, vacation clubs, vacation ownerships,* and *fractionals.* Very expensive timeshares have taken very expensive sounding names, *private residence clubs.* Names aside, timeshares remain poor real estate investments; resale is difficult. Another big negative: Coming to the same place during the same dates for 30 years has been eased with exchange clubs. ResortQuest International is among the largest. With the clubs, timeshare members are able to switch dates and locations with other timeshare holders across the globe. There is no guarantee of this, of course, and there are additional fees. Reciprocal, transferable memberships are possible with big developers who operate in several locations. Exchange options improve when the developer is a well-known chain operating globally.

The developer tries to sell each unit 50 times per year, once each week. An 80-unit timeshare might then have as many as 4,000 participants annually. For this illustration, a lucky developer could reap $80,000,000 to finance the project if all the units are presold at, say, an average price of $20,000 per unit per week. (The more desirable the period of use, in-season versus off-season versus shoulder season, the higher the initial timeshare cost.) That's a substantial amount of up-front money even if a mere percentage is sold, which is usually the case. In practice, two weeks or more is held back for maintenance. States such as California forbid the sale of a full 52 weeks. Unlike the condo, where the owner foots repair bills, timeshare repairs, services, and furnishings are supplied by the developer. Of course, additional housekeeping fees—

called T&T (that is, trash and towels)—and maintenance fees are charged during the weekly occupancy of each holder. Timeshare members are not responsible for furnishing the space, which may be nothing more than a single converted guest room. Currently, timeshare associations do not enjoy tax-exempt status.

With the legitimacy of the industry has come innovative changes. The first was the *deeded timeshare,* where buyers actually take title, just as they do with condominiums. Deeded timeshares can be resold (but not easily), gifted, exchanged, willed, or rented. They may even appreciate in value. But that is so unlikely that suggesting it to new buyers is forbidden by the American Resort Development Association, the timeshare industry's trade group. Limiting the number of participants is another idea being tested. Rather than 50 buyers per unit, the property is sold in, say, eight-week blocks to, say, six buyers. Rotating weeks is yet another innovation. It takes advantage of the two- to four-week break in the schedule. Buyers rotate throughout the years, so no one buys the best times and no one the worst. Of course, it might take a dozen years to get a one-time chance at Christmas or the Fourth of July weekend.

Timeshares and condominiums are discussed here as financing alternatives because they are sources of capital to new developers. Existing resorts can use the funds to upgrade and refurbish or to pay off outstanding debt. Sometimes, they just go into the owner's pocket. A basic occupancy from a group of permanent guests, who may now be partial owners, promises improved profits. Less advertising and possibly less housekeeping and repairs, depending on the agreement, mean savings in operations and improved profits. If kitchen facilities are provided, food and beverage costs may be reduced. If not, higher occupancy means higher F&B revenues.

Timesharing some, not all, of the facility in pieces is one option being tested by regular hotel operators. There are advantages to the seller/resort and less risk to the buyer/guest. And it may have a major impact on which way the industry develops.

➤*Joint Ventures.*   In several ways, the joint venture is similar to a partnership arranged between two or more individuals. However, with the joint venture, the individuals are one of several entities: corporations, partnerships, individuals, and even governments. For example, privately owned Radisson Hotels formed a three-way venture with the Russian Ministry for Foreign Tourism and a publicly owned U.S. business-center company, Americom. They opened the 430-room Radisson Slavjanskaya in Moscow.

Joint venture members invest in, share in, and create a new legal entity. Each participant brings its special capabilities to the joint effort: finance, marketing, operations, and so on. Since the joint venture is usually not taxed, each member reporting its own share of income, the duplicate taxation that the typical corporation faces is avoided.

Rising costs (land and construction), huge enterprises (megaresorts and developments), and specialization (finance and management) make the joint venture a perfect vehicle for the current business climate. A joint venture some years ago between Choice Hotels International and AIRCOA illustrates the point. The asset-management capabilities and real estate expertise of AIRCOA were merged with Choice's extraordinary sales, marketing, and reservation capability.

New and creative variations of the joint venture are on the horizon, hurried along by the explosion in gambling. Gaming management is a skill that new developers (Indian tribes, municipalities, and others) lack. Still, they want to retain the benefits that casino ownership represents. Joint ventures are the obvious compromise: Bring the skills and monies of the gaming management companies to the joint enterprise, while other members provide the sites, licenses, and political muscle.

➤ NEW MANAGEMENT PATTERNS

Our historical review has made clear that the era of the small innkeeper and the individual entrepreneur is waning. Erecting large, expensive buildings and competing in international markets require the management talent and the capital funding that only large, public companies—the hotel chains—can provide.

Chains

The very act of traveling evokes the unknown, the strange, the unfamiliar. Within such an environment, travelers must select a rather personal service—a bed for the night. Examining or evaluating the experience beforehand is not possible. So the hotel's reputation or its membership in a chain or affiliated group become the primary reason for the guest's selection.

Overseas, the environment is stranger still. Brand recognition is even more critical to the selection. That is why U.S. hotels developed abroad when the United States dominated the world's business scene. With international trade now more evenly balanced, foreign chains are appearing in the United States for the same reasons.

The combination of brand recognition and the inherent strengths of size and savvy management account for the chains' popularity and growth. And grow they have. The AH&MA publishes an annual *Directory of Hotel & Motel Companies* (chains). It defines a chain as any group of two or more properties operated under a common name (see Exhibit 2–12). Chain-controlled hotels now dominate the U.S. hotel industry. Some 75% of hotel rooms are under the umbrella of one chain or another. That figure was only 37% in the early 1970s, and there are almost 10,000 additional hotels today!

Modern business practices give chains an enormous operating advantage. Among their basic strengths are (1) expertise in site selection, (2) access to capital, (3) econ-

Brand	Parent
Best Western (International, Inc.)	
Choice (Hotels International)	
Days Inns (of America, Inc.)	Cendant
(Walt) Disney (World Resorts)	
Doubletree (Hotels Corporation)	Promus
Hilton (Hotel Corporation)	
Holiday Inn (Worldwide)	Bass
Hyatt (Hotels Corporation)	
Inter-Continental (Hotels and Resorts)	Bass
Marriott (Hotels, Resorts and Suites)	
Radisson (Hospitality Worldwide)	Carlson
Sheraton (Hotels, Inns, Resorts and All-Suites)	Starwood
Wyndham (Hotels and Resorts)	Patriot America

Exhibit 2–12 A baker's dozen, arranged alphabetically, of the nation's best known hotel names. Some companies *own* their hotels, some operate under *management contracts* or *lease* arrangements, and some license (*franchise*) their names. Many do all four. Some are owned by other companies.

omies of scale (purchasing, advertising, reservations, etc.), (4) appeal to the best management talent, and (5) brand recognition.

As this chapter has stressed, hotel chains are no longer hotel builders. Just as often, the builders are not the owners, and the owners are not hoteliers. So it is to the hotel chain that the builder/developers and owners turn for management skills. It is these very same skills that institutional lenders trust for the repayment of their loans. Obviously then, successful enterprises involve mutually supportive skills from several participants.

▶*Parties to the Deal.*   There are five different parties involved in the development and operation of a hotel. The confusion is compounded when one of the participants wears two or three hats. The *developer* (party number 1) sees the opportunity and puts the plan together. That developer could be one of the hotel chains, Marriott, for example. The hotel might be part of a larger development—one element in a shopping mall, or a business park, or a resort complex.

Financing is arranged from a bank, insurance company, pension plan, or other source. The *financier* is party number 2. As with all the participants, financing could come in total or in part from one or more of the other parties. The developer or the hotel management company might participate in the lending but more likely in the equity.

The equity—that is, the *ownership*—is party number 3. This party could be any of the others, a public corporation, a joint venture between one or more of the parties, or a separate entity making a passive investment.

If none of the participants is familiar to the consuming public as a hotel company, there will be no brand recognition. Then it is desirable that the group that manages the operation—the *management company* (party number 4)—have a recognizable logo. If the management company does not have a strong marketing presence, a franchise is licensed from a company (party number 5) that does (see Exhibits 2–13 and 2–14).

Company	Approximate number of:	
	Properties	Guest Rooms
American General Hospitality, Inc.	50	12,000
Beck Summit Hotel Management Group	50	10,000
Bristol Hotel Company	100	28,000
Interstate Hotels Corporation	200	43,000
John Q. Hammons Hotel, Inc.	50	13,000
Lane Hospitality	50	9,000
Larken, Inc.	25	4,000
Prime Hospitality Corporation	150	18,000
Remington Hotel Corporation	75	11,000
Richfield Hospitality Services, Inc.	125	38,000
Ritz-Carlton Hotel Company	100	23,000
Westmount Hospitality Group, Inc.	50	12,000
Winegardner & Hammons, Inc.	50	11,000

Note: The dynamics of aquisitions, consolidations, and sales limit names and numbers to best estimates at the time of publication.

Exhibit 2–13   A baker's dozen, arranged alphabetically, of the nation's best known hotel management companies. Competition has forced management companies into equity participation.

Hotel chains (see Exhibit 2–12) are likely to be a combination of all five parties. They help with development and financing, hold a piece of the ownership equity, and supply management talent. Chains provide the critical name recognition and the essential reservation system. Whereas the chain might be part of all five parties in a big development, small town projects use several different parties. The local business com-

Company	Approximate number of:	
	Properties	Guest Rooms
Americinn International, LLC (Americinn Brand Name)	100	4,000
Bass Hotels and Resorts (Crowne Plaza, Holiday Inn Brands, Inter-Continental)	2,300	400,000
Carlson Hospitality Group (Colony, Country, Radisson)	500	100,000
Cendant (Days, Howard Johnson, Knights, Ramada, Super 8, Thriftlodge, Travelodge, Wingate)	5,500	500,000
Choice Hotel International (Clarion, Comfort, EconoLodges, Friendship, MainStay, Quality, Rodeway, Sleep)	3,200	270,000
Hilton Hotel Corporation (Ballys, Conrad, Hilton)	250	100,000
Hospitality International (Downtowner, Master Hosts, Passport, Red Carpet, Scottish, Sundowner)	260	15,000
Marriott (Courtyard, Fairfield, Marriott, New World, Ramada, Residence, Ritz-Carlton)	1,300	200,000
Microtel Inns Suites Franchises, Inc. (Microtel Brand Name)	50	4,000
Promus Hotel Corporation (Club, Doubletree, Embassy, Hampton, Harrison, Homewood, Red Lion)	900	20,000
Sheraton Hotels, Inn, Resorts and All-Suites (Four Point, Sheraton)	400	125,000
Sholodge Franchise Systems, Inc. (Shoney's Brand Name)	100	10,000
Wingate Inns, L.P. (Wingate Brand Name)	50	3,000

Note: The dynamics of acquisitions, consolidations, and sales limit names and numbers to best estimates at the time of publication.

Exhibit 2–14   A baker's dozen, arranged alphabetically, of the nation's best known brand names. Name recognition enables them to license (franchise) their names. Sometimes they lease, own, and/or manage the properties as well. Some do all four. Most of the largest are owned by other companies, so they are not listed separately; among them Days, Knights, Ramada, Scottish, and Super 8.

munity may be the developer/owner but look elsewhere for the financing, the management, and the franchise.

➤ *Membership Organizations.*   The growth of chains and franchises, with their interlocking reservation systems and easy identifications, put independent operators at a competitive disadvantage. For a long time, independent hotels struggled to maintain their freedom. Of late, the question has shifted from "if and when" to affiliate to "how to choose the right organization."

Even European hotels, which are chiefly small, family inns, have begun examining possible affiliations. Almost three-fourths of European hotels are still independents. Affiliation for these fiercely independent hoteliers reflects the pressures of globalization and the appearance of the American franchise overseas.

Membership affiliation in a referral organization offers a way to compete with less loss of identity than with the franchise. Reservation referrals are cooperative structures initially designed to provide only one common service, marketing. Common reservation systems, standardized quality, joint advertising, and a recognizable logo were the original, limited objectives of most referral groups. There is no interlocking management, no group buying, no common financing—nothing but a unified sales effort. But this effort has proved successful enough for some referrals to broaden their activities.

The referral is a means by which the small entrepreneur can compete. It has been especially popular with small motel and motor lodge operators. After a while, they began to seek additional advice and assistance from the referral group. Some organizations expanded beyond their original intent, offering support in financing, technology, and management. They have retained their co-op structure, however, and some referral groups continue to operate as not-for-profit organizations.

Best Western International is by far the best known membership/referral group. Each of its nearly 4,000 properties in nearly 100 countries is individually owned. Members have voting status for the board of directors that operates the association. By maintaining standards, quality accommodations, and fair pricing, Best Western provides the traveling public with consistency among the properties, whose uniqueness reflects the individual ownership that is still maintained.

Management Companies and Management Contracts

A management contract is an agreement between a hotel owner and a management company (see Exhibit 2–13). The contract is a complex legal instrument by which the management company operates the hotel within the conditions set down by the contract. For this, the owner pays the management company a fee. Fees are paid whether or not there are earnings. Profits, if any, belong to the owner, but so do the losses. Since management fees are paid whether or not the property is profitable, management companies enjoy rapid expansion with little invested capital and almost no risk. Besides, most contracts provide increased fees for the management company if and when the hotel turns profitable.

Just as today's events explain the emergence of real estate investment trusts, history explains the success of the management companies. Professional management companies emerged as ownership separated from management. Management companies are especially important when owners know nothing about operating hotels. Such is the case, for example, when owners are real estate speculators. They know enough to seek professional management to maximize their investments.

Management companies have flourished during three unusual periods. In each instance, lenders took control of the hotels because owners were unable to repay their mortgage loans. Bankers know nothing about running hotels, but they know that the resale value of the properties is higher if the hotels are going concerns. So they hire management companies to run the hotels. This first happened during the Great Depression (1930s), resurfaced during the oil embargo (1970s), and repeated during the banking system collapse (1980s). Poor times for lodging operations are good times for hotel management companies.

Contracts can be negotiated at any time. If early in the development, the management company may provide advice on construction, on systems, on financing, and so on. When times were bad, owners accepted many restrictive terms in the contract in order to secure the management company's services. An improving economy has shifted the advantage. Lenders have disposed of their excess hotel inventory, and hotels have turned profitable. Simultaneously, the number of management companies has increased. This tight competition has forced concessions from the management companies as they bid for contracts. Owning companies are able to negotiate shorter contracts, less costly fees, and more capital investments from management companies.

A true management company is almost unknown now. Companies like those in Exhibit 2–13 have equity (ownership) stakes in the properties they manage. They wouldn't get the contract otherwise. A bigger change has come from consolidation. Chains, which have their own management talent, have taken over many hotels that would otherwise be operating under management contracts. The number of independent properties that require management talent is declining even as the number of management companies grows.

REITs are another piece of the changing environment. To be tax exempt, REITs must collect rents, not management fees. Management contracts are being squeezed out as the hotel lease has a rebirth.

➤*Leases.*   Contrary to the tone of previous pages, the hotel business has had some very good times. When profits were high, hotel companies owned and operated their own properties. Owning hotel real estate takes large sums of invested equity and significant risks from borrowing. Prior to management contracts, hotel companies began selling their properties, that is, the real estate, to nonoperating investors. But this was a time of profitable hotel operations. Hotel companies like those in Exhibit 2–12 wanted to retain the profits from operations. The lease, which is almost the opposite of the management contract, was introduced.

With a management contract, the owning company pays fees to the hotel operator. With a lease, the hotel operator pays rent to the owning company. Since the hotel is profitable, the hotel operator earns from the operations the rent that is due. That is the situation today with the REIT. The REIT, which owns the real estate, rents the property to an operating hotel company. The operating company pays rent, leasing the space from the REIT. The lessee (the one renting) might be a separate company or a paper-clip REIT.

Before the REIT, there was the sale-and-leaseback. In the 1960s, a profitable hotel company would sell (sale) its real estate to outside investors. These investors then leased (rented) the very property back (leaseback) to the company that had just made the sale. So the lease has had a long and successful history. Leases under REIT arrangement will not be the same, but the precedent exists.

The dynamism of hotel keeping is engrossing. Rarely do operators follow one pattern exclusively. In some instances, they own and operate hotels. Sometimes, it is a joint venture. Other times, hotel companies just manage, either their own properties or someone else's, for a fee. Another approach is the franchise.

Franchises

Franchising is not a new idea, nor is it unique to the hotel industry. Tires, speedy printing, diet clinics, and more are all franchised these days. With a franchise, the buyer (called the *franchisee*) acquires rights from the seller (called the *franchisor*). Those rights give the franchisee exclusive use (a franchise) of the name, the product, and the system of the franchisor within a given geographic area. Buying a franchise enables the small businessperson to operate as an independent but still have the benefits of membership in the chain. The franchise concept serves large absentee owners and small owner/operators equally well.

The franchisee pays a variety of fees to adopt the name and trademark of the franchisor (see Exhibit 2–15). In addition to an initial signing fee, the franchisee pays so much per room per night throughout the life of the contract. But that's not all. The franchisee also pays a rental for the company sign, a fee to access the reservation system, and a per reservation fee for each room booked. In addition, the franchisee buys amenities from the parent company in order to get the franchise logo. Extra fees are charged for required training and for participating in the frequent-guest program. Competition has encouraged some management companies to pay all or part of the owner's franchising costs in order to win the management contract.

Item	Representative Terms	Alternative Terms
Initial fee	The greater of $35,000 or $300 times the number of rooms	A lesser fixed amount plus a per room fee over, say, the first 100 rooms
Royalty	4% of room revenue	3% of gross revenue; *or* a minimum per room per night, say, $1.80
Advertising fee	1.5% of room revenue	1% of gross revenue; *or* a minimum per room per night, say, 50¢
Sign fee	1% of gross revenue plus continuing expenses: local licensing, insurance, repairs	None, except initial cost of installation plus continuing expenses
Training fee	0.5% of gross revenue, plus cost of schooling	None, but franchisee must bear costs of transportation and meals for employees sent to school
Reservation fee	3% of room revenue, plus $2 for each reservation	$4 for each reservation booked; *or* a minimum per room per night, say, $1.50
Computer terminal fee	$400 per month	None; *or* 0.5% of room revenue
Preferred guest program	0.5% of room revenue	May be included with advertising fee

Exhibit 2–15 Franchisors charge franchisees a variety of fees that might total as much as 8% of gross sales. The chart illustrates different methods of calculating those fees.

Fees have been rising, doubling in the past two decades to about 8% of gross sales, or approximately 9 to 10% of just room sales. If net earnings are, say, 20% of gross sales, the 8% figure equals close to 40% of net earnings! That's a great deal of money, making it one of the most expensive items in the hotel's profit and loss statement. On the other hand, brand affiliation can add 10 percentage points to occupancy and at least $5 to ADR. That, too, is a great deal of money.

With those fees come a variety of services. How many and which services depend on which franchise is purchased. The most extensive franchise might include feasibility studies, site selection advice, financing support, design and planning, mass purchasing, management consultations, advertising, and systems design. The central reservation system, discussed in Chapter 4, is the major reason by far that franchisees sign up. Estimates place the number of reservations coming through the system as high as 30% of the chain's total reservations and upward of half of all reservations for individual properties.

The franchise and its parent company are so alike that the guest cannot distinguish between them. The physical hotels look identical. It's the ownership and management structures that differ. The chain (the franchisor) does not own the franchise property, the operator (the franchisee) does. The franchisor does not manage the property, the franchisee does. If the franchisee elects not to manage, it could hire the franchisor as its management company under a separate management contract. Or instead, it could hire an entirely different management company.

The franchisor and its franchisees pursue independent goals. Both parties develop separately within the terms of the franchise contracts, although they appear to the public as one company. This physical similarity works to the advantage, or disadvantage, of both. Run-down properties destroy the image of the entire franchise and they may need to be severed from the logo. Some franchisees control more rooms or more hotels than the parent that sells them the franchise. Similarly, owners with multiple properties may have each hotel franchised by a different franchisor. In the end, the success or failure of a franchisee is determined by his or her individual business acumen.

➤ SUMMARY

Several important trends highlighted the lodging industry during the last half of the 1990s. Low borrowing costs, higher occupancy, and rising room rates heralded a return to profitability. To retain those gains, to maintain productivity and increased earnings, the hotel industry began to consolidate. In this respect, lodging followed the path of other U.S. industries. A new pattern of ownership, called the real estate investment trust, helped hotel companies grow larger as they merged, gobbled up, or joined with other hotel companies at home and abroad. The decline of the mom-and-pop was unabated.

Lodging's ownership pattern (consolidation) was in contradiction to its marketing pattern (segmentation). One study reported four dozen new national hotel brands plus many regional logos introduced in one year. Among them were Doubletree's Candlewood, Hilton's Garden Inns, and Sheraton's Four Points. Trying to meet every consumer's want, the hotel industry segmented its products and brands into smaller niches and subsegments: economy, all-suites, spas, and others.

Consolidation and segmentation have taken place in the global village of world economics. Globalization causes ideas and innovations to move swiftly from one continent to another. The speed and direction of their movement depends, in part, on the relative strength of currencies. As the U.S.

dollar dominated world trade, some special American concepts moved overseas. Franchising was one such idea. Hoteliers know that name recognition is the best way to attract a transient traveler who may never again come this way. Despite the high fees, franchising has joined the consolidation movement to help make lodging a global industry.

Whether internationally or domestically, the industry services two major markets. The inelastic commercial market continues to underpin the basic business of hotelkeeping. Coming on strong is the more elastic tourist market. World peace, prosperity, and freedom to travel promise to make the tourist/leisure guest an ever larger segment of the marketplace. Perhaps it will be the one to dominate the industry of the new millennium.

The final decade of the 20th Century reshaped the hotel industry for years to come. It proved that new patterns in products, markets, ownership, and management structures will emerge to keep the industry dynamic in servicing its growing customer base.

➤ QUESTIONS AND PROBLEMS

1. Identify the advantages and disadvantages to the personal career of a student who takes a job after graduation with a Hilton Inns franchise, and passes up an offer from Hilton Hotels, the parent company.

2. Why is Best Western International not listed among the large franchise companies of Exhibit 2–14? After all, Best Western has some 300,000 rooms in its brand! Explain in detail.

3. Someone once said, "If you try to be all things to every guest, you'll likely end up as every guest's second choice." Is that an accurate statement? Why or why not? Answer with special attention to the segmentation of the industry's product line.

4. Provide a rough estimate of the average-sized hotel operated by Carlson Hospitality Group, Hilton Hotels Corporation, Holiday Hospitality, Marriott, Super 8 Motels, and Travelodge. (The figures you need are provided within this chapter.) Compare your results to the discussion of hotel sizes in Chapter 1.

5. A traveler driving along Interstate 36 stops at two different hotels on successive evenings. Explain, and differentiate between, the signs posted by the front desk in terms of the text discussion about ownership, management, franchising, and joint ventures.

   Hotel A: This Hampton Inn is owned by Jerome J. Vallen and Sons, Inc., under license from Promus. Richfield Hotel Management.

   Hotel B: This Hampton Inn is owned by Promus. Jerome J. Vallen, General Manager.

6. Obtain a copy of a management contract from a local hotel, or review a book in the library on hotel management contracts. Discuss three terms (for example, life of the contract, payment, maintenance of the property, or investment by the management company) that intrigue you.

➤ NOTES

1. The lodging industry uses the term *segmentation* to mean product differentiation, that is, multiple products. Segmentation has a different, almost opposite meaning in marketing terms, that is, focusing on one product that is developed for one segment.

2. Female dress of the late 19th Century had ruffles and bustles, parasols, and numerous petticoats. The Saratoga Trunk, named for the spa, had a curved top to accommodate the elaborate wardrobes that were brought to the resort.

3. One chain recently identified its typical business guest as a male, age 25 to 44, holding a white-collar job that pays $54,400 annually. This traveler, who comes alone by air, holds a reservation and pays an average of $67.20 per night.

4. These are registered trademarks.

CHAPTER 3
The Structure of the Hotel Industry

Outline

Hotel organizations are structured—put together—in many different ways. That's because the organizational structure is a method of arranging the workforce to carry out the goals and functions of a particular company. And what a variety of goals, functions, and companies there is! Certainly, Chapters 1 and 2 made clear the immense range of operations, segments, markets, and locations that structure the numerous organizations under the single umbrella of the lodging industry.

Each organization takes final form from the patterns that make up the hotel industry. That's why the 1,000-room, chain-operated, convention hotel is no more like the mom-and-pop highway motel than is a seasonal, skiing resort like a casino hotel. And all these differ again from the conference center, the economy property, or the commercial hotel whose towers house residential guests.

Just as each hotel type calls for a different organizational structure, each calls for a different building structure, too. The ski lodge will probably have individual cottages or condos hidden in the woods. The resort may be a series of low-rise outbuildings surrounding the swimming pool. How different these structures are from the urban commercial giant, squeezed by high land costs, that adopts a high-rise configuration for its building design.

Differences notwithstanding, both the organizational structure and the building structure adhere to similar blueprints. Although differences distinguish the properties' lines, the basics are the same: the staff structured to serve the guest; and the guest room—the hotel's major product line—structured to accommodate the guest.

➤ THE ORGANIZATIONAL STRUCTURE

Hotels employ a vast number of persons with a variety of skills. Hotels have plumbers and accountants, bartenders and cooks, grounds managers and water purification experts, telecommunication specialists, and computer troubleshooters. The larger the hotel, the more specialized the tasks. Indeed, large hotels have bigger resident populations and provide more services than do many small towns.

Hotel organizations follow the pattern of other business or social institutions. They break up the workforce into separate departments, with each department entrusted with a share of the duties and services. Modern management techniques try to minimize the differences among the various departments because any one of them can destroy the best efforts of all the others. Coordinating the whole, unifying the different specialties, and directing their joint efforts is the job of the general manager.

The General Manager

Management titles vary from hotel to hotel, just as their organizations do. The large hotel chains use titles at the corporate level that are similar to other American businesses: CEO (chief executive officer), CFO (chief financial officer), and COO (chief operating officer).

General manager (GM, or The GM) is the favored title at the unit level—that is, for the individual hotel. This person is responsible for everything that happens in the hotel: for all the departments (see Exhibit 3–1) and for the general profitability of the whole works!

If the general manager is a senior member of the corporation that owns the hotel, his or her title might be President (of the corporation) and General Manager (of the hotel). Or the title might be Vice President and General Manager. The GM who sits on the corporate board of directors could be Director and General Manager, or even

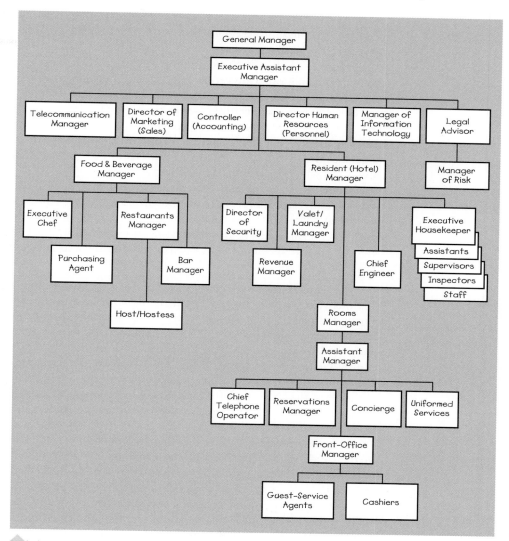

Exhibit 3–1   The organizational structure of hotels is changing, as is the hotel building's physical structure. Still, operations retain their traditional assignments with the rooms manager (resident manager, hotel manager, or house manager) responsible for all line operations except food and beverage.

Managing Director, but neither one is used very often. Managing Director has a European flavor (*directeur* is French for manager), so Managing Director may be used as much for ambience as for organizational clarity. If the manager and family own the hotel, Owner-Manager is standard terminology. Standing alone, the title of General Manager implies no ownership affiliation. Then the GM is the employee most responsible to ownership, corporate or otherwise, and the one accountable for the full scope of the operation.

When several properties of the same chain are located in one city and all are supervised by one person, the GM term might be assigned to that person rather than to the executives of the individual hotels. Chains use other titles as appropriate: *area vice president for operations: regional director of marketing:* and *food and beverage manager, eastern division.*

Whatever the specific title, the top executive of the hotel reports to ownership directly or through other divisional executives. Ownership vests its authority in that top executive and holds that person responsible for all that happens.

Large hotel organizations support the GM with specialized departments, and sometimes with an assistant, the *executive assistant manager*. Like the general manager, the executive assistant has complete jurisdiction over the entire house. That distinguishes the executive assistant position from that of the *assistant manager* (see Exhibit 3–1), which is a rooms department position only.

Hotels never close, and that places great demand on the energy and time of all hotel executives, but especially on the GM. Night, weekend, and holiday periods are covered in some hotels by rotating the entire management staff into a position called *executive on duty*. Every department head (see Exhibit 3–1) takes a turn. Thus, the reservoir of management talent is deepened and the experience of the individual manager is broadened.

➤*From Host to Executive.*   The many changes that were recounted in the previous two chapters have affected the position and person of the general manager. During the period of one-person ownership, the general manager personified the specific property. The GM of this era was either the actual owner or a representative who stood in the owner's place. He (and in those days, the positions were invariably held by men) was known as "Mine Host." His name was part of the advertising, his personality part of the aura; his presence part of the hotel's very identity. Hotels were smaller and the manager often visited with arriving and departing guests. The property reflected the host qualities, the personality, the leadership, the isms of this very special person (see Exhibit 3–2).

Whereas managers during this single-ownership period set the tone and standards for their individual properties, modern managers carry out the standardized expectations of a globalized chain. GMs of an earlier period put their marks on properties because they were in one location for a long time. Not so today, when rapid turnover, caused in part by personal decisions and in part by company transfers to other properties, is the expectation. Similarly, mass markets and one-time arrivals have made the individual guest less identifiable. Thus, the manager's role as Mine Host has been lessened, almost eliminated. Instead, managers have turned their human relation talents to a different type of "customer," the employee, and we examine this in Chapter 7. For their executive talents, managers turn to a growing list of nonguest issues. That shift in the manager's emphasis has been noted by observers, who worry that "the business of hotels" is not "the hotel business."

➤*Support Departments.*   The issues with which hotels contend multiply almost exponentially, it seems. Each new matter requires more knowledge and necessitates more expertise. Support staffs have grown apace with the issues: legal issues, employment issues, environmental issues, tax issues, zoning issues, and on without end. The support departments furnish the knowledge and expertise to the management team and to the operating departments. On occasion, support departments even make guest contact, as when accounting communicates with a guest about an overdue bill or engineering dispatches a TV repairperson to the guest room.

Marketing, human resources, purchasing, legal, and management information systems are part of a long list of support departments. The functions of some of these

Exhibit 3–2 The shift from hotel host to hotel manager is described lightly in this well-known ditty, which the authors have changed to modernize the phrasing.

What Has Become of Our Genial Hosts?

What was it in bygone days
That served the famous hoteliers?
Smiles and friendships, *bon mots* and more.
To know them, guests flocked through the door.

Schooled in the fine art of conversation
Made hotelkeeping an endless vacation,
Chatting and supping and drinking one's fill
While the cream of society fattened the till.

What has become of our Genial Hosts?
Alas, conditions have altered their posts.
They rarely see their fashionable clients.
Their careers have become mathematical science.

Occupancies, percentages, rooms income,
Wages, break-even, taxes, and then some!
Their carefree pasts have become archaic.
The innkeepers' life is today algebraic.

Each acts like an Einstein, a judge, and a foreman,
A housekeeper, a chef, an art critic, a doorman.
And there on the desk, a great volume about
Front-office management, titled *Check-In Check-Out*.

Consultants and salespersons vie for a visit
Then the new decorator with the latest what-is-it.
They're umpires and referees; they pacify all
From the board of directors to the charity ball.

And leaving the office, they find in the corridors
Anxious sales staffers and tired night auditors.
And if that's not enough, alack and egad
There's always the competitor's TV ad!

What's to be done about REITS and franchisees,
And what about the competition overseas?
Consolidation? Segmentation?
Rising prices of electrification?

Hearing the reverberations about minimum wage
Helped bring the change from host to sage.
Entertainment centers, computerization, what more?
Environmental concerns and a concierge floor.

What has become of our Genial Hosts?
What else: they're figments, relics, ghosts.
And when will they rest from their toil so hard?
When they hang o'er their tombs a "Do Not Disturb" card.

departments cross into the interests of the operating departments. For example, the rooms manager looks to human resources for help in filling job vacancies; to sales for help in filling empty rooms; and to accounting for help in credit-card control and settlement. Other support departments are not quite as pervasive, but every department looks for assistance from every other department at one time or another.

➤*Food and Beverage Department.*   Service made directly to the guest is the responsibility of two major departments. The rooms department, which is the thrust of this book, will be discussed in detail. Food and beverage is the other major operating department.

This department is headed by a *food and beverage manager* (see Exhibit 3–1) and divided into several subdivisions. Food preparation, which is the responsibility of the chef, is one of these. Foodservice falls under the jurisdiction of the restaurant manager (sometimes called the *maitre d'hotel*). The bar manager heads another area of this division, and the food and beverage purchasing agent still another.

Each of these department heads has one or more assistants who are responsible for certain areas of operation. The chef has a *sous* (under) chef and a steward (sanitation). Subordinate to the maitre d' are hosts and hostesses, who supervise the dining rooms. Bars are managed by head bartenders. So the organization grows, becoming larger and larger as lower organizational levels are added. At the bottom rung, doing the essential work, is the pot washer in the kitchen, the dining room attendant, the banquet porter, the kitchen runner, and the refuse handler.

The Hotel Manager

The *hotel manager* is the front-of-the-house counterpart of the food and beverage manager. All operating departments, except those dealing with food and beverage, report to the hotel manager. *Resident manager, hotel manager,* or *house manager* are the names most often used to designate this position. The jurisdiction may range from two to three departments in a medium-sized hotel to a half-dozen and more in a large property.

Exhibit 3–1 outlines the divisions of the front of the house at a medium-sized to large hotel and positions the hotel manager in relation to the balance of the hotel organization. Every department that deals with the guest falls within the hotel manager's purview. The job is one of coordination—presenting the services of several different departments as those of one company.

➤*Housekeeping.*   The manager of the housekeeping department, who is called the *housekeeper* or *executive housekeeper,* is one of several department heads reporting to the resident (or hotel) manager. In some instances, the housekeeper reports directly to the general manager. This might happen in a small hotel without a house manager, when the GM wants to emphasize housekeeping, or when additional duties are given to the housekeeper—responsibility for the laundry, for example. It is this kind of variation that accounts for the differences among hotels even though there is a standard organization that everyone follows. All hotels have housekeepers.

The housekeeping department has the largest number of employees.[1] It is charged with the general cleanliness of guest rooms, corridors, and other public space. Housekeeping in the food and beverage department is not normally the responsibility of the housekeeping department—that is assigned to the steward, not shown in Exhibit 3–1.

Working with the housekeeper (see Exhibit 3–1) are assistant housekeepers, floor supervisors, inspectors, and, at the end of the chain of command, guest-room attendants. Special attendants may be assigned to public washrooms, parlors, and bath-houses. Housepersons are available to do the heavier work and to move equipment.

Coordination between the front office and the housekeeper is essential. Hundreds of persons arrive at and depart daily from a large hotel. Rooms must be serviced quickly to placate waiting guests. Information on the status of rooms must be furnished accurately and immediately to the room clerks, who use the reports to make new room assignments.

The housekeeping department handles lost-and-found items, visits the sick, maintains linen storage and inventory, makes linen repairs, and issues uniforms to other departments. It handles all housekeeping assignments, from dry-cleaning draperies, to disinfecting after animals have been in residence, to the cleanup that follows a fire.

➤ ***Uniformed Services.*** The ranks of the service department—or uniformed services or bell department—are on the wane. At one time, this department included baggage porters, transportation clerks, and elevator operators for both guest and service cars. Now it is composed chiefly of bellpersons and door attendants, and even these are decreasing in number.

There are several reasons for this decline. Changing travel habits and licensing requirements have eliminated the service department's role in travel arrangements. Second, guests travel lighter today than they did a generation ago. Suitcases are built lighter (and many have wheels), and shorter stays mean less clothing. Self-service is expected in many facets of American life, so many guests carry their own luggage—all of which means fewer tips and less job appeal. Fewer workers seek such employment.

The decline in the number of uniformed employees has another explanation: management cost-cutting. Today, everyone must be paid minimum wage, whereas tips alone constituted the salary of an earlier era. Reducing the staff cuts labor costs and with them fringe benefits, which add as much as one-third more to direct labor costs. So the hotel that services the entrance door around the clock is rare, and the motor hotel without any of the uniformed services is the norm.

If bellservices are available, they will be the guest's first contact on arrival: if not a door attendant, perhaps a bellperson. Contact may be as early as the airport van driver, who is also a member of the service crew. In urban properties with separate parking, someone needs to be at the door to handle garaging and other auto services. Few urban hotels own their own parking spaces. They lease the space or have an outside contractor take a parking concession. (This outsourcing is still another explanation for today's smaller uniformed staff.)

Handling baggage for arriving and departing guests, including groups, is the major function of the service department. Laundry and valet service, ice, and transportation were once part of the department's duties, but they are less so today. Once roomed, few guests use bellservice. Loudspeakers, telephones, and computer systems have even replaced the paging and message-service roles of the department.

With guest arrivals and departures as their main function, bellpersons can be scheduled at a ratio of 1 bellhop per 65 anticipated hourly arrivals/departures. If they exist at all in small hotels, the bellstaff may also handle room service, lobby cleaning, and pool maintenance along with their other duties.

The title of the modern service department head is *manager of services,* or *superintendent of services,* not nearly as romantic as the more traditional terms, *bell-captain,* or its shortened version, *captain.* Recently, responsibility for the now-abbreviated service department has begun shifting to the *concierge,* a service-giver of a totally different type. If not organizational responsibility, which is still very tentative, certainly the services rendered are reminiscent of many previously provided by the uniformed services.

➤ *Concierge.*   A new front-office position has taken hold in the United States, but it has long been popular overseas, especially in France.[2] (In Great Britain where the front office is called the front hall, the concierge is the head hall porter.) Like a French idiom, translating the nuances of the job into Americanese leaves something to be desired. Many guests are uncertain what the position does, let alone how to pronounce it (*kon syerzh*).

The word comes from the Latin *con servus,* meaning "with service." Other translations offered are "fellow slave" or, more to the point, "building guard." According to the French, the *Comte de Cierges* (Count of Cierge) was in charge of the prisons, making him the keeper of the keys under the French monarchs.[3] Thus, the European concierge appeared as a door attendant (building guard) and from that to the keeper of the keys, porter, and provider of various services.

These duties are still part of the European concierge's job, particularly in the small hotels. Controlling the keys enables the concierge to watch the comings and goings of guests and thus to furnish a bit of extra protection and information. This is not the American interpretation of the job, except when a hotel offers a concierge floor, or luxury floor. Even then, the added security is a secondary objective.

The keeper of the door, the lobby concierge (see Exhibit 3–3), provides all types of miscellaneous information and a variety of personal, but minor, services. Information and service shape the basic description of the concierge's job. Travel information,

Exhibit 3–3   To assure accessibility, the concierge is usually located in the lobby. Some hotels limit concierge service to special floors with extra services but at a higher room rate. The pleasant working conditions and the aura of confident service are highlighted in this lobby photograph. *Courtesy of The Wynfrey, Birmingham, Alabama.*

Exhibit 3–4 The duties of the concierge, a guest-service position in large, upscale hotels, range from *A* to *Z*.

A...	as in	Art supplies and restoration
B...	as in	Babysitting services for vacating parents
C...	as in	Churches for all denominations
D...	as in	Dinner reservations at sold-out restaurants
E...	as in	Errand and courier services for speedy delivery
F...	as in	Flowers for that special occasion
G...	as in	Galleries for antiques and arts
H...	as in	Helicopter services
I...	as in	Interpreters for an international symposium
J...	as in	Jewelers from whom one can buy with confidence
K...	as in	Kennels for a cherished pet
L...	as in	Libraries for source materials
M...	as in	Maps to navigate the city or the subway
N...	as in	Newspapers from distant cities and foreign countries
O...	as in	Orchestra tickets at the last minute
P...	as in	Photographers for that spcial occasion
Q...	as in	Queries that no one else can answer
R...	as in	Restaurants of every specialty
S...	as in	Scuba diving sites and services
T...	as in	Transportation: air; auto; bus; limo; taxi; train
U...	as in	Umbrellas on a rainy day
V...	as in	Virtual reality equipment
W...	as in	Wedding chapels
X...	as in	Xeroxing a last-minute report
Y...	as in	Yoga demonstrations and instructions
Z...	as in	Zoo directions for an outing with the children

messages, tickets and reservations to a broad range of events, babysitters, language translation, and secretarial sources all fall within the purview of the concierge. Guests may ask the concierge to arrange for pet care, to provide extra chairs, to arrange flower delivery, to find lost items, to get medical care in an emergency, to recommend hair stylists, anything (see Exhibit 3–4).

As hotels retrench some services and automate others, the post of concierge becomes increasingly important. Guests can no longer turn to transportation desks, floor clerks, and elevator operators for questions and services. Those jobs no longer exist. Many of the gratuities that previously went to the uniformed staff have been redirected to the concierge desk. For services rendered, a concierge may be tipped by the guest and commissioned by the service company (theater, rentals, etc.).

The Concierge Floor.   The concierge floor is one amenity not discussed in Chapter 2. It is an extra service facility available at an extra charge. The concierge service is limited to guests on that special sleeping floor. Continental breakfast and evening cocktails are usually provided. As a premium floor, there are other extras. A terrycloth robe is furnished for the bath, shoes are shined, rooms are larger, arrival and departure procedures are expedited, and security is enhanced.

Access to the floor is limited and requires a special key for the elevator. The concierge is usually seated by the elevator, adding security as the floor clerk's position did before World War II.

All the upscale chains have concierge floors. Hilton calls theirs Towers after the famed Waldorf-Astoria Towers, which is part of the Hilton chain. Hyatt uses Regency club; Radisson, Plaza Club; and Omni/Dunfey, Classic Floors. Add these names to the frequent-guest programs, and the confusion of name segmentation increases dramatically.

The Asian invasion of the U.S. hotel business has brought pleasant additions to the concierge service. A floor butler, or floor steward, is available around the clock to handle personal services, including unpacking. Upscale Asian hotels have room bells or switches on the bed console to summon the butler.

➤*Telephone.*   The number of telephones in a large hotel often exceeds the number found in many of America's small cities. Nevertheless, computerization has reduced the size of this department just as automation has reduced the size of the uniformed services. Outgoing local and long-distance calls are handled by automatic, direct-dial equipment. Similarly, calls between guest rooms or from guest rooms to hotel departments, room service for example, no longer require a telephone operator to complete the call. Electronic billing automatically records the telephone company's charges on the guest's electronic bill, eliminating the old position of charge operator.

In no other department of the hotel has the introduction of costly and complex equipment been so rapid and so complete, and worked so well. Supervising the few employees left in the department is the head telephone operator, called the *chief operator* or *telephone supervisor*. Depending on size, there might be an assistant or shift supervisor.

Operators may still answer incoming calls and direct them to their proper destinations. The caller's sole contact with the property is the disembodied voice of the telephone operator, so incoming calls must be handled professionally and pleasantly. Some hotels still have incoming messages taken by the operator. More and more, the operator doesn't answer incoming calls and doesn't take messages. Incoming calls are handled by an electronic menu from which the caller chooses a service. If the service chosen is a guest room call, the operator intercedes. Hotels do not give out the room numbers or telephone numbers of registered guests. Messages are different. The telephone mailbox allows a caller direct access to the guest's in-room telephone, where the message can be left with privacy and without the mistakes of transcription for which the hotel is always blamed.

Even morning wake-up calls have been automated. And even this number has been reduced by furnishing an alarm clock in each guest room. Some guests still prefer the assurance of human intervention, so the telephone operator provides it with a morning wake-up call, probably an automated one.

➤*Other Departments.*   A previous paragraph noted the hotel manager's responsibility for all of the operating departments except food and beverage. This usually includes the hotel's numerous tenants. Among them are stores and shops (florists, beauticians, men's wear, etc.), businesses that rent office space, and airline or privately owned tour desks. The business center may be the hotel's, or it may be leased to still another tenant. Negotiating the lease and rental contracts by which these relationships are established falls to the office of the hotel manager.

Thousands of persons pass through the hotel in a week. Medical emergencies must be anticipated and preparations put in place. That's another job for the hotel manager. He or she must make arrangements, or have the concierge do so, in advance for both a physician and an ambulance. Many large cities throughout the country have some form of HotelDocs, a private medical service. The physicians come free to the hotel; the ill travelers pay for the care as they would at home.

Some hotels have the position of facilities manager. The post might be part of the engineering department, or even of housekeeping. Or it might be another responsibility of the hotel manager. The care and maintenance of the physical plant includes new construction, repairs and maintenance, window washing, carpet maintenance, technology, and employee health and safety.

Swimming pools are included among the hotel manager's responsibilities, although pool chemicals might be handled by the engineering department. Large operations have a pool manager who reports to the hotel manager. The pool manager may also be responsible for the hotel's spa. Reporting to the pool manager is a staff that includes lifeguards and pool attendants. They handle guest towels and other equipment, keep the area clean, do minor maintenance, and assure safe practices around the water. Pools are not viewed as profit centers, but guests may be charged for the use of certain cabanas, chairs, rafts, and other water equipment.

Security.   Automation and social changes have shrunk the size of several departments under the hotel manager's control, but not so with security. Responding to larger liability claims and increased crime, hotels have enlarged their security departments. The security staff ranges from one person walking night fire watch in a small hotel to a full-time police force, including plain-clothes officers, in larger properties. As crimes against persons and property increase, larger and better-trained security forces are needed. Chains have actually dropped franchised properties when they failed to address life-safety issues. Security training and physical modifications (sprinkler systems, room locks, in-room safes) have climbed high on the industry's priority list.

Security is charged with the protection of the guest and the employee. It is responsible for their property as well as their person. Losses are both ways. Guests are the victims, but so are hotels. Increased pilferage of towels, TV sets, and other room furnishings can be attributed to employees, in part, but guests often take home more than memories. Hotel guests run sophisticated scams against hotels, as other customers do against other businesses.

By common law, innkeepers are held to a higher level of security than are other types of businesses. Although safety, including fire control and prevention, is the department's major responsibility, there are plenty of sidelines requiring security's attention. Security helps the credit manager with lockouts and luggage liens. It handles drunks and prostitutes (*nightbirds* in hotel terminology), and maintains security logs for the hotel manager. Security officers handle accidents, make insurance reports, and carry out investigations of crimes, including deaths and suicides. The department is led by the chief of security, who reports to the hotel manager. Casino hotels have different security needs and, consequently, a different organizational structure. Every security department works closely with the local police. Hotel security serves first as a deterrent, then as a restraint, and only rarely as a police force. It must be an iron hand in a velvet glove.

➤ STRUCTURE OF THE FRONT OFFICE
What Is the Front Office?

Physically, the front office is an easily identifiable area of the lobby. Functionally, it is much less so despite constant reference to it as the "hub" and the "heart" of the hotel. The overuse of such terms should not detract from the real importance of the front office. It is in fact the nerve center of guest activity. Through it flow communications with every other department; from it emanate instructions for the service of the guest; to it come charges for final billing and settlement.

Organizational interdependence is not the only reason for the preeminent position of the front office. It is equally a matter of economics. Room sales produce over half the total revenue of the average hotel. For budget hotels, they produce all the revenue. And for others, much of the revenue that comes from food and beverage originates in meetings and convention groups, whose search for site selections begins with rooms. More revenue (about 66%) is derived from room sales than from the total of food, beverage, and telephone.[4] Furthermore, rooms are more profitable than these departments. Every dollar of room sales produces approximately 73 cents in departmental profit. Food and beverage combined average out to less than 21 cents departmental profit per dollar sale.

Hotel guests relate with the front office, and this adds to its importance. Guests who rarely see their housekeepers, who never see the cook, who deal with sales only on occasion, know the hotel by its desk. They are received at the desk and they depart from the desk. It is toward the desk that guests direct complaints and from the desk that they expect remedies. Guest identification, as much as profit or interdepartmental dependence, accounts for management's overriding concern with the front office.

Better to define the front office as a bundle of duties and guest services rather than as a fixed area located behind the lobby desk. Some divisions of the front office—reservations, for example—can be located elsewhere without affecting their membership in the front-office structure. Computerization's instant communication has reduced the need for all front-office segments to be within physical hailing distance of one another.

Someone once said that the front office was so named because it was close to the front door. Simple enough, but many hotels have substituted the term *guest-service area* in an effort to better define the role of the front office. By extension, the front-office manager becomes the guest-service manager; the front-desk clerk, a guest-service agent. Whatever their titles, the front-office managers and the guest-service agents operate the desk for the guest's convenience.

➤*Managing Rooms.*   How the front desk is managed and staffed depends on the hotel's pattern, its market segment, and its size. The organizational structure of a full-service hotel, for example, requires a very complete staff. Although few hotels have as complete an organizational structure as the full-service house, it serves as a model.

Full-service operations have three management positions on the hotel side (as differentiated from food and beverage or the support departments). The first of these positions, hotel manager (house manager, or resident manager) has already been discussed. Second is the *rooms division manager,* and then the *front-officer manager.* The front-office manager reports upward to the rooms division manager, who reports upward to the hotel manager, and thence to the general manager (see Exhibit 3–1).

When the organization is so complete, job responsibilities grow narrower down the organization's line. At the top, the hotel manager (the hotel manager is not the general manager) has responsibility for all operational functions except food and beverage. Included are departments that have not been discussed, such as maintenance and engineering, or laundry and valet. The hotel manager assigns responsibility for just the room functions to the rooms manager. That includes reservations, bellservices, telephone, and the front office. The front-office manager takes control of the front office—clerks, mail and messages, guest information, credit, and so on. Some properties add yet another management level, the front desk. The front-desk manager is a supervisor usually responsible for a single shift (see Exhibit 3–1).

Few hotels need three or four management positions, so the responsibilities of the positions remain but are handled by fewer persons. This chapter follows reality by including some of the rooms manager's duties under the headings of the hotel manager and the front-office manager. Remember: Many hotels just have one management level, or even none at all, between the employee on the desk and the general manager.

Whatever the manager's title, front-desk procedures require attention to detail. One study of the front-office manager indicated that performance and production are as important to success as is skill in dealing with people (see Exhibit 3–5). The fact is that performance and dealing with people are both the same at the front desk, since handling details is the best means of attending to customer and employee needs.

➤*Front-Office Clerks.* The room clerk (front-office clerk, guest-service agent) is still another organizational level. As suggested, numerous titles have been used in this position in an attempt to best represent the importance of the post. *Room clerk* and *front-office clerk*, which were American favorites, have been replaced largely by *guest-service agent. Receptionist* is the favored term outside the United States.

Titles aside, the front-desk clerk has a host of duties concentrated in four functions: room sales, guest relations, records, and coordination (see Exhibit 3–6). The guest-service agent is part salesperson, part psychologist, and part accountant. Moreover, as a first-line employee, front-office agents must carry out policies that have been established at higher levels. If an increase in rooms rates is mandated, it is the front-office clerk who must sell up to a price-conscious guest. It is the front-desk clerk who adjusts minor problems and buffers management from the first blasts of major complaints. It is the front-desk clerk who brings together the guest's reservation, the housekeeper's room availability, and the proper record of the guest's account.

A new front-office position, which emphasizes the guest service aspect of the desk, is appearing on the scene. The job has not yet been named, and it may disappear before it ever gets a title. With the introduction of computer-terminal registration, guests are able to bypass the front office and self-register using equipment similar to a bank ATM. To encourage reluctant guests, hotels have moved agents to the lobby side of the desk. Slowly walking guests through a learning process a time or two speeds up the work of the desk in the long run.

➤*Other Front-Office Functions.* There was once a front-office position called mail, key, and information clerk. Modern circumstances have eliminated the position and even some of the functions. What remains has been taken over by guest-service agents or is now done electronically. Today, for example, most guest mail comes by fax; guests don't stay long enough to get letters through the traditional post. Heavy metal hotel keys (and the front-desk traffic once generated by guests dropping them off and retrieving them later) have been replaced by electronic locks using disposable keys. Similarly, information and personal messages are handled today by electronic mail; in-room, closed-circuit television; and automated kiosks.

Electronic kiosks supply road and street maps, bus schedules, stock market quotes, theater offerings, weather reports, and information about events in town and activities within the hotel. Guests who have never used a computer keyboard are comfortable making one-touch inquiries, and hotels that have never staffed a concierge now have an electronic one in the lobby.

WYNDHAM HOTELS & RESORTS

MANAGER, GUEST SERVICES	*JOB DESCRIPTION*

DIVISION: Gardens
DEPARTMENT: Guest Services
REPORTS TO: General Manager
STATUS: Exempt

JOB SUMMARY

The Guest Services Manager is responsible for ensuring the operation of the Front Office in an attentive, friendly, efficient and courteous manner, providing all guests with quality service prior to and throughout their stay, while maximizing room revenue and occupancy.

QUALIFICATION STANDARDS

Education & Experience:
At least 5 years of progressive experience in a hotel or a related field; or a 2-year college degree and 3 or more years of related experience; or a 4-year college degree and at least 1 year of related experience.
Previous supervisory responsibility preferred.

Physical requirements:
- Long hours sometimes required.
- Light work - Exerting up to 20 pounds of force occasionally, and/or up to 10 pounds of force frequently or constantly to lift, carry, push, pull or otherwise move objects.
- Must have a valid driver's license from the applicable state.

Mental requirements:
- Must be able to convey information and ideas clearly.
- Must be able to evaluate and select among alternative courses of action quickly and accurately.
- Must work well in stressful, high pressure situations.
- Must maintain composure and objectivity under pressure.
- Must be effective in handling problems in the workplace, including anticipating, preventing, identifying and solving problems as necessary.
- Must have the ability to assimilate complex information, data, etc., from disparate sources and consider, adjust or modify to meet the constraints of the particular need.
- Must be effective at listening to, understanding, and clarifying the concerns and issues raised by co-workers and guests.
- Must be able to work with and understand financial information and data, and basic arithmetic functions.

DUTIES & FUNCTIONS

Essential:
- Approach all encounters with guests and employees in an attentive, friendly, courteous and service-oriented manner.

Manager, Guest Services, Page 1

***Exhibit* 3–5** The front-desk manager or guest-services manager has a broad range of responsibilities beyond guest services, including departmental management issues: staff, profits, legal, technical knowledge. This position has been combined and responsibilities shifted in some parts of the industry as a result of organizational restructuring during the low cycle of the early 1990s. *Courtesy of Wyndham Hotels & Resorts, Dallas, Texas.*

DUTIES & FUNCTIONS (cont.)

<u>Essential</u> (continued)

- Maintain regular attendance in compliance with Wyndham standards, as required by scheduling which will vary according to the needs of the hotel.
- Maintain high standards of personal appearance and grooming, which include wearing the proper uniform and name tag when working.
- Comply at all times with Wyndham standards and regulations to encourage safe and efficient hotel operations.
- Maintain a warm and friendly demeanor at all times.
- Establish and maintain attentive, friendly, courteous and efficient hospitality at the Front Desk.
- Respond to all guests requests, problems, complaints and/or accidents presented at the Front Desk or through Reservations, in an attentive, courteous and efficient manner. Follow up to ensure guest satisfaction.
- Motivate, coach, counsel and discipline all Guest Services personnel according to Wyndham S.O.P.'s.
- Ensure compliance to Wyndham Standard of the Week training, using the steps to effective training according to Wyndham standards.
- Prepare and conduct all Guest Services interviews and follow hiring procedures according to Wyndham S.O.P.'s.
- Conduct all 90 day and annual Guest Service employee performance appraisals according to S.O.P.'s.
- Develop employee morale and ensure training of Guest Services personnel.
- Maximize room revenue and occupancy by reviewing status daily. Analyze rate efficiency, monitor credit report and maintain close observation of daily house count.
- Attend all required Rooms Merchandizing meetings with all appropriate reports and documentation necessary to establish select sell guidelines and implement appropriate restrictions.
- Supervise the Night Audit function and monitor the House Charge Worksheet and Flash Report for accuracy.
- Participate in required M.O.D. program as scheduled.
- Ensure all end of the month report dates are met, i.e., Central Reservations, Market Segment, WynClub, AAdvantage, etc.
- Review Guest Services staff's worked hours for payroll compilation and submit to Accounting on a timely basis.
- Prepare employee Schedule according to business forecast, payroll budget guidelines and productivity requirements. Present with Wage Progress Report to General Manager weekly.
- Ensure that no-show revenue is maximized through consistent and accurate billing.
- Maintain Wyndham S.O.P.'s regarding Purchase Orders, vouchering of invoices and checkbook accounting.
- Ensure that Wage Progress, Productivity and the Ten Day Forecast are completed on a timely basis according to Wyndham S.O.P.'s.
- Maintain a professional working relationship and promote open lines of communication with managers, employees and other departments.
- Work closely with Accounting on follow-up items, i.e., returned checks, rejected credit cards, employee discrepancies, etc.
- Operate all aspects of the Front Office computer system, including software maintenance, report generation and analysis, and simple programming.
- Monitor proper operation of the P.B.X. console and ensure that employees maintain Wyndham S.O.P.'s in its use.
- Monitor the process of taking reservations ensuring that Wyndham courtesy and upselling techniques are maintained.
- Greet and welcome all guests approaching the Front Desk in accordance with Wyndham S.O.P.'s.
- Ensure implementation of all Wyndham policies and house rules. Understand hospitality terms.
- Operate pagers and radios efficiently and professionally in communicating with departmental staff. Ensure the proper use of radio etiquette within the department.

Manager, Guest Services, Page 2

Exhibit 3–5　Continued.

DUTIES & FUNCTIONS (cont.)

Essential (continued)
- Coordinate all aspects of the ongoing implementation of the Wyndham Way philosophy of service.
- Ensure correct and accurate cash handling at the Front Desk.
- Attend monthly all-employee meetings and any other functions required by management.
- Attend weekly staff meeting and provide training on a rotational basis using steps to effective training according to Wyndham standards.
- Perform any other duties as requested by the General Manager.
- Obtain all necessary information when taking room reservations.
- Ensure delivery of all messages, packages, and mail in a timely and professional manner.
- Be aware of all rates, packages and promotions currently under way.
- Follow and enforce all Wyndham hotel credit policies.
- Ensure that employees are, at all times, attentive, friendly, helpful and courteous to all guests, managers and other employees.
- Ensure participation by department in Wyndham Way monthly meeting.
- Focus the Guest Services and Housekeeping Departments on their role in contributing to the Guest Service Index (G.S.I.).

Marginal:
- Monitor all V.I.P.'s, special guests and requests.
- Maintain required pars of all front office and stationary supplies.
- Review daily Front Office work and activity reports generated by Night Audit.
- Review Front Office log book and Guest Request log on a daily basis.
- Assist the General Manager and Engineering Department in implementing and maintaining emergency procedures.
- Be familiar with all corporate sponsored programs such as airline mileage, Triple Upgrade, or V.I.P. programs, and the standards and procedures for each.
- Coordinate and maintain records for WynStar Program with the Wyndham Way Committee.
- Maintain an organized and comprehensive filing system with documentation of purchases, vouchering, schedules, forecasts, reports and tracking logs.
- Conduct meetings according to Wyndham standards as required by management.
- Perform, as necessary, all duties of Assistant Guest Services Manager.
- Other duties as required.

I HAVE READ AND UNDERSTAND THE JOB DESCRIPTION AS STATED ABOVE AND ACCEPT THAT ANY OF THE TASKS MAY BE MODIFIED OR CHANGED. I ACCEPT RESPONSIBILITY FOR KNOWING THE MODIFICATIONS AND / OR CHANGES IN THIS JOB DESCRIPTION. I CAN PERFORM THE ESSENTIAL FUNCTIONS OF THIS JOB AS LISTED ABOVE, WITH OR WITHOUT REASONABLE ACCOMMODATION.

_____   _____
Employee Signature   Date   Supervisor Signature   Date

Manager, Guest Services, Page 3

Exhibit 3–5   Continued.

Job Title: Guest-Service Agent

The hotel is personified by its agents. They receive the guests, service them throughout their stay, and handle their departures with efficiency and aplomb. A guest-service agent:

Acts as host(ess) and receptionist.

Accepts reservations.

Quotes rates and sells rooms.

Keeps records of vacant and occupied rooms.

Registers arrivals and assigns them rooms.

Ascertains creditworthiness of hotel guests.

Controls and issues keys.

Coordinates activities of both the bellservice department and the housekeeping department.

Helps protect the guest's person, and the guest's and the hotel's property.

Responds to guest inquiries and gives information about and directions to the hotel and the locale.

Dates, sorts, and files incoming mail, messages, packages, and telegrams.

Receives and acts on guest complaints.

Maintains guest bills by posting charges and credits to individual guest accounts.

Collects in cash or credit from departing guests.

Uses telephones, telewriters, pneumatic tubes, switchboards, video display terminals, and other computer equipment.

Exhibit 3–6   The job description of a guest-service agent (or room clerk) is broad ranging, requiring persons with good people skills, good organizational skills, and good communication skills, including those of salesmanship.

▶**Room Reservations.**   Reservations are requests for rooms from prospective guests who intend to arrive sometime in the future. These are received, processed, and confirmed by the reservations department, which is supervised by the reservation manager, who reports to the rooms manager (see Exhibit 3–1). Reservations arrive by letter, fax, and e-mail, or even directly across the desk occasionally. Most often, they are made over the telephone. Inquiries may come to the hotel's reservation office directly, but more likely they come through the chain's or franchise's central reservation office, the 800 or 888 number. In Chapter 4 we explain the procedure in detail.

The reservation department keeps records of who is arriving, at what time, and for how long. The information, including the type of facilities wanted, must be communicated to the front-desk clerk in anticipation of the guest's arrival. Tracking the number of rooms sold and the number still available for sale is the biggest responsibility of the reservation department. Groups and individual guests must be balanced to achieve a full house (100% occupancy) without overselling, which means not committing more rooms than are available. Reservations are maintained on a day-to-day basis for a year and in less detail for as much as three to five years ahead. Computerization has made the job easier and the decisions more accurate, as explained in Chapter 5.

➤*Cashiers.*   Cashiers are actually members of the accounting staff. Their location in the front desk and their relationship to many of the front-office positions place them in direct contact with the guest-service manager, who exercises control on a day-to-day basis.

Billing, posting (recording guest charges to the accounts), and handling cash and credit-card transactions are the major duties of this position. As the guest-service agent is usually the guest's first contact, the cashier is usually the guest's last. The cashier's window has been a frequent point of irritation because of long lines and lengthy check-out delays. With computer capability, including in-room check out through the TV set, management has corrected much of that bottleneck.

Several banking services have been handled traditionally at the front-office cashier's window. These include check cashing, cash advances, safe deposit boxes, and cash collections. Changes in the way we do business have made these functions far less important over the years. Hotels are reluctant to cash checks or even to take them in payment. Cash loans to guests are limited to small payments given to employees for tips or for other small charges, such as postage-due. Safes are provided now in many guest rooms, and most guests use credit cards, not cash.

Design of the Front Office

Like so many other aspects of the front office, its design and location are also undergoing change. The bank teller look of the old-fashioned office has given way to an open style that is less formal and more inviting (see Exhibit 3–7). New, computerized systems have reduced the amount of paper and much of the clutter that typified the old.

➤*The Lobby.*   Front-desk computers have also shrunk the amount of floor space previously needed for the front office. This has encouraged new designs and configurations, which are coming at the same time that the lobby itself is enjoying a renaissance. For decades, the lobby was once the gathering place for business and social activities.[5] Hotel lobbies are providing that service again after a half-century of designs that limited use and discouraged lingering.

Face-lifts and exciting interiors—interior architecture has gained new advocates among hoteliers—have shrunk the front office and introduced food, drink, and comfort to once sterile lobbies. The lobby is returning to its position of grandeur and to its role as a meeting place for all types of activities (see Exhibit 3–8).

New or old, the desk must serve its several purposes. It must be accessible to the guest but take a minimal amount of costly lobby space. Heavy pedestrian traffic and the high-priced realty that hotels occupy make ground-level shops important income producers. The more space taken for clerical use by the front office, the less available for rental. Good economics and better systems have shrunk the floor space of the front office.

Increased computerization will minimize the registration desk still further by furnishing each station with a complete set of electronic tools. Functions may even be separated—general front-office services from registration, check out from information.

The lobbies of economy, budget, and highway hotels remain compact and sparse. Upgrading such lobbies might improve occupancy. Comfortable-looking entry space captures some guests who stop impulsively but turn away if their initial impression is negative.

Exhibit 3–7 The modern front desk of a small hotel is open to the lobby to encourage a sense of welcome and enhance security. The work level is below the desk level to reduce fatigue and encourage eye contact. *Courtesy of Jerome B. Temple and* Lodging *magazine.*

Exhibit 3–8 The lobby, once sterile and unimaginative, has been revitalized as a meeting and eating place and as a social center. Hyatt pioneered the atrium concept. *Courtesy of Grand Hyatt Washington, Washington, D.C.*

➤*The Desk.*   The standard front-desk counter is about 3.75 feet high and approximately 2.5 feet across. The working space on the employee's side of the desk is lower by 0.5 foot or so. Reducing the height of the work space allows the room clerk to carry out clerical duties comfortably. It also drops the equipment below the guest's eye level, permitting the employee and the guest to have better face-to-face interaction (see Exhibit 3–7). Some hotels have experimented with lobby pods, where both the employee and the guest are seated (see Exhibit 3–9).

Security is another consideration in desk design. The cashier must be secured (see Exhibit 3–10) and the desk positioned to monitor elevator traffic. Security is enhanced when front-office personnel have an unobstructed view of the lobby. Atrium hotels have all guest rooms opening into an atrium, an advantage in security design. Hyatt introduced the atrium in the late 1960's, and it revolutionized lobby design, helping to restore the lobby as a social and business gathering place. They now range from a few floors to over 20 stories high and add a spectacular scene to the lobby (see Exhibit 3–8).

Internal communications is another consideration in the design. Despite the many new marvels in communication, face-to-face interaction at the desk remains an important means of handling the day's business. Most designs center the front-office clerk as the hub of activity. Exhibits 3–10 and 3–11 locate that position in the middle of the desk.

From this advantageous location, clerks coordinate the flow of business, from reservations to cashiering. Group arrivals are the exception. Hotels with heavy group

Exhibit 3–9   The stodgy front desk is "getting a life" as it moves into the lobby where guest–staff interaction is more accessible and more hospitable. *Courtesy of Delta Hotels & Resorts, Toronto, Ontario, Canada.*

Exhibit 3–10 Design schematic for the front office, but not to scale. Letter references key the positions and equipment to a front-office design before the advent of property management systems (computerization), as illustrated in Exhibit 3–11.

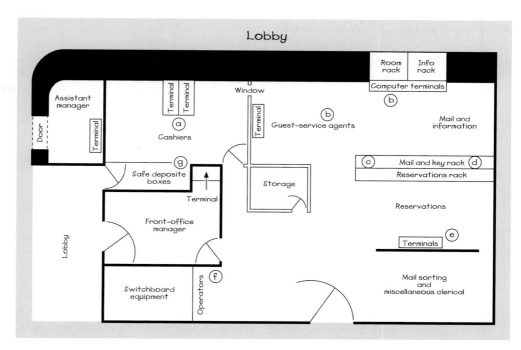

Exhibit 3–11 Design schematic of the front office, but not to scale. Letter references key the positions and equipment to a front-office design after the advent of property management systems (computerization), as illustrated in Exhibit 3–10. *Courtesy of Wilcox International, Inc., Division of American Hotel Register Co., Northbrook, Illinois.*

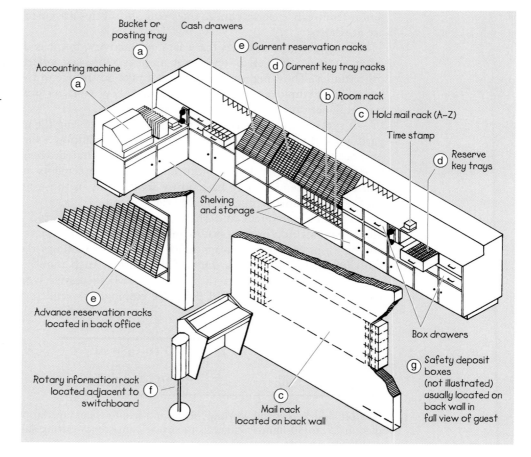

business often build satellite reception desks where busloads of arrivals can be accommodated without interfering with front-office traffic. Indeed, agencies handling group business are asking this of hotel companies.

Aesthetic as well as practical work space is the aim of modern desk design. Using lighting, form, and materials, architects must convey the image of the hotel: comfortable, open, organized, and professional.

Working Hours of the Front Office

Hotels never close. The legal definition of a hotel requires that they do not. Therefore, work schedules must provide around-the-clock staffing, at least at the front desk. Other departments (personnel or accounting) work a more normal workweek. Work schedules must also provide for the peaks and valleys that bring daily, sometimes hourly, fluctuations to the volume at the desk.

▶ *The Shift (or Watch).*   Most desk employees work an eight-hour shift, five days per week, with two successive days off. That creates three equal shifts per day. Although there are variations, the model (see Exhibit 3–12) follows the pattern of other businesses.

The day shift is preferred by most employees because it follows the usual workday. Bellpersons opt for the swing shift, when arrivals and tips are the heaviest. Even senior front-office clerks choose the swing shift if tips are customary, as they especially are at resorts.

The graveyard shift has the least guest activity, but it is during this shift that the night audit is completed. The night audit is more specialized than the other front-office duties. Thus, night auditors cannot take advantage of the general policy that allows senior employees to select their shifts. Few workers prefer graveyard, which is one explanation for the shortage of night auditors.

A special effort is needed to maintain morale during the graveyard watch. Graveyard work should be covered by formal policies. Employees must know that they are not locked into a career of night work. They are rotated when openings appear in the more desirable shifts. In the meantime, salary supplements are paid for night work, and careful attention may be paid to night meals in those hotels where the kitchen staff tends to shortchange the night crew's menu.

Rotating personnel and shifts whenever possible, and where union contracts allow, enables employees to know one another. It also reduces the chance of collusion among employees who always work together. Sometimes day and swing shifts are switched en masse. This is done at the start of each month as employees' days off allow. It is unwise to make the switch on two successive workdays. The swing shift would close at 11:30 PM, and the same employees would report for the day shift at

Day shift	7:30 AM–3:30 PM
Swing shift	3:30 PM–11:30 PM
Graveyard shift	11:30 PM–7:30 AM

Exhibit 3–12   Typical working hours at a front office. Overlapping jobs are often scheduled in 15- to 30-minute intervals to ensure consistency during shift changes.

7:30 AM the following morning. Not only is this a burdensome procedure in a large city, where employees need commuting time, but it may also be illegal under state labor laws. Shift rotations should always follow the clock: day, evening, graveyard, off; day, evening, and so on.

Most front-office positions follow the same work pattern. Cashiers, clerks, and even supervisors change shifts in concert. A 15-minute overlap offers a continuity that is lost with an abrupt change of shifts. If there are several persons in each job, individuals could leave in 15-minute intervals. If not, complementary jobs could be changed every quarter hour. Cashiers might change at 3 PM and billing clerks at 3:15 PM, for example.

▶*Forecast Scheduling.*   Proper scheduling begins with a forecast of business for the next week or longer, depending on the period of the work schedule. This information is a by-product of the reservation forecast discussed in Chapter 6. Schedules can be prepared once the demand on the front desk is known.

With forecasting and advance scheduling, employees are given their days off during the slowest part of the week. Several may be off on one day, and none on a busy day. Part-time personnel can cover peak periods, or hours of the workday may be staggered. Each technique is designed to minimize payroll costs and maximize desk coverage when required.

The amount of help needed varies during the day and even within the same shift. Cashiers are busy in the morning handling check outs and are less busy in the afternoon when the guest-service agents are busy with arrivals. Cashiers at a commercial hotel are slower on Mondays, when agents are busier, and busier on Thursdays, when agents are slower. An employee can be hired as a cashier for some days and as a clerk for others. Buyers of computer hardware should be certain that registration terminals are interchangeable with cashier terminals if job assignments are to be scheduled in response to traffic patterns.

The Split Shift.   The use of the split shift is limited to small and isolated hotels. But then it is not restricted to the front desk. The kitchen, the dining room, and the housekeeping departments schedule that way as well.

Unionization, wage-and-hour laws, and just plain physical distance have seen the decline of the split shift. Seasonal resorts still use it where wage-and-hour laws exempt seasonal workers. These resorts have remained free of unionization because of the short employment period and the transient nature of the workforce. Moreover, employees live on the resort property or nearby so that the major disadvantage of commuting is alleviated.

The split shift has a real advantage for the small resort where only one person staffs the desk. Employees need not be relieved for meals, but eat either before or after their shift. Exhibit 3–13 illustrates the long and short day commonly used at the resort desk. It is customary for employees A and B to switch shifts daily or weekly. The night auditor does not rotate watches.

Resorts that do turn-downs—replacing bathroom linen and preparing the bed for use—may require the room attendant to return in the evening for another variation of a split shift. In upscale urban hotels, turn-downs are handled by a second shift. It's a nice touch if the night attendant leaves on the pillow copies of all the messages that came in that day.

Employee A	7:00 AM–12:30 PM
Employee B	12:30 PM–6:30 PM
Employee A	6:30 PM–11:00 PM
Night Auditor	11:00 PM–7:00 AM

Exhibit 3–13   The split shift (or split watch) is used in resort hotels where labor laws allow and on-premise housing exists. Employees A and B swap shifts weekly.

➤ THE BUILDING STRUCTURE

As we note in the introduction of this chapter, there is a good deal of similarity between the hotel's organizational structure and the structure of the building that is the hotel. Moreover, both structures are very similar property to property. Every hotel offers guest rooms, the basic product that the industry sells, and every hotel has staff members to deliver that basic product. Yet the differences that exist among the hotels, differences in the physical building and differences in the organizational staffing, are what distinguish the many properties. It is these differences that account for the industry's segmentation into numerous parts.

The Old versus the New

Differentiating between hotels that were built before midcentury and those built since World War II is not difficult to do. Today's hotels take far more land—have a *large footprint* in real estate terminology—because they are more open and because the individual rooms are so much larger. Exhibits 3–14 and 3–15 make the contrast clear. Some very famous hotels in the old design still exist. Best known among them are New York's Waldorf-Astoria and Chicago's Drake.

Exhibit 3–15 represents the open design of the world's new hotels. Except for suites, room shapes and sizes are identical in this new group. To emphasize that point, contrast again the shapes and sizes of rooms in Exhibit 3–14 with those in Exhibit 3–15. Furthermore, the shape of today's room is standardized across the industry. Of course, room sizes are different. Size means floor area, and floor area is part of construction costs and hence of room rate. Older hotels required a wider range of room rates to differentiate the variety of offerings. Current designs have reduced the number of room rates from a dozen or more in the 1950s to between three and five classes a half-century later. This eases the front desk's job of quoting rates and assigning rooms.

➤**The Old: Inside Rooms.**   Inside rooms have followed the semiprivate (shared) bathroom (1930–1950) and the public (served the entire floor) bathroom (previous century) into oblivion. Rooms 58 to 97 in Exhibit 3–14 form a U shape of inside rooms around the light court. As illustrated, inside rooms are enclosed by wings of the building. Contrast this inside view to the outside rooms, numbered 02 to 28 and 72 to 98, or to the entire design of Exhibit 3–15.

The view from the inside room is down, and the roof on the lower floor is often dirty and unsightly. Inside rooms are affected by the changing position of the sun, which casts shadows into these rooms even early in the day. The light courts produce some unusually shaped rooms—rooms 60 to 66, for example. Of course, smaller rooms and inside rooms are more economical in construction and land costs.

►*The New: Suites and All-Suites.* The hotel suite has changed in meaning since the introduction of the all-suite concept. The traditional suite is a parlor (living room) with one or more bedrooms, illustrated in the modern Hotel by Exhibit 3–16 and in the more traditional hotel by Exhibit 3–14, rooms 72 and 74.

Larger suites add second or third bedrooms and additional living space. More luxurious accommodations include kitchens and formal dining rooms, saunas or

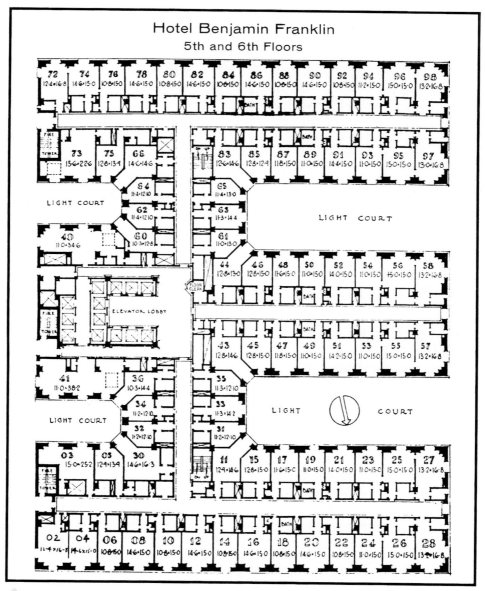

Exhibit 3–14 Typical of the decades 1925–1945, this upscale hotel offered accommodations in rooms smaller than today's budget inns. Light courts, designed to maximize land use, created odd-shaped rooms: 44, 61, and 63. (The building, the Hotel Benjamin Franklin, is a hotel no longer.)

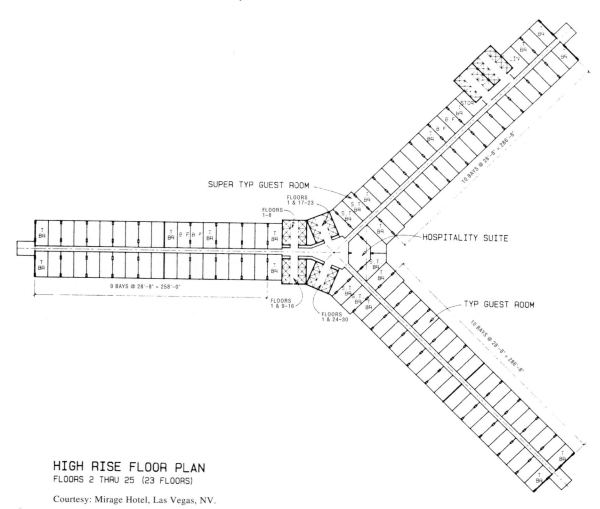

HIGH RISE FLOOR PLAN
FLOORS 2 THRU 25 (23 FLOORS)

Courtesy: Mirage Hotel, Las Vegas, NV.

Exhibit 3–15   The 21st-Century hotel is typified by the sweep of its open design and the standardization of guest room sizes and shapes. It takes a big footprint: compare it to Exhibit 3–14. *Courtesy of the Mirage Hotel, Las Vegas, Nevada.*

swimming pools, and even libraries. Almost every large suite contains a wet bar. Balconies and patios (lanai suites) are also common amenities. In the proper climate, suites have fireplaces. For a truly opulent experience, some hotels, especially casino hotels, offer a two-floor suite. So does America's heartland: The two-floor suite of the Netherland Plaza offers a panoramic view of Cincinnati.[6]

Specialty suites are named, although they may also be numbered as standard suites are. The *bridal suite,* the *presidential suite,* and the *penthouse suite* are common terminology. Historical figures or local references that emphasize the theme of the hotel—for example, the Kit Carson Suite—are other bases for choosing names.

Suites in all-suite hotels are a different product altogether. They are designed for a different market and a different use (Exhibit 3–17). The intent is for the all-suite to compete against the standard hotel room, not against the hotel suite. To compensate

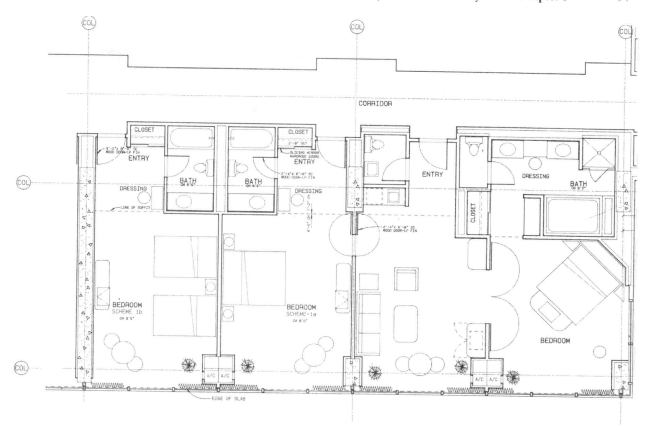

TYP END SUITE & GUEST ROOM PLAN
SCALE: 1/4" = 1'-0"

Courtesy: Mirage Hotel, Las Vegas, NV.

Exhibit 3–16 Folding doors separate the parlor and bedroom of this one-bedroom suite, which can be enlarged by unlocking the connecting door to the adjacent, second bedroom. Note the back-to-back plumbing and airconditioning (A/C) shafts. *Courtesy of the Mirage Hotel, Las Vegas, Nevada.*

for the extra square footage offered by the all-suite unit, public space is reduced. Forty percent of the typical hotel building is allocated to public areas. The all-suite hotel cuts that figure back by at least half.

All-suite and standard hotels alike employ a building technique that was invented by Ellsworth Statler in 1923. Back-to-back utility shafts reduce the amount of runs for piping, electrical, heating, and communication lines. There is economy in both the initial construction and continuing maintenance. It is not always possible, but kitchenettes, baths, and wet bars should be so constructed. Exhibits 3–14 and 3–16 show the baths back to back.

►*Corner Rooms.* Corner rooms are the most desirable rooms on the floor. They offer a double exposure and therefore command a premium price. To enhance the price differential, corner rooms get preferential treatment from the architect. They are usually larger rooms, and they are frequently incorporated into the suite. Corner

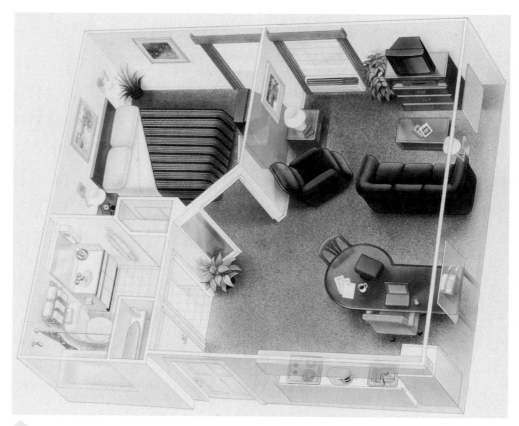

Exhibit 3–17   The large square footage of all-suite facilities is appealing to the modern traveler and to the longer-term guest, to whom the concept was originally marketed. Either a fold-out chair or a sofa bed in the parlor provides extra sleeping accommodations. Candlewood is one of the newest entries in what is presently the fastest growing segment of lodging. *Courtesy of Candlewood Hotel Company, Wichita, Kansas.*

rooms were an integral part of the older hotel because its design created them (see Exhibit 3–14). Modern hotels have fewer building corners and thus fewer corner rooms; round hotel buildings have none at all.

▶*Motor Inns.*   The highway hotel, child of the motel and grandchild to the tourist court, has its own, unique design. But it isn't one that is widely applauded. In general, these have been inexpensive properties to build. Since the price of land is usually less than the cost of erecting a high-rise building, motor inns are almost always low-rise: one, two or, rarely, three floors high. Consequently, they have the outline of a rectangle or a single strip of housing (see Exhibit 3–18). Providing easy access to outside parking, which is the aim of the highway property, necessarily limits design possibilities. Building an L or U shape helps with exterior appeal. Efforts are now being directed toward a more attractive exterior design, but the emphasis is on color and facing materials and on the entryway of the port-cochère rather than on changes in the basic rectangular configuration.

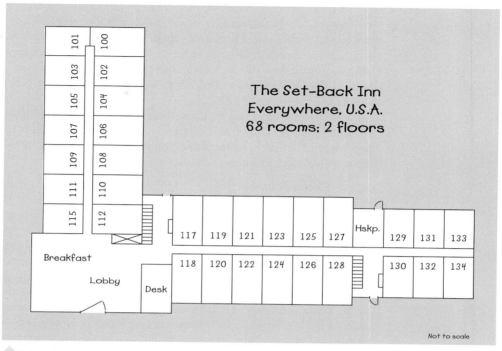

Exhibit 3–18   The typical design of the small, often two-story motor inn of 50 to 75 rooms is represented in this prototype. Ownership may still be mom-and-pop, but most motels are flagged with a franchise identity.

Numbering for Identification

Everyone uses the guest-room number for identification. Certainly, guests depend on the number to locate themselves. Desk personnel address guests by name, but within the front office, identification is always by number and then, if at all, by guest name. Hotel rooms are identified first by floor number and then by room number.

▶*Floor Numbering.*   Floors are numbered upward sequentially, but most Western hotels omit floor 13. New York City's Plaza Hotel is an exception: It has both a 13th floor and a room 13. Numbering systems reflect the culture of the hotel's location. Four is to the Orient as 13 is to the Occident. One never finds four in Asia as a room number, and sometimes not even numbers that add to four. Seven is a lucky number in the United States, as it is, along with six, in the Far East.

Americans number the first sleeping floor as floor one regardless of the number of levels between it and the ground. Mezzanine, upper-ground floor, and shopping level are interspersed without any standard order. The sequence adds an array of nonnumerical elevator buttons that confuse anyone who isn't a lifetime employee of the hotel. *M* is for mezzanine; *MM* is for the second mezzanine floor. Try to decipher *LM*, *SB*, and *S2* (lower mezzanine, sub basement, and sub basement 2).

The rest of the world begins numbering with the ground floor as floor number one. Even without the intermediary floors, what would be the 10th floor in the United States would be the 11th floor elsewhere.

A different numbering system needs to be used if the hotel is comprised of several low-rise buildings. Identically numbering each low rise unit of, say, three or four stories is one technique. Then each building is given a different name, and the keys for each are color coded. Others prefer to number the floors sequentially, moving in order from one building to the next. Guests get confused because only one unit has its ground floor numbered as floor one. Ground floors of the other units will have numbers in the teens or even 20s.

Hotels that have two or three towers have the same options. Either the towers are differentiated by name (the river tower) or direction (the east tower) with room numbers identical in each, or the floors are numbered sequentially with the bottom floor of the second tower using the next floor number in sequence.

➤ *Room Numbering.*   Assigning numbers to rooms is far more arbitrary than going up floor levels. Each hotel has a unique design, and that design determines where to begin numbering and what sequence to use. Sequential numbering is not even possible in an old floor plan like the one in Exhibit 3–14—too many corridors run at right angles to one another. Even one as simple as Exhibit 3–18 offers choices.

Rooms are frequently numbered odd and even along opposite sides of the corridor. The numbering might begin at the elevator bay and progress upward as the sequence marches down the corridor: 101, 103, 105 along one side; 102, 104, 106, and so on along the other. Of course, there is no rule that requires this. An atrium hotel such as the old Anatole in Dallas has rooms on only one side of the corridor and the numbering is sequential. All-suite hotel rooms are numbered in the usual manner because every room in the hotel is a suite.

Different floor designs present different numbering problems and require good signage. If the elevator empties into the center of the sleeping floor, the logic of any system begins to break down. The numbering system gets very confusing when a new wing or ell is added to the original structure. Rarely is the entire floor, old rooms and new, renumbered in sequence. The new wing may be numbered sequentially from the old, without concern about the interface with the old numbers. Sometimes the old numbers are duplicated in the new wing by adding an identifying suffix or prefix, like N for north wing.

Care in using certain numbers such as four and nine applies equally to room numbering as to floor numbering, as mentioned earlier. In Asia, correct positioning is also important. Many hoteliers there employ a fung shui (or feng shui) master who helps position the location of everything from doors and windows to desks and files and helps decide the most auspicious date to open a new hotel, a new dining room, or whatever.

Adjoining or Connecting Rooms.   Rooms that abut along the corridor are said to be adjoining rooms. Using the numerical sequence discussed above, 101, 103, and 105 would be adjoining rooms, as would 102, 104, and 106. If there is direct room-to-room access (a door between the rooms) without using the corridor (Exhibit 3–14, rooms 53, 55, and 57), the rooms are said to be connecting. Obviously, every connecting room adjoins, but not every adjoining room connects. Exhibit 3–16 shows adjoining rooms on the far left; adjoining/connecting rooms in the center.

Room Shape and Size

The guest room is the hotel's product. Therefore, its shape and size are critical to customer satisfaction. Size, especially, separates the industry into the several classes. Small rooms are associated with hard budget properties, huge rooms with deluxe accommodations. As the rate discussion in Chapter 9 points out, setting the different rate classes within the hotel also depends in part on the differences in the physical rooms.

►*Room Shape.*   There has been little overall change in the shape of guest rooms. As concave, square, and round structures are built, corresponding changes occur in the interior shapes and dimensions. Research may eventually show advantages in guest satisfaction or in reduced wear from certain shapes. Until then, the parallelogram remains the classic favorite, with the depth of the room approximately twice the width. The first increases in room size are made by adding to the depth. Width is improved next by increasing from 12 or 13 feet to 16 feet, which is a luxury-class room.

Other shapes, which might look interesting from the outside, present certain internal problems. A round building of small diameter produces rooms without parallel walls. The outer wall is circular, and the inner walls are angled to accommodate the bath and the central service core within the limited cross section of the small diameter.

The presence of full or false balconies and French or sliding doors gives a sense of spaciousness to any room. Balconies are often part of a facade that adds interest to the outside of a building.

►*Room Size.*   Room shape is primarily an architectural decision; room size is derived from financial and marketing factors. Although the trend has been toward larger and larger rooms, the economy segment has capitalized on smaller accommodations and smaller rates.

In the final analysis, the market determines the rate structure and consequently the average room size and its furnishings. That market varies from hotel to hotel, so that the twin double beds of the family-oriented hotel might be inappropriate to a property servicing the business traveler.

A comparison of international accommodations illustrates the danger of trying to identify hotels as one industry. As mentioned in Chapter 2, Japan's smallest budget rooms, called *capsule rooms,* are nothing more than sleeping accommodations. Guests change in a common locker area and crawl into a capsule approximately 5 feet high, 5 feet wide, and less than 7 feet long. That is less than 40 square feet (not even 4 square meters).[7] Most hard budgets are larger. The Ibis chain, a European entry into the budget market, builds rooms of approximately 130 square feet (approximately 12 square meters). Econo Lodges and Super 8s have rooms of almost 200 square feet (nearly 19 square meters).

The surprise comes when comparisons are made between today's budget accommodations and the rooms of the Benjamin Franklin hotel (Exhibit 3–14), which was a first-class facility in its era. The 150- to 175-square foot room of the prosperous 1920s was smaller than many of today's economy facilities, such as Choice Hotels International's Sleep Inn, at 210 square feet.

The Far East contributes to the other end of the scale as well. It has many of the world's opulent hotels, with large rooms and many extras. Hong Kong's Shangri-La Hotel offers a 500-square-foot facility (bath included). That size is immediately recognized as super luxury. (Guests do not get a feeling of luxury until the room size passes 400 square feet.)

The Four Seasons in New York City (370 rooms) compares favorably with luxury properties worldwide. Its rooms are 600 square feet (about 55.75 square meters), including a 120-square-foot bath. The standard American room measures between 250 and 350 square feet (approximately 23.3 to 32.5 square meters). So the Ramada International, another New York City hotel, is right on target at 350 square feet.

It's not enough to multiply the size of the room by the number of rooms to get the hotel's total square footage. Provisions must be made for service areas, public space, lobbies, offices, corridors, and so on. That requires almost a doubling of the total square feet needed for just the guest rooms. Even then, allowances must be made for the size, type, and class of hotel. A full-service, convention property might require a total of 900 to 1,200 square feet per guest room, although the room itself is only 350 to 400 square feet. An economy property with no public space might get by with as little as 600 total square feet per guest room, of which the room itself is 250 to 275 square feet. All of this bears on the amount of land needed to erect the property.

All-suite hotels provide a contrast in size, both to one another and in comparison with standard nonsuite properties. All-suite properties are segmented into economy, midmarket, and upscale: Room size is the major difference. Guest Quarters pioneered the extended-stay hotel with a 650-square-foot unit. All-suite hotels include bedroom, parlor, bath, and kitchenette, making a unit rather than a room the standard of measure. The budget room of AmeriSuites is about 380 square feet; Park Suites measure some 480 square feet. Fireplaces carry Homewood Suites to 550 square feet. Extended-stay suites that range from 400 to 650 square feet equate to the size of a standard apartment in many large U.S. cities!

How the Room Is Used.   Hotel chains use models to test guest acceptance and preview costs before proceeding with a new concept or with a major renovation of an existing property. The disproportionately high cost of building just one model room is offset by identification of design and furnishing flaws before the major project gets under way. For one thing, more thought is focused on how the room will be used.

Different kinds of guests use rooms in different ways. Within the same dimensions, a destination hotel furnishes proportionately more storage space than a transient property. A transient property allocates more space to sleeping and less to the living area than a destination facility. Such would be the case with New York City hotels, where the average use of the room is eight hours. Very cold or very hot climates increase usage of the room.

The use of the room also dictates the kinds of furniture required. A destination resort wouldn't need a desk, but the hotel rooms in China and the Middle East serve as company offices and are furnished as such.

Designers have become quite successful in making small rooms look larger. For example, nightstands can be eliminated by mounting bedside lamps on the wall. Mirrors do a good job of creating a perception of space. Wall-to-wall draperies and fewer patterned materials throughout the room add to the feeling of roominess. Designers also use mirrors and balconies to expand the sense of space. Nevertheless, it takes about 20 additional square feet (1.86 meters) before the occupant notices the larger size. That's the point where a rate increase could be justified if spaciousness is the only basis for the increase.

Clearly, there is no standard room. The hotel industry is moving in several directions at once. Miniprices use module units and measure 12 feet from center to center. Luxury operations opt for 15-foot centers and lengths of 30 to 35 feet. (The standard carpet sizes of 12 and 15 feet dictate the dimensions unless the plan calls for a custom job.) Costs of energy, borrowed money, and labor limit expansion even as competition pushes for more space. Comparisons, therefore, begin with the marketplace.

Bed and Bath

The increasing size of the bed—Americans are getting bigger—accounts in part for the increased size of the guest room. The new role of the bathroom—as a weapon in the competition wars—also contributes to the creep in total square footage.

▶***The Bed.*** Bed types, bed coverings, and bed sizes vary across the world and across time. Quilted bedding appeared in Japan about 1500. It is most certain that the nomads of the Middle East were using some form of stuffing in animal skins (early futons) to ease their sleep even earlier than the 16th Century. The modern American hotel room has gone through periods which favored, first, the double bed and then twin beds. Neither of these are popular today. The queen and king have taken over. If today's hotel wants a room with two beds, it opts for queen–doubles rather than traditional twin beds. Of course, larger beds mean larger rooms. Larger rooms mean higher construction costs and, hence, higher room rates.

Beds are being lowered as well as lengthened. The usual height of the mattress and box spring is 22 to 24 inches, in contrast to the average chair of some 17 inches. Lowering the bed to 17 inches makes the room appear larger because all the pieces are on the same horizontal plane. It also makes the bed easier to sit on, and lower hotel beds are used for that purpose. Adequate seating is needed to reduce the heavy wear on mattresses when beds are used as chairs. It is a real conflict: Lowered beds make the room appear larger, but the mattresses don't last as long. Mattress life can be extended substantially if the mattress is rotated and turned on a regular schedule of four times per year. Good housekeeping departments do this as part of their quarterly deep cleaning. The position of the mattress is tracked by a system of arrows attached to the side of the mattress.

If every hotel room were a replica of every other room, room assignments would be greatly eased. Every one would get the same room configuration, and the major decision for the desk would be which floor and what location within the floor. Although modern hotels are headed that way, as the earlier discussion on floor plans indicated, the front office still needs some shorthand symbols for designating different bedding and accommodations. These symbols, which were critical when hotels used room racks (see Exhibit 13–13), have been carried over into computer equipment.

Bed Sizes and Bed Symbols. The terminology used to describe the capacity of the room is often confused with the terminology used to describe the beds in the room. For example, a single room is one that sleeps one person, but that person could be in one of several different beds. *Single* and *double* refer with equal ambiguity to (1) the room rate, (2) the number of guests housed in the room, (3) the number of persons the room is capable of accommodating, or (4) the size and type of the beds. It is possible to have a single occupant in a double bed being charged a single rate although the room is designated as a double, meaning that it could accommodate two persons.

A single occupant in a queen double sometimes needs assurance that no additional charge is being made for the unused bed. The single-room configuration—that is, one single bed for one person—is unknown today. Thus, to the innkeeper, "single" means single occupancy or single rate.

SINGLE BED. A single bed, symbol S, sleeps one person. A true single is 36 by 75 inches, but is very rarely used; it is simply too small. Instead, the rare single room (room for one person) is furnished with a single twin or, most likely, one double bed. When the room is furnished with one twin, the symbol S is used, when furnished with a double bed, the symbol is D. Single beds must measure at least 39 by 72 inches to win an AAA rating.

TWIN BEDS. A twin room, symbol T, contains two beds each accommodating one person. (Two persons could also be roomed in a double, a queen, or a king bed). Twins measure 39 by 75 inches each and use linen 72 by 108 inches. The 75-inch mattress has been replaced in all bed sizes with a longer length, called a California length. The 39-inch width remains with the twin, but the length has been stretched to between 79 and 84 inches. Additional inches are added to the linen length as well.

Because of their flexibility, twins once accounted for 60 to 70% of total available rooms. The trend shifted as twins were replaced by double–doubles, and then queens, and then by queen–doubles. Single business travelers actually prefer a two-bedded room: one for sleeping and one for spreading papers.

Because the double–double and queen–double sleep four persons, they are also called *quads* or *family rooms*. Motel owners will offer couples queen–doubles at reduced rates with the stipulation that only one bed be used. A survey done some time ago by Sheraton's franchise division showed that the second bed of a double–double or queen–double was used about 15% of the time.

DOUBLE BED.   D is the symbol for double bed. The width ranges from 54 to 57 inches, and that's an important 3 inches. Like the twin bed, the length of the double has been stretching from 75 inches to the California 80-inch or more length. Linen sizes would be 90 to 93 inches wide and 113 inches long with a California mattress. Half a double bed is about 28 inches or so, narrower even than the single. That alone explains the double's loss of popularity among guests who are getting ever larger and heavier.

QUEEN AND KING BEDS.   Queen and king beds (symbols Q and K) are extra wide (60 and 72 inches, respectively) and extra long. They made popular the California length, which has also been called a *European king*. Although designed for two, three or four persons might squeeze in when the room is taken as a family room.

Both beds require larger rooms (the critical distance between the foot of the bed and the furniture—a 3-foot minimum—remains) and larger sheets, 108 by 122.5 inches. Since laundry costs are calculated by weight, larger sheets mean larger laundry bills. A larger room with extra laundry costs can only mean a higher room rate even without consideration for the extra, up-front costs of the larger bed, mattress, and linen.

HOLLYWOOD BED.   Two beds joined by a common headboard is called a hollywood bed. Hollywoods use the symbol of the twins, T, since that's what they are. They are difficult beds to make, because the room attendant cannot get between them. To overcome this, the beds are placed on rollers and swung apart, resulting in rapid carpet wear. Because the total dimension of these beds is 78 by 75 inches (two twins), they can be converted into a king by replacing the two mattresses with one king mattress laid across both springs.

STUDIO BED (ROOM).   A studio bed is a sofa by day and a bed by night. During the day, the bed is slipcovered and the pillows are stored in the backrest. There is neither headboard nor footboard once the sofa is pulled away from the backrest to create the bed. Today's guest room serves a dual bedroom–living room function, so studio rooms should be popular with business guests. They once were. Studios are not popular anymore because the beds are not comfortable and the all-suite hotel serves the same dual purpose.

The studio room, once called an executive room, has been used to redo small, single rooms in older hotels. *UP*, undersized parlor, is one of the symbols once used for studios. In Europe, a parlor that has no sleeping facilities is called a salon.

SOFA BED. A sofa bed is similar in function to a studio bed. It is a sofa first of all, which makes sitting more comfortable. It is usually 17 inches off the floor, whereas the studio bed may be as high as 22 inches. Unlike the studio bed, which rolls away from its frame, the sofa bed opens in accordion fashion from the seat. Since it unfolds, the sofa bed is less convenient and requires more space than the studio.

Parlors are generally equipped with sofa beds as part of a suite (see Exhibit 3–16), but a studio bed is usually a room unto itself. Sofa beds can be single, double, or even queen size, although the single is more like a three-quarter bed (48 by 75 inches).

Sofa beds are often called *hide-a-beds,* and thus carry an H designation. Large rooms that contain both standard beds and hide-a-beds are junior suites. Rooms in all-suite hotels offer a sofa bed in the parlor portion of the unit (see Exhibit 3–17).

ROLLAWAY BED (COT). A cot or rollaway is a portable utility bed that is added to the usual room furnishings on a temporary basis. A rollaway sleeps one person, and a comfortable one measures 34 by 75 inches and uses twin sheets. Cots usually come smaller—30 by 72 inches, with linen 63 by 99 inches.

Setting up cots is costly in housekeeping time, primarily because the cots are rarely located conveniently. Cot storage never seems to be high in the designer's priority.

WATER BED. In two decades, water beds jumped from a novelty to a hot item and then fell back again. The bed is rarely found in hotel rooms, although it offers an alternative to inner-spring and foam mattresses. Water beds have a long history, dating back to pre-Christian, nomadic tribes, which filled goatskins with water. Their use was rediscovered by a Californian who first tried starch and gelatin as fillers. The water bed is still primarily a phenomenon of the western states.

FUTON. The Japanese futon, which is a cotton-quilted bed, is another addition to the American sleeping design. Futons come in regular mattress sizes. The thick layers of batting are easily stored and readily adapted to service as a couch or bed.

MURPHY BED. Like many other copyrighted brands that identify generic products, *Murphy bed* has come to mean any fold-up bed. The popularity of fold-up-into-the-wall beds waxes and wanes. They're great for dormitories, but are not now in widespread use in the commercial lodging industry. Disappearing by day and appearing at night improves on the dual use of the guest room. With the bed folded, the room is usable as a meeting place or for the commercial display of goods. Fold-up beds have an edge on studio rooms because the bed is far more comfortable. One needs to look far, indeed, to find either of the two in commercial use.

And for the future? Possibly air beds—warm air cushions that support the sleeper without bed frame, mattress, or linen. What a revolutionary thing that will be! In the meantime, there is apt to be an increasing degree of choice. One day, guests will pick from a variety of mattresses: foam, spring, hard, soft, orthopedic, adjustable, vibrating, flotation, and futons.

▶*The Bath.* *Bath* is the industry's jargon for bathroom; it is not the guest's bathing accommodation, not the bathtub. Into the *bath*[room] goes the toilet (or water closet), the sink (or lavatory), and the tub (or bathtub) and shower. The hotel bath has undergone many changes throughout this century, but its position as a sound barrier between the room and the corridor remains. That location, abutting the corridor (see Exhibits 3–16 and 3–17) saves construction costs and leaves the desirable outside wall for windows or balconies. In more recent years, modular construction of the bath has gained some popularity. The bath is prefabricated away from the construction site and installed as one unit. Modular construction reduces the number of building trades required on the construction site and, some say, improves the quality of the work.

The bath accounts for about 20% of the room size. Thus, the baths in hard budget inns measure about 35 square feet and in midrange properties about 70 square feet. The luxurious Four Seasons, mentioned earlier, has a bath of 120 square feet. What a contrast this is to the hotel of a century ago, when public baths served whole floors or entire wings. (Very early hotels had all their baths in the basements because the mechanics of pumping water to higher floors was not yet in place.)

Stall showers, which occupy little space, gained favor as old hotels converted from rooms without baths. They fit easily into old, large closets or corners of renovated rooms. Tub and shower combinations were installed next when lifestyles changed again. Having both meets the cultural needs of all guests. The Japanese, for example, definitely favor tubs, just as they choose twin beds over all other choices. The bidet, which is installed in many other countries, has not found acceptance in the American home and thus not in the American hotel.

Upscale properties have cut back on low-cost amenities such as soap and shampoo. Strangely, they have gone all out in building larger bathrooms with expensive appointments: in-floor scales, in-bath telephones, electric shoeshine equipment, adjustable no-fog mirrors, and plush bathrobes. The Palmer House Hilton in Chicago, which was renovated several years ago, has 300 guest rooms with his-and-her bathrooms. The same Four Seasons mentioned above features bathtubs that fill in 1 minute!

Not only is the bath larger, but the ancillary space has grown as well. Dressing areas and second lavatories outside the bath proper have also increased the overall dimensions. Replacing closets with open hanger space has helped compensate. Consolidating furniture also saves space. One vertical piece incorporates several horizontal space users. Into armoires, for example, have gone television sets, bars and refrigerators, writing desks with telephones, and several drawers for clothing. Reflected in the new design is the two-night stay and garment-bag luggage of today's traveler.

▶ SUMMARY

Hotels need structure to carry out their historical assignment—selling and servicing accommodations. In Chapters 1 and 2 we outlined the variety of lodging accommodations that have emerged as innkeepers labor to meet these marketplace expectations. Hoteliers do this in part by altering both the structure of the hotel's organization and the physical room being offered for sale. Although the size, design, and accoutrements of today's room would surprise the historical innkeeper, the basic commodities of accommodations and service have remained unchanged.

The modern guest is housed in a hotel room of some 350 square feet of floor space, of which about one-fifth is assigned to the bath (the bathroom). Segmentation makes even a simple generalization like this one difficult to sustain. On the upscale side, room size exceeds 600 square feet, with suites measuring upward of 2,000 square feet. The hard-budget end of the continuum offers room sizes of less than 150 square feet. (Outside the United States, square meters—there are 0.093 square meters in 1 square foot—are the standard measure.) Similarly, upscale baths have sunken marble tubs, in-bath television sets, and dual lavatories, while hard budgets have no tubs, plastic bath curtains, and few amenities.

Hotel managers have looked as carefully at their staff structure as at their room structure. New societal expectations have wrought changes in service even as the increased physique of the modern traveler has changed the size of bedding. Guests are less willing to pay for, or wait for, individualized care, electing instead a degree of self-service. Less service demanded and less service offered have slashed the ranks of the uniformed services department, and automation has reduced the need for telephone and elevator operators. Electronics permit self-check in and check out, altering further the duties of the front office.

Organizational changes do not always mean staff reductions. Security departments have been enlarged again and again as concern for guest safety grows. Attending to governmental and environmental regulations requires staff attorneys where there had been none before. Changes in the workforce, in its size and in the laws that govern labor, necessitate large human resource departments, whereas a single personnel officer had handled the job a decade or two ago.

Some organizational changes have shifted responsibility rather than altering departmental size. Cashiers must deal with debit cards; concierges have new service responsibilities; integrated reservation systems have significantly altered the role of the reservations department. Indeed, reservations is probably the most dynamic of all the hotel departments. The function of the reservation system and the electronic-highway linkage that is its modern structure is discussed next, in Part II.

Hotel keeping has mutated and restructured over time. As long as the momentum continues, as long as the industry continually reorganizes and reinvents itself, it remains competitive and successful.

➤ QUESTIONS AND PROBLEMS

1. With special attention to front-office activities, prepare a list of duties carried out by one (or more) of the fictional staff in the book *Hotel* by Arthur Hailey (Garden City, NY: Doubleday & Company, Inc., 1965; also available through Bantam Books).

2. Using information provided in this chapter or acquired elsewhere, sketch to approximate scale a typical room with furnishings that Choice Hotels might be building in Europe. (That requires dimensions to be in meters and square meters.) Above the drawing list the several assumptions as 1, 2, 3, . . . *n* that your drawing relies upon. Cite references external to the text if used.

3. Using information provided in this book or acquired elsewhere, *estimate* the total square feet of New York City's Four Seasons Hotel. Show the several mathematical steps and label all of your figures.

4. Either as part of your travels this term or as part of a field trip, contrast the size, shape, bedding, price, and characteristics of two or more hotel rooms. Discuss.

5. Interview a hotel manager or a front-office employee. From the information obtained, construct the organizational chart of the front office, and prepare a description of any one front-office job, using Exhibits 3–5 and 3–6 as a guide.

6. Using the typical occupancy pattern of an urban hotel (see Exhibit 1–5), plot the bi-weekly work schedule for the desk of a 300-room hotel that has separate room clerk and cashier positions. The switchboard is not at the desk. Strive for efficient coverage with minimum payroll costs. All full-time employees receive two successive days off and work an eight-hour day, five days per week.

➤ NOTES

1. The housekeeping staff of the 4,000-room Excalibur Hotel (Las Vegas) numbers 750 persons.

2. The International Union of Concierges was founded in Paris, France, in 1952 and in the United States in 1978. Members wear the Golden Keys (Les Clefs d'Or) that are their symbol of professionalism.

3. The prison in Paris's Palais de Justice is the Conciergerie prison. Marie Antoinette was imprisoned there during the French Revolution.

4. The sequence is different in casino hotels, where casino revenue accounts for 60% of the gross and rooms only 15%. Food is 12%, beverage is 9%, and other is 4%.

5. President Ulysses Grant (1869–1877) frequently walked from the White House to the Willard, now an Inter-Continental Hotel, to have a cigar and a drink. Petitioners waiting to argue their constituents' positions hovered in the lobby—thus, the term *lobbyists*.

6. The two-floor Governor's Suite of the Fontainebleau Hilton (Miami Beach) is 20,000 square feet (the size of a dozen average homes) and has five bathrooms.

7. One square meter is 10.76 square feet. To convert square feet into square meters, divide 10.76 into the number of square feet. To convert square meters into square feet, divide the number of square meters by 0.093.

PART II

The Reservations Process

Chapter 4
Changing Methods for Making Today's Reservations

Chapter 5
Individual and Group Reservations

Chapter 6
Forecasting Availability and Overbooking

From the largest chains to the smallest independent operations, significant investment is being made year after year in better, faster, and more enhanced reservations technologies. Whether the investment is tens of thousands of dollars for an independent property or tens of millions of dollars for a chainwide system, the goal remains the same—to increase the accuracy, accessibility, and breadth of reservations venues for the property(s).

For the chain (or consortium of chains), the simple toll-free telephone reservations centers developed 40 years ago remain the foundation of the reservations process. However, through last-room availability technology, central reservations agents are now more informed and up to the minute in terms of space availability, rate structures, and even the ability to visualize (through

CD-ROM) each of the chain's properties. Through seamless connectivity technology, travel agents, airlines, and Internet providers offer additional options for making and taking a reservation. In almost all cases, the reservations are made in real time, directly to the chain's individual property being reserved. This saves the central reservation system (CRS) the task of forwarding reservations to the individual property and the property the task of updating its system with each CRS reservation received.

For the customer, these new technological enhancements lend ease, variety, and accessibility to the reservations process. In addition, the increasing sophistication of yield management technology is making the cost of a hotel room a real bargain for guests who are able to travel during the off-season, on the spur of the moment, or for those who are able to plan trip dates far in advance.

CHAPTER 4

Changing Methods for Making Today's Reservations

Outline

Global Distribution
The Airline Systems
Seamless Connectivity
Taking the Reservation
Other Electronic Reservations Trends

Automated Revenue Management Systems
The Yield Management Revolution
Automated Yield Management Systems

Hotel reservations technology has certainly come a long way since Kemmons Wilson first introduced Holiday Inn's central reservation system Holidex in 1965.[1] Although the Holidex central reservations system was the first of its kind in the lodging industry, it was founded on a simple idea. Give potential hotel guests and travel agents (who book a large percentage of all reservations) easy access to the company's rooms inventory. With one easy phone call, the purchaser of the product could learn about availability, location, and pricing of rooms.

The early central reservations systems had one practice in common: they were all based on use of the telephone. And since most households had access to a telephone in the 1960s, this vehicle proved practical and successful. Today, most households have access to a computer, and the computer (via the Internet) is rapidly replacing the telephone as the preferred means for booking a hotel reservation. Although it still represents a small percentage of total rooms reservations, on-line bookings have been growing at a compounded rate of 30% per month (see Exhibit 4–1).

➤ GLOBAL DISTRIBUTION

A complete understanding of today's complicated reservations technologies requires a look back to the beginning. In the beginning, even before the advent of Holidex, the airline industry was developing its own reservations systems. These airline systems proved to be an efficient and low-cost means for taking reservations. Based on these early airline successes, the lodging industry soon followed suit.

It is interesting to note that the lodging industry has historically followed airlines reservations technology ever since. The airlines have generally been the developers and

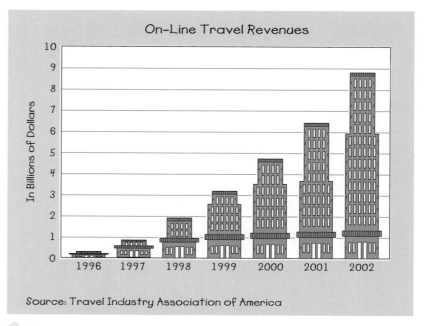

Source: Travel Industry Association of America

Exhibit 4–1 Booking travel reservations on-line is the fastest growing method—up 30% annually—of making travel arrangements. It is, in fact, among the fastest growing of all Internet-related businesses.

investors in new systems, while the lodging industry has demonstrated itself to be somewhat more conservative. By choosing to wait on the sidelines in the early stages of development, hotel chains have ultimately saved money by taking advantage of existing technologies and systems.

The Airline Systems

In the early 1960s, airlines began developing electronic reservations systems to ease the process for booking airline seats by in-house airline reservations clerks. Within a decade, the first airline reservations systems were being placed in travel agency offices. This was the first link in today's global distribution system networks.

You see, it makes sense to let someone else book the reservation. The airlines knew this back in the 1970s. Why have the travel agent call the airline to book a reservation when we have the technology to place the reservations system terminal right in the travel agent's office? In addition, since the travel agent is a one-stop source for hotel and rental car reservations, too, the new airline systems soon transformed into global networks.

It wasn't long before every possible airline had its hand in some reservations network. But these networks were expensive (American Airlines alone had invested well over $1 billion by 1985), and most airlines were financially or strategically forced to join together in developing central reservations systems (CRS) networks (see Exhibit 4–2). An excellent example of such a network is Worldspan, which joined together the systems originally owned by Northwest, Delta, and TWA Airlines.

Some of the most expensive components of airline CRSs were the individual terminals placed in travel agency offices. As such, larger agencies with access to more potential bookings received more terminals from the various airlines than did smaller agencies. A travel agency with a large assortment of different airline terminals had more options than did a smaller agency. This difference in size and accessibility to airlines became even more pronounced as the airlines began offering hotel rooms and rental car bookings directly through their systems. Larger agencies were now able to sell a complete trip, smaller agencies still needed to make their reservations by telephone.

Smaller travel agents weren't the only ones left out of the picture. Many major lodging chains were not connected to airline reservation systems either. Although they were able to join, some lodging chains thought the costs were prohibitive. A single hotel property in the chain would have had to pay three separate commissions for a single reservation: The hotel would have to pay the travel agent a 10% (or higher) commission; the airline would take a fee for access to the airline reservations system; and the hotel chain would take its normal fee for booking through the chain's central reservation office (CRO). Those chains that chose not to join the airline reservations system were still available to the travel agent by telephone, but in many cases telephone reservations just were not made.

To address this problem, many hotel chains began providing more efficient telephone reservation services to travel agents. In an attempt to encourage telephone bookings, hotel chains established private 1-800 toll-free numbers exclusively for travel agents. These private phone numbers were staffed by experienced reservationists who could answer questions and book reservations quickly. As efficient as this may sound, to many agents the telephone approach was not as appealing as the direct-access airline computer terminal.

Another issue that was apparent during these years was the fact that the hotel information listed on the airline reservations system was old news. Just as the hotel

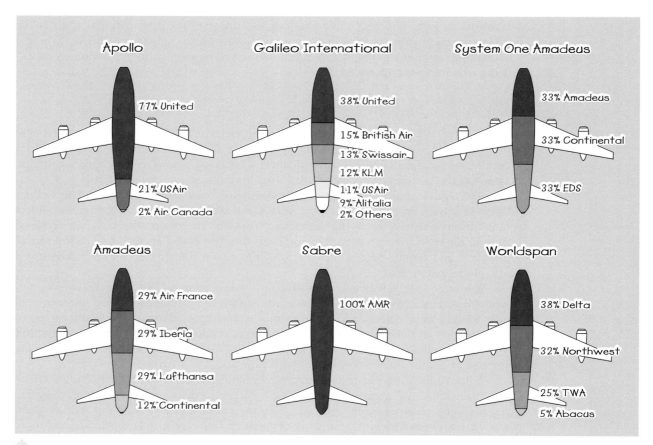

Exhibit 4–2 The size and cost of CRSs are staggering: approximately 400,000 terminals worldwide with corresponding technology and support. Ownership and operation require the resources of joint ventures like these. Only American Airlines' AMR Corporation (SABRE, now publicly traded) has been able to go it alone.

chain's CRO was not full-duplex at this stage, neither was the airline system. Hotels still needed to close availability when only a few rooms remained, they were still not able to alter rates at a moment's notice, and they were still only able to offer a few basic rate categories. In fact, many airline reservations systems only allowed a set number of changes to hotel information per day, and they required several hours' lead time. As a result, the risk of overbooking through the airline reservations system was high.

With the old-fashioned, one-way downloading of rates and availability, hotel chains and airline systems were constantly updating information. Not only was that labor intensive and prone to errors, but it created time lags between the creation of new data and its appearance on the CRS.

Seamless Connectivity

By the late 1980s, the quantity of transactions between the airline global distribution systems (GDSs) and the hotel central reservations offices[2] (CROs) began outpacing the unsophisticated half-duplex communication interfaces that were in place at the time.

Half-duplex systems (also known as *type B* systems) were basically one-way communication. A message would be sent in one direction, the response would be sent some time later. These type B systems required the travel agent to complete their rooms requests (or airline seats or rental cars) and forward them to the CRS. Minutes or even hours later, they received their confirmation. This delay was costly, frustrating, and prone to numerous errors and overbooking mistakes.

The introduction of full-duplex (also known as *type A*) communication in 1989 was a first step in solving this problem. Type A communication provided immediate confirmation of reservations requests (usually within about 7 seconds) and up-to-date rates and availabilities between the GDS and the CRO. Full-duplex communication between the GDS and CRS was an important landmark on the road to seamless connectivity. However, one key player was still not in the game—the hotel. The big question at this point was how the hotels themselves communicated their rooms inventory information to the chains' CROs?

►*Last-Room Availability.*   The old-fashioned central reservations offices of the 1960s through 1980s required constant manual updating of room availability between the hotel and the CRO. The hotel in-house reservations department was responsible for manually tracking the number of rooms sold by the CRO and calculating how many rooms still remained available for a given date. The CRO would continue blindly selling rooms until it was notified by the hotel to close room sales. In other words, the CRO never knew how many rooms were available at the individual property; it only knew that the hotel had rooms available.

This placed an important responsibility on the in-house reservationist to notify the CRO when room availability was tightening. This notification became an exercise in timing and forecasting; as often as not, mistakes were made. Sometimes the hotel's in-house reservationist closed rooms with the CRO too early; other times, rooms were closed too late. If the reservationist closed rooms with the CRO too early, there were still rooms available for sale and those remaining rooms became the responsibility of the in-house reservations department. Many times, the reservations department did not have enough in-house reservation activity and the date would come and go with several rooms remaining unsold. On the other hand, if the in-house reservationist closed the rooms too late, the hotel was overbooked.

Commonly referred to as last-room availability or full-duplex systems, today's CRSs offer on-line, two-way communication with all affiliated hotels in the chain. No longer a hit-and-miss game of guessing when the last room will be sold, modern CRSs can literally sell the very last room at any hotel. This is because the CRS now has on-line real information about the actual status of rooms at every hotel within the system. This is a significantly more efficient system because it allows the CRS more opportunities to sell every room without either underselling or overselling the hotel.

In addition, last-room availability technology is a necessary first step in providing an automated yield management system to the chain. Without on-line, full-duplex communication, a hotel's room rates are difficult to update. In fact, some older systems required the hotel to publish rates 18 months in advance without allowing changes throughout the entire year. The hotel literally had to forecast its levels of business and live with those forecasts no matter what might occur. As a result, the only way a hotel could alter its rates upward or downward during busy or slow periods was to close room availability with the CRO. Once closed, all rooms had to be sold through the in-house system, and rates could be changed as warranted. Today's on-line, last room availability systems allow the property to update rates with the CRS as often as necessary.

➤*Electronic Switch Technology.*   The road to seamless connectivity was now almost complete. At roughly the same time last-room-availability technology was being introduced between individual hotels and their respective central reservations offices, another brick was being paved between airline GDSs and travel agents. To understand why this brick needed laying, look back to the 1970s.

It was in the mid-1970s that the first airline reservations terminals were being placed in travel agency offices. As more airline reservations systems became available, more terminals were placed with travel agencies. Although that sounds good, this may be an example of when more is not necessarily better.

You see, a travel agent was now faced with numerous terminals and systems to learn and choose from. Not only did that mean memorizing a different set of codes for, say, American Airlines' Sabre system as opposed to United Airlines' Apollo system, but it also took up increased space at the travel agency. It was not necessarily more efficient to have more terminals, and travel agents often found themselves spending valuable time moving from terminal to terminal to research rates, dates, and availability.

It took a new innovation, switch technology, to get all the companies speaking the same language. Today, there are several major electronic switches available. One system, THISCO, was developed by 11 major lodging chains (Best Western, Choice, Days Inns, Hilton, Holiday, Hyatt, La Quinta, Marriott, Ramada, Sheraton, and Forte) in conjunction with Robert Murdoch's electronic publishing division. THISCO, which stands for The Hotel Industry Switching Company, was introduced in the early 1990s.

The switch functions like a clearinghouse. All reservations transactions are processed through the switch. The travel agent now needs access to just one terminal to communicate reservations requests and confirmations to literally any of thousands of airlines, hotels, car rentals, and other related products.

All of the benefits to the travel agent and hotel that accrue through last-room-availability systems are becoming available through airline reservations systems. Now, the travel agent is literally looking at the same hotel reservation data as the in-house reservationist; if there are special rates or packages, the travel agent can quote them as readily as the hotel's in-house reservationist. This is adding a new level of credibility to travel agents, who have often complained that their outdated data made them look unprofessional to the customer.

Another major advantage of the switch is the ability of the travel agent to learn just one set of procedures and to input just one set of codes. Switch technology functions as a translator as well as a real-time communicator. It translates codes into one hotel central reservations system or another. Now, when the agent is interested in booking a room with, say, two queens, the agent does not need to remember the exact input code. One chain might identify two queens with a QQ code, another chain might use 2Q or DQ for double queen. The electronic switch allows the user one system of codes and translates that information across each chain's central reservations system.

The introduction of the switch has allowed seamless connectivity across the spectrum of reservations. Now travel agents, airline reservationists, hotel central reservation agents, and in-house hotel reservations clerks access the same information at the same speed. All reservations are made in real time and update the rooms inventory the moment the reservation is confirmed.

➤*On-line Reservations Bookings.*   One of the fastest-growing means for personal access to the information superhighway is on-line subscription services. Such on-line companies as Prodigy, CompuServe, and America On-Line provide a direct link between the user and the server. Timely news and sports information, consumer and cinematic reviews, product ordering, and games are just a few of the common applications available to the on-line subscriber. Hotel reservations is another common application.

One of the more popular reasons for joining an on-line subscription service is to access major reservations systems (see Exhibit 4–2). Prodigy, for example, allows the subscriber a direct link to the Sabre network. Sabre, American Airlines' central reservations system, is able to provide useful information on most major airlines, hotels, and car rental companies.

Once on-line with Sabre, for example, the user can check air, rooms, and car availability; rates and discount plans; flight schedules; and additional pertinent data. After the guest has played with the options and made a decision, entering the reservation request is simply a matter of following the computer-generated prompts.

That is surprising to some users, because they wonder how the system can provide the same computer prompts when it is accepting reservations for a number of central reservations offices. For example, the input codes and data required for a Marriott reservation are quite different from the codes and data needed for a Sheraton reservation. The answer to this query lies in the sophisticated technology surrounding the switch.

Although the actual volume of on-line reservations is still quite small, it plays a greater role with each passing year. Most experts place current on-line reservations between 0.5 and 2% of all room reservations. With respect to the United States' $60 billion in rooms revenues, on-line reservations in the year 2000 probably accounted for less than $5 billion. But that is $5 billion more than just a few years before, when on-line reservations were nonexistent (see Exhibit 4–1).

Not only is the growth rate for on-line reservations astronomical, but there are some interesting trends with regard to who is using these services. Some of the best customers in the lodging industry are using on-line reservations technology. The profile of an average on-line user, who takes 25 trips per year, is an upper-income male with a high level of education!

Taking the Reservation

With the growing importance of the global distribution system will come changes to the way reservations are taken. Even as we write these words, the telephone is growing less important to the reservations process. Conversely, Web sites and on-line bookings are growing in importance. Only the future can tell what changes await the various players in the ever-changing reservations landscape.

▶**The Travel Agent.**   One certain shake-up will involve the world's travel agencies. Hotels are quietly developing systems that circumvent the 500,000 travel agencies worldwide. You see, hotels pay numerous commissions on each room reservation booked. For example, let's say a person visits a travel agent to book a ski trip. The travel agent (that's the first commission the hotel pays) books the lodging reservation through one of the switch companies (that's the second commission), which in turn is routed through an airline's global distribution network (that's the third commission) to the hotel chain's CRO (that's the fourth commission) and ultimately to the ski resort hotel itself. In an effort to save on all these commissions, hotels are developing direct booking vehicles (like Web pages), which book reservations directly into the hotel's in-house reservations department commission free (see Exhibits 4–3 and 4–4).

The airlines have already begun circumventing the travel agency. In recent months, several airlines have announced commission caps ranging from $25 to $50 on retail air travel bookings. Some have dropped on-line air reservations commissions to as little as $10. Indeed, Southwest Airlines recently announced that it would pay no commissions of any size to travel agents!

The Hotel–Travel Agent Relationship.   Travel agents are one of the major sources of hotel reservations. Travel agent bookings represent about 15% of all hotel rooms booked. Hotels pay a 10% commission—more in off-seasons to generate volume—for all rooms booked by a travel agency. Fees are not governmentally regulated. Amounts paid vary from property to property and even within the same property over time. *Overrides*, additional points of 10 to 15%, are paid to encourage high levels of business from one agency.

Guests pay no direct charge to the agency for its service, although some agencies have started to charge service fees. Neither do they pay for airline bookings made by

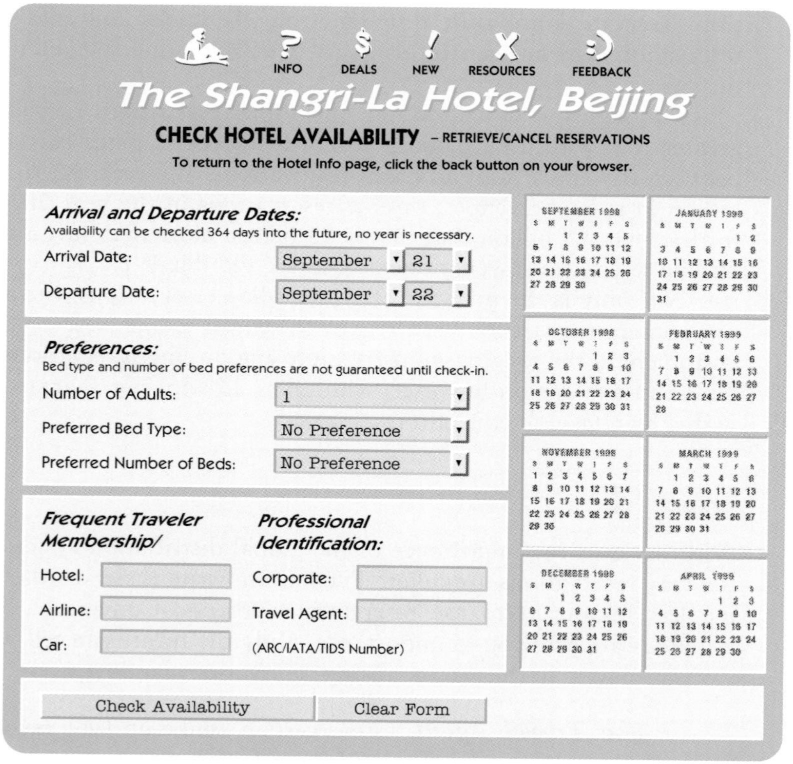

Exhibit 4–3a   Making reservations on-line is as easy as it is widespread (see Exhibit 4–1). This Shangri-La Hotels and Resorts on-line reservation form walks the guest through the process step by step. First we pulled up www.shangri-la.com. Then we selected Beijing, China. At that point, an availability screen popped up (Exhibit 4–3a). Once availability was assured, we were given a choice of many different room types and rates. Each room type was described, including rate, room description, bed type, and amenities, such as computer modem outlet, hairdryer, minibar, voice mail, and even shoe shine availability. Once we selected our room type, a "required fields" screen pulled up for us to complete and send the reservation (Exhibit 4–3b). *Courtesy of Shangri-La Hotels and Resorts, Hong Kong.*

Customer Information: *Required information fields are* **bolded.**

First Name:

Last Name:

Telephone:

E-Mail Address:
A reservation confirmation will be sent to the email address provided.

Street Address:

Suite or Apartment Number:

City:

State:

Zip/Postal Code:

Country: AFGHANISTAN ▼

Credit Information: *A credit card number is required to confirm/guarantee your reservation.*

Credit Card Type: American Express   Carte Blanche   Diner's Club
Discover   JCB   MasterCard   VISA

Credit Card Number:

Expiration Date (MM/YY):

Special Request Information:

Smoking Preference: Non-Smoking Room   Smoking Room

Comments:

Send Form — Click only once* | Clear Form

* *Please click "Send Form" only once to avoid the possibility of duplicate reservations.*
* *Please be advised that sensitve information, such as your credit card number, will be encrypted utilizing your browser's secured functions.*

Exhibit 4–3b

the agent in the guest's name. Two areas of contention emerge from this relationship. One is a marketing problem, the other a bookkeeping problem.

There are several marketing problems. Hotels complain that travel agencies (TAs) send business chiefly during the hotel's busy periods. Additional reservations are not needed then, and certainly not if they require a commission. According to the agents, hotels befriend them only when there is no business and ignore them and their customers—who incidentally are also hotel guests—as soon as volume recovers.

If the travel agent's repeat bookings are few and widely spaced, commission checks are small. Hotels find the cost of processing such checks greater than the commission. Hotels also have problems with some bookings when they originate with unknown agencies whose credit status is unproven. For these and for other accounting reasons that are reviewed in a later chapter, commission payments are not as prompt as TAs would like them to be. It is prompt, accurate payment that heads the agenda of every travel agency–hotel meeting.

Other key topics include the hotel's willingness to honor reservations and the reliability of its reservation system, including the frequency of overbooking. TAs are frustrated by these issues and by uncollected commissions, which they maintain total as much as half of all debt due. Whereas travel agencies actively solicit airline business,

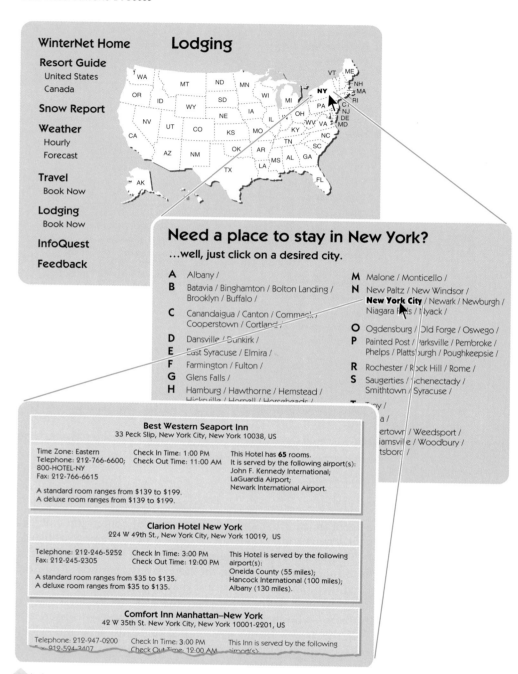

Exhibit 4–4   Booking rooms on-line is a snap. For this exhibit we searched using "WinterNet Lodging" and then clicked on the state we wanted to visit (New York). We then clicked on our destination (New York City) and were given a number of properties from which to choose. (Properties were listed alphabetically beginning with Best Western Seaport Inn.) *Courtesy of iiON Corporation, Fort Worth, Texas.*

they maintain that hotel bookings are made chiefly to accommodate their clients. That's hard to believe when one looks at the figures.

The macro view is rosier. Lodging industry payments to the travel industry increase each and every year. Hotels pay billions of dollars annually to the tens of thousands of individual agencies. Unfortunately for the client, those payments dictate which hotel the agency selects. If the guest has no preference (most do not), the hotel that pays commissions promptly will be the one the agency selects.

The system operates through a patchwork of informal relationships. Few formal agreements are in place. Many hoteliers believe that they are in direct competition with the travel agent, fighting for the same business and paying a commission to boot. That kind of thinking is being supported by the appearance of powerful mega-agencies and consortiums of agencies. Large-volume dealers stand toe-to-toe with national hotel chains. By securing the travel contracts of small and large corporations, these mega-agencies squeeze discounted rates from the national hotel chains anxious to get or retain a piece of the business.

➤*In-house Reservations Center.*   No matter what their affiliation or level of automation, all hotels have some system for accepting direct or in-house reservations. In certain properties, the number of in-house reservations is quite minimal. In other operations, however, the bulk of hotel rooms are sold through the in-house reservation center. This is especially true with nonaffiliated, independent hotels where there is no central reservations system (CRS) or where the CRS represents a small percentage of all reservations.

Direct or in-house reservations are also taken in quantity by hotels with large group sales business. Such business is generated by the hotel's own sales department, and those bookings bypass the CRS. For this reason, in-house reservationists have been incorporated into the sales departments of several hotel chains.

Experienced shoppers often call the hotel directly. The reservationist is more informed about the property. He or she has one hotel, whereas the CRS agent has hundreds or even thousands. If the hotel is full, reservations might be refused by the central reservation office but still be accepted on site.

A reservations manager, or supervisor, heads the division, which might number as many as a dozen persons. Large operations permit a degree of specialization, but the size scales downward until the room clerk alone carries out the function. Reports and room status computations may be the responsibility of one group of employees, and others may tend solely to tour groups. More often, several of these jobs are combined into one or two positions.

➤*Central Reservations System.*   The central reservations system (CRS) has historically been referred to as the central reservations office (CRO). Although there is a distinction between these two terms, today's jargon has made them almost fully interchangeable. Most managers refer to their central reservations center as the CRS.

In reality, the central reservations system (CRS) is the entire system, including all of the link-ups, software, switches, and nuances that will be described in this chapter. The central reservations office (CRO) is the hotel chain's portion of this overall system. The CRO is the actual office or site at which the chain's reservationists operate (see Exhibit 4–5).

Historically, most chains maintained one central reservations office. Guests accessed the office simply by dialing the 1-800 toll-free number the chain advertised. It was not uncommon for one central reservations office to receive several million phone calls per year. That is a lot of telephone activity!

Exhibit 4–5 Central reservation offices (CROs) like this one employ hundreds of reservationists in each of their multiple locations. Choice 2001, for example, has 4 U.S. and 18 international res centers. The typical center takes less than 3 minutes per call to field over 20 million calls annually. *Courtesy of Best Western International, Phoenix, Arizona.*

Therefore, CROs needed to locate in an area with a great capacity for telephone volume. This area was the Midwest. The Midwest, especially Omaha, Nebraska, developed into a major central reservations' hub because of the excess equipment in the area. The Bell System had unused capacity as a result of the massive defense grid built to accommodate the armed forces. With a promise of exceptionally good service and the support of the telephone system, hotel companies began opening reservation centers in the late 1960s. This created a specialized labor pool, making the area even more attractive.

Even today, midwestern cities such as Omaha and Kansas City house a large percentage of the nation's CROs. However, as call volumes rose in the 1980s, most chains found themselves establishing several CROs scattered nationwide. Today, the numbers are staggering. Some of the larger lodging chains boast over 2 million calls per month and book well in excess of 1 million reservations per month.

Processing the Call. Reservation agents receive the incoming calls and usually process them in 2 to 3 minutes. They are assisted with in-coming telephone calls by sophisticated telephone switching equipment. During busy call volume periods, automated telephone systems answer the call and may segregate the caller according to a variety of options. The caller is asked to listen to the options and then select by pressing a specific number on the telephone keypad. Large chains use the telephone system to segregate callers according to the hotel brand in which they are most interested. Another common way to separate callers is according to whether their reservation is for a domestic hotel property, a European hotel, an Asian property, a Latin American operation, and so on.

Once callers have been properly routed, they may be placed on hold for the next available reservationist. During the holding period, a recording provides information about the chain, special discount periods, new hotel construction, and the like. Automatic call distributor equipment eventually routes the telephone call to the next available reservationist.

Time is money, with labor and telephone lines the primary costs of CROs. So the reservation manager battles to reduce the time allotted to each call. A sign in one office read: "Talk time yesterday 1.8 (meaning minutes). During the last hour, 2.2. This hour, 2.1." Actually, more sophisticated devices are available. Some computer-management systems monitor each agent, providing data on the number of calls taken, the time used per call taken, and the amount of postcall time needed to complete the reservation. However, employee evaluations must not be judged on time alone. Systems should evaluate the percentage of the agent's calls that result in firm bookings and the relationship of the agent's average room rate to the average being sold by the entire center (office).

Res centers charge a fee for each reservation booked. Since the center is usually a separate subsidiary of the corporate parent, even company-owned properties pay the fee of several dollars per booking. Franchisors often get more than just the booking fee. A monthly fee on each room plus a percent of gross room sales may also be charged. Franchisees complain about the fee schedule, but the reservation system is the major attraction of franchising.

➤*The Hotel Representative.*   Although not normally done, hotels might maintain sales offices in distant cities, sending reservations from these offices to the hotel. Casino hotels usually maintain such offices in nearby cities: New York for Atlantic City, Los Angeles for Las Vegas. Reservations are among the services provided.

Hotels more often establish their presence in other locations through the use of a representative (rep). This person, or company, functions much as the traditional product representative, as a spokesperson and salesperson for many noncompeting brands. Utell International is one well-known rep.

When many noncompetitors (same-quality hotels from separate cities) associate with one particular rep, another alternative emerges: The independents band together to market the membership under one umbrella. Preferred Hotels and Resorts and Leading Hotels of the World are good examples of this group. These are not-for-profit affiliations.

The rep and the hotel negotiate a fee schedule, although a fee plus commission is not unusual. There may also be an initial membership fee. For that charge, the rep provides many sales and marketing services, including trade-show representation. Most important, the rep provides the central reservation office that the independent hotel lacks. Some international reps even service chains because the international rep provides language operators overseas and settles with travel agents in the currency of the local area. These are capabilities that the chain reservation office may not have.

Technology, with its access to travel agencies, transportation facilities, and company travel departments, is the key to the reservation business. Reps maintain their own systems, which they interface electronically with one or more airline computer systems, something the independent hotel cannot do.

▶ *Independent Reservation Services.* Membership in a central reservations system is one of the major advantages that chain-affiliated properties have over independent operations. The CRS provides each affiliated property access to sophisticated airline distribution systems, hundreds of thousands of travel agents, a convenient toll-free telephone number for potential customers, automated rate and inventory data, and a wealth of other automated benefits. Yet CRSs are extremely expensive, and the cost of developing a CRS is prohibitive for most small chains and independent operations.

Smaller chains can provide better guest service at a lesser cost by leasing the reservation service. Leasing from an independent reservation service is commonly referred to as *outsourcing*. It makes sense for independent properties and small and new lodging chains. For example, Fairmont, Meridien, and about 28 other chains use Tele-Service Resources; Preferred Hotels and Resorts uses Trust II; and Movenpick Hotels use ResCom Communications. (Interestingly, ResCom Communications is a subsidiary of the Holiday Corporation.)

One plan relinquishes the entire system to a res-center-for-hire. It is a new concept for hotels, but sharing telemarketing companies is not a new idea. Hotel clients are something that companies like J. C. Penney Telemarketing (Motel 6 and Hawthorne Suites) need to get used to. For hotel rep companies—Utell International, for example—the move is a natural extension of their primary role and should represent economies for each of their clients. UtellVision is a computerized reservation system for Utell member hotels. The system displays two screens simultaneously. The top screen is a series of high-resolution pictures of the member hotel and maps of the surrounding areas; on the bottom is an on-line reservations availability screen.

Independent hotels and small chains that join a private reservation service expect to gain efficiency and economies of scale, and they generally do experience a number of money-saving benefits. They save significant investment in hardware and software by joining rather than developing their own system. They save operating and training costs. Reservation processing is more efficient due to the massive computer capacity of the independent reservation service. And salesmanship is enhanced by joining a group of professionally trained agents.

Hotel chains have tried other, less dramatic restructuring in their search for electronic links and economy. Various affiliations have been tested as a means of broadening the market and spreading operating costs over a wider base. The affiliates have been other travel and lodging companies, but the umbrella has often been that of an independent entrepreneur. Some, like the Caribbean Hotel Reservation Service, have tried to develop space banks for an entire geographic area. Others are operated for one specific group: business travelers in luxury hotels, for example. Still others are quasipublic agencies such as tourist or convention bureaus.

Other Electronic Reservations Trends

In just one week, the average American adult is exposed to more information than a person living 100 years ago might have been exposed to in a lifetime. That statistical analogy speaks volumes in terms of the speed and quantity of information available today. And the trend will certainly continue. For example, the average processing power of a personal computer is expected to grow 1,000-fold over the next five years. In addition, information storage and retrieval capabilities of PCs are anticipated to grow at a compounded rate of 60% per year for the next five years. With these rapid advancements, central reservations offices are facing increasing opportunities for unique and more effective ways of performing their businesses. From voice recognition to "mapping" software, the future is anyone's guess.

▶*Voice Recognition.*   Amazing progress has been achieved in the area of automated voice recognition. Currently, there are systems in place that can recognize thousands of common words spoken by a host of various users. (Dragon Systems has a personal computer software application called DragonDictate which is capable of recognizing 30,000 words. Other systems are capable of as many as 60,000 words.)

There may come a time in the near future where straightforward rooms reservations are routinely handled electronically by voice-recognition and voice-synthesis (talking) systems. Indeed, thousands of voice-recognition systems are now at work across a myriad of other industries. AT&T uses voice recognition to assist the processing of directory assistance calls. Physicians' offices use voice recognition for transcribing detailed medical records. Business corporations use voice recognition for dictating letters.

The biggest argument in favor of such a laborsaving system is the overall repetitiveness of the reservationist's job. As unique as each reservation might seem, there are more commonalities than differences. Each reservation communicates the city, date, room rate and type, and other basic data. These are functions that a computer system could logically handle. In fact, the simplest of all voice-recognition software applications utilize a "command" system. This system recognizes several hundred words from a preprogrammed list of possible commands. On what day of the week a guest is traveling (7 possible words), the date of departure (31 possible words), type of credit-card guarantee (roughly 6 to 10 possible words), and credit-card number (10 possible words) are some of the common reservations commands a computer might easily recognize.

The voice-recognition reservations program would generate a series of questions for the guest to answer. With each response, the program would acknowledge the answer, allow the guest to make changes as necessary, and generate a new series of questions based on the previous response. In those situations where the computer could not recognize the guest's voice due to a strong accent or other impairment, a fail-safe system would be in place—the guest might press the zero button twice on the telephone keypad, for example, to alert an operator that personal assistance was needed.

The computer system could check availability, quote rates, suggest alternative dates, and thank the guest in a manner similar to the reservationist. Of course, such a system would be significantly less personal than dealing with an actual reservationist. On the other hand, it would surely be less expensive in terms of labor costs, and the computer system would never call in sick!

▶*Mapping Capabilities.*   As global distribution systems gain sophistication, options that were previously unavailable (or manually performed) are increasingly being automated. One example of an old manual format now available as an automated system enhancement is *mapping*.

Commonplace requests such as a hotel's physical address, its distance from a popular destination, or specific travel directions were once manual tasks. Central reservations agents, representing chains of hundreds or thousands of hotels, were required to look up such information in databases provided by member properties. This was a slow and generally inefficient method.

Today, modern mapping systems can provide comprehensive geographical, pictorial, and textual information about every member property. Best Western was the first company of its size to offer a mapping feature with its new central reservations system. Now central reservations agents have immediate access to geographically related questions about property locations, mileage, travel times, and so on.

Indeed, guests can retrieve the same information themselves automatically by calling any of the chain's 3,400 hotels worldwide. A call to the hotel's toll-free number from any location allows customers to determine the Best Western hotel that is closest to their desired destination and get specific directions to the property.

➤ *CD-ROM Reservation Technology.*   Another technological opportunity available to hotels through some of the airline reservations systems is CD-ROM. Both Sabre (through SabreVision) and Apollo (through Apollo Spectrum) offer CD-ROM technology to their listed hotels. CD-ROM is a high-tech way to see visual images of hotels and their surrounding communities.

Imagine a guest walking into a travel agent's office and asking to see pamphlets of hotels in Hawaii. Instead of merely showing pamphlets, the travel agent displays CD-ROM technology on the computer terminal. Now the guest is able to see color images of several hotels, maps of the surrounding community, and even take a tour through corridors, restaurants, and various features of the hotel. That is exciting, and many agencies experience booking rates three to four times higher with CD-ROM visuals.

Although rather expensive, the future looks bright for this new-wave technology. It allows the guest to make an involved and interactive hotel selection. And it saves on brochure printing costs!

➤ *Guest History Databases.*   Another benefit of the global distribution system is the ability for hotels to share guest history information. Database information is currently utilized only within chains. As the switch technology improves, guest history data may actually be shared across chains.

Even within the chain, hotels rarely take advantage of their wealth of data. Most property management systems allow a guest history function. Standard information required for the reservation becomes a marketing tool, if properly administered. After all, the hotel already knows the guest's name and address, the dates of the last visit, the rate paid, the room type, the number of guests, and the method of payment. Add a bit of marketing information such as the type of discount package purchased, the special rate or promotion used, and whether the reservation was over a weekend or was a weekend getaway package, and the manager has an enormous amount of marketing data.

From guest history databases to voice recognition, automation is changing the global distribution system and the way in which hoteliers manage the reservations process.

➤ AUTOMATED REVENUE MANAGEMENT SYSTEMS

An increasingly competitive and complex lodging industry has also changed the way hoteliers sell reservations. Rather than the old goal of simply "placing heads in beds," today's hoteliers need to selectively place the right heads into the right beds. You see, despite the large number of rooms that are available on an annual basis, every reservation request is not accepted. The decision depends on space availability and rate ranges available for the specific dates. An occupancy forecast determines the space situation for the day or days in question. Even if only one day of the sequence is closed, the reservation may be refused and an alternative arrangement offered. This is unfortunate if the declined reservation represented a request for a number of days. It is especially unfortunate if the period in question has only one sold-out date. Then the hotel is essentially trading a profitable, long-term reservation against a potential overbooking situation for one sold-out date. In many cases, the reservationist would override the system and book this type of reservation. Obviously, such a decision would be considered on a case-by-case basis.

In other situations, the salesmanship of the reservationist comes into play. The telephone provides a two-way conversation during which the reservationist can gauge the behavior of the guest. Some guests can be convinced to reserve their chosen date at a slightly higher nightly rate. Other guests' minds can be changed toward a slower occupancy period with the offer of reduced rates.

In any case, guests who cannot be accommodated represent lost revenues. The reservationist attempts to salvage lost reservations in a number of ways—offering premium rates during almost sold-out periods, offering different dates when rates are not as high, or even offering another sister property of the same chain in a nearby community. When all else fails, the reservationist can only thank the caller and ask him or her to try again another time.

Requests for accommodations are sometimes denied even if the house is not full. Most of the hotel's advertised packages are refused if the forecast shows that the house is likely to fill at standard rack rates. The inverse of this is also true. Reservationists must be taught to sell discounted packages or other reduced rates (weekend, commercial, governmental) only on request or when encountering rate resistance.

With a full house, requests from travel agents, to whom the hotel pays a commission, may be regretted. A low priority is assigned to requests from agents who are slow in paying. All reservations are refused if the caller has a poor credit rating, regardless of the occupancy forecast. Busy hotels give preference to higher-paying multiple-occupancy requests over single occupancy.

Casino hotels give preferential treatment to those who are likely to gamble, even to the extent of granting them free accommodations in preference to paying guests who don't play. Noncasino hotels do the same, allotting their scarce space to reservations from certain areas or markets that the hotel is trying to develop. Seasonal resorts quote in-season and off-season rates and frequently require a minimum length of stay on holiday weekends.

The Yield Management Revolution

Revenue management, the act of controlling rates and restricting occupancies in an effort to maximize gross rooms revenue, is most commonly referred to as *yield management*. In its simplest form, yield management has been around for decades. Any seasoned manager who increased room rates as occupancy for a given date rose, or who quoted higher rates for holidays and special event periods, or who saved the last few room nights for extended-stay reservations was using yield management. It is not the practice of yield management that is new, it is the incorporation of revenue managers into dedicated senior staff positions and the automation of yield management into complex property management systems that is new.

Organizations were downsized and labor costs reduced during the low cycle of the early 1990s. Despite the squeeze on profits, many hotels added revenue managers (or yield managers) to their organizations (see Exhibit 3–1). The move was easily justified by the revenue offset. Some 15 to 25% of recent ADR growth has been attributed to yield management, the specialty of these new managers. Thus, a 400-room property with an overall 10% increase in ADR from, say, $118 to $129.80 could attribute about $2 of the nearly $12 increase directly to the new yield team. Assuming 70% occupancy, that produces some $200,000 annually (400 rooms × 70% × 365 days × $2). That's a wonderful return on the costs of yield management hardware, software, and new hires!

► *Brief History of Yield Management.*   Like other businesses, hotel prices (room rates) have become more sensitive to customer wants and expectations. Yield management is market oriented, responding to sharper segmentation of guest identification. Until recently, hotel rates have been driven by financial and operating considerations alone (see Chapter 9). Rates were, and still are, expected to cover operational and capital costs and yet fall within the range of competition. It was the price sensitivity of certain market segments that made yield management practices successful in the first place.

The Airlines' Role.   Lodging has adopted yield management concepts from the airlines. Airline rate discounting was widespread in the early 1980s, and that contributed to the array of prices that the airlines found difficult to track. They began experimenting with adjusted rates based on demand forecasts. Discounted tickets purchased far in advance were used to establish a minimum level of seat occupancy and to forecast overall demand. Low and seasonal periods were also discounted. As the plane filled and departure time neared, higher and higher fares were charged. Full price was eventually charged for the remaining seats—a price that would have been virtually impossible to charge when the plane was empty.

Airlines and hotels are much alike. Both have a relatively fixed supply of product (seats and rooms), and both have products that perish with the passage of time. In the 1980s, airlines had one extra edge—large computer capability that was in place and was functional. It takes the capacity of these large systems to simultaneously track occupancy (seat or room) and the variety of price options that both industries market.

Price-sensitive concepts have been employed by hoteliers for a long, long time. Refining the practices and developing them into a program with rules and triggers, with a knowledge base and a strategy, awaited the superior computer capability of the airlines. Today, most major lodging chains have developed automated yield management systems that rival the best of the airline systems.

Market Demand.   Airlines and hotels did differ in one respect—their view of the guest. Hotels had previously operated on the belief that their customer was not a discretionary traveler. The guest who came, hoteliers felt, was someone who had to come. Guests did not come merely because the price was reduced enough to lure them into the purchase. Urban hotels, which cater to the least flexible guest, the commercial traveler, first evidenced the change. In desperate need of weekend business, these properties began to market weekend specials to discretionary buyers. The march to yield management had begun.

You see, yield management has an economic rationale. It assumes that all customers are price conscious—that they are aware of the existence of and the significance of price variations. Furthermore, it assumes that customers are price sensitive—that their buying habits respond to increases and decreases in price.

All things being equal, the guest is motivated by lower prices. Theoretically, when a similar room type is available for a significantly lower rate at an otherwise equal hotel, the guest will select the lower-priced accommodations. In addition, guests who might not have left home at the rack rate are inclined to visit hotels when rates are low. As a result, low-occupancy periods are generally accompanied by lower average room rates.

Each customer class has different degrees of price consciousness and price sensitivity. Earlier discussions on segmentation (see Chapter 2) indicated the wide range of guests to whom the industry appeals. In simple terms, these are the business (corporate) class, the leisure user, and the group buyer.

Corporate Guests.   The business or corporate customer is less sensitive to price—not unaware of price, just less sensitive to it. Businesspersons must travel when the need arises; they will not go merely because the price is reduced.

Business arrangements may be made only a few days or hours before arrival (see Exhibit 4–6). Location is very important, both to save travel time and to present the proper image. Business travelers need to be near the business center, which means high-priced real estate and high room rates. These travelers are away from home a good deal. They seek and probably merit a higher level of comfort than the occasional leisure traveler. In summary, business guests pay higher rates because they are less price sensitive. They have to be where they have to be at a given time, and that arrangement is often made suddenly, with little advance planning, and therefore little opportunity to obtain discounted rates.

Leisure Guests.   The leisure guest, as the name implies, is 180 degrees removed from the corporate traveler. With leisure guests, lead time is long. Reservation bookings are well planned, with adequate time to shop for the best room rates. This class of guest is flexible as to the time of the trip, the destination of the trip, and the stopping places. These guests may not even use a hotel. High prices might drive them into camping or park facilities. Poor price value might send them to the homes of friends

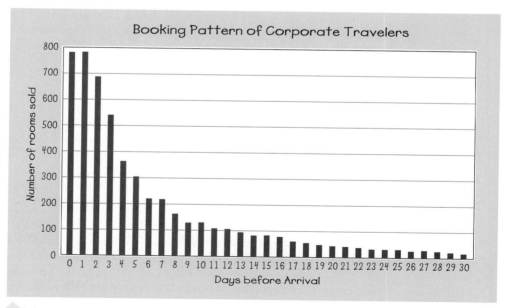

Exhibit 4–6   Booking pattern of corporate travelers during a 30-day period. Although some corporate guests book 30 (or more) days in advance, the majority reserve rooms within a few days of arrival. This 275-room hotel receives approximately 60% of its business from corporate guests.

or family. When prices of accommodations, fuel, toll roads, and gasoline are too high, this guest will just stay home.

Leisure travelers have been the major beneficiaries of the yield management approach offered by both the airline and the hotel industries. The leisure travelers' flexibility with regard to travel dates and itineraries allows them to take advantage of deep discounting during off-season and slow demand periods. It is not uncommon to find hotel rooms discounted between 50 and 80% during slow periods. A $250 hotel room in Australia's Kakadu National Park in the tropics, for example, may cost only $100 or so during the rainy season; a $400 golf package in Palm Springs may be discounted to $175 in the heat of the summer.

Group Guests. *Group business,* the last of the three general classifications, exhibits characteristics from both of the other two categories. That's because the group market forms from components of the business and leisure classifications. From the leisure category come social, fraternal, and hobby associations. From the business segment come professional, union, and governmental groups.

Both types of groups—leisure and business—have their own idiosyncracies. Generally, business-oriented groups are sensitive to date and place while being less sensitive to rate. That is because business groups usually meet the same week every year. Leisure-oriented groups are more rate sensitive and therefore tend to be somewhat flexible with regard to date and place. Profits can be increased if the sales department, based on good forecasting, can steer the business to the right (right for the hotel) time, place, and rate.

Yield management has changed the interface between the sales department and the group buyer. Based on information from the yield management program, sales must decide to take the business, reject the business, or try to negotiate a different time at a different rate. Saturday arrival for a group might actually prove more profitable at $90 per night, for example, than a Monday arrival (which replaces full rack rate corporate guests) at $115 per night. A well-programmed yield management system should provide the answer. (A more detailed discussion of group business and related automation is available in Chapter 5.)

At issue is whether the discounted room rates requested by the group, plus the value of the group's meeting room and banquet business, is valued at more or less than the forecasted income from normal guests who will be turned away. Yield management systems can answer that question. The discretionary decisions still remain for the salespersons to evaluate. For example, is other new business likely to spin off from this meeting? Is this a single event, or are we doing business with a meeting planner who controls 100 or more meetings per year?

Yield management means that function rooms are no longer booked on a first-come, first-served basis. Neither are guest rooms; there must be a price–occupancy mix.

▶ ***The Price–Occupancy Mix.*** Yield is calculated by multiplying occupancy (let's say 65% for a 250-room hotel) by average daily rate (let's say that the ADR is $75.00). In this example, yield is $12,187.50 per day. Yield can be increased by raising rates when occupancy (demand) is high. Rates are raised by refusing packages, requiring minimum lengths of stay, and charging groups full rate without discounts. When occupancy (demand) is low, prices are dropped by promoting the packages, seeking out the price-sensitive groups, and creating special promotional rates. That's the dichotomy of the lodging industry; when times are good (high occupancy), they are very good (because with high occupancy comes high rate). Conversely, when times are bad (low demand), times are very bad (because all of the hotel's competitors are also lowering their prices).

Since yield is the product of the two elements, equilibrium is obtainable by increasing one factor when the other decreases. Exhibit 4–7 illustrates the mathematics. Yield in all three cases appears to be identical. With the same room revenue, a management choice between high ADR and high occupancy needs to be made.

All managers will not view the values in Exhibit 4–7 as being equal. Some would prefer the higher occupancy over the higher rate. Higher occupancy means more persons. More guests translate into more food and beverage revenue, more telephone use, more calls for laundry and dry cleaning. More guests mean more greens fees, more amusement park admissions, or more money spent in the casino. For these reasons, some hotels charge the same rate for occupancy by one or two persons.

Another group of operators would prefer to strengthen their ADR. These managers feel that ADR is a barometer of a property's service and quality levels. With the lower occupancy that accompanies higher ADR, hotels save on variable costs like power, wear and tear on furniture and equipment, and reduced levels of staffing.

Clearly, price–occupancy mix is not a simple, single decision. Dropping rates to increase occupancy might not be the choice of every manager. Indeed, the manager might take that option at one hotel but not at another. Variations in the facilities of the hotel, in its client base, and in the perspective of its management will determine the policies to be applied.

Revenue per Available Room.   Yield is usually expressed in terms of gross revenue per day, per month or per year (see Exhibit 4–7). However, there is a special advantage to quoting yield in terms of revenue per available room (RevPar). RevPar (see also Chapter 1) combines occupancy and average daily rate into a single number. Continuing the illustration: A 250-room hotel at 65% occupancy and $75 ADR produces revenue per available room (RevPar) of $48.75 (65% × $75).

Before the popularization of RevPar in the mid 1990s, hotel managers tended toward one of the two camps described above. They migrated either toward higher occupancies or toward higher ADRs. Managers who work toward maximizing RevPar, however, must seek a balance or equilibrium between occupancy and rate (see Exhibit 4–8).

The only difference between calculating yield and RevPar is that yield incorporates the number of hotel rooms into the calculation, whereas RevPar looks at revenue per available room. In fact, if you take RevPar for any given day and multiply it by the number of rooms available in the hotel, the product is that day's yield. To demonstrate, take the $48.75 RevPar found above in our ongoing example and multiply it by

Hotel	Average Daily Rate	Percent Occupancy	Monthly Gross Yield	Potential Revenue	Yield Percentage
A	$ 75	65.00	$377,812.50	$620,000	60.9
B	100	48.75	377,812.50	620,000	60.9
C	50	97.50	377,812.50	620,000	60.9

Exhibit 4–7   Price–occupancy mix: yield is the product of occupancy times rate. Management decides whether a higher rate (ADR) or a higher occupancy is preferable. This exhibit assumes 250 rooms and a 31-day month. Potential revenue assumes 100% occupancy at an $80 ideal rate.

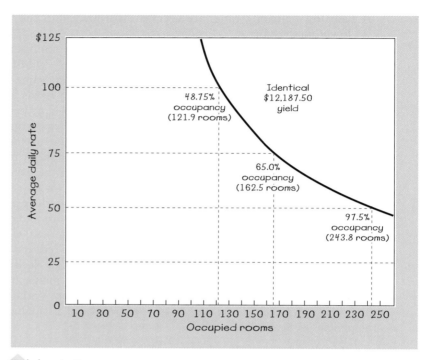

Exhibit 4–8 Referring to Exhibit 4–7, this graph demonstrates the infinite number of points that make up the daily yield curve.

the 250 rooms available. The product is the same $12,187.50 yield calculated several paragraphs above in the price–occupancy mix discussion.

The RevPar calculation is also beneficial to management as a quick-and-dirty glimpse into the hotel's success on any given day. If the hotel knows its fixed costs on a per room per day basis (fixed costs include administrative salaries, mortgage debt, fixed franchise fees, and insurance, to name a few), it can quickly gauge how much, if any, of the RevPar can be contributed toward variable costs and profits. In our ongoing example, if RevPar is $48.75 and fixed costs are $23.25, then $25.50 per available room can be contributed toward variable costs and profit. Management can readily see how well the hotel performed on that given day.

Automated Yield Management Systems

In a recent study of hotel sales and marketing departments, almost 80% of the respondents stated they use yield management technology to assist their decision process when booking group business.[3] The figure begins to approach 100% when individual hotel room nights booked through chains or large independent properties are included. Clearly, yield management is an expense worth incurring.

Automated yield or revenue management systems are tools that aid management decision making. Indeed, in the absence of management, these systems can automatically change rates, restrict rooms availability, and monitor reservation activity. Here's a brief list of the functions generally attributable to yield management systems. The yield management system:

➤ Establishes and monitors the hotel's rate structure

➤ Continually monitors reservations activity and sets inventory controls as needed (even in the absence of management approval)

➤ Aids rate negotiations with travel wholesalers and group bookings

➤ Monitors and restricts the number of reservations that can be taken for any particular room night or room rate/room type

➤ Allows reservationists the tools necessary to be salespersons rather than mere order-takers

➤ Matches the right room product and rate with customers' needs and sensitivities

Profits increase in all hotels that implement automated yield management systems. Certain properties, however, fare better than others. Generally, a property needs to have several characteristics in place to experience high returns on its investment in a yield management system. Some of these characteristics include a demand for rooms that can easily be segmented into distinct markets (see Exhibit 4–9), a long lead time for some types of reservations, a variety of room types and associated rates, and high-occupancy/low-occupancy periods throughout the year.

➤*Artificial Intelligence.*   Yield management systems allow for instantaneous response to changing conditions. Seven days a week, 24 hours a day, the system compares actual performance with forecasted assumptions and adjusts rates accordingly. To make these changes, advanced computer systems utilize either standard logical functions or state-of-the-art artificial intelligence operations. Artificial intelligence (AI) or expert systems use stored data that has been developed over a period of time to form rules that govern yield management decisions.

Today's expert systems are truly artificial intelligence. They literally think through demand, formulate decisions, and provide the user with an opportunity to talk with the computer. Below is a list of the special features generally found in an expert yield management system. The expert system:

| | | | | | | Market Segments (%) | | |
| | | | | | | | Group and Convention Rooms | |
Hotel	Percent Occupancy	Average Daily Rate	Corporate Guests	Leisure Guests	Casino Block	City-Generated	In-House	Wholesale Rooms
A	78.6	$117.62	43.0	10.0	18.0	15.5	13.5	
B	99.8	52.29	5.0	57.0	4.0			34.0
C	86.4	94.47	7.0	30.0	36.5	10.0	6.5	10.0
D	93.1	88.52	33.3	33.3	13.3	15.0		5.0
E	96.7	51.09		8.0	3.0	7.0	7.0	75.0

Exhibit 4–9   This hypothetical market mix might be valid for any number of gaming destinations (Las Vegas, Atlantic City, Reno, or Branson, Missouri). Notice the role that group, leisure, and wholesale rooms play in some hotels while being almost nonexistent in others.

1. Is able to deal not just with quantitative facts but with qualitative data as well
2. Includes an analysis of incomplete data when formulating a decision
3. Explains to the user how a given conclusion was reached
4. Allows a two-way communication interface with the user
5. Applies programmable rules and triggers to its set of facts
6. Can override basic rules and triggers when additional decision criteria warrant
7. Maintains a database of historical facts, including:
   - Demand for similar periods over a number of past years
   - Room nights lost (regrets) through both in-house reservations and chain (1-800) sources over a number of past years
   - Changes to demand (by various market segments) as forecasted reservations dates close in
   - The ratio and demand for transient (leisure) room nights versus corporate room nights over a number of past years
   - The demand for group room blocks (and the ratio of group room block "pickups") over a number of past years

➤*Rules and Triggers.*   The computer compares actual reservation activity with budgeted forecasts. When a particular date or period falls outside the rules for that time frame, the computer flags it. Once flagged, most systems will print a management report identifying periods that are exceptions to the forecast. In addition, expert systems will automatically change rates and other sales tools. The immediacy of the expert system is a major advantage. Hundreds and even thousands of dollars may be lost in the time it takes management to approve a given rate change. The expert system acts first and takes questions later.

To establish rules or triggers for the system to use, management must first segment the room count into market types. For example, a typical 250-room property might block 25 rooms for discounting to government guests or IT packages, 50 rooms for transient (leisure) guests, 100 rooms for business (corporate) customers, and the remaining 75 rooms for sale to tour groups and convention business (see Exhibit 4–9).

Different guidelines are then placed on each of these market segments. To illustrate, assume that management expects 25% of the transient room block to fill by, say, 181 days out (days before arrival). It also expects that 91 days before arrival, transient rooms will be 60% sold, and by 61 days out, the entire block will be 90% reserved. These are the parameters that management has forecasted for transient rooms; its expectations for business rooms may be completely different. Once these triggers are identified, they are programmed into the yield management system. The computer then evaluates the effects of changing demand and acts accordingly. If, for example, 181 days out the transient room block is 35% reserved, the computer would flag the date as a potentially busy period and increase rates for all remaining rooms. How much the rates increase is also subject to advanced programming.

➤*Centralized Yield Management.*   Although the majority of yield management systems are still property-based, the trend is toward centrally driven corporate systems. At the outset, centralized yield management looks much the same. As rooms are sold through in-house reservations (at the property) or the CRO, changes in inventory are automatically reflected in the centralized yield management system. As room types or dates begin to fill, the centralized system changes rates and inventory restrictions for the individual property. Similarly, if property-level management wishes to tap into its own yield statistics and manually alter rates or restrictions, nothing prevents that.

What appears quite similar on the surface actually affords the chain and individual property unique advantages. Through centralized yield management, the entire global distribution system (GDS) becomes a yield management tool. In essence, the in-house property management system (PMS), the CRS, and the GDS are all reading from the same page. The chain can run a whole series of reports, which improves its understanding of certain market segments, lodging categories, dates, and trends. Price-sensitive group room blocks can be moved to sister properties across the chain rather than being lost because one hotel in one particular city was not able to meet their price on a given date.

▶ *Yield Management Controls.*   Aside from simply adjusting the room rate, hotels have several other tools with which they work. One common tool is *boxing* the date. Boxing dates (no through bookings) is another control device open to the reservations manager. Reservations on either side of the boxed day are not allowed to spill into that date. For example, if Wednesday, April 7, is anticipated as a heavy arrival date, we might box it. Rooms sold for Monday or Tuesday must check out by Wednesday; rooms sold for Thursday or Friday cannot arrive a day earlier. Dates are blocked in anticipation of a mass of arrivals, usually a convention or group movement, that could not be accommodated through the normal flow of departures. With such heavy arrivals, no one is permitted to check in before that day and stay through the boxed day, even though there is more than enough space on those previous days.

Another tool available to the reservations department is closing a specific date to arrival. Dates that are closed to arrival allow the guest to stay through by arriving on a previous date. Closed to arrival is utilized as a technique for improving occupancy on preceding nights before a major holiday or event.

A final example of reservations sales tools is the minimum length of stay. This technique is designed to improve occupancy on nights preceding and following a major event or holiday by requiring guests to book a minimum number of nights. For example, if New Year's Eve has a three-day minimum length of stay, the hotel will probably improve occupancies on December 30 and January 1.

Nests and Hurdles.   Also known as *bid pricing, hurdle pricing,* or *inventory nesting,* this sophisticated yield management approach takes normal room allocations to a new level. By referring to Exhibit 4–10, let's assume that the Hurdle Hotel is experiencing an unusually high demand for corporate rooms and has sold out of the $120 rate (Monday) while still offering discounted and rack rate rooms. It would make little sense to turn down a corporate reservation request at $120 while still accepting discounted rooms at $60, but that is exactly what might happen if rooms allocations are not continually monitored. That's where inventory nesting comes in. By incorporating a set of nesting rules, the property can ensure that high-rate rooms are never closed for sale when lower-rate rooms are still open.

The newest trend in nesting does away with the old concept of rooms allocations by market segment. Instead, a minimum rate, or *hurdle point,* is established for each day. Reservations with a value above the hurdle are accepted, reservations with a value below the hurdle are rejected. In Exhibit 4–10, if the hurdle point were set at or below $60, all room types would be available. If the hurdle were raised to $100, the discounted rooms would be closed while corporate and rack rates remained available.

Data for the 250-Room Hurdle Hotel			
	Discounted Rooms	Corporate Guests	Rack Rate
Normal rate structure	$60	$120	$150
Normal room allocations	75	100	75
Current rooms demand			
Monday (hurdle price is $150)	60	100	57
Tuesday (hurdle price is $120)	53	82	48
Wednesday (hurdle price is $60)	34	51	22

Exhibit 4–10   Inventory nesting prevents higher-priced categories of rooms from being closed when lower-priced categories remain open. Hurdle pricing assumes that each business day has a theoretical rate floor against which reservation requests must be evaluated.

Rather than selling rooms according to unreserved market segment allocations, the hurdle concept sells rooms based on total property demand. When demand is low, the hurdle price is low. When demand is high, the hurdle price is high. In essence, the hurdle price represents the theoretical price of the last room expected to sell that day. If the hotel expects to fill, the hurdle point might be set at full rack rate. A person making a reservation who is only willing to pay a lower rate is worth less to the hotel than the future value of the last room, and therefore such a reservation would be denied.

The real beauty of hurdle pricing is that hurdles can be added for subsequent days. For example, in Exhibit 4–10, let's say that the hotel is close to full on Monday (hurdle point $150), somewhat less full on Tuesday (hurdle point $120), and wide open for Wednesday (hurdle point just $60). A guest wishing to stay Monday for one night only would need to pay $150 to get a reservation for the night. However, a guest checking in on Monday for three nights would get the benefit of adding the hurdles for those three nights. By adding $150 for the first night plus $120 for the second and $60 for the third night, this three-night reservation would pay a rate of $110 per night.

Fenced Rates.   A relatively new addition to the list of reservations sales tools has recently migrated to hotels from the airline industry. Fences or *fenced rates* are logical rules or restrictions that provide a series of options to the guest. Guests are not forced to select these options; their rate is determined by which (if any) options they choose.

As with yield management systems themselves, the airlines originated fenced rates. Examples of airline fenced rates might include the passenger who chose a lower but nonrefundable fare, a customer who purchased the ticket at least 21 days in advance to receive a special rate, or someone who stayed over on a Saturday night to take full advantage of the best price.

Fenced rates are relatively new to the lodging industry. However, the few chains using them seem quite satisfied with their results. It will probably be standard practice in the future to offer discounts for advanced purchases and nonrefundable and unchangeable reservations.

➤ SUMMARY

Sophisticated automation is changing the method in which reservations are requested and accepted. Never before have hotels had reservations coming into their properties from so many varied directions. The introduction of last room availability technology has started a revolution in hotel reservations management.

Last room availability is real-time communication between central reservations offices and property-level reservations systems. With last room availability, the entire global distribution system (GDS) can identify room types and rates at a member hotel and can literally sell to the very last available room. Electronic switch technology has afforded the industry increased access to member hotels. Travel agents, airlines, and subscription on-line services are all able to electronically access a property's reservations system.

With yield or revenue management (yield equals average room rate times the number of rooms sold), room prices change as a function of lead time and demand. Vacationing families, tour groups, and seniors often know as far as one year in advance their exact date and location of travel. These customers generally book early enough to take advantage of special discounts or packages; yield management works to their advantage. Conversely, corporate travelers frequently book accommodations at the last moment. In their case, yield management works against them by charging maximum rates to last-minute bookings when the hotel is nearing full occupancy.

➤ QUESTIONS AND PROBLEMS

1. On busy nights, it is not uncommon for a front-office manager to remove several rooms from availability. Usually, the manager creates a fictitious reservation, thereby "selling" the rooms and removing them from availability. By holding onto a few rooms, the manager feels in a better position to accommodate a special guest or request when the hotel is sold out.

   Granted that the reason management holds rooms may be very honorable, do you believe this practice undermines the very basis of last room availability technology? Explain your answer.

2. Central reservations systems are extremely expensive. Research and development, equipment, and staffing can easily run into hundreds of millions of dollars. How has this prohibitive cost structure changed the hotel industry? How will it change business in the future? And what options are available to the smaller and startup chains in the industry?

3. Several studies indicate quite clearly that reservation calls made to a travel agent, or to the res center, or directly to the hotel may result in three different rate quotes for the same accommodations at the same period of time. Explain.

4. Discuss the merits of higher rates with lower occupancy versus lower rates with higher occupancy if you were the manager of (a) a budget economy property, (b) a commercial convention property, or (c) an upscale resort property.

5. Yield management programs often discount rates to the benefit of one segment of guests but charge full rack rate to others who book at the last moment. With attention to the rewards and penalties that such policies carry, discuss a proposed policy that (a) deeply discounts rates for noncancellable reservations made 30 days in advance and (b) discounts rates for standby guests who are willing to wait until 7 PM for vacancies.

6. Develop a list of fenced rate restriction possibilities. This list may include those currently used by airlines, or create your own possible restrictions.

➤ *NOTES*

1. Sheraton Hotels introduced its central reservations system shortly after the Holidex system. But Sheraton was the first major chain to offer a toll-free 1-800 line to its customers.

2. Hotel central reservations offices (CROs) are also commonly referred to as central reservations systems (CRSs). These two terms are interchangeable.

3. In a 1998 study, PKF Consulting found that 83.7% of sales and marketing departments utilize automated rooms inventory controls and 79.8% of sales and marketing departments utilize yield management technology.

CHAPTER 5
Individual and Group Reservations

Outline

Components of the Reservation
Information Contained in the Reservation
Confirming the Reservation
Electronic Reservations
Reservation Coding

Convention and Tour Group Business
The Group Rooms Contribution
Categories of Group Business
Convention Reservations
Negotiating Convention Rates

Handling the Tour Group Reservation

➤ COMPONENTS OF THE RESERVATION

In this era of rapidly changing reservations technology, it is interesting to note a renewed appreciation for simply talking with the customer. Awash in technology, it is easy for a reservations center to lose sight of its basic task, selling rooms. After running the potential guest through a gauntlet of telephone queries, telephone keypad number punching, and recorded messages, the reservations agent can easily forget the person on the other end of the telephone. To avoid this oversight, one chain actually pastes pictures of real customers on the office walls to remind agents that those are real people on the other end of the phone.

Certainly there is room for increased efficiency—technology helps sort customers via certain critical parameters (for example, "domestic reservations please press 1," "international reservations press 2")—but not at the expense of customer service. The fastest reservation is not always the best reservation.

In a recent study of a major lodging chain's reservation office, reservationists experimented with changing their initial telephone greeting from the rushed monotone so often associated with call centers to a warmer, friendlier greeting.[1] The results were astounding. Customers responded positively to the inviting greeting they received, and their perceptions of the CRO improved dramatically (ultimately, the reservations booking rate should improve as well). It took very little extra time for the reservationist to be nice and to "smile" through the telephone. The friendlier greetings added a mere 300 extra seconds to each reservationist's day.

Today's hotel guests, whether corporate, leisure, or group, face more lodging choices than ever before. With so many options available, central reservations offices (and in-house reservations centers) are realizing that a well-trained reservations agent makes a significant difference in guest satisfaction, booking rates, and return business. Technology can get the average reservation down to 180 seconds, but a speedy "businesslike" attitude does not necessarily translate into a successful reservation!

Seasoned reservations managers realize that effective communication skills are more important than basic computer skills. Poorly trained reservations agents miss potential sales by failing to understand the guests' needs. Taking a step away from the rushed script allows the agent to develop a communicative information-gathering posture that may uncover personal information (needs) that can ultimately lead to the sale. Reservationists must realize that price is not the only factor that guests use in determining where to stay. Patiently answering questions, skillfully diffusing objections, and building personal rapport with the customer may prove as important to the decision process as the price of the room.

Training reservations agents to be salespersons is the key to success in the new millennium. That's because collecting the guest's reservation data is pretty much the same for all lodging chains. It's easy, too: Basic reservation content and each question that needs to be asked is right there on the reservations agent's computer screen. The computer literally prompts the agent through each step of the reservation.

Information Contained in the Reservation

The computer not only provides rapid input, it also prompts the reservationist to ask essential questions. As one question is completed, the lighted computer cursor automatically moves to the beginning of the next question. In this way, essential information cannot be overlooked. In fact, if the reservationist attempts to enter an incomplete reservation into the system, the computer will audibly beep and the cursor will blink at the beginning of the incomplete information field. Refer to Exhibit 5–1 for a glimpse at a sample reservation screen. See if you can identify which queries are essential and which are nonessential.

➤*Essential Reservation Data.*   The reservation process and especially the information obtained during the reservation are designed to improve the effectiveness of the front office. The facts communicated through the reservation form a valuable starting point from which the front-desk clerk can understand the guest's needs. Corporate guests may be placed away from the lobby in a quieter area of the hotel, while guests traveling with children may be roomed near the swimming pool. Late arrivals

Exhibit 5–1 All reservation screens are basically alike. They seek the same information in roughly the same order. See if you can identify which fields are "essential" and which are "nonessential." (ADR is an abbreviation for address.)

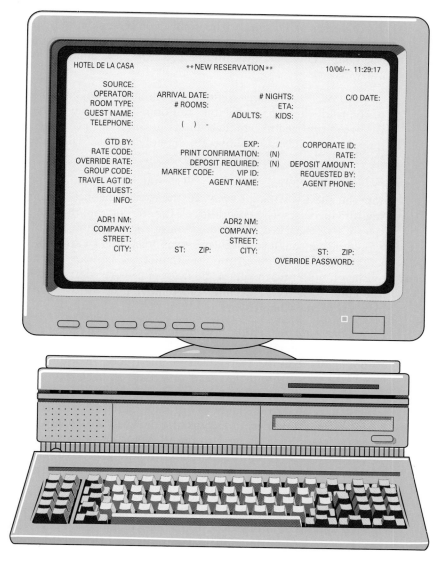

(see nonessential reservation data later in this chapter) are noted on the reservation screen so the front desk is better informed should it need to make difficult overbooking and walked guest decisions. Address information is collected so that the hotel can contact the guest for marketing or billing purposes or in the event the guest leaves behind a personal item.

Arrival and Departure Dates.   In the reservations centers for national chains, the questions of arrival and departure come third, after "What city?" and "What hotel?" Telephone time is not used to gather the details that follow unless the clerk is certain that space is available at the time and place requested.

Number of Nights.   This bit of redundancy forestalls later problems if the guest's count of nights is not in agreement with the time between the arrival and departure dates. A common miscommunication occurs when the guest counts the departure day in the number of nights.

Number of Persons.   The number of persons in the party and its structure help to clarify the kind of facilities needed. Two unrelated persons need two beds; a married couple could get by with one bed. Are there children? Is a crib required? A rollaway bed?

Number of Rooms Required.   Based on the size of the party and the types of rooms the hotel has available, additional rooms may be required. Most reservationists are authorized to handle requests for up to 10 rooms or so. As the number of required rooms increases above 10, the hotel's group sales department usually becomes involved.

Type of Rooms Required.   The question of room type is closely linked to the rate the guest is willing to pay. As the room type increases in luxury, the corresponding rate increases as well. Although the specific rate the guest wants to pay is the real question being asked, the reservationist certainly can't just offer a series of rates. That would be gauche. Instead, the reservationist offers a series of room types.

Generally, the reservationist attempts to sell from the top down. This is accomplished by offering the guest the most expensive room type first and then waiting for the guest to agree or decline before moving down to offer the next most expensive room type (see Chapter 8).

Corporate Affiliation.   Commercial hotels are very concerned with identifying all corporate guest reservations. The average corporate guest represents far more room nights than the average leisure guest does. In addition, corporate guests usually book their rooms with less lead time (and as such pay a higher average rate) than leisure guests do (see the yield management discussion in Chapter 4). As such, reservation data related to the guest's corporate affiliation is essential to the success of many commercial properties. In fact, asking the guest's corporate affiliation is often the first step in determining the rate to quote. Many corporate guests have negotiated a prearranged nightly room rate. Other corporate guests—usually less regular travelers to that particular hotel or region—are subject to the hotel's regular corporate rate.

Price.   The reservation (the sale) could be lost by the rate quotation. The agent may have no negotiating room if the yield management system has eliminated lower-priced options. Quoting the price is not enough. Distinctions between the prices must be accompanied by descriptive matter intended to entice the buyer to the better rate.

Name. The guest's name has become more important in recent years. In the past, the name was used for alphabetical filing of the reservation and was one of several means (confirmation number, date of arrival, etc.) by which the reservations agent or front-desk clerk could access the guest's reservation record.

Sophisticated reservation systems now use the customer's name as a means of gaining efficiency, saving time, and generating guest loyalty. Many systems integrate guest history into the reservations system. As the guest's name is entered into the reservation, a screen pops up for repeat customers showing the guest's address and phone; rate, room type, and number of nights stayed during the last visit(s); and other essential and nonessential information. With most information already in the system, the reservations clerk simply verifies that this is the same guest and asks if the information is still accurate.

Quality of the Reservation. The three quality types of reservations available—nonguaranteed, guaranteed, or advance deposit—are determined either by the guest or the reservationist. The reservationist, for example, may be restricted from accepting nonguaranteed reservations as a function of policy or unusually high business levels for the hotel. Similarly, the guest may not have a credit card with which to guarantee the reservation or may have a card but not be inclined to use it. In either case, the reservation may fail to materialize because of disagreement at this stage in the process. See Chapter 6 for a complete discussion of the quality of the reservation.

➤***Nonessential Reservation Data.*** Depending on the reservation system in place and/or the amount of reservation activity occurring in the reservation center at the time of the call, certain reservation information may not necessarily be required for each reservation. This less important information is categorized as nonessential or "nice-to-know" data. Examples of nonessential information include estimated time of arrival, special guest requests or needs, discounts or affiliations, and smoking or non-smoking room preference.

Although essential information must be complete for a reservation to be accepted into the computer system, nonessential information is not required. The computer will allow the input of a completed reservation into the system when nonessential data is missing. In fact, some computer screens display essential data in one color while displaying nonessential data in a secondary color. If time permits, the reservationist may request this additional data. Otherwise, it is often overlooked.

Estimated Time of Arrival. By knowing the guests' estimated time of arrival (ETA), the hotel can properly schedule front-desk clerks to assist with check in, van drivers to retrieve guests from the airport, and bellpersons to room them. More important, hotels that are filling to capacity can be certain to save rooms for guests who are going to be especially late.

Special Requests. Guest requests or needs run the gamut from simple, rather nonessential requests to extremely essential guest needs. That is why most reservationists provide guests with an opportunity to request any other items of importance before the close of the reservation process. If the request is essential (for example, a handicapped guest requesting a specially equipped room), the guest is usually certain to state the need. In other cases, the request (ocean view, near the Smith's room, below fifth floor) may be forgotten by the reservationist and the guest. That is the responsibility of the front-desk clerk—to handle each request on a case-by-case basis at the time of check in. Indeed, reservationists generally explain, "I'll note your request on the reservation, but I cannot promise you will get it."

Discounts or Affiliations.   Corporate, AAA (American Automobile Association), AARP (American Association of Retired Persons), or similar discounts or affiliations are usually handled during the room type and rate discussion earlier in the reservation. In fact, many such organizations (AARP, for example) require the guest to state his or her discount as a part of the reservation process. In such cases, the discount is void if the guest forgets to request it at the time of reservation.

Smoking Preference.   What was once merely a special request has become a standard reservation input field. Smoking preferences play an important role in guest-room satisfaction. Smokers and nonsmokers alike are very committed to their particular preferences. As such, practically all domestic hotels offer smoking and nonsmoking rooms for their guests' comfort. Some properties offer entire nonsmoking floors, and one small chain even experimented with complete nonsmoking properties.

With such a focus on smoking in today's society, it is surprising that the guests' smoking preference is still classified as nonessential reservation data. Given the amount of guest satisfaction and comfort riding on the smoking preference, it is even more curious that hotel reservations departments do not guarantee the smoking status of the reserved room—yet that's the standard in the lodging industry. The guest's smoking preference is noted and the hotel tries to accommodate the request, but there are no guarantees that a smoking guest will get a smoking room, or vice versa!

Address.   The guest address and/or phone number are requested by some hotels as a matter of record. Other hotels utilize the information to mail a confirmation card or confirmation letter (see Exhibits 5–2 and 5–3) when there is sufficient lead time. In the case of third-party reservations (as when a secretary or travel agent makes the reservation), the address and phone number of the person making the reservation is also requested. If unrelated persons share a room, both addresses may be requested. When several names are involved, the one under which the reservation will be claimed must be ascertained. The confirmation is normally mailed to that address.

Confirming the Reservation

A letter of confirmation or a confirmation card is usually printed by the computerized property management system (or central reservations system) using the information collected during the reservation (see Exhibits 5–2 and 5–3). There is a field on the reservation screen that asks "Print Confirmation? Yes or No." The system probably defaults to "No," requiring the reservations agent to actually enter "Yes" if a confirmation needs to be mailed (see Exhibit 5–1). Some properties ask the guest "Would you like us to mail you a confirmation?" Others do it as a routine activity when there is sufficient leadtime. Most properties, however, do not mail a confirmation. Instead, the reservationist closes the conversation by furnishing the caller with a confirmation number generated by the computer.

There is actually order to what appears to be random reservation numbers. First on the screen might be the scheduled arrival date, from 1 to 365. February 5, for instance, is 36. Then the individual hotel of the chain is identified by its own code. The agent's initials follow. Identification of the reservation concludes with the next confirmation number in sequence. The number, with the pieces set apart, may appear as 36 141 ABC 2366.

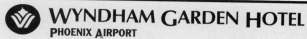

WYNDHAM GARDEN HOTEL
PHOENIX AIRPORT

April 30, _ _ _ _

Ms. Mary Watson
1020 1st Avenue, Northeast
Anytown, Texas 77001

Dear Ms. Watson:

Thank you for choosing the Wyndham Garden Hotel-Phoenix Airport for your next visit to our community.

We are delighted to confirm your reservation details as follows:

Confirmation #	75747 Guaranteed
Arrival Date	05/09/_ _
Departure Date	05/11/_ _ An early departure may result in additional charges.
Number of Guests	1 Adults 0 Children
Number of Rooms	1
Rate	$169.00

Please take a moment to review the following: Nonguaranteed reservations will be held until 4 PM on day of arrival. Guaranteed reservations can be canceled until 4 PM day of arrival. Failure to do so will result in a charge of one night's room and tax. For any amendments or additional information, please contact the reservations department at (602) 220-4400.

We look forward to welcoming you to the Wyndham Garden Hotel-Phoenix Airport and hope to make your stay a pleasant one.

Yours Sincerely,

Jeanne S. Tibbetts

Reservations Sales Agent

Exhibit 5–2 A letter of confirmation provides the same reservation detail as a confirmation card. Such letters are not individually written—this one was prepared as an automatic function of the hotel's Fidelio PMS. *Courtesy of Wyndham Hotels & Resorts, Dallas, Texas.*

Not every company follows this sequence. The reservation code might start with the first three letters in the guest's last name, and the clerk's identity might be dropped: VAL 36 141 2366. Or the number may be nothing more than the next digits in the sequence (Exhibit 5–3), accumulated by the month or year. In still other systems, the confirmation number is so complex it is almost impossible to decode.

Arrival	Time	Departure	No. Guest	Room Type	Rate
6/11/	GTD	6/14/	2	DELUXE KING	120

PLEASE CHECK FOR ACCURACY
Your Reservations Have Been Confirmed

Accommodations Requested

Special Request: OCEAN VIEW   Group Affiliation: WESTERN ATHLETES CONFERENCE

PAUL D. LIGAMENT
1234 ACHILLES TENDON WAY
WOUNDED KNEE
SOUTH DAKOTA   00000-0000

We require credit to be established prior to or at registration.
For your convenience we accept the following credit cards:
VISA, MasterCard, American Express, Carte Blanche,
Diners Club, and Discover Card.

A Guaranteed Payment Reservation:
Unless canceled, you will be responsible for payment of room accommodations reserved for one night with the remaining days being canceled.

A 6:00 PM Reservation:
Room accommodations and all remaining days will be canceled at 6:00 PM unless a deposit of $100.00 per room is received in advance.

Reservation #9821-017   **Toll-Free Reservations 800-555-5555**

Check-in time is 4 PM
Check-out is 12 noon

Exhibit 5–3   As with a letter of confirmation (see Exhibit 5–2), the "confirmation card" is prepared from information collected during the reservation. Confirmation cards are preprinted with hotel information. Blank spaces (including name and address, room type, etc.) are then filled in by the computer system. Confirmation cards may be mailed as postcards. This one is designed to be stuffed into a windowed envelope.

Electronic Reservations

Once entered into the system, the reservation appears electronically in a myriad of formats and printouts until the date of arrival. On that date, the reservation changes from a future reservation to an arriving reservation. On the date of arrival, the overall responsibility for the arriving or incoming reservation changes from the reservations department to the front-office staff (see Chapter 8).

An arrival list (Exhibit 5–4) is printed by the automated reservation system each night for the following day's anticipated check ins. The transfer of data is delayed until registration. The material is keyed in by the room clerk, and the transfer completed, but only after the guest arrives. Unlike the manual rack system (Exhibit 5–5), the computerized reservation system generally does not have a supporting correspondence file. Almost all supporting data is electronic in nature. Only under unusual circumstances will there be hard-copy support. Examples of these circumstances include reservation requests by mail or fax rather than telephone. Hard copies are also needed if the chain's reservation system does not have a last room availability interface with the hotel (refer to Chapter 4 for a more complete discussion).

With computerized property management systems (or a central reservations system), all the reservation information is stored in the computer's memory and can be recalled for viewing on the computer screen if the guest name and the date of arrival are known. In a perfect world, the reservation or confirmation number would be known, and that also would bring the information forward.

Although the majority of reservations remain undisturbed until the date of arrival, a great number of reservations are changed. Common alterations to reservations include a changed date of arrival or length of stay, a changed guest name (as when an

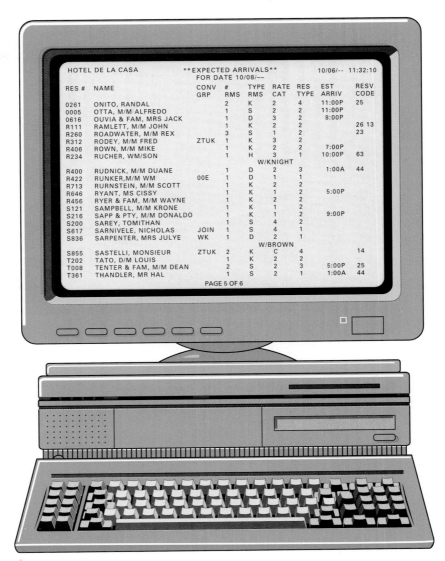

RES #	NAME	CONV GRP	# RMS	TYPE RMS	RATE CAT	RES TYPE	EST ARRIV	RESV CODE

HOTEL DE LA CASA   **EXPECTED ARRIVALS**   10/06/-- 11:32:10
FOR DATE 10/08/--

RES #	NAME	CONV GRP	# RMS	TYPE RMS	RATE CAT	RES TYPE	EST ARRIV	RESV CODE
0261	ONITO, RANDAL		2	K	2	4	11:00P	25
0005	OTTA, M/M ALFREDO		1	S	2	2	11:00P	
0616	OUVIA & FAM, MRS JACK		1	D	3	2	8:00P	
R111	RAMLETT, M/M JOHN		1	K	2	2		26 13
R260	ROADWATER, M/M REX		3	S	1	2		23
R312	RODEY, M/M FRED	ZTUK	1	K	3	2		
R406	ROWN, M/M MIKE		1	K	2	2	7:00P	
R234	RUCHER, WM/SON		1	H	3	1	10:00P	63
	W/KNIGHT							
R400	RUDNICK, M/M DUANE		1	D	2	3	1:00A	44
R422	RUNKER,M/M WM	00E	1	D	1	1		
R713	RURNSTEIN, M/M SCOTT		1	K	2	2		
R646	RYANT, MS CISSY		1	K	1	2	5:00P	
R456	RYER & FAM, M/M WAYNE		1	K	2	2		
S121	SAMPBELL, M/M KRONE		1	K	1	2		
S216	SAPP & PTY, M/M DONALDO		1	K	1	2	9:00P	
S200	SAREY, TOMITHAN		1	S	4	2		
S617	SARNIVELE, NICHOLAS	JOIN	1	S	4	1		
S836	SARPENTER, MRS JULYE	WK	1	D	2	1		
	W/BROWN							
S855	SASTELLI, MONSIEUR	ZTUK	2	K	C	4		14
T202	TATO, D/M LOUIS		1	K	2	2		
T008	TENTER & FAM, M/M DEAN		2	S	2	3	5:00P	25
T361	THANDLER, MR HAL		1	S	2	1	1:00A	44

PAGE 5 OF 6

Exhibit 5–4   Computer display of expected arrivals (reservations) list. Identical hard copies are provided on the day of arrival to the desk, the uniformed services, and even to the dining room if it is an American plan hotel. Note the estimated times of arrival and reservations codes (see Exhibit 5–6).

existing corporate reservation is to be claimed by a different employee), a changed room type or discount request, and a cancellation.

No matter what the alteration may be, the reservationist cannot make a change without first accessing the preexisting reservation. Only under unusual situations is the existing reservation difficult to locate. Difficulty in finding an existing reservation occurs when either the guest or reservationist has made a clerical error. Common clerical errors include incorrect date of arrival or incorrect spelling of the guest's name.

In many cases, these errors are found and rectified. In other instances, the existing reservation cannot be located. If, for some reason, the reservation cannot be found,

Exhibit 5–5   This outdated "reservation rack" demonstrates just how far we've come in a few short years. Actually, reservation racks are still in use in a number of hotels. They're still available for purchase, too, through suppliers such as the American Hotel Register Company. Reservation data was typed or handwritten onto slips, which were then inserted into these aluminum rack "pockets." The contents can be taken out and moved around as necessary. The rack shown here had 31 days (horizontal slots), each indicated by a black numbered pocket. Guests arriving on a given date were filed alphabetically. When that date eventually arrived, the entire rack was moved from the reservations department to the front desk.

the reservationist may actually take a new reservation. This is risky, because chances are there will now be duplicate reservations in the system.

➤*Advance Deposits.*   Guaranteeing the reservation by means of an advance deposit has grown more popular and less popular at the same time. If the request is for cash (check), the procedure has become less popular. Handling cash or checks requires a disproportionate amount of clerical time and postage relative to the economic gain.

The initial reservation procedure is similar whether or not a deposit check is requested. The reservation is confirmed, but only tentatively, since it contains notice that a reservation deposit is required. Two copies of the reservation confirmation may be mailed. The extra copy is to be returned with the check in the nonstamped, preaddressed envelope that is enclosed. More often than not, the hotel mails nothing. Instead, the customer is instructed to mail the deposit and to write the confirmation number on the check to ensure proper credit. With enough lead time, a receipt is usually returned to the guest. Most hoteliers, however, feel that the cost, time invested, and delay make the procedure unwarranted. This is especially true considering the widespread availability of credit cards.

Credit-Card Guarantees.   Even as requiring advance deposit checks has decreased in practice, guaranteeing by credit card is a procedure that has gained in popularity. The reservation clerk takes the credit-card number over the telephone and records it with the reservation. Nothing needs to be processed at this time. The charge will be forwarded only if the guest is a *no-show,* and then only if the hotel believes that collection is justified. In the usual sequence, the guest appears as expected and credit is established at registration.

Processing the credit card entails a fee that is not part of the cost of cash deposits. However, the fee isn't paid unless the charge is made. Check deposits have their own risk—they bounce.

Experienced travelers soon realize how much of a game the reservation process has become. Busy properties almost always insist on credit-card guarantees rather than on a 4 PM or 6 PM hold. Credit-card guarantees reduce the number of no-shows.

At the same time, guests know that many properties do not actually charge the card at the time of the reservation. With such properties, the guarantee is not processed until the expected night of arrival. A card that is charged at the time of the reservation requires another credit entry if the guest cancels in a proper and timely manner. So, to avoid making additional credit entries, many hotels wait to process the card until the night of arrival. The hotel's delay provides the traveler with a winning technique that costs the hotel unless the rooms manager is alert to what is happening.

Some unethical travelers play a credit-card game. They provide the hotel with an inaccurate credit-card number. In this way, if they fail to show, the hotel cannot charge them. On the other hand, if they do arrive and their false credit-card number is challenged, they can blame it on poor communication or a clerical error: They invent the false credit-card number by changing the sequence of one or two digits on their real credit card, which makes for a fairly believable excuse. For example, if their VISA card number were 4567 890 123 456, they could simply change the number to 4567 809 123 456. Now they have a believable excuse in the event they do show up for their reservation—but a fictitious number in the event of a no-show.

Most hotel chains and individual properties are wise to this game and intercept "errors" at the time of the reservation. They accomplish this by having an automated reservations system that is interfaced directly to a credit-card clearing center. During the several minutes the guest is on the telephone with the reservationist, the credit-card number is input and an approval verification is received. If the approval is denied, the reservationist gives the guest another opportunity to read the correct credit-card number.

➤*Cancellations.*   Like advance deposits, cancellations are special cases of reservation changes. They do not create unusual problems unless they are handled improperly. Handling anything at the front desk in an improper manner generates problems as well as bad public relations.

Encouraging cancellation calls is in the best interest of the hotel. Such calls reduce the no-show rate. Fewer no-shows generate more room revenue from walk-in guests and reduce complaints from the antiservice syndrome of overbooking.

The cancellation number, which is formulated like the confirmation number (discussed earlier), is the only major difference between a cancellation call and any other reservation change. Even then, its importance is limited to guaranteed reservations. The system must protect the guest who has guaranteed the room with a credit card (or other guarantee) from being billed if the reservation is canceled in a timely manner. The cancellation number is important when the process breaks down and the guest is billed as a no-show. If the guest is not billed, the number isn't needed or used. Nonguaranteed reservations are not generally provided with a cancellation number.

The cancellation number is important to the reservation count (see Chapter 6). Cancellations involving dates, number of rooms, and types of facilities affect room availability counts. There are other reservation changes that do not alter the count projections. Into this category fall the hour of arrival, the view or exposure, a request for a rollaway bed, and others.

▶ *Guest History Databases.*   Automation in the reservations department has created numerous efficiencies. What once was printed by hand, rewritten upon check in, and calculated manually is now a few computer keystrokes away. Automation has improved the speed and accuracy of the reservations department while leaving the basic task unchanged—unchanged, that is, until the introduction of guest history databases.

One of the ancillary benefits associated with speed and accuracy has been increased data storage capabilities. Customer information, collected during the normal flow of the room reservation, can be stored in guest history databases, manipulated, and used for marketing and guest service/recognition purposes. It makes sense that the hotel's use of guest history data has risen with increased computer storage and processing capabilities.

The guest history revolution has been fought primarily at the individual property level. Until recently, centralizing guest history information at the corporate level has been too unwieldy to justify. Guest history utilization at the property level is more manageable.

Guest history improves the most basic component of guest service: recognition. Hotels have always known that guests appreciate personal recognition. Imagine the unwavering loyalty that can be gained, then, if the guests' basic needs and requests are recognized in advance. That is the promise of guest history.

In its most common form, guest history is applied at the property level during the reservation process. As stated earlier in this chapter (see the section "Name"), the guest history function is utilized when the reservations agent pulls up a guest's previous stay information and saves them both the burden of repeating address, credit card, and room type/rate preferences. However, guest history can accomplish far more than that. In upscale corporate and luxury properties, guest history databases often inform front-office personnel of the various likes and dislikes of the guest. Simple preferences such as ground-floor room, feather as opposed to foam pillows, extra pears in the fruit basket, and so on, go a long way toward generating loyalty and a sense of belonging.

It makes good business sense, too. Not only does the hotel gain the benefits of enhanced guest loyalty, satisfaction, and repeat visitation, but guest history databases are valuable marketing resources as well. It takes little imagination to visualize the potential a mailed marketing campaign might have when focused on certain guest history parameters. For example, a hotel facing a slow autumn might mail a special promotion to those corporate guests who visited their property at least two times last year during September and October—now *that's* pinpointing the market.

Centralized Guest History.   Beginning around 1997, the industry saw increasing centralization of guest history information. What one property in Washington, DC knew about a particular frequent corporate traveler was now becoming available through the chain's central reservations system to, say, a sister property in Olympia, Washington.

Corporate travelers have been demanding improved guest service (recognition) to compensate for rising room rates. Chains such as Marriott Hotels and Resorts, Ritz-

Carlton, Preferred Hotels and Resorts, and Carlton Hospitality Worldwide saw the need to centralize guest history databanks and have taken the lead in this area of automation. These chains are banking on the premise that when frequent guests at one property are recognized like family in another of the chain's properties, the increased guest satisfaction will translate into increased brand loyalty.

Chain guest history databases have been developed from a variety of directions. Marriott's, for example, was designed around their existing Marriott Rewards frequent guest program. Since this program was already in place across their entire spectrum of properties, Marriott thought it made sense to use Marriott Rewards as the centralized starting point. As such, when the program rolled out (in October 1997), it already had guest profiles from more than 9 million members.[2] However, Marriott's guest history database system only stores basic guest information such as bed type and smoking preference.

Some of the smaller chains have an operational advantage over Marriott because of their relative size. Ritz-Carlton, for example, took the complete encyclopedia of guest history information they had developed at individual properties and integrated it into a centralized database. Ritz-Carlton calls this database its Customer Loyalty Anticipation Satisfaction System, or CLASS. Before the implementation of CLASS, regular Ritz-Carlton guests who were visiting a different Ritz-Carlton hotel for the first time would have been treated like first-timers. Now repeat customers at one property are repeat customers at all the Ritz properties.

Reservation Coding

The reservation's journey ends at the front desk (see Chapter 8). Sometimes the journey is long, as when the reservation was made a year in advance. In other cases, the reservation lead time is extremely short, as with reservations made minutes before arrival. In any case, the front desk is the final stopping point in the reservation's journey.

The first step in linking the reservation with the front desk is to change the status of the reservation from future reservation to arriving reservation. At the beginning of every new day, some set of future reservations becomes today's incoming reservations. In a computerized system, this change occurs automatically, either as the clock strikes midnight or as a step in the night audit process.

It is at this moment that guests' special requests and needs become the concern of the front desk. Armed with the knowledge of which rooms are clean and vacant, which rooms are due to check out, and which rooms are staying over, specific room assignments are developed in accordance with guest requests. Even in an automated property, the assigning of special rooms to match special requests is a manual operation. It is the clerk, operating with good judgment, who ultimately determines which requests can be met and which requests will be declined.

▶ *Special Coding.*   Whether operating under a manual or computerized system, certain reservations are different from the rest. They may be different in their method of payment, in the guests' specific requests, in the fact that they are *commissionable* to a travel agent, in their time of arrival, or in their affiliation. Whatever the case, the front-desk clerk needs to be alert and to treat these reservations differently.

The difference is generally highlighted somewhere on the reservation. In an automated system, a numerical coding scheme is commonly used. In this case, advance-deposit reservations will be indicated with one code number (see Exhibit 5–6, which

Computer Code	Internal System Meaning	Actual Printout on Guest Confirmation
11	VIP	
12	Group buyer	
13	Honeymooners	
14	Comp	
20	Connecting rooms	*Connecting rooms, if possible*
21	Adjoining rooms	*Adjoining rooms, if possible*
22	Rooms on same floor	*Same floor, if possible*
23	Need individual names	*Please advise names of individuals in your party*
24	PS	*Petit suite*
25	RS	*One-bedroom suite*
26	LS	*Two-bedroom suite*
30	Send liquor	
31	Send champagne	
32	Send flowers	
33	Send gift	
34	Send fruit	
40	Require deposit	*Please send one night's deposit to guarantee your reservation*
41	Due bill	
42	No credit, require advance payment	
43	Walk-in	
44	Late arrival	*Anticipated late arrival of guest*
50	Special rate	*Special rate*
51	Airline rate	*Airline rate*
52	Press rate	*Press rate*
53	Convention rate	*Convention rate*
54	Nonconvention rate	*Convention rate applies to convention dates only*
55	Travel agency	*Travel agency*
60	Cot	*Cot will be provided*
61	Crib	*Crib will be provided*
62	Bedboard	*Bedboard will be provided*
63	Wheelchair	*Wheelchair will be provided*
70	Casino guest	
80	See correspondence for very special instructions	
99	Print special message	*(Whatever that message is)*

Exhibit 5–6   Actual listing of reservations codes from a major hotel/casino operation. Code numbers correspond to an internal system description, policy, or abbreviation. Some codes (for example, code 54) print onto a special "comments" section of the confirmation form sent the guest. Other codes (for example, code 11) are designed for in-house use only.

uses code 40) and travel agent reservations another code (Exhibit 5–6 uses code 55). Following is a brief discussion about some of these special codes. For a more complete understanding of their impact on the guest check-in process, refer to Chapter 8.

Advance Deposits.   Reservations with an advance deposit need to be specially noted. If the deposit arrived, the front-desk clerk needs to be certain to post the credit on behalf of the guest. If the deposit never arrived, the front-desk clerk will probably cancel the reservation if the hotel is nearing capacity.

Late Arrivals.   If front-desk personnel know that a given reservation is due to arrive late, they will be less likely to assume it is a no-show as the evening progresses. Also, most late arrivals require a guarantee of some sort to hold the room past the normal 6 PM time frame for nonguaranteed reservations. (See Chapter 6 for a full discussion of the quality of the reservation regarding nonguaranteed and guaranteed reservations.)

Credit-Card Guarantee.   Rooms guaranteed with a national credit card are theoretically held for the guest all night long. If the guest fails to arrive, the night auditor will charge the credit card for one night's room (see Chapter 6).

Corporate Guarantee.   The right to guarantee rooms with a corporation's good credit must be prearranged with the hotel. In case of a no-show, the room charge is billed to the corporation's city ledger account (see Chapter 6).

Travel Agents.   Special-coding of travel agent (TA) reservations expedites the internal office procedure. After the guest departs, the hotel pays the travel agent's commission. (In those circumstances where the travel agent owes the hotel—an *account receivable*—the hotel bills the balance less the travel agent's commission.) When the reservation is placed, the agent identifies the agency, providing name, address, and *International Association of Travel Agents (IATA)* code number. Some hotels will not pay commissions, and the reservationist needs to explain that. If the customer wants the particular hotel, the agency will book the room and forgo its commission. Even if the hotel pays a commission, it may not do so on certain types of bookings. Deeply discounted rates (corporate or governmental, for example) are sometimes not commissionable.

Reservations are confirmed to the agency, not to the guest. In some cases, the hotel lacks the guest's address until registration time. To maintain accountability with the agency, the wise hotel manager sends a notice whenever one of the TA's clients fails to appear.

VIPs.   Very important persons (VIPs) are generally coded. These may be well-known dignitaries, celebrities, other hoteliers, or important members of an association that the hotel hopes to book later. VIP designations are made by a member of management or by the sales department. *Star reservation* is also used. A *contact reservation* is a VIP that should be met (contacted) and escorted to his or her room by the management.

Riding Reservation.   Reservations for which the date of arrival is vague may be allowed to "ride." The probable date is booked and then the reservation is carried until the guest shows or an allotted period of time passes, usually less than one week. Riding reservations are seldom used. They are generally found only at resorts or for VIP reservations.

Convention Delegate.   *Group affiliation* is a better term than *convention delegate* because the members of a group need not be part of a convention. Hotels cater to tours, company delegations, wedding parties, and other groups that need to be identified. Several codes are needed when different groups are booked at one time. For a more thorough discussion of group reservations, refer to the next section of the chapter.

➤ CONVENTION AND TOUR GROUP BUSINESS

The term *group business* represents a variety of venues. Group business can range from major conventions and expositions (trade shows), to midsized corporate meetings and conferences, to smaller incentive travel packages, tour groups, and corporate retreats. From large to small, group business is a major player in today's lodging industry.

For some properties, group business is almost nonexistent. Such hotels or motels may have limited or no meeting facilities, may be located in remote areas and face difficult group travel logistics, or may be so busy with leisure travel that there is no room for discounted group business. Conversely, major convention properties may derive upward of 90% of all hotel revenues from group activities. Although different types of properties have varying degrees of dependence on group business, the industry as a whole derives a significant portion of its revenues from this growing segment (see Exhibits 5–7 to 5–9).

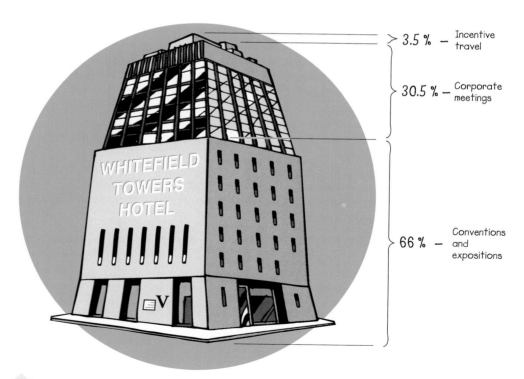

Exhibit 5–7   About two-thirds of group room revenues comes from conventions and expositions. The remaining one-third is composed primarily of corporate meetings (30.5%), with incentive travel (3.5%) making up the difference.

(a) Hotel rooms: 46.1% ($321.73)

(b) Retail stores: 13.0% ($90.44)

(c) City restaurants: 12.3% ($85.89)

(d) Hotel restaurants: 12.1% ($84.49)

(e) Local transportation, car rental, and gasoline: 6.0% ($41.73)

(f) Recreation, sporting events, sightseeing, and shows: 4.4% ($30.72)

(g) Hospitality suites: 3.3% ($23.09)

(h) Other: 2.8% ($19.92)

SOURCE: International Association of Convention and Visitor Bureaus, Washington, DC.

Exhibit 5–8　International conventions have a higher event expenditure per delegate ($895.57) than state or local conventions ($362.09). The average expenditure per delegate per convention for all conventions in the United States is $698.02. This exhibit shows how the average delegates spent their travel dollars.

Incentive travel, tour groups, conventions, and trade shows have become main-stays of hotel sales in the United States and abroad. Such gatherings are clearly defined as group business. Business meetings and corporate retreats, though smaller in scale, are included in this broad definition.

Depending on the hotel, smaller gatherings lose the distinction of being classified and tracked as group business. A small wedding party requiring only five or seven rooms, for example, may be considered an individual rather than a group reservation. Several executives meeting in a conference room for a few days are often handled through the hotel's in-house reservations department as individual rooms. Indeed, even a convention meeting planner visiting the property several weeks before the convention is probably handled as an individual (although complimentary) room. Techni-cally, the meeting planner's accommodations should be tracked as part of the overall convention count.

Group reservations are handled differently from individual reservations. One dif-ference is the central reservations office (or reservations link-up) may not be entitled to handle the group. Many chains require that group accommodations deal directly with the specific hotel property. Even at the hotel property, larger operations remove group reservations from the responsibility of the in-house reservations department.

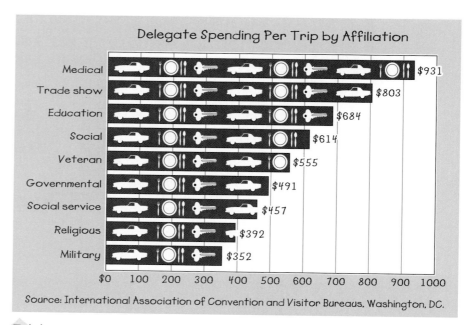

Delegate Spending Per Trip by Affiliation

Affiliation	Spending
Medical	$931
Trade show	$803
Education	$684
Social	$614
Veteran	$555
Governmental	$491
Social service	$457
Religious	$392
Military	$352

Source: International Association of Convention and Visitor Bureaus, Washington, DC.

Exhibit 5–9   Convention delegates have historically spent more per trip than corporate or leisure travelers. Depending on the type or purpose of the convention (medical vs. military), certain delegates spend more than others.

Most large properties have a group sales department designed to handle (among other tasks) group rooms reservations. Finally, depending on business levels, policies, and property characteristics, large groups may be granted special rates and discounts. These special deals are negotiated between the group's representative and the hotel's sales manager, with final approval granted by the general manager of the property.

Because of differing policies and definitions, group business is handled and characterized differently across various hotels and chains. Therefore, it is difficult to know exactly how great is the impact of group rooms activity on the lodging industry. A fairly large number of group activities are never counted. However, the convention industry (including conventions, expositions, corporate meetings, incentive travel, and trade shows) is conservatively estimated at $82 billion annually in the United States alone. According to the U.S. Department of Commerce, that places the convention industry roughly 17th in comparison to all industries in the United States! Of that $82 billion, about 66% of the revenues come from conventions and expositions, 30.5% come from corporate meetings, and 3.5% come from incentive travel (see Exhibit 5–7). Each of these categories has its own demographics and spending patterns. Some details related to convention visitor spending are shown in Exhibits 5–8 and 5–9.

The Group Rooms Contribution

The contribution of group rooms revenues to total rooms revenues depends on the type of hotel. Some properties—conference centers, for example—are exclusively group-oriented (see Exhibits 5–10 and 5–11). Other operations choose to accommodate groups during slow periods and off-seasons. There are very few hotels that refuse to accommodate group business altogether.

Exhibit 5–10   Convention and meeting facilities come in all shapes and sizes. These two examples range from a cozy roundtable conference room at the Adam's Mark Hotel in St. Louis to the 26,680-square-foot Plaza International Ballroom at the Peabody Orlando. This ballroom can seat 2,420 guests for a banquet! *Courtesy of the Adam's Mark Hotel, St. Louis, Missouri and the Peabody Orlando, Orlando, Florida. Used with permission.*

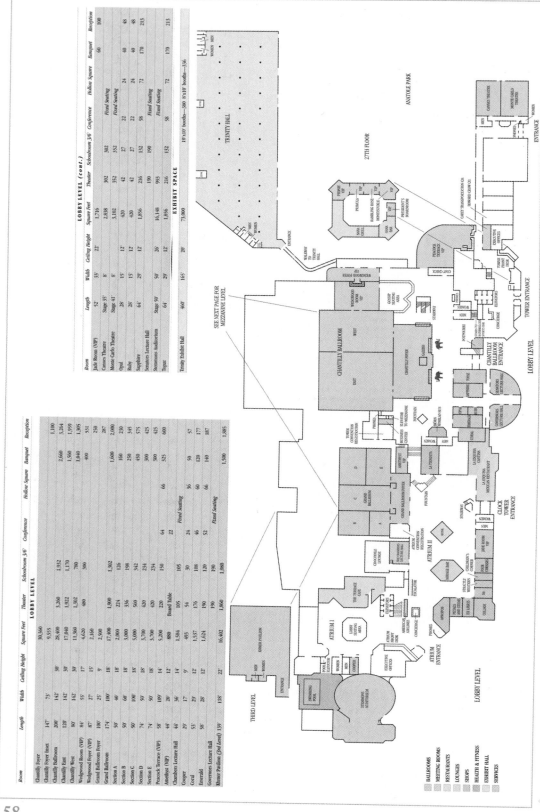

Exhibit 5–11 This exhibit illustrates the vast group capabilities of a major convention hotel. The Wyndham Anatole Hotel (Dallas) is the largest convention hotel in the Southwest. The hotel boasts over 300,000 square feet of meeting and function space (not shown here are facilities on the mezzanine level and in the Anatole Park). *Courtesy of the Wyndham Anatole Hotel, Dallas, Texas.*

▶ *Why Groups?*   There are three distinctions that separate group business from individual corporate and leisure travelers. These distinctions represent benefits (profits) associated with selling group rooms. Even though group rooms are usually sold at a discount from rack rate (as most things purchased in quantity are sold at a discount), it is still a very profitable venture for most hotels.

However, accepting a group booking for a given date is no simple matter. It must be evaluated in terms of the group's rooms revenues and related revenues (banquets, meeting room rentals, audiovisual equipment use, etc.), as opposed to displaced transient and corporate rooms business. Whether the group business justifies displacing normal hotel business (corporate and transient rooms) is a question for the hotel's yield management team (see Chapter 4).

There are three characteristics unique to group business that affect the hotel's interest in accepting group rooms:

1. Group business is a sizable market.
2. Groups provide certain economies of scale.
3. Group delegates spend more dollars.

The first point, "group business is a sizable market," was addressed earlier in the chapter (see Exhibits 5–7 to 5–9). There is no question that group business, an $82 billion industry, is "sizable," and depending on the type of hotel and the market in which it operates, some properties get more than their share of group business.

The second point addresses the incredible economies of scale associated with group business. *Economies of scale* is a term that denotes the economic benefits of mass production. Most items produced in mass quantities benefit from reduced per-item production costs. The same is true for the hotel industry. Selling a bulk of group rooms provides the operator with specific economies of scale. The sales department benefits from the reduced work in booking one large group as opposed to booking numerous smaller visits. The reservations department benefits from having a block of rooms set aside for the group. Even the front office, housekeeping, and uniformed services benefit from group room bookings.

With group arrivals and departures, business levels are clearly understood. With a five-day convention, for example, the front office is especially busy on the first and last days: During the first day, the front office is busy with heavy check ins; on the last day, it is busy with check outs. The middle days, however, are relatively slow for the front-office staff. During these slower middle days, the hotel saves labor costs by reducing its normal staffing levels. The same is true with the housekeeping and uniformed-services departments. In many hotels, the housekeeping department spends less time cleaning stayover rooms than it does cleaning check outs. Similarly, the bellstaff is busiest when assisting guests with luggage at check in and check out. Uniformed-service positions are very slow during the middle days of a convention.

The third reason hotels like group business is that group delegates have a higher worth than that of individual guests. No one understands this quite as well as the casino hotels. Interacting with other conventioneers often puts group delegates in a festive mood. The trip is not just business—in many cases there is fun and excitement in the excursion. And what better way to have fun than with an all-expenses-paid trip (see Exhibit 5–9).

Many convention, exposition, and related group delegates are visiting the event at no personal cost. Their company or business has funded most or all of the trip. Once at the hotel, delegates have a high likelihood of spending additional money. After all, their basic expenses (meals, lodging, transportation, and convention registration) have been paid. Therefore, they buy a round of golf that they might not ordinarily purchase if they were paying for the trip on their own. They may have an extra cocktail or two and buy more expensive "premium" brands. They may select a souvenir from the gift shop or even a painting from the gallery. And, of course, they might gamble a few extra (or a lot of extra) dollars. Even when delegates attend a convention at their own expense, there are favorable tax deductions that often reduce the real cost of the trip.

Casino Hotels. Casino hotels are an interesting breed in themselves. Casino hotels generally only accept groups that have a high likelihood of gambling. All things being equal, the casino manager may prefer a group of sanitation engineers, bottling managers, or morticians over a group of doctors, lawyers, or schoolteachers. In fact, the hotel may prefer a few empty hotel rooms over a hotel full of nongamblers. Therefore, even when space is available, certain groups will be refused by casino hotels.

Assuming that the sanitation engineers are considered to be good gamblers, the casino must decide how much they are worth. The question that must always be answered is: Will the group produce more casino revenues than the individual tourists the group is displacing? If the group has a strong reputation for casino play, it will be able to negotiate a better discount than a group with a lesser (or unknown) reputation.

Research shows that different delegates have different spending habits (see Exhibit 5–9). Industries in which delegates have higher annual salaries (say, physicians) usually see more spending per person during annual conventions than industries with lower annual salaries (say, military officers). This is not necessarily the case with casino gaming. With casino gaming, lower-income delegates may spend more on the casino floor than wealthier delegates.

The reason for this dichotomy can be found in such socioeconomic factors as education, aversion to risk, moral perceptions, and any number of other reasons for which a given delegate may or may not gamble. In the examples above, a casino operator may prefer the military over the physicians who have less propensity to gamble.

Why Some Hotels Refuse Groups. Not too many years ago, select resort operations were less inclined to accept group business than they are today. They refused group bookings for a number of reasons. The primary reason was because the group alienated nongroup guests staying at the property. That is still often the case. Staying in a hotel that is almost entirely occupied by a large group can be disconcerting to the individual, nongroup guest. Walking the halls, playing tennis, eating a meal, or sitting in the lounge can be rather self-conscious activities when the nonaffiliated guest is surrounded by loud and boisterous group delegates. Some exclusive resorts will not subject their individual guests to such an uncomfortable situation.

Hotels may be less interested in group business for several other reasons as well. Group business requires a certain investment from the hotel—there is the need for public meeting space (see Exhibits 5–10 and 5–11), audiovisual equipment, tables and chairs, food serving equipment, and so on. Also, there is the requirement of additional labor. Group hotels require a sales department staffed with one or more individuals, a convention and catering department, and food production areas. Finally, groups often negotiate discounted room rates. Hotels that find themselves in the enviable position of having strong year-round occupancy may be less interested in discounted groups.

Categories of Group Business

The need to communicate an ever-increasing amount of information has given extra strength to the convention market. Even as the information superhighway is being paved, the conventions market is larger than ever. Meeting and speaking with other delegates face to face offers certain benefits the impersonal computer, telephone, or Internet cannot provide.

Even as the convention market is growing, so is the group tour and travel market. Lacking the expense account and tax advantages of the conventioneer, the group tourist seeks economy above all else. Group tour and travel rates are often substantially lower than rack rates.

Whereas convention business is sold as a group and guests are handled individually, tour business is sold as a group and guests are handled as a group. One sale, one reservation, one registration,[3] one service, and one billing provide the savings on which the tour concept is built.

➤ ***Tour Groups.*** Tour groups are very convenient for the hotel, but that convenience comes at a price. Tour operators demand deep discounts. They get them because the entire burden is on the tour operator, with only minimal risk for the hotel.

The hotel deals with one party, the group tour company or wholesaler. The wholesaler leases the bus or plane, books the rooms, commits land transportation and entertainment, and then goes out to sell the package. Travel agents are the wholesaler's major sales outlets. Each agent receives a commission for the sale, and the wholesaler combines them into one group. In so doing, the workload of the front office is reduced considerably.

As much as 40% of the tour operator's original room estimate may be lost between the start of negotiations and the date of arrival, perhaps as long as one year later. Consequently, tour operators may be given the right to *sell and report* until as close as 7 to 14 days before arrival. Sell and report, also called *status control*, allows the wholesaler or tour operator to sell rooms and report back periodically. The right to this free sell is changed to sold-out status at the discretion of the hotel's forecast team.

Careful control is maintained over the right to sell and report because several agencies might be in that mode simultaneously. Specific dates are closed when the hotel is full and others may be closed to arrivals. Within the terms of the contract with the wholesaler, the hotel's forecast team can alter the closeout date for the tours, asking for the final rooming list one week, four weeks, or even five weeks before arrival. Nowhere in this process is the hotel's in-house reservation office involved. The wholesaler and that company's team of travel agents do all the selling. The deals are negotiated by the sales office, and the central reservations office is not generally involved.

➤ ***Convention Groups.*** Arrangements for the convention are made by a representative or committee of the organization and confirmed to the hotel with a contract of agreement. Large associations have permanent, paid executives in addition to the annually elected officers. These account executives are so numerous that they have their own organization—ASAE, the American Society of Association Executives.

If the organization is large enough to have a paid executive, he or she negotiates the arrangements with the hotel's sales staff. Details focus on many areas, including housing, meals, and meeting facilities. The organization (club, association, union) contracts with the hotel to buy meeting space (see Exhibits 5–10 and 5–11), banquet facilities, and rooms to house its own staff. It negotiates with the hotel for a block of guest rooms, but it does not pay for those rooms. Members deal individually with the hotel for accommodations.

The association sells function tickets to its membership for such events as banquets, cocktail parties, and luncheons. The money collected from these events is paid to the hotel at the negotiated price. If the association charges a higher ticket price, it will make a slight profit over the hotel's charge.

In addition, the group may also benefit from breakage (see Chapter 2) if it sells more tickets than the number of delegates who actually show for the event. On the other hand, if it guarantees a number higher than the number of delegates who show, the hotel will reap the benefit of breakage.

The organization is responsible for its own entertainment (although it may hire people through the hotel), its own speakers, films, and so on. For this, it charges the attendees a registration fee. Although some of the fee goes toward the costs of the program, the association usually profits here again.

Further gains may be made through the room rate arrangements. Sometimes organizations require the hotel to charge the attending members more than the negotiated room rate and to refund that excess to the group treasury. This raises many ethical concerns, particularly if the convention guest is unaware of the arrangement.

In no way does the association contract for rooms, except for those directly related to association headquarters, such as officers' and speakers' rooms. Room reservations are individually contracted between the hotel and each delegate. Billing is handled the same way, and collections become a personal matter between the conventioneer and the hotel.

►*Expositions and Trade Shows.*   Expositions and trade shows have many characteristics similar to conventions. In fact, trade shows are often held in conjunction with large conventions. The association (or trade-show entrepreneur) acquires space from the hotel or convention center and leases that space to exhibitors (see Exhibits 5–10 and 5–11). Those managing the trade show invite guests, exhibitors, and shoppers.

The average guest stay is longer with a show because the displays, which are costly and elaborate, require setup and teardown time. Otherwise, reservation and front-office procedures are the same as for a convention or an individual guest. More city ledger charges (delayed billing) may occur because the exhibitors are usually large companies that request that type of settlement.

Convention Reservations

Associations book conventions and expositions as much as 5 to 10 years in advance. Extremely large conventions (100,000 delegates or more) such as the National Association of Home Builders (NAHB) or the National Restaurant Show (NRS) may have unconfirmed bookings as far out as 20 years in advance. For small to midsized conventions, two to three years is the norm.

Initially, a blanket reservation is committed by the hotel and a rate is negotiated. For large conventions requiring more than one hotel, a citywide convention and visitor's bureau (CVB) negotiates the blanket reservation on behalf of participating hotels (refer to section entitled "Convention and Visitor Bureaus" following). The blanket reservation is little more than a commitment for a set number of rooms at a set rate for a set date. There is little additional detail until at least a year in advance.

►*Adjusting the Room Block.*   As the date approaches, some six months to a year in advance, the hotel begins to examine the blanket reservation or room block. After discussions with the association, the hotel may adjust the number of rooms required if the association predicts its convention size to grow or shrink that year. Meetings with neighboring hotels or the CVB may shed light on their management strategies with regard to the room block and the convention's ability to deliver the rooms committed. Finally, communication with other hotels where this group has previously been housed will give some sense of the group's attrition or casualty factor.

Convention hotels usually cooperate by furnishing each other historical information about the group—numbers, no-shows, and the like. They do this because conventions usually move annually. A hotel in one section of the state or nation is not competing with another if the organization has already decided to meet in another city. Similar information is available through local convention or tourist bureaus, which report to and have access to the files of the International Association of Convention and Visitor Bureaus (IACVB). The IACVB gathers data about the character and performance of each group handled by the member bureaus.

Reservation problems occur despite the best predictive efforts of the marketing and reservations departments. Association memberships change over time, and certain cities prove more or less appealing than previous sites. The casualty factor (cancellations plus no-shows) also varies from group to group, reducing the value of generalized percentage figures.

►*Convention and Visitor Bureaus.*   Convention and visitor bureaus are publicly funded, quasi-governmental agencies found in all large and most midsized or small cities. CVBs (sometimes known as convention and visitor authorities) are a centralized entity designed to represent the city's hospitality industries. Usually, CVBs are funded by local lodging or room taxes (see Chapter 9); they may also receive some government funding and some membership dues. Because the vast amount of funding comes from lodging taxes, hotels are viewed as paying "customers" of the CVB and the CVB is, in essence, working for the betterment of the hospitality industry.

The CVB represents the city in numerous group rooms bids each year (see Exhibit 5–12). Many of these bids are made directly to the ASAE or a regional counterpart of the same. Hotel sales managers from some of the larger properties (or key properties bidding on a particular piece of business) often accompany CVB representatives on national sales trips.

Expanded Services.   In recent years, CVBs have begun vertically integrating more and more group services. Such areas as transportation services (moving delegates to and from the airport and daily to and from the convention center), on-site registration assistance (temporary staffing of booths), database marketing (identifying who attended and from where they came), telemarketing (swaying potential delegates to attend the convention), promotion assistance (developing videos and print materials), and even special event or off-site banquet planning (managing extracurricular activities outside the convention center) are now being offered by some CVBs.

Meeting planners are generally pleased with the trend toward expanded bureau services. After all, any value-added service included with the price of convention space will ultimately make for a better convention and might even save the association money. But at what cost? Just as meeting planners are happy about the trend toward vertical integration of CVBs, independent meeting suppliers are less pleased. They

Conventions and Trade Shows	Dates	Attendance	Hotel(s)
Four Freshman	Sept. 17–20	500	Alexis Park
International Business Machines Corp.	Sept. 20–25	1,000	Caesars Palace
World Gaming Congress and Expo	Sept. 22–25	22,000	Las Vegas Hilton
International Foodservice Equipment Expo	Sept. 23–25	10,000	Las Vegas Hilton
Automotive Fleet and Leasing Association	Sept. 24–26	115	Bally's
Soldier of Fortune Magazine	Sept. 25–27	7,500	Continental
State Farm Insurance Co.	Sept. 25–Oct. 4	8,000	MGM Grand, Monte Carlo
American Institute of Hydrology	Sept. 27–30	200	Riviera
USS Albany Association	Sept. 27–Oct. 1	200	Showboat
International Association of Hydrologists	Sept. 27–Oct. 3	600	Riviera
USS Hoggatt Bay	Oct. 4–8	200	Imperial Palace
International Sanitary Supply Association	Oct. 6–8	10,000	Las Vegas Hilton
Association of Steel Distributors	Oct. 6–9	175	Bally's
Pony Baseball/Softball	Oct. 8–15	100	Luxor
General Federation of Women's Clubs	Oct. 9–10	200	Orleans
International Foundation of Employee Benefit Plans	Oct. 11–13	10,000	Las Vegas Hilton

Exhibit 5–12   A glimpse at this convention calendar (we started randomly with September 20) gives a sense of the wide variety of associations and affiliations that meet. Note the numbers of delegates and headquarters hotels listed. *Courtesy of the Las Vegas Convention and Visitors Authority, Las Vegas, Nevada.*

argue that CVBs are stepping outside their defined roles as convention and visitor bureaus. The job of the CVB, according to many meeting supply companies, is to bring business into the city. Once the CVB secures the business, independent meeting suppliers should be allowed to handle the details from there.

Certainly the CVBs' expanded role encroaches upon the independent meeting suppliers' hard-earned turf. When the CVB offers transportation services, that affects the ground-handling companies. When the CVB offers on-site registration assistance, that affects the temporary employment agencies. Others who may be affected by these expanded services include independent research and marketing consultants, video production and media print services, caterers, and regional tour operators.

The CVBs understand the problem but often opt for the greater good to the greatest number of persons. You see, if a convention threatens to be lost to a competing city because that city is including additional services, like it or not the CVB will have to match the bid. The alternative is to let the convention, and all its associated community revenues (see Exhibit 5–8), slip away. With conventions of 10,000 delegates representing some $7,000,000 to hotels, restaurants, transportation services, theaters, and shops in a community, CVBs cannot afford to lose business for the sake of a few independent meeting planners.

The Housing Bureau.   An important division or office within the CVB is the housing bureau (or housing authority). When the CVB is successful in bidding and committing citywide rooms to groups too large to be housed by one hotel, the housing bureau becomes involved. The San Francisco CVB's housing bureau, for example, handles well over one quarter million room nights per year. It offers its services once a convention reaches 1,000 delegates in three or more hotels.

Each hotel commits rooms toward the blanket reservation and a citywide commitment is made to the association. Rates remain the prerogative of the individual properties.

Reservation request cards (Exhibit 5–13) are returned to the CVB's housing bureau rather than to the individual hotel. The bureau relays to the hotel the guest's first, second, or third choice, depending on which hotel still has space. The hotel replies to the guest and sends copies of the confirmation to the housing bureau and to the association's headquarters.

Two properties may join forces if the convention is too large for one hotel but does not need a citywide commitment. The property that booked the business becomes the headquarters site and the booking office, with the second hotel (the overflow hotel) honoring the negotiated convention rate. This practice is now considered a violation of the antitrust laws. Joint housing of delegates is permissible, but each property should negotiate its own rates.

➤*Overflow Hotels.*   Some hotels require an advance deposit from convention delegates. This is especially true of isolated resorts where there is little chance that walk-ins will fill no-show vacancies. It is also true of overflow hotels.

Associated Tailors of America May 4–8, — — **Herald Square Hotel** **Reservation Department** Please make the following reservations quoted on European plan (no meals included). Reservations must be received by **Herald Square** no later than April 15. ☐ Guest Rooms—Single $82 ☐ Guest Rooms—Double $88 ☐ Suites: Petite $110 　　　　Deluxe $135 Will Arrive _____ Time _____ Will Depart _____ Time _____ Name _____ Address _____ City _____ State _____ Zip _____ Credit Card No. _____ Exp. Date _____ Reservations will not be held after 6 PM unless otherwise requested.	**Associated Tailors of America** May 4–8, — — **Herald Square Hotel** **Reservation Department** Please make the following reservations quoted on European plan (no meals included). Reservations must be received by **Herald Square** no later than April 15. ☐ Guest Rooms—Single $72 $78 $84 $90 ☐ Guest Rooms—Double $78 $84 $90 $96 　　　　(Please circle rate choice) ☐ Suites: Petite $110 　　　　Deluxe $135 Will Arrive _____ Time _____ Will Depart _____ Time _____ Name _____ Address _____ City _____ State _____ Zip _____ Credit Card No. _____ Exp. Date _____ Reservations will not be held after 6 PM unless otherwise requested.

Exhibit 5–13   Group confirmation cards showing run-of-the-house (flat) rates (left) and spread rates (right). Spread rates offer a range of choices not provided by the flat rates. (The hotel's address is on the other side of the card.)

Conventions are often too large to be housed in just one hotel. Therefore, the association finds additional properties to supplement the rooms available at the headquarters hotel. These supplemental properties are commonly referred to as overflow hotels.

Overflow hotels often require an advance deposit sufficient to cover the cost of all nights booked. This is because overflow properties may lose occupancy to the headquarters hotel during the second or third day of the convention. Because of cancellations and no-shows, the headquarters hotel often has vacancies at the outset of the convention. Rooms available at the headquarters hotel are very appealing to delegates housed at overflow properties. After all, for roughly the same rate, they can stay in the main hotel with all of the exciting hospitality suites and activities it has to offer.

Therefore, overflow properties need to protect themselves against delegates who check out the second day and move to the headquarters hotel. Overflow properties sometimes protect themselves by charging full advance deposits equal to the entire number of nights the delegate initially planned to stay. They may also change their cancellation policy to reflect 48 or 72 hours advance notice.

Negotiating Convention Rates

Convention rates are a unique breed because convention organizers bargain hard to obtain the best rates they can. Yet it is the individual convention delegate who actually reaps the benefit of the discounted rate when he or she pays the room bill. The association executive negotiates with the hotel(s) on behalf of the convention and all its delegates. The sales manager, the director of sales, or even the general manager negotiates on behalf of the hotel.

For most conventioneers, the hotel room is the largest expense item (see Exhibit 5–8). Therefore, the convention attempts to negotiate a favorable rate so as to attract the most delegates possible. Conversely, the hotel needs to keep its profitability and yield management policies in mind as it sets rate parameters with the group.

If the convention is planned during a slow season for the hotel, the sales department is willing to negotiate. The agreed-upon room rate is also dependent on the number (and profitability) of food and beverage functions planned in association with the convention. Other factors for the hotel to consider are the makeup or demographics of the convention, whether delegates have the potential to return as regular guests, and for casino hotels, whether delegates have a propensity to gamble.

Another factor the hotel will probably consider is the *attrition factor* for each particular group. Through contacts with other properties that have housed this group in the past, the sales manager gains an understanding of the attrition or *pickup rate* for this particular group. It makes no sense for the hotel to plan 800 rooms for five nights for the Associated Tailors of America conference (see Exhibit 5–13) if they'll be lucky to actually sell 650 rooms for an average of four nights. Associations have a tendency to exaggerate the number of rooms needed by delegates. Hotels must ascertain the attrition factor or pickup rate before committing to a specific room rate.

►*Attrition.*   The group's attrition factor and the group's pickup rate are actually reciprocals. They both provide the sales department with a measurement of the number of rooms actually reserved, in comparison to the number set aside in the reservation room block. They just derive this measurement in slightly different ways.

The pickup rate looks at the actual number of rooms sold to convention delegates divided by the number of rooms originally blocked. For an example, let's look back to the Associated Tailors' convention. Let's assume that the blanket reservation blocked 800 rooms for five nights—that's 4,000 room-nights. However, at the close of the convention, the hotel discovered it sold only 650 rooms for an average of four nights—that's 2,600 room-nights. The pickup rate was 65.0% (2,600 room-nights sold divided by 4,000 room-nights blocked).

Conversely, the attrition factor looks at the number of rooms that were not sold or not picked up. The attrition factor measures the remaining unsold delegate rooms by the number of rooms originally blocked. Again, let's look to the Associated Tailors' convention. If 2,600 room-nights were actually picked up against a block of 4,000 room-nights, 1,400 room-nights went unsold to convention delegates. These 1,400 room-nights may have ended up being sold to corporate or leisure guests, but only after the agreed-upon closeout date for accepting convention reservations. The attrition factor for this group was 35.0% (1,400 room-nights unsold divided by 4,000 room-nights blocked).

➤ *Comp Rooms.* Complimentary (comp or "free") rooms are one part of the total package. Complimentary rooms for use by the association are included at a rate of about 1 comp unit per 50 sold. The formula applies to both convention and tour groups.

Many hotels are beginning to take a hard look at how comps are earned and used. Attrition factors, no-shows, and cancellations are no longer counted in the computation. Credit is given only for the number of rooms actually sold; understays do not contribute to the count.

The use of comps is also being restricted. Comps are meant to be used by convention executives and staff during the dates of the convention and possibly several days immediately preceding or following the event. Comps are not designed for use months later as a personal vacation for the convention executive!

➤ *Rate Quotes.* Rates are quoted as flat or spread (see Exhibit 5–13). Under the *flat rate,* sometimes called *single rate,* all guests pay the same convention rate, which is usually less than the average rack rate. Except for suites, rooms are assigned on a best-available basis, called *run-of-the-house.* Some pay more for the room than its normal price, and others pay less. Run-of-the-house implies an equal distribution of room assignments. If half the rooms have an ocean view and half do not, the convention group should get a 50–50 split with a run-of-the-house rate. One Hawaiian hotel advertises "run-of-the-ocean" rates. A fair distribution includes an equitable share of standard, medium, and deluxe accommodations.

A *spread rate,* sometimes called a *sliding rate,* uses the standard rack rate distribution already in place. The level is reduced several dollars below the rack rates. Assignments are made over the entire rate spread according to individual preference and a willingness to pay. The range of wealth and interest among the attendees makes spread rates more attractive to larger groups.

Convention management companies, which sell all types of services to the association buyers, are flourishing as part of the trend toward third-party intermediaries. Their fees are paid by the hotel as a percentage of room rates, just as travel agents are compensated. Such commissionable rates reduce the rate-negotiating leverage that the convention group can exercise on the hotel.

➤ *Blanket Reservations.* As individual requests arrive at a hotel, they are charged against the blanket reservation. The hotel and the association reexamine the room commitment 45, 30, and 20 days before the convention begins.

Reservations received after the closeout date, 20 to 30 days before the convention starts, are accepted only if space remains—on an *availability basis only*. Reservations are confirmed individually, with an additional copy sometimes going to the association for count control.

Historically, handling group reservations, coordinating delegate rooms, and managing rooming lists has been a bit cumbersome. Housing bureaus collect convention delegate hotel preferences (see Exhibit 5–13) and prepare a list of delegates staying at each hotel. For smaller meetings, the company hosting the meeting probably develops the rooming list.

Once the names and addresses are prepared, the hotel may be responsible for sending a confirmation back to each delegate. This is where the cumbersome nature of rooming lists is most apparent. The housing bureau (or meeting planner) rooming list is usually delivered to each hotel on paper, requiring the hotel to hand-enter the data into its PMS system. That's where a lot of spelling and related errors occur.

New advancements on the market take advantage of the translation capabilities of switch technology (see Chapter 4) to download the information directly from the housing bureaus to each hotel, no matter which PMS system they may be using. One of the leaders in this new technology is THISCO's UltraRes system.

➤*Unidentified Delegates.*   Some delegates slip through the carefully planned system and appear to the hotel as regular guests unaffiliated with the convention. This is usually accidental, but some guests deliberately trick the hotel to gain rate or room advantages. Many delegates make room reservations by telephone and fail to mention they are with the convention. In addition, they do not mail back the reservation cards (see Exhibit 5–13).

One of two things may happen with these unidentified conventioneers: (1) the reservation might be denied (the convention block is open, but general reservations are closed), and the guest goes elsewhere; or (2) the reservation might be accepted as a nonconvention guest (both the convention blanket and the nonconvention categories are open). This second option leaves the hotel with duplicate space.

The situation takes a different twist when the conventioneer accepts space outside the blanket count because all the convention spots have been filled. Once housed, this guest argues to get the special, reduced, convention rate. Too many situations like that, and the carefully balanced yield management system goes awry.

➤*IT Packages.*   The inclusive tour (IT) package is the hotel's move into the lucrative group market. The hotel combines housing, food, and entertainment but no transportation to offer an appealing two- or three-night stay at greatly reduced rates. The IT package affects group bookings, but it is not a type of group business.

IT packages can and do compete with convention reservations. For large conventions, the yield management committee closes the remaining rooms to all but high-priced rates. When relatively few rooms of the hotel are assigned to the convention, all rate classes remain available, including the package, priced at less, and offering more, than the convention rate. Keen convention shoppers book the IT package.

Handling the Tour Group Reservation

The workload of the reservations department is affected relatively little by the demands of the tour group. Both the initial sale and the continuing contact rest with the hotel's marketing and sales department. That department may have a position called the *tour and travel desk.*

Yield management coordination is the major role for reservations during the time before the group arrives. Hotels doing a large tour and travel business maintain four-month horizons. Sell-and-report authorities are adjusted as forecasted demand equals, exceeds, or falls short of historical expectations.

Tour groups are almost always given shares-with rooms, since a premium is charged for single occupancy. The hotel gets a rooming list that shows each pairing. The entire block of rooms is preassigned. If the tour company brings in back-to-back groups, the very same rooms may be used again and again. Keeping the block together in the same floor or wing expedites baggage handling and reduces noise and congestion elsewhere.

Special group arrival sections, even special lobby entrances, reduce the congestion as the group arrives or departs. Transportation is by bus, even if only to the airport. These transfer costs are part of the fee and are arranged by the tour company. Bell fees are also included, levied by the hotel over and above the room charge.

➤ SUMMARY

Because reservations are in a sense contractual agreements, the hotel or corporate reservationist must be careful to document all pertinent information. Some reservation information, such as the date of arrival, number of persons and type of room, and guest's name and rate, is essential to the hotel. Other information, such as estimated time of arrival, special requests, and discounts, is less important to the reservation and may therefore only be collected in certain cases or by request of the guest.

Once the reservation has been agreed upon between the customer and the hotel or the central reservations office, its journey begins. In some cases the journey is short, as with those reservations made a few hours or days before arrival, and other times it is a long journey, as with reservations made many months—even years—in advance.

While electronic reservations are gaining popularity for individual bookings, group reservations require person-to-person negotiations with the property sales department. Unlike the individual reservation, where most requests are straightforward, a personal touch is required for groups negotiating bulk rates, dates, meeting requirements, meal functions, and other hotel services.

➤ QUESTIONS AND PROBLEMS

1. Many hotels are apprehensive about charging for corporate guaranteed reservations if a traveler fails to arrive. Even though a room was held and revenue was lost, the hotel is afraid to charge the no-show back to the corporation for fear of retaliation and loss of future business.

   Develop a series of strict—but fair—reservations policies that protect the hotel's interests while minimizing conflicts with the corporate account. In what instances would you charge the corporate no-show? When would you not charge?

2. The use of computerized reservations is far more efficient than the use of manual handwritten reservations. Compare the manual reservations approach to the automated collection of guest reservation information. List as many benefits (efficiencies) created by automated reservations systems as you can.

3. As a follow-up to Problem 2, are there any disadvantages associated with automated reservations systems? Why are many reservations managers retraining agents to be more patient, friendly, and helpful? Does this retraining have anything to do with the computer age in which we live?

4. Guests generally prefer the choice associated with spread rates. Hotels find it easier to manage rooms inventory when they use flat rates. Which would you use as a hotel manager? Explain your response in detail.

5. As a prominent hotelier, you have been asked by the CVB to appear before the county commissioners during a CVB budget-review session. The commission is angry that the local CVB spends public funds to maintain a convention housing bureau, and that those services are provided without a fee. Do the necessary research to provide hard facts to support your testimony in favor of the CVB.

6. The reservation of an unidentified convention delegate is treated like a corporate or leisure guest reservation. How might this lack of identifying the guest as a conventioneer affect the hotel? Could it benefit the guest? Could it hurt the guest?

➤ NOTES

1. Information related to the study of central reservations offices can be found in the June 1997 issue of *Lodging Magazine*.

2. Information related to Marriott's Automated Reservation System for Hotel Accommodations (MARSHA) can be found in the April 13, 1998 issue of *Business Travel News*.

3. Massachusetts was the last state to pass legislation allowing preregistration of groups. Prior to 1975, each member of a group had to register separately.

CHAPTER 6

Forecasting Availability and Overbooking

Outline

Forecasting Availability
Simple, Unadjusted Room Count
Adjusted Room Count

Overbooking
Reservations as Legal Contracts
Minimizing the Overbooking Problem

➤ FORECASTING AVAILABILITY

In Chapters 4 and 5, we have looked at various methods for making both individual and group reservations. We have seen the growing role of the global distribution system, the growth of on-line reservations, and the benefits associated with seamless connectivity. We have also learned the impact of group rooms on the hospitality industry and delineated some of the unique characteristics of group reservations. However, both individual and group reservations are dependent on one critical piece of information, which is still missing—the forecasted availability of rooms.

The concept behind rooms inventory is simple enough. There is a one-to-one match between rooms in the hotel and reservations accepted. Each reservation reduces the inventory until there are an equal number of reservations matched with available rooms. At that point, the hotel is sold out.

However, as additional factors begin to materialize, the simplicity is quickly complicated. Some guests stay over, others check out earlier than expected. Some guests with reservations cancel in advance of their arrival, others never show up to claim their reserved accommodations; indeed, some arrive a day or two early and still expect to receive their rooms. Add to these circumstances the chance for simple human error—"Oh, I thought he said July 14th, not July 4th"—and the situation is further complicated.

Simple, Unadjusted Room Count

It is beneficial to look first at a simple room count forecast, before incorporating the numerous complications that can affect the count. A simple room count is also called an *unadjusted room count*, because various adjustments (such as overstays, understays, cancellations, etc.) have not yet been introduced. They will be introduced later in the chapter. In this simple form, the unadjusted room count attempts to compare the rooms available in the hotel against the sum of stayovers and expected reservation arrivals. If any rooms remain uncommitted (that is, there are more rooms available than are committed to stayovers and reservations), they are available for sale that day.

➤ **Inventory Tracking Systems.**   At a moment's notice, the reservations department must be able to determine the number (and types) of rooms available for sale for a given date. With such pressing urgency, reservationists do not have the luxury of subtracting stayovers and expected reservations from rooms available to determine the room count. Therefore, they need to visualize the room count in some manner.

Even before the age of automation, reservations departments had a number of methods for keeping accurate and up-to-the-minute visual forecasts of rooms sold. Although these systems may appear cumbersome by today's computer standards, they served the purpose in years past. In fact, the basis for today's computerized rooms forecasting programs was found in the manual tracking systems of yesteryear.

For small hotels, a journal or reservations chart was developed. Each time a reservation was taken, it was plotted on the chart. When a cancellation was received, it was erased from the chart. For multinight reservations, it was necessary to plot each stayover night onto the chart.

This manual tracking approach worked especially well for smaller properties. Larger properties, with their added selection of room types, confused the situation. To solve the problem of tracking individual room types, larger properties used a manual *density chart* (see Exhibit 6–1). Similar to the journal or reservations chart, the density

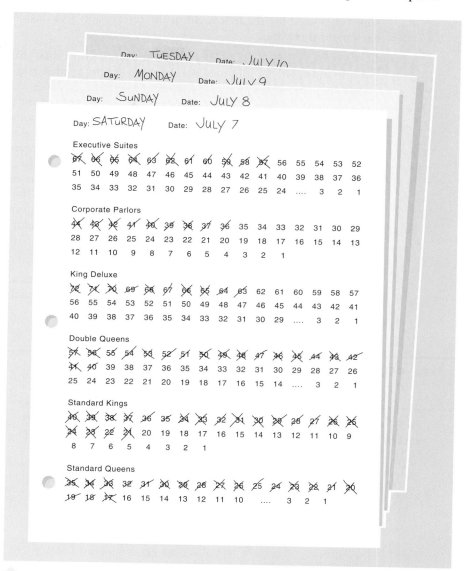

Exhibit 6–1 Both manual and electronic (Exhibit 6–2) density charts provide similar information. This manual example accommodates six different room categories. As rooms are reserved, they are checked off with an X (indicating the first day of arrival) or a slash (indicating subsequent days). The reservationist can quickly see, for example, that 20 kings are available and another 20 are already reserved.

chart required the reservations agent to plot the transaction each time a reservation was sold or a cancellation received. Unlike the earlier journals or charts, the density chart had separate pages for each date. Every time a room type was sold for a given date, the number of rooms remaining for that particular type was reduced by one. It was then a simple matter to look at a date and know just how many rooms of each category remained unsold. As with journals or reservations charts, multinight reservations were plotted for each stayover night. To indicate stayover nights, × marks were sometimes used for the first night of the reservation and slash marks (/) were used for each night thereafter.

Automated Systems. There are more similarities than differences between manual and automated room availability systems. Both track room totals by room type rather than by room number. A guest reservation is never assigned an actual room number until check in. Rather, a room type is reserved for the guest (see Exhibits 6–1 and 6–2). Infrequently, a guest may request a particular room number (that's where we stayed last year, or I like the location of room 165 because it's near the spa). In such cases, the hotel usually indicates the request on the reservation (see special requests discussion in Chapter 5) but offers no guarantees to the guest.

Automated property management systems offer various status reports under the reservations module. These reports are no different from the information available through manual counts—they're just faster and more accurate. Although status reports (see Chapter 13) are determined in part by the particular property management system, most are quite similar. Some of the standard status reports found in the reservations module include:

> A 7-, 10-, or 14-day room availability report provides a window of time for which each room type is listed and the number of remaining rooms available for sale are shown by date.

Business: MAY 25			1-Day Room Inventory						MAY 25 17:15:49	
			Mon MAY 25--							
Room Type	Room Cnts	Rooms Offmkt	Rooms Sold	Rooms Avail	Rates 1per	2per	Close Level	Host Status	CTA MLOS	
DDSU	15	1	5	9	85.00	85.00	4	Open		
DDSN	47	13	34	0	85.00	85.00	4	Closed		
KSU	10	0	5	5	75.00	75.00	2	Open		
KSUN	33	10	19	4	75.00	75.00	3	Open		
KHCN	3	0	1	2	75.00	75.00	1	Open		
DDHN	1	0	0	1	85.00	85.00	1	Open		
KEX	1	0	0	1	85.00	85.00	1	Open		
KEXN	5	2	1	2	85.00	85.00	1	Open		
D1HN	2	0	1	1	75.00	75.00	1	Open		
Totals:	117	26	66	25	56% Rack					

Action: 1 = Forward 1 Day   2 = Back 1 Day

Exhibit 6–2   An example of a one-day rooms inventory screen. This is an actual Multi-Systems, Incorporated Property Manager screen (PM Version 8.11) from a 117-room all-suite hotel. Notice that 26 rooms are off-market (out of inventory due to an in-house renovation project), 66 rooms are sold (either to incoming reservations or stayovers), and 25 rooms are available for sale. For information on CTA (closed to arrival) and MLOS (minimum length of stay), see Chapter 4. The various room types are listed in the first column from DDSU through D1HN. DD is two double beds, K is one king bed, S or SU indicates suite, EX stands for executive room-type, N means nonsmoking (in the absence of N, the room is smoking), and H or HC means handicapped accessible. *Courtesy of AmeriSuites Incorporated, Patterson, New Jersey and Multi-Systems, Inc., Phoenix, Arizona.*

➤ A current or one-day inventory report details all rooms in the hotel and their particular status. An example of such a report is shown in Exhibit 6–2.

➤ A reservations forecast report projects revenues and occupancies for each of several days into the future. Such a report usually displays the room and house count (number of guests in house) as well as projects the number of stayovers for each day. As the report reads further and further into the future (three to five days from today), the forecast becomes less and less accurate because it is based on each day's assumed check outs and stayovers.

➤ A general manager's daily report looks at the current day. Group rooms picked up, guaranteed and nonguaranteed reservations, anticipated stayovers, out-of-order and out-of-inventory rooms, walk-ins, early check outs, and more are all displayed in such a report.

➤ An arrivals list displays information about each reservation scheduled for that day's arrival. Each anticipated guest is listed alphabetically and can also be reviewed by affiliation: group reservations, travel-agent bookings, late arrivals, etc. (see Exhibit 5–4).

And more, depending on the size of the hotel and the sophistication of the property management system.

➤ *Simple Room Count.*   Whether the reservations tracking system is manual or automated (see Exhibits 6–1 and 6–2, respectively), exact room counts are performed several days prior to the actual date of arrival. By taking a more precise look at the next several days, the reservations department prepares itself for problems that may lie ahead. In fact, several room counts may be taken throughout the day of arrival. Common times to readjust the day's room count are before arrivals begin (around 6 AM), just after the check-out hour (around 11 AM for many properties), and immediately before and after 6 PM for hotels that allow nonguaranteed (6 PM) reservations.

A simple room count taken during these times provides management with a true understanding of the rooms inventory status for the day. If the hotel has rooms available for sale (a plus count), it is important to know the number and types of these rooms. Armed with this information, the reservations department and the front desk can better sell the remaining rooms in the hotel. Maximum rates are charged against the last few rooms available (a yield management approach).

The hotel also needs to know when there are no rooms remaining (an even or zero count). It is especially important to be forewarned when the hotel finds itself in an overbooking situation (a minus count)—when there are more reservations and stayovers than there are rooms available. With advance knowledge, the hotel can arrange supplementary accommodations at other hotels, alert its front-office staff to handle the sensitive situation, and encourage the reservations department to accept cancellations if and when they occur.

Even in a computerized system, where the room count is available at a moment's notice, managers still need to understand the components that form the total rooms available count. Specifically, managers wish to know the number of rooms occupied last night, rooms due to check out, and reservations due to arrive.

Committed Rooms.   The process works on commitments. The hotel is committed to guests staying over from last night and to guests due to arrive today. If the total of these (stayovers plus reservations) is less than the total number of rooms in the hotel, there is a plus count. If the hotel has more commitments than rooms available for sale, there is a minus count (overbooked).

The concept of overbooking (having a minus count) is discussed in detail later in the chapter. However, it is important to understand that it is not necessarily a mistake to overbook the hotel. Overbooking is often a strategic decision made by the reservations manager in concert with the front-office manager, the sales manager, and the general manager. The idea behind overbooking hotel rooms is much the same as the reason that airlines overbook flights. The airlines (and hotels) know that some percentage of their customers will not arrive (no-show) and others probably cancel. Therefore, the hotel reservations department plays a guessing game by projecting a series of adjustments onto the simple room count. The goal is to overbook the hotel just enough that the projected adjustments develop into a fully occupied hotel on the day of arrival. Too conservative a projection, and the hotel has unsold rooms; too aggressive a projection, and the hotel is forced to walk guests.

Refer to Exhibits 6–3 and 6–4. Exhibit 6–3 demonstrates a simple, unadjusted room count. The simple count looks at nothing more than rooms available, rooms committed to stayovers, and rooms committed to incoming reservations. These same figures are then reused in Exhibit 6–4. Exhibit 6–4, however, demonstrates an adjusted count. By including adjustments for overstays and understays, as well as for cancellations, no-shows, and early arrivals, the numbers are substantially different.

Adjusted Room Count

Mathematics carries an aura of exactness that deceives any reservations department that relies on unadjusted figures. Most of the figures must be modified on the basis of experience. The reservations department collects data over the years, and this information allows for more precise projections. But even the adjustments change from day to day depending on the day of the week and the week of the year. Percentages change with the weather, with the type of group registered in the house, and even with the news. Gathering the data is the first step and interpreting it is the second.

Given

A 1,000-room hotel had a total of 950 rooms occupied last night. Of those 950 rooms, 300 are due to check out today. In addition, there are 325 reservations for today. There are 5 rooms out of order (OOO).

The following table shows the calculation for this simple, unadjusted room count:

Rooms available in hotel		1,000
Occupied last night	950	
Due to check out today	300	
Equals number of stayovers		650
+ Today's reservations		325
Total rooms committed for today		975
Equals rooms available for sale		25 (with 5 OOO)

Occupancy percentage is 975 ÷ 1,000 or 97.5%.

Exhibit 6–3   Simple, unadjusted room count. By subtracting stayovers (650 rooms) and incoming reservations (325 rooms) from rooms available (1,000 rooms), the reservations manager knows there are 25 rooms available for sale today. Refer to Exhibit 6–4, where the same numbers have been adjusted to create a far different room count.

Given

A 1,000-room hotel had a total of 950 rooms occupied last night. Of those 950 rooms, 300 are due to check out today. In addition, there are 325 reservations for today. There are 5 rooms out of order (OOO).

Historical Adjustments

The hotel has developed the following historical adjustment statistics: understays, 6%; overstays, 2%; cancellations, 2%; no-shows, 5%; and early arrivals, 1%.

The following table shows the calculation for this adjusted room count:

Rooms available in hotel			1,000
Occupied last night		950	
Due to check out today	300		
Understays (6%)	+ 18		
Overstays (2%)	– 6		
Equals adjusted number of rooms to check out today	312 →	312	
Equals adjusted number of stayovers		638 →	– 638
Today's reservations	325		
Cancellations (2%)	– 7		
No-shows (5%)	– 16		
Early arrivals (1%)	+ 3		
Equals today's adjusted reservations	305 ⟶		– 305
Adjusted total of rooms committed for sale			– 943
Adjusted number of rooms available for sale			+ 57 (with 5 OOO)

Anticipated occupancy percentage is 943 ÷ 1,000 or 94.3%.

Exhibit 6–4 Using the same figures given in Exhibit 6–3, this adjusted room count incorporates a series of new calculations. Adjustments for understays and overstays are calculated as percentages of the number of rooms due to check out today (300). Adjustments for cancellations, no-shows, and early arrivals are calculated as percentages of today's reservations (325). The net result (+57 rooms) is far different from the +25 rooms found in Exhibit 6–3.

Each element in the projection can be refined over and over by using additional data or varying interpretations. Recomputing the count with these adjustments can make a substantial change in room availability.

➤*Computing Rooms Available.* The actual number of rooms available in the hotel (1,000 rooms for the continuing example shown in Exhibits 6–3 and 6–4) can change from day to day. For various reasons, rooms that were available for occupancy one day may be closed to occupancy on another day. If the removal is unexpected, removing the rooms from inventory can have an impact on the hotel's ability to accommodate guests with reservations.

When rooms are removed from availability, they are designated as being in one of two distinct categories: out of order or out of inventory. The difference between these classifications is of critical importance to management.

Out-of-Order Rooms.   A room placed out of order is generally repairable within a relatively short time. A minor problem such as poor TV reception, a clogged toilet, a malfunctioning airconditioner, or a broken headboard will usually classify a room as out of order (OOO). Out-of-order rooms pose a special problem to management because in sold-out situations they must be repaired and returned to the market quickly. In periods of low occupancy, management may wait several days before returning such rooms to the market.

Out-of-order rooms are, by nature, minimally inoperative—the problem that placed the room out of order is slight. As a result, in some situations out-of-order rooms are actually sold to the public: If the hotel is facing sold-out status and the few remaining rooms are out of order, management may choose to sell these rooms "as is" for a reasonable discount. A broken TV set may warrant a $10 discount; an inoperative airconditioner may warrant a $30 discount. No out-of-order room would ever be sold if it posed a hazard to the guest.

Because out-of-order rooms can be repaired and returned to the market, they are included in the total figure for rooms available for sale. In calculating room count statistics, out-of-order rooms are treated as if there were nothing wrong with them. Similarly, when calculating occupancy percentages, out-of-order rooms are left in the denominator as if there were nothing wrong with them.

In the continuing example, note that five rooms are out of order. Because out-of-order rooms are not removed from inventory, there are still 1,000 rooms available for sale in the hotel. The occupancy of 97.5% (see Exhibit 6–3) has demonstrated no change in the 1,000-room denominator.

Out-of-Inventory Rooms.   Out-of-inventory rooms cannot be sold "as is." Out-of-inventory rooms have significant problems that cannot be repaired quickly. Examples of major out-of-inventory (OOI) situations might include a flood that destroyed all carpet and floorboards in a room, a fire that has blackened the walls and left a strong odor, a major renovation that leaves half of the wallpaper removed as well as no carpet or furniture, and a murder investigation in which the police have ordered the room sealed until further notice.

By their very nature, out-of-inventory rooms are not marketable. The problem that placed them out of inventory is significant enough to remove the room from marketability until it has been repaired. These rooms, therefore, are not included in the total figure for rooms available for sale. In calculating room count statistics, out-of-inventory rooms are removed from the total of rooms available for sale. Similarly, when calculating occupancy percentages, out-of-inventory rooms are subtracted from the denominator.

In the continuing example, note that five rooms are out of order. To illustrate the points addressed above, let's see what happens if those five rooms were actually out of inventory. Remember, out-of-inventory rooms must be removed from the available rooms inventory. As a result, there will now be only 995 rooms available for sale in the hotel (1,000 rooms less 5 out of inventory). The room availability total of +25 will also change. There will now be only +20 rooms available for sale [995 rooms less (650 stayovers plus 325 reservations)]. Out-of-inventory rooms have an impact on occupancy percent as well. The rooms-sold numerator (975) remains the same, but the rooms-available-for-sale denominator would change to 995. The occupancy calculation (975 divided by 995) yields 98.0%. This is a different result from that in Exhibit 6–3, which showed 97.5%.

Exhibit 6–5 presents several additional examples of out-of-inventory and out-of-order computations.

►*Computing Rooms Occupied Last Night.* Rooms occupied the previous night is an exact figure except in those hotels where comp (complimentary) rooms are not listed as being occupied. Where policy excludes them from occupancy counts, the number of comp rooms must be added to the "Rooms occupied last night" figure to avoid an error in the projection. Similar errors pop up when the computer is programmed to count suites as two-room units even when the suite is not divided. The mistake comes in counting either two rooms as occupied or two rooms as checked out. In the ongoing problem, 950 rooms were occupied last night, but no comps.

1*a.* A 200-room hotel sold 125 rooms last night. If there were 10 rooms OOO, the occupancy would be as follows:

- Numerator (number of rooms sold):   125
- Denominator (number of rooms available for sale—remember, the denominator is not affected by OOO rooms):   200
- Equation: 125 ÷ 200
- Percent occupancy: 62.5%

  b. The same 200-room hotel sold 125 rooms last night. If instead the 10 rooms were OOI, the occupancy would be as follows:

- Numerator (number of rooms sold):   125
- Denominator (number of rooms available for same—remember, the denominator is reduced by the number of OOI rooms):   190
- Equation: 125 ÷ 190
- Percent occupancy: 65.8%

2*a.* A 460-room hotel sold 375 rooms last night. If there were 22 rooms OOO, the occupancy would be as follows:

- Numerator: 375
- Denominator: 460
- Equation: 375 ÷ 460
- Percent occupancy: 81.5%

  b. The same 460-room hotel sold 375 rooms last night. If instead there were 22 OOI rooms, the occupancy would be as follows:

- Numerator: 375
- Denominator: 438
- Equation: 375 ÷ 438
- Percent occupancy: 85.6%

Exhibit 6–5 Out-of-order rooms do not affect inventory (rooms available for sale), while out-of-inventory rooms do. These two examples illustrate the difference this distinction can have on the resulting occupancy percentage. Each example is calculated two ways: first the occupancy is calculated assuming that the rooms were OOO, then the occupancy is recalculated assuming that the rooms were OOI.

▶*Computing the Number of Stayovers.*   The number of rooms scheduled to check out today is not an absolute statistic. It is based primarily on the guests' initial plans at the time they were making their reservations. Even when a well-trained front-desk clerk reconfirms the departure date during the check-in process, changes still occur. Corporate guests may complete their business a day or two earlier (or a day or two later) than expected. Leisure guests may decide to sightsee in town a bit longer (or shorter) than originally planned. Emergencies also occur, where guests may need to catch the next flight home, regardless of their original plans.

Although these changes are difficult to project on an individual guest-by-guest basis, they generally form an historical trend over time. Although it is impossible to guess if Mr. Jones in room 2144 will stay an extra night, it is somewhat more certain to say that historically 2% of our scheduled check outs do not depart (they overstay) after all.

Each property collects historical data with which to project its understays and overstays. This data is usually expressed in terms of a percentage of the rooms due to check out that day. For example, in Exhibit 6–4, the understay percentage is 6% (0.06 times 300 rooms due out equals 18 understays) while the overstay percentage is 2% (0.02 times 300 rooms due out equals 6 overstays). Although these are both fictitious percentages, a real hotel would develop similar statistical projections over time.

Understays.   Some guests leave earlier than the hotel expected; they are known as understays. They are also sometimes referred to as *earlys*. When calculating the number of rooms due to check out, any understays will be added to the projected check outs.

Overstays.   Some guests stay past their scheduled departure date; they are referred to as overstays. They are also sometimes known as *holdovers*. When calculating the number of rooms due to check out, any overstays will be subtracted from the projected check outs.

Occupied last night		950
Due to check out today	300	
Plus understays (6%)	+ 18	
Less overstays (2%)	– 6	
Equals adjusted number due to check out today	312	–312
Equals adjusted number of stayovers		638

By including understays and overstays in the continuing example, the number of rooms due to check out changes substantially. In the simple, unadjusted room count shown in Exhibit 6–3, the number due to check out today was 300. Once understays and overstays are included in the computation, however, that number changes to 312, as shown in the preceding table and Exhibit 6–4. Similarly, the number of stayovers (650) demonstrated in the simple, unadjusted room count of Exhibit 6–3 changes with the inclusion of understays and overstays. In Exhibit 6–3 there are 650 projected stayovers. In the preceding table and Exhibit 6–4 that number changes to 638 projected stayovers.

▶*Computing Today's Reservations.*   Just as some departing guests change their plans and overstay or understay the scheduled visit, some expected guests do not adhere to their original reservations. As a result, guests often cancel reservations, arrive a day or two earlier than expected, or never arrive at all. Each of these variables is assessed and adjusted according to historical data, to represent a closer approximation of reality.

No-Shows.   Some guests who hold reservations never arrive at the hotel. These guests are referred to as no-shows. No-shows may be caused by a multitude of factors. A change in business or personal plans, inclement weather or closed roads, canceled or stranded flights, illness, or death may be some of the reasons a guest fails to arrive. Indeed, it is also possible that they simply forgot they had made a reservation.

No-shows present the hotel with a unique problem—namely, it is difficult to know when to classify the reservation as a no-show. For nonguaranteed reservations, the industry standard is 6 PM. Nonguaranteed reservations that fail to arrive by 6 PM are considered no-shows, and those rooms are remarketed to walk-in guests.

Guaranteed and advance-deposit reservations are another story. The very nature of these higher-quality guaranteed or advance-deposit reservations suggests that the hotel will hold a room all night long. Therefore, it is literally impossible for a hotel front-desk clerk to determine when a specific guaranteed reservation changes from an expected arrival to a no-show. A front-desk clerk or night auditor can be fairly certain that a reservation that has not arrived by 11 PM, midnight, or 1 AM is a no-show. However, there is always the chance that the guest has been detained and will still arrive in search of the reservation.

Asking for an estimated time of arrival on the reservation is one partial solution to this problem. By documenting the guest's expected arrival time, the desk clerk is better equipped to make difficult decisions about possible no-show guests. The earlier such decisions are made, the better the hotel's chances of selling the room to a walk-in.

Cancellations.   Although cancellations mean additional work for the reservations department and the front desk, they are still infinitely better than no-shows. Guests who cancel on the day of arrival are providing the hotel an opportunity to resell the room. The earlier the cancellation is received, the better the chance of reselling the room.

Cancellation policies usually require notice at least 24 hours in advance of the reservation's arrival date. Cancellations made on the day of arrival are treated like no-shows and charged one room-night. However, because cancellations (even last-minute cancellations) provide better information to the hotel than no-shows, many properties waive the one-night penalty to canceling guests. Even if the hotel charges a late cancellation fee of, say, $25, that is better for the guest than being charged one full room-night. That seems fair to all concerned, because a canceled room has more opportunity to be resold than a no-show room. As a courtesy, many corporate hotels allow business guests to cancel without penalty until 6 PM the day of arrival.

Early Arrivals.   Cancellations and no shows reduce the number of expected arrivals. Early arrivals increase the number of expected arrivals. Early arrivals are guests who arrive at the hotel one or more days prior to their scheduled reservation date.

There are a number of reasons why a guest might arrive at the hotel in advance of the expected reservation date. For example, the reservations department may have had a different date for the reservation than the guest understood, or possibly the guest's plans changed and he or she decided to arrive one or more days early. Whatever the reason, the front office will attempt to accommodate the guest.

Even in periods of 100% occupancy, the front-office personnel strive to find accommodations for the early arrival. Not only is that good guest service, but early arrivals often represent a number of room-nights to the hotel—many early arrivals stay through the end of their originally scheduled departure. An early arrival who arrives two days early for a three-night reservation may very likely stay all five nights.

Adjusting Today's Reservations.   The continuing example in Exhibit 6–3 shows an unadjusted reservations count of 325 rooms. Assuming a cancellation rate of 2%, a no-show rate of 5%, and an early arrival rate of 1%, the numbers change significantly (see the following table and Exhibit 6–4):

Today's reservations	325
Less cancellations (2%)	− 7
Less no-shows (5%)	− 16
Plus early arrivals (1%)	+ 3
Equals adjusted number of reservations	305

A certain amount of mathematical rounding is necessary in these equations. A 2% cancellation rate with 325 reservations gives 6.5 cancellations. It is necessary to round 6.5 cancellations to 7. Similarly, no-shows round from 16.25 to 16 and early arrivals round from 3.25 to 3.

The Adjusted Result.   With all the adjustment components in place, a look at the adjusted room count (Exhibit 6–4) shows a substantial change from the simple, unadjusted room count (Exhibit 6–3). The number of stayover rooms has been adjusted from 650 to 638 because the number of rooms due to check out has been adjusted with understays and overstays. The number of expected reservations has been adjusted from 325 to 305 because of estimated cancellations, no-shows, and early arrivals.

The count of 57 rooms available for sale shown in Exhibit 6–4 is significantly higher than the count of 25 rooms available shown in Exhibit 6–3. With the same five rooms out of order, the hotel can now accept 57 rooms as walk-ins (assuming it quickly repairs the five OOO rooms).

Exhibit 6–4 could just as easily have projected a change in the opposite direction. Second-guessing the actions of the guest is the reservations department's burden. Projections are made from the historical data gathered by the property and forecasted on the basis of experience. At best, it is a composite of many previous days and may prove disastrous on any given day. A cautious projection with too few walk-ins accepted results in low occupancy and empty rooms despite guests who were turned away earlier in the day. An optimistic projection allows the desk to accept so many walk-ins that the reserved guest who arrives late in the day finds no room.

This is the dilemma of overbooking: the need, on the one hand, to maximize occupancy and profits, and the pressure, on the other hand, to keep empty rooms for reservations who may never arrive. Hotels with heavy walk-ins, similar to the airline's standbys, are more flexible than isolated properties. Selective overbooking, 5 to 15% depending on historical experience, is the hotel's major protection against no-shows double reservations, and "guaranteed reservations" that are never paid. Conservative overbooking begins with a collection of data, made easier by a well-programmed computer and a regular update of projections.

Data collection must be structured and accurate so that the reservations office can rely on the figures. The computer can furnish the information if the database fo accumulating the report was planned for in the programming. Data must be accumulated in a chronological fashion, day of the week matching day of the week. It is important for the second Tuesday in April, for instance, to match the second Tuesday in April of last year, irrespective of the calendar dates of those Tuesdays.

Dates do have importance, of course. The Fourth of July holiday is a more important date than the day on which it falls. Similarly, the days before and after such a holiday must be identified with other before and after days of previous years.

▶ *Putting the Room Count to Use.*   Room forecasting starts with an annual projection and ends with an hourly report. In between are monthly, biweekly, weekly, three-day, and daily forecasts. Ten-day reports (see Exhibit 6–6) are sometimes used in place of the biweekly projections, but most reservation managers prefer to see two weekends included in a report.

Every department of a hotel uses the room count projections as a critical tool for labor planning. Each department makes sales and labor forecasts from the anticipated room count. Most departments depend on room occupancy for their own volume. This is certainly the situation with valet and laundry, room service, telephones, and uniformed services.

Housekeeping's schedule is also a function of room sales. So, too, there is a direct relation between the number of breakfasts served and the previous night's room count. Early work scheduling helps build good employee relations, and the two-week forecast is generally used for that purpose. A two-week lead time may be required in hotels covered by union contracts.

The reservations department should have its closest partnership with marketing and sales. Without that alliance, the property has little opportunity to maximize yield management policies. For example, how many discounted rooms has the sales department committed to wholesalers during a high-occupancy (thus, high-rate) period? The marketing department should be able to help reservations forecast no-shows, walk-ins, early arrivals, and so on, as they pertain to a particular group. Group figures differ from figures for independent guests and may vary from group to group.

Periodic Recounts.   The longer the period between the preparation of the forecast and its use, the less reliable it is. Without periodic updating, all the departments, but especially the desk, act on information that is no longer accurate. The three-day forecast permits a final push for sales and a tightening of labor schedules throughout the property to maximize occupancy and minimize costs.

By the time hourly projections are being made, responsibility has moved entirely to the front office. Overbooking problems, additional reservations, walk-ins, and stayovers are being resolved by front-office executives.

Periodic or hourly forecasts improve the system in two ways. Obviously, the information is more current (see Exhibit 6–7). Less obvious is the increased accuracy in percentage variations as the day wears on. Were it known, for example, that 80% of all the check outs were usually gone by noon, a better guess of understays and overstays could be made at noon each day than at 7 AM. Similar refinements are possible with cancellation percentages, no-show factors, and so on. In fact, it is possible to improve the accuracy of no show forecasts by separating the total reservations into three categories—advance deposit, guaranteed, and nonguaranteed—before applying a different no-show percentage to each.

Adjusting by Reservation Quality.   Returning to the continuing example illustrated in Exhibits 6–3 and 6–4, an improved adjusted room count is possible by

Occupancy Forecast Report

Santa Rae Ranch
Ann Parker

Occupancy Forecast Report
For the Period from 03-JAN- to 12-JAN-
Percentages Include Out of Order and Off Market Rooms
Percentages Exclude Tentative Group Rooms

	FRI JAN-03	SAT JAN-04	SUN JAN-05	MON JAN-06	TUE JAN-07	WED JAN-08	THUR JAN-09	FRI JAN-10	SAT JAN-11	SUN JAN-12
Total Rooms	236	236	236	236	236	236	236	236	236	236
- OOO	3	2	3	3	2	2	3	1	0	0
- OFF	0	0	0	0	0	0	0	0	0	0
Rooms Available	233	234	233	233	234	234	233	235	235	236
Rooms Occupied	94	90	83	44	33	27	21	30	42	27
- Non-Group Departures	11	18	34	14	4	5	17	2	13	4
- Group Departures	12	3	14	1	2	2	0	1	5	4
+ Non-Group Arrivals	18	13	9	4	0	1	15	14	3	0
+ Group Arrivals	1	1	0	0	0	0	12	0	0	0
Net In-House	90	83	44	33	27	21	31	41	27	19
+ Estimated Pickup	0	0	0	0	0	0	0	2	2	2
+ Excess Committed	82	60	1	0	0	0	19	9	14	0
+ Tentative Grp Rooms	5	0	0	0	0	0	2	0	0	0
Net Rooms Reserved	172	143	45	33	27	21	50	52	43	21
Net Rooms Available	61	91	188	200	207	213	183	183	192	215
Non-Group										
Projected Revenue	7113.00	6527.50	3438.50	2757.50	2446.00	1810.00	1341.88	4265.37	3415.99	2913.49
Avg. Rate	103.09	101.99	88.17	95.09	97.84	86.19	70.63	137.59	162.67	171.38
Group (Reserved)										
Projected Revenue	1064.00	965.00	221.00	175.00	47.50	0.00	1148.00	1100.50	590.00	190.00
Avg. Rate	50.67	50.79	44.20	43.75	23.75	0.00	95.67	100.05	98.33	95.00
Group (Excess Committed)										
Estimated Revenue	5340.00	3925.00	20.00	0.00	0.00	0.00	1945.00	845.00	1280.00	0.00
Avg. Rate	61.38	65.42	20.00	0.00	0.00	0.00	92.62	93.89	91.43	0.00
Group (Tentative)										
Estimated Revenue	375.00	0.00	0.00	0.00	0.00	0.00	150.00	0.00	0.00	0.00
Avg. Rate	75.00	0.00	0.00	0.00	0.00	0.00	75.00	0.00	0.00	0.00
Group (Totals)										
Projected Revenue	6779.00	4890.00	241.00	175.00	47.50	0.00	3243.00	1945.50	1870.00	190.00
Avg. Rate	59.99	61.90	40.17	43.75	23.75	0.00	92.66	97.28	93.50	95.00
Totals										
Projected Revenue	13892.00	11417.50	3679.50	2932.50	2493.50	1810.00	4584.88	6210.87	5285.99	3103.49
Avg. Rate	76.33	79.84	81.77	88.86	92.35	86.19	84.91	121.78	128.93	163.34
% Occupancy Reserved	38.63	35.47	18.88	14.16	11.54	8.97	13.30	17.45	11.49	8.05
% Including Commits	73.82	61.11	19.31	14.16	11.54	8.97	21.46	21.28	17.45	8.05

	TEN/ DEF	FRI JAN-03	SAT JAN-04	SUN JAN-05	MON JAN-06	TUE JAN-07	WED JAN-08	THUR JAN-09	FRI JAN-10	SAT JAN-11	SUN JAN-12
American Building Consult	DEF	30/0	20/0								
Bavarian Bakeoff	*DEF	0/1									
Bob's Bablo Island Tour	*DEF	5/4	0/3								
Brady Tours	DEF							5/0			
Cardinal Group	DEF	1/0	1/0	1/0							
Cups & China	DEF	10/0									
Honda	DEF							25/11	20/11	20/6	
MIPS	DEF	6/5	5/5								
Micro Data	TEN							2/0			
Presentations Now	DEF	5/0	5/0								
Sky Line Displays	TEN	5/0									
US Clowns Inc.	DEF	25/2	25/2								
US Water Polo Team	DEF	12/1	12/1								

* - This group's commitments must be cleaned up or all availability reports will be out of balance.

Exhibit 6–6 This computerized reservation forecast report displays a 10-day view of rooms activity. It details arrival and departure projections for individual as well as group rooms. Usually, such forecast reports also provide an estimate of each day's anticipated rooms revenues. (Note that unlike the treatment suggested by the authors, out-of-order rooms reduce rooms available. This technique boosts the percentage of occupancy and so reflects better on the rooms manager.) *Courtesy of Geac Computers, Inc., Tustin, California.*

Royal Hotel Weekly Forecast for February 3 to February 9							
	3	4	5	6	7	8	9
Rooms available for sale	1,206	1,206	1,206	1,206	1,206	1,206	1,206
Rooms occupied last night →	1,121	1,190	1,193	890	480	140	611
Less anticipated departures	444	396	530	440	350	55	20
Stayovers	677	794	663	450	130	85	591
Reservations	498	386	212	25	10	501	552
Estimated out of order	3	3					
Rooms committed	1,178	1,183	875	475	140	586	1,143
Estimated walk-ins	12	10	15	5		25	63
Rooms occupied tonight →	1,190	1,193	890	480	140	611	1,206
	Group Arrivals						
National Water Heater Co.	80	140					
Play Tours of America			68				
Chevrolet Western Division					5	183	
PA Library Association						251	396
Chiffo-Garn wedding party							23

Exhibit 6–7   Room availability forecasts grow less reliable the further the projected horizon. Each day's values build on estimates from previous days (see arrows). If the actual number of rooms occupied in any preceding day is different than the mathematical base—and it always is—later forecasts become less and less accurate since they begin with invalid figures.

separating nonguaranteed reservations from guaranteed and advance-deposit reservations. Instead of merely stating that 325 reservations are due in, it is more valuable to understand that, say, 100 reservations are nonguaranteed, 175 reservations are guaranteed, and 50 reservations are advance deposit.

If the hotel maintains statistical history by reservation quality or type, the accuracy of the entire projection is enhanced. In such hotels, the no-show percentage might be changed from the flat 5% for all reservation types to something more detailed. Assume that 20% of all nonguaranteed reservations are no-shows, 4% of all guaranteed reservations are no-shows, and 1% of all advance deposits are no-shows. The total number of no-shows would now change from 16 in Exhibit 6–4 to 28. This is calculated by taking 20% of 100 nonguaranteed reservations (20), plus 4% of 175 guaranteed reservations (7), plus 1% of 50 advance deposit reservations (0.5 rounds up to 1).

This same logic can be applied to early arrivals and cancellations. The more detailed the statistical history gathered by the hotel, the more accurate the daily projections will be.

Accuracy can also be improved by attention to the character of the market. The type of group clues the reservation department to the no-show percentage. For example, teachers are very dependable. Tour groups are nearly always full because volume is as important to the tour operator as to the innkeeper. That generalization must then be balanced by knowledge about specific tour companies. Allocations versus utilization should be computed individually on wholesalers, incentive houses, associations, and other group movers.

Market research may prove that bookings from certain localities are more or less reliable depending on transportation, weather, distance, and the kind of guest the hotel is attracting. Commercial guests have a different degree of dependability than tourists, who differ again from conventioneers or referrals. A large permanent guest population needs to be recognized in any percentage computation involving stayovers and anticipated departures.

The overall goal of any room count projection is to forecast the number of rooms available for sale. This is especially critical during high-occupancy periods. When the hotel is nearly full, it is important to forecast the number of rooms that may become available for sale due to understays, no-shows, and cancellations. By understanding the interrelationship of these adjustments, the front office has a better chance of filling the hotel.

➤ OVERBOOKING

Overbooking is standard practice in the lodging industry as it is in the airline industry. Overbooking means that a hotel knowingly sells more reservations than it has rooms available. When a hotel overbooks a sold-out date, it is taking a calculated risk that more guests will cancel or no-show than the number of rooms by which the hotel has overbooked. A conservative overbooking policy rarely places the hotel in a compromising situation. More aggressive overbooking, however, can force both the hotel and the unlucky guest(s) into an unpleasant situation.

Reservations as Legal Contracts

Courts consider room reservations to be legal contracts. The request constitutes the offer, and the promise of accommodations represents the acceptance. Either the promise to pay or the actual transfer of a deposit is the third important element of a contract: consideration. Such promises may be verbal (as with a telephone confirmation) or written (as with a letter of confirmation, see Exhibits 5–2 and 5–3).[1] The parties are competent; the transaction is legal; and there is a mutuality of interest. All the elements of a binding contract are in place.

If one party breaches the contract, the innocent party should be compensated for the injury. This has been the situation for many years. Recovery by either party has generally been limited to the natural or expected costs that the parties anticipated at the time of the agreement.

There have been few legal cases involving breach of reservation contract. That is because there is little to be gained by bringing suit. If the guest breaches the contract by failing to show up for the room, the hotel may have an opportunity to resell the accommodation. Even if the room cannot be resold, the monetary loss to the hotel is minimal. Similarly, if the hotel breaches the reservation contract by failing to provide a room, the guest is free to seek accommodations elsewhere. Even if a room cannot be found, the actual cost to the guest is still quite small (possibly limited to taxi fares and telephone calls expended in search of alternative accommodations). And courts are not willing to compensate the guest for inconvenience and depression.

In very few cases (usually involving group reservations or tour operators) have negligence or fraud in room reservations been alleged and then proven. The threat remains, however, especially for those hotels that overbook as a matter of operational policy. If the complaining guest can show that the hotel consistently overbooked, there might be adequate grounds to recover in a tort action.

This is also true in cases where the plaintiff can demonstrate foreseeable damage. For example, if the hotel overbooked and walked the guest during a sold-out period in the city (say, during the Olympics or the World Series, if either was being held in the city), the hotel could reasonably foresee the difficulty the guest would have in finding an alternative room. After exhausting all possibilities, if the guest decided to sleep in his or her car and was subsequently attacked and harmed, the hotel might be found liable for significant damages.

➤*Looming Legislation.*   Severe cases of overbooking, especially in isolated resort areas where no other accommodations were available, triggered initial interest by the Federal Trade Commission (FTC) in the early 1980s. Action by the FTC was held off, in part, by the industry's decision to act. Having witnessed the restrictive regulations the government placed on the airline industry, industry leaders took a proactive stance. In essence, they convinced the FTC of their ability to squelch the problem by voluntarily establishing their own internal policies and regulations. Today, overbooking penalties awarded to displaced guests are roughly identical among the major lodging chains.

Yield management may renew the government's interest—this time, probably at the state level. Several state attorneys general are again commenting that hotels are playing the same game as the airlines. Florida has already enacted such legislation. In addition to monetary penalties, the law requires the hotel to reimburse guests for prepaid reservations whether paid directly to the hotel or to a travel agency. New York requires travel agents to warn clients in the form of a rubber-stamped message that "this hotel has been known to overbook in the past" (see Exhibit 6–8).

Others at Fault.   Although states such as New York and Georgia have legislated mere refunds for unaccommodated guests, Pennsylvania, Michigan, and Florida permit punitive damages. Hawaii, Puerto Rico, and others have enacted eviction laws permitting the physical ejection of guests who overstay their reservation. That puts the ball in the hotel's court. No longer can the excuse for overbooking be laid on other guests.

The fault for overbooking is not the hotel industry's alone. Tour operators who earn commissions, conference committees who pledge room blocks, and individual travelers who don't show are all to blame. Each, the hotel included, attempts to maximize its own position at the risk of overbooking.

Tour operators who bring planeloads of tourists to a town contribute to the overbooking problem. The group is usually divided among several hotels, with the guest's selection of a particular hotel determining the cost of the tour. The tour operator is playing the odds, estimating that a given number of guests on each plane will choose hotels in the same ratio that the tour operator has committed rooms. When too many people select one property and too few select another, the hotel is blamed for overbooking. Guests are unaware that the hotel and the tour operator had agreed on the number of rooms months before.

Convention executives must be hounded to keep their numbers current. No-shows are reduced if the number of rooms saved for the convention is adjusted to the group's history at other hotels. If possible, convention groups should pair their members at the meeting site as the individuals arrive. This reduces the number of single rooms created when previously paired delegates do not show. Failing this, the hotel can levy a compulsory room charge for no-shows.

Our Pledge to You

We will not knowingly offer for rent, space on which we already have an advance deposit or credit-card guaranteed reservation from a customer. If, for any reason beyond our control, a room should not be available for a customer who has either an advance deposit reservation or a credit-card guaranteed reservation, we shall arrange for at least comparable accommodations at another hotel or motel in this area.

The Management

Exhibit 6–8　Nonoverbooking pledge. The American Hotel & Motel Association encourages all hotels to adopt similar policies. Reading between the lines, this pledge allows the hotel to overbook nonguaranteed (6 PM) reservations. That makes sense, in light of the extremely high no-show rate associated with nonguaranteed or "courtesy-hold" reservations. According to this pledge, however, guaranteed and advance deposit reservations are not to be oversold. *Courtesy of the American Hotel & Motel Association, Washington, DC.*

Guests, too, are to blame! They are notorious no-shows. Guests will make reservations in more than one hotel and, if they do show, will change their length of stay without notifying the desk. The reservation department is always second-guessing guests' moves, and this means occasional errors no matter how carefully previous statistics and experiences are projected.

▶ *Common Overbooking Policies.* The burden of *walking* an arriving guest—sending that person away—falls to the room clerk (see Exhibit 6–9). Too often management leaves it at that, making no provision to train the clerk and no provision to house the guest. Where this is a frequent affair, the staff grows immune to the protests and even finds a bit of humor in walking one guest after the other. In doing so, the staff reflects the apparent attitude of an unconcerned management. This is not the case in properties where quality assurance programs are in place (see Chapter 7). The situation is never treated lightly, even if a number of guests were walked that day.

No matter how well managed a hotel, no matter how well made the forecasts, overbooking will occur. Preplanning for overbooking reduces guest irritation and even offers some chance of retaining business.

Arranging substitute accommodations elsewhere is what the clerk should do. Providing the training to anticipate the incident is what management should do. Preparation includes preliminary calls to neighboring properties as the situation becomes obvious. Many satellite properties depend on this type of overflow for business.

Exhibit 6–9 An overbooked hotel is no laughing matter!

Affiliated properties usually refer to each other before overflowing rooms business to neighboring competitors—even to the extent that a full-service chain property may walk guests to one of the same chain's budget operations.

Managers need to be alert to unethical practices involving walked rooms. Some properties give a commission or kick back a payment to clerks of oversold properties when they refer walked guests their way. Even though the oversold hotel may specify to which properties guests can be walked, $10 or $20 from the unethical operation is incentive enough to disregard the rule. Indeed, such unethical clerks may begin referring walk-in customers to the other hotel even when rooms remain available at their own property.

Significant dollars are expended when walking a guest from those properties that have a quality assurance, guest-oriented policy in place. The hotel pays the round-trip cab ride to the substitute hotel. It underwrites the cost of one or more long-distance telephone calls. It also pays the room charge, regardless of the rate, at the alternative property. Some hotels give an outright gift (champagne, fruit basket, etc.) to apologize for the inconvenience. Others give a free room on the next visit as a means of bringing back a walked guest.

Assuming that those figures are cab, $20; telephone, $7; and room rate, $73, each incident costs $100. This computation ignores the value of lost sales in the other departments. Overbooking is not an everyday affair. If three guests per night are turned away 10 times per year, the hotel spends $3,000 (3 × 10 × $100) in remedies. Walking guests does not make economic sense. The cost of failing to achieve 100% occupancy on the 10 nights is certainly less expensive than the overbooking outlay, especially when goodwill is added into the equation.

Ignored in the economic computation above is the cost of public relations. The iceberg effect of one extremely unhappy guest can add up to untold costs. Plagued by bad publicity from overbooking, the Bahamas Hotel Association (BHA) formalized an areawide policy. The BHA recognized that being stranded on an isolated island without a room was not going to encourage tourism. The new policy carried the cab ride one step further, guaranteeing air taxi to another island if all accommodations in the host area were fully booked. A $20 cab ride is cheap compared with the cost of an air taxi!

Other localities have established programs to help themselves and the unaccommodated guest. Chambers of commerce or tourist authorities have set up hot lines. Many metropolitan areas have adopted a system that hooks participating properties together electronically and displays the city status on a lighted board (see Exhibit 6–10). Each morning and periodically during the day, the separate properties adjust their availability status. Referrals are easily made by reference to the lighted board; a light on means rooms are available; a light off means that particular hotel is full. Equally important, the desk can monitor what is happening throughout the city and adjust its own walk-ins based on citywide conditions.

Clearly, steps can be taken to ease the impact of overbooking. An industrywide policy of self-policing and public relations would minimize the incidence of overbook-

HOTELEX   NEW ORLEANS
AREA CODE 504

HOTELEX PO BOX 5286 REDWOOD CITY, CA 94063 **650-369-4171**	SHERATON 500 CANAL **525-2500**	HILTON 2 POYDRAS **561-0500**	HYATT RGNCY POYDRAS / LOYOLA **561-1234**	WESTIN 100 RUE IBERVILLE **566-7006**	FAIRMONT 123 BARONE **529-7111**
RADISSON 1500 CANAL **522-4500**	BOURBON ORL BOURBON / ORLEANS **523-2222**	MARRIOTT 555 CANAL **581-1000**	HLDY LE MYNE 301 RUE DAUPHINE **581-1303**	ROYAL SNSTA 300 BOURBON **586-0300**	QUEEN/CRSNT 344 CAMP **587-9700**
MONTELEONE 214 RUE ROYAL **523-3341**	CHATEAU SNSTA 800 IBERVILLE **586-0800**	BRENT HOUSE 1512 JEFFERSON HWY **835-5411**	HLDY FR QRTR 124 ROYAL **529-7211**	FR MRKT INN 501 DECATUR **561-5621**	LE PAVILLON 833 POYDRAS **581-3111**
		CROWNE PLZA 344 POYDRAS **525-9444**	INN BOURBON 541 BOURBON **524-7611**	PELHAM 444 COMMON **522-4444**	AVE PLAZA 2111 ST CHARLES **566-1212**
					FOR REPAIR CALL **1-(800)** **365-3106**

HAVALEX, INC.
P.O. BOX 5286
REDWOOD CITY, CA
(650) 369-4171

CHANGE: DATE: 08/21/

FILE: NNSO897

Exhibit 6–10   Hotelex is a citywide electronic referral service provided by Havalex, Incorporated to six U.S. cities including New Orleans (shown here). Sold-out hotels refer to the lighted boxes to know which competitors still have vacancies. This proves useful when walking guests on oversold nights. The system shown here is a simple on/off system displaying rooms availability status for same day walk-ins. Havalex will soon be introducing a touch-screen system which displays availability for up to 14 nights at as many as 62 properties. If a guest needs, say, nine nights, the system will scan availability for all listed properties and indicate only those hotels with vacancies all nine nights. *Courtesy of Hotelex Systems, Redwood City, California.*

ing and diminish the outcry from those cases that do occur. Success requires the support of each hotel and chain. A visible and concerted effort may serve to ward off renewed interest by the FTC. Apparently, governmental agencies perceive the issue more strongly than does the public. An AH&MA study on customer satisfaction ranked overbooking 19th in the frequency of guest complaints against hotels. The real problem lies with properties that do nothing. They are the true culprits. Even the FTC noted that it was not overbooking per se that concerned the commission. It was what the hotel didn't do to help when the guest was turned away. The FTC was criticizing the antiservice syndrome.

Overbooking and the Antiservice Syndrome.   While the majority of hotels are proactive in preparing their employees to handle oversold days, poorly managed properties simply place the "blame" on the guest. The common antiservice approach for such hotels is to act as if the reservation never existed. The clerk's pretense is what guests find the most frustrating part of the experience. To play out the charade, the clerk consults with co-workers, massages computer keys, and examines hidden room racks. Finally comes a proclamation. To the hotel, the guest is a nonperson without a record and one for whom the hotel is not responsible.

To the dismay of the entire industry, certain properties give no attention to the matter of overbooking. They set a low priority on the loss of goodwill because they either have little repeat business or they have more business than they can handle. What is unimportant to these properties is of grave concern to the majority of hotelkeepers. The majority act to minimize the frequency of overbooking. The minority exacerbate the problem to the detriment of all.

No-Show Policies.   Any overbooking discussion invariably gets around to no-shows—people who make reservations but never arrive and never cancel. No-shows, which reach as high as 25% in some cities on occasion, run about 8% industrywide.

There is a high correlation between the incidence of no-shows and the quality of the reservation. Reservations come in three qualities. Highest is the advance deposit reservation, next is the guaranteed reservation (guaranteed to either a credit card or corporate account), and lowest quality is the nonguaranteed reservation. The higher the quality of the reservation, the lower the likelihood of no-show.

That's why hotels are less willing to accept nonguaranteed reservations. Nonguaranteed reservations frequently no-show, and when they do, the hotel receives no compensation short of selling the room to a walk-in guest after the 6 PM hold. Hotels have a different option where guaranteed and advance deposit reservations are concerned.

Guaranteed and advance deposit reservations are penalized for failing to cancel or use their reservation. Guests are usually charged the cost of one room night (one room night plus tax is the common amount requested for an advance deposit). For advance deposits, it is a simple matter for the hotel to claim the deposit. With guaranteed reservations, the process is less certain. Collecting against guaranteed reservations is often quite difficult because guests are unwilling to pay the charge against their credit card or corporate account. This disagreement often results in a fight between the guest and the hotel over the amount of one night's lodging. Even when the hotel wins it loses because the guest may forever be lost as a valued customer.

Cancellation Policies.   Cancellation policies are another source of irritation to guests. After taking the time to contact the hotel and cancel the reservation, many guests are told they will still be charged one room-night. If the guest fails to contact the hotel within the limits established by the cancellation policy, the guest is still liable for one night's room charge.

Cancellation policies differ by chain, hotel, market, and destination. In addition, the cancellation policy often reflects the quantity of walk-ins experienced by the hotel. The most liberal cancellation policies allow the guest to cancel up until 6 PM on the day of arrival. Such liberal policies are generally found at corporate and chain-affiliated properties. If the guest fails to cancel within the time frame established, a one-night charge may be assessed. In contrast, many resorts and isolated destination properties mandate more stringent cancellation policies. Some request the guest to notify the hotel 24 to 48 hours in advance. Others require as much as 7 to 14 days notice. Indeed, more stringent cancellation policies may carry a weightier penalty: Some resort properties are known to charge the full prepaid stay.

The major credit-card companies mandate cancellation times for properties that guarantee reservations against their cards. Discover, MasterCard, and VISA all require properties to accept cancellations until 6 PM on the day of arrival (resort operations are given the option of requiring cancellations up to three hours earlier). American Express and Diners Club understand that different markets may require different cancellation policies. Therefore, these two companies allow hotels to establish their own cancellation times, provided that the hotels clearly explain the policies and procedures to all guests at the time of reservation. And oral descriptions are not necessarily sufficient. VISA, for one, requires written notice of cancellation policies for reservations made at least 72 hours in advance. Exhibit 6–11 charts the policies of the several credit-card companies.

Minimizing the Overbooking Problem

There are really no perfect solutions to the problem of overbooking. As long as hotels overbook to compensate for no-shows and last-minute changes in occupancy, there will always be walked guests. The answer is found not in eliminating overbooking as a management tool but rather, in minimizing the need to overbook on most occasions.

The issue boils down to this: A hotel overbooks because its guests change their minds. When guests change their minds, it often results in lower rooms occupancy than projected. Lower occupancy means less rooms revenue for the hotel. Therefore, in response to guest fickleness, the hotel has little choice but to second-guess the number of overstays, understays, cancellations, and no-shows for a given day. The operative word here is *guess*. And sometimes even the most scientific guesses go awry. That's when overbooking rears its head and guests lose confidence in the system.

Unfortunately, guests want the best of both worlds. They want the flexibility to understay or overstay as plans change, but they also want liberal cancellation and no-show policies for the times when they don't arrive. This leaves the hotel in a difficult position. If it charges a no-show guest for the unoccupied room night, the guest might never return to the hotel. If the hotel refuses a request for an overstay or tries to charge a fee to an early-departing understay, it may also create ill will. The answer is probably to be found in more restrictive reservations policies and third-party involvement.

▶ **Increasingly Restrictive Policies.**   Certainly, the airlines are strict about their flight policies. Most tickets are nonrefundable and must be paid at the time of reservation. Courtesy (nonguaranteed) holds on reservations usually expire within 24

Credit-Card Company

	American Express	Diners Club	Discover Card (Novus)	MasterCard	VISA
Name of guaranteed reservations program	Assured Reservations	Confirmed Reservation Plan	Guaranteed Reservation Service	Guaranteed Reservations	VISA Reservation Service
No-show charge policy	Will support no-show charge if "assured reservation no-show" is written on signature line	Will support no-show charge if "confirmed reservation—no-show" is written on signature line	Will support no-show charge if "no-show" is written on signature line	Will support no-show charge if "guaranteed reservation/no-show" is written on signature line	Will support no-show charge if "no-show" is written on signature line
Cancellation policy	Property may determine its own cancellation times	Cancellations by 6 PM (4 PM for resorts) on day of arrival	Cancellations by 6 PM (property may select up to three hours earlier) on day of arrival	Property may determine its own cancellation times	Cancellations by 6 PM if reservation made in past 72 hours; otherwise, property may set its own policy
Overbooking policy	Property must: • Provide and pay for room in comparable hotel for one night • Pay for one 3-minute call • Forward guest contacts to new hotel	Property must: • Provide and pay for room in comparable or better hotel for one night • Pay for one 3-minute call • Provide transportation to new hotel	Property must: • Provide and pay for room in comparable hotel for one night • Pay for one 3-minute call (if requested) • Forward guest contacts to new hotel • Provide transportation to new hotel	Property must: • Provide and pay for room in another hotel for one night • Pay for one 3-minute call • Provide transportation to new hotel • Neither hotel can charge guest for room or guaranteed reservation	Property must: • Provide and pay for room in comparable or better hotel for one night • Pay for one 3-minute call • Forward guest contacts to new hotel • Provide transportation to new hotel

Exhibit 6–11 Third-party reservation guarantees are supported by all five of the major domestic credit-card companies. If the room is guaranteed and the guest does not cancel within the established parameters, the hotel has the right to receive compensation for one night's stay. Of course, this means that the hotel must hold the room available for the guest until check-out time the following day. As long as hotels abide by the policies established by each credit-card company, they will be upheld by the credit-card companies in all but the most unusual

hours. No-show guests (and cancellations) face $50 or $75 "change" fees when they attempt to reuse their tickets. Indeed, unused tickets are only valid a year.

The lodging industry is slowly beginning to adopt similar policies. Merely adopting such reform, however, is not enough. The airlines went through a long period of guest education. And although the lodging industry will have a somewhat easier time educating their customers (because the airlines already broke much of the ground), competition between chains will surely affect the success of industrywide reservations policies reform.

Slowly, such changes are taking place. One chain puts its toe in the water, and soon another follows suit. Yield management fences (nonrefundable reservations, 21-day advanced purchase, and stay over Saturday night) are some of the first toes in the water (see the yield management discussion in Chapter 4). Early departure charges are also being tested.

Early Departure Fees.   Several major lodging chains, including both Hyatt and Hilton, have recently experimented with early departure charges. Although not terribly costly (most guests are required to pay between $25 and $50 as an understay penalty), such fees are designed to make guests think twice before departing early. Early departure fees are also expected to improve the accuracy of the reservation on the front end; once aware of an early departure penalty, guests will probably be more conservative in estimating the number of nights they plan to stay.

As with cancellation and no-show policies, early departure or understay fees must be clearly detailed at the time of reservation booking. Credit-card companies expect properties to explain the policy in detail at the time of reservation, include a comment about the policy with mailed confirmations, and have guests sign a statement reiterating the standard during the check-in process. When these procedures are followed, credit-card companies generally support the hotel with regard to guest disputes and chargebacks (see Exhibit 6–11).

▶ ***Third-Party Guarantees.***   There is some logic in removing the hotel from direct involvement with the guest when fees or penalties are involved. It is easier for the hotel to charge a credit-card company or travel agent the no-show charge than to assess it directly against the guest or the guest's corporate account. Although the guest still pays the charge in the end, the hotel is one step removed from the negative connotations associated with collecting such fees, and a third party is assigned that role.

Trip Insurance.   The increasing popularity of trip or travel insurance is predicated on this same logic. By placing a third party into the equation, some of the negative feelings associated with paying a penalty are assigned elsewhere and the hotel looks a little less the bad guy.

Although few domestic hotels actually recommend travel insurance with their reservations, it is somewhat more popular in Europe. At the time of reservation, or mailed with the confirmation, is some explanation about the benefits associated with travel insurance. The benefits are simple enough: For a small fee, a third party will become responsible for cancellation, no-show, understay, or reservation change fees assessed for a given trip. The reasons the guest may change their plans are usually described with the insurance and may include illness, death, a change in business plans, or even inclement weather.

The concept works something like this—with trip insurance, guests have no one to blame but themselves. You see, they should have purchased trip insurance (through a travel agent, tour operator, or trip insurance broker) if they thought their plans might change. Then, if they are charged a no-show, cancellation, change, or understay fee, the trip insurance will pay the cost. If they didn't buy travel insurance, how can they be mad at the hotel for charging them a fee clearly explained at the time of booking?

Credit-Card Guarantees.   Except for unusual circumstances, a credit-card is charged if the reservation has been guaranteed. Unfortunately, charging the credit card does not always equate to receiving payment. In many instances, the guest will dispute the charge.

When such disputes arise, third-party involvement by the credit-card company is necessitated. The credit-card company usually requires the guest to issue a statement in writing. Such statements as "I never made that reservation" or "I canceled that reservation well in advance" are difficult to prove.

That's why the costliest credit-card chargeback category is no-shows. Hotels should arm themselves against such disputes by following standard procedures. Best Western, for example, always provides separate confirmation and cancellation numbers (unlike some chains, which simply add an "×" to the confirmation number to signify cancellation). In this way, Best Western can insist that the credit-card company ask the guest to provide the cancellation number. No cancellation number (I lost it, I threw it away, they never gave me a number), no excuse. Similarly, Best Western doesn't accept the excuse "I never made the reservation." As a company, they find that excuse questionable—after all, how did the chain get the guest's name, address, phone number, and credit-card number?

Once the statement is in hand, the third-party credit-card company usually issues a temporary credit to the guest (and an offsetting debit to the hotel). This means that, temporarily, the guest does not have to pay the charge and the hotel does not receive the income.

At this stage, the statement is copied to the hotel and the property has an opportunity to respond. Many hotels stop at this point, believing that the case will never be settled in their favor. If the hotel chooses not to respond, the guest automatically wins the decision. Even when the hotel does respond, the case is still found in favor of the guest much of the time. Some critics of the system believe that credit-card companies uphold the guests because they want to keep them as customers. That is really not the case; if the hotel follows the credit-card company's standard procedure, they should never lose a chargeback dispute (see Exhibit 6–11).

Travel Agent Guarantees.   A different type of third-party guarantee utilizes the travel agent. When a guest makes the reservation through a travel agent, the hotel removes itself from dealing directly with the customer. In the event of a no-show, the hotel receives payment directly from the travel agent. Whether or not the travel agent then charges the no-show customer is the travel agent's problem.

The only weakness with this system is that the hotel must have a credit relationship with the travel agent. In today's fast-paced travel environment, there is rarely enough lead time for the travel agent to send a check and for the hotel to clear the funds.

➤ *Advance-Deposit Reservations.*   Probably the best of all methods for reducing the industrywide problem of overbooking is to encourage advance deposits. Advance-deposit reservations (also known as paid-in-advance reservations) have historically maintained the lowest percentage of no-shows. Guests who pay a substantial amount in advance (usually the first-night's room charge, although some resorts charge the entire payment up front) have a strong motive to arrive as scheduled.

However, advance-deposit reservations carry an extra clerical burden not found with other types of reservations. The reservation department, for example, has a tracking burden. If the guest responds by sending a deposit, the reservation must be changed from tentative to confirmed. If the guest doesn't respond, the reservation office must either send a reminder or cancel the reservation. Sending a reminder starts the tracking process all over again.

Handling the money, usually a check, involves bank deposits, sometimes bounced checks, and accounting records. Refunds must be made in a timely manner when cancellations are requested. Processing and writing any check represents a measurable cost of operation.

For many hotels, these operational burdens are inconsequential compared to the benefits that accrue from advance-deposit reservations. However, even those hotels using advance-deposit systems would probably switch if and when new guarantee systems become available. And that is apt to happen as new electronic systems and new innovations in money substitutes appear.

➤ SUMMARY

Accepting a reservation is really only half the battle. Tracking the reservation and forecasting house availability are also important components in a successful reservations department. Forecasting room availability is as much an art as it is a science. It is a simple matter to count committed rooms (those sold to stayovers and incoming reservations) as a means of forecasting the number of rooms available for walk-ins and short lead-time reservations. However, such a simple approach as counting committed rooms leaves untended a number of costly variables. Yet when the reservations manager begins to consider the potential for no-shows, cancellations, early arrivals, understays, and overstays, the art of forecasting becomes a bit like guesswork.

An error in predicting the number of cancellations and no-shows may prove disastrous to a nearly full hotel. Rooms may be overbooked, necessitating that guests be walked to a nearby property. When this is a rare occasion, the employees treat the situation with compassion and the walked guest is a satisfied one. However, when walked guests become a routine daily occurrence, the hotel is showing greed by purposely overbooking each day to compensate for the maximum potential no-shows and cancellations. In such cases, employees become jaded, guests receive little concern, and dissatisfaction inevitably results.

In reality, the lodging industry has done a superior job reducing overbooking complaints in recent years. Partially from fear of government regulation (as with airline overbooking policies), and partially from a desire to create lasting relationships and repeat business in a highly competitive industry, few hotel overbooking complaints have become public scandals in recent years.

➤ QUESTIONS AND PROBLEMS

1. What is the difference between out-of-order and out-of-inventory rooms? Explain why one of these designations affects the occupancy count while the other has no bearing.

2. Prepare a simple unadjusted plus count from the following scenario: A 700-room hotel had 90% of its rooms occupied last night. Of those occupied rooms, 260 are due to check out today. In addition, there are 316 reservations scheduled for arrival today, and 10 rooms are currently out of order.

3. The rooms forecast committee is scheduled to meet later this afternoon. You have been asked to prepare remarks on group no-shows. Contrast the likelihood of no-shows for (a) business groups, (b) tour groups, and (c) convention groups. How would your remarks differ if the group reservation had been made by (a) the vice president of engineering, (b) an incentive travel company, or (c) a professional convention management company?

4. The rooms forecast is a tool for managers throughout the hotel; it is not for the front office alone. List and discuss how several other nonroom departments (housekeeping, food and beverage, etc.) would use the rooms forecast.

5. A chain's corporate office launches a national campaign advertising its policy of honoring every reservation. Each property is notified that overbooking will not be tolerated. What policies can be implemented at the hotel level to meet corporate goals and still generate the maximum occupancies on which professional careers are built?

6. Two hours before the noon check-out hour, a walk-in party requests five rooms. The following scrambled data have just been completed as part of the desk's hourly update. Should the front-office supervisor accept the walk-ins?

General no-show factor	10%
Rooms in the hotel	693
Group reservations due (rooms)	250
Number of rooms departed so far today	203
Rooms occupied last night	588
Total reservations expected today from all sources (including group rooms)	360
No-show factor for groups	2%
Understays minus overstays as a percentage of occupied rooms	8%
Early arrivals expected	2
Nonsalable rooms and rooms that are out of inventory	7
Total forecasted departures for the day	211

➤ NOTE

1. Hotel reservations are legal contracts whether they are oral (see *Dold v. Outrigger Hotel and Hawaii Hotels Operating Company*, 1972) or in writing (see *Rainbow Travel Service, Inc. v. Hilton Hotels Corp.*, 1990). Although most cases show damaged customers or tour operators suing hotels for overbooking, hotels have also been known to sue guests for their failure to arrive (*King of Prussia Enterprises, Inc. v. Greyhound Lines, Inc.*, 1978).

PART III

Guest Service and Rate Structures

Chapter 7
Managing Guest Service

Chapter 8
The Guest Arrival Process

Chapter 9
Setting the Room Rate

The cyclical nature of the hotel business, with its peaks and valleys in sales volume, was explained in Part I. There it was pointed out that the cycle goes up and down frequently, as often, perhaps, as once a week. This short cycle appears on a graph as a wave moving across the chart between the highs and the lows.

Innkeeping, like other industries, has an additional cycle. All businesses go through life periods similar to that of the human body. These are far longer cycles during which an industry is born, matures, and ages. Long cycles do not graph as waves but rather, as extended trend lines with flat periods and gradual changes. Computers, for example, are in their youth, having been a major force for just a decade or two. Other industries, of which hotel keeping is one, are in more advanced, more mature, stages of development.

Strong competition is one characteristic of a mature industry. Numerous competitors offering similar but slightly different products battle for customers. If the product (bed and bath) being offered is pretty much the same from competitor to competitor, customers base their purchasing decisions on something other than the product. They buy because of price or because of service, or because of both.

Hotel managers were reawakened to the importance of guest service during the poor business cycle of the 1980s–1990s. Price cutting was widespread and its costs were disastrous. Hotelkeepers had focused on price, just one of the two issues. Something else was needed to differentiate one hotel's product from another's. Service competition was an alternative to price competition. In Part II we discussed guest history cards as one technique of service competition. With increased computer capability, hotels use guest databases to market, track visits, and improve service once the guest has arrived. However, real service is a personal experience that takes place between the guest and the service provider. Recognizing the role of the employee in the service act, hotel organizations have been restructuring around a new idea. Give line employees greater authority. Give line employees the power—empower them—to act immediately in the best interests of the customer.

Good service does not replace competitive prices. Nor can competitive prices offset unsatisfactory service. In Part III we examine these two alternatives: first, guest service, and then competitive prices and room rates.

CHAPTER 7
Managing Guest Service

Outline

Brief History of Quality Management
Quality Management in Manufacturing
Quality Management in Innkeeping

What Is Quality Management?
The Basic Product
Quality Management Defined
Quality Management Denied

Implementing Guest Service
Measuring Guest Service
Quality Guarantees
Complaints

Great guest service doesn't just happen; it needs to be managed. But it needs to be managed close to the action, not from afar. Shifting from a management-imposed culture to an employee-participation culture is slow, hard work. The first is traditional and long standing; the second is new and not at all familiar. Indeed, many workers are not interested in an additional job, that of managing guest relationships, which those employees see to be management's responsibility, not theirs.

The hotel industry continues its entry into an era of high-tech and increased self-service. In such an environment, some see personalized attention from employees as less pertinent. Service is not as important as increased telephone lines, or so goes that argument. High tech certainly can supplement, and already has in some functions, the industry's ability to serve its patrons. Fewer and fewer occasions of employee–guest contact increase—not decrease—the importance of those times when the employee and the guest come face to face. Globalization and industry consolidation emphasize, rather than depreciate, the importance of the industry's historical culture of guest service.

Hoteliers have begun managing guest service once again, although differently, of course, than they did when hotels were owner-managed. The innkeeper can no longer be the guest's immediate and personal host. The job of attending to the guest now sifts down through several organizational levels to the staffers on the floor. Getting those employees to recognize the importance of the task and having them take on the responsibility for doing it is the role of managing guest service. No easy task, that.

➤ BRIEF HISTORY OF QUALITY MANAGEMENT

Directing the personalized service that takes place between employees and guests is a difficult task for managers. To improve the quality of that interaction, management is encouraging employees, themselves, to take on the job. For managers who have risen through the ranks of accounting and taxation, mass marketing and real estate financing, the shift is an abrupt one. In little more than a decade, hoteliers have seen the introduction, maturation, and influence of human resources departments when there had been none before.

From the mid-1970s through the mid-1980s, the lodging industry passed through a period of rapid real estate growth and expansion. Hotels were targets of intense speculation, fueled in part by favorable federal tax legislation. Eventually, the heady expansion period waned and collapsed as tough economic times and changing tax laws, in part, took their toll. Like much of U.S. business, hotel keeping was reengineered—an apt euphemism for the self-inspection and rethinking that followed.

As the industry struggled to avoid wholesale bankruptcy, it abandoned its view of the hotel as a building and returned to its view of the hotel as a service business. Operations replaced financing as the focus of the 1990s. Hotel managers concentrated as never before on two aspects of operations: how to trim costs and how to build volume. From both needs came one answer: Attend to the guest.

Sensitivity to consumer needs and expectations is not special to innkeeping—it is a standard for all businesses. In one manner, then, lodging is like all business, just one industry among many. In other aspects, however, the hotel business is very different from heavy industry and even from other service industries.

Quality Management in Manufacturing

Worldwide markets, the advantage of globalization, come at the cost of worldwide competition. That competition grew intense as the world's economies blended into one. During this period, the quality of U.S.-made goods came into question. A reputation for quality, which the United States had held since the end of World War II, passed into other hands. Nearly a quarter century elapsed before the movement reversed again. A return to quality for all U.S. industries was signaled by Ford Motor Company's advertising slogan, "Quality Is Job One."[1]

The now popular emphasis on quality had its U.S. origins in the manufacturing industries. The decline in the reputation of U.S.-made goods forced manufacturers to reexamine production techniques and the workers responsible for that production. U.S. manufacturing responded, but it did not originate the movement toward quality management (QM).

Some work hard at tracing the origins of the quality management movement to Greek philosophers and Chinese mystics. Others attribute the entire concept to W. Edwards Deming, an American. Like so many evolving ideas, neither is all this nor all that. The Japanese, for example, invented quality control circles, which are teams of employees focusing on special issues.

Japan and Germany have been America's primary competitors in quality. Since much of Deming's work to upgrade quality took place during the 1950s in Japan, which was infamous then for very poor workmanship, Deming remains a central figure in the whole movement. Deming urged his disciples—and that term is warranted because of the intensity of his adherents—to follow the 14 points that he promulgated. Some of his points focused on the process and the product, others on the workers and the environment.

Check-In, Check-Out does the same. First, it is a process-oriented text, dealing with how-to: how to track reservations, how to set rates, how to improve yield management, how to expedite guest registration, how to record and control the sale of guest services, and how to facilitate guest departure. All of this is presented in sequence with electronic technology as one means of improving the product and the process. In this manner, the book concentrates on one of Deming's concerns.

Quality Management in Innkeeping

Locating this chapter on guest service right smack in the middle of the book is not accidental. It is here as a fulcrum, balancing the how-to with the other elements of quality service, the guests and the staff. Every topic that precedes this chapter and every one that follows carries a message, understood if not always expressed, about the importance of guest service throughout the hotel, but especially at the desk. Executive attention to rooms employees, and through these employees to the guests, is essential to the management of the front office. Attending to employee issues meets the second part of Deming's concept for the QM process.

Quality management (QM) has spun off other concepts, such as quality assurance (QA) and total quality management (TQM). The terms seem to be interchangeable now. The essence of all three terms is that every person in the company has the opportunity, and needs the ability, to make a positive impact on the customer. Just consider the terminology. Retailers speak of *customers,* various professionals refer to *clients* or *patients,* economists cite *consumer* trends, and galleries talk of *patrons.* Only the hotel industry calls its business clients *guests.*

Hoteliers have brought many innovations into the business. Bathtubs were added to hotel accommodations before they appeared in the White House. At one time, fans, radios, TV sets, elevators, telephones, clocks, and swimming pools were unique products, installed in leading properties to attract guests. They are standard expectations today. To the credit of the hotel industry, QM is viewed similarly. Quality management was an innovation when it first came to the hotel industry. Today, it is thought to be so basic an accommodation that no hotel can operate without it. Thus, the standard of the whole industry moves upward just as it does when every hotel room has a personal computer and fax.

➤*Examples of Quality Management.*   Hotels did not embrace QM terminology as early as manufacturing did. That fact doesn't distract from the lodging industry's long-held sensitivity to guest service. Guest service is an industry fundamental, although management's attention to it waxes and wanes over time. Industrywide interest in guest service peaked anew when the Ritz-Carlton Company, a hotel management company, won the 1992 Malcolm Baldrige National Quality Award. The award itself was new, established by Congress only five years earlier. It recognizes U.S. companies that achieve excellence by emphasizing quality. As the first hotel company to win the award, the Ritz-Carlton Company reawakened the entire industry to one of its basic tenets: Service the guests.

Winning an award in 1992 required the company to commit to excellence far earlier. Although the Ritz-Carlton Company set the pace, many other hotel companies also initiated formal quality management programs. The AH&MA held the first Quality Assurance Conference in 1988, and in that same year the Educational Institute of the AH&MA published the first text on the subject, *Managing Quality Services.*[2] Both the text and the conference flowed from the 1981 annual meeting when the AH&MA decided to create a *Quest for Quality* program. From that beginning, much of the industry came onstream.

Sheraton's Guest Satisfaction System (SGSS) began in 1987. Some Sheraton executives attribute part of the chain's increased occupancy and profits since then to the staff's heightened sensitivity to quality. The fundamentals of many of the programs are like Sheraton's. They begin with an emphasis on hiring the right people. SGSS calls that *HireVision;* the Ritz-Carlton Company calls it *Talent Plus.* All programs entail training, the delegation of increased authority to operative-level employees, and incentive awards to lubricate the smooth flow of the machinery. Training, delegation, and reward are the basic parts of quality management programs.

Radisson was another early convert to QM. It began a well-structured effort to implement a guest-service training program. Called *Yes I Can!* the program was installed in all Radisson-owned and Radisson-franchised properties. Radisson stretches its program of quality management beyond the guest, asking that each employee extend the same guest-oriented service to every other employee. Whether greeting or servicing a colleague, each staff member is to behave as if the other staff member were a guest.

Broadening the basic quality management program to other employees and even to purveyors is part of the explanation for the emergence of the term *total* quality management. TQM views everyone as part of the program: guests, staff, and purveyors. Companies that employ the TQM philosophy treat their purveyors as part of the excellence team but demand of them the same performance levels as the hotel itself is striving to achieve.

Each chain gives the basic idea, improved guest service and attention, its own twist. Ramada's *You're Somebody Special* program was launched in 1987. Doubletree calls its program *Continuous Improvement.* Lane Hospitality prefers the term *Employee Entrepreneurship* to illustrate its empowerment of employees. To empower employees is to give them the authority to settle a matter at their own organizational level. The Arizona Biltmore goes one step further: It provides each employee with a small budget that can be used to implement the empowerment.

Empowering employees has another advantage: Fewer supervisors are needed if staff members have the authority to decide on their own. But for this concept to work, better trained employees are needed to carry out the empowerment—and therefore, better salaries will need to be paid. There is no evidence yet that the hotel industry has accepted that rationale.

Whether a chain or an independent property, a conference center or a franchise company, most of the industry has adopted some form or process that could be called quality assurance. Formal quality assurance programs are expensive, ongoing, and successful only when top management is committed for the long haul. That commitment often waivers over time because, like advertising, QM costs are easily measured but results are not.

➤ WHAT IS QUALITY MANAGEMENT?

As we shall see shortly, there is no single, crystal-clear definition of quality management. At its core, QM seeks the cooperation of every staff member in achieving company goals, primarily those that stress guest service and guest relationships. In that, there is nothing new; management everywhere has such intent. Quality management brings a more formal tone, a more structured approach to the task. It recognizes, moreover, that guest service has many parts. Total quality management requires attention to all, not just some, of the parts. Among them is the physical product that the hotel delivers.

The Basic Product

Guests come to hotels to sleep. They willingly overlook missing amenities and poorly decorated lobbies if sleep, the hotel's basic product, is delivered. Above all else, hotel guests expect a good night's sleep. For quality management to achieve its goals throughout the hotel, guests must be satisfied with the delivery of the one product that they have specifically purchased. QM begins with the guest room. Dissatisfaction with this basic product cannot be redressed by a smiling desk clerk wearing a happy-face button as part of a structured quality management program.

To meet minimum guest expectations, hotels must maintain very high standards in bedding, cleanliness, room temperature, and noise. Other amenities could be counted easily enough, but none of the additional items (such as full-length mirrors, in-room coffee makers, or adequate lighting) is critical to the night's repose.

➤*Bedding and Cleanliness.*   The proverbial good night's rest requires, above all else, a comfortable bed. In Chapter 3 we provided information on bed sizes, which is the hotel's starting point for delivering its promise. The larger beds described there provide the extra 6 inches of mattress (6 inches longer than the average height of the sleeper) that some authors recommend.[3] Pillows need to be adequate in size, composition, and number. There should be two pillows for each occupant, either on the bed or in reserve in a drawer or closet. Many hotels offer a choice of hard or soft pillows, and most offer either feather-filled or synthetic pillows. The latter is an option that pleases guests with allergies.

Overall, the industry gets high marks for the quality of the mattresses and springs that complete the beds. Good hotel mattresses last as long as 10 years. Thus, experienced hoteliers make the initially higher investment, by buying matching mattresses and springs to ensure longer life. The quality of both is measured, in part, by the type, number, and gauge of the steel coils and by the method of tying them down. House-keeping must devise a system for turning the mattress at least four times annually. Equalizing wear this way ensures longer life. Providing comfortable chairs also adds to the life of the bedding because guests sit on the chairs and not on the mattress edges. Fire-resistant bedding has substantially reduced the number of in-room fires resulting from smokers falling asleep in bed.

Bedding must be clean! Unfortunately, clean sheets don't always look clean. There has been a shift away from ironing sheets to using a sheet of 50% cotton and 50% synthetic fiber, no-iron sheets. No-iron sheets are fine as fitted bottom sheets because the wrinkles are stretched out, providing the appearance of a smooth, ironed sheet—except fitted sheets are just not used. They are difficult to fold and handle, require extra storage space, and tear at the corners, increasing replacement costs. Because of this, many hotels use regular, not fitted, no-iron sheets, which wrinkle and leave the impression of less-than-clean bed linen.

Cleanliness is not limited to bedding. Guests are very sensitive to the quality of housekeeping everywhere, especially in the bath. Tub/showers, toilets, sinks, and bathroom floors require special attention to remove hair and dirt. Into the corners and behind the toilets take extra care. Chrome fixtures, particularly the sink and tub drains, must be cleaned and wiped daily. Vacuuming, the final step in cleaning the guest room, may take place only between guests. Rooms for stayovers are not vacuumed unless the room attendant or housekeeper thinks there is need to do so. Elsewhere, the policy might be to vacuum every day, check out or not.

Overall cleanliness, inside and outside the guest room, is taken for granted. Few guests ever compliment sanitation standards on guest-comment cards, but all will complain when it's missing.

▶ *Noise and Temperature.*   Noise is another reason that the industry fails to deliver its basic product, sleep. Even "road warriors" (business travelers who sleep away from home a great deal) complain about noisy rooms. Poor initial construction, which is not easily fixed after the fact, is high on a list of causes. Budget limitations force builders to ignore adequate sound barriers between rooms and in the utility and plumbing shafts. Back-to-back baths make for easy construction and maintenance, but play havoc in transmitting noises. In very bad cases, the plumbing is strapped inadequately, so noisy vibrations follow the opening of every faucet.

Poorly insulated rooms bring the neighbor's television set resonating into the sleeper's dreams. Everyday sounds from simple conversations to children playing come from rooms close by. Hallway noises, which include the whirr of ice-making machine motors, ice falling into buckets, ringing telephones, elevator doors, and late-to-bed revelers, add to the din. The worst noise offender is right in the room: the fan on the heating/airconditioning system. It is as much an annoyance as the room's temperature control.

Central heating and airconditioning systems are far superior to individual room units. Cost is, again, the determining factor. But some window units are not even temperature sensitive. They run all the time unless they're turned off completely. It's up to the sleeper to decide which is worse. Occasionally, the units don't run at all. Maintenance on the systems is minimal and on demand rather than preventative. Guests may be housed in rooms with nonworking units. Encountered occasionally are systems that deliver either heating or cooling, depending on the time of the year. No choice is available during swing months; guests get either heating or cooling, regardless of their own body temperatures.

The Ritz-Carlton chain has recently launched a new quality management program, *Care,* to reduce the number of in-room complaints. Among other ideas, it plans to refresh guest rooms once every three months. So the first hotel operator to win the Baldrige quality award sees a good deal of sense in managing the basic accommodation as its first quality concern.

Quality Management Defined

Defining quality management is as difficult a task as is delivering it. Some have tried explaining quality service by telling anecdotes, brief stories to illustrate the idea. Illustrations of this type are legend: A desk clerk makes certain that an important letter gets typed for a guest after hours; a bellperson delivers a forgotten attaché case to the airport just in time; a housekeeper takes guest laundry home to meet a deadline; a door attendant lends black shoes to a guest for a formal affair.

Despite the difficulties, formal definitions are the vogue. Everyone gives it a shot—the authors try their hand a few pages on—even if the results are incomplete. Along with hundreds of other publications, *Managing Quality Services,* cited earlier, says that, "QA is a management system that ensures consistent delivery of products and services." Another puts it this way, "TQM is a way to continuously improve performance at every level of operation, in every functional area of an organization, using all available human and capital resources."[4] Both of these descriptions, which represent the general run of QA definitions, fail to emphasize the duality of the issue: QM involves both the buyer–receiver of the service and the seller–giver.

Part I explained how segmented the hotel industry is; its customer base is equally fragmented. Thus, the desire to deliver quality originates with innumerable sellers, even as the search to find quality has many, many buyers. Each side and each member of that side sees the issue from a different perspective. No wonder variations abound in the delivery and receipt of service, and consequently in its definition. Quality service, and the management of quality service, have no objective measures. Definitions are necessarily vague, evaluations are obviously imprecise, and delivery is clearly inexact. Still, everyone knows it when they see it.

➤ *The Buyer's View.* From the guest's viewpoint, quality is the degree to which the property delivers what the guest expects. If the guest is surprised by a better stay than anticipated, the hotel is perceived as high quality. If the visit fails to meet expectations, the property is downgraded.

Advertising, word-of-mouth comments, price, previous visits and publicity create a level of expectation within the guest. Of course, that barrage of communications is received differently with different perceptions by almost every guest. Moreover, those very expectations change over time and place, even within the same guest. Influencing the guest's expectations are components that may be outside the hotel's control: a late flight, a rude cabdriver, a bad storm.

Guests hold different expectations about different hotels, even different hotels within the same chain. Quality is measured against the expectation of that particular property at that particular time more than against different hotels in different categories.

Driving up to an economy property with a loaded family van and a pet but without a reservation carries one expectation. Flying around the world to an expensive resort—a trip that a couple has planned for and saved for over many years—creates a much different level of anticipation. Coming to a busy convention property with a reservation made by the company's travel desk evokes still a third level of expectation. Each expectation must be met by the hotel with delivery at the highest level appropriate for the circumstances. Quality assurance attempts to do just that. It is a big, big order.

Consider two hypothetical properties. The first, an economy hotel offering minimal services, charges half its neighbor's rate. The neighbor, an expensive, upscale property and not a true competitor, has it all.

The economy hotel offers the following conveniences:

➤ No bellservice, but parking is convenient and many luggage carts are in the lobby.

➤ No room service, but the hotel is located near a well-known restaurant chain and has an exceptional choice of vending options.

➤ No health club, but the swimming pool is clean, open at convenient hours, and has a good supply of towels.

➤ No concierge, but the room clerk is knowledgeable and affable.

The upscale neighbor offers the following conveniences:

➤ Bellpersons, whom guests are urged to call on. But this hotel never schedules enough staff, resulting in long delays.

➤ Room service, but it is offered at limited times. This hotel suggests a pizza delivery company as an alternative.

➤ A well-reputed health club, but it is on lease, which means that this hotel charges for admission.

➤ A concierge, but the concierge has a recorded message that puts the guest on hold.

Extreme as the illustrations are, the point is obvious—quality is in the eye of the beholder. Managing for quality, therefore, must include standards set from the consumer's perspective. Doing so gives credence to the buyer's view of what quality service is all about. Management must first establish the systems and then the measurement standards for those systems—both to be based on the buyers' expectations. Management must also fix the procedure for achieving those standards. Successfully implemented, QM matches the buyers' standards with the sellers' ability to deliver. When done right, the guest/buyer knows that the hotel delivers quality guest service.

➤ *The Seller's View.*   Like every other policy and operating practice, QM originates with management. Either management makes deliberate decisions to implement particular ideas or it passively accepts ongoing procedures. So it is with quality assurance. Management creates and carries out a program of enhanced guest service or there is none.

Delivering quality requires management to focus on both employees and guests. The two are intertwined. Increasing guest services to satisfy the buyer's side of quality management requires special attention to operational issues, the employees' side of quality management. Staying close to the customer means stressing customer wants, ensuring consistency, remedying the mistakes that do occur, and concentrating on the whole with a passion that hints of obsession. But all of these are also operational concerns. Nothing can be accomplished without attention to the employees entrusted with the delivery.

Leadership. Adopting QM as a company philosophy forces major changes in the definition of management. Traditionally, management is said to be a series of functions. Planning, organizing, staffing, directing, and reviewing is the classic list of management's responsibilities. QM adds another element—leadership. Managing as a leader requires a change in both the style of management and the composition of the workforce being managed. When both components—management and workforce—focus on delivering quality above all else, the company is said to have a *service culture.*

With a leadership style, managers shift from their traditional position of review, which requires corrective action after mistakes are made, to a proactive style of supervision. Errors must be corrected, of course, but a proactive stance aims at error avoidance. Minimizing errors, whether on a production line or a registration line, is what QM is all about.

This fundamental shift in management style binds employees, supervisors, and management into closer relationships, certainly closer than they were previously, before quality management. Under the new organizational concept, management occasionally needs to share information that at one time may have been considered confidential. That comes from the broader scope of responsibility now being laid upon the staff. The interests and participation of operative employees has been enlarged. Consequently, staff members must be kept aware of activities in their own department and in other departments when functions overlap with their own.

Overlapping interests are reinforced through quality circles (QOs). Quality circles, which are discussed again later in the chapter, are employee committees. Representatives within each department and sometimes from several departments meet and work on problems. QOs at the front desk, for example, may have representatives from housekeeping, sales, telecommunications, and accounting. Each representative would then sit on a QO within his or her own department. Soon a network exists across the entire property. Quality assurance goals can be established to reflect the realities of the entire operation. Standards can be developed with input from other departments. Rewards for quality performance can be achievement driven.

Empowerment. Once so much of management's guarded interests are opened to the operating staff, the next step is almost anticlimactic. Some of management's power is given away, delegated down the line. Operative employees are authorized to make their own decisions as long as these fall within the scope of the individuals' job assignments. Entrusting the employee to act responsibly requires management to give that employee the authority to take action. Giving the workforce appropriate authority is empowerment.

Empowerment locates the problem solving and decision making at the source (see Exhibit 7–1). Line employees can act effectively once they have both the information and the authority to use it. Moreover, empowering employees creates leaner and flatter organizations. The pancake-like structures make each department operate almost as a small company, with greater responsibility and accountability, under the umbrella of general management.

The first response to empowerment involves individual actions by single employees. A misquoted rate is settled on the spot by the cashier as the guest checks out. Apologies for an unmade room are expressed with a small bouquet ordered by the desk attendant. Individual acts by employees bring immediate responses from the guests who experience them. But empowerment is more than guest relations.

GUEST QUARTERS®
SUITE HOTELS

Dear Guests:

Welcome to Guest Quarters Suite Hotels and Guest Quarters Magazine — an informative guide to this hotel's community, as well as interesting and entertaining reading on a variety of subjects.

I would like to take this opportunity to share something with you that is new and exciting at all Guest Quarters Suite Hotels. It's not a new amenity or special promotion — in fact, you can't touch or see this at all. But, when you stay at any Guest Quarters, you will sense what we are calling employee empowerment.

Employee empowerment means that at Guest Quarters, all of our employees have been trained and authorized to handle your inquiries on-the-spot. Whether it be a concern over our quality levels or a special request, Guest Quarters employees have been given the tools to make your stay flawless, without having to find a supervisor. (Of course, there are special situations which require the attention of a manager.)

Employee empowerment takes our award-winning service levels one step higher. It provides you with a more efficient and effective staff that is eager to serve you. Just as importantly, empowerment further demonstrates our confidence in our company's most valuable asset — our employees.

The results? I can't express how proud I am of how our employees have utilized empowerment. Rather than just exercise their decision-making privileges to address negative guest situations, Guest Quarters employees are going "above and beyond the call of duty" to provide unexpected touches and unanticipated acts of kindness. This is the true meaning of hospitality.

As we move forward in this decade which has been designated the "Decade of Customer Service," I am confident that Guest Quarters will continue to be one of the hotel industry's shining stars. I invite you to visit any of our 30 locations nationwide to experience impeccable service, coupled with the luxury of a suite.

Sincerely,

Richard M. Kelleher
President Guest Quarters Suite Hotels

Exhibit 7–1   With top management's support, employee empowerment is better for guests than amenities, better for profits than advertising, better for staff than yellow smiley pins, and better for the property than swimming pools. *Courtesy of Promus Hotel Corporation, Memphis, Tennessee.* (Guest Quarters Suite Hotels merged with Doubletree Hotels Corporation in 1993; Doubletree's merger with Promus occurred in 1997.)

A second and broader delegation of empowerment is that given to quality circles (QOs). Originally, QOs were merely asked to identify problems and to recommend possible solutions. Where QM has been implemented successfully, quality circles are actually executing their own ideas. They have been empowered to do so. QOs tackle two types of problems. One kind deals with guest relations, usually how-to's. The group considers how to speed check ins and check outs, how to reduce errors in reservations, how to expedite group baggage handling, and more.

The second type of issues faced by QOs also has an impact on quality service, but the relationship is less guest oriented. The attention is on in-house procedures (moving linen without tying up the service elevators), cost reductions (chargebacks by credit-card companies), or operational irritations (maintenance's slow response to requests for guest-room repairs). None of these has anything to do with immediate guest service, but all of them have everything to do with quality management.

The Employee.   Convincing supervisors to adopt a leadership style of management is but half the battle. QM requires employees to take on responsibilities, to accept the empowerment offered. Just as some managers and supervisors oppose the transfer of their power to employees, some employees decline to accept what's offered. Many prefer not to take on what they perceive to be a management job.

Similarly, the employer's willingness to share information about the business may not be matched by the employees' interest in receiving it—or receiving it, having the capacity to understand it, or the interest to use it. Even highly motivated employees may not comprehend what is offered or what is expected. Leadership requires followers; great leadership requires inspired and motivated followers. Quality management is burdened with the development of both leaders and followers; and that must be done within a workforce of great diversity in language, education, and cultural expectations (see Exhibit 7–2).

High job turnover is another reality of the hospitality workforce. Employees, and the term includes supervisors and managers as well, come and go at a costly pace. Many workers are in dead-end jobs. Boredom and monotonous repetition are blunted temporarily by moving to another property even though the new job has the same task routines. Turnover at the lowest levels of the organization, the spots where quality management could shine, exceeds 200% annually in some jobs of some hotels. Every employee is replaced twice each year! Events feed upon themselves: The very turnover taking place creates the jobs for those turning over. Less dramatic but equally disturbing turnover occurs among managers and supervisors. Establishing, maintaining, and improving a service culture is often put aside as resources are assigned to gathering and placing a turnstile staff.

It is far less costly to retain workers than to replace them. That's why retention plans, which have been in place in other industries for some time, are now finding their way into lodging. Stock options, year-end bonuses, and employee share ownership are relatively new concepts for this old industry. With them, workers are able to increase personal wealth by doing well the repetitive tasks that often make up hotel jobs. The low unemployment rate of the late 20th Century hastened the introduction of these industrywide changes. Of course, several chains, Marriott for one, adopted employee-participation plans years ago. Recent competition for labor, both from within the industry and from other industries, accounts for the renewed interest.

Rewards, financial and otherwise, are part of every QM plan. Incentives are especially useful at the front office, where QM programs demand a great deal from moder-

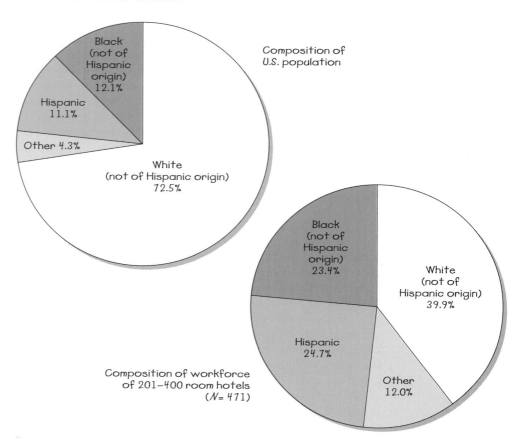

Exhibit 7–2   The workforce in American hotels differs ethnically and culturally from the composition of the national population and hence the probable mix of guests. Managers and staff need sensitivity to customs and expectations that differ from group to group. Diversity incorporates differences by embracing the cultures of its guests and staff. That's different from affirmative action, which focuses on hiring a predetermined number of minorities. *Courtesy of The American Hotel Foundation, Washington, D.C.*

ately paid personnel. Noncash rewards include inviting employee participation in quality circles, granting broad degrees of autonomy, selecting individuals for special cross-training, and awarding employee-of-the-month designations. Still, at operative levels, dollars and cents remain strong incentives. Although managers, especially supervisory managers, are not above cash rewards, the hotel industry has another incentive to offer them: time. Long hours on the job cause hardships in personal life for many nonhourly workers. Incentives for them may be nothing more than an extra day off!

Good staff at all organizational levels is the thread of the quality management weave. The commitment to finding and holding those persons is reflected in the salaries paid, the training offered, and the incentives rewarded. A company that concentrates on better human resources ensures a better delivery of quality service. The effort begins with selecting the right persons.

Selecting the Right Employee.   Managing guest services by empowering employees and enlisting their help requires a broad effort. It reaches beyond the immediate delivery of services, stretching backward to employment and forward to retention. Delivering quality service begins at the selection decision. How else can the right person be in the right place when the QM situation requires? Hoteliers knows this, so the personnel office has been the launch site for most QM programs. *Selecting*—QM programs avoid *hiring,* and stress that difference—intelligent, participative, and sensitive employees is fundamental to managing guest service. Friendly, interactive applicants, who have a sincere wish to help, solve problems of quality deficiency faster than do experienced technical workers who lack those qualities. Indeed, there are far more guest complaints about poor employee attitudes than about substandard facilities and broken TV sets.

Finding the right person even some of the time is a major hurdle that the hotel industry does not always clear. Once found, retaining the right worker, like retaining the right guest, would seem to be the very highest priority. Strangely, retention sometimes gets less attention than the original search. Yet retaining both the recruited guest and the recruited employee is at the very heart of QM. Retention is certainly less costly in time and money than is re-recruiting replacements. Induction, helping the new hire ease into the company, is a common pitfall in the hiring process. It's often a casualty of the pressure to get the new worker productive. After spending many dollars to recruit them, new employees are alienated in the very next step, entering the work door.

Even the right persons make mistakes in implementing whatever empowerment has been delegated. Chastising employees after an error has been made undermines the entire quality concept. Employees must take responsibility for their own actions, of course. However, QM replaces negative discipline with positive coaching, with direction and suggestions for the next time. In keeping with the concept of error avoidance, the need for coaching declines as up-front training increases.

Continuous training is one response to high turnover. Training brings about changes in behavior. One type of training improves work skills—better use of the front-office computer package, for example. Another type of training enhances interpersonal skills—meeting and greeting the arrival across the desk. Managing for service requires industry executives to provide both types of training. Providing them on a continuing basis, at no small cost, is a measure of management's commitment to a quality service philosophy.

▶*The Authors' View.*   The entire QM culture has been summarized in a brief phrase (an aphorism) that has become a favorite of the industry. "The answer is 'yes,' now ask me the question."[5] That clearly represents the type of employee (and management) attitude that QM programs are supposed to instill. Applications of the adage apply equally well to employee–guest interactions, employee–management interfaces, and employee–employee contacts. Under an umbrella of so broad a coverage, this brief saying offers a simple definition of total quality management.

Closer inspection proves QM culture to be very similar to the carefully cultivated culture of the concierge. With both, the attitude is expressed in Radisson's "Yes, I can!" Hotels that promote QM understand that the concierge is not a department, not even a staff. It is an attitude, the kind that one hopes all employees in a quality management program hold. Hence, the first part of the authors' definition: *Quality management is an attitude that has every employee acting like a concierge—*

Several times throughout this chapter the duality of quality assurance has been emphasized: The guest side (the display side) of the QM equation is balanced by the employee side (the operational side). Thus, the second phrase of the authors' definition of QM:—*and thinking like a manager.*

> *Quality management is an attitude that has every employee acting like a concierge and thinking like a manager.*

Quality Management Denied

The hotel business is part of a vast hospitality industry that includes food, beverage, and entertainment facilities. Within that definition, hotel leaders see their industry as a service industry, their product as hospitality, and their customers as guests. Because this position has been verbalized so often, hotel patrons are confused by the antihospitality–antiguest–antiservice syndrome that is part of some hotels.

Guest expectations, one component of quality delivery systems, were reviewed earlier. Guests recognize that every property is not charged with the same level of product despite its grouping under the common umbrella of lodging. But guests do not understand why minimal service means antiservice, and why a lack of personnel means a lack of courtesy. Management's failure to distinguish minimal service, justified by minimal rates, from antiservice, shown by employee negativism, has lead to the antiservice syndrome that some hotels demonstrate and many guests experience.

Quality management is the industry's response to antiservice. QM programs are designed to ferret out the problems, to train for the solutions, and to reward those who demonstrate the right response. Sometimes, however, the very structure of the operation thwarts the best of intentions.

➤**Who Knows Why?**   Every organization develops standard operating procedures. They are to business routines as personal habits are to individual routines. Some of them are new and meaningful; some are bad and in need of change. Along with the new and the good, guests encounter the old and the useless. Like all bad habits, old and useless ways are hard to discard. Hotels that insist on keeping them irritate their guests unnecessarily and undermine the concepts of quality service. To the observer, some practices seem to be almost intentional, as if inconveniencing the guest is easier than fixing the problem. For example, consider the following:

- ➤ Being roused out of bed by an alarm clock set by a previous occupant
- ➤ Paying fees for incoming faxes, despite free incoming telephone calls, including toll calls
- ➤ Experiencing half-day charges for late check outs even when the house has space
- ➤ Having unexplainable restrictions explained away as, "Sorry, company policy"
- ➤ Watching managers take the best parking places while guests walk the distance
- ➤ Facing dining room dress codes that are more rigid than accepted social standards
- ➤ Getting one room key whether one, two, or three guests occupy a room
- ➤ Understanding why the pool closes when guests are on hand and opens when most are away

➤ Reading instructions not to bring room towels to the beach, but finding no others available

➤ Hushing housekeepers who tap on the door hours before they come to clean

➤ Fighting check-out hours established around labor scheduling rather than the guests' comings and goings

➤ IMPLEMENTING GUEST SERVICE

The modern hotel services mass markets. How different that is from the individualized attention that was the norm a century ago. Smiling, courteous, concerned employees working in a democratic culture have replaced the rigid, serve-food-from-the-left, clear-drinks-from-the-right, white-gloved autocracy of a past era.

Hotel companies have shifted from the formal to the informal; from pretense to expedited service; from rigid procedures to empowerment. Much of the change can be explained by the public's new attitude toward service. Aware of labor costs, functioning in a self-service environment themselves, sensitive to the employees' expectations of equality, today's guests no longer expect a servile attitude. And employees no longer deliver it. Guests do expect—and are entitled to receive during each encounter—a friendly face, an attentive ear, and a twinkling eye. After all, quality service, as previously defined, is an attitude that shines through.

Measuring Guest Service

In Chapter 1 we discussed several measures for evaluating the industry's economic health. Occupancy percentages and average daily rates (ADRs) are the two basic measurements. Both figures rise or fall in response to the guest's experience with the service encounter. Happy guests mean good statistical results, and unhappy guests mean poor ones. Other factors also affect occupancy and rate. The state of the economy, the condition of the building, and the level of advertising are just some of the issues that cloud the results. Waiting for low occupancy and poor ADRs to warn of guest-service problems may be a matter of waiting too long. Management must look elsewhere and everywhere.

➤**Moments of Truth.**   Several years ago, a study was undertaken to measure the costs of poor service.[6] The amount of dollars and cents lost were calculated for each missed opportunity. Among the leading charges laid against the front office were overbooking, lost reservations, and discourtesy. Although one incident doesn't make a bankruptcy, poor service is insidious. Single episodes mushroom from minor, miscellaneous costs to staggering totals per week, per month, per year. Antiservice comes at a high cost.

Guests and staff interact more frequently in a hotel environment than in any other business setting. Hotel employees are asked to deliver an exceptional level of service over and over and over again each day. Exhibit 7–3 highlights the cumulative impact of having one's customers in residence.

With 70% occupancy and a double occupancy of 33%, employee-guest contacts number 2,800 per day. The figure soars to over 1 million per year for a hotel of only 300 rooms! The number multiplies even faster with full-service hotels, where more operating departments mean more employees. Not only are service expectations higher at the full-service property, so are the number of service contacts.

Number of rooms in the hotel		300
Percentage of occupancy		× .70
Number of rooms occupied each night	210	
Percentage of double occupancy		× .33
Number of guest-nights	280	
Moments of Truth		
Arrival	1	
Inquiry at the desk	1	
Bellperson	1	
Chambermaid	1	
Telephone operator	1	
Coffee shop host(ess)	1	
Server/busperson	2	
Cashier	1	
Newstand	1	
Total encounters per guest-night		× 10
Daily number of moments of truth		2,800

Exhibit 7–3   Moments of truth are the points at which the service provider and the service buyer meet eyeball to eyeball. Quality management makes certain that the employee will not need to blink.

Opportunities for meeting guest expectations—or failing to meet guest expectations—have been called "moments of truth."[7] It is during these encounters, when the service provider and the service buyer meet eyeball to eyeball, that the guest's perception of quality is set. Some say the first 10 minutes are the most critical.

How does the staff respond? Does the final guest of the shift receive the same attention as the first arrival? For many, only a smile and an appropriate greeting are needed. More is expected by the next guest: the one with the problem, the one with the complaint, the one with the special need. If the employee is empowered to act, to respond with alacrity, to evidence concern, it is a shining moment of truth.

Total quality management requires similar moments of truth between supervisors and staffers. Employees will not shine outwardly unless there is an inner glow. Supervisors will not get positive moments of truth if they always second-guess subordinates who have been empowered. Supervisors will not get positive moments of truth if staffers are irritated, say, by late work-schedule postings that frustrate personal plans. Good results from service encounters begins with a good working environment. Shining moments of truth come best from a total quality program.

▶*Quality Control through Inspection.*   Review and evaluation are essential parts of the management function. That's no less true in managing guest services than, say, in managing cash. Cash management requires standards and procedures to account for the control of money. Service management, too, has standards and procedures for maintaining quality. Quality control (QC) enables hotel companies to maintain even standards throughout all the properties of a far-flung chain. Guests rely on these standards, identifying them through corporate logos. To ensure the consistency promised by the logos, chains use inspectors to make on-site visits and evaluations.

Quality control has become more commonplace, therefore, as the size of individual properties grows and the range of franchising spreads.

Some chains have their own inspectors; others hire outside firms. Visits from the home company are both announced and unannounced. External inspectors usually come anonymously. Although there for a different purpose, inspectors from AAA, Mobile Travel Guide, and others are also on the road. In most cases, the inspectors provide a verbal report to the unit manager before filing the formal, written document with central headquarters. Tit for tat, managers may also file reports on inspectors. Generally, standards are enforced more stringently in company-owned or company-managed hotels than in franchised properties.

Each chain has its own policies. Hilton aims for three inspections per year. Choice Hotels International sets a minimum of two visits; Super 8 Motels, four visits per property per year. Franchise contracts also differ, allowing the franchisee a range of 30 to 180 days in which to remedy serious defaults before the franchise is canceled. Radisson culls from the bottom up, using several criteria, including the comment cards that will be discussed soon. Differences among the chains account for the variations in procedure. For example, about 90% of Radisson's hotels are franchised, compared to, say, the 75% or so of Hilton's.

Quality control has many parts. One is an inspection of the physical facility. This involves a wide range of issues, from the maintenance of the grounds, to the quality of the furniture and equipment, to the cleanliness of the property. Are there holes in the carpets, burns in the bedspreads, paper in the stairwells? Check sheets used by the inspectors deal with a variety of details: working blow driers, cleanliness of air vents, number of hangers in the closet, and even the rotation of mattresses (see Exhibit 7–4).

Food is tasted and drinks are sampled in all the food and beverage outlets, including room service. Large properties require several days for a full visit. Mystery shoppers, as inspectors are sometimes called, also check employee sales techniques. Does the room clerk sell up? Does the bellperson promote the facility? Does the telephone operator know the hours of the cabaret?

Security is another QC point. Both guest security (keys, locks, chains, and peepholes)[8] and internal security (staff pilferage from the hotel and theft from guests) come under scrutiny during the visit. Do bartenders ring up every sale? Does cash paid to room service waiters reach the bank deposit? Security shopping is designed to uncover dishonesty and criminal acts. That's far different from the intent of the typical inspection visit and may even require special state licensing.

Mystery shoppers are not police. Neither are they consultants or critics. They are reporters of the scene. Evaluating service and employee attitude and testing the staff's mettle during moments of truth are the purposes of quality inspections. Quality is maintained when management acts on the QC reports, using them to reinforce good habits. Training, not punishment, follows when reports are negative. When that really is the intent of the practice, the staff learns about the mystery shoppers in advance, and the inspectors' evaluation sheets are made available to all. How else will the standards that management hopes to establish be known?

Quality Guarantees

Quality guarantees (QGs) are simply assurances that the hotel will deliver on its promise of quality service, or else. . . . With QGs, the company puts its money where its advertising mouth is. Guaranteeing a satisfactory level of product and service takes gumption. It contradicts the not-my-fault phenomenon currently evident across the

INSPECTION REPORT

Auditor _____   Hotel _____

Identification no. _____   City _____

                                        Date(s) _____

	Excellent	Good	Fair	Poor	Comments
Registration					
1. Waiting time		×			About 2 minutes
2. Greeting	×				Used my name in conversation
3. Friendliness		×			
4. Efficiency			×		PMS was slow
5. Staff on hand	×				Other clerks handled telephone
6. Grooming		×			Except for Grace's hair
7. Accuracy	×				
Rooming					
1. Bellperson offered				×	No, had to call housekeeping
2. Elevator wait	×				3:00 PM
3. Floor signage	×				
4. First impression			×		Not too clean; stale odor
Guest Room					
1. Hangers	×				
2. Paper products			×		Facial tissue box nearly empty
3. Sanitation			×		Shower curtains need attention
4. Desk	×				
5. Telephone and book	×				Displayed card with fees listed
6. Bed and linens		×			
7. Lighting				×	Bulb burned out, standing lamp
Services					
1. Call housekeeping		×			Delay in acquiring extra pillow
2. Send fax to self	×				Prompt, no charge to receive
3. Get maid to let in				×	Took $3 tip and let me in
4. Ask for second key		×			Clerk remembered me, or said so
5. Ask for toilet repair			×		38-minute delay

Exhibit 7–4   Secret shoppers making quality-control inspections uncover operating weaknesses that management and staff must attend to.

United States. Service guarantees take responsibility for everything that happens. QGs announce unequivocally to customers and employees alike that management is confident enough to stand behind its advertising. It is a courageous stand and a sign of management's confidence in the programs it has implemented. Sure, it backfires at times.

QGs are not like discounted rates, used and discarded as occupancy declines and recovers. Quality guarantees become part of the operating philosophy of the business:

They are the very essence of the operation. Such a potent tool must be introduced carefully as the ultimate result of an ongoing and succes l program of quality management. Guarantees fail miserably when they evolve fi ɔ i an advertising need rather than an operational plan.

Several years ago, a well-known hotel chain jumped on the QG bandwagon with a promise of "complete satisfaction." No modifiers or limiting exceptions—just complete satisfaction guaranteed. An incident arose when a guest relying on that policy stopped at one of the properties. There was no hot water for a shower on the morning of departure. Citing the well-advertised guarantee, the guest asked for a free room or an allowance against the standard charge. The member property declined, explaining that the malfunctioning boiler was beyond its control. So much for a guarantee of complete satisfaction.

QGs need to be narrowly defined at first. Once a standard is established, the guarantee can be aimed at a target and delivered accordingly. Implementing guarantees in stages, by specific expectations within certain departments as capabilities come on line, announces to guests and staff that service quality is in place. Marriott, for example, guarantees to deliver room-service breakfast within 30 minutes. Failure to do so means a free breakfast. Wrapped up in this simple promise is an advertisement, a departmental promotion, an employee empowerment, an assurance of quality, and a willingness to be measured.

Other hotel companies offer different guarantees—the no-overbooking policy of Westin's, for example. Each Westin hotel keeps open enough empty rooms to ensure the property's compliance. Strict enforcement minimizes cash restitutions because guests are almost never walked. Obviously, there is still the cost of empty rooms that might have been rented. From a practical side, however, the guarantee is inexpensive to deliver. Hotels do not reach full occupancy very often. When they do, careful counting can almost always accommodate every reservation. Only on a few occasions will rooms be left vacant in order to meet the guarantee.

Quality guarantees are a two-edged sword. Failing to pay off after announcing a guarantee alienates guests far more than the incident itself. Guarantees must be unambiguous, limited in scope, and focused on specific objectives that are easily understood. With such guarantees, a failure to deliver is evident to all. There is no quibbling about payment, which—when made promptly—leads to guest loyalty and positive word-of-mouth advertising.

Nothing highlights operational weaknesses more than having to pay off guarantees that arise from legitimate complaints.

▶*Americans with Disabilities Act.* The Americans with Disabilities Act (ADA) is a quality standard of a special nature. It was enacted into law in 1990 and became effective in 1992. The ADA provides for changes in physical structures and hiring practices to accommodate the disabled, be they guests or employees. The ADA applies to all industries, including lodging, which is covered by Title III of the act. Certain levels of quality service are guaranteed by law to some 43 million disabled Americans. Unlike the guarantees of hotel companies, the law levies stringent penalties, under civil-rights legislation, for failure to comply.

Actual enforcement with fines and penalties didn't take place for several years. The further away from the law's effective date, the greater has become the Justice Department's expectations for compliance. What previously had been resolved informally is now finding its way to the desks of many assistant U.S. attorneys. In part, the change in emphasis follows the boom in hotel construction. New facilities must be in compliance, and the law holds responsible both landlords and tenants. There have even been some efforts to add franchisors to the list. Savvy hoteliers have minimized penalties by working with private groups (for example, the Society for the Advancement of Travel for the Handicapped) to identify and correct barriers, by increasing training sessions for staff and management, and by keeping records of actions taken to comply.

The federal government's ADA and the lodging industry's QM converge on the same two subjects: Both treat guest and employee issues. The one legislates changes and the other implements them as a matter of good business. Hotel companies hired handicapped employees long before the law was enacted, although less was done to accommodate disabled guests. Radisson was an early employer of the disabled, and so was the Ritz-Carlton Company. Holiday Inn, especially its Worldwide Reservation Center, was still another. Companies like these now include ADA awareness and training as part of their quality assurance efforts. Embassy Suites calls the ADA segment of its QM program "Commandments of Disability Etiquette."

All departments of the hotel, including the rooms division, are affected by the legislation. Each responds with a different solution. Housekeepers learn to leave guest's personal belongings exactly in place. Cashiers count cash aloud, announcing which denominations are being returned. Folios and registration cards are enlarged to further help the visually handicapped. Similar alterations in procedures and space accommodate handicapped workers. Equipment might be modified or even totally replaced. Enhanced lighting, power to recharge wheelchair batteries, or other alterations are sometimes warranted. Hiring practices and other personnel procedures are often more difficult to change than the equipment or work area. Included in these special human resources needs are revised approaches to hiring, testing, job structures, position descriptions, and more.

Physical Accommodations.   Federal and state ADA laws have been confusing, frustrating, incomplete, and contradictory. It wasn't until 1997, for example, seven years after federal passage, that the rules of California and the federal government were finally reconciled. The language of the ADA is very open ended. Rules and their interpretations were to come later. For the physical plant, terms such as *undue hardship* were and still are subject to interpretation. Employers had to translate an equally ambiguous word, *disability*. Innumerable and frivolous lawsuits continue to hammer out the meaning of such terms as *reasonable expectations* one court case at a time.

Early efforts concentrated on the physical barriers because they were easy to measure and confirm. ADA regulations define them in unequivocal mathematical terms. The number of handicapped parking spaces is one evident result of the regulations. Everyone understands measurements, understands the meaning of an inch. Door thresholds must be less than 0.5 inches, roll-in showers a minimum of 36 by 60 inches, stalls in public rest rooms no less than 42 by 48 inches, drinking fountains no higher than 36 inches from the floor. Exhibit 7–5 lists a sample of the accommodations that lodging operators must make to comply with the Americans with Disabilities Act.

Guest bathrooms remain high on the unsatisfactory list. Redoing baths is an expensive proposition, so hotels prefer waiting until that need is evident before making wholesale changes. Exhibit 7–6 provides a summary of bathroom changes being implemented throughout the industry. Hotels built after 1992 are required to have 5% of the rooms for the physically impaired, 5% for the vision impaired, and 5% for the hearing impaired.

Communications

Telephones for the hearing impaired

Public telephones at proper height

Telecommunication devices for the deaf (TDDs)

Guest-room telephones

Visual alert to a ringing telephone

Easy dialing for those with reduced muscle control

Large telephone buttons or replacement pad

Voice-digital phone dialing

Safety Equipment

Visual alert to smoke detectors

Visual alert to door knocks, bells, and sirens

Visual or vibrating alarm clocks

Low viewports on doors

Low location of room locks

Lighted strips on stairwells

Contrasting color on glass doors and handrails

Dual handrails on ramps

Automatic door openers

Slower times on elevator door closures

Access

Handicapped parking spaces

Ramp access to and within the building

Minimum thresholds

Adequate door access

Levered hardware, or adapters

Bathroom access (see Exhibit 7–6)

Lowered drinking fountains with accessible controls

Closed-caption decoders for TV and VCR

Assisted listening systems for meetings

Mattresses on frames rather than pedestal beds

Lower light switches and thermostats

Two-level reception desks

Curb cuts in sidewalks

Replacing high-pile carpeting

Accommodating seeing eye and hearing ear animals

Closet rods and drapery controls accessible

Extension cords for recharging wheelchairs

Lifts: elevators, vertical and incline platforms

Portable devices when facilities are not permanent

Eggcrate cushions for arthritics

Graphics

Size, color, and illumination

Braille and raised lettering in elevators

Braille and raised lettering behind guest-room doors

Recessed or projected graphics where appropriate

Verbal recitation of bill denominations when making change

Exhibit 7–5   The Americans with Disabilities Act established a range of specifications to improve accessibility for disabled guests and staff. (For a reference, see the *American with Disabilities Act Accessibility Guidelines, ADAAG.*)

Innkeepers were not pleased with the passage of the ADA. Much of what they feared has come true. Meeting architectural standards has been costly despite assurances from the bill's supporters that they wouldn't be. Governmental intervention got another beachhead in industry, and a nest full of scam artists have hatched many punitive lawsuits. As with the Occupation, Safety and Health Act (OSHA), the ramifi-

Building roll-in showers with folding seats
Replacing faucet knobs with lever hardware
Installing grab bars in tub and toilet areas
Elevating sinks to accommodate wheelchairs
Insulating pipes on the underside of the sinks
Raising toilet seats
Lowering towel bars
Enlarging bathrooms to provide turnaround space
Providing transfer seats at the tub
Designing clearance space to get through the door
Lowering mirrors
Including hand-held showers with adjustable height bars

Exhibit 7–6   Alterations to and new construction of bathrooms require changes from previous standards to meet the minimum accommodations established by the Americans with Disabilities Act, which became effective in 1992.

cations of ADA's passage will not be known for years, not until the regulations and their legal interpretations work their way through the bureaucracy of federal and state governments and the delay of the courts. Improved treatment for handicapped employees has been the plus side of ADA. Unfortunately, no significant increase in travel among the handicapped is evident as yet.

Signage.   The ADA brought renewed attention to signs. Lack of signage or just plain poor signage are irritants for all visitors, not only the handicapped. By requiring compliance for braille and raised lettering as well as a host of other requirements, the law helped focus the entire issue of good signage. The American Automobile Association has joined in with its own signage requirements as part of its rating system, but theirs does not include handicapped accommodations for meeting or recreational facilities.

Signage for the visually handicapped must be provided inside and outside elevators, on guest-room keys when requested, and on the outside of handicapped rooms. Audible elevator signals (once for up; twice for down) supplement the traditional Braille or raised numbers. Some properties are testing audio signs that are broadcast from small transmitters to the handicapped guest's receiver. The audio signal tells guests where they are and how to proceed to a room or to the elevators.

Guests who are handicapped by other than sight rely on signs for different reasons. The wheelchair symbol used by tourbooks indicates special parking; wheelchair accessibility to the lobby, the desk, at least one food-and-beverage outlet, and of course, to and in the guest room.

Good signs and directions are not special to handicapped guests. Managers must "walk" their properties, get out from their offices, and note—not just see—what guests encounter as they enter and proceed through the property as strangers. Are there fire-exit signs? If the exits are alarmed, a sign should say so. Are no-smoking rooms and floors marked? Is the entire ambiance of the hotel destroyed by a bunch of supplemental handwritten signs? Can one actually find a guest room following the posted directions? Are some rooms named rather than numbered? Are all the bulbs in electric signs functioning? Exterior signs on the building are often forgotten and lack maintenance and repair.

The alert manager should question the staff at the desk, in uniform, or on the guest floors about the location of certain sites. Employees who have no reason to be in particular areas of the hotel are often unable to direct guests to a banquet facility, the swimming pool, the spa, or the guest laundry.

Every cloud has a silver lining, and ADA's requirements have focused attention on signs as part of the overall picture of guest service.

Complaints

Complaints are another tool for directing management's attention to troubled service areas. Unfortunately, too few guests actually complain. Most merely mumble quietly, never to return. That's why those complaints that are registered must be resolved quickly and corrected for the future. Measuring customer unhappiness is like trying to compute the costs behind the moments of truth. Neither offers any mathematical accuracy, but both make many believable points.

Putting dollar values to the cost of complaints requires some assumptions. These assumptions have never been proven, but they are quoted frequently nevertheless. It is said, for example, that 10% of guests would not return to the property of their most recent stay. Using the same values as in Exhibit 7–3, a hotel would lose 21 guest-nights each day (300 rooms at 70% occupancy times the 10% loss). That totals a whopping 7,665 guest-nights per year for a 300-room hotel. Based on an assumed average daily rate of, say, $65, the failure to resolve complaints in this example would be nearly $500,000 per year (7,665 guest nights at $65). The figure stretches into the stratosphere of nearly $5 million when 3,000-room hotels such as those of Exhibit 1–6 are involved.

Some argue, moreover, that labor-intensive industries such as lodging increase productivity only by improving service encounters. The failure to do so represents additional labor costs as well as costs from lost business. Here, too, there is not much empirical evidence to support the hypothesis.

Every complaint has an impact on the bottom line, but not every complaint takes dollars to resolve. One major investigation reported just the opposite: Only one-third of all written complaints involved a financial issue. Money is more often at stake with face-to-face encounters. Exhibit 7–7 offers another tidbit: Better to spend a bit to hold that guest than to invest five times the amount soliciting a new customer.

➤ *Still Another Calculation.*   Still another calculation is shown in Exhibit 7–7. Like the others, it begins with a bunch of widely quoted but vaguely grounded assumptions. Still, the conclusions are startling.

> *Premise 1:* 68% of nonreturning guests stay away because of indifferent service. (Deaths, relocations, competition, and poor products account for the other 32%.)
>
> *Premise 2:* 5% or less of dissatisfied guests actually voice their unhappiness. There is an iceberg effect here. Below the surface floats the vast bulk of complaints, never voiced and never resolved. Of this silent majority, it is said that well over half will not patronize the hotel again. Worse yet, they will tell 10 to 11 others not to do so; some tell as many as 20 others. This fact is so irrefutable in the view of many that a "rule" has been created, the 1–11–5 rule. One unhappy guest will tell 11 others, and each of the 11 will tell 5 more.

Loss of Guests

68% of nonreturning guests quit because of indifferent service.

32% is lost to death, relocation, competition, and poor products.

Complaints

Less than 5% of dissatisfied guests speak out—so for every one that does there may be twenty who do not.

Over half of the silent majority refuse to return—an iceberg floating beneath the surface.

Noncomplaining guests do complain to friends and acquaintances.

10 to 11 others will hear of the mishap.

13% of the group will gripe to 20 others.

Two-thirds of the iceberg could be won over if they were identified—about half of these could become boosters.

Costs

It costs over $10 to write a complaint letter (including the cost of writing time, follow-up time, and postage).

It costs five times more to get a new customer than to keep an existing one.

Exhibit 7–7 Widely quoted, but rarely referenced, figures emphasize the importance of a proactive stance in handling complaints.

Premise 3: About two-thirds of the icebergs can be warmed and won over by resolving the complaint. About one-third of complainers can be converted from blasters to boosters if their complaints are handled quickly and properly. Implicit here is the guest's willingness to speak up. Guests will when they are very angry or when management creates an environment that encourages guests to register complaints.

➤ *Preventing the Complaint.*   Identifying the reluctant complainer is a challenge. It will not be met by asking departing guests the rote question, "How was everything?" Desk personnel and managers from all operational and organizational levels must ask direct and specific questions. That means talking to guests, whether in the lobby, by the pool, or elsewhere. The dialogue may start with pleasantries: an introduction, a comment on the weather, an inquiry about the frequency of the guest's visits. But then the conversation must elicit the negatives, if there are any. "Did you use room service?" opens a chain of related questions. "How was the bed?" directs the conversation in a different direction. "Can you tell me about any especially pleasant (or unpleasant) experiences you have had here?"

Issues that flow from these solicitations are not complaints in the truest sense, but they give management direction for improving service and preempting complaints from someone else later on. More important, they bring out the guest's concerns and give the hotel the opportunity to redirect the dynamics and make friends. Many of the issues raised require no immediate actions, no costs, no allowances. They form the base for operational changes and they build the relationships that promote returning guests, especially if the questioner follows the brief interview with a letter of thanks to the candid guest.

Management must be knowledgeable if it hopes to prevent complaints. Executives who don aprons and get to ground zero by working in different departments, say once a month, do more than create public-relations photo-ops. They learn, for example, that the location of the dishmachine is the cause for high breakage, that the housekeepers' vacuums really don't work, or that customer service warrants the front-desk purchase of umbrellas for guest use.

Early Warning.   Complaints can be forestalled if the staff is honest with the guest and tells it like it is. Alerting guests to bad situations allows them to decide whether or not to participate. So the reservation department explains that the pool is closed for repairs during the dates under consideration. A request for connecting rooms is impossible to promise, so the request is noted but no guarantee is made by the reservationist. And that is so stated, not just implied.

Similarly, sales executives must warn small groups about other large parties in the house during the anticipated booking period. Room service reports elevator problems and thus some delay before the order will be delivered. Room clerks offer special rates in a certain wing because ongoing renovations there are noisy at times and create extra dust.

Complaint management acknowledges how the "squeaky wheel" gets the best results. Attending promptly to the squeak may mean better service for all. Observant guests often side with the hotel when an obnoxious squeaker rolls up the desk. They will cede their priority in line to get the pest out of the way. Similarly, handling families with tired or irritable children outside the sequence actually improves service for others.

Preventing the complaint by anticipating the problem and providing unsolicited accurate information is far preferable to assuaging angry guests after the fact. Explaining the circumstances makes guests feel better about the situation and forestalls their complaints. "The maid will not get to the room before luncheon, so we can accommodate your early arrival but not before 1 o'clock."

If a policy of candor works wonders in reducing complaints, the opposite is also true. Misleading information, either directly or by implication and omission, enrages guests who feel they have been cheated—as they have.

Comment Cards.   An ongoing debate continues about the effectiveness of guest comment cards. But the battle to improve guest service needs every weapon that can be mustered. Comment cards are just another device for getting guest input. Like other information-gathering techniques, they have advantages and disadvantages. Innovative approaches to this old standby strengthen the instrument and improve its quality. The better the questionnaire, the more information available for managing guest services.

Hoteliers complain that guests use questionnaires to gripe. Guests do not balance the good and the bad, hoteliers protest, but concentrate their comments on operating weaknesses. Actually, that's good. Uncovering and remedying shortcomings is what QM programs are all about. As noted earlier, too few guests ever bring their concerns to the hotel's attention. Guest comment cards help overcome the iceberg effect, the reluctance of the complainer to complain. Management's grumbling about the disproportion of positive and negatives probably has its origin in their personal promotion and bonus decisions, which often include comment-card data.

Critics attack the validity of comment cards on the basis of very low response rates, typically 1 to 2% of the guest population. Long, detailed questionnaires account for some of the low numbers. Guests just won't take time to answer. Small cards with a narrow focus, one that changes periodically, improve the overall response rate. It might be done in one of two ways. Short, themed questionnaires about a single concern, cleanliness or courtesy for example, could be distributed throughout the entire hotel. Separate, specialized forms for use within each department is another means of shortening and focusing the inquiry.

Just asking guests to participate increases the number of returns. Some of the best results come during the check-out procedure, when response rates improve tenfold. Locating touch-screen terminals in the lobby near the cashier solicits direct responses from departing guests. Even here, though, the number of questions and the speed with which the guest can respond is critical to success. Marriott's Fairfield Inns call their exit survey the Score Card System. Strategic placement of the equipment encourages adult use and dissuades random input from children, another criticism that is occasionally voiced.

Participation rates increase when guests have an incentive for completing the cards. The rate of return goes up with every dessert coupon the desk issues. (It also gets guests into the coffee shop.) Similarly, room upgrades for the next visit combine incentives with room promotions. Immediate upgrades are given when the solicitation is made during registration.

Awarding elaborate prizes from a drawing of comment-card participants is another incentive for guests to complete them. It also flags the importance that the property attributes to quality assurance. Moreover, contest information enables the hotel to match guest names with comments. That isn't always possible otherwise because some guests prefer anonymity.

Modern communications have taken questionnaires to another level. Hotel companies have followed other industries by providing and advertising toll-free telephone numbers for disaffected consumers. The additional costs of doing this are balanced by the additional demographic data obtained. Besides, immediate attention to consumer complaints builds enormous goodwill quickly. Provided, that is, that the call is answered by an actual person, who has the ability to resolve the issue and the personality to make friends of the caller. Like so much of the QM concept, it is easier to create the system than it is to implement it effectively.

Every comment card or telephone call should receive an immediate and personal response from someone with authority to act. Guests then know that they are getting the highest level of attention. Telephone calls suggest a sense of urgency and often elicit further details of the incident. Carefully done, very carefully done, a letter supposedly originating with the employee involved may produce exceptional results. Far too often the hotel's response is a bland, standardized letter or a generic apology that fails to address the issues raised by the guest.

Comment cards and telephone calls, including courtesy calls by the hotel following a guest's stay, help uncover unexpected problems. Complaints can be forestalled once management has the facts. Getting the information may require active solicitation: a personal request to fill out the questionnaire. It may take a bonus such as a free in-room movie or a glass of wine with dinner. Better results may depend on nothing more than smaller questionnaires that can be answered with a check mark. Guests who prefer to do so can write additional comments.

However done, management gathers the information and analyzes it for trends in operating weaknesses and strengths. A good system does more than establish customer goodwill. It helps measure service and identifies functions that are working well or poorly. Checking off complaints over a given period on a simple spreadsheet highlights those areas that appear over and over again on the comment cards. Different information is treated differently. Management cannot always act immediately. This must be explained to staff members who sit in quality circles working to improve the hotel's QM efforts. Sometimes the issue is operational and action can be taken immediately, adding an emergency telephone to the exercise room, for example. Other information is more strategic and involves serious budget concerns, building additional elevators, for example.

After going to great lengths to obtain information, management must assure its accuracy. Using input from comment cards for employee service awards encourages employees and their friends to complete the forms or to tell guests what to write. At other times, the forms are shortstopped somewhere. Housekeeping throws away those that are left in the rooms. Room clerks pocket those that reflect poorly, and unit managers withhold those that sound too negative. Providing postage-paid cards with the chief executive's address prevents incorrect handling and emphasizes the questionnaire's importance to the company.

Quality Circles.   Quality circles, or quality teams, are still another method of getting information. Circles are small groups of employees who meet regularly as quasi-permanent teams to identify issues in delivering quality service. The terminology differs, but guests are occasionally added to the teams, especially at resorts. If the circle catches problems before complaints are registered, QM is working perfectly. Sometimes the remedies come after the fact, arising from management's referral of a series of complaints.

Quality circles in the service industry are very much like those in manufacturing. Small, continuous improvements—creative changes—are the goals. Spectacular breakthroughs or innovations are not customarily part of the circle's design. Consequently, the group's composition is taken from all levels and across departmental lines. Delays in room service at breakfast, for example, may prove to be housekeeping's fault— moving linen between floors ties up the elevators just when room service demand is highest!

Total quality management requires each employee to service other departments as if they were guests. A cross-departmental team, therefore, has members who are internal customers of one another. Teams may function in several capacities, or different teams may be organized for specific, corrective action. In addition, there are focus groups (short-term, one-issue teams) and ongoing self-managing units.

American culture emphasizes the individual and not the group. Circles have been very successful in some hotel environments and have flopped terribly in others. Like comment cards or lobby interviews or toll-free calls, the circle serves as another piece in the quality mosaic. It is both a source of information on which to act and a means of finding the solution with which to act.

▶ *Handling the Complaint.*   Quality assurance aims for error-free service, but that is a goal more than a fact. Experience keeps a tight rein on reality, making complaint-free environments desirable but very unlikely. Only the number, timing, or place of the complaint is uncertain, not whether one will occur. As QM programs reduce the number, the remaining complaints gain in importance. Besides, not all complaints are subject to quality management solutions. Systems, procedures, and training aside, the unexpected will always happen. Door attendants do lose car keys.

Preparing for Complaints.   Preparing for complaints begins by acknowledging their likelihood. Training programs must first emphasize the probability of a complaint. Employees with a proper mindset, those not caught unaware, recognize the importance of attitude in receiving and resolving complaints. Proper preparation minimizes the impact and cost of the complaint. Preparing properly means making the best of the worst. Readying employees to receive and resolve complaints has become an integral part of quality management programs.

Although the specifics differ, complaints follow a theme in each department. This gives quality circles an effective role in training. Within the circle, members share their individual experiences and solutions, and the group adopts the best ideas as departmental standards. Employee empowerment, the authority to accept responsibility and to remedy the situation, is implicit.

For front-desk employees, common themes spring from specific encounters. What is the proper response to a departing guest who protests a folio (guest bill) charge? What should be done with an irate arrival whose reservation has been sold to another? What accommodations can be made if the guest tenders a travel agent's coupon that is not acceptable to the hotel? Common situations all, playing themselves out time and again in a fixed pattern if not an exact duplication. None are rare, unexpected encounters. A series of options must be readied and employed as needed (see Exhibit 7–8).

Directing employees to kick the problem upward is an option required by certain circumstances. Even empowerment programs limit employee authority to certain decision levels. Preparing employees for the complaint must include information about when and why and to whom to refer the matter. Rarely do the sessions train for the next (frequently necessary) step: What is to be done when the next level of authority is not available? Leave the fuming guest to wait . . . and wait . . . and wait?

Complaints may arise because the spread between guest expectations and service delivery widens dramatically after arrival. But complaints are not always of the hotel's doing. Hotel staff may just be the most convenient recipient of the guest's bad day. Tired and grumpy travelers, those who have done battle with family members or business associates, who have fought against canceled flights and lost luggage, may find the hotel employee—especially an inexperienced one who dithers and dathers—an ideal outlet for a week of frustrations. Preparing for the complaint means understanding this.

Preparing for the complaint means putting up with drunks and being tolerant of the show-off and the braggart performing for the group. Preparing for the complaint allows one to overlook exaggerations, sarcasm, and irony. Preparing for the complaint recognizes that senior persons sometimes berate younger staff in a replay of the parent–child relationship. Preparing for the complaint means understanding that some persons can never be satisfied whatever the staff may try.

Responding to Complaints.   No complaint is trivial in the eyes of the guest. What the hotel's representative perceives as trivial often originates from a series of small, unattended-to issues that smoulder until management's casual attitude fans the fire of dissatisfaction. Suddenly, the trivial explodes into a major configuration.

By Listening.   To bring about change, the complaint must be received and understood. Complaints are communicated only if the complainer speaks and the listener listens. It is not enough for the complaint-taker to hear passively; he or she must listen actively. Careful listening is fundamental to resolving every complaint. Full attention to the speaker moves the problem toward prompt resolution even before the explanation is complete. Experienced complaint-handlers never allow other employees, guests, or telephone calls to distract them from hearing out the complainant.

Hotel Anywhere, U.S.A.
Internal Memorandum

To:	Guest-Service Agents
From:	Holly Wood, Rooms Manager
Subject:	Empowerment Guidelines
Date:	January 1, 20--

Effective this date, all guest-service agents who have completed the four training hours have authority to make the following adjustments using their own discretion. Managers and supervisors are always available for consultation.

An Apology is the First Response! Apologies are free; we give away as many as necessary, but be sincere and listen carefully.

Where appropriate, verify information before acting

Issue	Intermediate Response	Maximum Response
Noisy room	Relocate, if stayover	Upgrade now or next visit, gift to the room
Incorrect rate	Correct the paperwork	Allowance for the difference, ticket to club or spa
Engineering problems: Heat and AC, TV, plumbing	Send engineer, change rooms	Upgrade, up to 25% off rate
Protest charges: Telephone	Allowance for local	Allowance for long distance
In-room film	Allowance	One per day
Valet parking	Allowance	Full amount

Exhibit 7–8 Managers and staff must prepare for the inevitable complaint by establishing guidelines that help empowered employees make the right decision for the circumstances.

Complainers do not always begin with the real issue—which is true, of course, with many conversations. Questions are appropriate provided that they are not judgmental, but interrupting unnecessarily angers the speaker and pushes the conversation to another level of frustration before all the facts are in hand.

Listening requires good eye contact and subtle supportive body movements. Appropriate nodding, tsh-tshing, mouth expressions, and hand movements encourage the speaker and convey attention, sympathy, and understanding. It is important to remain in contact with the speaker and empathetic toward his or her experience throughout the recitation.

Small mishaps end in court cases when the listener makes short shrift of the incident and of the person voicing the grievance. Lawsuits are the invariable results of leaving the resolution of small accidents entirely to the security staff. Aggrieved guests want management's attention and evidence of its concern. They want a sympathetic listener to hear them out.

Guests do not like being rushed along; they want the whole story to come out. The listener must be sensitive to his or her own body language, careful that negative signals are not halting the complainer or dropping a cold blanket over the encounter. Watching for the guest's nonverbal signals helps interpret the guest's readings of one's own signals.

IN A PROPER VENUE.   Complainers who grow hostile or overly upset, loud, or abusive must be removed from the lobby. Shifting to a new venue should be done as quickly as possible. Don't wait for the issue to intensify or the time committed to the situation to outgrow the lobby discussion. Perhaps the pretense can be that of comfort: Let's sit down in the office; we'll be more comfortable there, and there will be no interruptions.

Walking to the new location offers a cooling-off period. It provides an opportunity to shift the topic and to speak in more conversational tones. Walking changes the aggressive or defensive postures that one or the other might have assumed in the lobby. The office location adds to the manager's authority and prestige.

The louder the guest growls, the softer should come the response, which usually brings an immediate reaction: Loud complainers quiet down to hear replies that are given in near whispers. A harsh answer to abuse or to offensive language only elevates the complaint to a battle of personalities. Above all, the hotel wants the guest to retain dignity. Divorcing the interaction from personalities helps do that. The facts are at issue, not the persons; certainly not the employee, who may be the original target of the guest's ire.

Ultimately, the manager may refuse to discuss the issues further unless the guest modulates language and tone. The hotelier tells the complainer that he or she is being addressed politely and the listener expects the same courtesy. In a worst-case scenario, say with a drunk or drug-crazed guest, the hotel may need to call the police.

BY MAKING A RECORD.   Asking permission to record the complaint by taking notes indicates how seriously management views the matter. It also allows the guest to restate the issue and have it recorded with accuracy, at least from the guest's point of view. The hotel's representative gets an additional opportunity to express concern and sympathy as the issues are restated aloud. It also slows the conversation, helping to cool emotions. Contributing to the written report makes the complaining guest sense that already something is being done. Thus, the stage is set for resolving the problem.

Front offices maintain permanent journals of the day's activities, including complaints. These logs improve communications with later shifts since the issues often carry over. The documentation helps the participants recall the incident later, provides a basis for training, and supports legal proceedings if the matter goes that far. Serious accidents are documented again by security and by the hospital or the police, depending on circumstances.

The recordkeeping goes further. Getting the guest's folio, registration card, or reservation data helps the manager understand what happened. Calling an employee into the office or on the telephone in the guest's presence broadens the investigation, clarifies the facts, and mollifies the complainer. Employees should get as much courtesy as the guest. Training or discipline, if appropriate, is done elsewhere in private. Both the staff member and the guest should be addressed with civility, certainly using surnames and appropriate titles: Mr., Mrs., Dr., Ms.

WITH A SETTLEMENT.   Once registered, the complaint must be settled: resolved somehow and closed. The complainant expects some satisfaction or real restitution for the embarrassment. The hotel wants to keep the customer, strengthen the relationship, if possible, and send the guest forth as a booster who tells the world how fairly he or she was treated. Still, the hotel doesn't want to give away the house atoning for mistakes that caused no harm and little damage.

Apologies are free—we can give away as many as needed; and indeed, only an apology may be needed. Apologies are in order even if the complaint seems baseless or unreasonable. The effectiveness of the apology depends on the guest's reading of the manager. And that reading often reflects the importance of and the guest's involvement in the delivery of the service. A transient family views situations differently than a family celebrating an important anniversary. A business traveler's anger increases directly with the importance of the message that wasn't delivered.

Does the unhappy guest see the hotelier as truly contrite or merely mouthing niceties as a means of getting a quick solution? There are different ways of apologizing, but none are effective unless they ring true. The standard, "I am sorry, and I apologize on behalf of the hotel," goes a long way toward settling minor issues quickly and satisfactorily. "I am sorry" can take on different nuances with different levels of emphasis—"I *am* sorry"—additional words—"I am *so* sorry"—or deleted words—"I'm sorry."

Guests listen for subtle connotations in words and voice. Voices can be shaped and honed through practice to carry just the right intonations and emphases. Concern, belief, and self-disparagement can be communicated irrespective of the words. Other standbys, although often repeated, have a proper place in the list of apologies: "I know how you must feel"; "Yes, that is distressing"; and "I would have done the same."

Although it is not necessary to fix blame for the incident—and doing so may be counterproductive—the hotel's staff clearly may be at fault. When pertinent, admitting as much helps to set the tone, as long as the admission doesn't include minimizing the incident or offering lame excuses. Use a simple statement about "our" mistake.

Managers who want to go beyond the apology send gifts to the room. The traditional fruit basket, or a tray with wine and cheese, or even a box of amenities serve this function. Apologies appear on the card once again.

Complaints that are settled with apologies are the least expensive kind and often prove to be the most satisfying for both sides. Subsequent telephone calls or letters reinforce the apologies that were expressed during the face-to-face encounters.

After hearing out the guest, quieting down the situation, and offering appropriate sympathy, the hotel manager must provide restitution and lay the issue to rest. The quicker the problem can be resolved, the better. That is what happens with most complaints. But serious items are not settled that easily. Smashed fenders, dentures broken on a bone, or snagged designer's dresses are not remedied on the spot. Insurance companies, or law firms in more serious instances (a fall in the tub), work their wares slowly. Nevertheless, sympathy, concern, and prompt, on-the-spot action reduce the longer-run consequences and costs.

More concrete solutions are needed when apologies are not enough. A list of options should be identified for the hotel's representative as part of the preparation process (see Exhibit 7–8). Heading the list are items that cost the hotel little or nothing, as would an upgrade. Even here, there are degrees: Should we upgrade to another level? To the concierge floor? To an expensive suite? The upgrade is offered for this visit or for another. If for another, the manager's card with a direct number—"call me personally and I'll arrange it"—reinforces the special nature of the solution. Some managers preface every offer by hinting that the arrangements are special. By implication, deviating from standard procedure recognizes the guest's importance and the hotel's desire to make things right.

Annoying but inconsequential incidents can be handled with small gifts. Tickets to an event that is being held by the hotel are welcome. Athletic contests (tennis tourneys), presentations (distinguished speakers), theater-style entertainment, and the like are almost without cost if seats are plentiful.

Admission to the hotel's club or spa, tickets to local activities such as theme parks or boat rides, or transportation to the airport in the hotel's limousine are other options. Cash refunds are the last choice, but they may be the only appropriate response. Damage to property requires reimbursement, and extraordinary circumstances necessitate an allowance against folio charges.

Usually, the situation is less serious. The guest has twice before reported an inoperative television set. Or, the guest's request to change rooms has been ignored. Or, the long delay in getting a personal check cleared for cashing is irritating and embarrassing. Complaints of this type need fast and certain action. Once the solution is resolved, a wise manager explains what is to be done and how long it will take. Better to overestimate the time—then a more rapid turnaround will impress the guest with the hotel's sincerity.

By Asking the Guest.   Guest demands soften if the episode is handled well and if the guest feels that the treatment is fair. To get that kind of response, the hotelier needs to get into the guest's head, to view the situation from the other side. If the interview appears to be moving favorably, the guest can be brought into the decision loop. Carefully, the hotel's agent elicits the guest's expectations, which often are less than the hotel's, and draws the guest into formulating the remedy. The complainer becomes part of the solution, and the process gains momentum toward a quick and satisfactory conclusion.

All of which is easier said than done. Standing near an experienced complaint-handler—listening to what is said and how it is said—is the best learning experience the manager can have. It is especially helpful if the claim is denied.

Customers are always right! Except sometimes they aren't. The first reference is to the attitude with which management hears the guest's complaint; the second reference is to the context of the complaint. Management can listen attentively, sympathize completely, and communicate caringly, but still *say no* to outrageous requests based on nonevents.

Refusing compensation—remember, apologies are always in order—may cost the customer's patronage. It is a fine judgment call, as repeat patronage may already be lost. In denying restitution, inexperienced managers resort to "company policy" as the reason. Company policy is a great turnoff! Better to explain the answer in terms of fairness, of safety, of service to other guests, of economic reality, or of past experience.

Unhappy guests may request the intervention of higher authority. If that is appropriate, the next manager must be formally introduced and the issue recapped aloud to expedite the meeting. Thereafter, the first interviewer remains silent unless questioned and allows the second conversation to progress without interruption.

Complaints that are resolved quickly and equitably make friends for the hotel. Resolved or not, management's attitude, as expressed in words and movements, goes far toward minimizing (or aggravating) the damages.

➤ SUMMARY

There are as many definitions of quality guest service as there are positions arguing its value. The goals of quality service are simple to express and extremely difficult to implement. Two parties, guests and employees, structure the modern view of guest service. Managing for the first, the guests, is not new; it is part of the industry's heritage. Bringing employees into the process, which the contemporary approach does, is the fresh idea.

Changes have been made even in guests' treatment. Traditionally, hoteliers have attended to guests' needs within the accommodations that the host was offering. Today, hotels provide what the market wants to buy, not what management wants to offer. As that happens, the guest's perception of quality and the reality of the quality offered move closer together. Quality is provided not from management pronouncements and advertisements but from the employees' delivery of courtesy, appreciation, and honest representation.

Success in providing what the customer wants rests ultimately in the hands of those closest to the guest. Moments of truth are guest–employee, not guest–management, interactions. Enlisting the wholehearted support of the workforce requires changes in the methods of managing employees and the work environment. Winning staff commitment is a slow process. It cannot be dictated; it must come from a willingness to participate. Employees join the effort when their roles have been redefined to make clear their contribution to the total. Empowering staff members to make decisions within their own level of authority is one of the most dramatic redefinitions that management has taken.

The fundamentals of managing for quality have changed in the past two decades. With these changes have come new terms and new expressions. If history is any guide, the language of quality management, quality circles, quality guarantees, and so on, will soon fade away. Such is the experience with other management innovations. Fads in management come and go like other fashions. Hotel managers must retain the vision and principles behind the management of guest services even as the words behind them fade and disappear.

➤ QUESTIONS AND PROBLEMS

1. Using the computer, create a simple spreadsheet showing the form and functions that management can use to summarize and analyze complaints originating within departments of the rooms divisions.

2. Prepare and briefly discuss a list of three quality guarantees that are defined narrowly enough to be communicated easily and achieved successfully: for example, room service breakfast delivered within 30 minutes. Be certain to include the penalty to be paid by the hotel if the guarantee is not met.

   a. Explain why Marriott's guarantee of breakfast is, in the words of the authors, "an advertisement, a departmental promotion, an employee empowerment, an assurance of quality, and a willingness to be measured."

3. Compute how many moments of truth occur in a full-service convention hotel of 630 rooms during a typical month. Comment.

4. From readings and personal experience, discuss six of the most difficult elements of resolving a complaint.

5. You are the hotel's liaison with the architects designing guest rooms for a new tower. Present them a list of the 10 most important items that must be provided if the hotel is to meet its obligations under the Americans with Disabilities Act.

6. List five incentives that a hotel might offer to get guests to complete a guest comment card. Make a special effort to have the incentives encourage cross-advertising, by which one department awards incentives for use in another department.

➤ *NOTES*

1. Trademark of the Ford Motor Company.

2. Stephen J. Shriver, *Managing Quality Services* (East Lansing, MI: Educational Institute of the AH & MA., 1988).

3. Robert J. Martin and Thomas J. Jones, *Professional Management for Housekeeping Operations,* 2nd ed. (New York: John Wiley & Sons, Inc., 1992).

4. Shriver, p. 3; Bruce Brocka and Suzanne Brocka, *Quality Management: Implementing the Best Ideas of the Masters* (Burr Ridge, IL: Richard D. Irwin, Inc., 1992).

5. Rick Van Warner, in *Nation's Restaurant News,* October 26, 1991, attributes the aphorism to Keith Dunn, who cites Don I. Smith as the original source.

6. Stephen Hall, *Quest for Quality: Cost of Error Study* (n.p.: American Hotel & Motel Association and Citicorp Diners Club, n.d.).

7. The term *moments of truth* has been attributed to Jan Carlzon, former chairman of SAS Airlines.

8. To be approved for inclusion in AAA's lodging guide, hotel rooms must have deadbolts, automatic locking doors, and peepholes, and provide facilities for the disabled.

CHAPTER 8
The Guest Arrival Process

Outline

➤ THE ARRIVING GUEST

In many hotels, the guest arrival process appears to be a simple affair. The guest is greeted, information is verified, payment is initiated, and a room is selected. Most guests move through their arrival and registration process without a second thought to the intricacies and choreography of the front-office functions involved. Yet the entire check-in process is important enough to be evaluated as a substantial part of the hotel's overall rating by both Mobil and AAA. Exhibit 8–1 gives a glimpse of the complexity of the arrival process.

An ideal check in goes unnoticed by the guest because all hotel and front-office functions flow smoothly. From the valet attendant who parks the car to the doorperson who greets the guest, from the front-desk personnel who handle the arrangements to the bellperson who handles the luggage, all systems work in unison. Within just 3 to 5 minutes, the guest is happily on the way to the room.

Aside from the actual reservation (which may or may not have been made by the guest), this is the guest's first opportunity to see the hotel in action. First impressions are critical, and that is why the arrival and check-in process is often referred to as a moment of truth. The front-office staff does not get a second chance to make a good first impression.

A Moment of Truth

Different segments of the lodging industry offer differing levels of service. At no time is this difference in service as pronounced as it is during the arrival and check-in process. Limited-service properties offer no employee interaction between the porte-cochere (the canopy in front of most hotel lobbies under which arriving guests temporarily park their vehicles) and the front desk. In a limited-service property, the guest may not see or speak with any employee other than the guest–service agent. In fact, for hotels that offer self-check-in terminals or kiosks, limited-service guests may not see any employee at all upon arrival to the hotel.

Full-service hotels, on the other hand, place several ranks of employees between the front door and the front desk (see Exhibit 8–1). The guest may encounter a valet parking attendant, a doorperson, and a bellperson before ever arriving at the front desk.

➤ *The Valet Parking Attendant.*   The first employee that guests often encounter in a full-service hotel is the valet parking attendant. The parking attendant greets the guests as they pull their vehicles under the porte-cochere, opens their car door(s), assists with placing luggage on the curb, and takes responsibility for parking and securing the vehicle (see Exhibit 8–1).

Valet parking is an amenity or service provided by many fine hotels. However, not all full-service hotels offer valet parking. It is most commonly found in urban, city-center hotels where space is at a premium and guest self-parking is inconvenient (see Exhibit 8–2).

This department is a revenue center for some hotels. By charging the guest a fee for parking each day, the valet parking department generates income to help defray the costs of maintenance and insurance on the parking lot or parking structure. The parking fee (which runs as high as $50 or $60 per day in city-center hotels) is added directly to the guest's folio or account. In addition, many guests tip the attendant each time their car is returned.

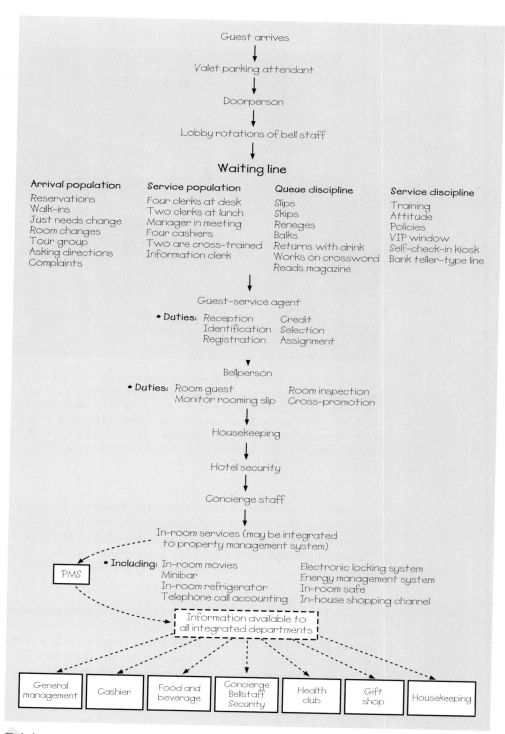

Guest arrives
↓
Valet parking attendant
↓
Doorperson
↓
Lobby rotations of bell staff
↓
Waiting line

Arrival population	Service population	Queue discipline	Service discipline
Reservations	Four clerks at desk	Slips	Training
Walk-ins	Two clerks at lunch	Skips	Attitude
Just needs change	Manager in meeting	Reneges	Policies
Room changes	Four cashiers	Balks	VIP window
Tour group	Two are cross-trained	Returns with drink	Self-check-in kiosk
Asking directions	Information clerk	Works on crossword	Bank teller-type line
Complaints		Reads magazine	

↓

Guest-service agent

• **Duties:** Reception   Credit
       Identification   Selection
       Registration   Assignment

↓

Bellperson

• **Duties:** Room guest   Room inspection
       Monitor rooming slip   Cross-promotion

↓

Housekeeping
↓
Hotel security
↓
Concierge staff
↓
In-room services (may be integrated
to property management system)

PMS

• **Including:** In-room movies   Electronic locking system
       Minibar   Energy management system
       In-room refrigerator   In-room safe
       Telephone call accounting   In-house shopping channel

Information available to
all integrated departments

General management	Cashier	Food and beverage	Concierge Bellstaff Security	Health club	Gift shop	Housekeeping

Exhibit 8–1 The guest arrival process is a complex choreography of departments and responsibilities. When their efforts come together seamlessly, the guest has a positive "moment of truth." Shown here is an arrival flow pattern for a full-service corporate hotel. Luxury resorts might add several functions to the flow pattern (golf, dinner reservations, or table assignments for an American plan resort). Limited-service properties might provide none of the services displayed here.

Exhibit 8–2   Example of a hotel offering both doorperson and valet parking services (note the sign to the right of the doors). At the Wedgewood Hotel, doorpersons and parking attendants are one and the same. Although most small four-diamond hotels would probably not offer both services—the Wedgewood has just 60 luxury rooms, 30 suites, and 4 penthouses—its rack rate ($160 to $440) is sufficient to warrant them. *Courtesy of the Wedgewood Hotel, Vancouver, British Columbia, Canada.*

Hotels may lease or subcontract the operation of this department to a private parking company. With leased operations, a private company takes the responsibility for parking the guest's car, insuring it against damage, and staffing the department. They also pay the hotel a monthly lease for the privilege of using their parking lots and garages. In such cases, the guest is unaware that valet parking is a contracted department.

▶*The Doorperson.*   Not all full-service hotels (or even resorts for that matter) offer a doorperson. In an era of rising labor costs, that's one position easily eliminated. This is especially true when you realize that it is a non-revenue-producing department. As a result, only the finer hotels can afford to provide doorpersons. And as such, the doorperson makes a statement both about the opulence of the hotel and about its concern for providing the finest in guest service.

To many guests, no position represents the hotel quite like the doorperson. The uniformed services position of doorperson is part concierge, part bellperson, part tour guide, and part friend all rolled into one. The doorperson may offer the guest suggestions, point out interesting historic sites, explain difficult directions, and hail a taxi. For newly arriving guests, the doorperson assists with removing and securing luggage from the car until the bellperson retrieves it for delivery. In addition to all these tasks, the doorperson also opens doors! (See Exhibit 8–2.)

Guest Registration

After being greeted at the curb and the front door, the guest arrives at the front desk (see Exhibit 8–1). In a small property, the desk itself is small and probably staffed with just one or two agents. Each of these agents is capable of handling the full range of functions the guest requires. In larger properties, however, the front desk may be literally hundreds of feet long, with 20 to 30 or more clerks working (see Exhibit 8–3). In large hotels, each clerk has a distinct responsibility. Although each line or queue is clearly marked with a sign, arriving guests are usually on their own in deciding which clerk to approach or in which line to stand. For arriving guests, the sign might say "reception," "registration," "check in," or "arrivals." For further information, see the discussion on queuing theory later in the chapter.

Two types of guests present themselves at the front desk: those with reservations and those without. Those with reservations are generally handled without problem. The agent reconfirms the accommodations requested, the guest signs the registration card, a method of payment is secured, a room is selected, and some pleasantries are exchanged. In a computerized property, the entire reception process can be handled quickly—say, in 2 or 3 minutes.

Guests holding reservations may encounter two problems: no record of the reservation and no space available. The arrival and reception should go quickly, even if the reservation has been misplaced, provided that space is available. As unobtrusively as possible, the clerk elicits the reservation information again and makes the assignment. No reference to the missing paperwork is made. Far more composure is necessary if

Exhibit 8–3   Here's a look at the front desk of the Opryland Hotel in Nashville. The Opryland is among the largest independent, unaffiliated hotels in the world. It boasts 2,879 rooms and 222 suites. *Courtesy of the Opryland Hotel, Nashville, Tennessee.*

the clerk is to handle an overbooking situation successfully. With proper training, the emergency procedures described in Chapters 6 and 7 are implemented, and the moment of truth is achieved without incident.

A lower level of expectation exists for guests who have no reservations. If space is available—and in most hotels there is space—the procedures take a little longer. Information that was available to the agent from the reservation must now be obtained and checked against availability for the first night and succeeding nights. The same questions posed by the reservationist must be asked by the room clerk. How many nights? How many rooms? How many in the party? Like the reservationist on the telephone, the room clerk offers the walk-in alternative accommodations if the exact request cannot be met.

▶*Registered, Not Assigned.*   Very early arrivals, especially those who appear before the day's check-out hour, may be required to wait until a departure creates a vacancy. Even then, the room must still be cleaned. Baggage-check service is offered to all guests who must wait, and a complimentary beverage may be given to some if the hotel is responsible for the wait. In anticipation of an upcoming vacancy, the clerk may have the guest register. The account is marked RNA (registered, not assigned) and kept handy until the first appropriate departure takes place. The assignment is made but the guest is kept waiting until housekeeping reports the room ready for occupancy—guests are not sent to unmade rooms.

Guests who arrive after the room is vacated but before it has been cleaned by housekeeping—a status called *on change*—are assigned at once but not provided with a key until the room has been cleaned and inspected. This is not an RNA.

RNAs occur whenever the hotel is very full with simultaneous arrivals and departures of large conventions, or when tour groups overlap. Busy holidays cause RNAs at the type of resorts where arrivals come early and departures stay late.

Waiting for the room is a distressing experience, especially as the hours tick away. On some occasions it may be necessary to assign guests temporary rooms, changing them to a permanent assignment later. This type of costly duplication should be avoided except in special circumstances. Most front-office systems, including computerized ones, allow RNAs to create charges even though no room identification is possible.

In corporate hotels, RNAs are less frustrating. Corporate guests who arrive early in the morning are happy to register and leave their luggage secure. They then go about their business until the workday ends later that afternoon. Upon returning to the hotel, they find their room number has been assigned and their luggage is waiting for them in the room.

Early Check-in Policies.   Generally, hotels have rooms available from the night before. Even when last night's status was "sold out," there are usually rooms available. That's because a few of last night's rooms probably never arrived (for a discussion of no-shows, see Chapter 6). The hotel received its revenue by billing the no-show guest, but the room itself was never occupied. Therefore, a guest checking in at, say, 7 or 8 AM is likely to find a room available.

The real question is: Will the front-desk clerk allow the guest to check in? Check-in time for most hotels is between 1 and 4 PM, allowing housekeeping ample time to clean check-out rooms. A guest checking in at noon or 11 AM is no big deal, but a guest who wants access to the room at 7 or 8 AM poses a problem for some hotels—their policies do not allow early check-in without imposing a fee. Similar to a late check-out fee (for guests who stay beyond 2 or 3 PM), the idea behind an early check-in fee is that the guest is using the room for a number of hours before the start of the official "day."

Imposing such a fee does more harm than good. The guest feels taken advantage of. Moreover, letting the guest into the room early will probably result in a few breakfast meals and some telephone revenue as well. Crowne Plaza Hotels and Resorts encourages early check in for corporate members of its Priority Club Worldwide. They advertise corporate check ins beginning at 7 AM (and late check outs until 3 PM) without extra charge!

▶ *Waiting Lines.*   Early check in and RNA policies do more than get the guest into the room early; they get the guest out of line, too. Few check ins occur early in the day, and therefore the front desk should accommodate such guests whenever possible. Otherwise, those guests may return during the busiest check-in times. For corporate hotels, the busiest check-in times are usually from 5 to 8 PM. The busiest check-out periods are 7 to 9 AM.

There is probably nothing more frustrating after a long day of travel than to arrive at a congested front office. From early in the morning, the traveling guest has been waiting—waiting to park the car and get a parking stub, waiting to have the airplane ticket validated, waiting for the plane to begin boarding, take off, land, and deplane, and waiting to be shuttled to the hotel. Imagine the frustration walking into the lobby of your home away from home to see yet another waiting line. Indeed, that is one of the appeals of the new self-check-in kiosks, discussed later in this chapter.

It is the job of hotel management to adequately staff busy check-in periods. Hard to do, because guests can (and do) arrive at literally any hour. Add to this uncertainty the constrictions of a limited budget, union and nonunion labor laws (meal breaks and the like), employees who are not yet fully trained, sick call-ins, and the problem becomes amplified. It becomes even more exaggerated when you realize that the industry is larger and busier than ever before. How else can you check thousands of guests into a megaresort except one guest at a time?

Long Lines Equal Poor Service.   Some theorists suggest that today's guests are more impatient with check-in lines than ever before. The blame, they say, is on the computer industry, which has created a "get it now" society. Through modern technology, we can communicate at lightning speed, send documents by modem, and reach cellular phone customers wherever they happen to be. Maybe that's why guests are so impatient.

Whatever the reason guests are so impatient, it is in the hotel's best interest to minimize the wait. That is because the check-in process—and its accompanying wait in line—is one of the most memorable moments of the guests' stay. A long wait can ruin the check in and ultimately the entire stay. The check in is probably the first, or one of the first, face-to-face encounters the guest has with hotel staff. The first encounter should be memorable, and a long wait in line certainly is memorable (just not the kind of memory we wish to instill). In addition, arriving guests have little else to occupy their mind. They quickly become restless and critical of the front-office operation. Finally, guests have a certain expectation with regard to the check-in process. A limited wait is reasonable, a long wait becomes synonymous with a poorly run hotel. That is especially true when there are few guests in line. When the wait is due to some hidden element, guests become indignant.

To empathize with the waiting guest, management needs to understand and train for three important factors:

1. Empty minutes go faster when the guests' time is filled with something to do.
2. For waiting guests, not knowing how long they'll be waiting is worse than knowing an estimated length of wait, even if the wait is expected to be quite long.
3. Anything the guest(s) can do to make the whole check-in process more efficient is understood and appreciated. Guests want to help.

Queuing Theory. In the early 20th century, A. K. Erlang, a Danish mathematician, introduced a theory called *telephony.* Originally designed as a mathematical model for solving telephone traffic line usage, the theory found other applications during World War II. Each modification resulted in other names as the application changed slightly. Erlang's traffic theory has been renamed *queuing* (also spelled *queueing*) theory, congestion theory, and for its application to lines, waiting line theory. The uses are manifold: toll booths, 911 calls, traffic lights, airports, parking lots, hospitals, data processing, and more.

Queuing theory is a mathematical tool that management uses to obtain an optimum rate of customer flow. It balances the costs of making customers wait against the costs of serving them more rapidly. Queuing theory attempts to quantify the dilemma regarding ideal levels of guest service.

Too little service and the guest waits in line, or waits on the reservation telephone line, longer than expected. Dissatisfied guests, formal complaints, a low percentage of repeat business, or lost revenue from guests who leave are the consequential losses from too little service.

Responding to too little service (a definition that varies with the class and pattern of the hotel), management adds more registration windows, more employees, more computer terminals, and self-check-in kiosks. The guest is served more rapidly but at a significant cost in labor, equipment, and lost lobby space.

Queuing theory requires an understanding of probability statistics as well as of differential and integral calculus. Computer programs are available to do the computations. Four key elements must be quantified: arrival population, service population, queue discipline, and service discipline (see Exhibit 8–1). The quality of the assumptions and facts behind these four components dictate the level of success that the final solution takes.

ARRIVAL POPULATION.   A number of factors affect the size of the population arriving at the desk. Certain hours of the day and certain days of the week are busier arrival times than others. The quantity of group business has an impact, as does the method of handling them. Are they registered at the desk or in a separate area? All guest transactions are not the same. Guests stand in line to check in, to ask questions, to complain, to get change, and to obtain and return keys (see Exhibit 8–1).

SERVICE POPULATION.   The kind and number of available agents and their configuration behind the desk is the service population. Intrinsic to this component are several special issues. The ability of the clerk; the number of clerks, and whether that figure is fixed or variable; and the assignment of duties (does each position handle every request, or are there special windows for special needs?) are all elements of the service population.

QUEUE DISCIPLINE.   Queue discipline refers to the behavior exhibited by the guests who are waiting in line. This is the element that changed waiting line theory from mathematical science to a behavioral one. Guests cry "Social injustice!" when some one who arrived after them is served before them. Skips and slips are the most infuriating to waiting guests. Skips and slips, which are opposite sides of the coin, take place when another guest skips ahead of the waiting guest, who then slips behind.

Queue discipline addresses the guest's reaction to the line: Does he or she refuse to join the line because of the length (a "balk")? Does a guest switch lines as the respective lengths vary? If a guest leaves the line (a "renege") after waiting for some time, is that decision determined by the length of the line, or is it a random move? Do others allow the line jumper back in? Little is really known about the behavior of hotel guests standing in line to be registered.

SERVICE DISCIPLINE.   Service discipline is the last of the four key elements. It examines the server's attitude and approach as the queue discipline questions the guest's behavior. Are guests handled on a first-come, first-served basis? How are interruptions fielded from a "one-quick-question" interloper? Is priority treatment provided for special VIPs and frequent-guest members?

Creative Solutions to Long Lines.   Responses to the problem of long waits have come from all industries. Banks have addressed the problem by implementing a single waiting line so that waiting customers don't have to be frustrated by picking the slowest clerk. Grocery chains have developed an approach that solves the problem and also serves as a marketing tool. They advertise: We'll open a new line whenever more than two customers are waiting. Fast-food chains, airlines, and many others send an employee to the rear of the line to take orders and ease the bottleneck at the cash register. Customers respond as much to the company's demonstrated concern as to the actual solution.

Some solutions can be, and have been, borrowed from other industries. The single waiting line is the most apparent. Snaking the line back on itself, as is done in theme parks, makes the line appear shorter, but it does take up costly lobby space. Telling the guest the estimated waiting time recognizes the human behavior part of waiting, but it does nothing to speed up the process. Neither does another technique, which merely assuages the guest's irritation from waiting. Borrowing from pizza-delivery philosophy, guests who wait in line longer than 5 minutes get a monetary reward: cash, reduced room rate, or an upgrade.

Radio-assisted registration has been tried, but only the largest hotels are able to work this out. Customer-service staff work the rear of the registration line or catch new guests as they enter the lobby. The reservation information is radioed to back-office computers. Using a different computer provides temporary relief to the property-management system and to the front-office crew. The guest is directed to a special window to sign the form and pick up the key.

Separating certain guests from the regular line saves time for both those separated and for those remaining. A concierge or executive check in that accommodates special categories such as guaranteed reservations, negotiated corporate accounts, and frequent-guest patrons are sample categories.

But some of the best ideas are the most creative. The Mirage Hotel and Casino in Las Vegas boasts a 20,000-gallon saltwater aquarium behind its front desk. It's hard to get bored when live sharks are swimming just a few yards in front of you. Other major hotels transform the wait into a party. They bring in jugglers, magicians, and comedians who perform for the waiting guests. And of course, the amusement parks have it down to a science. Which of the following ideas can the lodging industry adopt from the theme parks?

- *Pre-shows:* an informative video describing various aspects of the resort and designed to run on a continuous loop
- *Time signs:* describing the approximate wait in line from this point forward
- *Live entertainers:* as with the jugglers, magicians, and comedians described above
- *Segmented queues:* allowing guests to see just a small section of the queue at a time to create the illusion of short lines
- *Video screens:* entertaining video clips of various topics
- *Interactive participation:* guests decipher codes, draw graffiti on walls, converse with robots, and so on
- *Themed environments:* aquariums, jungles, pyramids, and the like to give guests plenty to look at while waiting in line

➤*The Registration Card.* Registration is not essential to the common-law creation of a legal guest–hotel relationship. In several states it is not even a statutory requirement. In contrast, other countries not only require registration cards but use them as police documents. Guests furnish foreign innkeepers with passports and a great deal of personal information that has value only to the authorities (see Exhibit 8–4). Indeed, hotel registration in Brazil requires the guest to fill in the names of both mother and father. Age, gender, date of birth, next destination, previous stop, and nationality are never found with registration information collected in the United States.

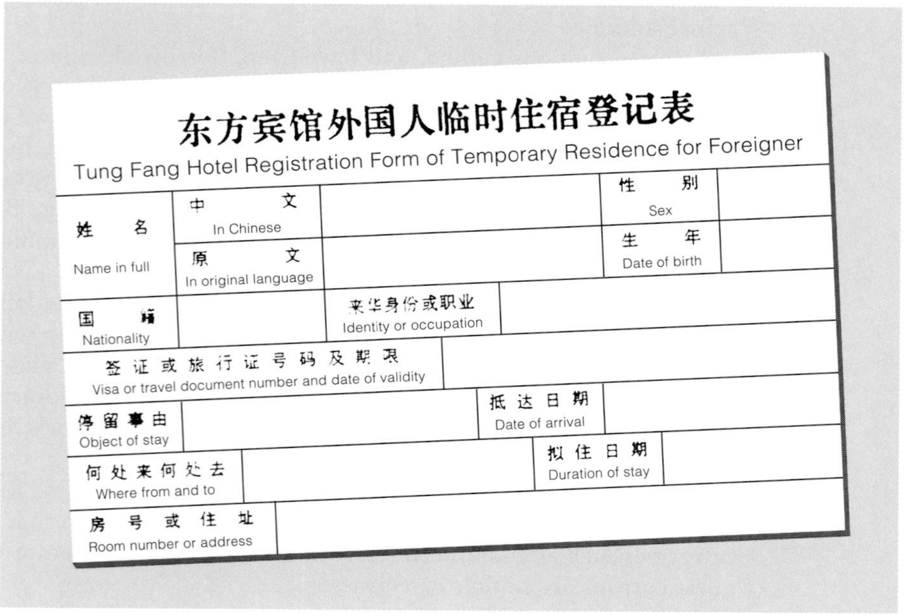
东方宾馆外国人临时住宿登记表
Tung Fang Hotel Registration Form of Temporary Residence for Foreigner

姓 名 Name in full	中 文 In Chinese		性 别 Sex	
	原 文 In original language		生 年 Date of birth	
国 籍 Nationality		来华身份或职业 Identity or occupation		
签证或旅行证号码及期限 Visa or travel document number and date of validity				
停留事由 Object of stay		抵达日期 Date of arrival		
何处来何处去 Where from and to		拟住日期 Duration of stay		
房号或住址 Room number or address				

Exhibit 8–4 Domestic hotels would never think of asking age, gender, travel plans, or names of the guest's mother and father. However, these types of questions are asked of guests on many foreign registration cards, including this one from the People's Republic of China. That may be due, in part, to their use as police documents in some foreign countries.

In manual (nonautomated) properties, registration information is collected by handing the guest a blank registration card to complete. Today's property management systems (PMSs) have eliminated the need for manually collecting guest information. For the most part, information collected at registration is the same as information collected during the reservation. Automated properties preprint registration cards from the information collected at the time of reservation (see Exhibit 8–5). Now instead of burdening the guest with completion of an entire card, the front-desk clerk merely asks the guest to verify accuracy of information and sign at the bottom of the card.

Number in the Party.   The number of persons (the house count) has importance for statistics that are developed during the night audit. In addition, the number of persons in the room determines the rate charged. When indicating the number of guests in the room, many hotels separate adults from children (see Exhibit 8–5). This is especially true in an American plan hotel that probably charges less for young children's meals than for adult meals.

Name and Address.   An accurate and complete name and address is needed for credit and billing and for the development of mailing lists for future sales promotions. A complete address includes such things as ZIP codes, apartment numbers, and even state of residence, for the names of many cities are common to several states. Commercial hotels often ask for the patron's business address and organizational title in addition to the residential address (see Exhibit 8–5).

Greater credit can be extended to a guest whose address has been verified through an exchange of reservation correspondence than to a walk-in. Whereas those

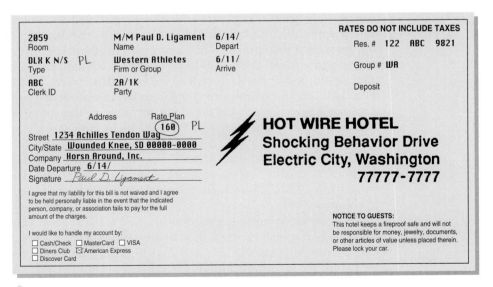

Exhibit 8–5 With a computer-prepared registration card, all a guest need do is verify the accuracy of the information, read the disclaimers, and sign. A detailed and accurate reservation saves the hotel duplicate work. Assuming that the name has been spelled properly, the address is correct, etc., the information collected at the time of reservation is reused again and again (on the letter of confirmation, the folio, the rooming slip, the arrivals list, etc.) (see Exhibit 5–3).

intent on fraud will use false addresses, vacant lots, or temporary box numbers, unintentional skippers (people who forgot to check out or inadvertently left a portion of their folio unpaid) can be traced, billed, and subsequently collected from if an accurate name and address is on file.

Room Number.   Even as the hotel industry seeks higher levels of courtesy and guest service, the guest is known as much by room number as by name. Once the guest is registered in the property management system and a room number has been assigned, all subsequent transactions are referenced and billed to the room number rather than to the guest's actual name. The room number is the major means of locating, identifying, tracking, and billing the guest. Even before the guest arrives, the reservation number (or with some systems a preassigned folio number) is used to locate the guest and credit advance deposits.

Date of Departure.   The guest's expected date of departure is of critical importance during the check-in process. By double-checking the guest's departure plans, the front office ensures the accuracy of future room availability figures.

Many front offices require the guest to sign a statement or initial the registration card next to their date of departure (see Exhibit 8–5). This is especially true for busy periods when a scheduled departure is necessary to provide the room to a newly arriving reservation (see Exhibit 8–8). Of course, plans change, and some percentage of guests will invariably depart earlier or later than they originally thought. In such cases, the front office strives to accommodate the guest. There is usually no extra charge for early departures and most unscheduled stayovers are accommodated (see the section entitled "Early Departure Fees" in Chapter 6).

Discounts or Corporate Affiliations.   Another issue resolved during the check-in process is the guest's corporate affiliation or qualified discounts. The corporate affiliation (if applicable) is often logged and tracked by the front desk on behalf of the sales and marketing department. This corporate information is critical to the sales department because many companies have accounts with individual and chain properties. By tracking corporate guest visitation, the sales department is able to continue offering discounts and special rates to companies who frequent the property. Many corporations have agreements with the chain (or with an individual hotel) to stay a certain number of room nights per year. Tracking use is critical to the success of such ongoing relationships.

Even when a corporate guest's company has not negotiated a special room rate, the hotel is usually willing to grant a standard corporate discount. Such discounts range from 10 to 20% or higher depending on the type of hotel, the date, and season of visitation.

Even noncorporate guests may qualify for discounts. Leisure guests are often members of national or worldwide organizations such as AAA or AARP. AAA (American Automobile Association) and AARP (American Association of Retired Persons) are two of the largest membership organizations in the world. Most hotels grant AAA and/or AARP discounts to qualified guests. A complete discussion of rate discounts is found in Chapter 9.

Clerk Identification.   The front-desk clerk who checks the guest into the hotel is automatically identified in the property management system from the password the clerk used when logging onto the computer. Clerk identification is important in case a problem or other issue arises. By knowing who checked the guest in, management can return to that clerk and ask related questions. Possibly the guest was pleased with the process and complimented management on the clerk's performance. On the other hand, maybe the clerk provided an insufficient discount, was rude, or forgot to establish a method of payment.

Folio Numbering.   All hotels assign a unique folio number to the guest's account. In a computerized property, this account number is provided at the time of reservation. The number is assigned early in case the guest sends advance payment. The folio (or account) number references the guest's automated file just as readily as the room number or guest name.

Computerized numbering serves as a control device when one employee is clerk, cashier, and supervisor all in one. It is possible for such an employee to sell the room as clerk, pocket the money as cashier, and cover the discrepancy as night auditor. When the staff grows large enough to permit a separation of duties, numeric form control becomes less important.

Another major advantage to a computerized property management system is the ease of storing records. While according to some management consultants the standard is seven years (three years for registration cards), many properties find themselves storing folios, registration cards, and accounting records for even longer periods. In an electronic hotel, storage is easy when daily records are downloaded onto tape or disk. In a manual property, storage consumes considerably more space.

Disclaimer of Innkeeper Liability.   Almost every registration card carries a statement concerning the hotel's liability for the loss of guest valuables. Such a disclaimer is shown in Exhibit 8–5. The form and content of the statement are prescribed by state statute, and consequently, these vary among states. If the innkeeper meets the provisions of the statute, and public notice on the registration card is usually one such provision, liability for the loss of valuables is substantially reduced. Were it not for the dollar limits set by state legislatures, innkeepers would have unlimited liability under common law.

Common law is far more stringent than statutory law; it makes the hotel responsible in full for the value of guests' belongings. Most states, but not all, limit the innkeeper's liability to a fixed sum even when the guest uses the safe provided. Other statutes prevent recovery against the hotel if the guest fails to use the safe, provided that the hotel has complied with every provision of the law (see Exhibit 8–6). State legislatures have extended this principle of limited liability to checkrooms and to goods that are too large for the ordinary safe—salesperson's samples, for example.

Notices, which must be posted in the rooms, must include the maximum rate charged for the room (see bottom Exhibit 8–6). Charges sometimes exceed that figure when a yield management system is in operation or when rates are changed frequently. The hotel may charge what it wishes, but there is a danger in not changing the permanent rate schedule that must be posted in each guest room.

Catering to Pets.   Over the past five years or so, the number of pet owners who travel with their pets has increased from 30% to 65%.[1] Pet owners are becoming a sizable market, one not overlooked by the lodging industry. Many pet owners think "it's the cat's meow" when luxury properties cater to their pets. The Chicago Ritz-Carlton, for example, offers a gourmet room service menu for dogs and cats, a "Pet Recognition Program" that provides a treat to the guest's pet each time they visit, and even an on-site grooming and pet-walking service. The Four Seasons hotel group offers similar services at some of its properties. Holiday Inn, Ramada, Motel 6, and a growing list of other chains also accommodate guests' pets.

NOTICE TO GUESTS
ARIZONA INNKEEPERS' LAWS

NOTICE is hereby given of the provision of Section 33-302 of the Arizona Revised Statutes provided as follows:

§33-302. Maintenance of fireproof safe

A. An innkeeper who maintains a fireproof safe and gives notice by posting in a conspicuous place in the office or in the room of each guest that money, jewelry, documents and other articles of small size and unusual value may be deposited in the safe, is not liable for loss of or injury to any such article not deposited in the safe, which is not the result of his own act.

B. An innkeeper may refuse to receive for deposit from a guest articles exceeding a total value of five hundred dollars, and unless otherwise agreed to in writing shall not be liable in an amount in excess of five hundred dollars for loss of or damage to property deposited by a guest in such safe unless the loss or damage is the result of the fault or negligence of this establishment.

C. An innkeeper shall not be liable for loss of or damage to merchandise samples or merchandise for sale displayed by a guest unless the guest gives prior written notice of having and displaying the merchandise or merchandise samples, and acknowledges receipt of such notice, but in no event shall liability for such loss or damage exceed five hundred dollars unless it results from the fault or negligence of this establishment.

D. The liability of an innkeeper to a guest shall be limited to one hundred dollars for property delivered to this establishment to be kept in a storeroom or baggage room and to seventy-five dollars for property deposited in a parcel or checkroom.

NOTICE is hereby further given of the provisions of Section 33-951, and 33-952, Arizona Revised Statutes, as amended, which provided as follows:

§33-951. Lien on baggage and property of guests

Hotel, inn, boarding house, lodging house, apartment house and auto camp keepers shall have a lien upon the baggage and other property of their guests, boarders or lodgers, brought therein by their guests, boarders or lodgers, for charges due for accommodation, board, lodging or room rent and things furnished at the request of such guests, boarders or lodgers, with the right to possession of the baggage or other property until the charges are paid.

§33-952. Sale of property; notice

A. When baggage or other property comes into the possession of a person entitled to a lien as provided by §33-951 and remains unclaimed, or the charges remain unpaid for a period of four months, the person may proceed to sell the baggage or property at public auction, and from the proceeds retain the charges, storage and expense of advertising the sale.

B. The sale shall not be made until the expiration of four weeks from the first publication of notice of the sale, published in a newspaper once a week for four consecutive weeks. The notice shall contain a description of each piece of property, the name of the owner, if known, the name of the person holding the property, and the time and place of sale. If the indebtedness does not exceed sixty dollars, the notice may be given by posting at not less than three public places located at the place where the hotel, inn, boarding house, lodging house, apartment house or auto camp is located.

C. Any balance from the sale not claimed by the rightful owner within one month from the day of sale shall be paid into the treasury of the county in which the sale took place, and if not claimed by the owner within one year thereafter, the money shall be paid into the general fund of the county.

NOTICE is hereby further given of the provisions of Section 12-671; and 13-1802; Arizona Revised Statutes, as amended, which provide as follows:

§12-671. Drawing check or draft on no account or insufficient account with intent to defraud; civil action; definition of credit; prima facie evidence

A. A person who, for himself or for another, with intent to defraud, makes, draws, utters or delivers to another person or persons a check or draft on a bank or depositary for payment of money, knowing at the time of such making, drawing, uttering or delivery, that he or his principal does not have an account or does not have sufficient funds in, or credit with, such bank or depositary to meet the check or draft in full upon presentation, shall be liable to the holder of such check or draft for twice the amount of such check or draft or fifty dollars, whichever is greater, together with costs and reasonable attorneys' fees as allowed by the court on the basis of time and effort expended by such attorney on behalf of plaintiff.

B. The word "credit" as used in this section shall be construed to be an express agreement with the bank or depositary for payment of the check or draft.

C. Proof that at the time of presentment, the maker, issuer or drawer did not have sufficient funds with the bank or depositary, and that he failed within twelve days after receiving notice of nonpayment or dishonor to pay the check or draft is prima facie evidence of intent to defraud.

D. Where a check, draft or order is protested, on the ground of insufficiency of funds or credit, the notice of formal protest thereof shall be admissible as proof of presentation, nonpayment and protest and shall be prima facie evidence of the insufficiency of funds or credit with the bank or depositary, or person, or firm or corporation.

E. "Notice", as used in this section, means notice given to the person entitled thereto, either in person, or in writing. Such notice in writing shall be given by certified mail, return receipt requested, to the person at his address as it appears on such check or draft.

F. Nothing in this section shall be applicable to any criminal case or affect eligibility or terms of probation.

§13-1802. Theft; classification

A. A person commits theft if, without lawful authority, such person knowingly:

1. Controls property of another with the intent to deprive him of such property; or

2. Converts for an unauthorized term or use services or property of another entrusted to the defendant or placed in the defendant's possession for a limited, authorized term or use; or

3. Obtains property or services of another by means of any material misrepresentation with intent to deprive him of such property or services; or

4. Comes into control of lost, mislaid or misdelivered property of another under circumstances providing means of inquiry as to the true owner and appropriates such property to his own or another's use without reasonable efforts to notify the true owner; or

5. Controls property of another knowing or having reason to know that the property was stolen; or

6. Obtains services known to the defendant to be available only for compensation without paying or an agreement to pay such compensation or diverts another's services to his own or another's benefit without authority to do so.

B. The inferences set forth in §13-2305 shall apply to any prosecution under the provisions of subsection A, paragraph 5 of this section.

C. Theft of property or services with a value of one thousand dollars or more is a Class 3 felony. Theft of property or services with a value of five hundred dollars or more but less than one thousand dollars is a Class 4 felony. Theft of any property or services valued at two hundred fifty dollars or more but less than five hundred dollars is a Class 5 felony. Theft of property or services with a value of one hundred dollars or more but less than two hundred fifty dollars is Class 6 felony. Theft of any property or service valued at less than one hundred dollars is a Class 1 misdemeanor, unless such property is taken from the person of another or is a motor vehicle or a firearm, in which the theft is a Class 6 felony.

THE MANAGEMENT

RATES ON THIS ROOM

THE ABOVE RATES ARE SUBJECT TO ADJUSTMENT FOR SPECIAL NEGOTIATED OR SEASONAL RATES.

Registering pets has some serious potential costs, including the discomfort of other guests. Some hotels refuse all animals except Seeing Eye dogs. Others, as explained above, seek pet owners as a distinct portion of their market. Most pet owners appreciate the innkeeper's problems and make restitution for damages. Additional protection is provided when a contract (and/or a deposit) is signed by the owner agreeing to pay for any damages that occur.

Points of Agreement.   Even as management strives to expedite the process, extra reading matter is being added to the registration card. The content of these extra messages differs among hotels and chains. Each has different problems and legal experiences. The presence of the messages meets legal requirements, but it is doubtful whether any guest actually reads messages during the hurried moments of registration. The message is repeated on the rooming slip, however, and that slip is left with the guest (see Exhibits 8–14 and 8–15).

Despite the printed comments that guests are supposed to read, legitimate misunderstandings (about the rate, the date of departure, etc.) do occur. To minimize the likelihood of misunderstandings, hotels often train front-office personnel to elicit the guest's agreement on several of the more sensitive issues.

The room rate is one such issue. Although it is bad form to mention the guest's rate aloud, it is important to reach agreement on the nightly charge before rooming the guest. Rather than discussing the rate aloud, it has become standard practice to ask the guest to initial the rate. Usually, the clerk circles the rate (see Exhibit 8–5), passes the registration card to the guest, and asks for the guest's initials. If there are any disputes about discounts or special pricing arrangements, now is the time for the guest to mention them.

Another point of agreement sometimes stressed on the registration card is the smoking status of the guest's room. Smokers and nonsmokers alike are adamant about their personal preferences. Nonsmokers want a fresh room without the stale odor of smoke; smokers want a smoking room complete with ashtrays and matchbooks.

Hotels can spend considerable funds making nonsmoking rooms truly smoke-free. Window and wall coverings, bedspreads, and carpet have never been exposed to smoke. Should a guest smoke (or allow a friend to smoke) in such a setting, it could cost the hotel hundreds of dollars to make the room smoke-free again. As such, nonsmokers are sometimes asked to initial the nonsmoking status (N/S in Exhibit 8–5) as a reminder to keep the room smoke-free.

Also frequently included on the registration card is a statement by which the guest agrees to stand personally liable for the bill if some third party (the company, the association, or the credit-card company) fails to pay (see Exhibit 8–5).

Going Green.   The environmental programs offered by the hotel are also sometimes mentioned on the registration card. Although more likely to be included on the rooming slip (so the guest has more time to read about them), hotels are beginning to promote the "greening" of their workplace more and more regularly.

Exhibit 8–6   (on page 248) When this notice to guests is correctly displayed (line three) in each room, the innkeeper's liability is drastically reduced. This state (Arizona) limits innkeeper liability to between $75 and $500 depending on how the item was stored (storage, baggage room, or safe—see section 33-302 items B, C, and D). Other states provide different levels of protection. This document is incomplete until the property fills in the various room rates at the bottom of the notice.

Not only is the greening of our industry the politically correct thing to do these days, but it is also quite profitable. It is profitable in two ways: from a marketing standpoint as well as a cost-savings one. Environmental consciousness is great for public relations and generates positive feedback from hotel guests. Although guests may be slightly inconvenienced by the green programs in place, hotels that offer such initiatives say that guests rarely complain. In fact, they become involved. By hanging-up wet towels to use again (see Exhibit 2–7), initialing an agreement to have bed linens laundered every other day,[2] and walking into a warm room because the aircon-ditioning adjusts to an energy-savings mode when unoccupied, the guest takes an active role in the hotel's green consciousness.

Although the more sophisticated energy, water, and waste management savings systems are usually engineered into the initial design of the facility, there are many conservation opportunities available to hotels for little or no investment. For a discussion of automated energy management systems, see that section in Chapter 14; see also Exhibit 8–7.

Simple low-investment programs usually concentrate on saving money through energy and water conservation. Hotels are different from other businesses because

Exhibit 8–7   Because of its isolated location on an island in Australia's Great Barrier Reef, the Hayman Island Resort designed its entire operation around energy savings and conservation. For fresh water, the resort has its own desalination plant. For electricity, it has its own power plant. *Courtesy of Hayman Island Resort, North Queensland, Australia.*

lights stay on 24 hours a day. Merely turning off unnecessary lighting, changing 100-watt incandescent bulbs to 20-watt fluorescents, and putting exterior lighting on timers will save considerable money and help the environment.

Retrofitting guest-room showers, faucets, and toilets pays for itself quickly with the savings in water consumption. Even low- or no-investment policies such as serving water in the restaurant only upon request or laundering linens less often (see above) makes a big impact when multiplied over hundreds of guest rooms (see Exhibit 8–7).

➤ COMPLETING THE REGISTRATION

At registration time, many things are going on simultaneously: The reservation is being located; the guest is being welcomed; accommodation needs are being determined or reevaluated; some small talk is taking place; the clerk is trying to sell up; the guest's identity, including the correct spelling of the name and address, is being verified; certain public rooms or services in the hotel are being promoted; the anticipated departure date is verified; both the guest and the clerk are completing their portions of the registration card; the credit card is being validated; and mail or messages are handed over. Finally, a bellperson is called and the guest is roomed.

All this normal activity notwithstanding, the clerk must remain alert to special cases. Room clerks issue the coupons that accompany each IT package, and there could be a dozen of them. Room clerks are the point position for advertising contracts (rooms traded for advertising), for travel agency vouchers (the guest has paid the travel agency that booked the room), and for special rates. Conventions, for example, sometimes have reduced rates before and after the convention dates and sometimes they don't. And of course, if it's a mystery shopper checking in, a few more curves will be thrown at the overworked front-desk clerk (see Chapter 7).

Throughout the procedure, which could take anywhere from 1 to 15 minutes, the clerk must remain calm, dignified, and friendly. Some feel that the clerk's attitude is the most important part of the whole registration, reception, and room selection process.

The Room Selection Process

Early each morning, front-desk clerks look at the rooms they expect to have available for sale that day. Rooms that were not occupied last night are immediately available; rooms that are due to check out today will eventually be available (assuming that they actually check out; see Exhibit 8–8). By comparing the housekeeper's report against the property management system, the clerk identifies all available rooms. A determination is made at this point as to how many additional walk-ins will be accepted. The decision will be revised many times throughout the day (see the discussion in Chapter 6).

➤ *Blocking Rooms.*   Every room has distinct features, and a well-trained desk clerk understands these distinctions. Not all double–doubles are the same. Some are better than others because of location, view, newer furnishings or paint, or any number of other enhancements. The task of the front desk is to align reservations with available rooms.

Blocking, or preassigning rooms to guests, ensures a high level of certainty that special requests will be accommodated. When the room count identifies a high number

Just a Reminder

Ms. Angelica Chuckee   Room 3308

You indicated upon checking in that you would be departing today. Your room is reserved for an incoming guest and your check-out time is 12 noon.

Should you need to stay in New York City an additional day, please contact our assistant manager, located in the main lobby or on Ext. 123. The assistant manager will make the necessary arrangements to reserve a room for you in a nearby hotel, as all our rooms have been reserved for today.

You can also make reservations for your next hotel stop before departure through our worldwide central reservation service.

Thank You.

Exhibit 8–8   Check-out reminders like this may be printed on cards or letterheads and placed under the guest's door or on the pillow the night before. Reminders are used only when the hotel expects an overbooking situation the following day.

of rooms available for sale, few rooms will be preblocked. For example, there is no purpose in blocking a standard queen reservation when there are numerous standard queen rooms available. Conversely, when the room count is tight (few rooms available to walk-ins) all incoming reservations will be blocked against the list of available rooms. In this way, the few unblocked rooms remaining are easily identified for walk-in customers. In the event that the house count is negative (the hotel is overbooked), a priority list is established. Management-made reservations, VIPs, and guaranteed reservations head the priority list—the rest of the reservations will probably be filled on a first-come, first-served basis.

Regardless of projections, a careful rooms manager always blocks special cases early in the day. Included in this category are connecting rooms, early check-ins, handicapped rooms, management-made reservations, suites, and VIPs. If the house is very crowded, even special request assignments may need to wait for check outs. The desk knows who the anticipated departures are, although it's never really certain. The desk does not know what time the departures are leaving relative to the arrival of the new guests. So special requests are assigned first to vacant rooms (if the rooms meet the requirements of the request), and then to rooms as the guests depart.

The numbers of the preassigned rooms are entered into the PMS. This prevents the room's assignment to another arrival. It also provides immediate display for the clerk when the guest approaches and requests the reserved accommodations. Changes in the original assignments are made throughout the day as new information surfaces. If the arriving guest reports a change in the size of the party, or in the date of departure, or if the party appears before the preassigned room has been vacated, changes will need to be made.

➤*Assigning Rooms.* Whenever possible—and it's possible more than it's practiced—the agent should attempt to *sell up*—to sell the guest a higher-priced room than was originally reserved. Good selling is the key to rooms profits (see Exhibit 9–18).

The best way to sell up (or up-sell) the product is to show it. At resorts, where longer stays are the norm, guests may prefer to see the room before signing in. That can be done—and has been done—with a screen monitor at the desk. With sophisticated reservations systems, the same image can be projected into the home to sell the reservation directly to the buyer via the Internet. The use of a front-desk photo album is another common (and inexpensive) way to demonstrate to the guest the various differences in room types.

Obviously, the better the clerk knows the product, the more rapidly and satisfactorily the assignment will be made. It has been jokingly said that the fewer the rooms available, the easier it is to make assignments. With few rooms, the guest must take what's offered or have nothing.

Property Management System Algorithms. The computer uses an algorithmic function to search its memory for appropriate room assignments. Algorithms are a series of "if-then" statements by which the computer arrives at the proper response. The algorithm comes into use when the computer displays an arrival list, an over-the-credit-limit report, or similar statements. It does the same with room assignments, but the program is more sophisticated.

Suppose that a double–double is to be assigned to the arriving party. The system can be made to display the first choice (the computer's first choice), and the room is then assigned. Or, if the clerk wishes, the screen will display all the double–doubles, including those ready, those on change, and those that are out of order (see Exhibit 8–9). Management can control the display—the first double–double displayed is the one that management wants sold first, and the final room on the list is to be sold last. In this manner, management controls rooms to accomplish any of several goals: to rotate room use equally, to concentrate occupancy in newly refurbished rooms at a higher rate, to restrict wings or floors to save energy, and others.

Upgrading. Upgrading a room assignment—giving a better accommodation for the original rate—is one technique for resolving complaints. It has other applications as well. Upgrades might be given to frequent-guest program members, to VIPs, to businesspersons from companies with negotiated corporate rates, and even to guests as a reward for patiently queuing.

Upgrades are also used if there are no rooms available at the rate reserved. In such cases, a well-trained and motivated front-desk clerk tries to up-sell the guest. More frequently, the guest is given the better room at the lower rate, but the upgrade is explained. If the differential is significant, the guest is moved the following day

```
Date: 06/06/__ 10:37                    THE LODGE AT RIVER'S EDGE
                                           Room Status Report
```

Room Number	Discrpncy	Room Type	Clean Sectn	Hskpg Credits	# of Guest	Room Status	Description
102		DDSN	R1	1	0	VACANT, CLEAN	RIVER N/S CONNECT 103
103		DDSN	R1	1	2	OCCUPIED, CLEAN	RIVER N/S CONNECT 102
105		KEX	R1	1.5	0	VACANT, CLEAN	RIVER S
106		KKEX	R1	1.5	2/2	OCCUPIED, CLEAN	RIVER S
107		KN	N1	1	2	OCCUPIED, CLEAN	POOL N/S
108		DDN	N1	1	0	VACANT, DIRTY	POOL N/S
109		KK	N1	1	2	VACANT, CLEAN, BLOCKED	POOL S
110		KEX	N1	1.5	0	VACANT, CLEAN	POOL S
111		PEXN	S1	2	0	VACANT, DIRTY	MTN VIEW N/S CONNECT 112
112		DDN	S1	1	0	VACANT, CLEAN	MTN VIEW N/S CONNECT 111
115		QSN	S1	1	0	VACANT, CLEAN	MTN VIEW N/S
116		DDSN	S1	1	2/3	OCCUPIED, CLEAN	MTN VIEW N/S
117		K	S1	1	3	VACANT, CLEAN, BLOCKED	MTN VIEW S
118		QS	S1	1	0	VACANT, CLEAN	MTN VIEW S
119		K	S1	1	2	VACANT, CLEAN, BLOCKED	MTN VIEW S
120		DD	S1	1	1	VACANT, CLEAN, BLOCKED	MTN VIEW S
121		PEXN	P1	2	1	OCCUPIED, CLEAN	SPA N/S
123		PEXN	P1	2	2	OCCUPIED, DIRTY	SPA S CONNECT 125
125		PEX	P1	2	1	VACANT, DIRTY, BLOCKED	SPA S CONNECT 123

```
MORE
Due check out: 30       Dirty: 67       Occupied: 114       Occupied/dirty: 52       Occupied/clean: 62
     Blocked: 24        Clean: 193      Vacant: 146         Vacant/dirty: 15         Vacant/clean: 131
```

Exhibit 8–9 This room status report displays rooms in numerical sequence. Other options allow the clerk to call up rooms by status and room type (display only clean, executive parlor, nonsmoking rooms—PEXN). With a computer algorithm, the system might call up rooms in reverse numerical order, or even randomly.

when the lower rate opens. The costs of moving, to both the guest and the hotel, warrant leaving the upgraded assignment for a few nights if the rate spread is small.

Did Not Stay.   A party that registers and leaves is a DNS—a did not stay. Dissatisfaction with the hotel or an incident with a staff member may precipitate the hasty departure. The guests sometimes seek remedy first, or they may leave without saying why. The cause isn't always the hotel. Emergency messages may be retrieved upon arrival, or a telephone call might come in soon after the room assignment. As a courtesy and to ensure good guest relations, usually no charge is levied if the party leaves within a reasonable time after arrival, even if the room was occupied for a short period.

As a control device, DNS guests are referred to the rooms division's supervisory staff. Upon further investigation, supervisors may uncover poorly trained employees, a weakness in the reservations system, or some other root problem as a result of the DNS complaint. Although the vast majority of DNS situations (which don't occur all that often) are legitimate, some caution is urged.

The most common DNS ruse happens when a conventioneer finds an open room at the headquarters hotel down the street. That's why caution is always urged with overflow guests housed in another hotel. Some managers actually ask the complaining DNS guest (who probably said something like "this room does not meet my standards" or "I've received an emergency call and must leave immediately") to wait a moment. The manager then phones the headquarters hotel and asks if they are holding a reservation for the guest (say Dr. Brown). If the response is "yes," the manager will explain to the DNS guest that the hotel must charge him for a one-night stay. When such guests realize their trickery has been uncovered, they usually settle down and spend the night(s) in the hotel after all.

Cash-Only Guests.   Although all guests are asked to establish credit at check in, few actually pay their bills in advance. Instead, most guests imprint a credit card or utilize their corporate account to establish credit against charges to be incurred during the visit. Only a small percentage of guests choose to pay cash (or a cash equivalent like a traveler's or personal check) at check in.

Under the law, hotel room charges may be demanded in advance. In addition, the law provides innkeepers with the right to hold luggage for nonpayment. This prejudgment lien is under court challenge. Rather than testing the issue, hotel keepers rely on the credit card and on their right to collect in advance.

Paid-in-advance or cash-only guests are "flagged" to prevent charges being made from other departments. Once the room is paid in advance, other departments must also collect cash for services rendered. Communicating that to the other departments often results in costly errors. You see, few hotel guests are cash-only customers. Even those who prefer to pay with cash at check out are encouraged to leave their credit card on file during the visit. In this way, explains the front-desk clerk, they can charge various expenses incurred around the property back to their hotel room account—it's far more convenient. Later they can replace the credit-card charges with cash upon check out, if that's their preference.

As such, few hotel guests are paid-in-advance customers (it is common in budget properties). Therefore, other hotel departments (restaurants, lounges, golf courses, health spas, clubhouses, gift shops, etc.) are relatively unaccustomed to dealing with cash-only guests. These other departments often forget to check their point-of-sale systems (which are usually interfaced with the property management system) to verify the guest's credit standing. In the end, they inadvertently deliver room service meals, extend access to tennis courts, and even allow merchandise charges to cash-only guests.

This places the burden of payment back on the shoulders of the front desk. A guest who has "charged" a $50 room-service meal must now pay for it. Some front-office managers will phone the guest's room and explain that a bellperson is coming up to collect payment; others leave a less intrusive message to please settle the account with the front desk. If the incident was accidental, the money is forthcoming. But those guests who were trying to defraud the hotel make themselves scarce at this point and never settle their account!

By the way, telephone charges are a common source of lost revenues from paid-in-advance guests. When checking in the paid-in-advance guest, with so much else on their minds, front-desk clerks sometimes forget to deactivate the in-room telephone from outgoing calls. Only during the night audit shift does the hotel then realize it has a cash-only guest owing $35.00 in long-distance charges. Certainly, the desk can't wake the guest at 2 AM, so they leave a note for the morning crew. When the morning desk staff follows up, they find that the guest has already departed.

VIP Guests.   Reservations may carry the designation VIP (very important person), SPATT (special attention required), Star Guest, or some other similar code. All these mean that the guest is an important person and the clerk should provide service in keeping with the visitor's stature. The guest could be the executive officer of a large association that is considering the hotel as a convention site, a corporate officer of the hotel chain, or perhaps a travel writer.

Such a designation sometimes requires the assistant manager to accompany the arriving guest to the room. It sometimes means that the guest need not register. It may also mean that no information about the guest will be given out to callers unless they are first screened.

There is a difference between a VIP and a DG (distinguished guest), according to one professional publication. The VIP represents either good publicity for the hotel or direct business, whereas the DG is honored because of position rather than economic value. Presidents, royalty, movie stars, and celebrities rate a DG designation. Meeting planners, company presidents, or committee chairpersons get the VIP treatment and then only during the tenure of their office. VIPs are treated to comp rooms, baskets of fruit, or bottles of liquor. Thoughtfulness and imagination sustained by personal consideration are more important to the DG than the amount of money spent.

▶ *Self-Check-in Kiosks.*   Even as hotels strive to provide higher levels of guest service, automated devices enable the guest to perform more and more front-office functions. The best example of customers serving themselves is self-check-in/self-check-out terminals or kiosks. Located in the lobbies of some of the finest hotels in the world, guest-operated terminals are no longer viewed as a reduction in service. Instead, self-check-in devices provide the guest with another long-awaited option. Rather than queuing at the front desk for an undetermined length of time, today's sophisticated traveler can opt for a self-check in (see Exhibit 8–10).

Integrated directly into the property management system, the self-check-in/self-check-out terminal offers choices much like a guest–service agent would. The guest can select room numbers and room types from an on-line inventory of clean and available rooms. In addition, many of these machines are portable, thereby allowing the hotel to strategically locate the terminal in busy areas (say, for a large group check in). Some hotels even locate the system in their shuttle vans for registration en route from the airport. Other hotels staff front-desk receptionists at airport luggage claim areas.

Exhibit 8–10 AutoCheck is an excellent example of a self-check-in kiosk. At the touch of a screen, this full-color system retrieves the guest reservation, verifies credit, authorizes in-house charges, checks the guest into the PMS, assigns a room, generates a keycard, prints the room number and directions, produces amenity coupons, and activates the phone, voice mail, movie, and energy management systems. *Courtesy of Multi-Systems, Incorporated, Phoenix, Arizona.*

While guests are waiting for their luggage, they can register using a hand-held terminal, and the room key is waiting upon arrival.

Prerequisites. Most self-check-in terminals require the arriving guest to hold an advanced reservation and a valid credit card. Although that is the current standard, these prerequisites are changing. Some of the newest self-check-in devices now provide an option for walk-in customers. However, the self-check-in process becomes more detailed for the walk-in guest. All of the basic information obtained during the reservation process (name, address, length of stay, etc.) must be input by the guest into the terminal. Some self-check-in terminals now accept cash. These are especially popular in limited-service motels that continue to sell rooms after hours via automated terminals.

Features. Some self-check-in systems display an electronic map of the property. In this way, guests can knowledgeably select rooms most convenient to them. In addition, it is possible for the terminal to display messages, promote certain aspects of the hotel, and even to up-sell the guest to a higher-priced room!

Most self-check-in/self-check-out terminals feature a built-in printer that provides the guest with a receipt of the transaction. This receipt may actually be used as a guest identification card during the stay. Some of the newer self-check-in systems even utilize touch-screen technology. Rather than using a keyboard or computer mouse for data entry, the guest need only touch the monitor. For example, if the computer provides a selected list of room types, the guest merely touches the list next to the room type of choice.

Self-check-in terminals also provide the guest with a room key. While some of the older systems required the guest to visit the key clerk at the front desk, most of the more recent terminals include an automated key function. At the end of the self-check-in process, the system dispenses a key or prompts the guest to remove a blank key card from the stack and swipe it through the electronic key writing slot. As an added bonus, many systems allow guests to use their personal credit cards as the room key.

Case Study.   Numerous chains have introduced self-check-in systems over the last few years. Hyatt Hotels' Touch and Go system is available at almost all of its non-resort properties. HFS (now Cendant) has built its AutoCheck system into every one of its Wingate Inns. The list, including Promus, Hilton, Choice, and others, continues to grow.

Choice Hotels created a whole new chain based around the premise that some guests prefer efficiency over service. This new chain, MainStay Suites (there are currently 15 all-suite properties with rates ranging from $50 to $110), doesn't even have a front desk! Instead, guests proceed to a kiosk, where they choose the language (English, Spanish, or French) with which they prefer to check in. They then select a task from one of four icons: check in, check out, other hotel services, or community information.

During the check-in process, an automated voice takes the guest through each step. The voice asks the guest to swipe the same credit card used to make the reservation. The card number then accesses the reservation particulars from the central reservation system, Choice 2001. The voice then asks a series of questions related to departure date, room preference, and rate. Once the particulars are verified, the system asks the guest to create and confirm a PIN number. This number is used to access the MainStay Suites system during the remainder of the guest's stay.

At this point, the self-check-in kiosk dispenses a key (or keys), displays a bird's-eye view of the property, and prints an advance folio. The folio reiterates the room rate, check-in and check-out dates, and the room number. It also tells the guest how to find the room and where best to park. The folio is the only place where the guest is addressed by name or room number—for security reasons, the system never displays the guest's name or room number except on printed receipts. When everything is concluded, guests press the "finish" button, and the system wishes them a nice visit.

Establishing Guest Credit

Accurate identification at check in is so important as to be mandated by many local statutes. By accurately knowing the guest, the hotel protects itself and provides a valuable service to local law enforcement agencies. Information about transient visitors can be of critical importance. In Rhode Island, a guest was found murdered. The hotel had obtained no identification at check in, and it took authorities many days to identify the victim.

Proper identification also serves to protect the hotel. When cash customers are allowed to check in without producing identification, the hotel opens itself to a number of potential problems. A classic case in Arizona illustrates the point. A guest checked into a one-story motel, paid cash for the room, and signed the registration card with a phony name. In the dead of the night, the guest proceeded to load his van with all of the room's furnishings. The next day, the guest was gone, the motel room was bare, and the motel had absolutely no recourse, having failed to obtain proper identification. (And the room was truly bare. The guest had taken everything—the TV set, bed, and dresser, as well as the toilet, tub, and carpet!)

Even if the guest has no intention of stealing, securing guest identification aids the hotel in a multitude of ways. Knowing the guest's name and address allows the hotel to return lost and found items, bill and collect late charges, and maintain a valuable database.

➤*Credit Cards.*   Every registration card asks the guest to identify the method of payment (see Exhibit 8–5). If a personal or company check is the answer, credit approval must be obtained from the rooms division manager. More likely, a credit card is tendered. If there is a choice, the desk should always request the card for which the hotel has negotiated the best merchant fee (see Chapter 12).

With a PMS, the credit-card data is entered into the electronic folio either through the computer keyboard or by means of a credit-card reader. Using a credit-card reader, the room clerk gets a simultaneous authorization about the validity of the card from the credit-card company. The terminal reads the magnetic strip and communicates that number electronically to the credit-card clearinghouse. Use of electronic credit-card scanners integrated with property management systems saves about 40 valuable seconds during the check-in process. The number can be punched in manually if the strip signal is damaged or inoperative. Back comes an authorization number (or a denial), which appears on the screen of the credit-card reader. The authorization number is the hotel's guarantee that the credit card is legitimate.

An approval number can also be obtained by telephone. The clerk talks either to a computer or to an actual person. The telephone method is time consuming and prone to error. Forty digits must be verbalized, including the number of the card, the expiration date, the merchant's number, and the amount of the sale. Still, it is better than the technique used some 20 years ago in which the clerk scanned printed lists of invalid numbers before accepting the card. Under current procedures, the burden of approval is on the card company.

Part of the communication between the credit-card company and the hotel involves the amount of charges that will be added to the guest's balance. Limits exist for both the hotel and the individual. These "floor limits" are explained in Chapter 12. That discussion also includes the next steps in the credit-card story: processing the card at departure and collecting from the credit-card company.

➤*Back-Office Records.*   Front-office records post departmental charges incurred by the guest against the credit established at check in. Back-office records track those charges through the bank or credit-card company until payment has been received. Credit cards are just one of several records initiated by the front office but completed by the back office. Final settlement of travel agency bills clears through the back office, although the reservation and paperwork begin at the front. Frequent-guest records and frequent-flyer partnership records are another front-office/back-office relationship. The disposition of these various records is explained in Chapter 12. It is not a matter that concerns the clerk at the point of registration.

Record keeping for frequent-guest or frequent-flyer programs is a new job for the front office. It has just recently been incorporated into the PMS at many properties. Guests using automatic-teller registration may still be required to go to the desk to get frequent-guest credits.

➤ *THE ROOMING PROCESS*

While the guest registration process nears completion, a bellperson may arrive to escort the guest to the room. As the guest moves into the realm of the bell department, a number of critical functions are accomplished. The bellperson explains various locations and departments throughout the hotel, details a list of current hotel activities and promotions, and serves as final inspector before the guest prepares to occupy the room.

Uniformed Services

The bellstaff is part of a much larger department commonly referred to as uniformed services. Throughout the guest's visit, the uniformed services department attends to various needs and services. Valet parking, doorpersons, concierges, hotel security, and the bell staff all play a key role in enchancing the property's image. No other department has the degree of personal one-on-one time with the guest as does uniformed services.

Like all members of uniformed services, the bellstaff are goodwill ambassadors who turn an ordinary visit into a warm and personable experience (see Exhibit 8–11). By developing close, professional relationships with the guest, a well-trained bellperson successfully promotes a number of hotel services. Suggestive selling and gentle persuasion are invaluable skills for a bellperson to possess.

Exhibit 8–11   The legendary elegance of the Fairmont Hotel, built atop San Francisco's Nob Hill in 1907, is embodied in the bell department. A large bellstand (centered in the lobby just behind the bellman standing in the photo) staffs more than 20 bellpersons for this 600-room property. *Courtesy of The Fairmont Hotel and Tower, San Francisco, California.*

➤ *Guest Communication.*   Bellpersons, like all members of the uniformed services staff, are encouraged to engage the guest in conversation. Whenever staff members see a guest, they should make the effort to smile and at least offer a simple greeting (see Exhibit 8–12). By taking such steps, the guest comes to know and trust one or more members of the uniformed staff.

It is interesting to watch which uniformed personnel are attracted to which guests. Sometimes it is a matter of personality type or due to a relationship formed during the rooming process. Whatever the reason, many guests develop a favorite

---

Among the requirements for a Four- and Five-Diamond ranking by the American Automobile Association are the following services expected of bellpersons:

All Bellpersons Must:
__ Be neatly uniformed.
__ Wear tasteful nametags.
__ Be friendly, courteous, and helpful.
__ Be knowledgeable of hotel and area.
__ Make good eye contact with guests.
__ Acknowledge the presence of guests (e.g., when passing in corridors).

On Guest Reception:
__ Welcome guest to the hotel.
__ Address guest by name (should pick up on name from desk or luggage tags).
__ Explain food and beverage department, recreational and other facilities.
__ Hang garment bag in closet.
__ Take out and set up luggage rack; suitcase should be placed on luggage rack, not on bed or floor.
__ Explain operation of lights, TV, and thermostat.
__ Offer ice at a Four-Diamond, expected to be automatic at a Five-Diamond.
__ Point out emergency exits or diagram.
__ Offer to open or close drapes.
__ Explain any unusual features within the room.
__ Explain turn-down.
__ Check bathroom supplies.
__ Offer additional services.

On Check Out:
__ Arrive promptly (wait should not exceed 10 minutes).
__ Check around room and in bathroom for belongings that might be left behind.
__ Offer to arrange for car delivery.

Source: "Highly Effective Bell Staff Enhances Your Property's Image." *Hotel & Resort Industry*, May 1988, pp. 84–89.

Exhibit 8–12   AAA inspectors rate hotels based on a number of criteria. Here are the bell guidelines for four- and five-diamond properties.

among the bellpersons or other uniformed services staff. Such relationships, as long as they remain in the boundaries of professional behavior, are encouraged by management.

By developing such personable relationships, the bellperson is well situated to know when the guest's visit has gone awry. The bellperson can then approach the guest and solicit the complaint. Careful training places the bellperson in the critical role as bridge between the dissatisfied guest and the responsible department. When management works to keep open these lines of communication, the bellperson performs a key function in the hotel's quality assurance program.

➤*The Importance of Training.*　Although a professional dialogue is encouraged, it is often difficult to monitor and maintain. All uniformed services staff (but especially the bellperson) have ample opportunity to speak with the guest on an intimate level. By design, bellpersons have a great deal of autonomy. During the rooming process, driving the airport shuttle, and at other times, the bellperson can be with a guest(s)—and out of management's sight—for 10 or 15 minutes at a time. Therefore, it is difficult for management to know what is actually being discussed with the guest during these one-on-one conversations.

There are numerous examples of bellpersons stepping over the line of acceptable behavior. Distraught with the job, a bellperson might bad-mouth the hotel or senior management to the guest. Disappointed with the lack of gratuities that day, a bellperson might boldly ask for a more generous tip from the guest. There are even cases where bellpersons dealt drugs and prostitution to the guest! Minimizing such occurrences begins with proper hiring and continues with constant training.

Mystery Shopper Services.　Because it is so difficult to assess the bellperson's professionalism while he or she is rooming the guest, many managers stress its importance with secret shopper services. Such services work on the premise that employees act differently when they sense that management is watching. On the other hand, a secret shopper posing as a hotel guest is able to truly observe the employee's professionalism on the job.

Secret shoppers visit the property and stay one or more nights (see Chapter 7). During this time, they attempt to engage employees in a number of usual and sometimes unusual activities. Although employees are probably forewarned that secret audits may be conducted, they usually have no idea they are being observed. As a result, secret shopper services are an excellent way to monitor the effectiveness of employee training—especially in the uniformed services department.

The Bell Staff

Several innovations have affected the uniformed services department's functions and means of earning income. Self-service icemakers and vending machines on the floor, and in-room refrigerators and minibars, have reduced the kind and number of service calls that bellpersons make. Group arrivals and self-check-in kiosks, in which individuals room themselves, further reduce the service functions of this department.

➤*Rotation of Fronts.*　Tips comprise the bulk of the bell department's earnings. According to a study done by the American Hotel & Motel Association, the bellperson's cash salary was the lowest of any hotel employee. Despite this, total earnings usually exceed that of other front-office employees, including some management positions.

The bellperson who comes forward to take the rooming slip and room the guest is called a *front*. Fronts rotate in turn. The one who has just completed a front is called a *last*. Lasts are used for errands that are unlikely to produce gratuities. Cleaning the lobby is a responsibility of the last. Lasts are also assigned dead room changes, with no chance of a gratuity, such as lockouts and moves carried out in the guest's absence.

Between the front and the last, positions rotate in sequence, moving forward in the rank as each new front is called. Each position in the sequence should be represented by a particular post in the lobby. One station might be by the front door to receive incoming luggage; another across the lobby; a third by the elevators. Staffing requirements for a full-service bell department run approximately one bellperson for every 40 to 50 estimated check ins (see Exhibit 8–11).

The procedure is much less formal today. Fronts wait by the bellstand, which is visible from the front desk. As the clerk completes the registration, the front is summoned to the desk by lights or signals or verbally by the clerk calling "Front!" Aware of the routine, the front rarely needs prompting.

With a property management system, remote printers located at the bellstand print the rooming slips, so the bellpersons approach the guests aware of their names. By coding the printout, the desk communicates additional information (VIP, heavy luggage, etc.) to the bell department. The PMS also maintains a record of fronts.

A record of fronts assures each person a proper turn, although the sequence may be altered if a guest requests a specific person or if a last is still away on some long-term errand. The record, maintained at the bellcaptain's desk, tracks the crew, which is the most mobile department in the hotel. By noting the bellperson's presence on various floors at various times, the record offers protection from accusations in the event of theft or other trouble. It fixes responsibility about the rooming procedure or lost luggage. The comings and goings of the bell staff, the purposes of their errands, and the times elapsed are recorded and maintained.

➤*Responsiblities of the Bell Staff.*   Depending on the level of service for the particular hotel, there may be no uniformed services department at all. In many small hotels, the bell staff is a catch-all department that performs a multitude of tasks. Small operations may ask the bellperson to drive the shuttle van, act as doorperson, make room-service calls, deliver cocktails to guests relaxing in the lobby, and even aid the front-desk staff during meal-break periods.

Certain responsibilities are outside the scope of the bell department's duties. Bellpersons do not quote rates or suggest room assignments. They call the room clerk for a second assignment whenever the guest is dissatisfied with the room.

Bellpersons, or just the captains, share in other incomes. Auto rentals, tickets to local attractions, and bus tours are available at the captain's desk. Each of these companies pays a commission (usually 10 to 15%) that more often accrues to the uniformed services than to the hotel. This may also hold true when the hotel contracts an outside laundry or dry cleaner for guest service.

Luggage.   The doorperson, or just as often the guest, carries in the baggage from the cab or car. It stays on the lobby floor until the guest is finished registering. The room clerk gives a rooming slip to the bellperson, who now takes over the guest's service. Jointly, the guest and the bellperson identify and retrieve the luggage and head toward the elevator. The guest, the bellperson, and the baggage might ride up together. Or the bellperson might leave the guest in order to transport the luggage on the service (rear) elevator, while the guest rides the guest (front) elevator. They meet at the elevator lobby on the guest's assigned floor.

Final Inspection.   Rooming guests is the primary task of the bell department. Although many individuals room themselves, it is preferable to go in the company of a staff member. Guests who are in the company of a bellperson avoid the embarrassment of walking in on an occupied room. Service personnel always knock and wait before unlocking the door.

Once inside, the bellperson performs another inspection function. First, the bellperson hangs the guest's loose clothing and hefts the baggage onto the luggage rack or bed (see Exhibit 8–12). Temperature controls are checked, and the room is inspected for cleanliness, towels, soap, toilet tissue, facial tissue, and other needs. Lights, hangers, television sets, and furnishings are examined. Special features of the hotel are explained—the spa or the operating hours of room service, for example.

Self-service items are pointed out—the ice machine, or the in-room refrigerator. Connecting doors are unlocked if the party is to share several connecting rooms. Unless there is a special request for service, the bellperson leaves the key and the rooming slip and accepts the proffered tip, if any. Before leaving, there may be a final sell for a particular dining room or lounge and a final "good day."

Group Luggage Handling.   Tour groups are easy for the bellstaff to handle and are generally quite profitable. Using the guest list furnished by the group, the desk preregisters the party (see Exhibit 8–13). Roommates, whom the tour company has identified, are assigned, and keys are readied in small envelopes for quick distribution (see Exhibit 12–3). Similar key envelopes are prepared for rapid distribution to airline crews when permanent reservations have been negotiated with the airline.

The property management system can print the key envelopes (coded by groups), the rooming lists (knowing who is with whom and where is very important to the tour guide or the company meeting planner), identification cards for in-house use, baggage tags, and every other form needed for a successful group meeting. All of these items are derived from the same basic information, which is fed into the computer only once.

Final instructions to the tour members are given on the bus. Communication is impossible once the captive audience is lost. Tour members are reminded that charges not included in the tour price will need to be settled individually with the hotel. A notice to that effect is also included in the key envelope (sometimes called the key packet). The envelopes are distributed in the lobby (or on the bus) by the desk, the tour coordinator, or sometimes the bellstaff. Guests find their own rooms without help from the bell department while the baggage is being unloaded from the bus.

Group baggage can be a headache as well as a backache for the uniformed services if bags are improperly marked or hard to identify. Putting some procedures in place makes the task easier. The tour company should provide each traveler with brightly colored tags to attach to the luggage before departure. The color identifies the group, expediting baggage handling in and out of the airport and the hotel. The individual's number is written on each tag, and that number corresponds to that person's place on the master rooming sheet (see Exhibit 8–13). Copies of the list should have been given to every hotel on the tour. The number, which is easier to read than a name, helps the bellstaff match the bags with room numbers.

Refer #	GUEST NAME		ROOM	GROUP	ARRIVAL	DEPART	COMPANY LINE	# PERS
	HMS32G	FINNERMAN					VAIL SKI MEADOW'S LODGE	2/05/
1	ADAMS	ADAM	609	NEWMEX	2/05	2/08	NEW MEXICO ST. SKI TEAM	1
2	BURTON	BOB	607	NEWMEX	2/05	2/08	NEW MEXICO ST. SKI TEAM	1
3	CURTIS	CHARLES	612	NEWMEX	2/05	2/08	NEW MEXICO ST. SKI TEAM	1
4	DILARDO	DALE	612	NEWMEX	2/05	2/08	NEW MEXICO ST. SKI TEAM	1
5	ELAN	EVAN	616	NEWMEX	2/05	2/08	NEW MEXICO ST. SKI TEAM	1
6	FEINSTEIN	FRED	613	NEWMEX	2/05	2/08	NEW MEXICO ST. SKI TEAM	1
7	GRAY	GARY	604	NEWMEX	2/05	2/08	NEW MEXICO ST. SKI TEAM	1
8	HARRIS	HARRY	606	NEWMEX	2/05	2/08	NEW MEXICO ST. SKI TEAM	1
9	INGOLS	IAN	616	NEWMEX	2/05	2/08	NEW MEXICO ST. SKI TEAM	1
10	JEFFREYS	JEFF	606	NEWMEX	2/05	2/08	NEW MEXICO ST. SKI TEAM	1
11	KASTLE	KRIS	604	NEWMEX	2/05	2/08	NEW MEXICO ST. SKI TEAM	1
12	LANGE	LOUIS	605	NEWMEX	2/05	2/08	NEW MEXICO ST. SKI TEAM	1
13	MORRISON	MORRIS	602	NEWMEX	2/05	2/08	NEW MEXICO ST. SKI TEAM	1
14	NORDICA	NEWT	605	NEWMEX	2/05	2/08	NEW MEXICO ST. SKI TEAM	1
15	OLIN	ORSON	609	NEWMEX	2/05	2/08	NEW MEXICO ST. SKI TEAM	1
16	POWELL	PAUL	607	NEWMEX	2/05	2/08	NEW MEXICO ST. SKI TEAM	1
17	QUAIL	QUINN	618	NEWMEX	2/05	2/08	NEW MEXICO ST. SKI TEAM	1
18	ROSSIGNOL	ROBERT	602	NEWMEX	2/05	2/08	NEW MEXICO ST. SKI TEAM	1
							TOTAL PEOPLE:	18

Exhibit 8–13 A group rooming list showing names (and reference numbers), room numbers assigned, arrival and departure dates, and group affiliation is initially prepared by the tour operator or meeting planner. This list serves as the reference document for baggage, billing, and group communication. Small groups such as this are usually housed on the same floor to ease luggage handling.

There is another variation: Each bag can be marked with the correct room number from a computer printed list of adhesive-backed labels. The bellperson removes the room number from the printed list and slaps it on the bag for delivery.

All hotels that cater to tour and meetings business use similar techniques for delivering group baggage. Although it has the appearance of antiservice, delivering the group's luggage in bulk is really the only efficient manner for handling the task. By eliminating the one-on-one rooming of each guest, the bell department can move through luggage deliveries quickly. Aside from being escorted to their rooms, group guests don't miss much else. Information normally shared during the rooming process—hours of the restaurant, for example—is shared by a desk clerk or bellcaptain during a short presentation to the captive audience on the bus. This frees the bell department to get right to luggage deliveries. Within 30 to 45 minutes, most small and midsized groups will have received their luggage.

Group luggage is the bellpersons' bread and butter. That's because the bell department is paid a small stipend for every group guest arriving and departing that day. Group contracts include a negotiable charge commonly referred to as "baggage in and baggage out." Group baggage handling rates run as little as $2 per person in and $2 per person out, to as much as $6 per person each direction. Group baggage handling rates may be a factor of unionization (unionized bell departments may set a minimally acceptable rate), the time of year the group arrives, the room rate paid, and so on. The entire fee (both in and out) is paid at the time of contract, and a hotel that handles a lot of group business can easily supplement paychecks by several hundred dollars per bellperson per week.

►*Rooming Slips.*   The rooming slip serves as a vehicle for communication between the front desk and both the bellperson and the guest. The bellperson uses the rooming slip to better understand the guest and the rooming situation. The slip provides the bellperson with information related to the guest's name, the guest's affiliation or corporate name (if appropriate), the room number assigned, the guest's home city (great for making small talk), and the number of nights reserved. As explained earlier, the rooming slip also serves as a support document to prove the bellperson's whereabouts during a specific period in question.

Although not intended for that purpose, the slips have been used by the Internal Revenue Service. Estimating the average tip per front and counting the number of fronts according to the rooming slips provides a fair estimate of tip income. The estimate is then compared to that reported by the employee.

Content.   The guest uses the rooming slip for two purposes: as a receipt and as guest identification. As a receipt, the rooming slip provides the guest with an additional opportunity to verify the accuracy of information. For example, the rooming slip may show that the guest's name has been misspelled. The room rate, date of check out, or some other information may also be inaccurate. Many rooming slips restate hotel disclaimers as a means of strengthening the hotel's legal relationship with the guest (see Exhibit 8–14; see also Exhibit 8–15).

Overseas hotels use the rooming slip as a sales tool for their own property and for local, noncompeting businesses. Few American hotels sell such advertising space. With their more extensive services and facilities, they need all the space themselves.

The American rooming slip is an interesting mix of selling, services, and legal safeguards. Depending on management's inclination, the rooming slip is either a simple slip of paper or a complete, elaborate sales tool in a variety of colors. Caesars

Informative
 Floor plan of the property
 Aerial view of the property
 Telephone directory of services
 Kinds of lobby shops
 Foreign language capabilities of the staff
 Airline, taxi, and limousine telephone
  numbers
 Local sites to see and things to do
 Airport bus: times of operation and rates
 Currency exchange capabilities
 Map of the city with highway designa-
  tions

Marketing
 List of restaurants: prices, hours of operation, and menu specialties
 A message of welcome or a note of appreciation
 WATS number for other hotels in the
  chain
 Recreational facilities: tennis, golf, pool,
  sauna

Regulatory
 Check-out hour and check-in hour
 Rate of gratuity applied to the room
  charge
 Regulations for visitors
 Limitations on pets

 Dress code
 Availability of the safe for valuables
 Settlement of accounts
 Expectations for guaranteed reservation
  holders
 Deposit of room keys when leaving the
  property
 Fees for local telephone calls

Identification
 Clerk's identifying initials
 Identification of the party: name, number
  of persons, rate, arrival and departure
  dates
 Room number
 Key code—where room access is con-
  trolled by a dial system key

Instructional
 Express check-out procedure
 Electrical capacity for appliances
 What to do in case of fire
 How to secure the room
 Notification to the desk if errors exist on
  the rooming slip
 How to operate the in-room films; their
  cost
 How to operate the in-room refrigerator;
  cost
 Rate of tax applied to the room charge

Exhibit 8–14   The size and breadth of the property dictates the size and breadth of the rooming slip. Small hotels may provide little more than a simple receipt to the registered guest. Other hotels, anxious to market in-house services, local attractions, paid advertisers, and legal disclaimers, may provide a multipage rooming booklet (see Exhibit 8–15). This exhibit demonstrates the variety of content found on rooming slips in the United States.

Palace in Las Vegas has a rooming booklet of 20 pages! Exhibit 8–14 lists the range of information that a hotel might try to communicate to the guest.

Color-coded rooming slips, like that of Hyatt's Passports, may also serve as a guest identification card. The color tells the cashiers in the bars and dining rooms whether the guest is a paid-in-advance guest, a tour group member, a VIP, and so on.

Although the guest is just arriving, check-out information and a check-out form are frequently provided in order to plan for a quick departure. Quick check out has been in place far longer than self-check-in/self-check-out terminals. Innovative departure systems that did not need computer hardware were inaugurated as early as 1975. However, they all require the guest to use a credit card or other form of advance credit.

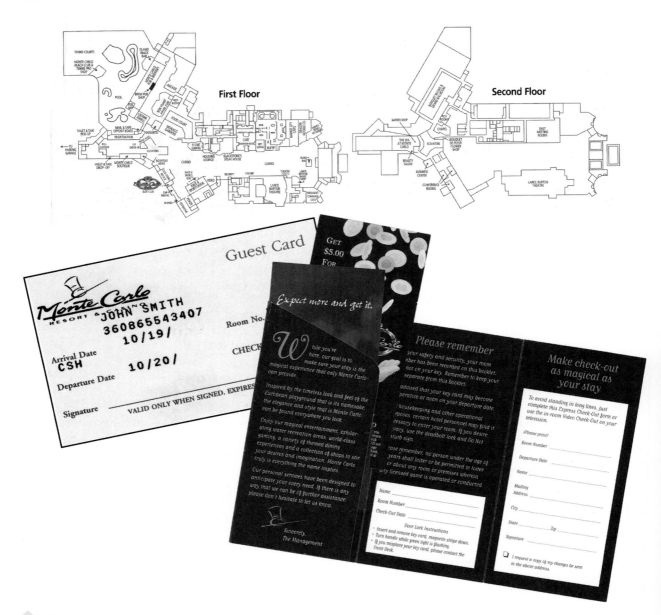

Exhibit 8–15   Example of a rooming slip and packet presented to arriving guests at the Monte Carlo Resort & Casino. Not only are arrivals given a guest card for making room charges across the property, but they are also presented a welcome packet. Included in the packet is a property map; a few gaming, food, and beverage coupons; an express check-out form; and assorted legalistic statements. *Courtesy of the Monte Carlo Resort & Casino, Las Vegas, Nevada.*

➤ SUMMARY

Arriving guests face a number of opportunities to meet members of the uniformed staff. Valet parking, the doorperson, guest service agent, and the bell department all play critical roles in the arrival process. The first impressions made by these employees create a positive (or negative) lasting effect on the guest's perception of the hotel operation.

The check-in procedure represents an especially sensitive segment of the arrival process. The front-desk clerk communicates with the guest in an unscripted fashion where few rules dictate their interaction. A wise front-desk clerk evaluates the guest and attempts to understand unique requirements. Too rapid a check in and the guest leaves with a sense of rudeness or having been rushed. Too slow a check in and the guest perceives inefficiency in the hotel operation. Add to this sensitivity the need for the desk clerk to retrieve payment, extract additional information, get a signature on the registration card, ask credit questions, and attempt to up-sell to a higher-priced room, and the check-in process can be a tense several minutes.

The bell department spends the last moments with the arriving guest. Rooming the guest is a complex process of small talk, suggestive selling, room inspection, and overall guest service. Oh yes—bellpersons carry the luggage as well.

➤ QUESTIONS AND PROBLEMS

1. Reorganize the following jumbled list of events, persons, and job activities into a logical flow from start to finish of the guest arrival process:
   (a) Room selection
   (b) Establishing guest credit
   (c) Registered, not assigned
   (d) Bellperson
   (e) Valet parking attendant
   (f) Rotation of fronts
   (g) Room assignment
   (h) Obtaining guest identification
   (i) Rooming slip
   (j) Upgrading and/or up-selling
   (k) Rooming the guest
   (l) Preblocking rooms
   (m) Doorperson
   (n) Registration card
   (o) Check-out reminder
   (p) Room status report
   (q) AAA discount
   (r) Pet deposit

2. Foreign registration cards often require significantly more personal information than is required for domestic registration cards. Some management personnel feel that this extra data amounts to an invasion of the guest's privacy. Other managers, however, believe this extra information aids the hotel in providing better security and service levels to the guest. With whom do you side? Why might a hotel legitimately need to know your future and past destinations, your mother's maiden name, and your date of birth?

3. Intentional bias can be programmed (through computer algorithms) into the room-selection sequence of a property management system. Rooms will then appear in a prescribed order rather than in sequence or at random. Certain rooms can be offered first, or not, depending on management's criteria. Give examples explaining why management might wish to decide which rooms appear in which sequence in order to direct the clerk's selection.

4. A local merchant, whose attempts to service the hotel's guest laundry and dry cleaning business have been frustrated, visits with the new rooms manager. (The laundry of this 600-room, commercial hotel does not clean personal guest items.) The conversation makes the rooms manager realize that she has never seen commission figures on any of the reports. She learns that the bellcaptain, who doesn't seem to do any work—that is, he doesn't take fronts—gets the commissions.

   The rooms manager initiates a new policy. All commissions from car rentals, bus tours, ski tickets, laundry, balloon rides, and so on, will accrue to the hotel. An unresolved issue is whether or not the money will go into the employee's welfare fund.

   A very angry bellcaptain presents himself at the office of the vice president of the rooms division. Explain with whom you agree (the rooms manager or the bellcaptain) and prepare an argument to support your opinion.

5. Some hotels upgrade corporate guests to nicer rooms when space is available. Usually, the guest need not even ask for this courtesy—it is offered as standard operating procedure. Managers of such properties believe that the corporate guest appreciates the courtesy and the nicer room. And since the room is not likely to sell anyway, why not make someone happy?

   The reverse side of this argument, however, suggests that the guest comes to expect this treatment and even feels slighted if only standard rooms are available. In addition, hotels that give upgrades away free are doing themselves a disservice in terms of up-selling corporate guests to a higher rate. After all, why should corporate guests ever select higher-priced rooms (or concierge floor rooms) when they are given at no extra charge as a matter of standard practice? How would you respond to these arguments?

6. Ten weary, footsore travelers,
   All in a woeful plight,
   Sought shelter at a wayside inn
   One dark and stormy night.
   "Nine beds—no more," the landlord said,
   "Have I to offer you;
   To each of eight a single room,
   But number nine serves two."
   A din arose. The troubled host
   Could only scratch his head;
   For of those tired men, no two
   Could occupy one bed.
   The puzzled host was soon at ease—
   He was a clever man—
   And so to please his guests devised
   The most ingenious plan:
   | A | B | C | D | E | F | G | H | I |
   In a room marked A, two men were placed;
   The third he lodged in B.
   The fourth to C was then assigned.
   The fifth went off to D.
   In E the sixth he tucked away.
   In F the seventh man;
   The eighth and ninth to G and H.
   And then to A he ran.
   Wherein the host, as I have said,
   Had lain two travelers by.
   Then taking one—the tenth and last,
   He lodged him safe in I.
   Nine single rooms—a room for each—
   Were made to serve for ten.
   And this it is that puzzles me
   And many wiser men.

   —Excerpted from *Hotel News,* Winnipeg, 1935.

   Does it also puzzle you? How was the ingenious host able to lodge ten men in only nine rooms?

➤ *NOTES*

1. According to the American Hotel & Motel Association (AH&MA), pets are welcome in more than 23,000 U.S. lodging establishments, up from 10,000 hotels in 1994. Additional information can be found in *Accommodations Offering Facilities for Your Pet,* published by the American Automobile Association.

2. The experience of one 291-room full-service property demonstrated savings of 6,000 gallons of water and 40 gallons of detergent per month just by laundering bed sheets every other day. And that was for an optional program in which not all guests chose to participate.

CHAPTER 9

Setting the Room Rate

Outline

➤ *FACTORS IN ESTABLISHING THE ROOM RATE*

In recent years, average room rates have risen from two to six times the national rate of inflation. There are a number of reasons why rates are rising so quickly. Inflation is certainly part of the answer. But also to blame for recent rate increases are higher daily operating costs (including rising labor rates) and an increased consumer demand for hotel rooms. The result of these factors is an industry whose prices are sometimes suprisingly strong.

In 1975, roughly 25 years ago, the average hotel room in the United States was selling for just $17.29. An average room in the year 2000 is projected to sell for $89.76! That equates to a 6.81% compounded rise in average room rates over 25 years (see Chapter 1). A similar growth over the next 25 years will see the average American spending $465.98 per room night in the year 2025—a frightening thought. How old will you be in 2025? Will you be able to afford $466 for a night at the Holiday Inn?

Hotel Room Demand

Probably the biggest culprit in the industry's flight to higher room rates is the nation's economy itself. The late 1990s represented the greatest nonwartime boom that the world, especially the United States, has ever experienced. A natural result of a booming economy is an increased demand for hotel rooms. To respond to this demand, the industry has been building hotels at a feverish rate. Today, there are more hotel rooms available in the United States than ever before, but room demand is higher than ever before, too.

The result is a form of inflation—inflation at a microeconomic level, affecting just the travel industry. Inflation occurs when too many dollars are chasing too few goods. The result from such a dilemma is a rise in consumer prices; and the entire travel industry (hotels, air travel, rental cars, and restaurant meals, to be specific) has experienced an inflation of prices over the past several years (see Exhibit 9–1).

The amazing thing about the great economic boom of the late 1990s is that most other industries demonstrated extremely low inflation. The national Consumer Price Index (CPI) reflected low single-digit inflation during most of the boom years (generally 2 to 3%). Most products, the travel industry excepted, cost little more today than they did, say, five years ago—but not so with hotel rooms. Hotel rooms represent a microcosm of the overall economy; and a unique microcosm at that. When the whole economy is booming, salespeople are traveling; companies, both large and small, are hosting more lavish corporate retreats; and conferences are boasting record attendance. The leisure travel market, flush with its own sense of wealth, is also traveling more.

The result is increased rooms demand. And of course, increased demand means higher average rates. That's the uniqueness of the situation—the rest of the economy is booming but inflation is staying in check, while the hotel industry is seeing rapid rate increases—increases that are averaging about twice the inflation rate of other industries (see Exhibit 9–1). The thing about "averages," however, is that there are highs and lows. Some markets (mostly major urban areas) are seeing rate increases even higher than those described above. Other markets are stagnant in terms of room rate inflation.

➤*Competition.*   Just as operating costs dictate the minimum a hotel can afford to charge, competition sets the maximum it can expect to get. External competition

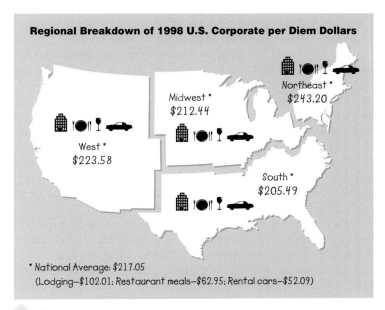

Regional Breakdown of 1998 U.S. Corporate per Diem Dollars

Northeast *
$243.20

Midwest *
$212.44

West *
$223.58

South *
$205.49

* National Average: $217.05
(Lodging–$102.01; Restaurant meals–$62.95; Rental cars–$52.09)

Exhibit 9–1   In the year 1998, all four regions in the country broke through the invisible $200 per diem (per day) barrier—for the first time ever. Hotel rooms, restaurant meals, rental cars, and other travel expenses rose at roughly 6% per year in the late 1990s—surprising increases when inflation was hovering at record lows, about 3% per year.

from neighboring facilities prescribes the general price range. Internal physical differences within the rooms determine the rate increments.

Supply and demand, the degree of saturation, and the extent of rate cutting in the community fix the rate parameters. Customers comparison shop, and hotel management should do the same. Differences in both the physical facilities and the range of services offered justify higher rates than the competition. The physical accommodations are easier to compare; they are there for the looking. Swimming pool, tennis courts, meeting rooms, restaurants, and a lobby bar head a long list of differences that give one property a competitive advantage over its neighbor. Room size, furnishings (bed and bath types), location, and exposure differentiate the internal product.

The condition of the facilities can offset their competitive advantage. "Clean and neat" sends an important subliminal message. Hotels with burnt-out bulbs in the hotel sign, wilted flowers in the planters, and dirty glass on the entrance door lose out to hotels with lesser facilities that look fresh and new.

Differences in service are more difficult to discern, but they add to the room rate charge as substantially as do other components. Twenty-four-hour room service, pool guard on duty, and an extensive training program for employees begin another, less visible list of competitive advantages. Like the capital outlays of the physical accommodations, these costs must be recaptured in the room rate as well.

►*Room Rate Elasticity.*   Elasticity is the change in demand (rooms sold) resulting from a change in price (room rates). If demand increases with a drop in price (or decreases when price is raised), demand is elastic. If demand appears unaffected by drops or increases in price, demand is inelastic. Hotel room rate reductions in an elastic market generate new business (higher occupancy). Hotel room rate reductions in an inelastic market generate little or no new business.

The hotel industry has always believed that reductions in rate produce less new business than is lost from lowering the unit price, thereby suggesting that room demand is somewhat inelastic. The supposition was supported by actual experience. Room income (occupancy multiplied by average daily rate) actually rose during the low-occupancy periods of the past decade because increased room rates did not drive away significant amounts of sales (occupancy). It did not, goes the reasoning, because room demand is inelastic (see Exhibit 9–2).

Elasticity of demand for hotel rooms is exceedingly complex. An inelastic property can actually increase rates during an economic slump with profitable results. Rate changes can be disastrous—or very beneficial—depending on the elasticity of demand and the direction of change chosen by management.

Different markets have different degrees of sensitivity. Tour properties are more elastic, and commercial demand is more inelastic. Hotels experience different degrees of elasticity throughout the year. That is what the demand pricing behind seasonal rates is all about. A given hotel may have numerous seasons throughout its annual cycle.

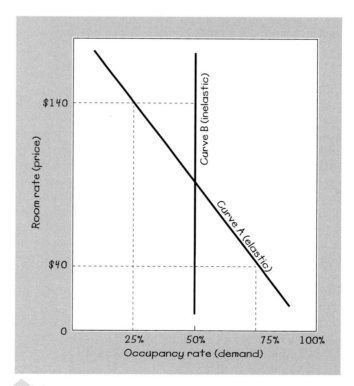

Exhibit 9–2   Curve A represents a normal elastic demand curve, characteristic of the leisure market. As room rates fall, room demand increases by the leisure market. When the rate is reduced from $140 to $40, occupancy jumps from 25% to 75%. The corporate travel market, on the other hand, is considered inelastic (curve B). Corporate travelers are little concerned with rate, so a reduction in room price will not create increased demand.

Elasticity of demand was the catalyst for major change throughout the travel industry between the 1970s and 1990s. During this period, customer profiles began to form into distinct buyer segments. The airlines—after deregulation—were the first to capitalize on the emerging distinctions between corporate travel and the leisure market. The hotel industry wasn't far behind.

This parameter shift was the beginning of a conscious attempt to segregate buyers by their price sensitivity, the concept behind yield management. Both industries discovered that demand was elastic for the leisure market and inelastic for the business segment in terms of both time and price. Demand is a little of both for the group rooms market.

The art of managing these distinct markets cannot be taken lightly. Success from discounting to the leisure market (where lower rates result in incremental increases in occupancy) does not hold true with the corporate market (where lower rates are not offset with increased occupancy). Similarly, offering alternative dates to move the guest into discounted low periods of occupancy works well with the leisure market (whose vacation periods are relatively flexible) but poorly with corporate guests (whose travel dates are on a need-to-go basis). Discretionary leisure buyers may even change location to save the lodging budget, while corporate guests are last-minute shoppers with extremely little flexibility (see Exhibit 9–2).

Complicated as this may seem, group rooms business throws yet another dimension into the picture. Tour groups, which are usually price sensitive, take on many of the characteristics of the leisure segment—elastic in terms of rate, flexible with regard to date. Conventions, trade shows, conferences, and corporate retreats generally demonstrate the characteristics of the corporate market—inelastic with regard to rate, inflexible in terms of travel dates. But remember one thing, even an inelastic market becomes elastic at some point. There may be little or no difference in corporate occupancy when the rate fluctuates between $80 and $160. But if the rate becomes too high, say $260, some sensitivity will ultimately result.

Rate Cutting.   According to many industry experts, there is a distinct difference between rate cutting and discounting. Rate cutting functions in an inelastic market. Unwarranted rate cuts generate new business for one property only by luring the customer away from another property. Discounting, on the other hand, attracts new customers to the industry, benefiting all properties. Discounting seeks out the stay-at-home customer, the visit-friends-or-family customer, and the let's-camp-out customer. Rate cutting aims at the guest already staying in a competitor's hotel across the road or down the boulevard.

Competitors, who are the source of the new business, counter with rate cuts, and the price war is on. A decline in price per room and in gross sales, rather than the hoped-for increase in occupancy, is the net result. Some resort localities outlaw price wars by making it a misdemeanor to post rates outside the establishment. Printed rate schedules are permitted; it is advertising on the marquee that is not allowed. Conversely, other communities actually require room rates to be posted outside the property. In such cases, the lowest and highest posted room rates on the marquee establish the rate parameters that the customer can expect to pay. This reduces the unsavory practice of "sizing up" the walk-in guest before quoting a room rate.

The long list of special rates (discussed later in the chapter) proves that not all rate variations are viewed as rate cutting. Perhaps they must merely stand the test of time. The family plan, in which all children roomed with their parents are accommodated without charge, caused dissension when it first appeared (see Exhibit 9–9). It is today a legitimate business builder. So, too, is the free room given to convention groups for every 50 or 100 paid rooms. Like any good sales inducement, special rates should create new sales (elasticity), not make the product available at a lower price. For once sold at a lower rate, it is almost impossible to get the buyer to pay the original price.

Once established, rates are not easily adjusted. Increases must be undertaken slowly if they are not to affect patronage. It does not matter that the rate was too low to begin with. Rate reductions will bring no complaints if the initial rates were too high. Opening with rates that are too high may do devastating damage before the adjustment is made. Excessive rates create bad word-of-mouth advertising that takes time and costly sales promotions to counteract.

➤ *Elasticity of Lodging Taxes.*   One rate component over which hotel managers have little or no control is local lodging taxes. Also known as bed, room, or hotel taxes, these guest charges often provide significant revenues for the local municipality (see Exhibit 9–3). Operating with increasingly tight budgets, cities are lured into the easy money available from taxing out-of-towners. After all, it appears politically correct to increase the tax revenue base without actually raising the taxes charged to local citizens.

But the reality of the situation is not so straightforward. Several concerns are not initially apparent. First is the ethical debate. Many antagonists of the hotel tax believe it is wrong to charge out-of-town visitors for city services and improvements that are

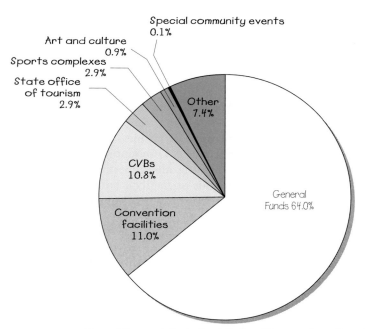

How Travel-Related Sales Taxes Are Used

Exhibit 9–3   Someday, tourists may complain "No taxation without representation" as loudly as at the Boston Tea Party. That's because travel-related taxes generate about $8 billion a year for local municipalities. Yet little of these visitor-paid taxes find their way into improved tourist-related facilities. The bulk of lodging tax revenues is deposited into community general funds.

not tourism related. For example, how can one justify charging a bed tax that's earmarked for improving and building new schools and local sports field complexes (as shown in Exhibit 9–3)? The visitor clearly does not benefit from the taxes paid—it is taxation without representation.

Second, several careful studies have demonstrated that an increased lodging tax actually hurts the local economy. More revenue may be lost in other taxes than is actually gained in room tax. For example, New York City had the highest lodging tax in the United States (an effective 21.25% rate). They at one time suffered a decrease in convention business by as much as 30%. With 30% fewer convention visitors, that was 30% fewer purchases of souvenirs, arts and crafts, meals and drinks, clothing, and related purchases. Each of these purchases generated tax revenue (sales tax) in its own right. Therefore, an increase in the lodging tax had negative repercussions—a decrease in related sales tax revenues—for New York City. Today, New York City's lodging tax doesn't even rank in the top five cities across the United States (see Exhibit 9–4).[1]

Taxing Demand. Although the individual traveler rarely considers the rate of local taxes, group business has become increasingly conscious of this vexing premium. Carefully negotiated group rates seem purposeless and inconsequential if the city then slaps an additional 21.25% levy on rates that have been shaved by just five to ten dollars. Bed taxes have become deterrents to the marketing efforts of numerous convention and visitor bureaus. Taxes in the 10 to 12% range seem acceptable to most consumers. Rates above 14% meet resistance among some groups and associations. Yet, Houston, Washington, DC, and Detroit—well recognized destinations for groups—struggle with room taxes in the 15 to 17% range (see Exhibit 9–4).

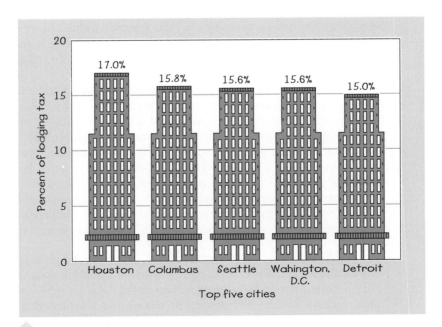

Exhibit 9–4   A study of the largest cities in the 50 states (and Washington, DC) identified the highest bed taxes in the United States. Across the country, the average lodging (bed) tax is 11.65%. High tax rates, yes, but not as bad as many foreign countries—Hungary charges hotel guests some 59 separate taxes, totaling a whopping 39% of the hotel bill!

The trend may be changing, however. More and more hotel managers are joining together to battle rising bed taxes in their cities. By forming one cohesive and vocal group, hotel managers represent a formidable opponent to city councils bent on raising the tax. And with the domino effect that develops when fewer visitors come to the city, it is not difficult to garner additional support from local merchants.

The lodging industry stands firmly against the proliferation of bed taxes. To fight increasing taxation, various industry associations have begun conducting research and educational campaigns aimed at local politicians who see the tourism sector as an easy place to find tax revenues without actually having to face the taxpayer. This research has generated some interesting findings. Twenty-five years ago, total room taxes (state and local sales and bed taxes) were just 3 to 4% of the room charge. Today, the national average is 11.65%—better than a threefold increase (see Exhibit 9–4). The rise in bed taxes may be the highest increase in taxation of any industry in the United States, except possibly the gaming industry. The lodging industry pays about twice the tax rate imposed on most other goods and services.

Research by the American Hotel Foundation discovered that an increase in the bed tax has negative repercussions on rooms demand (elastic rooms demand will decline when the total room rate including tax increases). A decrease in rooms demand doesn't just affect the hotel industry. Tourists and corporate travelers who stop coming can't buy meals, rent cars, take home souvenirs, or play at golf courses, to name a few complementary visitor services. In fact, a hypothetical 2% increase in the lodging tax results in a 5.1% reduction in room sales and associated visitor spending.

Discounts Off Rack Rate

All hotels have a rack rate against which other pricing structures are designed (see Exhibit 9–5). A hotel's rack rate is the quoted, published rate that is theoretically charged to full-paying customers. In essence, the rack rate is the full retail rate. However, just as customers rarely pay the sticker price for a brand-new automobile, guests rarely pay the rack rate for a hotel room.

Although reservationists try to offer the customer full rack rate, shrewd guests never accept it. Corporate discounts, affiliation discounts (AAA and AARP, for example), frequent-travel discounts, advanced and nonrefundable purchases, and a host of other possibilities have all combined to erode the hotel's ability to charge full price.

Proof of discounting is most evident in the average daily rate computation. Hotels with an average rack rate of, say, $78 probably never actually attain a $78 ADR. Instead, the property's ADR is a reflection of the vast discounting taking place throughout the property. Corporate meetings, tour groups, discounted transient travelers, and corporate guests negatively affect the hotel's ability to sell rooms at rack rate. As a result, a hotel with an average rack rate of $78 probably receives an ADR closer to $68.

▶ *Examples of Discounted Rates.*   Discounted or special rates come in a variety of shapes and sizes. Some merely provide a slight discount from the rack rate, as when a hotel offers a 10% price reduction for AAA or AARP members. Other special rates, such as volume discounting programs and seasonal price reductions, are quite significant, reducing the posted rate up to 50%, 75%, or even more.

The reordering of rates is part of the shakeout of segmentation. Rates are a function of supply and demand, and in a perfect economy these two variables move toward equilibrium. However, for now, *special rates*—a term that is preferable to *dis-*

INN & RESTAURANT

GUEST ROOM RATES

	Single	Double
Deluxe Double Queen	$ 91.00	$ 97.00
Deluxe Double Queen with Patio or Balcony	93.00	99.00
Deluxe King with Patio or Balcony	93.00	99.00
Courtyard Double Queen with Patio or Balcony	97.00	103.00
Courtyard King	97.00	103.00
Deluxe Poolside King with Patio or Balcony	101.00	107.00
Family Suite	103.00	109.00
Executive Suite	105.00	111.00
Parlor Suite	109.00	115.00
Executive Suite with Balcony	109.00	115.00
Luxury Suite	115.00	121.00
Presidential Suite	250.00	250.00

No room tax.

No charge for local calls.

Children 12 and under stay free.

$8.00 for each additional adult.

Cribs/Rollaways available.

Non-smoking rooms available.

Bathtub available upon request.

Special Rates are available for

Large Groups • Senior Citizens • AARP

Corporate Travelers

AAA Members

Route 1, Box 777 • Coalinga, CA 93210
(209) 935-0717 • 1-800-942-2333 • FAX (209) 935-5061
www.harrisranch.com
Midway between San Francisco and Los Angeles
On I-5 at Hwy 198
Effective 8-24-98

Exhibit 9–5   Hotels distribute printed rack rates but provide for special discounts, including families, AAA and AARP members, and corporate travelers. Moreover, many now charge the same rate for both single and double occupancy. Note the number of different room types and facilities at this upscale property. *Courtesy of Harris Ranch Inn and Restaurant, Coalinga, California.*

counted rates—are in. The list of those entitled to special rates is limited only by the imagination of the marketing department.

One hotel chain has special rates for teachers; another for students. Most have discounts for senior citizens; almost all allow children in the room with their parents at no charge. The *Worldwide Directory* of Holiday Inns advertises a sports rate for U.S. amateur and professional teams. Special introductory rates are a common tactic for launching a new hotel. The same tradition that gives police officers discounts in the coffee shop gives other uniformed groups such as the clergy and the military discounts off the room rack. And so the list grows.

Travel agents and travel writers usually get free accommodations while they are on familiarization (fam) trips. At other times, the special rate is a standard 50% discount, unless, of course, they come during the height of the busy season.

Hawaii's *kamaiina* rate (literally, "oldtimer's rate") is an interesting case of special rates. A class-action suit was filed by a Californian on the grounds that the 25% discount granted to Hawaiian residents was discriminatory. The argument was denied by the court. The judge found that "offering a discount to certain clients, patrons, or other customers based on an attempt to attract their business is [not] unlawful." The decision is important because it shows the other side of the issue. Rates that are raised to discourage business from certain persons might well be judged as discriminatory. Rates that are lowered to attract certain persons are viewed quite differently, at least by one court.

All rate discounts should be aimed at the development of new markets and should be phased out as that market stabilizes. It does not work that way in practice. Over time, many special rates become part of the established rate structure. Here are some of the more common examples of discounted rates found in most hotels:

Seasonal Rates.   Posted rack rates can be changed, or they can include seasonal variations (see Exhibit 9–5). Season and off-season rates are quoted by most resort hotels, with incremental increases and decreases coming as the season approaches and wanes (see Exhibit 9–6). The poor weekend occupancy of urban hotels has forced them to offer a seasonal rate of sorts—a discounted weekend rate.

Hotel capacity in many resort communities is vast, able to handle great numbers of tourists during periods of peak demand. Because of this glut of hotel rooms available for high-season demand, low-season rates are often deeply discounted—so steeply in fact, that many resort properties once closed their doors during low-occupancy seasons. This practice changed some 10 or 15 years ago. Today, very few resort properties actually close for the off-season. The expense of reopening the facility, training and hiring new staff each year, and operating a skeleton crew to maintain the closed facility combined to change the economics of closing the property. Instead, resorts remain open, steeply discounting rooms to value-conscious guests.

Weather-related Discounts.   When it comes to negotiating group rates, even nature gets involved. A growing trend designed to reduce the length of the low or shoulder season at certain resorts is a weather discount factor. Credits or discounts against the rate are offered guests for each day it rains or stays unseasonably cool.

Obviously, this is risky business, and few resorts are yet offering such plans. But select Hiltons and Marriotts are currently on the bandwagon, and others are sure to follow. Indeed, at least one Marriott resort offers a "temperature guarantee" package that they have insured through Lloyd's of London!

SPLENDID SECLUSION

Nestled in the high Sonoran Desert foothills north of Scottsdale, The Boulders offers the enchantment of a dramatic location created by the forces of time. Spectacular rock outcroppings that captivate everyone who steps within their spell. Ancient saguaros silhouetted against the clear Sonoran sky. And a world-famous resort which blends so easily with nature that the local wildlife might never notice it was there.

The private country club features two 18-hole championship golf courses built right into the desert, as well as a tennis garden and the new Sonoran Spa…which offers a variety of signature body treatments using the natural herbs of the desert along with a fully equipped cardiovascular and weight room, aerobics classes, and a variety of nature hikes and other stimulating programs.

Just a short stroll from the resort is el Pedregal, a festival-style marketplace of intriguing shops, restaurants, and galleries. And all around The Boulders is the enticing tranquility of the lush Sonoran Desert with its breathtaking natural views.

RESORT CASITAS

At The Boulders there's no such thing as a typical guest room. Instead there are 160 guest casitas shaped into the dramatic terrain, each decorated with natural wood and Mexican tile. Among the pleasures of these individual casitas are fully stocked mini-bars, a woodburning fireplace for cozy evenings, and a private patio or balcony overlooking the spectacular desert terrain.

CASITA DAILY RATES

European Plan (no meals included)	Single	Double	Triple	Modified American Plan (breakfast and dinner included)	Single	Double	Triple
Jan 2–18, May 1–28, Sept 28–Dec 9	$325	$350	$375	Jan 2–18, May 1–28, Sept 28–Dec 9	$375	$450	$525
Jan 19–April 30, Dec 22–Jan 1	$425	$450	$475	Jan 19–April 30, Dec 22–Jan 1	$475	$550	$625
May 29–June 25, Sept 1–27, Dec 10–21	$200	$225	$250	May 29–June 25, Sept 1–27, Dec 10–21	$260	$335	$420

PATIO HOMES

Patio homes at The Boulders are ideal for families or groups of friends who want to make themselves at home in a setting more spacious than one of the traditional casitas. Along with all the same services and amenities as the casitas, each Southwestern-style patio home features a fully-equipped kitchen, spacious dining area and living room, fireplace, private patio, laundry facilities and garage, with a choice of one, two, or three bedrooms.

PATIO HOME DAILY RATES

Dates	1-Bedroom Plus Den	2-Bedroom	2-Bedroom Plus Den	3-Bedroom
Jan 2–18, May 1–28, Sept 28–Dec 9	$450	$650	$700	$750
Jan 19–April 30, Dec 22–Jan 1	$550	$750	$800	$850
May 29–June 25, Sept 1–27, Dec 10–21	$325	$400	$450	$475

Courtesy: The Boulders Resort, Carefree, Arizona

Exhibit 9–6   The Boulders Resort in Carefree, Arizona publishes the year's high-, mid-, and low-season rates on one brochure. Notice the wide price disparity between seasons. Add in the fact that such hotels are often more restrictive to certain discounts during high season and less restrictive during low season, and the disparity grows even wider.

Weekly Rates.   Weekly rates, which are less than seven times the daily rate, are offered occasionally. Improved forecasting and increased revenues in all the other departments compensate for the reduction in room revenue.

Both the daily rate—assume $170—and the weekly rate—assume $1,050—are recorded by the clerk on the registration card and, later, on the guest bill. The $170 rate is charged daily until the final day, when a $30 charge is posted. In this way, the daily charge is earned until the guest meets the weekly commitment. If one-seventh of the weekly charge were posted daily, the hotel would be at a disadvantage whenever the guest left before the week was up, as frequently happens. One variation on weekly rates leaves the daily rate intact but discounts services such as valet, laundry, and greens fees.

Corporate Rates.   America's corporations do a great deal of business with the nation's hotels. Corporations and hotel chains are synergetic. Corporations have offices and plants worldwide. Employees at all levels (management, personnel, sales, engineering, accounting) travel in vast numbers. They visit the very countries and cities in which the hotel chains have opened their properties worldwide. The synergism works when the employees of a certain corporation stay in the hotels of a given chain. By guaranteeing a given number of room-nights per year, the corporation negotiates a better rate, a corporate rate, from the hotel chain.

Reducing room rates is only part of the discount. Reducing the number of rooms needed to close the deal is a more subtle form of discounting. Not many years ago, corporate rates required 1,000 room-nights per year. Recent figures place the level as low as 50.

The figures were pushed lower by the appearance of third-party negotiators rather than by the astuteness of corporate travel desks. Corporations with numbers that were too small to negotiate on their own were included under the umbrella of room consolidators. Third-party volume buyers who were in no business other than negotiating discounts with hotels (and airlines) represented numerous companies and developed a tough rate-negotiating base. Hotels responded by dealing directly with the smaller corporate accounts, bypassing the travel agents and the consolidators.

Technology has altered the corporate discount picture as well. In the past, major corporations negotiated favorable rates by promising a large annual room volume with a given chain. However, no one really counted, and room volume (actual or anticipated) was never verified. With the increasing sophistication of CRS systems, most major hotel chains are now able to accurately track a corporation's total room volume chainwide. Corporate room activity at franchised properties, parent properties, and through the CRS are all combined into a quarterly volume report. Renaissance Hotels, for example, produces quarterly reports for more than 1,800 of its major corporate accounts. These reports take the guesswork out of room rate negotiations and give both the hotel chain and the corporation an accurate picture of utilized volume.

Corporate rates are now one of the panels in the mural of discounting. But their implementation has left still another irritant between travel agents and hoteliers. Slashing rates low enough to compete for corporate business leaves the hotel little margin for paying commissions. Travel agents get no commission when they book rooms for corporate clients who have negotiated special rates with the hotel. The agent who makes the reservation to accommodate the corporate client is in a dilemma. Either book the room and get no commission or tell the corporate clients to book their own rooms.

Commercial Rates.   Commercial rates are the small hotel's answer to corporate rates. Without the global chain's size to negotiate national corporate contracts, smaller hotels make arrangements with small commercial clients. Such understandings might account for 5 or 10 room-nights per year for a manufacturer's representative or salesperson traveling on a personal expense account.

Under the commercial rate plan, a standard low rate is negotiated for the year. This standard rate provides the commercial guest with two advantages. First, the rate is guaranteed. Even during periods of high occupancy, most small hotels honor the commercial rate. Second, when demand is mild, the commercial guest is granted an upgraded accommodation at no additional charge. This small courtesy costs the hotel nothing, yet generates substantial loyalty on the part of the guest. Few hotels actually distinguish between corporate and commercial rates. The two terms are effectively synonymous.

Government Per Diems.   Federal, state, and local governments reimburse traveling employees up to a fixed dollar amount. This per-diem (per day) cap is made up of two parts: room and meals. Reimbursement is made on the actual cost of the room (a receipt is required) but no more than the maximum. Anyone traveling on government business is reluctant to pay more than the per-diem room allowance, since the agency will not reimburse the excess. Meal reimbursement is a given number of dollars per day and generally requires no receipts (see Exhibit 9–7).

Key cities, those with higher costs of living, are given higher caps (see Exhibit 9–7). The General Services Administration (GSA) of the federal government publishes the per-diem rates that apply to federal employees. The distinct market segment covers all federal civilian employees, military personnel, and recently, cost-reimbursed federal contractors.

Difficulties may arise when the per-diem guest encounters the desk. Some chains accept the government rates, but individual properties may not. And if they do, the yield management decision may reject these heavily discounted rates for that particular period. Moreover, since per diems, like some other special rates, are on a space-available basis, some central reservations systems will not quote the rate for confirmation. *Space available* means that rooms are not confirmed until close to the date of arrival. Over all these hurdles, the guest must then prove per-diem entitlement. Without a standardized form, letter, or procedure, the individual room clerk makes a discretionary call based on whatever evidence the guest can provide.

In recent years, a controversial repeal of a previously mandated government regulation has left the lodging industry wondering what is fair in terms of per-diem rates. The debate revolves around the Hotel and Motel Fire Safety Act of 1990. This act was proposed after a U.S. Treasury agent perished in a fire at the Dupont Plaza Hotel in San Juan, Puerto Rico, on New Year's Eve 1986.

In an effort to protect government employees traveling on business, the 1990 act mandated that hotels must comply with certain smoke detector and sprinkler regulations if they wished to sell rooms to government employees traveling on per diem. Complying with this act costs the lodging industry over $1.2 billion per year! Some 17,000 hotels and motels across the country (about 38% of all hotel and motel rooms nationwide) complied with the Fire Safety Act.

These hotels made the fire safety investment because they believed that compliant properties would be the only ones allowed a piece of the lucrative government market. In late 1996, however, the government—just as it was about to begin auditing all ho-

How to Use the Per Diem Tables

The maximum rates listed in the table are prescribed by law for reimbursement of per diem expenses incurred during official travel within CONUS (the continental United States). The amount shown in column a is the maximum that will be reimbursed for lodging expenses, including applicable taxes. The "M&IE" rate shown in column b is a fixed amount allowed for meals and incidental expenses covered by per diem. The per diem payment for lodging expenses plus the M&IE rate may not exceed the maximum per diem rate shown in column c. Seasonal rates apply during the periods indicated. Unless otherwise specified, the per diem locality is defined as "all locations within, or entirely surrounded by, the corporate limits of the key city, including independent entities located within those boundaries."

Requests for per diem rate adjustments should be submitted by the agency headquarters office to the General Services Administration, Office of Governmentwide Policy, Attn: Travel and Transportation Management Policy Division (MTT), Washington, DC 20405. Agencies should submit their requests to GSA no later than May 1 in order for a city to be included in the annual review.

Georgia		Column *a*	*b*	*c*
Albany	Dougherty	56	30	86
Athens	Clarke	44	26	70
Atlanta	Clayton, De Kalb, Fulton, Cobb (see also Norcross/Lawrenceville, GA)	81	38	119
Augusta	Richmond; Savannah River plant	50	26	76
Brunswick	Glynn	42	26	68
Columbus	Muscogee	48	26	74
Macon	Bibb	47	30	77
Norcross/Lawrenceville	Gwinnet (see also Atlanta, GA)	81	38	119
Savannah	Chatham	49	30	79
Warner Robbins	Houston	43	26	69

Source: GSA, Washington, DC.

Exhibit 9–7   The General Services Administration (GSA) of the U.S. government prints annual per-diem tables for official travel within CONUS. Shown as an example is the state of Georgia.

tels to verify their compliance with the act—pulled the plug on the policy by removing the audit requirement. Today, hotels are still urged to provide adequate fire safety protection, but the government is not auditing their actual compliance—a move that has been deemed unfair by the thousands of hotels who spent billions of dollars bringing their fire safety systems up to code in the early 1990s.

Employee Courtesy Rates.   Special rates are extended to employees of the chain when they travel to other properties. Indeed, for the large chains, this is actually a market segment. Substantial discounts from the hotel's minimum rate plus upgrade whenever possible result in a very attractive bargain. Special rates are always provided on a space-available basis. Employee-guests are accepted only if rooms are vacant when they present themselves (some chains allow reservations a few weeks before arrival if projected occupancy is below 75% or so). The Federal Deficit Reduction Law of 1984 reinforced this by taxing the employee for the value of any free room if paying guests were turned away.

Offering complimentary or discounted employee rooms is an inexpensive way for chains to supplement their employee benefits packages. Because such rooms are provided on a space-available basis, there is little associated cost (aside from housekeeping) to providing the employee a free or deeply discounted rate. And many chains find some real benefits in increased morale and motivation as employees take advantage of the chain's discounted rooms.

Indeed, some chains actually listen to their employees. They request visiting employees to fill out evaluation forms complete with comments and suggestions for improvement. If carefully monitored and tracked, such a "secret shopper" program can have enormous advantages to the chain.

It Pays to Pay Rack Rate.   Although not really a discount, some upscale chains are experimenting with added perks for guests who actually pay full rack rate. The perks include such valuable amenities as free use of a cellular telephone, limousine service to the airport and nearby shopping, free dry cleaning, and even free food items. Several Ritz-Carlton properties allow full rack–rate guests an extended check out until 6 PM. Four Seasons hotels give deluxe accommodations (a free upgrade) to rack rate guests.

Senior Citizen Rates.   Every 7 seconds, another person reaches age 50. There are currently better than 65 million Americans over the age of 50, and that number will jump to about 100 million by the year 2010. In addition to these age-related statistics, it is important to note that senior citizens (defined as 50-plus years of age by some organizations) represent the fastest-growing travel market.

Although seniors are by no means a homogeneous group, they have certain features and expectations in common. First, people over the age of 50 are the best money savers in the world. As such, when they travel (and they love to travel), they're careful with money. They try to find travel bargains, and they can find them, because they have such flexible travel schedules.

When asked about their preferences, seniors listed discounted buffet breakfasts, complimentary newspapers, and free cable television as their top lodging amenities. They also seem to appreciate hotels where grandchildren stay free, low-cholesterol and low-sodium menu items are offered, bathtub grab bars are provided, and large-digit alarm clocks and telephones are available. Chains such as Ramada Inns, Howard Johnson's, and Hilton, to name a few, are among the leaders in marketing to senior travelers.

Infinite Other Discounts.   There are an unlimited number of additional rate discounting possibilities. Large groups such as AAA, Discover Card members, or the like no longer have a monopoly on special rates. Any sized group that can produce even a few room-nights per year is negotiating discounted rates.

One growing midsized market is bank clubs. Members of credit unions or banks and holders of numerous credit cards now find discounted rates part of their incentive package. Some of these groups charge for the service, others provide it free as a means of attracting and holding bank customers.

The Entertainment Card, Quest International, and other travel clubs carry more clout today than ever before. By providing members with deep discounts (usually about half of rack rate) for traveling during off-peak periods, such clubs provide a win–win–win product. The travel club wins because it charges members a fee to join, members win by gaining access to substantial travel discounts, and hotels win when rooms fill (albeit at discounted rates) during less busy periods.

Hotels must be extremely careful, however, to limit the use of such discounts to the slower periods of the year. It's a costly mistake replacing a full-paying rack rate or corporate guest with an Entertainment Card customer on a sold-out night. On the other hand, it makes good sense to attract such deeply discounted business on nights when the hotel is unlikely to fill. Yield management is the tool for making the decision.

Auctioning is a form of discounting that is gaining popularity even at the smallest market level—the individual traveler. Auctioning allows hotels, airlines, and rental car agencies to enter a product-available database marketed directly to the traveler through technology available to the average person (see Exhibit 9–8). The guest—say, Carl Jones—decides where he is traveling to, the dates and times he wishes to travel, and any specifications (must be a four-star property, a midsized car, etc.) related to the trip. He is then asked to quote his own rate!

If a hotel, airline, and/or rental car agency informs the database that this is a reasonable offer, Jones gets the deal as bid. He never knows until the offer is accepted which airline he will fly, which hotel will accommodate him, or which rental car he

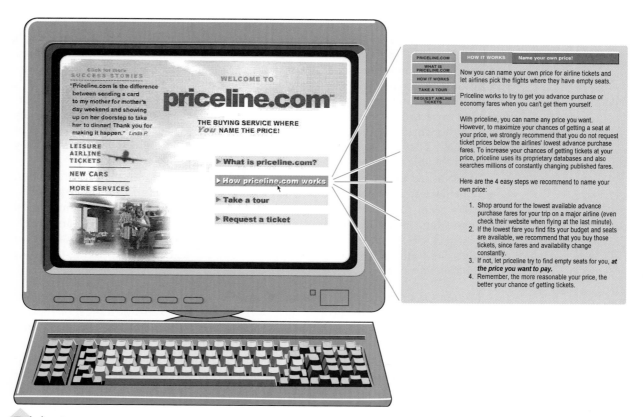

Exhibit 9–8 On-line travel discounts and auction services such as priceline.com may be the wave of the future. Other on-line services provide last-minute bargains from tour group packages that didn't quite fill. If price is the only motivation and the customer is willing to travel any hour, day or night, on-line is certainly the place for bargains! *Courtesy of priceline.com, Stamford, Connecticut.*

will drive. If the bid is too low, Jones places a time limit on his offer and waits to see over the next few days whether the various travel components in question will respond favorably.

Companies such as priceline.com, Bid4Travel.com, and others are in the early stages of developing auctioning. As it continues to grow, inventory auctioning will set a new standard for rate discounting in the industry.

►*Complimentary Rooms.* Hotel managers should be as reluctant to give away complimentary (comp) rooms as automobile sales managers are to give away free cars. But both the perishability of the room and the low variable cost of housing an occupant change this reality. Comps are used for business promotion, as charitable giveaways, and as perks.

By custom, complimentary rates are extended to other hoteliers. The courtesy is reciprocated, resulting in an industrywide fringe benefit for owners and senior managers. Such comps rarely include food or beverage (costs are too high) even in American plan hotels. As mentioned earlier, another portion of the travel industry—travel agents and travel writers—are comped during fam trips. Deregulation permitted fam trip comps by the airlines, which have now joined the hotel industry in developing site inspection tours for the travel industry.

Site inspections are also made by association executives, who are considering the property as a possible meeting place. Site visits are comped even though some association executives have been known to abuse the industry standard by using site inspection opportunities to vacation with their families. Comp rates as part of the group's meeting were discussed previously, and these are considered to be acceptable standard practice.

Comps are given to famous persons whose presence has publicity value. Comps are used as promotional tools in connection with contests in which the winners receive so many days of free accommodations. In gambling casinos, comps extend to food, beverage, and even airfare from the player's home. Parking is so difficult in Atlantic City that it too has become part of the high-roller's comp package. After all, in a brief period of table play, a high-roller can lose many times the cost of these promotions, which on close inspection prove to be surprisingly inexpensive.

Posting the Comp. Internal control of comps is important! In most hotels, the night auditor is required to submit a report of comps granted each day and by whom. To that end, the actual room rate is recorded in the rate block on the registration card and marked "COMP." Daily, or at the end of the stay, the charge is removed from the folio with an allowance (see Chapter 10). Under this procedure, a daily room charge is made so that the room and the guest are both counted in the room and house counts. The total allowances at the end of the accounting period provide statement evidence of the cost of comps.

Some casino hotels have the comp paid by a paper transfer to another department (sales, casino, entertainment). The departmental manager has accountability, and the amount of comps appear on that departmental budget.

Recording no value in the rate square but only the word *COMP* is another method for handling free accommodations. No dollar value is charged each day and, therefore, no allowances are required to remove the charges. Neither is a permanent dollar record of comps available. Comps are not usually recorded in room and house counts under this procedure.

The night auditor prepares rate-discrepancy reports for all types of discounts and comps. They are a quick product of a property management system (see Chapter 13). The PMS has all the rack rates in memory. Every room assigned at a special rate is identified and reported to management.

Additional Rate Variations

Not all variations to the rack rate involve discounting. Factors such as the charge for additional guests in the room, negotiating a group rate years into the future where inflationary pressures must be considered, and periods of extremely high occupancy provide managers with opportunities to flex their rate muscles.

▶***Premium Periods.***   Some hotels find themselves in the enviable position of having too much business—too much demand during certain premium periods. These premium periods are generally characterized by a national or regional holiday, major sporting event, or other sizable attraction. For example, when Indianapolis hosts the Indianapolis 500, when New Orleans celebrates the Mardi Gras, or when Los Angeles enjoys the Rose Bowl, hotel rates rise dramatically.

Premium rates are charged when normal demand significantly exceeds room supply. In such cases, hotels have been known to charge several times their standard rack rate. Such rate adjustments may be based on "gut feel" and a knowledge of what other properties are charging, or yield management software may be utilized to assist with the decision-making process.

Indeed, rate alone is not the only adjustment the guest will be forced to accept. Other standard practices include closing specific dates to arrival and requiring certain minimum lengths of stay (see Chapter 4). By carefully following such practices, a manager can extend a sold-out day—say, Super Bowl Sunday—into a sold-out weekend or three-day event.

▶***Double Occupancy.***   Double occupancy refers to the use of the room by a second guest. Traditional rules increase the single-occupancy rate by a factor (normally not twice) whenever the room is double-occupied. However, the price spread between single and double occupancy has been narrowing. One rate is being used more frequently because the major costs of a hotel room are fixed (debt service, taxes, depreciation). Having a second or third occupant adds relatively few incremental costs (linen, soap, tissue). Although far from universal, one charge for both single and double occupancy is gaining favor.

Convention rates are almost always negotiated with double occupancy at no extra charge. The more persons in the hotel, the more the hotel benefits from sales in other departments: banquet, bar, casino. Suite charges have also followed that pattern. The room rate is the number of rooms that comprise the suite, not the number of guests who occupy it. The room, not the guest, becomes the unit of pricing.

Several arguments support the movement toward a single room price. The fewer the rate options, the less the confusion, and the more rapidly the telephone reservationist can close the sale. Price is a critical issue in package plans or tour bookings, and rates can be shaved closely because the second occupant represents a small additional expense. A third occupant adds a still smaller incremental cost. The incremental cost is almost unnoticed if the extra person(s) share existing beds. That is what makes family-plan rates attractive. An extra charge is levied if a rollaway bed, which requires extra handling and linen, is required. Suite hotels are popular because the extra hide-abed is permanently available.

Unless the family-rate plan has been quoted, a charge is generally made for the third and subsequent occupants to a room (see Exhibit 9–9). Even in hotels where single and double occupancy is charged the same rate, a third or fourth guest probably pays an additional fee. Usually, that added charge is a flat fee—say, $20 per extra person.

Many hoteliers find a flat $20 fee illogical in light of the numerous room types available at the property. Where $20 may be fine for a $100 standard room, it does not seem high enough for a $150 deluxe or a $200 executive parlor. Indeed, if the hotelier can make the argument that we charge for extra guests because they cost the hotel incremental expenses, that argument is doubly true in premium rooms.

Controversy is growing among American hotelmen about the family rate plan method of basing hotel rates upon occupancy by adults only. Children of 14 years or less, accompanying their parents, are not charged for occupancy of rooms with their parents. For example, one adult and a child are charged a single rate for the double occupancy of the room. Two adults and children are charged a double rate for a room, or two single rates if two rooms are engaged. There are various other modifications of the plan, but fundamentally it represents complimentary accommodation of children below a certain age level.

At least three leading hotel chains have adopted the plan and report great success from the higher occupancy attributable to it. Why, then, the controversy? Certainly when hotel chains of the stature of the Statler, Eppley, and Pick chains favor the family rate plan, it is well on its way to becoming a standard practice for most other hotels in the country.

The controversy rests on the issue of whether this plan is a form of rate cutting—the most disagreeable word in the hotelman's language. In this era of downward adjustment from high wartime levels of occupancy, naturally hotelmen are sensitive to any indirect methods of reducing rates. No hotelman wishes to see any kind of repetition of the rate-cutting practices of the 1930s.

In an attempt to evaluate the plan in its rate-cutting connotation, we believe that most hotelmen would be hardpressed to define a rate cut in exact terms. For example, is the commercial rate to traveling men a type of rate reduction? Does a convention rate involve a hidden discount? We can remember the time when it was standard practice to compliment the wife of a traveling man, when a week's stay at a hotel resulted in having the seventh day free of charge, and when the armed forces, clergy, and diplomats got lower rates.

In our opinion, rate cutting is practiced only when hotels depart from their *regular* prices and tariff schedules in order to secure patronage from prospects who are openly shopping for the best deal in room rates. If, therefore, it is regular practice for hotels to have special rates for group business, this does not seem to represent rate cutting; and the same principle should apply to the family rate plan. If this plan becomes widely adopted—as seems very likely—then it falls into the category of any other special type of rate for special business.

In some respects the plan is a form of *pricing accommodations by rooms instead of by persons*. In many resort hotels a room is rated regardless of its occupancy by one or two persons, and a similar concept is used in apartments and apartment hotels.

Although the arguments for or against the family rate plan must be decided by hotelmen themselves, a strong point in favor of the plan is found in its adoption by other vendors of public service—the railroads and airlines. Family rates, weekday rates, seasonal rates, special-type carrier rates, etc., have been in vogue for several years. If the hotels adopt the family rate plan, it seems that they will be falling into line with a national trend rather than venturing alone into a new and untried experiment in good public relations.

Source: The Horwath Hotel Accountant.

Exhibit 9–9 A circa-1958 article discusses the controversy surrounding the family-rate plan. Note in the third paragraph that rate cutting (e.g., discounting) is referred to as "the most disagreeable word in the hotelman's language." Also note the names of old chains that are no longer in business.

In a standard room, extra guests (whether the second, third, or fourth occupant) cost the hotel in a variety of ways, including extra water and electricity, additional amenities, more towels and linens, and, of course, some wear and tear. These costs are not identical from a standard room to a deluxe accommodation. Hotels outfit deluxe rooms with larger bathtubs, more expensive personal amenities, heavier-quality linens, and higher-quality furnishings. An additional person in a deluxe room has a higher incremental cost to the hotel than does an additional person in a standard room.

A flat $20 rate represents a declining percentage of the rate as the quality of the room increases. In the $100 standard, $20 reflects a 20% surcharge. Yet in the $200 executive parlor, $20 reflects only a 10% surcharge. In fact, if the $100 standard guest is willing to pay $20 for an extra occupant, it makes sense that the $200 executive-parlor guest would be equally willing to pay something like $40 for an extra guest.

▶*Projecting Convention Rates.* Even as the hotel manager is concerned with establishing rack rates, discounted rates, and premium rates for today, tomorrow, and the short term, there are pressures to forecast rates far into the future. These pressures are created by the sales and marketing department, which may be selling convention room blocks 5, 10, even 20 years into the future. And just as rate is an important factor to groups today, it is also a major criterion for selecting accommodations 10 years hence.

Room rate inflation is a very real concern for group business. A $125 negotiated group rate today can easily become a $250 group rate in 15 years. Inflation isn't the issue; it's whether, say, $250 will be a fair price in 15 years.

Groups are asking for contract language that protects the room rate. Statements are stipulating that rates will be no more than X times the basic rate, or Y percent off the rack rate, or no more than the best rate (the lowest rate) charged at the time of the convention.

Time Is Money

While the actual date of arrival and departure is the primary consideration for establishing the guest charge, the number of hours of occupancy may someday play a role in rate determination. In simple terms, time is already a rate criterion in many hotels.

▶*Arrival Time.* The day of arrival is listed on the reservation, the registration card, and the guest folio. The time of arrival is also indicated on the folio by means of an internal electronic clock operating in the property management system. Assuming that the clock is accurate, the actual minute of check in is recorded on the electronic folio.

The actual time of arrival is more critical to the American plan hotel, where billing is based on meals taken, than to the European plan operation. American plan arrivals are flagged with a special meal code.

The hour of arrival at a European plan hotel is less critical. An occasional complaint about the promptness of message service or a rare police inquiry might involve the arrival hour. Very, very late arrivals, such as a guest who arrives at 5 AM are the exceptions. Somewhere in the early morning hours (5 to 7 AM) comes the break between charging for the night just passed and levying the first charge for the day just starting.

Check-in hours are difficult to control. Guest arrivals are dictated haphazardly by travel connections and varying distances. Still, many hotels have established check-in hours. The termination point of a night's lodging is more controllable, so every hotel posts an official check-out hour.

➤*Departure Time.*   Check-in and check-out hours are eased or enforced as occupancies fall or rise. Setting the specific check-out hour is left to each hotel. It might be established without any rationale, or it might be the same hour that nearby competitors are using. The proper hour is a balance between the guest's need to complete his or her business and the hotel's need to clean and prepare the room for the next patron.

Seasoned travelers are well aware that check-out extensions are granted by the room clerk if occupancy is light. Under current billing practices, the effort should be made cheerfully whenever the request can be accommodated. If anticipated arrivals require enforcement of the check-out hour, luggage should be stored in the checkroom for the guest's convenience.

Resorts are under more pressure than commercial hotels to expedite check outs. Vacationing guests try to squeeze the most from their holiday time. American plan houses usually allow the guest to remain through the luncheon hour and a reasonable time thereafter if the meal is part of the rate. Some 90% of the resorts surveyed in an AH&MA study identified their check-out hour to be between noon and 2 PM, in contrast to the 11 AM through 1 PM range used by transient hotels. These same properties assigned new arrivals on a "when-available" basis.

Special techniques in addition to that shown in Exhibit 9–10 have been tried to move the guest along. On the night before departure, the room clerk, the assistant manager, or the social host(ess) calls the room to chat and remind the guest of tomorrow's departure. Even today, this task could be assigned to a computer. A more personal touch is a note of farewell left by the room attendant who turns down the bed the night before. A less personal touch can be seen in Exhibit 9–11.

Incentive Rate Systems.   Incentive rate systems have been suggested as a means of expediting check outs. First, the check-out period for a normal day's charge would be established—say, between 11 AM and 1 PM. Guests who leave before 11 AM are charged less than the standard rate, and those who remain beyond 1 PM are charged

CHECK-OUT TIME: 1 PM

We would like to ask your cooperation in checking out by 1 PM so that we may accommodate travelers who are beginning their stay. If you require additional time, you may request a two-hour grace period (until 3 PM) from the assistant manager or the front-office manager. If you wish to check out later, we regret that there must be a $12-per-hour charge, from 3 until 5 PM, for this added service. An additional half-day rate will be charged to guests who delay their departure until between 5 PM and 8 PM. After 8 PM, a full-day rate will be charged. Of course, you are then welcome to remain until the following afternoon at 1 PM.

As an incoming guest, your comfort and convenience depend on these stipulations. We hope you will visit again soon.

Exhibit 9–10   Permanent bureau tent card left in each guest room. Many hotels place a similar statement on the registration card.

more. Flexible charges of this type require a new look at the unit of service, shifting from the more traditional measure of a night's lodging to smaller blocks of time.

Unlike other service industries, hotels have given little consideration to time as a factor in rate. Arrival and departure times establish broad parameters at best. We can expect these to narrow as hotelkeepers become more concerned with the role of time in rate structuring. Taken to the other extreme, it is conceivable that the hour will

Exhibit 9–11   An excerpt from "The Late Check-out," in the March 1997 issue of *Lodging Hospitality*. Written by Megan Rowe, Senior Editor, and used with permission.

Recently, while staying at one of the San Antonio Marriotts, I had occasion to make this request. I would be in meetings all morning, and I wasn't scheduled to leave until 3 PM. I figured I could have lunch, go back to my room and dig out my winter coat and boots, then check out.

The night before I was to leave, I made my request. The clerk asked me what time I wanted to check out. "Three o'clock," I answered.

"You can stay until three, but we'll charge you for a half-day," he said.

At first, I was stunned by the sheer greed this response implied. When I recovered, I asked whether this was an arbitrary decision on his part or a policy of the hotel.

"It's our policy," he said, defensively.

"Is it a *new* policy?" I responded, trying to keep a smile on my face, "because I've never heard of such a thing."

"No, it's not new, and I don't know what kind of hotels you've been staying in, but it's very common."

First deny my simple request, then try a subtle insult. Good thinking.

This kind of treatment would probably have bothered me in any hotel, but it seemed terribly out of place at a hotel with an otherwise extraordinarily friendly and accommodating staff.

The next day, I visited the front desk, posed the same request—hypothetically—to a different employee, and asked how he would handle it. He said he would ask how late, check to see if the room was booked, and possibly okay it based on whatever information he got from the reservations system. If he wasn't sure, he would check with someone in the back office, and they would most likely okay it. Standard operating procedure, in my experience.

eventually become the basic unit for constructing room rates. Under current practices, a stay of several hours costs as much as a full day's stay (see Exhibit 9–12).

The total length of stay may also be an issue in the guest's level of satisfaction with the hotel. Guests with few hours to visit scarcely get enough time to sleep and bathe. It is the guest with sufficient leisure hours who truly enjoys the property by taking advantage of relaxation and recreational activities (see Exhibit 9–12).

A popular journalist once observed facetiously that the length of time one spends in a hotel room is inversely proportional to the quality of that hotel room. When you arrive at, say, 1 AM and need to get some rest for a 7 AM flight the next morning, the room will be lavish—there will be vases of roses, trays of food and drink, soft music, a Jacuzzi tub, and candlelight. Conversely, when you have no time commitments and all day to spend in the hotel, it is invariably a poor-quality establishment—there will be no restaurant or lobby, fuzzy TV reception, and a drained swimming pool!

►*The American Plan Day.*   Meals are part of the American plan (AP) rate, as they are with the modified American plan (MAP). Accurate billing requires an accurate record of arrival and departure times. Arrivals are registered with a meal code reflecting the check-in time. For example, a guest arriving at 3 PM would be coded with arriving after lunch but before dinner.

A complete AP stay technically involves enough meals on the final day to make up for the meals missed on the arriving day. A guest arriving before dinner would be expected to depart the next day, or many days later, after lunch. Two meals, breakfast and lunch, on the departing day complete the full AP charge, since one meal, dinner, was taken on the arriving day. MAP counts meals in the same manner, except that lunch is ignored.

Guests who take more than the three meals per day pay for the extra at menu prices, or sometimes below. Sometimes, guests who miss a meal are not charged. That is why it is very important to have the total AP rate fairly distributed between the room portion and the meal portion. Meal rates are set and are standardized for everyone. Higher AP rates must reflect better rooms, since all the guests are entitled to the same menu.

AP and MAP hotels have a special charge called *tray service*. It is levied on meals taken through room service. European plan room service typically contains hidden charges as a means of recovering the extra service. Menu charges are greater than the usual coffee shop prices when the food is delivered to the room. This device is not available to the American plan hotel because meals being delivered to the room are

Guest	Rate Paid	February 14th Arrival	February 15 Departure	Total Hours
1	$100	1 AM	6 AM	5
2	100	2 PM	11 AM	21
3	100	8 AM	3 PM	31

Exhibit 9–12   Shown are three different room utilization schedules. Three guests, paying the same $100 rate, experience three significantly different lengths of stay. The first guest arrives very late (1 AM) and checks out early (6 AM) the next morning. The second guest exactly parallels the hotel's standard check-in and check-out times (2 PM and 11 AM, respectively). The third guest extends arrival and departure times by taking advantage of light occupancy and normal front-office courtesies.

not priced separately. Instead, a flat charge of several dollars per person is levied as a tray service charge.

➤*Day Rate Rooms.*   Special rates exist for stays of less than overnight. These are called *part-day rates, day rates,* or sometimes *use rates.* Day rate guests arrive and depart on the same day.

Day rates obviously make possible an occupancy of greater than 100%. Furthermore, the costs are low. Nevertheless, the industry has not fully exploited the possibilities. Sales of use rates could be marketed to suburban shoppers and to small, brief meetings. Unfortunately, better airline service has cost hotels day rate business, although capsule rooms at international airports have had some success. Airport properties have promoted their locations as central meeting places for company representatives coming from different sections of the country.

A new day rate market is becoming evident. Motels near campsites and along the roadways are attracting campers as a wayside stop during the day. A hot shower, an afternoon by the pool, and a change of pace from the vehicle are great appeals when coupled with the low day rate.

Check-in time is often early morning. Corporate guests prefer to start their meetings early, and truck drivers like to get off the highway before the 8 AM rush hour. If clean rooms remain unsold from the previous night, there is little reason to refuse day rate guests early access to the room. Indeed, they may order room-service coffee or breakfast as an added revenue bonus.

Since rooms sold for day use only are serviced and made available again for the usual overnight occupancy, the schedule of the housekeeping staff has a great deal to do with the check-out hour. If there are no night room cleaners, the day rate must end early enough to allow room servicing by the day crew. On the other hand, low occupancy would allow a day rate sale even late in the day. Nothing is lost if an additional empty room remains unmade overnight.

There are no rules as to what the hotel should charge for the day room. Some purists suggest that it must be half the standard rack rate. Others appreciate the extra revenue and are willing to charge whatever seems appropriate. Corporate hotels must remember that their day rate rooms compete with their convention and meeting facilities. A small group of executives might prefer meeting in the day rate guest room with its attached bathroom and access to room service rather than the larger impersonal convention meeting room. This can prove detrimental to the hotel if the meeting room sells for two or three times the day rate room.

➤ DETERMINING THE PROPER ROOM RATE

Because a sound room rate structure is fundamental to a sound hotel operation, every manager is sooner or later faced with the question of what is the proper room charge. It is a matter of exceeding complexity because room rates reflect markets and costs, investments and rates of return, supply and demand, accommodations and competition, and not least of all, the quality of management.

Divided into its two major components, room rates must be large enough to cover costs and a fair return on invested capital, and reasonable enough to attract and retain the clientele to whom the operation is being marketed. The former suggests a relatively objective, structured approach that can be analyzed after the fact. The latter is more subjective, involving factors such as the amount of local competition and the condition of the economy at large. There is little sense in charging a rate less than what is needed to meet the first objective; there is little chance of getting a rate more than the competitive ceiling established by the second limitation.

Yield management, the balancing of occupancy and rate, has emerged as the number one component of rate making. In Chapter 4 we examined the questions with which a yield management system deals. Yield management deals with timing: At what occupancy level are discounted rates, or premium rates, triggered (see Exhibit 9–17)? Yield management deals with volume: How many rooms should each rate class have, and what percentage of each should be shifted upward or downward (see Exhibit 9–16.) Yield management deals with marketplace: Shall we cater to the corporate guest or the golden club tour? Yield management deals with horizons: What decision is to be made six months out? Three months out? Today? Yield management deals with displacement: Is the group booked Saturday through Tuesday at a discounted rate displacing more or fewer dollars than the traditional business traveler of Monday and Tuesday? Yield management deals with lead time: What is the lead time of conventions (one to three years), groups (one to three months), and individuals (one to three days) (see Exhibit 4–6).

Yield management has attracted attention because it introduces two new concepts to room pricing: (1) the industry is selling rooms by an inventory control system for the first time, and (2) the pricing strategy considers for the first time the customer's ability and willingness to pay. This discretionary market, with a sensitivity to price, is itself a new phenomenon.

In years past, the rate structure was built from the standpoint of internal cost considerations. Yield management has not eliminated that focus. Important as they are, customers are not the only components of price. Cost recovery and investment opportunity are reflected there as well. Depreciation and interest as well as taxes and land costs are outside the hotel–guest relationship but not external to the room charge.

The more traditional components of rate deal with recovering costs, both operating and capital. They deal with profits and break-even projections. Mixed into the equation are competition, price elasticity, and rate cutting. And in the end, the average daily rate earned by the hotel is partly determined by the ability of a reservationist or room clerk to sell up.

Traditional Rate Calculations

Hotel room rates are derived from a mix of objective measures and subjective values. Expressing room rates numerically gives the appearance of validity, but when the origins of these numbers are best-guess estimates, the results must be viewed with some measure of doubt or uncertainty.

Facts and suppositions combine together when hotel managers calculate the room rate. As useful and respected as the following mathematical formulas may be, they are still merely an indication of the final rate. Fine-tuning the formula, establishing corporate and double occupancy prices, and adjusting the rate according to the whims of the community and the marketplace are still the role of management.

➤ *The Hubbart Room Rate Formula.* The Hubbart room rate formula[2] offers a standardized approach to assigning room rates. The Hubbart formula sets rates from the needs of the enterprise and not from the needs of the guests. The average rate, says the formula, should pay all expenses and leave something for the investor. Valid enough—a business that cannot do this is short-lived.

Exhibit 9–13a illustrates the mechanics of the formula. Estimated expenses are itemized and totaled. These include operational expenses by departments ($1,102,800

	Example
Operating Expenses	
Rooms department	$467,400
Telecommunications	60,900
Administrative and general	91,200
Payroll taxes and employee benefits	178,200
Marketing	109,800
Utility costs	138,900
Property operation and maintenance	56,400
Total operating expenses	$1,102,800

Taxes and Insurance	
Real estate and personal property taxes	67,200
Franchise taxes and fees	112,200
Insurance on building and contents	37,200
Leased equipment	56,400
Total taxes and insurance	$ 273,000

Depreciation (Standard Rates on Present Fair Value)	Value		Rate			
Building	$_____	at	_____%	168,750	
Furniture, fixtures, and equipment	$_____	at	_____%	126,000	
Total depreciation					$ 294,750

Reasonable Return on Present Fair Value of Property	Value		Rate		
Land	$_____	at	_____%	
Building	$_____	at	_____%	
Furniture, fixtures, and equipment	$_____	at	_____%	
Total fair return				$ 414,000

Total	$2,084,550

Deduct—Credits from Sources Other Than Rooms	
Income from store rentals	14,850
Profits from food and beverage operations (if loss, subtract from this group)	131,400
Net income from other operated departments and miscellaneous income (loss)	(7,050)
Total credits from sources other than rooms	$ 139,200

Amount to be realized from guest-room sales to cover costs and a reasonable return of present fair value of property	$1,945,350

(a)

	Example	
1. Amount to be realized from guest-room sales to cover costs and a reasonable return on present fair value of property [from part (a)]		$1,945,350
2. Number of guest rooms available for rental		150
3. Number of available rooms on annual basis (item 2 multiplied by 365)	100%	54,750
4. Less: Allowance for average vacancies	30%	16,425
5. Number of rooms to be occupied at estimated average occupancy	70%	38,325
6. Average daily rate per occupied room required to cover costs and a reasonable return on present fair value (item 1 divided by item 5)		$ 50.76

(b)

Exhibit 9–13   (a) Although the Hubbart room rate formula was introduced in 1952, it is still used to compute zero-based room rates. By dividing fixed costs, variable expenses, and a reasonable return on the property by the estimated number of room sold, the Hubbart formula provides a fairly reliable minimum average rate calculation. (b) Computing the divisor, the estimated number of rooms sold, requires an occupancy projection, which is applied to the number of available rooms per year. *Courtesy of the American Hotel & Motel Association, Washington, DC.*

in the illustration), realty costs ($273,000), and depreciation ($294,750). To these expenses is added a reasonable return on the present fair value of the property: land, building, and furnishings ($414,000). From the total expense package ($2,084,550) are subtracted incomes from all sources other than room sales ($139,200). This difference ($1,945,350) represents the annual amount to be realized from room sales.

Next (see Exhibit 9–13b), an estimate of the number of rooms to be sold annually is computed. Dividing the number of estimated rooms (38,325) to be sold into the estimated dollars ($1,945,350) needed to cover costs and a fair return produces the average rate to be charged ($50.76). The computations are simple enough; the formula is straightforward enough. Deriving the many estimates is where the weakness lies.

Shortcomings of the Formula.   Like many such calculations, the Hubbart room rate formula is only as accurate as the assumptions on which it was projected. Several such assumptions come immediately to mind for the Hubbart formula: What percentage is "reasonable" as a fair return on investment? What occupancy rate appears most attainable? What are the cost projections for payroll, various operating departments, utilities, and administrative and general?

The formula leaves the rooms department with the final burden after profits and losses from other departments. But inefficiencies in other departments should not be covered by a high, noncompetitive room rate. Neither should unusual profits in other departments be a basis for charging room rates below what the market will bring.

There is some justification in having rooms subsidize low banquet prices if these low prices result in large convention bookings of guest rooms. (Incidentally, this is one reason why the food and banquet department should not be leased as a concession.) Similar justification could be found for using higher room rates to cover unusually high dining room repairs and maintenance, or advertising costs. The trade-off is wise if these expenditures produce enough other business to offset lost room revenue resulting from higher room rates.

Additional shortcomings become apparent as the formula is studied. Among them is the projected number of rooms sold. This estimate of rooms sold is itself a function of the very rate being computed. How can a hotel estimate the number of rooms it will sell before first knowing the average rate for which it will sell each room—yet that is exactly what the Hubbart formula requires! Rate, in turn, is a function of double occupancy. Yet the increased income from double occupancy is not a component of the Hubbart formula. Neither component (the impact of rate on occupancy and the impact of double occupancy on rate) is projected.

The average rate that is computed ($50.76) is not the actual rate used by the hotel. Hotels use a number of rate classes, with various proportions of the total number of rooms assigned to each classification (see Exhibits 9–5 and 9–6). The actual average rate will be a weighted average of the rooms occupied. Reflected therein are the range of accommodations the hotel is offering and the guest's purchase of them based on nearby competition.

Square Foot Calculations.   To compensate for the fact that the Hubbart room rate formula provides no rate detail by room type classification, some managers use a square foot calculation. The basis for this is the fact that more expensive and higher-quality guest rooms are invariably larger than standard rooms at the same property. Therefore, rather than calculating the Hubbart room rate per room sold, this variation calculates the rate on a per-square-foot basis.

To illustrate, assume that the hotel presented in Exhibit 9–13 has a total of 56,250 square feet of space in its 150 guest rooms. With occupancy of 70%, there would be an average of 39,375 square feet sold per day. With an annual required return of $1,945,350, the daily required return is $5,329.73 ($1,945,350 divided by 365 days). Therefore, each square foot of rented room space must generate $0.1354 per day ($5,329.73 divided by 39,375 square feet sold per day) or almost 14 cents in daily revenue. As a result, a 300-square-foot room would sell for $40.62 (300 square feet times $0.1354) and a 450-square-foot room would sell for $60.93. Assuming that the hotel sells all room types in equal ratios to the number of rooms available in each type, this square foot calculation works as well as any other means for determining individual room type rates.

▶*The Building Cost Room Rate Formula.*   Time and repetition have created an industry axiom saying that rate can be evaluated by a rule of thumb (the building cost rate formula): The average room rate should equal $1 per $1,000 of construction cost. For a 250-room hotel costing $14 million (including land and land development, building, and public space but excluding furniture, fixtures, and equipment), the average rate should be $56 ($14 million ÷ 250 rooms ÷ $1,000).

The building cost yardstick is about as reliable as an old cookbook's direction to the chef: "Flavor to taste." Despite some very radical changes throughout the years, the rule is still being quoted on the theory that rising construction costs are being matched by rising room rates. Higher construction costs are a function of room size as well as building materials and labor. This generation of rooms is 100 to 200% larger than rooms were even 25 or 30 years ago.

Cost of construction includes other factors: type of construction, location, highrise versus low-rise buildings, and the cost of money. Luxury properties can cost five or six times as much per room as economy hotels. Land costs vary greatly across the nation. Comparing California and Arkansas is a lesson in futility. New York City may be stretching toward a $300 per-night room rate, but that is not the expectation of the manager in Dubuque, Iowa.

Economy chains have stopped advertising a minimum national rate. Each locale has its own cost basis for building, borrowing, taxing, and paying labor. Budgets aim only for a percentage rate below that of local competitors. Advertising a single rate as part of the national company logo is no longer feasible.

Increases in room construction costs are startling. Marriott's typical room cost runs between $100,000 and $200,000 today. Its figure was $8,000 in 1957. Consider what has happened in Hawaii over 20 years. Twenty years after the Mauna Kea was built at $100,000 per room, it was sold at $1 million per room! And the hotel was two decades older by that time.

The situation is the same in New York. Regent Hotels, a superluxury chain, has a 400-room hotel in New York with an average cost of $750,000 per room. With an actual average daily rate of $400, the hotel is far from the $750 ADR dictated by the rule-of-thumb standard.[3]

The Hotel Bel-Air in Los Angeles is another hotel that breaks the mold. With only 92 rooms, the property sold for a record $110 million (or approximately $1.2 million per room) to a Japanese hotel concern. Despite its incredibly high average daily rate ($375), the hotel earns far less than the $1,200 per average room-night that the building cost rate formula dictates.

These examples are special cases of "trophy hotels." Viewing the trophy as an art asset, which gives satisfaction and pleasure to the owner, offers some perspective on the price. Like an art piece, these eyebrow-raising prices are justified as long-term investments and by their uniqueness (location). In retrospect, the excessive prices of a generation ago have proven to be good deals.

In fact, no one actually expected the Japanese hotel company that purchased the Hotel Bel-Air to make an operating profit. Profit, if any, would come from selling the resort several years down the road. The Japanese buyer was one of four interested parties willing to bid in excess of $1 million per room for the Hotel Bel-Air. And the company that sold the hotel made an enormous profit, having purchased it just seven years earlier for $22.7 million.

Trophy hotels are extreme examples that do not set the rule for the remainder of the industry. With economy hotels costing less than $50,000 per room, and standard properties less than $80,000 per room, advocates of the rule take heart. Lower costs and lower rate figures maintain the spread between actual rate and rule-of-thumb rate close enough to keep the rule alive.

Conditions seesaw, first supporting the rule and then undermining it. The general rise in land and construction costs has been offset by improvements in design and reductions in labor force. The rise in financing costs has been offset by the lower costs of older hotels still in use. Since building costs are tied to historical prices, older hotels have lower financing costs (and probably lower real estate taxes, too) to recover. That is true, at least, until they're sold.

The building cost formula, a standard whose first known reference was in 1947, is still as roughly accurate today as it probably was back then.[4]

The Cost of Renovation. The costs of additions, property rehabs, or new amenities such as pools fall within the scope of the $1 per $1,000 rule. First, the cost of the upgrade is determined on a per room basis. The installation of an in-room air-conditioner might be priced at $1,500 per room. A general-use item such as a sauna would need a per room equivalent. The cost (assume $150,000) would be divided by the number of rooms (100) to arrive at the per unit cost.

Exhibit 9–14 illustrates an example of a major hotel renovation program. This exhibit assumes that a 200-room hotel spends $1,303,240 renovating its rooms, for an average cost of $6,516.20 per room. The problem assumes the hotel has a 12% cost of funds (interest rate). With a $6,516.20 expense per room at 12% interest and 15 years of debt repayment, $956.74 is the annualized cost of principal and interest per room per year. Therefore, the rule of thumb established in the building cost rate formula suggests that the hotel needs to charge an additional $0.96 (96 cents) per occupied room-night to compensate for the expense incurred when renovating its facility. With that kind of information, management can evaluate the likelihood of the additional investment being competitive in the eyes of the guest who is asked to pay the increased price.

▶ *The Ideal Average Room Rate.*   The firm of Laventhol & Horwath designed the ideal average room rate as a means of testing the room rate structure. According to this approach, the hotel should sell an equal percentage of rooms in each rate class instead of filling from the bottom up. A 70% occupancy should mean a 70% occupancy in each rate category. Such a spread produces an average rate identical to the average rate earned when the hotel is completely full—that is, an ideal room rate.

Exhibit 9–15 illustrates the computation used to derive the ideal rate. This formula assumes that each room type (standard, executive, deluxe, and suite) fills to the same percentage of rooms sold as every other room type. At a 70% hotel occupancy, 70% of the standard rooms will be sold, 70% of the executive rooms will be sold, 70% of the deluxe rooms will be sold, and 70% of the suites will be sold.

Once calculated, the manager is armed with a valuable figure, the ideal average room rate. As long as rates remain constant and the ratio of double occupancy does not change, the manager has a valid ideal rate. If the actual average rate on any given day or week is higher than the ideal average rate, the hotel has failed to provide a proper number of high-priced rooms. Such a hotel's market appears to be interested in rooms selling above the average, so room types and rates should be adjusted upward.

An average room rate lower than the ideal, and this is usually the case, indicates several problems. There may not be enough contrast between the low- and the high-priced rooms. Guests will take the lower rate when they are buying nothing extra for the higher rate. If the better rooms do, in fact, have certain extras—better exposure and newer furnishings—the lack of contrast between the rate categories might simply be a matter of poor selling at the front desk (discussed later in the chapter).

Check in at the front desk represents the last opportunity to up-sell the guest to a more expensive room accommodation. Good salesmanship coupled with a differentiated product gives the hotel a strong chance to increase middle-and high-priced room sales. Such comments as "I see you have reserved our standard room; do you realize for just 12 more dollars I can place you in a newly refurbished deluxe room with a complimentary continental breakfast?" go a long way toward satisfying both the guest and the bottom line.

A faulty internal rate structure is another reason that the ideal room rate might not be achieved. The options, the range of rates being offered, might not appeal to the customer. Using the ideal room rate computation, the spread between rates could be adjusted. According to the authors of the formula, increases should be concentrated in

1. Renovation Project Parameters

	Guest rooms: Cost per Room	Hallways: Cost per Door	Meeting Space: Cost per Square Foot	Lobby: Cost per Square Foot	F&B Outlets: Cost per Seat	Total Project
Soft costs[a]	$ 515	$ 194	$ 2	$ 3	$ 212	N/A
Hard costs[b]	3,305	755	5	18	1,342	N/A
Subtotals	$764,000	$189,800	$105,000	$73,500	$170,940	$1,303,240

2. Basic Hotel Information

- A 200-room full-service airport hotel
- 15,000 square feet of convention space
- 3,500 square feet of lobby space
- One 110-seat restaurant and bar
- 12% cost of funds interest rate
- Total renovation cost $1,303,240 (as shown above)

3. Project Cost per Average Guest Room

- $1,303,240 project divided by 200 rooms equals $6,516.20 per room.
- Assume that the $6,516.20 project cost per average room is to be repaid over 15 years at a 12% cost of funds rate.
- The combined principal and interest charge is $956.74 per room per year.

4. Impact of the Building Cost Room Rate Formula

- The $956.74 annualized cost per average room divided by $1,000 rule-of-thumb formula equals $0.96 increase per average room night sold.

[a]Soft costs include professional and contractor fees, sales tax, and shipping fees.
[b]Hard costs include construction costs, labor, materials, and all FF&E.

Exhibit 9–14 Figures developed in this exhibit come from an actual renovation project of a 200-room full-service hotel. Applying the $1 per $1,000 building cost room rate formula standard to this project results in roughly an added 96 cents in required per-room revenue.

Room Type	Number Rooms by Type	Percent of Double Occupancy	Single Rate	Double Rate
Standard	140	30	$ 80	$ 95
Executive	160	5	105	105
Deluxe	100	25	120	140
Suite	75	70	160	160
Total rooms	475			

Calculation Steps

1. Multiply all standard rooms (140) by their single rate ($80) to get a product of $11,200. Then take the double occupancy percentage for standard rooms (30%) times the total number of standard rooms (140) to get 42, the number of double-occupied standard rooms. Next, take the 42 double-occupied standard rooms times the differential between the single and double price ($95 double rate minus $80 single rate equals $15 differential) to get $630. Finally, add the room revenue for standard rooms calculated at the single rate ($11,200) to the additional room revenue received from standard rooms sold at the double rate ($630) to get the full-house room revenue for standard rooms, a total of $11,830.
2. Follow the same procedure for executive rooms: 160 rooms times $105 equals $16,800. The differential between single and double occupancy for executive rooms is zero, so there is no added revenue for double occupancy. The full-house room revenue for executive rooms is $16,800.
3. Follow the same procedure for deluxe rooms: 100 rooms times $120 single rate equals $12,000. In terms of double occupancy, there are 25 deluxe rooms (25% double occupancy times 100 rooms equals 25 rooms) sold at a $20 differential ($140 double rate minus $120 single rate equals $20 differential) for a total double occupancy impact of $500. The full-house room revenue for deluxe rooms is $12,500.
4. Follow the same procedure for suites: 75 rooms times $160 equals $12,000. The differential between single and double occupancy for suites is zero, so there is no added revenue for double occupancy. The full-house room revenue for suites is $12,000.
5. Add total revenues from standard rooms ($11,830), executive rooms ($16,800), deluxe rooms ($12,500), and suites ($12,000) for total revenues assuming 100% occupancy—ideal revenues. That total ($53,130) divided by rooms sold (475) is the ideal average room rate of $111.85.

No matter what the occupancy percentage, the ideal average room rate remains the same.

Try this problem again, assuming, say, 70 percent occupancy. The end result will still be an ideal average room rate of $111.85.

Exhibit 9–15   Although Laventhol & Horwath, the firm that developed the ideal average room rate, is no longer in business, the formula lives on. Follow these steps to develop an ideal average room rate for any hotel. *Courtesy of Laventhol & Horwath, Philadelphia.*

those rooms on those days for which the demand is highest. That begins with an analysis of rate categories.

Rate Categories. The discrepancy between the rates the hotel furnishes and those the guests prefer can be pinpointed with a simple chart. Guest demands and the hotel offerings are plotted side by side.

Guest demands are determined by a survey of registration card rates over a period of time. The survey should not include days of 100% occupancy when the guest had no rate choice. Special rate situations would also be excluded. Using elementary arithmetic, the percentage of total registrations is determined for each rate class. Exhibit 9–16 illustrates the contrast between what the guest buys and what the hotel offers. It also points to the rates that need adjustment.

Exhibit 9–16 assigns 40% of the hypothetical hotel to the average room rate. Two additional categories of 20% and 10%, respectively, appear on both the lower and upper ends. It is the sad history of our industry that hotels fill from the bottom up. Lower-priced rooms are in greatest demand. This means that low occupancy is accompanied by a low average daily rate. It is felt, therefore, that there should be more categories at the lower end of the price scale. These lower categories would be bunched together, while the higher rates would be spread over fewer categories. That might be the reason that Hilton advises its franchises to concentrate on the minimum single rate as the key in competition.

The Impact of Up-selling and Discounting

Although a well-trained front office staff pays for itself day after day through the incremental rooms revenue it generates by up-selling, training is only half of the story. The market in which the hotel operates has a great deal to do with its success as well. In those markets where demand is strong, competing hotels continue to push rates to new ADR heights. Hotels find it easier to sell expensive rooms, and price-sensitive guests find few properties willing to bargain on rate.

This is not the case in all markets. In markets where demand is soft, the industry tears down the very prices it worked so hard to build. And like anything, it is easier

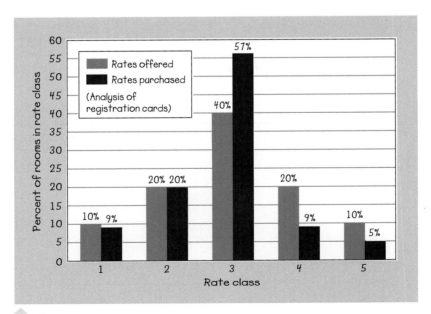

Exhibit 9–16   This exhibit highlights the need for rate adjustments by contrasting the supply and demand of different rate categories.

and faster to destroy than to build. In markets where discounting is rampant, the only sure winner is the customer who buys a quality product for a fraction of the price. If and when occupancy demand finally catches up to rooms supply, the industry finds itself dug into a deep hole. After becoming accustomed to discounted rates, customers perceive full rates as a very poor value. It is hard to pay $250 during a high-occupancy period when just a few weeks ago you received the same room for $100!

►*The Discounting Dilemma.*   Hotel customers are becoming increasingly aware of the room rate discount game. Travel articles tout the same bottom line to the customer—shop around for your best rate. Many customers have trained themselves to ask for the discount when booking lodging accommodations. This creates the image that standard prices are unfair and that the industry needs to discount because the quality of the product does not warrant full price.

Discounting Profitability.   Room discounting is designed to increase occupancy at the cost of a lowered room rate. If the resulting occupancy increase is sufficient, it covers the lost revenues from reduced rates. In such a situation, both parties are happy—the guest pays less for the room and the hotel makes a higher profit from having created more room demand.

However appealing these potential profits are, rate discounting has a negative side as well. In fact, the whole idea of discounting rates to increase demand is somewhat suspect. Let's assume that a given hotel property was operating at an annualized occupancy of 60% with a $70 ADR. Because the property decides it wants to increase occupancy, it establishes a rate discounting program. Exhibit 9–17 shows that for this example, a 10% rate discount (second column of Exhibit 9–17) requires occupancy to rise to 66.67% in order to gross the same revenues as previously earned. That's an 11% increase in occupancy required to offset a 10% discount in price—just to gross the same revenues!

An increase of 11% may not be easy in a community experiencing, say, only a 3.0% demand growth. To accomplish an 11% increase, some other lodging operation(s) will lose customers. Herein lies the biggest problem: As competing lodging properties catch wind of your discounting program, they too will begin to discount. Ultimately, a rate war will ensue, and the only winner will be the customer who pays the reduced rate.

Current Occupancy (%)	Percent of Rate Discount			
	10%	15%	20%	25%
50	55.56	58.82	62.5	66.67
55	61.11	64.71	68.75	73.33
60	66.67	70.59	75.00	80.00
65	72.22	76.47	81.25	86.67
70	77.78	82.35	87.5	93.33
75	83.33	88.24	93.75	100.00

Exhibit 9–17   Substantial increases in occupancy are required to offset discounted rates. Figures in columns two through five (listed as 10% through 25%) reflect the changes needed to maintain gross revenues. For example, a hotel that discounts rates by 20% must increase occupancy from its current 65% level to 81.25% or room revenue will fall.

➤*Up-selling Premium Accommodations.*   The room rate policy faces a moment of truth when the front-office employee and the buying public come face to face. Fashioning a room rate policy is a futile exercise unless management simultaneously prepares its staff to carry out the plan. The selling skills of reservationists and clerks are critical to the average daily rate until the house nears capacity. Since nearly full occupancy is a rare occasion, earning a consistently higher ADR on the 60 to 70% day is achieved only when a program for selling up is in place.

The hardest sell comes from the guest-service agent. A guest who approaches the desk with a reservation in hand has already decided to buy. Already committed, the new arrival is susceptible to a carefully designed and rehearsed sales effort (see Exhibit 9–18). The hardest job comes from the reservationist who doesn't even see the buyer. Too hard a sell, too firm a price, and the guest is lost early on. Teamed up, the reservationist and the room clerk deliver a one–two punch to the ADR, although they could be 1,000 miles and 30 days apart.

A firm sale begins with product knowledge. That's why good sales executives travel to the central reservation office to brief the operators there. On property, both the reservationists and the room clerks need continuous training about the facilities and accommodations of the hotel. This is rarely done. Few hotels ever assign 15 minutes per day for staff visits and inspections. Hotels spend millions of dollars upgrading rooms and modernizing facilities, but the room clerk never sees the changes. A simple and consistent training program assures management that reservationists and front-desk clerks know their product.

If the desk staff knows the product, a repertoire of reasons can be developed to up-sell. A 10% up-sell of $10 to $20 is not a large increment in terms of today's rate (see Exhibit 9–19). Since every dollar of the increment goes to the bottom line, it represents a large annual figure, even if only a portion of the attempts are successful. The focus might be to move the commercial guest from standard service to a concierge floor. The weekend shopper of that commercial hotel needs a different approach. This discretionary buyer may turn away if the rates quoted at check in fail to reflect the package plan originally booked at the time of reservation.

Each guest looks at the incremental dollars differently, and so does the employee. Management must be cognizant that the basic room rate and especially the incremental up-sell seem excessive to employees working for an hourly wage. Part of the training must attend to the employee's frame of reference. Having some type of incentive plan for the employee does help change attitudes.

Incentives to Up-sell.   Motivated room clerks are better selling tools than cut rates and giveaways. They are less expensive, too, even with an incentive-pay plan. And it takes a good incentive plan coupled with proper training to make the system work.

Incentive systems stimulate interest and emphasize the goals of management. Rewards are especially important during heavy discounting periods, when guests know that low rates are available and sales resistance is high. Unlike some other places of the world (see Exhibit 9–19), clerks in the United States do not share in any mandatory service charge. Therefore, a special cash pool is needed for incentive distributions.

Incentive systems require an accurate and easily computed formula. Flat goals can be established, or the focus can be on improvement from last year, or last month, or last week for that matter. Most front-office incentives are keyed to average daily rate. Occupancy is a factor in total revenue, which suggests other bases for setting goals.

Most systems establish a pool that is shared by the team. Individual competition is restricted to the clerks, but selling up is a function of the reservation office, the tele-

---

Mastering the Basics of Selling

1. **Impressing the Guests**
   - Maintain an appealing physical appearance, including good posture. Don't lean or hang over the front desk. Bring to the job your own sense of spirit and style.
   - Organize and keep the front-desk area uncluttered.
   - Get to know your property's every service and accommodation type thoroughly. Make frequent forays around the property to learn firsthand about each kind and category of room so that you can better describe the facilities to potential guests.
   - Memorize or keep close at hand an up-to-date list of the locations and hours of operation of all food and beverage facilities; entertainment lounges; recreational and sports rooms; and banquet, meeting, exhibit, and other public areas.
   - Learn the names and office locations of the general manager and all department heads, including directors of marketing, sales, catering, convention services, and food and beverages.
   - Be friendly to guests, greeting them warmly and, whenever possible, by name and title. For instance, when requesting a bellperson's service, ask him or her to take "Mr. Smith to room 340." (To ensure the guest's privacy, be discreet in mentioning the room number to the bellperson.) Call the bellperson by name as well.
   - Give guests your undivided attention.
   - Answer all questions completely, but concisely and accurately, based on your in-depth knowledge of hotel operations. Refrain from boasting about accommodations and services; instead, offer simple, to-the-point descriptions of features.
   - Assume a polite, patient manner in explaining the various options available—for example, the size of rooms, kinds of reservations (confirmed or guaranteed), and the terms *American, European,* or *modified American plan.*

2. **Winning the Guests**
   - Expand prospects' accommodations horizons with descriptions of the room and service possibilities awaiting them. Potential guests may think of a hotel as simply a building filled with bedrooms, but you know better. So inform them about rooms with views, rooms near the health spa, twin-bed rooms, suites, rooms furnished according to a certain historical period, or ultramodern accommodations with Jacuzzis. Lay everything out for prospects, dwelling on the positive, distinctive appeals of each choice. Throw in the tempting intangibles associated with each type of room; for instance, the prestige of having a room on the same floor as the hotel's exclusive club for special guests, or the pleasure of staying in a room equipped with a VCR or a fireplace.
   - Attempt to sell a room to suit the client. Observe people and try to read their particular hankerings. If a guest is new to the hotel, a room with a nice view might be impressive. Business travelers might prefer a quiet room at the back. Guests with children, people staying for an extended visit, honeymooners, and celebrities are among those who might be interested in suites.
   - Sell the room, not the rate. If a guest asks flat out for rates, avoid quoting a minimum or just one rate; instead, offer a range, portraying in detail the difference in accommodations that each rate affords.

Exhibit 9–18   Mastering the basics of selling. Commonsense advice from the Foundation of the Hospitality Sales and Marketing Association International's pamphlet entitled *The Front Office; Turning Service into Sales. Courtesy of the Hospitality Sales and Marketing Association International, New York.*

- Should a prospect look unsure or reluctant to book a room, suggest that the guest accompany a hotel employee on a walkthrough. A tour of the premises gives guests a chance to settle any doubts they might have and demonstrates the hotel's policy of goodwill and flexibility.
- Keep abreast of special sales promotions, weekend packages, and other marketing strategies, and dangle these offerings to prospects. (To make sure you're informed, you might ask your sales department to hold regularly scheduled presentations to front-office staff on their latest schemes.)
- Look for opportunities to extend the sale—there are many. If a guest mentions that he or she is hungry or arrives around mealtime, promote the hotel's dining facilities; if a guest arrives late, talk up the entertainment lounge or room service. As the person most in contact with guests throughout their stays, you are in the enviable position of being able to please both your guest and hotel management. You can delight guests merely by drawing their attention to the multitude of services your hotel offers, whether it's quick dry cleaning or a leisurely massage. And you can thrill the boss by advancing a sale and hotel revenues through your promotion of in-house features.

3. Wooing the Guests

- When a guest arrives, upgrade the reservation to a more luxurious accommodation whenever availability allows, ask whether the guest would like to make a dinner reservation, and ask whether he or she would like a wake-up call.
- Record and follow through on all wake-up call requests.
- Deliver mail and messages promptly.
- Avoid situations that keep guests waiting. For instance, if you're unable to locate a guest's reservation and a line is beginning to form on the other side of the counter, assume that the hotel has plenty of the desired accommodations available and go ahead and book the guest. Finish registering anyone else who is waiting, and then search for the missing reservation.
- Should mishaps occur, whether a reservation mix-up or a housekeeping error, handle the matter with aplomb without laying the blame on any individual employee or department.
- Dispatch each departing guest with a favorable impression of the hotel. In other words, treat the guests with care and courtesy during check out. Regardless of whether guests enjoyed their stay, they will remember only the hassles experienced at check out if you allow them to occur. Therefore, don't. That is, be sure there are useful, comprehensive procedures for dealing with guests who dispute postings and payments, and follow those procedures with assurance and professionalism.

phone operators, the bellpersons, and others. That's why the pool, with its spinoff in morale and teamwork, is preferred.

The cash pool is generated from a percentage—say, 10%—of room sales that exceed projections. Management projects either the total room sales or the average daily rate. Management projections might be based on the ideal room rate (see Exhibit 9–15) or the budget forecast. If actual sales exceed target sales, the bonus becomes payable. The bonus period is important. It must be long enough to reflect the true efforts of the team but short enough to bring the rewards within grasp.

Higher ADRs are a win–win–win situation. The clerk wins by receiving increased payroll as an incentive for up-selling. Management wins because up-selling contributes

Top Dozen U.S. Cities for Hotel Room Rates

Rank	City	Average Room Rate
1	New York City	$225.00
2	Boston	178.00
3	Washington, DC	178.00
4	Chicago	177.00
5	Dallas	168.00
6	Los Angeles	163.00
7	Phoenix	158.00
8	San Francisco	154.00
9	Fort Lauderdale	150.00
9	New Orleans	150.00
11	Houston	146.00
12	Philadelphia	139.00

Top Dozen International Cities for Hotel Room Rates

Rank	City	Average Room Rate (U.S. dollars)
1	New Delhi	$420.00
2	London	399.00
3	Hong Kong	394.00
4	Monte Carlo	369.00
5	Moscow	359.00
6	Bombay	354.00
7	Budapest	335.00
8	Manila	334.00
9	Buenos Aires	328.00
9	Paris	328.00
11	Tokyo	323.00
12	Santiago	321.00

Source: "Corporate Traveler Index" (1998) published annually by *Business Traveler News* since 1985.

Exhibit 9–19   Even expense-account guests are reluctant to pay more for upgraded rooms, especially in international locations where the average corporate rate is twice that of U.S. cities. Intensive training plus incentives can remake guest–service agents into top-notch salespersons. Convincing just 10% of recalcitrant buyers to upgrade will produce incremental profits even after funding incentive bonuses for the front-office staff.

proportionately higher profits to the P & L Statement. And the guest wins by receiving exactly the room desired—this is where training is so important. The clerk isn't forcing anything on the guest that the guest doesn't want. Guests are more than ready to pay top dollar for better and better accommodations. That's been demonstrated time and again over the past decade as room rates and room quality continue to rise.

➤ SUMMARY

A proper room rate is as much a marketing tool as it is a financial instrument. That's because the room rate needs to be low enough to attract customers while being high enough to earn a reasonable profit: Easier said than done. Even in this day of sophisticated computer technology, calculating the room rate still involves plenty of guesswork and gut instincts. There is an unquantifiable psychology involved in the room rate. An attractive rate for one person may appear too high or too low to another guest. For some, high rates suggest a pretentious operation; for others, a low rate suggests poor quality.

Searching and working toward the perfect rate is difficult, indeed. Even after the rate has been determined and established, it is immediately changed. Rates fluctuate by season, they change according to room type, they vary with special guest discounts, and they shift as a function of yield management.

Although there are some well-established methods for calculating the proper rate, these should never be used to the exclusion of common sense and market demand. The Hubbart room rate formula and the building cost rate formula are two of the most common means for determining the rate. In addition, the ideal average room rate formula adds a dimension of retrospection to understanding the appropriateness of a rate in terms of the local marketplace.

➤ QUESTIONS AND PROBLEMS

1. Assume that the ideal average room rate for a given property is $87.25. Month after month, however, the hotel consistently outperforms its ideal average room rate by at least $5 to $10. You are the general manager of the property, and you know you can extract much information from this data. Based on the fact that the hotel's actual ADR is consistently higher than its ideal average room rate, what do you know about the front-office staff's ability to sell rooms? What do you know about the price sensitivity of your customers? And what do you know about rate tendencies in the surrounding marketplace? Armed with this data, what type of action might you now consider?

2. Up-selling at the front desk is paramount to enhancing hotel profitability. Yet up-selling also has the potential to cause the guest discomfort and to appear pushy or aggressive. There is a fine line between professionally up-selling the room and appearing as if you are "hustling" the guest. How might you attempt to up-sell each of the following types of guests? Acting as the guest–service agent prepare a professional up-selling dialogue for each of these situations (make up your own room types and rates as necessary):

   (a) Standing before you is an executive on your corporate-discount plan. He is stretching and yawning from a hard day of air travel and local meetings.

   (b) About to check in is a mother with her three young children. She is alone—her husband doesn't arrive until tomorrow. The kids are obviously excited about the prospects of swimming and running around the courtyard.

   (c) Two gentlemen from a recently arrived bus tour are standing in front of you. Even though the rest of the tour group is housed in standard queen doubles, these men are commenting that their room is much too small.

   (d) A female executive with an extended-stay reservation is currently checking in. She comments on the fact that she must stay in your hotel for at least 10 days. How can she possibly survive 10 days away from home?

3. A commercial hotel offers a deeply discounted rate on Friday, Saturday, and Sunday nights. Discuss what should be done or said in each of the following situations:

(a) A guest arrives on Saturday but makes no mention of the special rate and seems unaware of the discount possibilities. The desk clerk charges full rack rate. On check out Monday morning, the cashier notices the full rate charged for two nights, but the guest (after reviewing her folio) says nothing.

(b) The situation is the same as that in part (a), but this time the guest does comment that she thought a discounted rate might apply.

(c) A corporate guest stays Wednesday through Wednesday on company business. He receives a slightly discounted commercial rate for all seven nights, but his rate is still much higher than the special weekend rate available to anyone off the street. He knows about the special rate and asks that his three weekend nights be reduced accordingly.

(d) Create a fourth scenario of your own.

4. Explain why hoteliers differentiate between discounting practices and rate cutting. Create a list of similarities and differences between discounting and rate cutting. Then conclude whether you believe they are substantially different activities or really two different statements for describing exactly the same practice.

5. The Hubbart room rate formula calls for an average room rate that will cover expenses and provide a fair return to the investors. Compute that rate from the abbreviated but complete set of data that follows:

Investment (also fair market value)	
Land	$ 3,000,000
Building	25,000,000
Furniture and equipment	6,000,000
Nonappropriated expenses, such as advertising, repairs, etc.	$ 1,200,000
Income from all operating departments except rooms, net of losses	$ 3,200,000
Rooms available for sale	563
Nonoperating expenses, such as insurance, taxes, and depreciation	510,000
Desired return on investment	16%
Interest on debt of $25,000,000	14%
Percentage of occupancy	71%

6. Using the data from Problem 5, compute what the typical room charge should be according to the building cost rate formula.

➤ NOTES

1. The International Hotel Association (IHA) published a study entitled "IHA Taxation Survey—A Comparative Survey of Taxation on the Hospitality Industry." This study offers an analysis, country by country, of the taxes levied against hotels and restaurants.

2. *The Hubbart Formula for Evaluating Rate Structures of Hotel Rooms*, 1952, is available from the American Hotel & Motel Association, 1201 New York Avenue, NW, Suite 600, Washington DC 20005, and is used here with the association's permission.

3. Although the business world regularly uses the term *rule of thumb* to denote an industry standard, one origin of this term is far from being politically correct. The expression may derive from Anglo-Saxon common law, where little more than 100 years ago, a man's wife and children were his personal property, his chattel. If he was so motivated, he could beat them, as long as the weapon he used was no larger in diameter than his thumb—hence one possible origin of the phrase. Another origin is that of a unit of measure. The length of

the thumb from knuckle to tip of a 10th Century English king named Edgar the Peaceful was a unit of measure (roughly an inch)—hence the other common explanation of the term.

4. An August 1995 letter to the editor of the *Cornell Hotel and Restaurant Administration Quarterly* stated that the earliest reference the author (Bjorn Hanson) could find was a 1947 publication of the *Horwath Accountant* (a newsletter from a now defunct accounting firm). The author of this newsletter (Louis Toth) stated that for the

$1 per $1,000 rule of thumb to work, several things needed to be in place: (1) The rule referred only to the cost of the building, not the entire project; (2) the hotel needed to receive rents from concessionaries to cover debt service and taxes on the land itself; (3) the hotel needed a 70% occupancy; (4) the cost of FF&E could be no more than 20% of the cost of the building; and (5) income before fixed charges must be at least 55% of room sales.

PART IV

The Hotel Revenue Cycle

Chapter 10
Billing the Guest Folio

Chapter 11
Cash Transactions

Chapter 12
Credit and the City Ledger

The sequence of the text is designed about the flow of guests as they pass through the several stages that structure their relationship with the hotel. First comes reservations, which are described in the three chapters of Part II. Modern telecommunications have changed the mechanics of reservation requests, and modern technologies have improved the hotel's techniques of forecasting and processing room availability. Once the reservation contract is agreed upon, the hotel confirms the understanding and begins tracking the expected arrivals through its reservation system.

In Part III, the guest arrives, sometimes carrying the reservation made in Part II and sometimes unexpectedly as a walk-in. The mechanics of that arrival, including room rate decisions, rooms assignments, and the rooming process, are examined thoroughly in this middle section of the book. Here, too, are discussed the special guest-service relationships that set the tone during the arrival time (Part III) and throughout the subsequent sale of services (Part IV).

Part IV brings us to the reason for the guest's visit: the sale of services, especially room sales, by the hotel. Selling services is only one part of this section. Recording the sales, collecting the amounts, and establishing the accounting procedures make up the content of Chapters 10, 11, and 12. In Part V, the cycle closes, and the guest checks out. There are still records to keep after the guest's departure—as there were throughout the guest's entire stay. Part IV attends to the records of the sale and Part V to the accuracy of the record.

Computerization has improved the techniques of recording and reviewing the records from guest sales and services. Fundamental to the process is an accounting base, whose essential rules have remained unchanged despite the speed and accuracy of computerization. In Part IV we review the rules of basic accounting over and over again. This teaching technique—the recitation of rules—helps the student clear the hurdles of accounting's debits and credits. In this manner, Part V establishes a firm base for understanding the ideas behind accounting even if the reader lacks formal courses in the subject. Too often the nonaccountant rejects the accounting explanations as being too difficult. Not so; the repetition of the rules will indicate how narrow an understanding of accounting is needed to be accounting wise about front-office folios.

In part, the business environment for hotels is a noncash one with credit, credit cards, debit cards, and smart cards the new media of exchange. We explain this in Chapter 12. Despite the popularity and convenience of the cards, cash retains its hold on many business activities. In Chapter 11, we review the money form of cash as well as its substitutes, old standbys such as traveler's checks and personal checks. The economic impact of the new cash that's coming, the euro, is unknown as yet, but its form is introduced in Chapter 11. Before we examine cash and credit cards, an overview of the entire billing process is provided in Chapter 10.

All of the preceding carries the guest (and the text) to the final stage of the sales/collection process, the audit. In Part V we emphasize the changes in audit techniques that computerized property management systems have brought. For one, they have reduced the piles of paper and make possible the megaproperties (hotels of 2,000 rooms and up) that have appeared in the past decade.

CHAPTER 10
Billing the Guest Folio

Outline

There's a tempo, a rhythm, to the flow of guests through the hotel. Reservations sounds the first beat. Then the guests arrive and register. The melody ends with the stay and the eventual departure. Between check in and check out, guests enjoy the facilities of the hotel. The sale of those facilities is what the business of innkeeping is all about. Hotels sell rooms, food, and beverage, along with minor departmental services such as telephone and laundry.

Hotels and their customers (guests) have a different relationship than do other retailers and their customers. Hotel customers register as they arrive. Their names, addresses, and credit-card numbers, and often their business associations as well, are known to the innkeeper. Consequently, the sale of services can be completed without immediate payment. Unlike other retail transactions, which require immediate settlement, the merchant/hotel waits for payment. Sometimes the wait is a few days, sometimes a week. In the meantime, the amounts due are recorded on a bill, which is presented to the guest as he or she departs. Hotel professionals call that bill a *folio*.

The folio is an accurate and current statement of how much the guest owes the hotel. It is available at the front desk on demand. Whereas other businesses send their customers monthly statements, the hotel's statement is ready on a moment's notice, even though the exact moment of departure is unknown. Indeed, even the day of departure may be uncertain. Of course, the hotel is as anxious as the guest to have an accurate folio available. Incorrectly charged items delay the check-out procedure and create ill feelings. Charges not on the folio statement are difficult to collect after a guest has departed. Collecting these *late charges* by mail after the guest has left is expensive, both in administrative costs and in guest relations.

➤ *ACCOUNTS RECEIVABLE*

Except at the retail level, most commerce is carried on without immediate payment. Businesses buy and sell to one another without a direct exchange of money. Payment is delayed until a more convenient time in order to complete the sale as quickly as possible. Hotels also work that way. Guests are not disturbed during their sleep in order to collect the room rates! Instead, charges are made to the folio and collections are made later. Guests usually settle at check-out time. During the period between the sale (room, food, beverage, etc.) and the payment (at departure), the guest owes the hotel. A customer who owes a business for services that have not been paid is known as an *account receivable*.[1]

Types of Accounts Receivable

Hotels have two types of accounts receivable because guests can be in two different categories. Guests who are currently registered and occupying rooms in the hotel are transient guests. Hence, the amounts they owe are classified as *transient accounts receivable*. Persons or companies that owe the hotel for services, but are not registered, are not currently occupying rooms, are city guests. Hence the amounts they owe are classified as *city accounts receivable*. Both types of debtors are receivables (the hotel is to receive payment). Transient receivables are presently in the hotel; city receivables are not.

Guests can and do change status. Usually, the shift is from transient to city. A transfer takes place, for example, when a transient guest checks out and uses a credit card—as most do—to settle the debt. The debt is still owed, but the guest is no longer in the hotel. The debt of the transient guest is now a debt of the credit-card company.

But the credit-card company is not a registered guest, not a transient guest, not occupying a room. The credit-card company falls into the city category: a hotel receivable that is not occupying a room.

➤ *The Ledger.*   There are numerous accounts receivable in both the transient and city categories. Hotels as large as the Luxor, which is illustrated in Exhibit 1–1, might have 5,000 guests registered, with as many as 2,000 or 3,000 folios. Accountants call that combination of folios a *ledger*. They call any combination of records a ledger. Since all the parties are registered, that is, transient guests, this particular group of records is called a *transient ledger*. The individual folios of transient guests are viewed as one record, a transient ledger.

City accounts receivable are combined similarly. The total records of city accounts, that is, debtors to the hotel who are not registered currently, is called a *city ledger*. The individual accounts of city guests are viewed as one record, a city ledger.

The Transient Ledger.   *Transient ledger* is shorthand for the transient accounts receivable ledger. Hotel professionals use other jargon to identify this particular ledger. Because the ledger (that is, the total record of debt to the hotel by registered guests) is available at the front office, it is frequently called the *front-office ledger*. Since it is made up of registered guests, it is also called the *guest ledger*. Room rates are the largest source of charges to guest folios, so *rooms ledger* is still another term used for the transient ledger.

The variety of terms used to identify the transient ledger spills over to the folios that make up this ledger. Thus, the single transient folio may be called *folio*, or *guest folio*, or *front-office folio*. Since the folio is a record of the guest's account with the hotel, the folio is also called an *account card* or *guest bill*.

The City Ledger.   There are numerous subcategories of the city ledger as explained in Chapter 12, but there is but one general term, *city ledger*. That makes city-ledger references easier to remember than the variety of labels (guest ledger, rooms ledger, front-office ledger) used for the transient ledger.

Other than terminology and location (guest ledger at the front desk; city ledger with the accounting office), timing is the chief difference between the two ledgers. Charges, which are the records of services rendered, are *posted* (recorded) immediately to the guest ledger since the guest might choose to leave at any time. City guests, who must establish credit in advance, are billed periodically. This permits some delay in posting city-ledger charges. Like many other businesses do, hotels bill city accounts monthly. Often, a three-day cycle is used for the first billing. These variations in timing are accommodated by different ledger forms as well as by different posting and billing procedures.

➤ *What Is and Isn't Accounted For.*   Each folio is an account receivable, a record of the guest's debt to the hotel. Since folios deal only with accounts receivable, persons who pay cash for services received, as they might in cocktail lounges and restaurants, are not part of the front-office billing procedure. It makes no difference whether the buyer is a guest or a stranger; there is no account receivable, no debt owed, when settlement is made immediately with dollars. For purposes of a chapter entitled "Billing the Guest Folio," there is no record made when customers purchase services for cash. We have more to say about cash transactions in Chapter 11.

Strangers, nonguests without front-office folios, can still purchase food and beverage on credit. They do so with credit cards. A credit-card charge creates an account receivable within the city ledger, not the front-office ledger. It is, of course, an account for the credit-card company, which is a nonregistered debtor. That's the definition of city ledger. As a result, the nonguest owes the credit-card company and the credit-card company owes the hotel as a city-ledger account.

Hotel guests, like strangers, use dollars at times to pay for meals or other services. Since that is a cash payment, no account receivable record (no folio) is involved. Also like strangers, registered guests may elect to use credit cards to pay for services. Then, just as it happens with strangers, the credit-card record becomes part of the city ledger.

To summarize, both registered guests and strangers pay for services in one of two methods: method one, they pay cash; method two, they charge services to personal credit cards. Guests have a third option of payment, one not available to nonguests: Method three, guests charge services to their rooms, to their front-office folios. By merely signing for the charge, the guest acknowledges the debt. The amount is then posted to the folio. Payment for the folio with all its charges comes later, usually as the guest checks out. Much of this chapter concentrates on this third method of paying for services.

The Folio: The Individual Account Receivable

Folio, bill, guest account, account card, guest account card, and guest bill are used interchangeably to refer to the individual account receivable that is opened for each registered guest. Of course, one folio may serve a party of several persons, as it does with a family, for example. *Visitor's account* is the European terminology for folio.

➤*Location and Filing of the Folio.*   Modern hotels have adopted computerized folios almost without exception. Computerized folios (see Exhibit 10–1) are maintained in electronic memory and are visible only when printed. Therefore, the desk needs input and output devices (keyboards, screens, and printers) to input and access the information. Older, hand-prepared, pencil-and-paper folios (see Exhibit 10–2) had to be physically stored at the desk (see Exhibit 10–3).

Whether electronic or hand prepared, maintaining the folio record is a responsibility of the front-office cashier. Hand-prepared folios generated such large quantities of paper that a billing clerk, or posting clerk, was often used to support the cashier. As we explain later, much of the electronic posting is done at computer terminals in the various food and beverage outlets. The result is fewer desk employees and fewer errors. As front-office jobs are combined, guest-service agents with broader responsibilities take on what was the job of the cashier.

➤*Number of Folios.*   The size of the hotel determines the number of folios in use, more or less. Essentially, there is one for each occupied room. There are exceptions, however. Several friends sharing one room might request several folios, and a single person occupying a four-room suite may need but one.

The number of city-ledger accounts is not determined by the number of occupied rooms. City-ledger accounts are established for individuals and companies who want credit privileges with the hotel. In pre-credit-card days, large hotels had thousands of city-ledger accounts. Not so today, when almost everyone carries national credit cards. Now, the bulk of the city ledger can be accounted for in a half-dozen national credit-card accounts. Electronically tying city-ledger accounts to the computers of credit-card companies and banks speeds processing and reduces administrative costs.

HI-JINKS HOTEL
A Vallen Corporation Property
☐V

1000 NOAH VAIL
ROTTEN PUMPKIN POND
MASSACHUSETTS 01266
1-800-555-5555

RES#   43 RLG 1234   ACCT# 5941

IN   11-02-   OUT   11-04-

NAME: Iona Carr

ADDRESS: S.N. Eaky Rd.
Mousie, KY 40288

RATE 100   ROOM   444

DATE	DESCRIPTION	REFERENCE		CHARGES	CREDITS	BALANCE
						100.00
11/02/	ROOM	444	18-1	100.00		105.50
11/02/	ROOM TAX	444	18-2	5.50		119.48
11/03/	COFFEE SHOP	444	38-1	13.98		130.58
11/03/	TELEPHONE	444	43-2	11.10		136.58
11/03/	FAX	444	43-3	6.00		159.18
11/03/	LOUNGE	444	26-2	22.60		-0-
11/04/	VISA#1111111	444	50-4		159.18	

. . . . If you were a Vallen ☐V Associate Member,
you would have earned 320 Club Membership points.

TRANSFER TO CITY LEDGER
I AGREE THAT MY LIABILITY FOR THIS BILL IS NOT
WAIVED, AND AGREE TO BE PERSONALLY LIABLE IF
THE INDICATED PERSON, ASSOCIATION, OR COMPANY
FAILS TO PAY ANY PART OF THESE CHARGES.

_____
SIGNATURE

For Reservations: 1-617-555-5555   •   Fax: 1-617-555-5554   •   E-mail: vallen@hotel.com

Exhibit 10–1   Representative, computerized guest bill (folio) printed at the end of a guest's stay. Note especially the reservation number, arrival and departure dates, rate, and room number at the top. In this chapter we focus on the meaning of the postings.

ROOM NO.	409					E69080		

m M/M Art E. Fishal
86 Bates Boulevard
Hitchcock, Texas 01020

ARRIVED	RATE	PERSONS	COT	REG. CARD #	PREV. INV. #	CLERK
12/23/	78	2	N/A	69080	N/A	SB

DATE	12/23/		12/24/													
BROUGHT FORWARD			99	24												
ROOM	78	–														
TAX	6	24														
RESTAURANT	15	–														
"																
TELEPHONE-LOCAL																
-LONG DISTANCE																
TELEGRAMS																
LAUNDRY & VALET																
CASH ADVANCES																
"																
NEWSPAPERS																
TRANSFERS from 407 #69081			84	24												
TOTAL DEBIT	99	24	183	48												
CASH																
ALLOWANCES																
CITY LEDGER																
ADVANCE DEPOSITS																
CREDIT CARDS			183	48												
TRANSFERS																
BALANCE FORWARD	99	24	0													

ALL ACCOUNTS ARE DUE WHEN RENDERED

Exhibit 10–2   The left and right illustrate two pencil-and-paper folios, normally prepared with a carbon copy that is given to the guest. Compare the formats to Exhibit 10–1. Refer to this illustration again later in this chapter when the text explains two types of transfers: Room 407's folio-to-folio transfer of $84.24, and Room 409's guest-ledger to city-ledger transfer of $183.48.

▶***Master Accounts.***   Tour operating companies, trade associations, conventions, and single-entity groups incur charges that are not billable to any one person. Business expenses such as these are charged to another folio, called a *master account*. Master accounts allow group charges to be distinguished from personal charges. The master account is its own person, much like a business corporation has a legal identity separate from that of its individual owners. Master accounts are not city-ledger ac-

ROOM NO. _____407_____   **E69081**

m ___Benny Fishal___

12345 Education Avenue
Reading, Pennsylvania 98765

ARRIVED	RATE	PERSONS	COT	REG. CARD #	PREV. INV. #	CLERK
12/23/	78	2	N/A	69081	N/A	SB

DATE	12/23/		12/24/													
BROUGHT FORWARD			84	24												
ROOM	78	–														
TAX	6	24														
RESTAURANT																
"																
TELEPHONE-LOCAL																
-LONG DISTANCE																
TELEGRAMS																
LAUNDRY & VALET																
CASH ADVANCES																
"																
NEWSPAPERS																
TRANSFERS																
TOTAL DEBIT	84	24	84	24												
CASH																
ALLOWANCES																
CITY LEDGER																
ADVANCE DEPOSITS																
CREDIT CARDS																
TRANSFERS TO 409	#69080		84	24												
BALANCE FORWARD	84	24	0													

ALL ACCOUNTS ARE DUE WHEN RENDERED

counts. As long as the group is in the hotel, its master account is a standard guest folio at the front office. Master accounts are often transferred to the city ledger for direct billing after the group has departed.

Decisions about master account billing are made well in advance of the group's arrival. The hotel and the organization settle sales and credit terms as part of the group contract. How the charges are distributed is decided by the group, not the hotel. A company holding a meeting of its employees (that is, a single-entity group) might have all the charges of every delegate billed to its master account. It's different with convention delegates because each represents a different company or organization. Since no one master account is applicable, each convention delegate pays his or her own room and personal charges. However, the association that stages the convention

Exhibit 10–3   The cashier's well (bucket or pit) separates pencil-and-paper folios by sequential room numbers. Computerized properties use the bucket to separate and locate preprinted folios, correspondence, or vouchers.

has a master account for banquet costs, cocktail parties, and meeting expenses. Other general costs such as telecommunications or room charges for invited speakers are also charged to the convention's master account.

Tour groups have master accounts but they differ from master accounts of convention groups. Convention attendees pay their own bills. Tour-group participants pay the tour company in advance, and the tour company negotiates with the hotel. So the tour company is responsible for payment of all charges included in the package. The tour company's master account includes the room charges for everyone in the group, plus whatever else was sold with the package: meals, drinks, shows, golf, and so on. Personal expenses—those not within the package—are charged to the guest's personal folio.

Each group and association has its own way of doing things. That makes for numerous variations in billing the master folio. Under one plan, the full room rate for everyone is included on the company's (single-entity) master account. Another might include only the single rate. Then delegates with attending partners would be charged the spread between single rate and double rate on their individual folios.

A flat dollar allowance per room is another modification. Onto the master folio goes a per diem allowance that includes any type of charge (room, meals, bar). Charges that exceed the lump-sum figure are entered on the personal folio. Additional complications arise from American plan billing, from compulsory service charges, and from room-based taxes.

Large companies and affiliated allied members are among the attendees of most conventions or trade shows. They cover the expenses of their own staffs with a master account, which is separate altogether from the master account of the group putting on the event. The hotel will have numerous, unrelated master accounts to track. Posted to these accounts are the expenses of the affiliated companies for cocktail parties and host suites, and even meals provided for the total convention by the sponsoring affiliate. Such sponsorship is an accepted means of public relations for the allied members.

Those responsible for the master accounts might settle the bill at check out. More frequently, it is transferred to the city ledger and settled by mail and telephone over the next 30 days. In Chapter 12 we resume the discussion at the point of transfer.

Split Billing.   The distribution of the charges between the master account and the guest's personal folio is called *split billing* or *split folios.* Both the master folio (often called the *A folio*) and the guest or *B folio* are standardized forms of the types illustrated throughout the chapter. A and B are used merely to distinguish the group entity from the individual person. The A folio is the major folio where the large charges of the association, tour company, or business are posted. Sometimes, the hotel itself is the A folio. Such is the case with casino comps and frequent-stay customers.

Casino Comps.   Casino hotels sometimes provide complimentary (free) accommodations to "high rollers" (big players). Split billing is used to account for the comps. To the A folio is posted all the charges that the hotel/casino will comp. Depending on the size of the guest's credit line, the comp could be for room only, or for room, food, beverage, and telephone. Even the airfare might be reimbursed. Items not covered are posted to the B folio, which the guest pays at departure.

Preferred-guest Programs.   Preferred-guest (or frequent-traveler) programs employ the flexibility of split billing. Two different folios are opened when a guest checks in with frequent-traveler points. The full rate of the room is charged on the A folio. On departure, the guest pays the nonroom charges, which have been posted to the B folio. The A folio is transferred to the city ledger, and either the parent company or the franchisor is billed. According to the frequent-traveler contract, one of these is now the account receivable obligated to pay the room charge.

The actual amount paid to the hotel under the preferred-guest program is always less than the rate quoted to the guest. Most programs pay full rack rate only if the occupancy of the hotel is above a given figure—90% perhaps. Below that figure—and the hotel is usually below that figure—the program reimburses the participating hotel for its operational expenses: linen, labor, and energy. So the reimbursement may be set anywhere from $20 to $50. No provision is made for recovering fixed costs such as taxes, interest, or fair wear and tear.

The burden falls heaviest on resorts. Where else would one expect the frequent traveler to use the points—at the same corporate hotels where the points were originally accumulated? Or at a luxury resort with friends and relatives? The burden of preferred-guest program redemption is especially onerous to resorts if the program reimburses, as some do, on a sliding scale based on the previous month's average daily rate. Resorts discount rooms during the off-season or the shoulder periods. This produces a low ADR. Yet the next month, when the season starts and when the frequent travelers cash in their points, the parent company reimburses on the basis of the previous month's low ADR.

Understanding Debits and Credits

Familiarization with accounting and with its system of debits and credits gives a big assist to those staff members responsible for front-office records. A knowledge of debits and credits is especially helpful in understanding how front-office records (the transient ledger) interface with back-office records (the city ledger). Unfortunately, many guest-service agents lack even a rudimentary knowledge of the subject. Therefore, front-office forms, including folios, are designed as if the user was not literate in accounting. Care in employing the forms properly ensures accuracy even though the user lacks an understanding of debits and credits.

► *The Meaning of Debits and Credits.*   Accounting language speaks of debits and credits. *Debits* (often called *charges*) and *credits* are the terms that accountants use to indicate increases and decreases in the values of accounting records. The records discussed in this chapter are folios. That increase/decrease idea is reinforced on some folios that use + (plus) and − (minus) signs (see Exhibit 10–12). Some persons find it helpful to visualize debits and credits rather than merely speaking about them. If so, think of a T-shaped record with the left side called *debit* and the right side called *credit*. Here's one for an account receivable named Justin Case:

Justin Case: Account Receivable

Debit $s	Credit $s

The format of Exhibit 10–4 reflects that very design. The T shape is formed by a horizontal line of 1 inch or so under both "Charges" (read debits) and "Credits." A vertical line between the two columns completes the T. The first figure, $9.00, is placed in the debit (Charges) column, the left side of the column pair. That increases the amount that the account receivable owes. Ten lines down, $241.58 appears in the right (or Credits) column, and it reflects a reduction of the guest's debt to the hotel. The two postings can be summed up in two rules:

Increases in accounts receivable (folios) are made with debits (the $9.00).

Decreases in accounts receivable (folios) are made with credits (the $241.58).

The two rules are part of a broader application because accounts receivable fall into the broader category known as *assets*.

Assets.   An asset is something a business owns. Hotels own many, many assets. Buildings, land, furniture, kitchen equipment, autos, and so on are the start of a long list. Only two of the numerous assets that make up a hotel are important to understanding the discussion that follows. Accounts receivable, which are debts that customers owe the hotel, is one of the two assets important to this and the four chapters that follow. Cash (money in the bank or at the front desk, or in the bar till) is also owned by the hotel. Cash is the second asset important to the balance of the text. Cash grows less important as more and more guests use credit cards, that is, accounts receivable, to pay for purchases.

We have already outlined the rules that apply to accounts receivable. Those rules actually apply to the entire asset class, of which cash and accounts receivable are but two. Looking back two paragraphs supplies the rules for all assets:

Increases in assets, including accounts receivable and cash, are made with debits.

Decreases in assets, including accounts receivable and cash, are made with credits.

If a guest gives the hotel cash (money), the hotel's assets increase and that requires a cash debit. Conversely, if the hotel gives a guest money (cash), the hotel's assets decrease and that requires a credit. Similarly, a guest who buys services (room, food, beverage, etc.) by charging the folio owes the hotel more. That account receivable is increased with a debit, the $9 on line 1 of Exhibit 10–4. Conversely, if the

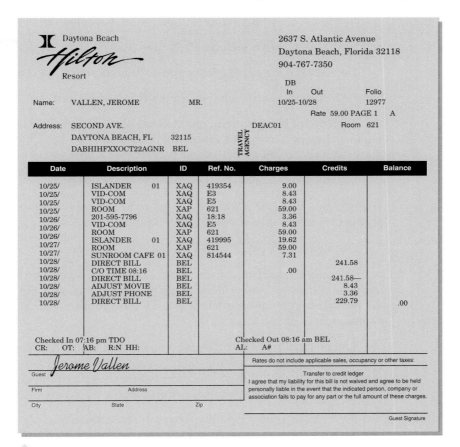

Exhibit 10–4 Debits (charges) and credits (payments) can be visualized within a "T": debits on the left column, credits on the right. Mentally draw the line between the columns and then draw a horizontal arm across the two columns. Note the similarity of format and content to Exhibit 10–1. The final entry involves a direct, city-ledger billing to the sponsoring organization. *Courtesy of Daytona Beach Hotel Resort, Daytona Beach, Florida.*

guests pays off the debt, the account receivable is reduced, as it is with the $241.58 of Exhibit 10–4. Reviewing:

Increases in assets, including accounts receivable and cash, are made with debits.

Decreases in assets, including accounts receivable and cash, are made with credits.

Sales or Incomes. Hotels are in business to sell services. It's those sales that produce incomes and eventually profits for the business. The sale of rooms is the hotel's major product. Depending on the size, class, and type of property, income is also earned from the sale of food, beverage, telephone, laundry, spas, golf, and others.

As we have just seen, guests can pay by charging services to an account receivable. Of course, they can also pay with cash. They're both the same service, but paid for differently. The record of service is different from the record of payment, so the debit/credit rules are different. Just as all the assets follow one asset rule, so all the incomes follow one income rule. Increases/decreases in incomes (or sales) are opposite from increases/decreases in assets:

Increases in incomes (sales of room, food, beverage, etc.) are made with credits,

but Increases in assets, including accounts receivable and cash, are made with debits.

Decreases in incomes (sales of room, food, beverage, etc.) are made with debits,

but Decreases in assets, including accounts receivable and cash, are made with credits.

Sometimes, but not often, incomes are decreased. Go back mentally to Chapter 7. Assume that as a result of a serious mistake on the hotel's part, the guest's room charge is waived. The room income was recorded yesterday with a credit:

Increases in incomes (sales of *room,* food, beverage, etc.) are made with credits.

Today, when the error is uncovered, the room charge is to be removed. Removing (reducing or decreasing) a room sale (any sale) requires a debit:

Decreases in incomes (sales of *room,* food, beverage, etc.) are made with debits.

By using a room sales debit today, the guest-service agent balances the room sale credit of yesterday. The original credit is washed out with the subsequent debit, and the net result is no change to the guest's folio. Both postings, which reflect the two events, remain on the folio.

Equality of Debits and Credits.   Each accounting event has two parts. For example, two things happen when a guest pays a bar bill with cash: (1) the hotel has more cash (money) in the till than was there before the sale of the drinks; and (2) bar sales, some prefer the term *bar income,* has also increased. Apply the rules:

Increases in assets, including accounts receivable and *cash,* are made with debits.

Increases in incomes (sales of room, food, *beverage,* etc.) are made with credits.

Thus, an accounting entry with two parts has been created. Every accounting event is recorded under this dual-entry system. Dual-entry accounting always requires equal dollar amounts of debits and credits.

If the same guest elected to charge the bar bill to the folio, the asset increase is with accounts receivable, not with cash. Accounts receivable would have the debit rather than cash. It is still the same bar sale, so the credit remains the same.

Increases in assets, including *accounts receivable* and cash, are made with debits.

Increases in incomes (sales of room, food, *beverage,* etc.) are made with credits.

This sale to a registered guest requires posting to the account receivable, the front-office folio. The previous illustration, the sale for cash, would *not* pass through the front-office folio! The front-office folio is an account receivable (the guest owes the hotel). Sales paid in cash create no debt; no folio posting.

There *is* a cash transaction that does involve the folio: a departing guest who elects to settle the account with cash at the time of check out. As a result of earlier postings to the folio, room sales each night, and the bar charge just discussed, the guest is an account receivable. We know that accounts receivable are assets (debits) owned by the hotel. The cash taken in from the check-out transaction is also an asset. So the equality of debits and credits is maintained by an increase to one asset, cash, and a decrease to another asset, accounts receivable. Since the guest just paid, there is no longer an account receivable debt. Because the guest paid the account, and the debt is no longer due, the account is closed, balanced off—zeroed out—with a credit.

Increases in assets, including accounts receivable and *cash,* are made with debits.

Decreases in assets, including *accounts receivable* and cash, are made with credits.

The next several pages illustrate folio applications of the several rules. A variety of folios from various hotels with different folio formats is used. In every case, the same rules apply:

1. Every accounting event requires equal dollar amounts of debits and credits.
2. Increases in assets, including accounts receivable and cash, are made with debits. Decreases in assets, including accounts receivable and cash, are made with credits.
3. Increases in incomes (sales of room, food, beverage, etc.) are made with credits. Decreases in incomes (sales of room, food, beverage, etc.) are made with debits.

➤ POSTING TO ACCOUNTS RECEIVABLE

Because hotels identify arrivals through the reservation and registration procedures, they extend credit to their guests. Except in unusual circumstances, explained in Chapter 8, guests are permitted to charge their room folios with the goods and services they purchase throughout the property. The discussion continues about registered guests (accounts receivable) who buy with the credit that hotels extend.

Front-office folios are the records of those accounts receivable. As we have stressed continuously, folios do not reflect sales made for cash or sales made with credit cards in any of the hotel's restaurants, lounges, or other outlets. Cash and credit cards do have a role at the front desk. They are used at check-out time to settle the account receivable (folio) that arises from charge sales made in the outlets.

Room charges and charges for in-room telephone calls always sell on credit. There is no practical way for the hotel to collect cash for these sales. Telephone charges are posted automatically by a tie-in with the telephone company. Room charges are posted nightly by the night auditor. The guest awakens to find the folio balance larger by the value of the night's stay plus taxes.

Overview of the Billing Procedure

Electronic folios gained popularity from the mid-1980s on. Pencil-and-paper folios (see Exhibit 10–2) were the norm during the previous half-century. Progress during that period focused on the development of better carbon paper and then on duplicating paper without messy carbon. Stationery companies were able to package forms with carbon and carbonless paper. These packages reduced the duplication required to write and rewrite the information over and over again. The computer does much the same. It retains the information in memory and prints it again and again as needed.

➤ ***Preparation of the Folio.*** The folio is created when the guest arrives and registers. Computers format the folio from the registration data entered by the desk clerk as the arrival procedure unfolds. Some systems preprint the folio the night before arrival from reservation information. Pencil-and-paper systems required an additional step to copy registration information onto the folio.

Many bits of information appear on the folio. The bottom of Exhibit 10–4 indicates the time of the guest's arrival, and eventually the time of departure is printed. Usually, that information appears at the top of the folio, as it does in Exhibit 10–5, where the arrival time is 12:29. Also shown there is the group's identity, *American* (top left), and its code number, *6566* (top right). Exhibit 10–5 includes other typical data.

Radisson Hotel Ottawa Centre

100 Kent Street, Ottawa, Ontario, Canada K1P 5R7 Telephone (613) 238-1122

LA RONDE FINE CUISINE   **CAFE TOULOUSE**   **Lautrec's**

ROOM / CHAMBRE	NAME / NOM	RATE / TAUX	DEPARTURE / DEPART	TIME / HEURE	
2228	STEIN, FRANK N.	75.00	14/10/		ACCT# 20539

ROOM / CHAMBRE	FIRM OR GROUP / COMPAGNIE OU GROUP	PLAN	ARRIVAL / ARRIVEE		
1K1A	AMERICAN		09/10/	12:29	

					GROUP 6566
54	P.O. BOX 1211 DB				
	LANSING MI 90125-0012				

CLERK COMMIS	ADDRESS / ADRESSE		METHOD OF PAYMENT MODE DE PAIEMENT		

DATE	REFERENCE/RÉFÉRENCE		CHARGES	CREDITS / CRÉDITS	BALANCE DUE / SOLDE DÛ
09/10	ROOM	2228, 1	75.00		
09/10	ROOM TAX	2228, 1	3.75		
10/10	TOUL POS	000000	17.12		
10/10	LNG DIST	315-386-	.57		
10/10	ROOM	2228, 1	75.00		
10/10	ROOM TAX	2228, 1	3.75		
11/10	ROOM	2228, 1	75.00		
11/10	ROOM TAX	2228, 1	3.75		
12/10	LNG DIST	315-386-	1.14		
12/10	LNG DIST	315-386-	1.14		
12/10	ROOM	2228, 1	75.00		
12/10	ROOM TAX	2228, 1	3.75		
13/10	TOUL POS	000000	9.86		
13/10	TOUL POS	000000	16.58		
13/10	ROOM	2228, 1	75.00		
13/10	ROOM TAX	2228, 1	3.75		
					440.16

FIRM / COMPAGNIE   ADDRESS / ADRESSE

CITY VILLE _____ PROV. _____ POSTAL POSTALE _____

ATTENTION _____

GUEST SIGNATURE SIGNATURE DU CLIENT X _____

I AGREE THAT MY LIABILITY FOR THIS BILL IS NOT WAIVED AND AGREE TO BE HELD PERSONALLY LIABLE IN THE EVENT THAT THE INDICATED PERSON, COMPANY OR ASSOCIATION FAILS TO PAY FOR ANY PART OR THE FULL AMOUNT OF THESE CHARGES.

IL EST CONVENU QUE MA RESPONSABILITÉ DE CETTE FACTURE N'EST PAS ABROGÉE ET JE CONSENTS A L'ASSUMER DANS L'ÉVENTUALITE OU LA PERSONNE INDIQUÉE, SOCIÉTÉ OU ASSOCIATION REFUSE DE PAYER LE MONTANT EN TOTALITÉ OU EN PARTIE.

Courtesy: Radisson Hotel Ottawa Centre, Ottawa, Canada.

Exhibit 10–5   Computer-prepared folio showing group affiliation, *American;* group identification, *#6566;* the clerk's identification, *#54;* the account number, *#20539;* and the guest agreement for ultimate liability of the bill. *Courtesy of the Radisson Hotel Ottawa Centre, Ottawa, Ontario, Canada.*

Illustrated are room assigned (2228), rate charged ($75), clerk's identity by name or number (54), and dates of arrival and anticipated departure (9/10 and 14/10).[2] Included, of course, is the guest's name, Frank N. Stein, and address. The number of persons in the party is usually shown, but not in Exhibit 10–5 (see Exhibit 10–9).

Folios are numbered sequentially as a means of identification and accounting control. The folio account number of Exhibit 10–5 is 20539. Folio numbers are especially important for internal control when the hotel uses pencil-and-paper folios, and almost always appear in the upper right corner, Exhibit 10–2.

As society grows more litigious, information of all kinds is being added to the folio to protect the hotel from unwarranted lawsuits. Notice of the availability of a safe for the protection of the guest's valuables is one such disclaimer. This fits better on the registration card (Chapter 8), which the guest sees on arrival, rather than on the folio, which the guest normally sees at departure.

Nearly every folio now carries at the bottom of the page a statement about liability for the bill (see Exhibit 10–1 and others). With so many persons (employers, associations, credit-card companies) other than the guests accepting the charges, hotel lawyers want to make certain that eventually someone pays. The odd part about the statement is how rarely the guest is asked to sign it.

Filing the Folio.   Electronic folios are maintained in memory. There is nothing to see except on the computer screen unless one wishes a hard (printed) copy. Pencil-and-paper folios are filed in the cashier's work area in a file box or recess in the desk called a cashier's *well,* or cashier's *pit,* or cashier's *bucket* (see Exhibit 10–3). Within the well, folios are separated by heavy cardboard dividers. Guest accounts are kept in room-number sequence because room numbers, even more than guest names, are the major means of guest identification.

Not all hotels have done away with the cashier's bucket. A need still exists for filling paper information by room number even with PMSs. The communication section, which follows, explains this.

Presenting the Bill.   Common law protects the innkeeper from fraud by requiring guests to prove a willingness and an ability to pay. Credit is, therefore, a privilege that management may revoke at any time. Nervous credit managers do just that whenever their suspicions are raised. The folio is printed and presented to the guest with a request for immediate payment. Even the traditional delay until the guest checks out is revoked. Motor hotels may go one step further by collecting in advance either in cash or with a signed credit-card voucher.

Since most guests are not credit risks, bills are normally presented and paid at check-out time. It works that way for the vast majority of guests who stay several nights. Two hard copies of the folio are printed on demand. The guest takes away one copy and one stays with the hotel. Of course, with a PMS, any number of copies could be printed—or none at all. If a hard copy isn't needed, guests can view the folio on a front-office monitor, or more leisurely, on the TV set in the room.

Long-term guests are billed weekly, and they are expected to make prompt payment. Irrespective of the length of stay, bills are also rendered whenever they reach a predetermined dollar amount established by management. The class of hotel, which reflects room rates and menu prices, determines the dollar figure of this ceiling. Using the same ceiling set by the credit-card company for that particular property simplifies the process. Credit-card companies also limit the total amount that the individual guest can accrue. Charges over that figure void the hotel's protection and cause the credit manager to present the bill.

► *Communications.*   A guest can buy and charge services as soon as the folio is open, even before going to the room. Although this was always possible, electronic communications has increased the speed and accuracy of the process. This portion of the chapter explains how it was once done and how it is now done.

Guests buy services from dining rooms, bars, room service, newstands, and so on. Every one of these services is delivered some distance from the front desk where the folio is maintained. Getting the information from the point of the sale to the front desk is critical to the accuracy and completeness of the billing process.

Before the Age of Electronics.   With a pencil-and-paper system, the communication between the department making the sale and the desk recording the sale depended on close cooperation and fast footwork. As an example, follow the sequence of a guest who eats breakfast in the coffee shop and signs the check. By so doing, the guest requests the coffee shop to charge the meal to the folio. The coffee shop cashier verifies the guest's identify by looking at the guest's key or identification card (see Chapter 8). Usually, no verification at all is made.

As a precaution against the loss of the signed restaurant check, a handwritten record, called a *departmental control sheet,* is prepared at the department (the coffee shop) selling the service (see Exhibit 10–6). The signed coffee shop check, now called a *voucher,* is sent by the coffee shop cashier to the front desk. The voucher includes the guest name, room number, signature, and the amount due. The same information is on the control sheet as a backup in case the voucher is lost.

The front-desk cashier/billing clerk hunts through the pit until he or she finds the correct folio (follow the explanation with Exhibits 10–2 and 10–3). Then in the proper vertical column, today's date, horizontally opposite the proper charge, $15 restaurant in this illustration, the dollar amount is posted. The folio is refiled in the well sequentially by room number. The coffee shop charge will be paid as part of the entire folio when the guest checks out.

Sending the voucher to the desk is easier said than done. Hand-carried vouchers are slow because the cashier must await the availability of a runner: busperson, foodserver, bellperson. To minimize the inconvenience—and also because the cashier lacks

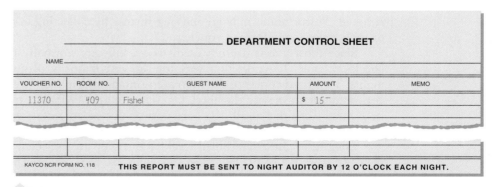

Exhibit 10–6   Portion of a control sheet, where guest vouchers are hand recorded (as a protection against loss) before being dispatched to the front office for posting. Compare this technique to the electronic communication of Exhibit 10–7. *Courtesy of Kayco Systems, Lake Elsinore, California.*

authority over the runners, several vouchers are accumulated before the cashier summons help. That delays the folio posting. Employees sometimes forgetfully pocket the voucher as they go off to do their regular duties. So any of a number of causes result in delays at the front office. Vouchers that appear at the desk after the guest checks out, called *late charges,* are very difficult to collect.

To minimize the number of late charges and lost vouchers, hotels have adopted systems that are more reliable than the runner but less reliable than the PMS. Communication between income-producing departments and the front desk can be expedited by using remote printers, telephones, or pneumatic tubes to carry the vouchers. Each has advantages and disadvantages.

With Electronic Systems. The computer, the hotel's property management system (PMS), has done away with vouchers, control sheets, runners, and late charges. Communication is electronic. The distant department is tied electronically to the front desk by means of the PMS. Cashiers in the dining rooms, lounges, and room service enter the check into an electronic cash register, called a *point-of-sale (POS) terminal* (see Exhibit 10–7). Instantaneously, the information enters computer memory. The guest's folio is always current and late charges are minimized. Moreover, the PMS gives the departmental cashiers additional capability to verify guests' identities and their right to charge.

Property management systems with point-of-sale terminals are expensive installations. Management might make an economic decision to leave certain minor departments, which generate a small amount of revenue, without POS capability. Therefore, some hotels have a mixture of electronic and pencil-and-paper systems.

Exhibit 10–7   Point-of-sale terminals (POS) are located at various revenue centers (restaurants, lounges, gift shops). Each POS interfaces with the hotel's property management system (PMS) electronically posting transactions to guest folios; this is the location for the screen shown in Exhibit 13–3.

Posting Debits (or Charges) to Accounts Receivable

Debits (increases to accounts receivable folios) and credits (decreases to accounts receivable folios) are posted (entered on the folios) to keep guest accounts current. Debits to accounts receivable, often called charges, are the more common folio entries and will be treated first.

▶ *Understanding the Line of Posting.*   Each accounting event requires equal debits and credits, as stressed in an earlier portion of the chapter. That equality is not immediately apparent on guest folios. Each departmental charge appears as a single line rather than the two parts that one would expect from a debit and a credit. Exhibit 10–8 contains a variety of departmental charges, all in the one-line pattern. Among them are room income (line 1), telephone income (line 4), and restaurant income (line 5, the Woodlands).

Although there is but one line, there are two entries. Every line on a folio refers to accounts receivable. The folio is an account receivable! So any posting on the folio impacts on the balance owed by that guest. The single line identifies the cause of that impact: room, food, beverage, and so on. The balancing value in the other account required by the dual-entry system is always accounts receivable.

Examine Exhibit 10–8. Each line there must be read as two parts, one of which is always accounts receivable. The rules are applied as follows:

Increases in assets, including *accounts receivable* and cash, are made with debits.

Increases in incomes (sales of *room, food, telephone,* etc.) are made with credits.

Note that lines 2, 3, 8, and 9 are not incomes. They're sales taxes, and that discussion is several paragraphs ahead. In Exhibit 10–8:

Line 1	Debit accounts receivable, credit room sales for $89.
Line 2	Debit accounts receivable, credit sales taxes payable for $6.19.
Line 3	Debit accounts receivable, credit occupancy taxes payable for $2.67.
Line 4	Debit accounts receivable, credit telephone sales for $0.75.
Line 5	Debit accounts receivable, credit restaurant sales for $24.03.
Line 6	Debit accounts receivable, credit telephone sales for $0.75.
Line 7	Debit accounts receivable, credit room sales for $89.
Line 8	Debit accounts receivable, credit sales taxes payable for $6.19.
Line 9	Debit accounts receivable, credit occupancy taxes payable for $2.67.

Each of the folios illustrated in the chapter carry the same format. There is a single line entry for each activity. The printing on that line identifies the source of the change in the account receivable. The opposite, balancing debit or credit—and it usually is a debit—is to accounts receivable. Every folio entry involves a posting to accounts receivable.

Reference Numbers.   Exhibits 10–4, 10–5, 10–8, and 10–9 display reference numbers on each line of posting. These numbers identify departments in the hotel's chart of accounts. A chart of accounts is a coded numbering system by which the hotel classifies its records. Each department within the hotel is identified by code, but it isn't a secret code. Having codes makes record keeping easier. There is no uniform coding system among hotels, but there is consistency within the individual property and sometimes within the chain.

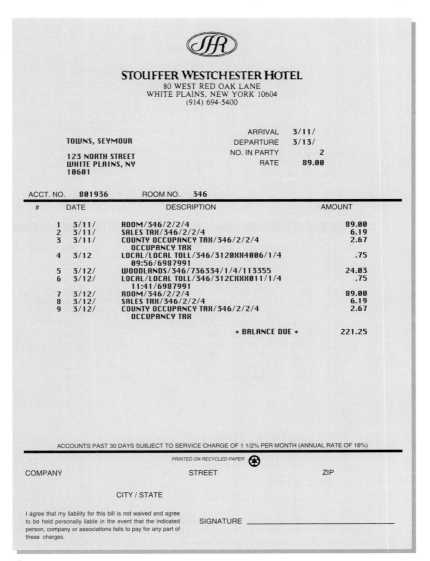

Exhibit 10–8 All electronic folios provide the same general format for posting departmental charges. Note the sale tax posting on lines 2 and 3, 8 and 9. "Stouffer" is no longer a hotel chain; Stouffer properties have been renamed Renaissance. *Courtesy of the Stouffer Westchester Hotel, White Plains, New York.*

Exhibit 10–9, lines 2 to 11, first displays in the description column the number assigned to the account receivable. The account receivable, the folio, is the room number, 2315. Following that comes a second number. It represents the department affected by the posting. Lines 2 to 4 reference the number 5 as the rooms department. Hence, 5–18 is room sales, 5–19 is room tax, and 5–20 is room tax to a second governmental agency. Similarly, lines 6 to 8 reference 59 as beverage sales with 59–96 the

HAWAII PRINCE HOTEL

W A I K I K I

PRINCE HOTELS

Hawaii Prince Hotel, 100 Holomoana Street, Honolulu, Hawaii 96815
Telephone: (808) 956-1111 Facsimile: (808) 946-0811

A-STANDARD

DECAT, M/M BILL
1234 PENNSYLVANIA AVENUE
WASHINGTON, DC
56789-0000

ARRIVAL DATE 6/21
DEPARTURE 6/22
NO. IN PARTY 2
RATE 125.00

ACCOUNT NO. 67877 ROOM NO. 2315

NUMBER	DATE	DESCRIPTION			AMOUNT
1	5/31	ADV DEP VISA MASTER		4000 0000 0000 0000	$130.21CR
		1NT RM/ST TAX		67877	
2	6/21	ROOM	2315	518	$125.00
3	6/21	EXCISE TAX	2315	519	$5.21
4	6/21	ROOM TAX	2315	520	$6.25
5	6/21	LOCAL PHONE	2315	621XXX9005	$.75
		13:57 9564902		67877	
6	6/21	PROMENADE DECK	2315	5996	$23.00
7	6/21	PROMENADE DECK	2315	5996	$3.00
8	6/21	PROMENADE DECK	2315	5996	$.96
9	6/22	PRINCE COURT	2315	1382	$18.00
10	6/22	PRINCE COURT	2315	1382	$2.00
11	6/22	PRINCE COURT	2315	1382	$.75
		* Balance Due *			$54.71

SIGNATURE

I AGREE THAT MY LIABILITY FOR THIS BILL IS NOT WAIVED AND AGREE TO BE HELD PERSONALLY LIABLE IN THE EVENT THAT THE INDICATED PERSON, COMPANY OR ASSOCIATION FAILS TO PAY FOR ANY PART OR THE FULL AMOUNT OF THESE CHARGES.

Exhibit 10–9 The folio illustrates an advanced deposit made by credit card (line 1). Note references to the chart of account numbers: 2315, the guest's room number—debit the account receivable 2315; and the credit references: 518, 5996, 1382, etc. for each charge. This is one of only a few hotels that use dollar signs within the postings because of a large international customer base. *Courtesy of the Hawaii Prince Hotel, Honolulu, Hawaii.*

Promenade outlet. Food is referenced with number 13, lines 9 to 11, and telephone with number 6.

Exhibit 10–8 follows the very same pattern. The debit, accounts receivable, is first identified by its room number, 346. (Traditional accounting always records the debit before the credit.) Then, just as in Exhibit 10–9 come a series of numbers identifying the credit accounts. 2/2/4 are obviously the room and sales tax accounts, corresponding to number 5 of Exhibit 10–9.

The references of Exhibit 10–4 do not follow the same pattern. The ID column is quite likely the person doing the posting. The Ref. No. column may refer to the number on the voucher that gave rise to the charge. That idea is supported by the sequential numbering of the two Islander postings, 419354 on 10/25 and 419995 two days later, on 10/27.

►*Getting the Posting onto the Folio.* Charges are posted throughout the day as the guest uses the hotel's services. Often, the same charges appear again and again as they do for food (see Exhibit 10–9, lines 9 to 11), beverage (lines 6 to 8), or telephone. Depending on the type and class of hotel, additional charges may be generated in the laundry/valet department or in any of a variety of other minor departments. Among the others are garage or parking fees; saunas and health clubs; in-room safes, bars, and films (see Exhibit 10–4, lines 2 and 3); and sports and recreational charges such as green fees, ski-lift tickets, skeet shooting, horseback riding, and more.

In every instance, the charge must be communicated to the desk from the distant department providing the service. Either the desk accesses the information from the computer or receives it in paper-and-pencil form. In the first case, the department uses a POS and the communication is electronic. If there is no POS, the voucher is delivered by hand, telephone, or remote printer, and the guest–service agent enters the charge into the PMS through the front-office terminal.

The Rooms Department. The rooms department is an exception to the procedure. Room charges are posted but once each day by the night auditor during the early hours of the morning. Folios are kept at the desk, so there are no vouchers.

With a pencil-and-paper system, the night auditor removes each folio from the well (see Exhibit 10–3), writes the room charge and tax on each, and totals the account (see Exhibit 10–2). This is a very time-consuming and error-prone procedure.

Property management systems keep the room rates in memory, compute the taxes automatically, post and total electronically, and print on demand. With a PMS, the night auditor initiates a program that posts the room rates and taxes to all the folios, as illustrated in Exhibit 10–9, lines 2 to 4, and in other illustrations throughout the chapter.

Four exceptions, all infrequent ones, require room rates to be posted during the day rather than by the night auditor. Exception one is the day rate: Guests arrive and depart the same day—leaving before the night audit even takes place. Late check outs are another example. The previous night's room charge is posted in the normal manner by the auditor, but the premium for staying beyond the check-out hour is added by the cashier as the guest departs. It's something the auditor has no way of knowing. Situation three is a recent innovation. Guests who check out earlier than the guarantee on their reservations are compelled to pay a penalty, which is posted by the guest–service agent on duty. Again, the auditor has no way of knowing about the early departure.

Paid-in-advance guests, say those without luggage, are the final exception. Often, but not always, room charges are posted at the same time the guests make payment—that's even before they go to the room. With this procedure, guests get receipts at check in and do not return to the desk at check out, having already settled their accounts. At the time of the audit, the night auditor finds that the folios have already been posted.

Regardless of when postings are made, room charges, like food, beverage, and telephone charges, increase the accounts receivable with a debit to the folio. However, every folio posting is not a debit; there are also credits to accounts receivable. Before we discuss accounts receivable credits, let's conclude the debit folio postings with a special case, sales taxes.

Sales Taxes. Taxes levied by local, county, and state governments on room sales are universal to hotel keeping. Governments find taxing visitors easier than taxing residents. Making the hotel collect the tax just adds insult to the injury. With rare exceptions, every room charge is followed by a tax posting. In collecting the tax, the hotel acts for the government. The entry debits accounts receivable—increasing the guest's debt to the hotel—and credits sales taxes (payable).

Taxes payable is a debt that the hotel owes to the government. Until the quarterly payment is made, it is due and payable. In other words, the hotel is an account receivable of the government just as the guest is the hotel's account receivable. Logically enough, one becomes an *account payable* when situated on the other side of the owe–owed relationship. Collecting taxes from guests as an arm of the government makes the hotel liable to (owing) the state and/or local agencies. The amount due is labeled as *taxes payable*. Exhibits 10–4 and 10–5, 10–8 and 10–9 reflect those tax entries. One reads the folio as: debit accounts receivable (the guest owes the hotel) and credit taxes payable (the hotel owes the government what will be collected eventually from the guest).

Posting Credits (or Payments) to Accounts Receivable

As the guest folio is increased by charges, so it is decreased by payments. As each charge results in a debit to the account receivable's folio, so each payment results in a credit to the account receivable's folio. Paying the bill reduces the guest's debt to the hotel.

Decreases in assets, including *accounts receivable* and cash, are made with credits.

As we have noted, charges occur and are posted numerous times throughout the day. Payments, on the other hand, usually wait until the end of the stay. Of course, guests can and do make payments during the stay. With reservations, payments are often made in advance, prepaid. Irrespective of when and how the payment is made, the transient folio (the guest bill, the front-office account) *must* always have a zero balance at check out! That is, total debits posted throughout the stay and total credits, whenever posted, must equal at departure. Departed guests can have no transient folio balance if they are no longer registered. In the first few pages of the chapter we made clear that only registered guests can have accounts in the transient ledger.

▶ ***Three Means of Settling Accounts.*** Hotels have many services to sell and that results in a range of charges being posted to the folio beginning with room, food, and beverage. Credits are easier to track because accounts can be settled in only three ways. Guests have only three credit options, although two or three options can be used simultaneously. That's a good rule to remember: There are only three methods by which the guest can "pay" the hotel.

Guests may pay with cash, although very few do. In accounting terminology, cash means any kind of money: bills and coin, foreign currency, domestic and international traveler's checks, personal checks, and bank or cashier's checks. Paying with cash is discussed thoroughly in Chapter 11.

Credit cards are the preferred method of settling guest accounts. Actually, that is a settlement by transfer, one of several types of transfers. Guests transfer their debt to someone else, usually but not always a credit-card company, which eventually pays the hotel.

Allowances, reductions to the guest's bill, is the third method of settling. One recent study suggests that billing errors that require allowance adjustments might occur as often as one posting in four.

▶ ***Allowances.***   Just as retail stores allow the return of unsatisfactory goods, hotels give credit for poor service, misunderstandings, and mathematical errors. The retailer's exchange of merchandise is the hotel's allowance. Legitimate adjustments to guest complaints are considered so important that lease provisions usually give the hotel authority to grant allowances for unsatisfactory service by concessionaires renting space in the hotel.

Even computerized properties use paper-and-pencil allowance vouchers, also called *rebate slips*. A written record requiring an authorized signature highlights the issue both for the guest and for the company anxious to minimize errors in guest service (see Exhibit 10–10). Improving weaknesses in the operation starts with knowing what the failures are.

An allowance report is prepared daily as part of the night audit. As hotels empower employees (Chapter 7) to make decisions such as granting allowances, reports to management increase in importance as a control technique. Employee empowerment aside, good fiscal management requires a supervisor's signature when the value of the allowance exceeds a given amount. That limit would vary with the class of the property.

Allowances are given to adjust the bill after the fact. Problems brought to management's attention early enough will be corrected. Allowances are warranted only if it is too late to rectify the complaint. A range of circumstances require allowances: a higher room rate is posted than appears on the guest's rooming slip; a charge belongs on someone else's folio; a guest room never receives service from housekeeping; the hotel fails to deliver promised services or a basic commodity such as hot water; or a complimentary (comp) guest.

Comp Allowances.   Only a few executives have "power of the pen"—the authority to compliment rooms or other services. Comps are subject to abuse, and top management should require a daily compilation of comp charges. If, as is done in many instances, the comp guest is not registered, not charged a rate, or counted in either the house count or the room count, there is no accounting record of the stay and,

Exhibit 10–10 Prenumbered allowance vouchers provide pencil-and-paper records of guest complaints and company errors. *Courtesy of Kayco Systems, Lake Elsinore, California.*

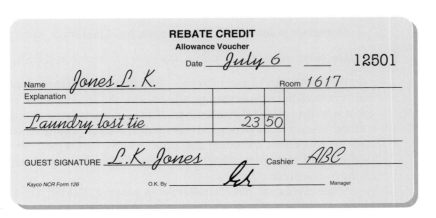

consequently, no control. It is far better to charge the guest in full and grant an allowance at the end of the stay to cover the charge on the room.

Good accounting for comps starts with a daily posting of the full room rate. To allay the guest's concern, the rate that appears on the top of the folio is marked *comp*—for example, 140 COMP. At departure, an allowance—one of the three methods of settling (crediting) accounts receivable—is prepared. The allowance is valued at the same amount that was posted to the folio each day by the night auditor using the following rules:

Increases in assets, including *accounts receivable* and cash, are made with debits.

Increases in incomes (sales of *room,* food, beverage, etc.) are made with credits.

The allowance negates the original room income postings by reversing the night auditor's work:

Decreases in incomes (sales of *room,* food, beverage, etc.) are made with debits.

Decreases in assets, including *accounts receivable* and cash, are made with credits.

Net result, no charge to the guest (although some jurisdictions require the room tax to be paid) and no income to the hotel. Now, however, there is a record of the visit and the comp.

The decrease in room income from the allowance could be charged as a direct offset to room income. Opening a special account in the chart of accounts for complimentary room sales is a better approach. It enables the hotel to separate courtesy comps from room allowances necessitated by hotel operations. Similar results are obtained when a special room allowance account is established for adjustments to frequent-guest programs (FGPs). The chart of accounts for rooms would then have separate allowance records (debits) for: Rooms–allowances, Rooms–comp, and Rooms–FGP.

Allowances for Poor Service.   Who has not witnessed coffee poured into a customer's lap or a pair of hose snagged on a cocktail booth? A suit is lost by a valet; a shirt is scorched by the laundry; the cot for the child is never delivered. Countless irritating events are bound to occur in hotels that serve hundreds or thousands of visitors each day.

If the problem is not caught immediately, there is little management can do but reimburse for the loss. The account receivable is credited (reduced) and the department being charged (food, rooms, laundry) is debited (its income is reduced).

Decreases in incomes (sales of room, *food,* beverage, etc.) are made with debits.

Decrease in assets, including *accounts receivable* and cash, are made with credits.

Allowances to Correct Errors.   Handling small late charges is one of several clerical errors requiring correcting allowances. A late charge is posted to the folio of a guest who has already checked out. If the charge is large enough to pursue by mail, a transfer—soon to be explained—is used. If the late charge is too small to warrant the costs of collection, including guest annoyance, it is wiped off. Accounts receivable is credited and the hotel absorbs the error (debit the department from which the late charge originates).

Some errors are just carelessness in posting. Exhibit 10–11 shows the allowance for 99 cents that was inadvertently posted as part of the room charge by the night au-

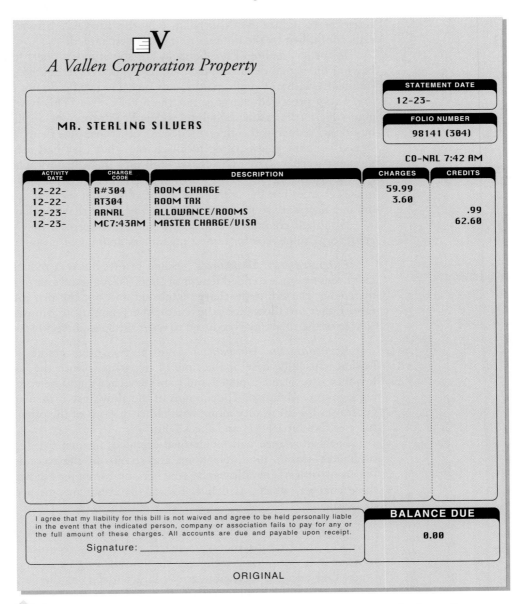

A Vallen Corporation Property

STATEMENT DATE					
12-23-					

MR. STERLING SILVERS

FOLIO NUMBER
98141 (304)

CO-NRL 7:42 AM

ACTIVITY DATE	CHARGE CODE	DESCRIPTION	CHARGES	CREDITS
12-22-	R#304	ROOM CHARGE	59.99	
12-22-	RT304	ROOM TAX	3.60	
12-23-	ARNRL	ALLOWANCE/ROOMS		.99
12-23-	MC7:43AM	MASTER CHARGE/VISA		62.60

I agree that my liability for this bill is not waived and agree to be held personally liable in the event that the indicated person, company or association fails to pay for any or the full amount of these charges. All accounts are due and payable upon receipt.

Signature: _____

BALANCE DUE

0.00

ORIGINAL

Exhibit 10–11   The folio is zeroed out (see lower right corner) using both an allowance and a credit-card transfer, two of the three means of settling an account (see Exhibit 10–13 for an illustration of the third method). Note the sequential folio number on the right top.

ditor. Exhibit 10–4 (third line from the bottom) adjusts for a dual posting of an in-room film (lines 2 and 3).

Many errors originate in misunderstandings or lack of attention. For example, a couple arrives for several days but one spouse leaves early. Although the desk is aware of the situation, the double occupancy rate continues for the entire stay. An allowance is needed to reduce the debit balance by the difference between the single and double rates multiplied by the number of nights overcharged.

In theory, it should not happen, but sometimes a guest folio is carried one night beyond the actual departure day. An allowance corrects the error. This happens most frequently with one-night, paid-in-advance guests who do not bother to check out.

Every protested charge is not the hotel's error. This is why having old vouchers accessible to the cashier is helpful. (New PMS programs display vouchers from previous days, reducing the time needed to otherwise search manually.) When shown a signed voucher, guests often recall charges that they had vehemently protested only moments earlier. Large bar charges fall into this category when viewed with a sober eye the following day. This also happens when two persons share a room and one makes charges but the other pays. Especially when the first guest has already checked out is it necessary to prove to the remaining guest that the charge was made.

Although computers reduce the number of errors, they do not compensate for guest forgetfulness or for honest misunderstandings or mistakes.

Extended-stay Allowances.   Some resorts allow a reduction in daily rate if the guest remains an extended length of time. To make certain of the guest's commitment to remain, the full daily charge is posted and not the pro rata charge of the special rate. Either an allowance is given on the final day to adjust the weekly rate or the charge of the final day is reduced to meet the special weekly total.

Recording the Allowance.   Like the two other credits (cash and transfers), allowances usually arise at the time of departure. Once the issue that triggers the allowance is resolved, a pencil-and-paper voucher might be completed and an authorizing signature obtained. The amount of the allowance is then credited to the folio. The guest uses the allowance along with either or both of the other methods of settling the bill (see Exhibit 10–11) and checks out.

Each allowance will be charged (debited) against the department from which it originates—room, food, telephone, and so on—by the accounting department, not by the front office. The allowance vouchers or computer records serve as the basis for these charges, which, as debits, reduce the credit income accounts of the operating departments.

➤*Transfers.*   Transfers are one of three methods for settling folios. Like allowances and cash payments, transfers are usually recorded as the guest departs. A transfer is an accounting technique that moves a figure from one record (folio) to another. One account receivable grows larger (debit) as the new amount is added. The balance of the other folio gets smaller (credit) as the same amount is removed. Each folio changes by the same value. The rule that was set down earlier still applies:

Every accounting event requires equal dollar amounts of debits and credits.

All or part of a folio balance can be transferred. Transfers can be made between accounts in the same ledger (registered guest to registered guest in the transient ledger) or between accounts in two ledgers (registered guest in the transient ledger to city account in the city ledger). The first transfer type, registered guest to registered guest, is easier to track because both folios are available to the front-office staff. Transfers between transient folios and city accounts, usually credit-card companies, appear incomplete to the front-office staff because the city ledger is not at the front desk for viewing. It is maintained by the accounting office.

Both transfer types involve the same accounting entry. The result is a debit to one account receivable (an individual or company) and a credit to a second account receivable (an individual or company).

Increases in assets, including *accounts receivable* and cash, are made with debits.

Decreases in assets, including *accounts receivable* and cash, are made with credits.

Transfer of Transient Ledger to Transient Ledger.   The two pages of Exhibit 10–2 illustrate transfers recorded on pencil-and-paper folios. Note that both parties have folios, and both stay one night, December 23 (the first vertical column). Both folios have room and tax charges of $84.24 ($78 + $6.24). When the new day, December 24, starts, both have beginning balances, BROUGHT FORWARD. The BROUGHT FORWARD value is larger in Room 409 than in 407 because of the restaurant charge. As the day unfolds, Room 407 gives (transfers) its balance to Room 409. Both check out before the day's end. Room 409 pays the total amount. That total payment of $183.48 is the second of the two transfer types: transfer of transient ledger to city ledger. It is discussed next.

Room 407 clears the bill with a transfer. By so doing, the folio balances out to zero (see Exhibit 10–2). Earlier, we stressed that every check out must have a zero balance: credit payments (the transfer) equaling debit charges, $84.24.

The same transfer sequence can be seen in Exhibit 10–12, line 009, illustrated here on PMS folios. Guest Berger, room 301, settles his account with a credit transfer to guest Meade, room 723. Meade's account increases and Berger's decreases by the same value, $230.80. With the credit transfer, Berger's account is zeroed out as required of all check outs.

Folio Formats.   Folios are formatted differently but are easily understood. The folios of Exhibit 10–12 use + and − signs to indicate debits and credits to accounts receivable. Compare that to Exhibit 10–9, where all figures are debits to accounts receivable unless specially marked with a credit, $130.21CR (line 1). Still another method of distinguishing debits and credits can be seen in Exhibit 10–5 and 10–11. They're the easiest because two separate columns are used.

Transfer of Transient Ledger to City Ledger: Credit Card.   Credit cards are the most common method of settling transient folios. The guest "pays" the transient folio by transferring the balance to a credit-card account in the city ledger. The front-office cashier sees the transient folio brought to zero and leaves collection from the credit-card company to the accounting office, which is covered in Chapter 12.

Three exhibits illustrate the mechanics. Exhibit 10–11 shows a credit card used in conjunction with an allowance. The two credits of $63.59 balance the debit total of $63.59. Note the zero balance on the bottom right. Now the hotel must collect from VISA, the city-ledger account.

Similar transfers are highlighted on Exhibits 10–2 and 10–12. After the transient folio to transient folio transfer, a second transfer is made. On Exhibit 10–2, Art E. Fishal's transient folio balance, $183.48, is transferred to the credit card. Thus, Fishal's account is zeroed. Same with Exhibit 10–12, where Meade shifts the $435.85 balance to American Express.

Transfer of Transient Ledger to City Ledger: Direct.   Exhibit 10–2 shows an old-fashioned pencil-and-paper folio. This illustration is especially helpful in visualizing the several transfer options available. The lower portion, the credit segment, of

Canadian Pacific ◄ Hotels & Resorts

Hotel Macdonald

10065 - 100 Street
Edmonton, Alberta   T5J 0N6
Tel. (403) 424-5181   Fax (403) 424-8017
G.S.T. Registration # 100769686

RECYCLED PAPER   PAPIER RECYCLÉ

ARRIVAL/ARRIVÉE	FOLIO NUMBER/No DOSSIER
WED 12 JUN	**006562**
DEPARTURE/DÉPART	BALANCE/SOLDE
FRI 14 JUN	**.00**

INTR2 KG /B 301   **FOLIO/DOSSIER**

NAME/NOM	NIGHTS/NUITS	STATUS/STATUT	DATE	TIME/HEURE	ID
Mr. Hamilton Berger	2	**Ck Out**	**14 JUN**	**1:34p**	**RU**

ADDRESS/ADRESSE

GUARANTEED BY/GARANTI PAR
AX

REMARKS/REMARQUES
CAN

LINE No. No LIGNE/	DATE	ROOM CHAMBRE	DESCRIPTION DEPARTMENT	REFERENCE RÉFÉRENCE	AMOUNT MONTANT	ID
001	12JUN	01/301	Room Charge	Rm 301	95.00+	DU
002	12JUN	01/301	Room Tax	Rm 301	4.75+	DU
003	12JUN	01/301	GST Room	Rm 301	6.65+	DU
004	13JUN	01/301	Room Charge	Rm 301	95.00+	SS
005	13JUN	01/301	Room Tax	Rm 301	4.75+	SS
006	13JUN	01/301	GST Room	Rm 301	6.65+	SS
007	14JUN	/301	Library Bar	2135	16.97+	
008	14JUN	/301	GST Library	2135	1.03+	
009	14JUN	01/301	Guest Ledger 006573 Meade, Vincent		230.80-	RU

Goods & Services Tax (GST) Summary

A	0.0000	.00	13.30+	13.30+
B	0.0000	.00	1.03+	1.03+
Grnd Tot		**216.47+**	**14.33+**	**230.80+**

Guest's signature
Signature du client   X _____

I agree that my liability for this bill is not waived and I agree to be held personally liable in the event that the indicated person, company or association fails to pay for any part or the full amount of these charges. Over due balance subject to a surcharge at the rate of 1.5% per month after one month. (19.56% per annum).

Je me porte personnellement responsable du règlement total de cette noté au cas ou la compagnie, l'association ou son représentant désigné en refuserait le paiement. Les comptes en souffrance sont sujets à un intérêt de 1.5% par mois après un mois. (19.56% par année).

Exhibit 10–12   Line 9 of both folios illustrates a transfer from room 301 to room 723. With the transfer, room 301 zeros the account and checks out. Room 723 transfers the total balance to an American Express account in the city ledger. Note the plus (debit) and minus (credit) signs in the amount columns. Sales taxes (GSTs) are summarized on each folio. *Courtesy of the Hotel Macdonald, Edmonton, Alberta, Canada.*

Exhibit 10–2's folios displays four possible transfer options that are not immediately visible on any PMS folio.

The folio illustrates settlements by cash (line 7 from the bottom), by allowances (line 6 from the bottom), and by four different transfers (lines 5, 4, 3, and 2 from the bottom). Line 2 from the bottom—transient to transient transfer—has already been illustrated with Benny Fishal's transfer to room 409. Line 3 from the bottom—transfer to credit cards—has already been illustrated with Art E. Fishal's transfer to the credit card of the city ledger. Although not used for the Fishal family, lines 4 and 5 from the bottom of Exhibit 10–2 illustrate two additional transfer possibilities. They are non-

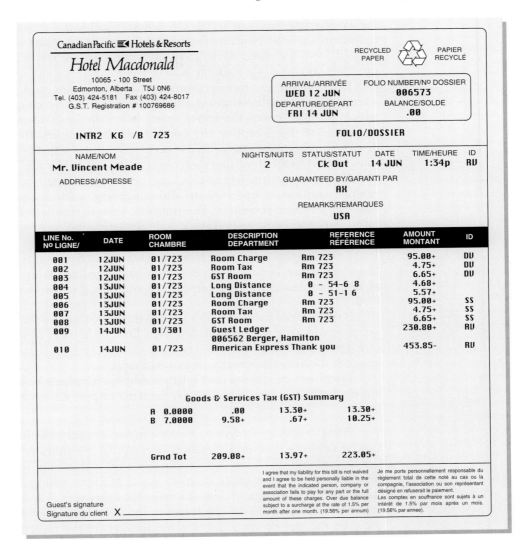

Canadian Pacific ◄ Hotels & Resorts

Hotel Macdonald

10065 - 100 Street
Edmonton, Alberta   T5J 0N6
Tel. (403) 424-5181   Fax (403) 424-8017
G.S.T. Registration # 100769666

RECYCLED PAPER   PAPIER RECYCLÉ

ARRIVAL/ARRIVÉE	FOLIO NUMBER/Nº DOSSIER
WED 12 JUN	**006573**
DEPARTURE/DÉPART	BALANCE/SOLDE
FRI 14 JUN	**.00**

INTR2 KG /B 723   **FOLIO/DOSSIER**

NAME/NOM	NIGHTS/NUITS	STATUS/STATUT	DATE	TIME/HEURE	ID
Mr. Vincent Meade	2	**Ck Out**	**14 JUN**	**1:34p**	**RV**

ADDRESS/ADRESSE

GUARANTEED BY/GARANTI PAR
AX

REMARKS/REMARQUES
USA

LINE No. Nº LIGNE/	DATE	ROOM CHAMBRE	DESCRIPTION DEPARTMENT	REFERENCE RÉFÉRENCE	AMOUNT MONTANT	ID
001	12JUN	01/723	Room Charge	Rm 723	95.00+	DV
002	12JUN	01/723	Room Tax	Rm 723	4.75+	DV
003	12JUN	01/723	GST Room	Rm 723	6.65+	DV
004	13JUN	01/723	Long Distance	0 - 54-6 8	4.68+	
005	13JUN	01/723	Long Distance	0 - 51-1 6	5.57+	
006	13JUN	01/723	Room Charge	Rm 723	95.00+	SS
007	13JUN	01/723	Room Tax	Rm 723	4.75+	SS
008	13JUN	01/723	GST Room	Rm 723	6.65+	SS
009	14JUN	01/301	Guest Ledger 006562 Berger, Hamilton		230.80+	RV
010	14JUN	01/723	American Express Thank you		453.85-	RV

Goods & Services Tax (GST) Summary

A	0.0000	.00	13.30+	13.30+
B	7.0000	9.58+	.67+	10.25+

Grnd Tot   209.08+   13.97+   223.05+

I agree that my liability for this bill is not waived and I agree to be held personally liable in the event that the indicated person, company or association fails to pay for any part or the full amount of these charges. Over due balance subject to a surcharge at the rate of 1.5% per month after one month. (19.56% per annum).

Je me porte personnellement responsable du règlement total de cette note au cas ou la compagnie, l'association ou son représentant désigné en refuserait le paiement. Les comptes en souffrance sont sujets à un intérêt de 1.5% par mois après un mois. (19.56% par année).

Guest's signature
Signature du client   X _____

credit-card transfers to the city ledger (line 5 from the bottom, and transfers back FROM the city ledger, advance deposits (line 4 from the bottom). First, let's discuss the city ledger transfers that are not credit cards.

Direct city-ledger transfers are no different in form or procedure than credit-card transfers. The distinction lies in the debit posting to the city ledger. In the case of credit cards, the city-ledger designation (debit) is VISA, American Express, and so on. Final settlement comes from one of the credit-card companies. Direct city-ledger transfers result in a debit to a personal, city-ledger account—an individual's, an association's, or a company's. Usually, such credit has been preapproved.

Master accounts are the best example of direct city-ledger transfers. The firm, association, or group is billed at the conclusion of the event. Doing so saves the hotel the service costs of using a credit-card company. When the group leaves, the master account—the A folio in the transient ledger—will be credited (see Exhibit 10–4) and the association's account in the city ledger is debited. In Exhibit 10–4, the $229.79 balance is credited (with a transfer credit) in the transient ledger and subsequently debited (with a transfer debit) to the association in the city ledger. Billing and collection then take place through the mail.

Direct city-ledger transfers sometimes involve coupons. A guest who is booked by a travel agent or airline may pay the transient folio with a coupon. This is a receipt by which the third party, the travel agent, acknowledges that it has already been paid by the guest. By accepting the coupon, the hotel agrees to directly bill the travel agency or other third party. This is accomplished by transferring the transient guest's folio (credit) to the third-party's account in the city ledger (debit) and billing by mail.

Despite improved credit-checking procedures, hotels still experience *skippers*, persons who leave (*skip*) the hotel without paying. Some skippers are accidental or the result of misunderstandings. The transient folio is transferred to the city ledger and billed. Since honest guests leave a trail of reservation and registration identification, collection takes place without difficulty.

Real skippers make their living by skipping. Their moves are intentional and deliberately planned even though the states have legislated skipping as a prima facie case of intent to defraud the innkeeper. Because it is a crime, a police report should be filed.

It often takes a day or two to verify the skip. Charges for additional room nights are posted during that period. It makes little difference, actually, since collection is rare. Once discovered, the room is checked out. The folio balance is transferred to city ledger and eventually written off as a bad debt.

Telephone companies may rebate credit for telephone calls made by skippers and not paid. There are never too many, since the skipper has no wish to leave a traceable trail.

Transfer of City Ledger to Guest Ledger: Advanced Deposits.   Transfers of advanced deposits flow in a direction opposite to the other two interledger transfers. Credit-card and direct city-ledger transfers shift the account receivable *from* the transient ledger (the front-office folio) *to* the city ledger. Billing is then made by the accounting office. Advanced deposits move the other way. The balance starts in the city ledger and moves from the city ledger to the folio in the guest ledger. Since the deposit precedes the guest's visit, the transfer appears on the folio's first line (see Exhibits 10–9 and 10–13, lines 1). But how does the deposit get into the city ledger to begin with?

Guaranteed reservation's require a deposit, either a credit-card deposit (see Exhibit 10–9) or a cash deposit (see Exhibit 10–13). The hotel receives the asset, either the account receivable with the credit-card company or the cash by means of a check, and records it:

Increases in assets, including *accounts receivable* and *cash*, are made with debits.

Receipt of the payment cannot be recorded on the guest's front-office folio. There is no folio because the guest has not yet arrived! Only registered guests can have transient folios, so the hotel opens a city-ledger record, Advanced Deposits (for guests who have yet to arrive). Advanced deposits from all guests are accumulated in this one city-ledger account.

Obviously, the hotel has collected payments from guests who owe nothing. Therefore, the hotel is liable for (owes) services to be provided sometime in the future. Just as the hotel has a liability for room taxes it collects from guests and has not yet

Exhibit 10–13 An advanced deposit paid with cash starts the folio with a credit balance. Another cash payment at check out completes the sequence, illustrating one of the three methods of settling a folio. (See Exhibit 10–11 for the other two means of settling an account, allowances and transfers.) *Courtesy of the Sydney Renaissance Hotel, Sydney, New South Wales, Australia.*

30 PITT STREET
SYDNEY NSW 2000 AUSTRALIA
TELEPHONE: (02) 259 7000
FACSIMILE: (02) 252 1999
TELEX: AA127792
A.R.B.N. 003 864 908

SYDNEY

RENAISSANCE
HOTEL

GUEST			
VALLEN, M/M J	ROOM		2003
EASTER PACKAGE	RATE		170.00
2ND AVE BEACHSIDE APPTS	No. PERSONS		2
BURLEIGH HEADS QLD 4220	FOLIO No.		152490
	PAGE		01
	ARRIVAL		04/12/
CH-A BUNNY	DEPARTURE		04/16/
	DEPOSIT		$680.00

DATE	REFERENCE No.		DESCRIPTION	CHARGES / CREDITS
19				
		00754	DEPOSIT	680.00CR
APR12	401	01859 99	LOCAL CALL	.70
APR12	011	02003 00	ROOM CHG	170.00
APR13	131	04071 61	BRASSERIE	22.00
APR13	401	02145 99	LOCAL CALL	.70
APR13	011	02003 00	ROOM CHG	170.00
APR14	181	02003 43	MINI BAR	2.50
APR14	011	02003 00	ROOM CHG	170.00
APR15	401	01736 99	LOCAL CALL	.70
APR15	011	02003 00	ROOM CHG	170.00
APR16	001	00001 23	PAID CASH	26.60CR
			TOTAL-DUE	.00

TRAVEL AGENCY	I AGREE THAT MY LIABILITY FOR THIS BILL
LOVE TRAVEL	IS NOT WAIVED AND AGREE TO BE HELD
JENN	PERSONALLY LIABLE IN THE EVENT THAT
SH8 HIGH ROAD	THE INDICATED PERSON, COMPANY OR
SOUTHPORT QLD 4215	ASSOCIATION FAILS TO PAY FOR ANY
CHARGE TO	PART OR THE FULL AMOUNT OF THESE
	CHARGES.
	SIGNATURE

SYDNEY RENAISSANCE HOTEL - INSPIRED BY THE PAST, DESIGNED FOR THE FUTURE. SM.
FOR RESERVATIONS: AUSTRALIA (008) 222 431, IN SYDNEY (02) 251 8888 ● BANGKOK 02 236 0361
HONG KONG (852) 311 3666 ● JAPAN (0120) 222 332, IN TOKYO (03) 3239 8303 ● KUALA LUMPUR
(03) 241 4081 AND (03) 248 9008 ● SEOUL (02) 555 0501

AUSTRALIA • CANADA • CARRIBEAN • CENTRAL AMERICA • CHINA • EUROPE • HONG KONG • INDIA
INDONESIA • JAPAN • KOREA • MALAYSIA • MEXICO • MIDDLE EAST • PAKISTAN • SRI LANKA
THAILAND • UK • USA   FORM No. FO 001 12/92

Courtesy: Sydney Renaissance Hotel, Sydney, Australia.

paid to government, so it has a liability to provide services for guests who have paid in advance of service delivery:

Increases in liabilities, including taxes payable and *advanced deposits* payable, are made with credits.

Equality of debits and credits is created by the two entries made when the deposit is received:

Increases in assets, including *accounts receivable* and *cash*, are made with debits.

Increases in liabilities, including taxes payable and *advance deposits payable*, are made with credits.

The record of the hotel's city-ledger liability, advance deposits (credit), remains in the city ledger until the guest arrives, days or weeks later. Upon arrival, the balance is transferred *from* the city ledger *to* the guest's newly opened transient ledger folio. As with other transfers between ledgers, the guest–service agents at the front office may see only the transient-ledger half of the entry.

The hotel still owes the guest; the transfer has not changed that. The guest purchases various services during the visit. These purchases are applied against the original deposit until the deposit is used up. By the end of the stay, either the hotel still owes the customer, or the customer owes more than the original deposit. A refund is necessary if the guest still has unused deposit, and that case is treated in Chapter 11. More likely the guest checks out owing additional amounts—deposits usually ask for only one night's room rate. Then the cycle begins again. Payment on check out can be made by an allowance, with a transfer (credit card) or with cash (see Exhibit 10–13).

➤ SUMMARY

Selling services such as room, food, beverage, and telephone is the business of hotel keeping. Most of these transactions are sales to registered guests, called transient accounts receivable. (Accounts receivable buy without paying immediately. By charging, accounts receivable owe the hotel.) Hotels also do charge business with guests who are not registered. They are called city accounts receivable. These individual accounts receivable can be combined into ledgers. When registered, they are combined into the front-office (transient or guest) ledger. Individual city guests are combined into the city ledger.

Accounts receivable in both ledgers are increased by accounting entries called debits and decreased by accounting entries called credits. Explanations of business transactions are simplified when professional terminology is used. Each sale of service produces changes in the amount accounts receivable owe and, simultaneously, in the amount of income generated to the hotel through that sale. Incomes are decreased by debits and increased by credits. That's the opposite of the accounts-receivable rules. As a result, a dual system of equal debits and credits is created. Each sale increases accounts receivable with a debit and increases sales (or income) with a credit.

Individual accounts receivable are maintained on personal records called *folios*. Each registered guest has a folio that reflects the increases (debits) brought about by the guest's purchase of hotel services. This folio must be settled (credited) when the guest checks out.

There are three methods of settling a folio debt: by cash, by a reduction of the amount due (called an allowance), or by transferring (shifting) the bill to some other person or some other company (usually a credit-card company) to pay. However the settlement is made, every front-office folio is brought to a zero balance when the guest departs. Credits balance the debits that have been generated throughout the guest stay.

This chapter has focused on debits and credits developing from accounts-receivable transactions. In the next chapter we look at cash transactions, including their effect on accounts receivable.

➤ *QUESTIONS AND PROBLEMS*

1. Differentiate the following:
   (a) Debit from credit.
   (b) Master account from split account.
   (c) A folio from B folio.
   (d) Transient guest from city guest.
   (e) Charge from payment.

2. Use a word processor to replicate the folio that would be produced when the Arthur Jones family checks out. Mr. and Mrs. Jones and their infant son, George, reside at 21 Craig Drive in Hampshireville, Illinois 65065. Their reservation for three nights at $125 per night plus 5% tax was guaranteed May 17 with a $200 cash (check) deposit for one night, indicating that they will arrive late. They check in at 10 PM on June 3 and take one room (1233).
   (a) Breakfast charge on June 4 is $12.90.
   (b) Mrs. Jones hosts a small luncheon meeting for her company, and a $310 charge for the meeting room and meal is posted to the folio.
   (c) The family decides to leave earlier than planned and notifies the desk of a 7 PM check out.
   (d) A long-distance call of $8 is made.
   (e) The family checks out. They raise the issue of no clean linen—the laundry had a wildcat strike—and argue for an allowance. One is given—$25. The rooms manager then charges 30% of the normal room charge for the late departure.
   (f) Payment is made with an American Express card, no. 33333333333.

3. Create a pencil-and-paper folio; use Exhibit 10–2 as a guide. Post the events of Problem 2 as they would appear on a hand-prepared folio.

4. Under which of the following circumstances would management grant an allowance? How much would be the value of that allowance? What else might be done if an allowance were not granted?
   (a) Guest sets the room alarm clock, but it fails to go off, which causes the guest to miss a meeting that involves thousands of dollars of commission.
   (b) Same circumstance as part (a) but the guest called the telephone operator for a morning call, which wasn't made.
   (c) Guest checks out and discovers the nightly room charge to be $15 more than the rate quoted two weeks earlier by the reservations center.
   (d) Same circumstance as part (c) but the discrepancy is discovered soon after the guest is roomed.

5. How would the following transfers be handled? (Answer either by discussion, by offering the accounting entries, or both.)
   (a) A departing guest discovers that a $60 beverage charge that belongs to another guest, who is still registered, was incorrectly posted yesterday to the departing guest's account.
   (b) Same circumstance as part (a) but the $60 beverage posting was made today.
   (c) Same circumstance as part (a) but the other guest has departed.
   (d) Two days into a guest's four-day stay, the reservation department realizes the guest's advance deposit was never transferred to the front-office account.

(e) Same circumstance as part (d) but the discovery is made by the guest, who writes to complain about the omission one week after check out.

6. Check your understanding of accounting by proving the debits and credits for each of the following situations, which were not discussed in the text.

 (a) The hotel pays the quarterly sales taxes of $8,925.00 due the local government, the city of Popcorn, Indiana.

 (b) The hotel receives a check from Diners Club for payment of credit-card balances due of $1,000.

(c) Same as part (b) but Diners Club withholds 4% for a fee.

(d) The hotel receives a check from its parent company for $1,500, representing the total payment due for several frequent-stay guests who used their points at your hotel. The amount of room charges generated by those guests was $5,500.

➤ *NOTES*

1. Remember the spelling rule for rec*ei*vable: Place *i* before *e*, except after *c*, or when sounded like *a*, as in n*ei*ghbor or w*ei*gh.

2. Exhibit 10–5 is a Canadian folio. Contrary to the U.S. style, the days are written before the month. 9/10 is the 9th of October, not the 10th of September.

CHAPTER 11
Cash Transactions

Outline

Handling Cash Transactions
Cash Paid-outs
Cash Receipts
House Receipts and Expenses

The Cashier's Daily Report
Preparing the Cashier's Report
The Income Audit

Cash and Cash Equivalents
Counterfeit Currency
Check-Cashing Safeguards

➤ *HANDLING CASH TRANSACTIONS*

In today's electronic age, very few hotel room folios are actually paid in cash. Instead, guests opt for credit cards, debit cards, or other forms of electronic payment. After all, cash is bulkier than credit cards, less secure, it provides a less detailed transaction trail than credit-card purchases, and it requires an exchange to local currencies when visiting foreign countries. For corporate guests, an added step is required when using cash. Either the corporate guest must get a cash advance before beginning travel or be out-of-pocket the amount of cash expended until the company makes reimbursement for the travel costs. No wonder so few guests pay cash at the front desk.

In the front office, the term *cash* includes all transactions involving foreign currency, traveler's checks, and personal checks as well as U.S. currency. Because cash is a negotiable commodity, cash transactions are documented separately from credit-card, direct bill, and other noncash activities. Separate documentation gives management added detail with which to follow the cash trail. The amount of money involved, the guest's name, room number, date and time, and clerk identification are all details provided through the property management system. As an added control, hotels also require cashiers to reconcile their cash drawers on a shift-by-shift basis.

The reduced use of cash has not diminished the special care that it requires. Although guests pay with cash less frequently now, hotels must still keep adequate balances on hand because cash transactions do not always involve inflows. Guests expect to cash traveler's checks, even personal checks at times. They may need to change large bills. We should expect that foreign currency conversions at U.S. hotels will increase substantially with the introduction of the euro, the single European currency. Front desks also handle cash advances to guests and provide up-front money for many hotel uses. So cash is not going to disappear into a cashless society.

Even as cash grows less popular as a means of folio settlement, its security grows more problemsome. Cash is very negotiable, easily pocketed, and a continuing target of the bad guys. Counterfeiters, bad check artists, photocopiers and short change manipulators work their wares at hotel desks. They would rather try the hotel desk than busier retail outlets. Guest-service agents handle less money than most other retailers, and are, therefore, less able to search out and identify bogus paper. Moreover, there are internal employee losses as well as external ones. When speaking of money, eternal vigilance is trite but true.

Cash Paid-outs

Cash at the front desk flows two ways. Cashiers receive money, but not frequently, and then it is as a folio settlement from a guest who is checking out. Cashiers in the operating departments also have *cash receipts,* but these are for services provided. Some guests pay cash at the various outlets (restaurant, gift shop, clubhouse). Unlike the cashiers in the operating outlets, front-office cashiers take cash only for settlement of accounts receivable.

Increases in assets, including accounts receivable and *cash,* are made with debits.

Decreases in assets, including *accounts receivable* and cash, are made with credits.

Front-office cashiers have no product to sell. Conversely, outlet cashiers have no record of accounts receivable and are not able to accept payments from departing guests. Each cashier type accepts cash from guests but for different reasons.

Cash paid-outs are a function of the front-office cashier. Except for tips paid to employees, no paid-outs are ever made by cashiers in the operating departments.

Whereas front-office cashier take in and pay out cash, other hotel cashiers make no advances. Paid-outs to guests are, in fact, small loans, and they increase the guest's debt to the hotel. The payment requires a cash outlay, which decreases the cash on hand.

Increases in assets, including *accounts receivable* and cash, are made with debits.

Decreases in assets, including accounts receivable and *cash,* are made with credits.

Tips to employees are the most common paid-out, but there are others as well.

➤*Tips to Employees.* Tips are the most common cash advance. They are paid to an employee upon request of the guest. A signed check from the dining room or bar is the usual method of request. The amount of gratuity is added to the check by the guest when signing for the service. When the signed voucher reaches the clerk, the departmental charges are separated from the tip. The tip is posted under the cash advance category, not the food or beverage category. After all, the tip is not departmental income, so it must not appear under a departmental heading.

Acting on the guest's signature, the front-office cashier pays the tip to the server, who signs for the money on a cash advance voucher. The cash advance voucher is then posted to the guest's folio along with the departmental charge (food, beverage, or whatever). At the end of the shift, this paid-out appears on the cashier's balance report as a reduction to the cashier's drawer.

Since the procedure is not an unusual one, a traffic problem could develop at the front desk if employees from all over the hotel came to collect their tips. To forestall this, tips are paid by the cashiers in the various dining rooms and bars. In a way, the problem handles itself. Most tips are added to national credit cards. Charges to national credit cards do not usually come to the front office. Only charges to the guest's folio, whether there are tips or not, flow through the front-office procedure. Even a credit-card charge (restaurant, bar) made by a registered guest will not pass through the guest's folio, but rather, will be deposited as income directly by the department involved.

Front-office cashiers still process tips to front-of-the-house employees: bell, housekeeping, and delivery persons. Most hotels pay their employees' tips on receipt or at the end of the shift. This is wonderful for the employee, but it can often result in the hotel subsidizing its employee gratuities in three common ways: float (that is, the time value of money), merchant discount fees on credit cards, and potential noncollectible accounts. Granted, it may be a minimal sum of money when considered on a per employee basis, but over time (and in large properties with hundreds or thousands of employees) it can quickly add to a significant amount.

Float. Because of the time value of money, it is expensive to prepay an employee's tip before the guest's bill is paid. Yet this is exactly what happens with many paid-out tips. To illustrate the point, let's follow the payment cycle for a newly arriving guest, Diane Green.

Upon arrival, Green asks the front desk to issue a $10 tip to the bellperson as a paid-out against her folio. Because this is the first day of a lengthy visit, let's assume that Green's folio will not be settled for nine days. In this example, the hotel has ostensibly paid the bellperson with money it will not receive for nine days.

To add insult to injury, Green's bill will probably be settled by a national credit card. Certain types of credit-card companies take weeks before they pay the hotel. It is conceivable therefore that the hotel has paid the bellperson a tip with money it will not receive for some 20 or 30 days! That is a costly employee benefit (see Exhibit 11–1).

*Schedule of Hypothetical Costs Associated
with Paying Employee Tips Upon Receipt*

1. **Assumptions**
   - Hotel staffs 7 bellpersons per day, who average $20 per day in charged tips.
   - Hotel staffs 22 waitpersons and room servers per day, who average $45 per day in charged tips.
   - Hotel staffs 4 bartenders per day, who average $40 per day in charged tips.
   - Some 75% of all charged tips are paid by credit card. The average merchant discount fee for all types of credit cards is 2.25%.
   - The average time for settlement of the bill (including those who pay by credit card, those who pay by direct bill, and those who pay by cash) is 2 weeks past date of check out.
   - Approximately 0.5% of all folios are noncollectible.

2. **Float-Related Costs**
   - Total employee tips paid out per day are $140 for bellpersons, $990 for waitpersons, and $160 for bartenders. That's $1,290 for 365 days equals $470,850 per year.
   - Assuming a 9.0% internal rate of return and an average 2 weeks before collection, the hotel's cost of floating employees' tips equates to $1,629.87 per year.

3. **Merchant Discount Fees**
   - Assuming $470,850 per year in total employee tips and that 75% of all tips are paid to credit cards, the total amount of tips paid by credit cards is $353,137.50.
   - If the average merchant discount fee is 2.25%, the hotel's annual cost of paying employees tips in full (rather than discounting them) is $7,945.59.

4. **Noncollectible Accounts**
   - Assuming $470,850 per year in total employee tips and that 0.5% of all folios are noncollectible, the hotel pays employee tips of $2,354.25 but never receives payment from the guest.

5. **Grand Total Annual Costs**
   - The hotel's cost of floating employees' tips equates to $1,629.87 per year.
   - The hotel's cost of paying the employees' share of the merchant discount fees is $7,945.59.
   - The hotel's costs of paying employee tips on noncollectible accounts is $2,354.25.
   - For this hypothetical scenario, the total cost to the hotel for paying employee tips in full is $11,929.71.

Exhibit 11–1 Employee tips are customarily handled as paid-outs on the same day they are charged to folios or credit cards. This costly practice is, in fact, an employee compensation benefit and should be explained that way and so treated during wage negotiations.

Merchant Discount Fees.   National credit-card companies charge merchants a fee for accepting their credit card. The merchant discount fee may range anywhere from 2 to 5%, depending on the sales volume of the hotel, the credit card in question, and a number of other variables (see Chapter 12). In Green's example, she settled the bill with an American Express card. Let's assume that the hotel pays a 2% fee for the use of American Express.

A 2% fee on all American Express card sales means that the hotel receives $98 from American Express for every $100 charged at the hotel. Therefore, American Express will only reimburse the hotel $9.80 for the bellperson's $10 tip, which the hotel has already paid in full.

Although 20 cents sounds trivial, it adds up over time and volume. After all, that's 20 cents for just one tip to one bellperson; imagine dozens of tips to possibly hundreds of employees per day (see Exhibit 11–1).

Noncollectible Accounts.   The most blatant example of subsidizing employee paid-out tips is when the guest folio becomes uncollectible. Whatever the reason for the uncollectible account, the hotel loses more than the departmental revenues. Whether the uncollectible folio was a direct bill account gone bad, a personal check with insufficient funds, or a fraudulent credit card, the hotel also loses the amount of the paid-out tip.

Some hotels attempt to recover uncollectable tips from their employees. But collecting from the employee months after the service was rendered is quite unlikely. In addition, it negatively affects morale to collect what the employee perceives as a rather trivial sum of money.

Another Look at Employee Tips.   Exhibit 11–1 demonstrates the hidden costs to the hotel of paying employee tips upon receipt. For example, while visiting the hotel, Ms. Green might charge a few meals (and tips) to her folio, she might call the front desk and ask them to pay the bellperson a tip on her behalf, and she might charge cocktails (and tip) in the lounge one evening as well. Although Ms. Green has yet to check out (and when she does her bill might not be settled for many weeks), the employees will all receive their tips on the days she makes the various charges. This is a costly employee benefit for the hotel.

Yet almost all hotels conduct this practice. There really is no other way to handle employee tips without creating additional burdens. Hotels could refuse to allow guests to charge tips against their folio. Although this would save hotels the cost of the merchant discount fee, the practice would create far more ill will than it would save in expenses. Similarly, hotels could wait to pay employee tips until the guests' bills actually cleared. This would save hotels those expenses related to both float and noncollectible accounts. It would, however, create such an accounting and tracking nightmare that it would be hard to justify. Hotels look upon tip expenses as another cost of doing business, a costly one at that.

Exhibit 11–1 assumes that a full-service hotel pays tips to bellpersons, waitpersons, and bartenders. They are but 3 of numerous commonly tipped positions (clubhouse staff, banquet staff, etc.). These and a number of other assumptions are discussed in Exhibit 11–1.

▶ *Cash Loans.*   Loans to hotel guests are generally quite rare, occurring under unusual circumstances and only to those guests well known by the hotel's management. Advancing money to the guest as a paid-out (debit) against the folio runs the same costs and risks discussed above (float, credit-card merchant discount fees, and potential losses from uncollectible accounts). However, just as few hotels charge processing fees to employees who receive tips against credit cards, equally few hotels charge fees to guests desperate for a cash loan (see Exhibit 11–1).

It is now more difficult to cash a check than it was to obtain a cash loan years ago. This is especially true on weekends when banks are closed. Some hoteliers believe that it is better to have a small loan skip than to have a large check bounce, so they grant the former if forced to choose. Companies that use the hotel on a regular basis may establish "loan" arrangements for their staffs by guaranteeing the advances. Preferred-guest programs provide just such check-cashing privileges.

Third-Party Sources of Cash.   A number of new options have surfaced as a result of the hotel industry's unwillingness to act as banker for the millions of domestic and international travelers. Among these options are automatic teller machines (ATMs), credit-card advances, and expedited money order services. Each of these options provides cash to the guest without jeopardizing the hotel or putting it into a business for which it lacks expertise.

Credit-card advances (for example, Comcheck) and money order services (for example, Western Union's FlashCash) transfer the related costs and risks (float, credit-card discount fees, and potential losses from uncollectible accounts) from the hotel to the guest. In essence, guests send themselves money and pay their own costs. For example, by calling Western Union and using a national credit card, guests authorize payment to themselves. The guest gets the money, but Western Union, not the guest, is now the hotel's account receivable.

These financial services don't come free. Fees paid by the guest to the third parties range from 5 to 10%, depending on the amount and the company plan. Guests who would howl at the hotel for charging such usury pay up without a whimper.

Automatic Teller Machines (ATMs).   By far the most common method used by today's guests for generating cash is the automatic teller machine (ATM). The use of ATMs (see Exhibit 11–2) is not limited to the United States: ATMs are rapidly becoming the accepted norm for quick currency worldwide. The two most popular overseas networks, Cirrus (linked to MasterCard) and Plus (linked to VISA), can be accessed by over 90% of the ATM bank cards in circulation in the United States. Another attractive benefit to using worldwide ATMs is that the ATMs' foreign exchange rate is often lower than the rate charged by local banks.

Corporate travelers are depending more and more on automatic teller machines. ATMs are available 24 hours a day, 365 days a year. And with hundreds of thousands of machines available (see Exhibit 11–3[1]), an ATM is usually just a step away. This limits the amount of money corporate travelers need to carry for a long trip. In addition, it minimizes the risk of financial loss if the guest's wallet is stolen or lost.

Although this is the age of credit cards and electronic payments, travelers still need to carry cash for expenses such as taxicabs, tips to skycaps or bellpersons, newspapers, and incidental items. Corporate travelers have historically received cash advances prior to departing on business trips. Yet cash advances are costly, running as much as $20 or more to process each corporate travel advance because of the number of staff involved. The traveler needs to fill out the cash advance request, the manager needs to approve it, an accounts payable clerk processes it, and a financial manager cuts the final check.

In recent years, many firms have begun using ATMs exclusively. The traveler uses the corporate credit card to secure cash for the trip, getting additional cash when necessary along the way. At the end of the trip, whatever cash remains unspent can be

Exhibit 11–2   Advanced ATM machines offer many more features than the standard ATM cash machines including check cashing for personal, corporate and payroll checks with no risk to the hotel or merchant. Risks are minimized by the Mr. Payroll ATM, which uses a security system based on facial recognition. With biometrics technology, the ATM "never forgets a face." *Courtesy of Mr. Payroll Corporation, Fort Worth, Texas.*

Company	Number of Worldwide ATMs	Fee per Transaction
American Express	130,000+	2 to 5% of the transaction amount
Cirrus (MasterCard)	175,000+	Rates set by the issuing bank
Diners Club	195,000+	4% of the transaction amount, or $6
Plus (VISA)	175,000+	Rates set by the issuing bank

Exhibit 11–3   Corporate and leisure travelers have benefited in recent years with the growing number of available ATMs. This is especially true in foreign countries, where travelers gain the convenience of local currency at the touch of a button without the concern of exchanging just the right amount of money. Also, using international ATMs allows the traveler to float the currency exchange for some 20 or 30+ days.

redeposited directly back to the ATM account. Even considering the fees charged by the ATM network this is a considerably cheaper way of handling cash advances.

ATMs in Hotel Lobbies.   Lodging chains are quickly realizing the benefits associated with installing ATMs in hotel lobbies. Such chains as Choice, Crowne Plaza, Doubletree Club, Embassy Suites, Hilton, Holiday Inn, Radisson, Ramada, and Sheraton have ATMs in place in some of their hotel lobbies. Not only do these machines provide for guest convenience, they have become a new revenue center for the hotel as well.

Prior to 1996, there was no incentive for hotels to install ATM machines, because banks did not charge the user a fee per transaction. Instead, all ATM network costs were paid internally by the banks themselves. In April 1996, VISA and MasterCard eased their restrictions on surcharging cash ATM transactions. Following this change in policy, ATM users pay a surcharge of $2 to $5 per transaction (depending on card, location, bank, and amount of transaction).

A number of ATM manufacturers also provide hotel service contracts. In exchange for a place to install the ATM (usually in a secure high-traffic area such as the hotel lobby) and access to thousands of guests, the service provider agrees to purchase, install, and maintain the machine; load it with cash on a regular basis; and split surcharges with the hotel. Pay telephones and cigarette machines are installed under similar contracts.

Not only does the hotel benefit from this new revenue source, but it also reduces or eliminates the need for the front desk to cash personal checks. In addition, with more cash in their hands, guests may spend more in the gift shops, restaurants, bars, and casinos. Also, the newest ATMs are fast becoming important new marketing tools for hotels and local merchants. ATMs promote products through coupons and/or on-screen graphics. Many ATMs allow a hotel to custom-design one or more coupons for the back of the guest receipt. A coupon might be worth a free drink in the bar or a free appetizer in the restaurant. In addition to this approach, ATMs can flash messages and promotional screens to the guest while waiting for the transaction to process.

➤ **Paid-outs to Concessionaires.**   Full-service hotels often arrange for local merchants to provide guest services the hotel is unable to offer. These merchants may actually have an outlet inside the hotel (for example, a beauty salon, florist, or gift shop), or they may contract services off-premise (for example, a travel agent, valet cleaning, or a printing shop). These private vendors are commonly referred to as *concessionaires;* their shops are known as *concessions.*

The concessionaire–guest relationship often mandates that the hotel act as middleman. In circumstances where the hotel relays the goods on behalf of the guest (laundry is usually delivered to the guest's room by the bellstaff, for example) or where the concessionaire looks to the hotel for collection (say, when a guest charges her hairstyling to the room folio), the hotel is acting as an intermediary. As such, the hotel is sometimes entitled to a fee or commission for its part in the process. It is not uncommon for hotels to earn 10 to 20% of the laundry and dry cleaning revenue (the other 80 to 90% accrues to the vendor) as their share of providing laundry bags, bellstaff pickups and deliveries, storage, and collections.

The hotel also finds itself stuck in the middle when dealing with problems or complaints. When a piece of clothing has been lost or destroyed, the guest is not interested in learning that the laundry service is a private concession. Quality guest service dictates that the hotel solve the problem on behalf of the guest!

Accounting for Paid-outs to Concessionaires.   The hotel also acts as intermediary in terms of disbursing revenues to the concessionaire. Payment is made to the merchant when the service is completed and charged to the guest's folio as a paid-out. Specifically, the clerk debits accounts receivable (a paid-out on the guest's folio) and credits cash. The clerk then removes the cash from the drawer in the amount of the paid-out (remember, the paid-out charged the guest may be different from the amount of cash handed over to the concessionaire, because the hotel may keep a portion of the proceeds as its share of the transaction). The concessionaire then signs the paid-out voucher and the money is handed over.

At the end of the shift, the cashier's balance report reflects the reduction of cash in the money drawer. In essence, the hotel has loaned the money on behalf of the guest and awaits repayment when the guest checks out. Of course, all of the costs associated with float, credit-card discount fees, and uncollectable accounts are issues for negotiation between the hotel and the concessionaire.

Paying the concessionaire in cash each time the service is used is expensive and time consuming, for the merchant as well as for the hotel, since the concessionaire must wait for the cash and sign the paperwork. In many cases, a different plan is arranged. The hotel bills the guest just as if the concessionaire were a department of the hotel, collects on check out, and reimburses the merchant periodically. In such cases, the guest's folio looks a bit different. Rather than reflecting a paid-out posting, the charge instead is posted to an actual department (say, laundry or valet). The net effect—the guest owes the hotel—remains unchanged.

➤*Refunds at Check Out.*   On occasion the hotel owes the guest a refund at the conclusion of the stay. This happens in one of several ways. Either there was a substantial deposit with the reservation, or a large payment on account was made on (or after) arrival. If the guest shortens the stay, or the hotel adjusts the rate downward, there could be a credit balance at the time of departure. Paid-in-advance guests who leave additional deposits to cover other charges to their rooms (such as for telephone calls) may also show a credit balance.

At check out, the hotel pays the guest. Zeroing the credit balance of the account requires a debit or charge entry. A paid-out voucher is prepared for the guest's signature in the amount the hotel owes. At the end of the shift, the computerized cashier's balance report subtracts the amount of the paid-out from the total cash remaining in the money drawer.

Cash is never refunded if the original payment was not made in cash! If the guest's personal credit card were the source, for example, the hotel would issue a rebate against the credit card. Similarly, large cash deposits made by the guest may not be refundable on check out. Before receiving the large cash deposit, the clerk should explain hotel policy regarding paid-outs. Some hotels restrict the size of the paid-out to, say, $100. Anything above that amount requires a check to be processed by the hotel accounting department and mailed to the guest's home. This prevents guests from depositing illegitimate traveler's checks, personal checks (discussed later in this chapter), or counterfeit money and then attempting to collect legitimate cash against that amount the following day.

Cash Receipts

We have already emphasized that cash paid-outs are limited to front-office cashiers. Cash paid-outs are advances to accounts receivable. Eventually, those advances are repaid by the guest, the account receivable, right back at the front desk. That normally takes place when the balance of the folio is settled, typically at check out. Guests settle their folios, as Chapter 10 stressed, in one of 3 methods: with cash, with credit card, or with an allowance. Cash paid by the guest and received by the hotel is the thrust of this chapter.

Increases in assets, including accounts receivable and *cash*, are made with debits. Decreases in assets, including *accounts receivable* and cash, are made with credits.

➤*Cash Receipts at Check Out.* Only a small percentage of check outs elect to settle with cash. Most guests pay by credit card or request direct billing through the city ledger. Very few use cash, traveler's checks or personal checks.

Posting cash paid to the folio has the opposite effect from posting a cash paid-out to the folio. Whereas the paid-out increases the amount owed by the guest (debit to accounts receivable), cash receipts decreases the amount owed by the guest (credit to accounts receivable). In all cases, the amount collected from the guest is the exact amount required to reduce the folio balance to zero.

It is a quick procedure: The computerized property management system maintains a cumulative balance, which indicates the amount due. Some hotels display the folio on the computer screen for the guest to scan, others deliver preprinted hard copies to all departing guests, and still others encourage self-check out via the television screen (see Chapter 13).

Whatever the method, all cashiers are trained to inquire about very recent charges that may still be unrecorded. Catching unposted telephone or breakfast charges minimizes the number of late charges, with their high rate of uncollection and guest displeasure.

➤*Cash Receipts on Account.* Payments may be requested at any time, not just at departure. Long-term guests are billed weekly, as a means of improving the hotel's cash flow and keeping the guest as current as possible. Guests who exceed certain credit limits or guests who generate too many charges (especially items normally paid for in cash) are billed at the hotel's discretion. Sometimes, guests themselves decide to make payments against their accounts.

At check out, departing guests are given a copy of the zero-balance folio as a receipt for their cash payment. Similarly, guests who make cash payments on account are given a copy of the folio to serve as a receipt of the payment. The only difference is the timing: the folio given in the middle of the stay is probably not a zero-balance folio. In fact, paid-in-advance customers usually maintain a credit balance on their folios throughout some of the visit.

The desk is frequently faced with a guest—especially one who hasn't traveled extensively—who tries to pay on the day before departure. Because of possible late charges, the desk tries to discourage guests from making payment too early. In fact, day-early payments require special attention by the cashier, who must be certain to collect enough to cover the upcoming room-night and room tax that will not be posted until the auditor arrives. So the employee convinces the guest to wait until the next day rather than paying in full the previous day in anticipation of an early departure. Naturally, many guests find it incomprehensible that they are dissuaded from concluding their business until the next morning. This is much less a problem in modern hotels, which provide the guest with a number of rapid automatic or self-checkout options.

➤*Cash Receipts at Check In.* All guests are asked to establish credit at check in. Most simply proffer their credit card and the desk clerk verifies it for a predetermined floor limit. Direct bill guests are not asked about credit at check in because their company has a previously established account on file with the hotel's accounting department. Only cash guests, then, are actually asked to pay their room charges up front. Cash guests include those paying with currency, traveler's checks, and personal checks (if allowed).

Unless an additional deposit is made, no other room charges are allowed against a paid-in-advance guest, who often departs the hotel without stopping at the desk. An additional room charge is made and collected each succeeding day the customer remains. Unless this is received, someone on the desk automatically checks out advance payments by the check-out hour of the following day. Some limited-service properties may actually lock out guests who remain beyond the check-out hour. Less extreme measures, including telephone messages, are usually used to communicate with the paid-in-advance guest.

Automatic check out of a paid-in-advance guest requires coordination and communication. The front desk must be careful not to prematurely show as vacant any room that was paid in advance. Prior to automatically checking the guest out, a bellperson or housekeeper is asked to inspect the room. Only after they communicate that the room is truly empty should the front desk complete the check out.

▶ *Reservation Deposit Receipts.*   Just as cash is seldom used to pay the folio at the front desk, so is cash rarely used when requesting an advance deposit. Most guests simply guarantee the reservation with a credit card. Still, some hotels (particularly resorts where reservation lead time may be several months in advance) request advance deposits in order to hold the reservation. In such cases, the easiest means of collecting the deposit is simply to charge the guest's credit card upon taking the reservation.

Some properties, however, do not choose to collect deposits against guest credit cards. Who can blame them? When there is sufficient lead time, a mailed-in deposit (check or money order) has no merchant discount fee associated with it. For the hotel that collects an entire season's worth of advance deposits, this small distinction may represent thousands of dollars in savings.

Different hotels handle these deposits in different ways, usually as a function of the size and sophistication of their accounting systems. The easiest but least businesslike method assigns the check to the front-office cash drawer. There it stays, unrecorded, until the guest arrives weeks or months later. The check is then applied to a newly opened folio as if the money were just received that day. This procedure simplifies the bookkeeping, especially if there is a cancellation, but it has little additional merit even for a small hotel. Lack of a proper record and the failure to clear the check through the bank indicate poor management of both procedure and funds.

Sometimes the actual folio that is to be assigned the guest on arrival is opened when the deposit check is received. This procedure is extremely cumbersome for manual or semiautomated properties that utilize prenumbered folios. However, in computerized properties, this procedure works quite satisfactorily. That is because one major difference between manual and computerized properties is the timing as to when they assign the guest folio. In a manual property (unless a reservation deposit is received), the folio is not assigned until check in, which may be months later. In a computerized property, a folio identification number is assigned immediately, at the moment of reservation.

Establishing a City-Ledger Account.   The most common method for handling reservation deposits uses the city ledger (see Chapter 12 for a complete discussion of the city ledger). An account is established in the city ledger for advance-deposit receipts. Guest deposits are credited to that account and later transferred to the folio on guest arrival.

With a city-ledger advance-deposit account, the front-office cashier sees only one side of the transfer, the credit made to the account of the arriving guest. The debit portion to the city-ledger advance-deposit account is made by the accounting office, not by the front-office cashier.

As an additional control, the reservation office keeps both the front-office cashier and the city-ledger accountant current with the names and amounts of advance deposits. Each day's anticipated list is compared to the actual arrivals, and oversights are corrected. Deposits applied that day by the front-office cashier become the basis of the city-ledger debit entry made by the accountant. Some unclaimed deposits will be returned because of timely cancellations. Others will be forfeited to pay for the rooms that were saved for the no-shows.

House Receipts and Expenses

Although the front-office cashier is primarily responsible for handling rooms-related revenues and disbursements, other responsibilities are assigned as a function of convenience. Due to the fact that the front desk is centrally located and accessible to all departments of the hotel, the cashier in the small hotel takes on a set of hotel-related cash responsibilities, both house receipts and house expenses.

➤ *Assorted City- and General-ledger Receipts.* Some hotels, especially small properties that lack a full accounting staff, elect to funnel all cash and check receipts through the front office. This adds another person and record to the process, which strengthens the internal control. It also adds another set of responsibilities to the front-office cashier.

Examples of assorted city- and general-ledger receipts that are not affiliated with the rooms division include receipts for meetings or banquet functions, reimbursement or rebates for overpayment to vendors, refunds or credits from taxes, and lease revenues from merchants or concessionaries. In small hotels, the front-office cashier might serve as dining room or lounge cashier. Magazines, newspapers, and candy may be sold across the desk. Coin collections from vending machines or sales of miscellaneous items such as kitchen fat (to tallow-rendering plants) or container deposits may all flow through the front desk. Meal tickets in American-plan resorts are also commonly sold at the front desk to nonguests.

Depending on the accounting system in place, the cashier records a credit to some type of general account and a debit to cash on the front-office documentation. The specific detailing of the general account (each affected account must be updated) later handled by the accounting department on an item-by-item basis.

➤ *Assorted House Paid-outs.* Just as some of the cash receipts collected by the front-office cashier are not actually transient guest receipts (rather they are city- or general-ledger receipts), some of the paid-outs made by the front-office cashier are not actually guest paid-outs (rather they are house paid-outs). The front-office cashier acts, on one hand, as a depository for the accounting department and, on the other hand, as the accounting department's disbursing agent.

Unlike guest paid-outs, which have an impact on the cashier's drawer, house paid-outs do not. As such, house paid-outs are not posted to the property management system—guest paid-outs most certainly are. The reason house paid-outs do n affect the cashier's drawer is because the cashier treats house paid-outs (petty cash disbursements) just like cash.

The person receiving the money (say, the bellperson who just purchased $30 worth of flour for the kitchen) signs a petty cash voucher (see Exhibit 11–4). The voucher is kept in the cashier's drawer and treated as if it were cash. It is cash, because the accounting department's general cashier will buy the petty cash voucher at some later point. The purchase of this voucher by the general cashier reimburses the front-office cashier and leaves the cash drawer intact—as if the petty cash disbursement had never been processed in the first place.

The Imprest Petty Cash Fund.   If the front-office cashiers are reimbursed daily, the petty cash fund is administered by the accounting department's general cashier. If the front-office cashiers are only reimbursed when petty cash vouchers reach a sizable sum or at the end of the month, it is known as an imprest petty cash fund. An imprest fund authorizes the front-office cashier to hold petty cash vouchers in the drawer day after day.

The cashier holds the house petty cash vouchers until some predetermined point is reached. This point is usually a function of both time and amount. A cashier is assigned a limited bank from which to conduct all the day's transactions. If the cashier's ability to make change and serve the guest is compromised by a large petty cash holding, it is time to sell the vouchers to the general cashier. Some hotels have a specific policy when the total petty cash vouchers in a given cashier's drawer reaches, say $25, the amount must be turned over to the general cashier. Petty cash vouchers are also cleared from front-office cashiers at the end of each accounting cycle, usually the last day of the month.

A wide range of small expenditures are processed through the petty cash fund. Salary advances to good employees or termination pay to employees the hotel wants immediately off the premises might be paid by the fund. Some freight bills need immediate cash payment under ICC regulations. Stamp purchases, cash purchases from local farmers or purveyors, and other payments (see Exhibit 11–4) are handled through the front office of a small hotel.

```
                    PETTY CASH

 AMOUNT  16 37                    Date  Dec. 18

 FOR  One Hotel T-shirt —
 Promotional gift to Sunshine Tours Leader


 CHARGE TO  Director of Sales and Marketing

              SIGNED  Mary Noel
 KAYCO FORM NO. 1046
```

Exhibit 11–4   Petty cash vouchers are usually simple, handwritten forms. When available, a store receipt documenting the exact amount of the purchase should also be attached. *Courtesy of Kayco Systems, Lake Elsinore, California.*

➤ THE CASHIER'S DAILY REPORT

Every cashier in the hotel, whether at the front office, the dining room, the bar, room service, or the snack bar, prepares a daily cash report. With the report, the cashier turns in the departmental monies. These funds (plus any that clear through the general cashier) constitute the hotel's daily deposit made to the bank.

The daily deposit is supported by a flow of cash records. The records of the front-office cashiers (see Exhibits 11–5 and 11–6), are first reviewed by the night auditor because they contain accounts receivable information. They are processed again the following day through the income audit. The income audit combines the front-office cash records with the records of the other departmental cashiers. This creates a support document (see Exhibit 11–7) for the bank deposit.

Preparing the Cashier's Report

The front-office cashier's report is much more complicated than standard cashier reports found in other departments. This is due to the two-way flow of front-office cashier's responsibilities. Whereas departmental cashiers only receive payment from guests, front-office cashiers both receive funds and pay them out.

➤ **The Cashier's Bank.**   Each cashier receives and signs for a permanent supply of cash, called the *bank*. The amount varies depending on the position and shift that the cashier has. A busy commercial hotel needs front-office banks of as much as

---

CASHIER: ARDELLE   **REPORT DATE: 03/09/--**   **15:27:30**

CASHIER'S BALANCE REPORT

CODE	ROOM	LAST NAME	FIRST NAME	ACCOUNT	RATE	TIME	AMOUNT
→ 0001	217	JOHNSON	LINDA	CASH	RACK	06:57:23	48.52
0026	1171	VANLAND	TOM	VISA	GRP	07:11:10	179.37
0024	678	HARRISON	GEORGE	DSCV	TOUR	07:12:12	87.50
0025	456	LENNON	JOHN	MC	TOUR	07:16:44	87.50
→ 0011	319	WILSON	BILL	CHCK	DISC	07:17:17	82.50
0011	337	ADAMS	JOHN	CHCK	RACK	07:21:50	67.21
0031	902	GREENBACKS	LOTTA	POUT	RACK	07:24:01	-17.50
0026	842	STUART	LYLE	VISA	GRP	08:10:15	161.40
0024	212	JONES	ROBERT	DSCV	DISC	08:34:20	242.59
0011	711	GREGORY	GARY	CHCK	TOUR	09:10:10	111.77
0011	315	GONNE	CONNIE	CHCK	RACK	09:44:30	96.20
0031	107	MOORE	MANNY	POUT	TOUR	10:10:15	-20.00
0025	371	ORTIZ	RAUL	MC	RACK	10:40:29	68.57
0011	211	JACKSON	ANDY	CHCK	DISC	11:04:41	46.31
0011	551	WASHINGTON	BOB	CHCK	TOUR	11:57:01	1,278.71

Exhibit 11–5   In the "Account" column of this cashier's balance report are shown cash, checks, city ledger (credit cards), and paid-outs. Follow the arrows marking Ardelle's cash guests, Johnson and Wilson, Exhibits 11–6 and 11–7.

```
CASHIER: ARDELLE        REPORT DATE: 03/09/--              15:28:41
                    CASHIER'S BALANCE REPORT BY CODE
```

CODE	ROOM	LAST NAME	FIRST NAME	ACCOUNT	RATE	TIME	AMOUNT
→ 0001	217	JOHNSON	LINDA	CASH	RACK	06:57:23	48.52
TOTAL	CASH		0001				48.52
→ 0011	319	WILSON	BILL	CHCK	DISC	07:17:17	82.50
0011	337	ADAMS	JOHN	CHCK	RACK	07:21:50	67.21
0011	711	GREGORY	GARY	CHCK	TOUR	09:10:10	111.77
0011	315	GONNE	CONNIE	CHCK	RACK	09:44:30	96.20
0011	211	JACKSON	ANDY	CHCK	DISC	11:04:41	46.31
0011	551	WASHINGTON	BOB	CHCK	TOUR	11:57:01	1,278.71
TOTAL	CHECKS		0011				1,682.70 ←
TOTAL	AMERICAN EXPRESS		0021				0.00
TOTAL	CARTE BLANCHE		0022				0.00
TOTAL	DINERS CLUB		0023				0.00
0024	678	HARRISON	GEORGE	DSCV	TOUR	07:12:12	87.50
0024	212	JONES	ROBERT	DSCV	DISC	08:34:20	242.59
TOTAL	DISCOVER		0024				330.09
0025	456	LENNON	JOHN	MC	TOUR	07:16:44	87.50
0025	371	ORTIZ	RAUL	MC	RACK	10:40:29	68.57
TOTAL	MASTERCARD		0025				156.07
0026	1171	VANLAND	TOM	VISA	GRP	07:11:10	179.37
0026	842	STUART	LYLE	VISA	GRP	08:10:15	161.40
TOTAL	VISA		0026				340.77
0031	902	GREENBACKS	LOTTA	POUT	RACK	07:24:01	-17.50
0031	107	MOORE	MANNY	POUT	TOUR	10:10:15	-20.00
TOTAL	PAID-OUTS		0031				-37.50

Exhibit 11–6 Cashier's report by code (the hotel's chart of accounts). This portion of the report shows payment methods against which the cashier reconciles cash, checks, and charges. This report shows payment by room. Departmental cashiers show activity by departmental sales (telephone, restaurant). This exhibit is the second in a continuing series of interrelated Exhibits 11–5 through 11–9, follow the arrows of cashier Ardelle.

REPORT DATE: 3/10/--

CASH RECEIPTS SUMMARY REPORT

DEPARTMENT	CASHIER	CASH SALES	COLLECTION TRANSIENT RECEIVABLES	COLLECTION CITY LEDGER RECEIVABLES	TOTAL CASH RECEIPTS	PAID-OUTS TRANSIENT	PAID-OUTS CITY LEDGER	NET CASH RECEIPTS	ADD:OVERAGES LESS:SHORTAGES	TURN IN FOR DEPOSIT
FRONT OFFICE	ARDELLE		452.51 →	1,278.71 →	1,731.22 →	-37.50	0.00	1,693.72	-.76	1,692.96
FRONT OFFICE	BABETTE		1,171.14	622.50	1,793.64	-49.00	-25.00	1,719.64	1.20	1,720.84
FRONT OFFICE	CHARLES		850.19	1,460.51	2,310.70	-11.50	-5.00	2,294.20	0.00	2,294.20
FRONT OFFICE	DIANE		67.10	0.00	67.10	0.00	0.00	67.10	0.00	67.10
FRONT OFFICE	EDWARD		572.46	604.27	1,176.73	-12.90	0.00	1,163.83	-2.41	1,161.42
FRONT OFFICE	FRANCES		934.72	210.58	1,145.30	-18.65	-14.00	1,112.65	.87	1,113.52
GIFT SHOP	GARY	687.14	0.00	0.00	687.14	0.00	0.00	687.14	0.00	687.14
GIFT SHOP	HARRY	901.73	0.00	0.00	901.73	0.00	0.00	901.73	-1.47	900.26
LOUNGE	ILONA	1,262.85	0.00	0.00	1,262.85	0.00	0.00	1,262.85	1.01	1,263.86
LOUNGE	JEROME	2,411.59	0.00	0.00	2,411.59	0.00	0.00	2,411.59	0.00	2,411.59
RESTAURANT	KATE	816.44	0.00	0.00	816.44	0.00	0.00	816.44	-.25	816.19
RESTAURANT	LOUISE	1,017.55	0.00	0.00	1,017.55	0.00	0.00	1,017.55	-.61	1,016.94
SNACK BAR	MARC	469.68	0.00	0.00	469.68	0.00	0.00	469.68	2.71	472.39
SNACK BAR	NANETTE	371.02	0.00	0.00	371.02	0.00	0.00	371.02	0.00	371.02
DAILY TOTALS		7,938.00	4,048.12	4,176.57	16,162.69	-129.55	-44.00	15,989.14	.29	15,989.43

Exhibit 11–7 This cash receipts summary recaps records of all departmental cashiers and serves as the source document for the income auditors' daily bank deposit. Information shown for Ardelle corresponds with Exhibit 11–6, from which Washington, a city-ledger collection, appears in column 5 above. The total of the other cash collections, Johnson through Jackson, appears as transient collections. Paid-outs (column 7 above) originate in the bottom three lines of Exhibit 11–6.

$10,000, but the night cashier at the same hotel might get along with $250. It is partly a question of safety and partly a question of good financial management. Excessive funds should not be tied up unnecessarily; temporary increases can be made for busy periods.

A careful review of all house banks may release sizable sums for more profitable use. One major accounting firm reported that the total of house banks and cash on hand is about 2% of total sales (about $600 per room). An excessive percentage suggests that cashiers are borrowing from their banks or that daily deposits and reimbursements are not being made, which means that extra funds are required to operate the banks. There are other reasons, of course—infrequent reimbursement of the petty cash fund, for example, which makes the fund unnecessarily large.

Cashiers lock their banks in the safe or hotel vault after each shift. The cashier's bank may not be used for personal loans. To ensure that all funds are properly held in the cashiers' bank, the accounting office sporadically schedules surprise counts. When the cashier comes on duty, he or she will find the safe deposit box inaccessible—access to the safe deposit box requires two keys, one is the cashier's key and the other is the accounting office's master key. To open the box, the cashier needs to summon an auditor, who takes a few minutes with the cashier to count and verify the contents.

Unfortunately, common banks for several employees to share are not unusual. These are seen in every department from the bar to the front office. With shared banks, control is difficult to maintain, and responsibility almost impossible to fix. Custom and convenience seem to be the major reasons for continuing this poor practice, although it obviously requires less hotel funds to stock shared banks.

Everyone handling money should be covered by a bond. Bonds are written to cover either individual positions or as blanket coverage, whichever best meets the hotel's needs.

The bank must contain enough small bills to carry out the cashiering function. There is no value in a bank comprised of $100 bills. Two examples follow: with a $500 bank for the text discussion, and a $1,000 bank for the separate discussion of the exhibits.

▶*Net Receipts.*   Net receipts represent the difference between what the cashier took in (receipts) and what was paid out. Since only front-office cashiers are permitted to make advances, net receipts in the bar and coffee shop are the same as total receipts except when tip advances are made. Net receipts at the front office are computed by subtracting total advances (paid-outs), city and transient, from total receipts, city and transient. House paid-outs and miscellaneous receipts are not included because they're counted as cash (as discussed earlier in the chapter).

For discussion, assume the totals of the front-office cashier's balance report to be:

Receipts	
Transient receivables	$2,376.14
City receivables	422.97
Total receipts	$2,799.11
Paid-outs	
Transient ledger paid-outs	$ 107.52
City ledger paid-outs	27.50
Total paid-outs	$ 135.02

The front-office cashier accesses this information through the cashier's balance report. See Exhibits 11–5 and 11–6 for examples of a cashier's balance report. Note, however, that this current example (total receipts of $2,799.11 and total paid-outs of $135.02) does not correlate to the figures shown in Exhibits 11–5 through 11–9. For an example of a net receipts calculation using the figures found in Exhibits 11–5 and 11–6, see Exhibit 11–8.

Some balance reports provide only summary data such as that described in this section—total transient ledger receipts, total city ledger (and general ledger) receipts, total transient ledger paid-outs, and total city ledger paid-outs. Other balance reports are very complete, telling the cashier exactly how much net receipts to have in the drawer.

Whether the system provides detail for net receipts or not, this figure is a simple number to compute. In this example, net receipts are total receipts ($2,799.11) less total paid-outs ($135.02) equals $2,664.09 in net receipts.

▶*Over or Short.*   No cashier is perfect. The day's close occasionally finds the cash drawer over or short. Sometimes the error is mathematical, and either the cashier finds it without help or it is uncovered later by the auditor.

Cash errors in giving change are usually beyond remedy unless they are in the house's favor. Guests may not acknowledge overpayments, but they will complain

---

Given
1. A starting bank of $1,000
2. The cashier's balance report shows:

Cash receipts (both transient and city ledger)	$1,731.22
Paid-outs (both transient and city ledger	37.50

3. Count in the cash drawer at the close of the watch

Checks	$1,682.70
Currency	821.00
Coin	177.26
House vouchers	12.00
	$2,692.96

Computation
1. Net receipts (gross receipts minus advances)
   NR = $1,731.22 – $37.50 = $1,693.72
2. Overage and shortage (what should be in the drawer minus what is in the drawer)
   O&S = ($1,000 + 1,693.72) – 2,692.96 = $0.76 short
3. Turn-in (checks, vouchers, other nonnegotiable items, and all cash except the bank)
   TI = $1,682.70 + 12.00 = $1,694.70
4. Due bank (amount needed to reconstitute the bank)
   DB = $1,000 – (821.00 + 177.26) = $1.74.
5. Verification (the excess of the turn-in over the amount due)
   DB = $1,694.70 – ($1,693.72 – .76) = $1.74.

Exhibit 11–8   Preparation of the front-office cashier's report requires an understanding of the computations. This exhibit is based on the figures shown in Exhibits 11–5 to 11–7 and 11–9, and not on the text discussion.

DEPARTMENT CASHIER'S REPORT

DAY *TUE*   DATE *3-9*

CASHIER *Ardelle*

DEPT *F.O.*

SHIFT *8:00* A.M. ☑ P.M. ☐ TO *4:00* A.M. ☐ P.M. ☑

		AMOUNT	✓
CURRENCY	$1.00		
"	$5.00		
"	$10.00		
"	$20.00		
"	$50.00		
"	$100.00		
COIN	1¢		
"	5¢		
SILVER	10¢		
"	25¢		
"	50¢		
"	$1.00		
BAR STUBS:			
PAID-OUTS:			
VOUCHERS AND CHECKS:			
New York Exchange-Wilson		82	50
Cleveland Trust-Adams		67	21
Chicago 1st Natl.-Gregory		111	77
Bank America-Gonne		96	20
Natl. Bank of St. Louis-Jackson		46	31
First Interstate-Washington		1278	71
Postage Stamp Voucher		12	—
TRAVELER'S CHECKS			
LESS SHORT		76	
TOTAL AMOUNT ENCLOSED		1694	70
NET RECEIPTS WITH O & S		1692	96
DIFFERENCE		1	74

Exhibit 11–9   Cashier's envelope for preparing the turn-in at the close of the shift. Exhibits 11–5 to 11–8 show the source of the figures that appear on the envelope, but note that the net receipts figure includes the $0.76 shortage. *Courtesy of Kayco Systems, Lake Elsinore, California.*

soon enough if they have been shortchanged. Restitution after the fact is possible if the cash count at the end of the shift proves this to be so.

Overages and shortages become a point of employee–management conflict when cashiers are required to make up all shortages but turn in all overages. Better systems allow overages to offset shortages, asking only that the month's closing record balance. Both procedures encourage the cashier to reconcile at the expense of ethical standards. Shortchanging, poor addition, and altered records accommodate these management requirements. It is a better policy to have the house absorb the shortages and keep the overages. A record of individual performance is then maintained to determine if individual overages and shortages balance over the long run. They should, unless the cashier is inept or dishonest.

Over or *short* is the difference between what the cashier should have in the cash drawer and what is actually there. It is the comparison of a mathematically generated net total against a physical count of the money in the drawer. The cashier *should* have the sum of the bank plus the net receipts. What money is on hand in the drawer is what the cashier *does* have. Over or short is the difference between the *should have* and the *does have*.

In our continuing example, the front-office cashier should have $3,164.09 on hand at the close of the shift. This is calculated by taking net receipts of $2,664.09 (see discussion page 369) plus starting bank ($500) equals $3,164.09.

Should Have on Hand	
Net receipts	$2,664.09
Starting bank	500.00
Total of should have	$3,164.09

Once the cashier knows how much should be in the drawer, it is a simple matter of comparing that total with the actual cash on hand. The cashier's drawer probably contains personal and traveler's checks, currency, coin, and petty cash vouchers. Credit cards are not included in this discussion of the cashier's drawer because they are often electronically deposited to the hotel's bank or handled by the accounting department as a city ledger accounts receivable. A full discussion of credit-card processes is included in Chapter 12

Does Have on Hand	
Checks (personal and traveler's)	$2,704.60
Currency	356.00
Coin	62.13
House petty cash vouchers	42.50
Total cash on hand	$3,165.23

The cashier apparently has more in the drawer than there should be. In such a case, the cashier has an overage. If the amount of cash on hand were actually less than what there should be, the cashier would be short. The amount of the overage or shortage is simple enough to compute—just subtract the amount there should be ($3,164.09) from the amount of cash on hand ($3,165.23). The net total ($1.14) is the amount of overage. A positive net number is always an overage; a negative net number is always a shortage.

▶ ***The Turn-in.*** When the cashier has calculated net receipts, determined the amount there should be, and counted the actual cash in the drawer, it is a simple matter to compute the turn-in. However, in many hotels, the cashier is not responsible for counting the drawer. In such operations, cashiers are not allowed to count the drawer even if they wish to.

Cashiers who total receipts and count drawers know exactly how much they are over or short. Overages can be very appealing to unscrupulous cashiers. If allowed to calculate the amount of overage, some cashiers will pocket the difference. That is troublesome, but it becomes double trouble when the cashier's calculations were in error. If the cashier bases the overage amount on an error and then steals that amount, the mistake (and the theft) is likely to be uncovered by the night auditor. This is a common way in which hotels uncover employee embezzlement.

For this reason, many hotels limit the employee's access and knowledge regarding the correct amount of the day's deposit. Instead, the employee rebuilds the starting bank with currency and coin and then deposits everything else remaining. In such operations, the front-office cashier functions no differently than a departmental cashier.

The Front-office Turn-in. The turn-in of the front-office cashier is more complicated than the turn-in of the departmental cashiers. The front-office bank is used to cash checks, make change, and advance cash as well as to accept receipts. Assume, for example, that nothing took place during the watch except check cashing. At the close of the day, the bank would contain nothing but nonnegotiable checks. It would be impossible to make change the next day with a drawer full of personal checks. So the cashier must drop or turn in all nonnegotiable items, including checks, traveler's checks, foreign funds, large bills, casino chips, cash in poor condition, vouchers for house expenses, and even refund slips for inoperative vending machines.

The objective of the cashier's turn-in is to rebuild the starting bank in the proper amount and variety of denominations to be effective during the next day's shift, and "drop" the rest of the contents of the cash drawer. Sometimes, there are enough small bills and coins in the cashier's drawer to rebuild tomorrow's bank quite easily. At other times, there are too many large denomination bills or nonnegotiable checks and paper to effectively rebuild tomorrow's bank. In such cases, the cashier must turn in all of the large bills and nonnegotiable paper, leaving tomorrow's bank short. That's OK, because the income audit staff will leave currency and coin in requested denominations for the start of tomorrow's shift. By adding these new funds to the short bank, tomorrow's drawer will be both accurate and effective.

Our continuing example helps to illustrate the concept of turn-in or drop. Remember that the cashier has a total of $3,165.23 on hand, comprised of checks ($2,704.60), currency ($356.00), coin ($62.13), and house petty cash vouchers ($42.50). The cashier must turn in all of the nonnegotiable paper, including checks ($2,704.60) and house petty cash vouchers ($42.50), which equals a $2,747.10 total turn-in.

▶ ***Due Bank.*** At this point it is quite obvious that the cashier does not have enough negotiable money to rebuild tomorrow's $500 starting bank. In fact, tomorrow's bank will be short by $81.87. This shortage is commonly referred to as the *due bank*. It is also known as the *due back, difference returnable, U-owe-mes,* or the *exchange*.

The due bank is calculated subtracting the amount of money retained by the cashier, $418.13 (356 in currency plus $62.13 in coin) from the amount needed to open the next day's bank, $500.

Due Bank Computation	
Original bank	$500.00
Cash on hand	418.13
Due bank	$ 81.87

Since the cashier always retains the exact bank, it is apparent that the turn-in includes the overage or allows for the shortage. The hotel, not the cashier, funds the overages and shortages. A due bank formula, which produces the same due bank figure as the simple subtraction computation, mathematically illustrates the hotel's responsibility for the over and short.

Due Bank Formula
Due bank = turn-in − (net receipts ± over
  or short)
Due bank = $2,747.10 − ($2,664.09 + $1.14)
Due bank = $2,747.10 − ($2,665.23)
Due bank = $81.87

To keep their banks functional, cashiers specify the coin and currency denominations of the due bank. There is little utility in a due bank of several large bills. For the very same reason, the turn-in may be increased with large bills to be exchanged for more negotiable currency. More often, the change is obtained from the general cashier before the shift closes, or from another cashier who has coins and small bills to exchange.

Exhibits 11–8 and 11–9 offer a second example complete with cashier's turn-in envelope, but with different values from the text discussion.

The Income Audit

Income auditors and general cashiers are members of the hotel's accounting department. They usually perform the income audit each morning to process the cashier drops made the preceding day. One purpose of the income audit is to verify that each department's (and indeed each shift's) cashiers have accurately dropped (turned in) the amount indicated on the deposit envelopes (see Exhibit 11–9). Although this function is performed in a vault or safe room, there are several general cashiers present and the audit may even be videotaped as an additional safeguard.

The income audit generally has two purposes: to audit the day's incomes from cash and accounts receivable sales, and to prepare the hotel's daily bank deposit. During this function, every deposit envelope from every department cashier is opened, verified, and added to the growing pile of cash, checks, traveler's checks, foreign currency, house vouchers, and so on. Every form of payment except credit cards is counted, totaled, and added to the hotel's daily deposit. Credit cards are the exception because hotels electronically deposit many national cards (for example, VISA and

MasterCard). Other credit cards are billed through the city ledger (for example, American Express) placing them directly in the hands of the accounting staff.

The income audit includes both front-office cashiers (who probably calculate the exact amount of their turn-in and know shift by shift whether they are over or short) and departmental cashiers (who may or may not precalculate their turn-in before preparing the deposit envelope). In the case of departmental cashiers who rebuild their starting bank and blindly drop the rest of their money, the general cashier merely counts and verifies the contents of the drop. Whereas the general cashier attends to the actual count of the cash turned in, the income auditor focuses on the accuracy of the amounts reported by the various departmental cashiers. Together, the general cashier(s) and income auditor(s) make up the day audit team.

➤*Paying Off the Due Bank.*　　Many cashiers turn in more money than necessary. The excess amount of their drop is the due bank. As discussed above, due banks are caused by a variety of factors: there may have been a large house paid-out that used most of the drawer's cash; there may have been too many large denomination bills and too few small ones to effectively rebuild tomorrow's starting bank; or there may have been too many checks cashed to leave sufficient money for tomorrow. Whatever the reason, the income audit staff pays each cashier's due bank from the growing pile of turned-in cash before preparing the hotel's daily deposit.

Most operations use a signature and witness system to facilitate returning the due banks to each cashier. One main cashier (often a front-office cashier) is given a series of due bank envelopes with the name of each cashier to whom the envelope is owed. The departmental cashier then signs for the sealed envelope in the presence of the main cashier and adds the contents of the envelope to the department's starting shift bank. Of course, the sealed envelopes were prepared during the cashier audit and were therefore witnessed by several general cashiers as to the correct amount sealed inside. Although simple, these signature and witness systems are generally quite effective.

➤*Paying Off the House Vouchers.*　　In hotels that utilize an imprest petty cash fund, front-office cashiers are asked to hold their house vouchers until they build to some predetermined amount (say, $25). Front-office cashiers write house vouchers for a soda machine refund ($0.75), a video game refund ($0.50), and a tank of gas for the shuttle van ($19.50). These are kept in the cash drawer until they exceed the predetermined amount ($25). Even at the close of the shift, as the cashier is building tomorrow's starting bank, the vouchers are still kept by the cashier. Tomorrow, however, if the cashier writes a few more house vouchers (say, a gallon of sour cream was purchased from the grocery store for $4.59), the entire sum of all vouchers will be turned in.

In this example, the sum to be turned in is $25.34. The cashier turns in all of the house vouchers, not merely the one or two vouchers that put the total over the predetermined amount. The income audit staff counts the house vouchers as cash and credits the drop envelope with the amount of house vouchers. In some cases, a due bank may be caused by an extremely large house voucher (say, a large C.O.D. shipment arrived).

➤*Tour Package Coupons.*　　Hotels that operate in busy tour and travel markets often incorporate the redemption of package coupons and certificates into their cash drawer procedures. Such coupons or certificates are found primarily in departmental cashier turn-ins, but front-office cashiers may also have an opportunity to redeem them under some circumstances.

Generally, package tours provide the guest with substantially more than just a hotel room. Breakfast each morning of the visit, two free rounds of golf, a discount in the gift shop, several free drinks, and a dinner show are all examples of products that might be included in a packaged tour. In order to identify themselves as members of the tour, guests are presented with a coupon booklet that contains redeemable certificates.

As an example, when a couple arrives at the dining room for breakfast, the wait-staff and cashier may not be aware they are tour customers. In fact, they are treated like any other customer until the end of the meal. Then, instead of paying for the breakfast in cash, credit card, or room charge, the tour couple need only redeem their complimentary breakfast coupons.

It's at this point that many accounting systems break down. Departmental cashiers forget to collect tour coupons with the same determination that they show when collecting cash. After all, the cashier thinks, the meal is complimentary; if the tour guest accidentally forgets the coupon booklet in the room, what's the harm? This overlooks the fact that someone is paying for the guest's complimentary meal (golf, drinks, or whatever). In fact, the redeemed coupon serves as documentation to the travel wholesaler for payment. Redeemed coupons are proof that goods (breakfast in this case) were exchanged and become the basis for the account receivable. That's why redeemed coupons often become part of the departmental cashier's daily turn-in.

▶ *Foreign Currency.*   Foreign currency (see Exhibit 11–10) is not regularly accepted in the United States. Overseas, U.S. currency is widely accepted. Even the Canadian dollar, with its stability and similarity of value, experiences exchange problems as it moves southward from the U.S.–Canadian border. But international tourism is growing at an amazing rate, with more to come in the years ahead. More foreign currencies are being tendered across hotel desks, and more language capability is being encouraged among front-office staffs.

Nevertheless, relatively few American hotels have followed their international counterparts into the foreign-exchange business. This is a service that U.S. hotels would prefer to have done by another agency. Thus the growth in foreign-exchange facilities has been outside the hotel lobby.

Cities with large numbers of foreign tourists, such as New York and Miami, have developed adequate exchange facilities to accommodate the international tourists. These currency-exchange companies, privately owned, have been supported by local tourists bureaus, chambers of commerce, and the U.S. National Tourism Organization, which see the importance of the international tourist to the balance of trade. Exchange agencies allow the hotels to service the currency needs of the international guest with a reasonable ceiling on costs.

Servicing the guest is all that American hotels appear to do. It is a limited service at that—limited to a very few hotels that deal only in a few popular currencies because they have identified a well-defined international market segment for themselves. Overseas, foreign exchange is a profit center for the hotel. There is a profit to be made because both domestic and foreign hotels exchange currency at something less than the official rate. That's a double insult because even the official rate, which is determined by open market bidding, provides a spread between buy price and sell price.

Since it is not desirable to inventory money from all around the world, hotels do not provide for the reconversion of local currency into foreign funds as the visitor prepares to go home. Therefore, the hotel's concern is only with the bid rate. Money bro-

Country	Currency	Country	Currency
North America		**Caribbean, Bahamas, and Bermuda**	
Canada	Dollar	Bahamas	Dollar
Mexico	Peso	Bermuda	Dollar
		British Virgin Islands	Dollar
Central and South America		Curacao	Guilder
Argentina	Peso	Jamaica	Dollar
Bolivia	Boliviano	Martinique	Franc
Brazil	Real	Trinidad	Dollar
Chile	Peso	**Africa**	
Colombia	Peso	Egypt	Pound
Costa Rica	Colon	Ethiopia	Birr
Ecuador	Sucre	Ghana	Cedi
El Salvador	Colon	Libya	Dinar
Guatemala	Quetzal	Morocco	Dirham
Honduras	Lempira	South Africa	Rand
Nicaragua	Cordoba	Sudan	Dinar
Peru	New Sol	Tanzania	Shilling
Uruguay	New Peso	Zambia	Kwacha
Venezuela	Bolivar		
		Mideast, Far East and Pacific	
Europe's EMU		Australia	Dollar
Austria (schilling), Belgium	Euro	Bahrain	Dinar
(franc), Finland (markka),	(phased	China	Renminbi
France (franc), Germany	in 1999–	Hong Kong	Dollar
(mark), Ireland (punt), Italy	2002)	India	Rupee
(lira), Luxembourg (franc),		Indonesia	Rupiah
Netherlands (guilder),		Israel	Shekel
Portugal (escudo), and Spain		Japan	Yen
(peseta)		Jordan	Dinar
		Kuwait	Dinar
		Lebanon	Pound
Other Europe		Malaysia	Ringgit
Czech Republic	Koruna	New Zealand	Dollar
Denmark	Krone	Pakistan	Rupee
Greece	Drachma	Philippines	Peso
Hungary	Forint	Saudi Arabia	Riyal
Malta	Lira	Singapore	Dollar
Norway	Krone	South Korea	Won
Poland	Zloty	Syria	Pound
Slovak Republic	Koruna	Taiwan	Dollar
Sweden	Krona	Thailand	Baht
Switzerland	Franc	Turkey	Lira
United Kingdom	Pound	United Arab Emirates	Dirham

Exhibit 11–10   Shown are most of the world's currencies. Conversion rates for major currencies are quoted in local newspapers and in *The Wall Street Journal*. See the text for additional discussion on the European Economic and Monetary Union's (EMU) euro.

kers quote both a buy (bid) rate and a sell (ask) rate. The desk buys foreign currency from the guest at a rate that is lower than the broker's bid rate, reselling later to the broker at the bid rate. The hotel might buy Canadian dollars, for example, at 8 cents less than it sells them for, although the official spread might be only 4 cents. The extra spread between buy and sell may be further enriched by a supplemental exchange fee. This fee, which currency dealers call *agio,* provides the hotel with additional funds to pay for bank charges or to offset unexpected variations in foreign currency value. The latter makes it especially important to process foreign currency quickly and to include it in the turn-in every day.

Obtaining daily quotes and avoiding banks that are not brokers themselves (that is, middlemen) will maximize foreign exchange profits. In fact, the hotel could become an intermediary broker by also converting funds for taxi drivers, bellpersons, and servers throughout the community in addition to its own personnel. Of course, this opens a whole new business with the large risks that accompany foreign exchange.

If the hotel is dealing in foreign currencies, the accounting office must furnish the cashier with a table of values for each currency traded (see Exhibit 11–10). (Several airlines quote currency rates, including rates on foreign traveler's checks, as part of their reservation system service.) If currency values fluctuate over a wide range, a daily or even hourly quote is necessary to prevent substantial losses. More likely, the hotel will just refuse that particular currency.

Canadian currency poses less of a problem than most other kinds. It is similar in form, divisions, and value to the U.S. dollar. Consequently, hotels close to the border have accepted Canadian dollars at a par with the U.S. dollar. Although this practice involves an exchange cost to the hotel, it has been a good advertising and public relations gimmick that has more than offset the expense.

The EMU Euro.   In an attempt to become more competitive on a global basis and to simplify currency transactions in closely related countries, the European Economic Monetary Union (EMU) created a new form of currency. In 1999, prior to the introduction of the new euro banknotes (see Exhibit 11–11), all EMU member countries were given a choice to join the new monetary system. Several countries opted out of the euro, including Denmark, Sweden, and the United Kingdom. One other country, Greece, did not qualify to join the euro system because of significant government and public debt.

The new euro was introduced in January 1999 and will become the sole currency for 11 countries (see Exhibit 11–10) by January 2002. Many experts predict that the euro will become the dominant force in international tourism, in part because the euro reflects more assets and GNP than does even the U.S. dollar.

The euro will certainly simplify matters for the lodging industry. Currency exchange rates with the euro will be far less volatile and easier to track than were the currencies of 11 separate countries. In addition, currency exchange rates among the 11 EMU countries will be eliminated, saving tourists the cost and inconvenience of exchanging various monies. But best of all, the new euro will make much of Europe seem almost borderless as tourists travel country to country with little more difficulty than Americans travel from state to state.

Example from the Land of Nod.   Let's see what needs to be done when a guest from the Land of Nod tenders a ₦ 1,000 bill in payment of a $34 account. Each ₦ (Nod dollar) is exchanged at 5 cents U.S. money by the hotel, although the official rate may be somewhat higher—say, 5.1 cents. Therefore, the ₦ 1,000 is exchanged at

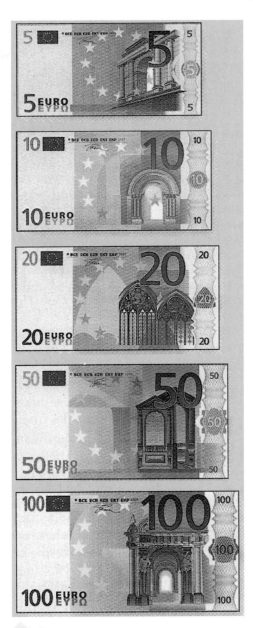

Exhibit 11–11   The obverse of each of the seven euro banknotes (not all are shown here) features architectural styles from the seven ages of Europe's cultural history. The reverse features seven different European bridges. Each bill is a unique color, and the size of the note increases with the denomination.

$50, which is $1 less than the official rate of exchange. The cashier would return $16 U.S. in exchange for the ₦ 1,000 and the charge of $34. (Change is given only in U.S. dollars even if the cashier has Nod dollars.) If, on the other hand, the guest had offered only a ₦ 500 bill, the cashier would have collected an additional U.S. $9 to settle the $34 account in full. What if it were a ₦ 2,500 bill, and the cashier had on hand 1,500 Nod dollars? What would be the change? (Answer: The cashier would give U.S. $91 in change. Remember: Foreign currency is never returned even if it's available in the cash drawer. That would give away the profit earned on the exchange rates.)

Rare indeed is the hotel that will accept a foreign check. However, if payment were made by foreign check, the hotel makes an additional charge, passing on to the guest the bank's fee for foreign exchange. The amount of the fee is a function of both the size of the check and the variation in the rate of exchange.

Foreign traveler's checks (especially Canadian traveler's checks) are more readily accepted than personal checks. Although cashiers are cautioned to use the same level of scrutiny with foreign traveler's checks as they use with U.S. traveler's checks (accepting traveler's checks is discussed in depth towards the end of this chapter), there is an additional catch. Foreign traveler's checks look identical to U.S. traveler's checks, with one simple difference: Instead of stating "Pay to the order of (name) in U.S. dollars," the foreign traveler's check states "Pay . . . in Canadian dollars" (see Exhibit 11–16), or whatever currency. Many a time has a clerk accidentally cashed a foreign traveler's check thinking it was payable in U.S. funds. This can represent a considerable loss to the hotel.

► CASH AND CASH EQUIVALENTS

Even as the ratio of guests' folios paid with cash and cash equivalents (traveler's checks, personal, and corporate checks) is decreasing, the incidence of counterfeiting and forgery is at an all-time high. Due to advances in technology and print quality, computers are responsible, in part, for the rise of cash-related crimes proliferating nationwide. The busy hotel, with its hundreds or thousands of new guests each day, creates the perfect haven for such crimes. That's why it is of paramount importance that managers be trained in the secure handling of cash and checks.

Hotels are likely targets for professional counterfeiters for several reasons. First, agents are often rushed with numerous small transactions, allowing the professional counterfeiter easy access and egress. Second, hotel cashiers are inundated with so many guests that they would probably have a difficult time remembering (much less describing or identifying) the professional counterfeiter.

Finally, as discussed earlier, hotels handle relatively little cash as a percentage of all sales volume. Although that may sound contradictory, counterfeiters often seek establishments that deal in little cash. That's because cashiers who handle lots of cash become very adept at spotting a phony. Conversely, hotel cashiers (who handle relatively little cash) are poorly prepared to spot fake currency.

Counterfeit Currency

According to the U.S. Secret Service, there may be over $1 billion in counterfeit currency in worldwide circulation. In the United States, the number is far less (about $35 million). But as the U.S. dollar has become increasingly accepted worldwide, the incidence of counterfeiting has also been rapidly increasing. You see, just as hotel front-office cashiers (who handle relatively little cash) are likely targets for counterfeiters, so are international cashiers, who probably handle even fewer U.S. dollars. And according to the Secret Service, whereas the most popular counterfeit bill in the United States is the $20 bill, overseas the most popular counterfeit is the $100 bill!

As computer technology has improved, the counterfeiting problem has compounded. Recently, a high school student in New Mexico made $1, $5, $10, and $20 bills by scanning the real currency into her home computer and printing the money out as a school project. She then asked classmates to tell the difference, and several students later spent the currency at local stores. Another case includes a 16-year-old West Virginia boy who scanned his own portrait over Ben Franklin's, and successfully passed the $100 note.

Virtually anyone willing to spend the few hundred dollars necessary to purchase a color printer/scanner can enter the counterfeiting business. In just four short years, computer-generated counterfeit money has risen from 0.5% (half of one percent) to over 44% of all counterfeit money in circulation.

➤ *Detecting Counterfeit Currency.*   Beginning in 1996, the U.S. Treasury began issuing currency with new security features. The $100 bill (see Exhibit 11–12) was the first, with new denominations being introduced at the rate of about one per year. The redesigned notes take advantage of new technologies to make them more secure from counterfeiting as well as easier to recognize when passed (see Exhibit 11–13). Since the first series of notes was introduced in 1861, U.S. currency has continually evolved in an attempt to thwart counterfeit activities. Despite many previous alterations, this most recent design change is probably the most noticeable.

Exhibit 11–12 details the eight new features embedded in bills introduced since 1996. Hold a new $100, $50, or $20 bill to the light and notice some interesting enhancements. For example, a polymer security thread runs top to bottom down the bill, just to the left of the portrait. A watermark, to the right of the portrait, is visible from both the obverse and reverse of the bill. These two features are difficult to replicate on counterfeit bills. The most difficult of all, however, is the color-shifting ink found in the numerical denomination of the bill at the bottom right corner. Looking at it head on, the number appears green. Bringing it up under your eye and turning the bill away from you, you'll notice that the green color shifts to black. None of these three features can be successfully scanned into even the most sophisticated computer systems available today.

Other Cashier Applications.   Hotel cashiers may also be interested in a number of relatively inexpensive counterfeit detection devices that have hit the market in recent years (see Exhibit 11–14). These detection devices utilize two additional technologies in their search for counterfeit currency. One of the most popular devices is a detector shaped like a marker pen made by companies such as Dri-Mark Products of New York. This pen is popular with major retailers (such as Disney) because it is simple to use. In essence, it employs a chemical reaction to indicate whether the currency in question has authentic cotton fibers. All U.S. currency is made from 100% cotton rag—there is no paper content. As such, detector pens that react with starch (found in paper products) turn counterfeit bills brown.

A second detection technology searches the bill for magnetic ink. Magnetic ink has been used by the Federal Reserve since 1932. The ink is found on the portrait and around the edges. Counterfeit currency created on copiers or printing presses lacks the magnetic ink (see Exhibit 11–14).

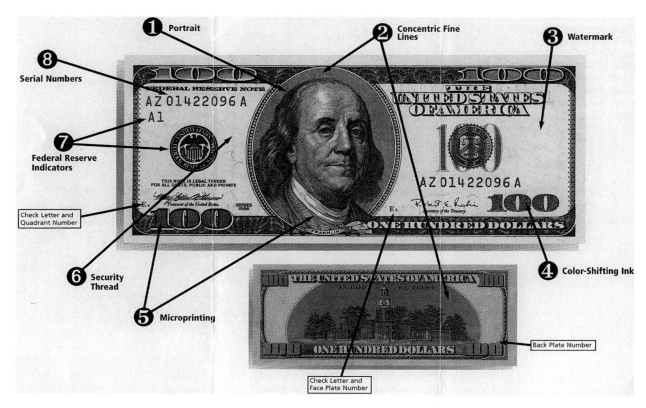

❶ Portrait The enlarged portrait of Benjamin Franklin is easier to recognize, while the added detail is harder to duplicate. The portrait is now off-center, providing room for a watermark and reducing wear and tear on the portrait.

❷ Concentric Fine Lines The fine lines printed behind both Benjamin Franklin's portrait and Independence Hall are difficult to replicate.

❸ Watermark A watermark depicting Benjamin Franklin is visible from both sides when held up to a light.

❹ Color-Shifting Ink The number in the lower right corner on the front of the note looks green when viewed straight on, but appears black when viewed at an angle.

❺ Microprinting Because they're so small, microprinted words are hard to replicate. On the front of the note, "USA 100" is within the num-

ber in the lower left corner and "United States of America" is on Benjamin Franklin's coat.

❻ Security Thread A polymer thread is embedded vertically in the paper and indicates, by its unique position, the note's denomination. The words "USA 100" on the thread can be seen from both sides of the note when held up to a bright light. Additionally, the thread glows red when held under an ultraviolet light.

❼ Federal Reserve Indicators A new universal seal represents the entire Federal Reserve System. A letter and number beneath the left serial number identifies the issuing Federal Reserve Bank.

❽ Serial Numbers An additional letter is added to the serial number. The unique combination of eleven numbers and letters appears twice on the front of the note.

Exhibit 11–12 What's new about U.S. currency since 1996. Similar security features are included on the new $50 and $20 bills.

1. Don't return the bill to the passer. It will just encourage the person to leave the scene.
2. Delay the passer, if possible.
3. Observe the passer and any friends, colleagues, or vehicles (license numbers) to provide authorities with a description.
4. Call the police or the local office of the Secret Service.
5. Write your initials and date on the blank portion of the note, but handle the bill as little as possible (for later fingerprinting).
6. Place the bill in a clean envelope as soon as possible.
7. Surrender the note only to a properly identified police officer or Secret Service agent.

Exhibit 11–13   Seven immediate steps that front-office cashiers should take when counterfeit bills are passed.

Whatever their approach, hotels are urged to use caution when accepting currency. Counterfeit currency can cost a hotel a considerable amount of money in a relatively short amount of time because counterfeiters usually pass a number of bills in quick succession. Counterfeit bills are like ants, you never find just one! And when the hotel finally realizes what has happened and calls the police or the Secret Service, they are in for another shock—the counterfeit bills will be confiscated without restitution.

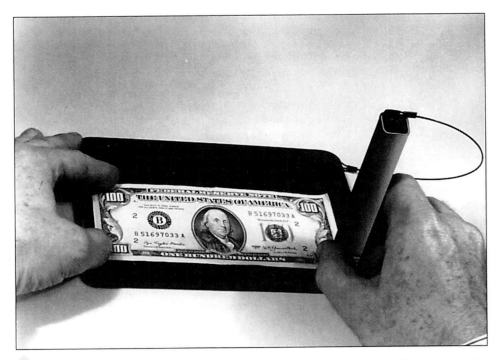

Exhibit 11–14   Detection devices like Vistatector supplement front-office training designed to recognize bogus currency. This system works on the magnetic ink in all U.S. currencies; other systems work on the starch in counterfeit paper. *Courtesy of Vistatech Enterprises, Ltd., New York.*

Check-cashing Safeguards

Even in the smallest hotel, management cannot make every credit decision every hour of the day. Instead, it creates the policies and procedures that will minimize losses and retain customer goodwill. A credit manual or credit handbook is the usual manner of communicating management's position. Each company reflects its own approach in policies, but procedures for handling personal checks (and traveler's checks) are much alike from hotel to hotel and from handbook to handbook.

Hotels train their front-office personnel to be pleasant, courteous, and accommodating. Check scam artists are usually loud, rude, and threatening. By pushing in during rush hours, harassing the clerks who have been taught to "take it," and pressuring for service, passers of bad checks walk away with millions. Losses can be reduced when certain procedures are put in place.

▶ **Procedures for Minimizing Fraud.**   Hotel operations are 100 times more likely to lose money to forged and fraudulent checks than they are to armed robbery! Using proper check-cashing procedures is critical to avoid significant losses from this form of theft.

As with counterfeiting, computer technology has made check-cashing forgery a simple crime for anyone to perpetrate. Basic desktop publishing and scanning equipment is all one needs to ably copy and alter personal checks. And since checks are paid by computer automation as well, the altered check will clear provided the account has sufficient funds.

Unfortunately, hotels that accept forged or worthless checks have little recourse. Banks are not responsible for losses incurred from bad checks passed against them. The hotel ends up holding the bag—prevention is the only cure.

The Old "One–Two–Three."   Prevention is as easy as "one–two–three." That's because the vast majority of faulty checks can be detected by front-office cashiers with three simple observations.

First, is the check perforated? All legitimate checks are perforated on at least one side (except for the small percentage of checks that are government checks, checks printed on computer card stock, and counter checks). Because perforation equipment is so bulky and expensive, few check forgers bother with this detail.

Second, do the Federal Reserve district numbers 1 to 12 match the location of the issuing bank? Cashiers should compare the Federal Reserve district number located between the brackets along the bottom of the check with the restated district number printed (in smaller type) in the upper right-hand corner of the check (see Exhibit 11–15, item 9). Many check forgers change the Federal Reserve district numbers at the bottom of the check to a different district. In this way, the check is sent for clearing to the wrong district, gaining the forger several valuable days. Remember, if the numbers don't match, the check is a forgery.

Third, is the routing code printed in magnetic ink? The routing code found at the bottom of the check (Exhibit 11–15, item 8) must be printed in dull, flat magnetic ink. If the ink is shiny or raised, the check is a forgery.

Although these are the three critical questions for a cashier to observe, there are others. A comprehensive check-cashing checklist has been developed and is discussed later in this chapter. It provides management with a more thorough understanding of the check-cashing process.

Simple Deterrents.   Every weapon available must be employed in the battle against check fraud. Closed-circuit television in banks and photographing procedures

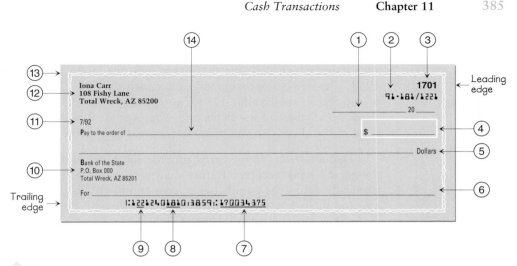

Exhibit 11–15   Fourteen locations flag a possible bad check: (1) Is the date current? (2) Do the routing numbers correspond to the magnetic numbers? (3) Has the account existed for some time? (4) Is the amount more or less than the statutory definition of grand larceny? (5) Are the values of the handwritten dollars and the numerical dollars identical? (6) Does the signature correspond to the registration card or the endorsement? (7) Are the account numbers in agreement with a bankcard that is being proffered? (8) Is the magnetic ink dull or reflective? (9) Is the number of the Federal Reserve region accurate? (10) Does the bank directory list this bank as shown? (11) When was the account established? (12) How does the maker's identity compare with the hotel's records? (13) Is the check perforated? (14) Is the payee a third party, a corporation, or cash?

elsewhere affirm a hotel's right to use similar equipment. Dual-lens cameras, which simultaneously record a picture of the instrument being negotiated and of the check passer, are available. Other systems allow the development of latent fingerprints without the use of ink or other messy substances. Just a sign explaining that such equipment is being used serves as a deterrent, as does a printed warning citing the penalty for passing bad checks.

Other hotels collect a check-cashing fee, which is used to offset worthless checks. The rationale of penalizing honest guests is open to debate. It would be better to adopt and enforce a stringent procedure, irritating as it is to the honest guest, than to collect an unwarranted fee. The procedure may include a telephone call at the guest's expense to his or her office or bank according to the circumstances and time of day. Using a check-cashing service may cost the guest a similar fee, but it puts the hotel in a better light.

Endorsements.   Procedural protection requires proper and immediate endorsement after the check is received. This is particularly true with open endorsements containing only the payee's name. The cashier should use a rubber stamp that reads as follows:

For Deposit Only
The ABC Hotel

The stamp should contain space for identification, credit-card number, room number, and the initials of the person approving the check.

Invariably, bank endorsements blot out much of the information recorded on the rear of the check. The data is unusable when needed most, if the check comes back. This issue, which was one that every industry faced, was addressed by Congress in 1988. The legislation that emerged assigned the first 1.5 inches from the trailing edge of the check (see Exhibit 11–15) to endorsements. In that space on the rear of the check go all the endorsements and whatever identification will fit into the area. The front of the check can still be used if more data is needed.

Debit Cards. Debit cards provide the hotel with immediate payment through the guest's bank account. Rather than writing a personal check, the debit card electronically debits the guest's bank account and credits the hotel's. Payment is immediate, and the risk associated with accepting personal checks is removed. For additional discussion on debit cards, refer to Chapter 12.

➤***Check-Cashing Checklist.***   No single set of rules covers every circumstance, but a list of limitations and restrictions is a helpful guide to those responsible for approving checks. Such a list follows. Modifications depend on the class of hotel, the source of authority, and the circumstances surrounding the particular request:

1. Accept checks only for the amount of the bill. Be particularly alert for the cashback technique, by which cash as well as services rendered are lost.
2. Allow no one to be above suspicion on weekends, holidays, and after banking hours.
3. Refuse to accept any check that is altered, illegible, stale (older than 30 days), postdated, poorly printed, or from a third party.
4. Be suspicious of checks slightly smaller than the statutory measure of grand larceny. If $100 separates petty larceny from grand larceny in the state, a $107 check is less likely to be counterfeit than is a $94 one.
5. Compare the signature and address on the check with those on the registration card: Are they similar? Should they be? Compare the signature on the front with the endorsement on the rear. Ask the same questions!
6. Compare the age of the guest with the birth date on the driver's license. Has the license expired? Compare the person's listed height and weight, hair and eye color, and the photograph, if available, to the person standing before you. More and more state driver's licenses and identification cards are being manufactured with tamperproof technology. When identification data has been altered, the card disintegrates in some conspicuous manner. For example, with Pennsylvania's driver's licenses, the state seal disintergrates if the card has been altered.
7. Pay special attention to endorsements. Accept no conditional, circumstantial, or restrictive endorsements. Challenge endorsements that are not identical to either the printed name (in the case of a personal check) or the payee (in the case of a third-party check).
8. Require endorsements on checks paid to the bearer or to cash. Require all endorsements to be made in your presence, repeating them when the check is already endorsed.
9. Refuse a check payable to a corporation but endorsed by one of the officers seeking to cash it.
10. Obtain adequate and multiple identification and record in on the rear 1.5 inches of the trailing edge along with any other information that can help if

the check is refused: address, telephone number, credit-card number, license plates, clerk's initials.

11. Verify business names in telephone directories or listings such as Dun & Bradstreet, Inc. Obtain military identification. Call local references. Request a business card.

12. Create fictitious information or names of company officers and see if the guest verifies them.

13. Make certain that the check is complete, accurate, and dated. Watch for misspellings and serial numbers of more than four digits.

14. Keep a bank directory and check the transit and routing numbers against it. Verify the name of the bank with the directory listing, giving special attention to the article "the" and the use of the ampersand (&) in place of the word *and*. "City Bank of Laurelwood" is not the same as "The City Bank of Laurelwood"; "Farmers and Merchants Bank" is not "Farmers & Merchants Bank."

15. Check for perforations. All legitimate checks have at least one side that is perforated.

16. Remember, cashier's checks (checks drawn on the bank by one of its officers) are spelled with an apostrophe *s,* are full size, never pocket size. Watch it! These checks can be stopped at the bank of issue up to 72 hours after being validated. (Trust companies issue treasurer's checks, not cashier's checks.)

17. Be cautious of certified checks, since most persons do not use them.

18. Check the signatures on bank drafts (a check drawn by a bank on its correspondent bank) with the bank directory, and verify the bank's correspondent bank at the same time.

19. Note that because of withholding, payroll checks are almost never even dollar amounts.

20. *Read* identification—don't just look at it! Ask questions: "What does your middle C stand for?" Don't offer the answer: "Is your middle name *Charles?*"

21. Determine whether the guest is registered from the same city as the one in which the bank is located.

22. Be familiar with bank locations: The 12 Federal Reserve districts are numbered from 1 in the east to 12 in the west. Locate the magnetic code on the lower left of the check. The first two digits following the bracket (|:) identify the Federal Reserve bank handling the commercial paper. Numbers greater than the 12 Federal Reserve districts are fakes. This is not true of NOW accounts or similar noncommercial checks.

23. Watch the calendar: Most bad checks are passed during the final quarter of the year, the holiday season.

24. Expect the magnetic code to be dull; shiny numbers that reflect light have been printed with other than magnetic ink. Preestablish firm limits on the value of the checks to be cashed.

25. Question emergencies. If airfare is needed to fly home unexpectedly, why can't the airline take the check?

26. Ignore evidence of identity that consists of social security cards, library cards, business cards, or voter identification cards. These are easily forged or reproduced, and they generally carry no photo.

27. Personally deliver the check to the cashier without allowing the guest to retrieve it once it has been approved.

28. Watch check numbers. Low digits mean a new account where the danger is greatest. The larger the number, the safer the check. New accounts generally begin with number 101, and 90% of all "hot" checks are written on accounts less than a year old (numbered 101–150).

29. Look for the small date on the left upper section of the check (when available). This indicates the date the account was opened.

30. Do not write the check; insist that the check be written by the guest.

31. Machine, color-copied checks can be smeared with a wet finger; real safety-paper checks cannot.

32. Remember that bank cards do not cover cash losses, only merchandise purchased. Limit check cashing to the front-desk cashiers.

33. Note that credit managers have been known to eavesdrop on guest telephone calls.

34. Ask yourself how difficult it would be to create the identification offered.

35. Compare the numerical amount of the check with the written amount.

36. Watch the value of foreign traveler's checks. Foreign checks are issued in foreign currency. Don't cash 20 marks or francs as a U.S. $20 value (see Exhibit 11–16).

►*Traveler's Checks.* American Express (AmEx) pioneered the traveler's check, and it has retained its preeminent position ever since. VISA and MasterCard entered the field in the late 1970s and early 1980s as extensions of their credit-card business. Several banks and travel agencies round out the slate of participants. It is a competitive business. However, due primarily to the proliferation of ATM machines (discussed earlier in the chapter), the traveler's check industry has stagnated in recent years. With easy access to electronic cash, travelers feel even more secure carrying their plastic ATM cards as opposed to dozens of bulky traveler's checks. As such, the traveler's check industry stalled in the late 1990s at about $50 billion per year. It will probably decline in volume over the coming decades.

Traveler's checks are purchased by the consumer prior to the trip. They are used as if they were cash, with the issuing company guaranteeing their replacement against loss or theft. The charge is usually 1%, but the checks are often issued without charge. Even without charge, there is plenty of competition for the business. Large sums of interest-free money are available for investing. The time lag (the float) between the purchase of the traveler's check and the use of the check might be months. Some 15 to 20% of traveler's check sales are never claimed. No wonder AmEx advertising encourages buyers to hold their checks for some distant emergency.

Buyers sign the checks at the time of purchase and countersign when they cash the instruments. Signature comparison is the main line of defense against fraud. Checks must be countersigned under the scrutiny of the cashier or resigned if they were initially endorsed away from the cashier's view. Some traveler's checks provide for dual countersignatures (usually to accommodate a husband and wife team), yet only one signature is required to cash the check.

Traveler's checks are very acceptable and some hotels will cash them even for nonregistered guests. Other hotels are extra cautious and require additional identification or compare signatures to registration cards. Comparing signatures is all that's required. In fact, many issuing companies do not even want the cashier to ask for addi-

Exhibit 11–16 Foreign traveler's checks look similar to U.S. traveler's checks. Although there are variations in color, an unwary cashier can easily confuse currencies. This is especially true when the check is payable in dollars, which are used by a number of countries including Australia, Canada, Jamaica, Hong Kong, Singapore, and the United States.

tional identification. That is because extra identification takes the cashier's focus away from the signature line. And the identification may also be invalid—in more than half the instances of stolen traveler's checks, the identification has also been stolen!

Prompt refund of lost or stolen checks is their major appeal. Hotel desks, with their 24-hour service, represent a logical extension of the issuing company's office system. Hilton entered into such an agreement with Bank of America. It is both a service to the guest and a marketing device for the chain.

Traveler's Checks Deterrents.   The best defense is to carefully watch the guest sign the traveler's check. Cautious cashiers should never remove their eyes from the check being signed. Indeed, some cashiers never even remove their hand from the check, always holding onto one corner while the guest is signing. It is a simple matter for someone to produce a stolen traveler's check, pretend to sign it while the cashier's attention is focused elsewhere, and then quickly substitute a previously signed traveler's check with a well-forged signature.

Like their commercial brothers, traveler's checks employ a magnetic code on the lower left portion of the paper (see Exhibit 11–16). In the United States, the first digits are always 8000, which tells the clearinghouse computer that it is a traveler's check. The next portion of the code identifies the type. For example, 8000001 is Bank of America, 8000005 is American Express.

Although forgers can easily alter the clearinghouse transit codes, they cannot easily copy the high-quality, high-speed laser images major companies print in their traveler's checks. These images can be seen when holding the traveler's check to the light (don't confuse these highly detailed laser imprints with simple watermarks found in paper). MasterCard and Thomas Cook, for example, show a Greek goddess on the right side of the check. Similarly, Citicorp displays a Greek god's face on the right of the check. Bank of America uses three globes (which supplement the other globes already visible). And VISA provides a globe on the left with a dove in the upper right of the check.

American Express utilizes a somewhat different safety approach. Red dots are visible in the check if held up to the light, but a wet finger is the acid test. It will smear the check when applied to the denomination on the back left side but will not smear the back right side.

The components of this chapter—cash, cash paid-outs, and cash equivalents—represent a small percentage of the transactions that occur at the front desk. Most transactions are handled by credit card or credit transfer to a city ledger account. In Chapter 12, the focus changes to the issues of credit. Because credit cards and credit equivalents represent the lion's share of front-office transactions, poor or lazy procedures can harm front-office profitability. In Chapter 12 we explain credit-handling procedures and caution managers to treat credit transactions with the same care as cash transactions.

➤ SUMMARY

Even as the quantity of cash circulating in hotels declines, the need for careful cash-handling practices increases. This is especially true for front-desk cashiers because they not only receive cash but pay it out as well.

Front-office cashiers receive cash from a number of potential sources. Guests may pay cash on their room folio at check in, at check out, or in the middle of their stay. Cash is also received at the desk on behalf of other departments (as when a customer pays for a banquet) and for auxiliary revenue centers such as soda machines or video games.

Cash is paid out by the front-office cashier for a number of reasons as well. On check out, the guest who overpaid the folio may receive a refund.

Employees may receive charged tips in cash, concessionaries may receive charged purchases in cash, and guests themselves may receive cash advances against the folio. Add to this list of paid-outs the use of an imprest petty cash account and the front-office cashier's job becomes a complicated and sensitive task.

To make the job even more difficult, cashiers must remain alert to potential check-cashing, credit-card, or cash transaction frauds. Hotel front desks are favorite targets for counterfeit currency, forged checks, or stolen credit cards. Front-office managers need to carefully train cashiers to identify situations where fraudulent practices are occurring.

➤ QUESTIONS AND PROBLEMS

1. Industry experts suggest the amount of cash in the banks of hotel cashiers should equal some 2% of gross revenues, or about $600 per available room. For a 100-room hotel that grosses $3 million annually, this equals $60,000 in cashiers' banks.

   As a new general manager, you are concerned with the sizable amount of outstanding cash in your cashiers' various banks. You know that if it were released from the banks, the cash could return significant revenues or interest income.

   Be creative as you identify three distinct methods for identifying which banks have excess cash or other means for releasing some of the $60,000. However, remember to maintain cash bank security as you brainstorm new methodologies.

2. An international guest tenders $171 in U.S. funds and #2,000 from his native land to settle an outstanding account of $206.20. #s are being purchased by the hotel for 51.50 per U.S. dollar. What must the cashier do now to settle the account? Assume that the guest has more U.S. dollars; assume that he doesn't. The hotel cashier has no foreign funds in the drawer.

3. Explain how international tourism helps balance the trade deficit of the United States. How does international tourism worsen the deficit?

4. Sketch and complete a cashier's envelope for October 11 showing the details of the turn-in and the amount of due back. (City-ledger collections are handled by the accounting office. No provisions are made for cash over or short; the cashier covers both.)

   Given for Problem

House bank	$1,800.00
Advances to guests	$181.15
House vouchers	$16.20

Vending machine refunds	$0.50
Received from guests	$7,109.40
Cash in the drawer exclusive of other cash listed below	$1,721.00
Traveler's checks	$2,675.00
Personal checks:	
Washington	$75.25
Lincoln	$310.00
Jefferson	$44.98
Carter	$211.90
Kennedy	$55.00
Others	$1,876.85
Bills of $100 denomination	10 each
Torn and dirty currency	$62.00
Coins	$680.14

5. Imagine that your hotel operates in a community where the incidence of counterfeiting is quite high. Develop a procedure for all front-desk cashiers in terms of accepting U.S. currency. Remember to be sensitive to the amount of time it takes to examine a bill properly and the fact that the cashier may be busy with other guests in line. Also, discuss whether the procedure should be eased for smaller denominations: $50s?, $20s? What if the cashier knows the guest from previous hotel visits? Be certain that your policy distinguishes between the newer currency (introduced in 1996) and the older currency (which will be in circulation for many years to come).

6. Some hotels prevent cashiers from knowing their net receipts. Without knowing net receipts, the cashier turns everything in from the day's drawer except the bank. If the drawer is significantly over for the shift, the cashier is none the wiser and is not tempted to steal the amount of the overage. Do you support such a policy? Are there any drawbacks to not allowing cashiers access to their net receipt figures?

➤ NOTES

1. Exhibit 11–3 assumes an annualized growth rate for ATMs worldwide of roughly 10%. Actually, international ATMs have been growing at a more rapid rate than domestic ATMs in recent years.

CHAPTER 12
Credit and the City Ledger

Outline

The City Ledger
Credit Cards
Other Cards
Other City-Ledger Categories

Managing Credit
Cost–Benefit Decision
The Management Function
Managing Three Specifics

Mechanics of the Entry
Transfers from *Guest Folios*
Transfers to *Guest Folios*
City-Ledger Postings without Transfers

Notwithstanding the cash discussion of Chapter 11, guests rarely pay with cash. In fact, front-office managers get suspicious when guests indicate that they'll settle that way. They know that skippers leave no incriminating identification. Legitimate guests favor and hotels prefer credit cards. Indeed, credit cards seem to be everyone's favorite these days. And much like the hotel industry with its new products and new logos, the credit-card industry continues to fashion old offerings into more appealing consumer products. The credit revolution that began during the last half of the 20th Century gains momentum still.

Credit in innkeeping predates current usage by centuries. Proprietors of the Roman mansiones (as the Biblical inns were called) and colonial innkeepers (1,500 years later) issued tokens, like today's traveler's checks. Because the tokens were redeemable anywhere on demand, their value fluctuated with the creditworthiness of the hotelkeeper. Earlier still, knights used wax impressions of their signet rings to guarantee payments to the innkeepers. Freed from the need to carry coins, they traveled with greater ease along the dangerous roads populated by highwaymen.

Buying on credit, that is, promising to pay later, is how America does business. The rest of the world is gradually adopting the idea. Both commercial and retail trade start out as credit transactions. Commercial businesses usually settle their credit purchases by cash, mailing checks at the end of the month, but even that is changing. Credit-card companies have aggressively marketed corporate procurement cards that are used in lieu of cash. MasterCard has BusinessCard, for example,[1] but it is only one of an estimated 200 commercial cards. Retail guests, including hotel guests, usually settle their purchases with personal credit cards. With billions of credit-card transactions taking place annually, expecting cash at the front desk is out of sync with the realities of the marketplace.

Customers who have not yet paid are called accounts receivable. In Chapter 10 we explained that hotels have two types of accounts receivable. Registered guests who owe the hotel for services are called *transient* (or *front-office*) *accounts receivable*. Those who owe the hotel but are not registered are called *city accounts receivable*.

Most city receivables (debtors who are not registered) start out as transient receivables (debtors who are registered). For example, a registered guest using a credit card to complete a speedy check out becomes a city account. Once the guest is no longer registered, the receivable, which is still owed, becomes a city-ledger receivable. City-ledger records are not limited to individual persons or credit-card companies. Associations, wholesalers, or client companies become city accounts when their front-office folios, often master accounts, are transferred to the city ledger for billing by mail.

Transferring from front-office accounts to city accounts is just one of three methods for settling the folio at check out. Allowances and cash are the other two options. In Chapters 10 and 11 we examined them in detail along with the postings that create the front-office account. A hotel guest buys services (rooms, food, beverage, etc.) on credit, charging the amount to the guest-room folio. Then, at the end of the stay, settlement is by cash, allowances, or transfers. Transfers shift the debt from the front-office ledger of the guest's individual account to some category of the city ledger.

➤ THE CITY LEDGER

Ledgers are accounting records that group similar activities. Hence, registered guests who owe the hotel for services are grouped together in the transient (or front-office) ledger. Accounts receivable who are not registered are grouped in the city ledger. Just as the front-office ledger contains many individual account folios, each identified by room number, so the city ledger is subdivided. Of course, city-ledger accounts have no room numbers, but they do have account numbers for ease in identification and posting (see Exhibit 10–11), line 4: MC7:43AM).

In Chapter 10 we discussed the front-office ledger and the individual accounts (or folios) that are maintained there. This chapter focuses on the city ledger and the kinds of accounts that comprise it. Chief among them is credit cards. No hotel merchant can do businesses without accepting credit cards. Consequently, even the smallest hotel maintains a credit-card category within the city ledger. It may be the only type of credit used by a small hotel. More likely, several methods for extending credit are used. Although they may not be actual, separate, city-ledger groupings, they are viewed separately here for discussion purposes.

Credit Cards

Estimates of credit-card use range from one-third to two-thirds of all room, food, and beverage sales. More important than the specific figure is the upward trend in the number of credit-card transactions. Even Europeans, who have traditionally favored cash, have started using cards.

➤*Brief History of Credit Cards.*   Hotels were dabbling in credit cards as early as 1915 when Western Union (the telegraph company) and the railroads issued special cards to preferred customers. In 1950, a New York attorney, supposedly embarrassed at being short of cash in an upscale restaurant, founded Diners Club. Within a year, gross billing reached 1 million 1950 dollars, although it was circulated in and around only New York City. American Express, which had dominated the traveler's check business since 1891, introduced the American Express (AmEx) card in 1958. Both Diners and AmEx were stand-alone enterprises. It wasn't until 1960 that the banks entered the fray, when the California-based Bank of America (B of A) launched BankAmericard. The B of A eventually franchised the concept, which resulted in the present-day VISA system, now the world's largest credit-card issuer. MasterCard, also fathered by the banking system, was a 1970 union of MasterCharge and MasterCard. As the action heated up, the lodging industry's big chains began issuing their own credit cards—but not for long.

Hotel credit cards were short-lived. Costs of administration and borrowing were too high. Chains were much smaller in the middle of the century and they lacked the computer capacity and financial depth to stay the course. Besides, broad-based cards were finding more general acceptance. Many hotel chains have recently returned to the arena through affinity-card partnerships with VISA or other international cards.

Hilton's experience is a good example of the ambivalence that the whole industry had toward credit cards. Between 1959 and 1962, Hilton twice converted its system. All Hilton and Statler cardholders (Hilton bought the Statler chain in 1954) were switched from company cards to Carte Blanche and back again to company cards only. Undoubtedly, part of the problem was Hilton's choice of Carte Blanche as the partner. Carte Blanche was a small player in the national scene and unknown internationally. It was acquired in 1978 by CitiCorp, which broadened the global coverage of Carte Blanche by adding Diners Club in 1981. Diners Club still has a strong international presence because it franchises outside the United States.

By the 1970s, the lodging industry had come to understand that credit cards were financial instruments, not marketing tools for hotel chains. With some relief, the industry left the credit-card business to the credit-card companies. So another agency wedged itself between the hotel operator and the guest. As a third-party intermediary, the credit-card company plays a role similar to the third-party reservation agency, the third-party marketing group, or the third-party telephone company.

➤*Kinds of Credit Cards.*   All credit cards are not the same, except they're becoming so. Although the number and variety of cards seem endless, credit cards fall into three general types. *Bank cards* are the most common, followed by *travel and entertainment cards* (T&Es). Everything else, and there are many spin-offs, falls into category three, *private label cards.*

The credit-card industry is very competitive. Initially, each of the three types was designed for different consumer markets. To some degree, this is still true. However, competition has forced each type of credit card to spread beyond its original concept. The differences between bank cards and T&Es blur as banking deregulations allow and competition forces each to take on attributes of the other. No longer are there sharp distinctions. Bank cards now charge an annual fee, although they were initially offered without charge. T&Es, which traditionally required merchants to wait for reimbursement, have introduced express deposits like the bank cards. Prestige cards with high spending limits and special privileges are offered now by bank cards to the affluent, who were the original customers of the T&E cards. Both are racing to develop smart cards to broaden usage and reduce fraud. The battle has been joined.

Bank Cards.   VISA and MasterCard are the best known examples of this card class. Bank cards are issued by banks to anyone, depositors and nondepositors alike. Bank agencies cross the country searching for customers willing to take another card. Solicitations are estimated at an astonishing 3 billion cards annually. There are more cards in the United States than there are residents!

The first bank cards went to economic groups that were unable to qualify for the more stringent credit references of the T&E cards. Recall that T&E cards preceded bank cards by some 2 to 10 years. Banks, which are in the business of lending money, encourage lower economic groups to take the cards and gradually pay them off. Bank-card purchases can be financed over time with interest due on the outstanding balance. Just another form of bank lending. At first, there were no annual fees, and with some customers, there are none still. Wise cardholders make prompt payments in full to avoid the high finance charges, up to 1.5% per month. At that rate, card companies are lending at some 18% per year while borrowing at about half that. It's a good business!

Discover Card is a special kind of bank card because it is issued and processed through only one bank. Although it offers the ultimate reward to cardholders, cash refunds of up to 1% of annual purchases, and charges merchants the lowest fees, Discover lacks the image of the snazzier cards.

Travel and Entertainment Cards (T&Es).   Best known of the T&E cards are American Express (AmEx) and Diners Club. Travel and entertainment cards are not part of the banking system; they do not encourage slow payment with high interest. The user is expected to settle in full each month. Failure to do so evokes penalties, one of which is interest. If late payment persists, the card may be revoked or some incentives may be withheld, frequent-flyer points for example. T&E card holders pay larger annual fees and face more stringent credit checks. Higher card fees, fewer bad debts (about 0.25% lower than the bank cards), and higher discount fees from merchants, not interest, are the T&Es major income earners. And in those higher discount fees lie the cause of the credit-card wars that are discussed later.

T&E's are slower than bank cards in reimbursing merchants/hotels. This provides another means of earnings, called *float*. If collection is made from cardholders on day 1 and payment to the merchants is delayed until day 11, the credit-card company has interest-free use of the money for 10 days. What is aggravating to the merchant waiting for several hundreds or even thousands of dollars is very big money to the T&E working with tens of millions of dollars. Everyone—credit-card company, merchant, business user, and consumer—chases the float. Float is one explanation for the increased use of credit cards by businesses. The business has interest-free use of the money for 30 to 60 days, between dates of purchase and payment to the credit-card company.

Bank agreements have shut out T&Es from the banking system. MasterCard and VISA prevent member banks from issuing T&E cards even if they want to. AmEx and Discover have challenged them and the government's investigation has carried the matter to court. Overseas, where there are no such restrictions, travel and entertainment cards are issued by banks. Other international competition comes from the en Route Card (Air Canada's national airline) and Japan's JCB (Japanese Central Bank) card.

Private Label Cards.   Private label cards are best illustrated with the hotel's own card. Such cards have very limited use; other merchants will not accept them. Promoting customer loyalty has been their chief purpose, but the 1.5% monthly charge on overdue accounts (see Exhibit 10–8) certainly helps the hotel's bottom line. Sales promotion rather than credit control has been the objective of private label cards since Hilton bailed out of the business. So where the cards do exist, credit verification is minimal. There is no urgency for the industry to return to private labels because frequent-guest programs now provide the same marketing information. Moreover, the credit-card companies, AmEx in particular, provide merchants with helpful customer analyses.

Gasoline companies (Arco, Texaco, etc.) marketed private label cards for many years. Consumers once carried a variety of gas cards as they carry a variety of credit cards today. Billing and payment were handled through the corporate gas companies. The oil embargo of the 1970s changed the retail gasoline industry dramatically and contributed to the disappearance of these private label cards.

Department stores have fared better. They still issue private label cards but have replaced their policy of selling only with company cards by now accepting national credit cards as well.

➤*The Credit-Card Wars.*   Fierce competition has all the credit-card companies fighting to gain and hold market share. Broadening the product line has been one technique. New card types have been created, much like the lodging industry has done with new subbrands. For example, AmEx introduced the Optima card, which grants revolving credit and so competes directly with the bank cards—no need to pay off monthly after all. Even within Optima there are several options, and Optima is but one of American Express's line of products. AmEx has some three dozen consumer and business cards. Some are student directed, some are corporate directed, some are consumer directed. Each company offers a line of credit cards: a personal card, a platinum card, a procurement card, a limited-use card, and so on. Limited-use cards protect the business by allowing only limited, specific use, employee travel being the most common. The limited-use Air Travel card, for example, does not permit ATM withdrawals.

Both card types have gone international in their quest for market share. AmEx started with a stronger base because it already had a worldwide system of travel agencies. It captured that global market by pioneering an emergency hotline for prescription drugs, legal referrals, baggage insurance, check cashing, accident insurance, guaranteed reservations, worldwide message, and passport replacement. MasterCard responded by forming a partnership with Thomas Cook Group PLC, AmEx's international competitor in the travel business. Domestically, both card types include life insurance coverage on air tickets and minimum auto collision on car rentals as long as prepayment has been made with the card.

In keeping with its upscale market target, American Express cards have no preset spending limits, although the company monitors balances as a percentage of the cardholder's average volume. Bank cards have very specific spending ceilings, but good customers can have them raised on request. Limits become important when one is traveling a great deal or buys a big-ticket item like a cruise. On the one hand, AmEx sells exclusivity—per cardholder its customers spend two to three times more per year than do bank-card users—and on the other hand encourages the card's use at everyday locations such as gas pumps and grocery counters.

Friendly competition intensified to all-out war over two issues. VISA and MasterCard fought in court and won the right to issue "gold cards," a term that AmEx had coined almost 20 years earlier. Another skirmish broke out in 1991 after MasterCard and VISA decided to fight American Express rather than one another. The restaurant industry of Boston was the battlefield. A group of restauranteurs there refused to accept American Express cards. The discount rate, the amount credit-card companies charge merchants, was too high at 3.5% of sales. Bank-card fees were 1 to 3%. A 2% difference for an upscale restaurant doing $2.5 million per year is $50,000 out of the owner's pocket. The battle was fierce and grew more tumultuous when VISA started paying legal fees for the restaurant owners. American Express capitulated, reduced fees, and increased advertising expenditures. Probably as a result, AmEx fees have generally fallen everywhere from 3 to 5% of sales (3.25% average) to 2.7 to 4% of sales (2.75% average). Helping with advertising for the Boston restaurant scene wasn't really special because American Express already promoted specific restaurants and restaurant cities.

Many small businesses avoid the higher rates of T&E cards; they just don't take them. Bank cards advertise that fact widely: "AmEx is not taken there." Other merchants accept the T&Es but discourage customers from using them. AmEx fights this battle because it has a contract provision that forbids merchants from doing just that. There is no law requiring merchants to sign on, but the contract is clear: Sign on and you may not discourage the user. Most merchants protest quietly by posting T&E logos at the bottom of their credit-card displays. Grumbles aside, the number of T&E outlets grows, part of the general increase in credit-card use.

New Products.   In their continuing quest for market share, credit-card issuers such as Advanta, Capital One Financial, and First USA have reduced interest rates and tested new packaging ideas. Popular among these are *affinity cards* and *co-branded* cards. Among the bank-card issuers, MBNA specializes in affinity cards with low-finance charges, achieved by targeting only good customers.

Affinity cards carry two designations: the name of the affiliated group and that of the credit-card company. Almost any organization that offers the credit-card company an extensive mailing list can affiliate. Charities, professional organizations, public-service television stations, environmental groups, and so on, add their names to the already established national card. The card company gets a list of possible new card users. Affinity cards are supposed to sharpen the group's identity and get members to use the card for the benefit of the organization. To encourage membership use, the affiliated organization gets a small signing bonus, typically a few dollars for each name on the list and a percentage of every sale, typically 0.5%. The money is used to save the whale, or fund scholarships, or build homes for the needy, according to the group's inclination.

Affinity cards have not proven successful with every organization. Big groups such as AAA or medical associations seem to do best. Affinity cards ask individual members to give up their own promotional awards for the benefit of the group. Rewards for purchasing with the card were small at first: a road map or a ice chest. Then users began earning points for larger gifts or for savings bonds or, best of all, for frequent-flier points. (Airlines sell points to banks and other buyers for between 1 and 2 cents per mile.) As personal reward gifts got better, affinity support faded.

Co-branded cards, the ultimate in rewards, appeared several years ago with a promise of changing the credit-card business. It hasn't happened. In fact, several of the major co-brands have abandoned their participation. The co-branded card grew from the basic idea of giving something to the user for each dollar charged. General Motors co-branded with Household International to offer points that reduced the cost of GM autos. Ford did the same with CitiCorp's Citibank. Liabilities grew too rapidly even for companies as large as these giants. Almost as quickly as their boisterous appearance came their quiet demise.

➤ *How the System Works.*   The system works because there is something in it for everyone. Customer-users can buy even if they have no money. If payment isn't financed, at least it's delayed with a float of 30 to 60 days. Card issuers profit through annual fees, interest charges, float, and discount fees. Merchants go along even though they pay much of the financial costs. Merchants make sales that may otherwise be lost and simultaneously reduce their credit risks, so much so that hotels have done away with the front-office position of credit manager. Local banks have no float, but they earn interchange fees for handling the transactions.

Credit-card companies charge merchants a discount fee that begins with the bank card's minimum of 1 to 2% and the T&E card's top of 3 to 5%. Like any business expense, discount rates are subject to negotiation. Large-volume merchants such as hotel chains negotiate smaller discount fees, but competition among the bank cards gives even the small hotel some negotiating space. Besides, banks and hotels have other business relationships, and from these, merchants gain additional negotiating leverage. Franchise systems combine the credit-card volume of the members, providing a competitive edge over independent hotels. Umbrella organizations have attempted to gain the same advantage for independents, but administrative costs have offset the gains from quantity discounts.

Dollar volume and card types are not the only components of the fee. Handling, authorization, and settlement procedures are determinants as well. At one time, banks handled all the support services for bank cards. Costs have been unbundled recently, and banks have given the job of sales and card processing to third parties. T&E companies still handle merchant transactions directly. Because several, separately identified, third-party costs (as much as 2 to 3% more) are now added to the discount fees, bank-card costs total very close to those of the T&E cards. Thus, effective rates for small operators reach 3 to 5% even for bank cards. Among the special fees are charges per transaction, charges for equipment installation, telecommunication charges, equipment rental fees, authorization fees, and capture fees.

Costs are higher still if the credit card is manually processed. Point-of-sale terminals in food and beverage outlets save processing fees, as does swiping the card through an electronic scanner (see Exhibit 12–1) for front-office authorization. Room clerks who fail to swipe the card during registration incur extra fees for the hotel if the information needs to be verified manually later on. All "nonmag" alternatives (manual handling, telephone authorization, and communication by mail) result in higher discount fees. Savings from electronic processing are offset somewhat by charges for the electronic equipment, but one terminal can be used for all cards.

A final fee, a chargeback fee, is levied when a charge is dishonored because of disputes or errors. In addition to the fee, the hotel doesn't collect the basic charge. Loss of income and costs of fees from chargebacks are compounded when the charge contains tip advances to employees (see Exhibit 11–1). An uncollectible charge leaves the hotel with out-of-pocket costs for both the sale and the cash-advanced tip. Staffers are expected to refund such tips, but rapid turnover and employee ill will reduces the likelihood of the hotel's recovery. Folio charges made by guests for concession and lobby shop purchases raise similar issues. When such purchases are charged to the folio, the

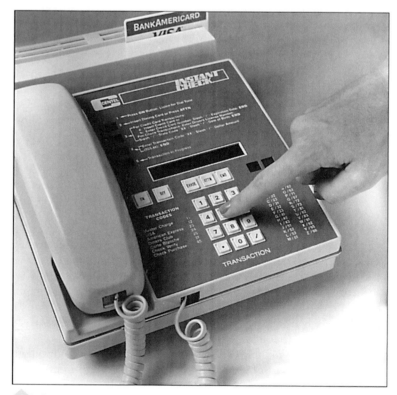

Exhibit 12–1 Card swipe (horizontally across the top) permits electronic credit-card verification, which is faster and less costly per transaction than manual input by Touch-Tone telephone. Merchants/hotels buy or rent the equipment, but costs are offset somewhat by lower discount fees. *Courtesy of Centel Transaction Services, Las Vegas, Nevada.*

hotel pays the credit-card fees if the folio is settled with a card. Worse still is a folio charge that is dishonored. Credit-card fees and dishonored charges must be negotiated as part of the concessionaire's rental lease.

A new fee on the horizon is pointed at the card user. Several issuers have started levying fees on customers who fail to charge a minimum amount. There's an additional fee if the card is canceled. It's reminiscent of the lodging industry's charges for early check out or for failing to cancel a reservation 72 hours (3 days!) in advance. Neither makes any friends.

Hotels deal directly with the credit-card companies for T&E charges. At one time, this was done with individually signed vouchers mailed in and individually prepared checks mailed back. Today, it is electronically driven. Even so, reimbursement from T&E cards is slower than from the banking system. Payment can be hurried for an extra fee, which offsets the credit-card company's loss of float time. Conversely, bank discount rates can be reduced if the hotel delays accessing its deposits. That gives the bank more float time, which it repays with lower discount rates.

Credit-card processing is easier with bank cards because a local bank is in the loop. Manually or electronically, the hotel deposits the sales records of its bank-card transactions in its own, local bank. The hotel's bank account receives almost immediate credit for the day's total (see Exhibit 12–2). Discount fees are usually charged at month's end. The hotel's bank gets reimbursed from the cardholder's bank, which may be some distance away. This fund transfer takes place through an interchange system that MasterCard and VISA own and operate. MasterCard and VISA are owned, in turn, by a group of large banks. Interchange centers function for bank credit cards like the federal reserve banks function for check-clearing facilities.

Other Cards

Major changes in the use of plastic money are becoming more and more evident. Credit cards are no longer used exclusively for credit. Large numbers of cardholders are substituting credit cards for cash. They are using the card not as a credit instrument but as a convenient replacement for pocket money. Full, prompt payment converts credit plastic into some other kind of plastic. *Secured credit cards* are good examples because they are not "credit" cards even though they are called that. Users with no credit secure their charges by depositing cash with a card issuer. The "credit card" is used then to charge up to the predeposited amount. It is a means for bad debtors to get the convenience of a card.

Convenience and float, not only credit, are now major considerations in the use of credit cards. Take a few steps ahead and convenient credit cards become *debit cards*. Further ahead still, they become *smart cards,* cards with embedded computer chips. Credit cards, debit cards, and smart cards offer the same in convenience. So something else is needed to switch users from the credit card's float to the debit card's instantaneous bank withdrawal. Several such factors are at work, including new fees on users who pay promptly, costly interest charges on those who don't, expensive discount fees to merchants, controversial ATM charges, acceptance of the new cards by more merchants, and limitations on the storage capacity of the magnetic strip cards.

➤*Debit Cards.*   Despite their place here in a chapter dealing with credit, neither debit cards nor smart cards are categories of the city ledger. Debit and smart cards are issued by the same companies that issue credit cards, and that's what places their discussion here. Debit cards transfer funds electronically (EFT, electronic funds

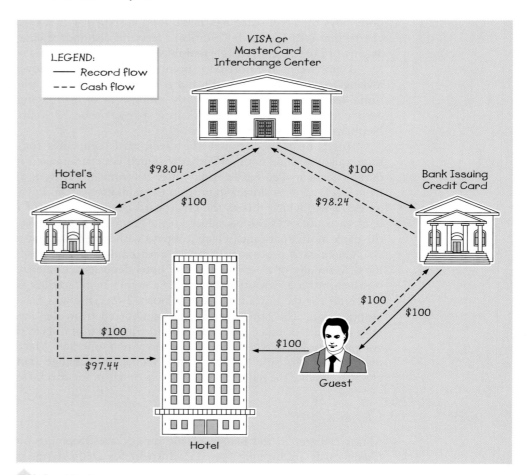

Exhibit 12–2   Diagram of the bank interchange system outlines the flow of records, cash, and fees as credit-card charges pass through the system. The merchant/hotel ultimately pays the total cost of $2.56 or 2.56% ($100 the hotel provides in service less the $97.44 it receives in cash).

transfer). The money is switched instantaneously from the cardholder's account to the merchant's account. Immediate settlement means that there is no debt and hence no account receivable for the city ledger to maintain. Debit cards are cash settlements as explained in Chapter 11, but cash settlements without risk from dishonest employees, from overages and shortages (no one makes change), or from bounced checks.

Debit cards are to merchants what automatic teller machines (ATMs) are to cardholders. With an ATM, the user gets the cash in hand. With on-line debit cards, the merchant or hotel gets cash into its account as quickly as the swiped card passes through the reader.[2] There is no time lag, no question about the user's ability to repay, and no float. No float is a negative for the consumer, but a positive for the hotel. Smaller fees, less than 50 cents per transaction, is another plus for the merchant. Lower collection costs will remain because fraud is lessened with debit cards.

Debit cards are good for merchants, but they will not replace credit cards until something as good as the float is offered to the users. Current regulations do not permit merchants or hotels to levy surcharges on credit cards. Moreover, rebates for cash (debit cards) are limited to 5% under current usury and truth-in-lending laws. In other words, there is no way for a merchant to reward customers using debit cards and no means of penalizing those using credit cards. Prices cannot be cut for cash or raised for credit-card purchases. With no price differential and the float still in place, most customers remain credit-card fans. Marketing efforts including co-branded, affinity, and business debit cards are working to turn around the perception. Debit cards are the ultimate in the cashless society that futurists predict. EFT means savings in processing expenses, time, paper, and accounting costs for both the merchant and the user. More and more retailers are signing on as debit-card use accelerates, but widespread adoption awaits more direct benefits to the customer. Convenience is one such benefit, but it goes only so far in offsetting the perceived value of float.

►*Smart Cards.*   Smart cards were introduced in France during the 1950s. Perhaps that is why they are more popular in Europe than in the United States. All U.S. credit-card companies, which are in some stage of smart-card development, are playing catch-up. Even VISA and American Express, the traditional enemies, are cooperating in a joint European research project. Progress is slow because a universal system is essential. One can expect the magnetic stripe to be in place for some time, with a hybrid card containing both stripe and chip used during the transition.

Smart cards have followed a developmental pattern that began with *stored-value cards*. Stored-value cards are a cross between cash and debit cards. Users pay for the card in advance with cash, usually in denominations from $25 to $100. In Europe this *electronic purse* carries up to five different national currencies. Loaded with cash, the user swipes the electronic purse through computerized terminals (telephone use is very popular) until the prepaid amount is used up. Marriott is testing stored-value cards in some of its campus operations; Burger King and McDonald's in some of their retail outlets. The card is either tossed away or reloaded by a second cash purchase at the bank's ATM or even through telephone hook-ups to the bank.

Smart cards, the next level of sophistication, are miniature computers scarcely different in size and appearance from a standard credit card. They have an electronic chip instead of the magnetic stripe of present-day cards. That's why they're also called *digital cash* or *chip cards*. Unlike credit cards, smart cards carry a sizable quantity of storage in their microchip databases. The typical card has 8K of memory, roughly 15 pages of typed data. The memory can be accessed by card-reader devices that quickly scan and use information from the card. Smart cards are seen to be the future because they are everything in one. They are credit cards, stored-value cards, identification cards, debit cards, door keys, medical and insurance records, ATM cards, and more, all rolled into one. Smart-card use will gain momentum as Internet commerce rises and better methods are needed for paying across the Web. Smart-card use will require additional investments in equipment at the merchant/hotel level.

Retailers are already using low-level smart cards to track customer demographics and loyalties. These cards provide marketers with customer names and addresses, with purchasing patterns, income levels, and hobbies. Understanding customer habits and lifestyles enables retailers to better market products and services. Customers receive discount coupons, special advertisements, and bonus points as their payoffs.

The hotel industry has had the very same information for years. The customer's identity, company, room preference, and frequency and length of stay are available to any hotel with a property management system. Making use of the information is another issue; few hotels do, but many say they are starting. How pleased a guest would be with a birthday card from a favorite hotel, with a thank-you note for staying five times in the past three months, or with a favorite bottle of wine waiting at check in. Intense competition demands a level of service beyond the industry's norm. Smart cards and credit management will help bring that to reality.

Other City-Ledger Categories

Every hotel has a credit-card category in its city ledger because credit cards are universal. Not so with other types of city-ledger receivables. Depending on its market, a hotel may have none, some, or many other kinds of city accounts. Charges arise from a variety of individual party givers (weddings, for example), or from a wide range of group activities (single-entity incentive groups, for example). Some city accounts, such as local charities that rent the ballroom, never even register as guests. Other city accounts come only from registered guests, who transfer their front-office folios as they check out. Among the more common transfers are master accounts, groups and packages, and travel agencies.

> ►*Master Accounts.*   Master accounts accumulate charges for group activities. The master account is a folio, but the guest is a convention group or a trade association, not an individual person. Large hotels frequently have several master accounts going simultaneously.[3] According to the group's instructions, room charges, entertainment, banquets, room rentals, cocktail parties, and room service might be charged to the master folio. Sometimes, even outside vendors, florists, or bands are paid by the hotel and charged to the master account. In Chapters 10 and 11 we explained how these charges are posted to the folio. At the end of the event, the account receivable is transferred from the front-office ledger to the city ledger for billing and collection.

Functions that involve hundreds of persons using rooms, rental space, and banquets represent very large sums of money. The hotel wants prompt payment. To ensure this, the master account folio is carefully reviewed by the client (the meeting planner, the association executive) and by the hotel (the sales manager and the accountant). Errors in master account folios may be substantial, but even meeting managers concede that they are not always in the hotel's favor. Even so, there are four common errors that irritate meeting planners. Attending to these beforehand expedites the billing, the settlement, and the eventual payment. Preventing the complaint is what good service is all about.

Error 1 is split billing. Meeting planners complain that charges are incorrectly split between master accounts and individual, personal accounts. Charges for group events should appear on the master folio and not on the personal folio of the executive who signs the tab. Front-office employees grow careless despite specific, written instructions from the client.

Error 2 is unauthorized signatures. Meeting and convention groups have many bosses. In addition to the elected board of directors, the officers, and the paid professional staff, there are informal leaders and past officers. Not all these persons are authorized to sign for charges. Meeting planners complain that unauthorized charges with unauthorized signatures appear on master accounts despite an advanced list of authorized signatures having been provided.

Error 3 is the sequence of posting. The breakfast charge of day 2 of the meeting should not appear on the folio before the dinner of day 1. Picky clients require the entire bill to be reposted to show each event in sequence. Comparisons to the original contract and to the function sheets are facilitated thereby. That pleases the meeting planner, but the hotel could have done it beforehand.

Error 4 is comp rooms. Complimentary rooms are given to the group according to a widely used formula: 1 free room-night per 50 paid room-nights. Meeting planners complain that hotels deduct the lowest room rates against the free markers instead of the highest room rates. Comp rooms go either to VIPs or to staff members working the convention. Therefore, when making the adjustment, the best rates should be comped, says the client. Specifically, if the group has a secretary in one room and a keynote speaker in another, the hotel should match the one comp room allowed against the speaker's higher room rate, not the staffer's lower room rate.

Although it is best to resolve billing differences while they are still fresh, it may not be possible to do so before the group departs. Agreed-upon items should be resolved and billed promptly without waiting to reach accord on the few differences. Otherwise, a small sum keeps thousands of master-account dollars unpaid.

►*Groups and Packages.*   Master-account billing is also used for wholesale packages and groups such as single entities. Single entities include athletic teams, company product shows, and incentive travelers. In each case, one buyer, one account receivable, is responsible for the master account. Accompanying the master account are the names and room numbers of the individual members. Further identification of the membership is shown on the room rack: with color on the manual racks; with code on the computer racks.

In keeping with the group's instructions, the hotel may post every charge (room, food, beverage, and incidentals) to the master account. Then everything is paid for by the group. Split folios are the more likely design. Major items such as VIP rooms and banquets are posted to the A folio, the master account, to be paid by the group. Personal incidentals are charged to the many B folios, to be paid by individuals. In that case, a notice, which may be computer generated, is often inserted in the key envelope (see Exhibit 12–3) to remind each member that personal charges must be settled indi-

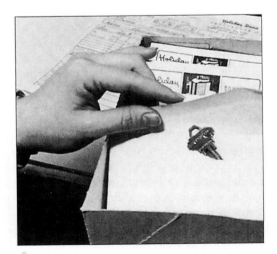

Exhibit 12–3   Key envelopes readied for distribution to an arriving group. Discount coupons, convention/group information, and reminders about settling personal expenses (B folio charges) may be included along with the key. *Courtesy of Holiday Inn, Minneapolis, Minnesota.*

vidually upon departure. The master folio may also be paid at departure but is more likely to be transferred to the city ledger for billing and later collection from the contracting group.

Who pays for what is more clearly understood with tour packages. The package has been marketed and sold with certain services included or not. Services that are not included are posted to the guest's individual folio. Coupons are issued to the guests for those services included in the package. The coupons are color-coded and dated to limit their use to the particular package. Guests pay for breakfast, drinks, tennis—whatever is part of the prepaid package—with the appropriate coupon. Cashiers in the various hotel departments treat the coupons as part of their turn-in (see Chapter 11).

Coupons are charged to the tour operator's master account, so breakage accrues to the tour operator. That is, the tour operator collects from the guest for the entire tour but pays the hotel only for actual tickets returned to the master account. By not using the services they have purchased, guests create additional profit for the promoter. The hotel also creates additional profits for the promoter if it handles the vouchers carelessly. Vouchers are not just colored slips of paper that can be lost or thrown away; they are debts that the promoter must pay if the hotel has them to account for the services.

In the hotel's own inclusive tour (IT) package, breakages accrues to the hotel. The package is sold to the guest and the money is collected in advance (minus commissions if it goes through a travel agency). If the guest fails to use the coupon, the hotel has gained. Accountingwise, the hotel distributes the single payment received from the guest among the departments, allocating a portion to room sales, food sales, tennis sales, bar sales, and so on.

▶ *Travel Agencies.*   Hotels and travel agencies have a strong love–hate relationship. That antipathy springs from the industry's view that travel agents, as third parties in the reservation process, get paid for supplying hotels with their own customers. For the travel agents, not getting paid—vigorously denied by the lodging industry—is only part of a whole issue of abuse. Heavily solicited when business is slow, agencies feel neglected when occupancy strengthens. There is no need to pay commissions if the house fills without agency business, so hotels deny reservations from agency customers—who are also hotel guests, remind the agencies. Notwithstanding some industry-to-industry complaints, individual hotels and individual agencies develop strong professional relationships that profit both. For the most part, the lodging industry is pleased to take travel-agency business and pay the 10% commission.

A travel agency becomes an account receivable in the city ledger when the agency collects for the room in advance of the guest's arrival. Thus, the agency in a distant city has payment for the room that the hotel must deliver. Eventually, the hotel is reimbursed, less commission. Commission payments are always a point of contention. The agency is entitled to its commission even if it does not collect in advance. Then the agency must wait until the guest checks out and the hotel computes the commission and forwards the check, the mechanics of which are explained several pages ahead.

Rapid improvements in travel technology are redefining both the travel agent's role and its income stream. The biggest changes involve agency–airline relationships, but the spillover affects lodging as well. Some time back, airlines reduced and capped the amount of commissions per ticket that agencies could earn. Prior to that, commissions were costing the airlines as much as they paid for equipment maintenance. The profitability of travel agencies is also threatened by Web shopping, satellite ticket purchases (convenience stores in Japan sell domestic airline tickets), and ticketless travel. Economic pressure is forcing agencies to find new revenue sources or face extinction, commissions alone will not sustain them. Agencies are consolidating, diversifying, charging fees to customers, servicing commercial accounts, or disappearing from the hotel's city ledger.

▶*Standard City-Ledger Accounts.* Credit-card charges, master accounts, and travel agency activities involve third-party receivables. This segment of the city ledger is much larger in dollar volume than the occasional city-ledger charge accumulated by individual guests. That has changed from the ledger's original form, which was debt owed to the hotel by local (hence, *city*-ledger) customers. Standard accounts still exist, but they have been replaced on the whole by the widespread use of credit cards. What accounts there are may no longer have their origin in the front-office ledger and are not necessarily local. Standard city accounts include individuals and companies that preestablish credit in order to use the hotel's facilities. A local business, for example, might use guest rooms for its visitors and public rooms for business meeting and social affairs. Once credit has been established, the authorized user merely signs for the charges. Monthly or sometimes more frequently, bills go out directly to the individual or company.

Airline crews are a good example of the standard city-ledger account. They are much sought after by hotels as basic occupancy even though the average daily rate is very low. Layover crews charge rooms to the airline's city account, and once a month the hotel bills. Airline contracts sometimes require the hotel to accommodate stranded travelers as well as crews. Typically, the airline pays for the facilities by giving the passenger a miscellaneous charge order (MCO) (see Exhibit 12–4). The stranded passenger pays with the MCO, which the hotel uses to balance the front-office folio. The account receivable is transferred to the city ledger and the airline is billed. MCOs are also used when the airline acts as a travel agency and books the guest into a prepaid room. The MCO becomes a travel agency voucher, as explained later.

▶*Banquet Charges.* Credit cards have also replaced open-book credit (based solely on a signature) that was once the norm for banquet charges. Party givers and banquet chairpersons once expected to sign for the party leaving the hotel waiting for collection. Catering managers still give open-book credit in limited cases. When open

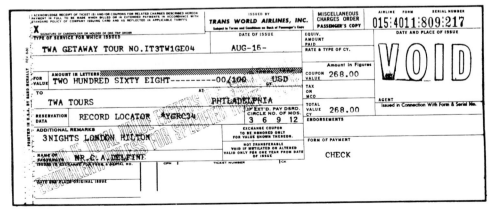

Courtesy: Trans World Airlines, Inc.

Exhibit 12–4 The miscellaneous charge order (MCO) is a special voucher used by airlines to pay hotel charges, as they might do with stranded passengers. *Courtesy of Trans World Airlines, Inc., St. Louis, Missouri.*

credit has not been cleared beforehand, collection is arranged in advance with a credit card or check. When open credit has been cleared beforehand, a bill is presented and signed at the close of the event. The value of the function is charged to a one-use, city-ledger account and billed within three days, which follows the billing pattern for speedy check outs and master accounts.

Pay-as-you-go functions are much riskier affairs. The group may be known, but there is no financial security behind it. Included in this category are school proms, political dinners, charitable fundraisers, and other speculative functions that base payment on ticket sales. A portion of the estimated bill should be collected in advance, and a ticket accounting system should be part of the up-front agreement. The credit department should review the contract and establish the identity and creditworthiness of the responsible individual.

▶*Late Charges.*   Late charges are among the more frequent, individual city-ledger postings. Late charges are departmental charges such as food and beverage that appear on the folio after the guest has checked out. Either they were entered late from the point-of-sale terminal, or they did not arrive at the front desk in a timely manner. Late charges are irritants to both the guest and the hotel. Guests may need to modify expense accounts after the late charge arrives in the mail, and hotels may need to absorb the costs because guests often refuse to pay after the fact. If the charge is small, the hotel might not even bill. The cost of processing and the loss of guest goodwill might cost more than the amount sought.

Collections are easier when the folio of the departed guest has been transferred to the city ledger. Then the front-office folio is retrieved, updated with the late charge, and transferred to the city ledger along with the earlier folio charges. The process is not even noticeable with express check outs. Accurate folios arrive when the guest is copied by mail some three days later and the total shown agrees with the amount submitted to the credit-card company.

The discrepancy is sharper if the guest settled at the cashier's window with a signed credit-card voucher. Then the copy that the guest carries away will be smaller than the amount that the credit-card company bills. If the card company does not permit after-the-fact additions to a signed charge slip, the hotel bills the guest directly using the reg card's address. The hotel has a second chance at collection, but that doesn't minimize the guest's anger. Direct billing of late charges is the only option for guests who settle with cash, checks, or traveler's checks. There is no option at all if there is a corrected or dishonored charge from a nonregistered guest who used the bar or dining room. Not registered means that the guest's address is not known to the hotel and credit-card companies will neither release the cardholder's address nor allow altered charge slips.

Late-Charge Procedures.   Late charges are identified by *LC* (late charge) or *AD* (after departure). Small late charges—$15 and under, perhaps—are wiped off with an allowance. The folio of the departed guest is reopened and the late charge posted. Immediately, the new balance is zeroed by means of an allowance. That procedure creates a permanent record of the transaction:

Decreases in incomes (rooms, food, beverage, etc.) are made with debits.

Decreases in assets, including *accounts receivable* and cash, are made with credits.

A second procedure is also used. A new, separate late-charge folio is created, on which all small late charges are posted. Daily, the total late-charge balance is cleared with one allowance, obviously a less burdensome procedure for the desk. Either way, management should get a daily allowance report, which is one of the exception reports prepared during the night audit (see Chapter 13).

Notwithstanding these provisions for allowancing late charges, efforts to collect them should be conscientiously pursued. In that case, the late charge could be posted to the guest's closed folio and immediately transferred to the city ledger for billing.

►*Delinquent Accounts.*   Into the delinquent (or bad debt) division of the city ledger go all receivables that are awaiting final diposition. Such is the case with large, uncollectible late charges, which were not treated as allowances. They, and other unrecoverable debts, are eventually written off the books as bad.

Returned checks (bounced checks) also account for a portion of delinquent receivables. Rather than reestablishing the customer's old records, returned checks are viewed as new debt and tracked separately. Checks come back for many reasons. Chief among them are insufficient funds, no such account, account closed, illegible signature, and incorrect date. Since passing bad checks is a criminal offense, hotels should support the police in prosecuting offenders even when restitution is made.

Credit-card chargebacks, guests who skip (intentionally leave without paying), and judgmental mistakes in extending open credit comprise the remainder of the delinquent division. For most hotels, credit-card chargebacks, skips, and open credit errors represent a negligible operating cost. Hotels that show significant costs in these areas should reevaluate their credit policies.

►*Executive Accounts.*   Hotel executives can be city ledger receivables in their own hotel. Management people use the hotel for personal pleasure as well as for house business. Company policy dictates how charges are to be made. House entertainment might be distinguished from personal charges on the guest check by an "H" (house business) or an "E" (entertainment) added under the signature. Without the H symbol, the accounting department bills the person as a regular city account. Many times, though, the billing is only a percentage of the actual menu price, depending on the employment agreement.

►*Due Bills.*   Since the 1930s, hotels have traded room nights for advertising. The deals have involved radio and television stations and billboard, newspaper, and magazine companies. Sometimes the trades are with manufacturers for capital goods such as beds and lamps. Evidence of the hotel's obligation to meet its half of the bargain is shown on a contract called a *due bill*. Due bills are also called *trade advertising contracts, trade-outs,* or *reciprocal trade agreements.* Temporary accounts receivable are needed in the city ledger when the other party in the swap checks in to take advantage of the "free" facilities.

Rationale for Due Bills.   Airlines, theaters, arenas, and the media deal in highly perishable products. So do hotels. There is no means of recapturing an unsold airline seat or an unused television spot for resale another day. The same is true with the lodging industry. All of these businesses have the same problem: There is no way to inventory the product for resale at a later time. Once the newspaper is printed, that day's advertising space is lost. Once the night has passed, that night's empty hotel room cannot be sold again. Trading the lost inventory for something useful is mutually beneficial when both parties have unsold, perishable products.

The hotel would like to restrict the products it trades to its most profitable item, rooms, and have the occupant pay in cash for the less profitable items, food and beverage. This is understandable from the hotel's point of view. The cost of providing an otherwise empty room is minimal; the cost of food and beverage is high. Moreover, unused food and beverage, unlike unused rooms, can be sold the following day. The advertising media set restrictions too, making no promise as to where the hotel's ad will appear in print or at what time it will be heard on the airwaves.

Whereas the hotel would like to limit the due bill to rooms, to use by certain individuals, and to given days of the week with advance reservations required, the facts of life may be otherwise. It is a matter of negotiation.

Some due bills are so negotiable that they are traded on an open market. Discount brokers buy the bills from the original receiver, or negotiate directly with the hotel, at reduced prices. The due bills are resold to a third, or even a fourth party, each time with an additional markup. In due course, they are used at the hotel by the final buyer in lieu of cash. The hotel accepts the bills at face value, which is still greater than the price paid by the user.

The concept works, and so does the series of marked-up resales, because two prices are involved. Both the hotel and the media (or other swapping party) deliver the due bill at retail prices but deliver the goods or services at cost. If the media accepts a $100 room for a $100 TV spot that costs $40, the TV station can resell the room at $60 and still make $20. There is even greater impetus when we remember that the room and the air time would have gone unused anyway.

Due bills are favored during periods of low or moderate occupancy and are less popular during busy periods. The oil embargo of the 1970s and the poor economy of the early 1980s brought a rebirth of due bill usage. Conversely, the good times on both sides of the millennium meant fewer vacant rooms and fewer due-bill deals.

Processing the Due Bill.   Due bill users must present the actual due bill agreement at the time of registration. This permits the guest–service agent to assign the most expensive accommodations. (The hotel's cost of delivering an expensive room is almost the same as delivering an inexpensive one.) The clerk also verifies the expiration date of the agreement. Amounts unused after that date are lost to the due bill holder. When that happens—and it does frequently—the hotel gets the advertising (or whatever), but the media company never gets to use all of its due bill.

The due bill is attached to the registration card and the rate is marked "Due Bill" along with the dollar room charge. A standard guest folio, or sometimes one specially colored or coded, is used. The actual due bill is filed at the front desk during the guest's stay. After the value of the accommodations used has been recorded on the due bill, it is returned to the holder at check out.

The transient folio, which was used to accumulate charges during the due bill user's stay, is transferred to the city ledger in the usual manner. However, the city ledger account is treated differently. There is no billing. Instead, the account is charged off against the liability incurred by the contract. At the time of the agreement, a liability was created by the hotel's promise to furnish accommodations to the media or other trader. As hotel accommodations are furnished, that liability is decreased. It is balanced off against the city ledger account that was created from the transfer of the guest folio at the time of check out.

➤ MANAGING CREDIT

Organizing and processing credit charges through the city ledger, the first segment of this chapter, is but one component of credit. Management must attend to a long list of other functions, including bad-debt management, check processing, internal procedures, and collections. But first of all, management must decide what its credit policies are.

Cost–Benefit Decision

There is no perfect credit policy. Any business that extends credit is vulnerable to loss. Each credit decision weighs immediate, determinable benefits against possible, uncertain costs. Recognizing that, the hotel industry has reduced its level of open credit. More reliance is now placed on credit cards and credit investigations. Open credit still has traditional uses—for advances to concessionaires, outlays for tips, payments for C.O.D. packages, and even some convention/banquet sales.

Successful credit policy cannot be measured by accounting figures alone. Hotels with small amounts of bad debts (or small ratios of bad debts to accounts receivable) are not necessarily the best managed ones. A conservative credit policy will mean few credit losses, but it may also cause substantial losses from business that was turned away. Low credit losses are easily measured on the books; lost business has no entry. Profits might have been improved by taking the business that an ultraconservative credit policy denied. The conundrum is that the increase might not have been achieved; there's no way to know.

The issue is not black and white—always credit/never credit. Every full-service hotel offers some amount of credit. The question focuses on how much, when, and under what circumstances credit is offered. The answer is not always the same, even for the same credit manager in the same hotel. With different conditions, credit could be severely curtailed, moderately administered, or liberally issued, even to the same customer with the same credit standing (see Exhibit 12–5).

Good occupancy, the first item of Exhibit 12–5, permits the hotel to adopt a conservative credit policy. There is no reason to replace low-risk guests with those of uncertain credit standing. When occupancy is high, a bad debt loss is the sum of full rack rate plus administrative costs, not just the marginal cost of providing a room during low occupancy.

Food and beverage sales, which have a high variable cost, are different. Far more caution is needed to justify banquet sales during a low period than room sales during a low period. A banquet bad debt may well cost the hotel two-thirds or more of the

Severely Curtailed	Moderately Administered	Liberally Issued
High occupancy	-	Low occupancy
In-season	-	Off-season
No competition	-	Price cutting
Established property	-	New hotel
High interest rates	-	Low interest rates
Reputable hotel	-	Disreputable hotel
Item of high variable cost	-	Item of low variable cost
Inexperienced lender	-	Low losses from debt-recovery
Hotel overextended	-	Good credit rating

Exhibit 12–5   Factors other than the creditworthiness of the guest explain why credit tightens and eases over time even for the same guest at the same hotel. It also explains why a guest in need of credit may be denied at one property and welcomed at another a short distance away.

bill (food, call-in labor, flowers, special cake, favors, etc.). Room losses are substantially less, both in percentage (25%) and in absolute dollars.

Hotels reduce rates when occupancies are low. These would also be the times for a more liberal credit policy. In fact, the more liberal credit policy might be traded for the lower room rates. Too dismal a circumstance, and the hotel will need to give both to get the business. Fighting for market share or competing with better appointed properties are additional reasons for liberalizing credit (see Exhibit 12–5).

The most obvious cost of poor credit is the out-and-out loss from nonpayment. Bad debts generate other hidden costs, the loss of customer goodwill among them. Administrative costs such as record keeping, application forms, printing, credit checks, postage, telephone, and employee time are never charged against the debt and rarely are they toted up. In contrast, bank charges, attorney fees, and collection costs are usually identifiable. That fact does not make them any less expensive, however.

The offsetting benefit is that of expanded sales volume. There is also profit to be made from lending. If the hotel's credit rating is good, it can borrow at low rates, or even self-finance. Extending credit at 18% annually (1.5% per month) provides an opportunity to profit from the interest spread.

The Management Function

Establishing and monitoring credit is a broad-based management function coordinated by the credit manager. If there is no credit manager, the controller takes on the task. Some responsibilities are handed off to other managers, who then form a credit committee. The rooms manager assumes an active role in front-office credit, and the sales/catering executives do the same for banquets and group business.

The credit manager/controller must support a credit policy that encourages a healthy marketing approach even as it strives for prompt payment and bottom-line returns. This is best done by viewing credit in three subfunctions: extending credit, monitoring credit, and collecting receivables.

▶*Extending Credit to Arriving Guests.*   Prescreening for credit approval is not always possible in the lodging industry. Lead time may be inadequate, as it is with a walk-in guest; reservations may not originate with the hotel, which is the case with central reservation systems. Nevertheless, after-the-fact collections depend on before-the-fact procedures.

Collecting overdue accounts begins with identifying the receivable, either at registration or earlier. Credit management is a pervasive function that merely begins at the desk. Like marketing or security, credit is everyone's responsibility. Housekeeping must report light or missing luggage, uniformed services must be wary of suspicious activities, and food and beverage personnel must obtain legible signatures and room numbers when guests sign for services.

Reservation Arrival.   Identification is more reliable when the guest has a reservation that involved correspondence. Then, the name, address, and perhaps even the company identification have been verified by mail. At registration, complete name and address are reconfirmed. That means given name, not initials; and street address, not post office box, office building, or city alone.

Early suspicions can be confirmed quickly. ZIP code directories help identify false addresses. Some hotels have the bellperson record the guest's car license number on the rooming slip. Illegible scribbles on the reg card are clarified before the guest leaves the desk. An inexpensive telephone call to the guest's supposed office puts many issues in perspective.

Credit procedures put stress on the clerk–guest interchange. Specific information must be elicited but done under the quality assurance umbrella. Tact in selecting the right words and care in applying voice intonations—often ignored in training programs—must be taught and practiced. Many factors, such as a tired guest or a misplaced reservation, exacerbate an already awkward situation. If baggage is missing or light, the clerk will need to press for more complete details. If the guest is nervous or poorly dressed, the clerk may insist on photocopying a driver's license. The line between information gathering and invasion is a thin one, as is the line between guest understanding and anger. Front-office clerks need to be masters of diplomacy.

No magic formula separates safe risks from poor ones. But collection is possible only if the hotel can identify the person and the address. Returned checks, late charges, credit-card chargebacks, and other open accounts cannot be collected, regardless of the guest's sincerity, without these essential facts. Unlike most industries, innkeeping has the opportunity to get the data. Procedures should be in place to ensure its collection.

Walk-in Arrival.   Because walk-ins pose additional credit risks, every hotel flags them with a special identification: *NR* (no reservation), *OS* (off-the-street), and *WI* (walk-in) are common symbols for alerting desk personnel. Recent telephone reservations, particularly those directed through the central reservation system less than 24 hours before arrival, must be classified as walk-ins for credit purposes.

The reg cards of walk-in guests are not always filed immediately. Some properties wait until the credit manager has inspected them. The credit manager uses telephone directories, credit-card companies, city directories, colleagues, and direct-dial telephone calls to verify information about guests, be they walk-ins or otherwise.

Suspicious guests can be required to pay in advance—credit card or not. Paid-in-advance guests are usually denied credit throughout the house. Extreme measures like these do not build guest loyalty. Few walk-ins intend to defraud the hotel. The extra caution needed to protect against some should not disintegrate into antiservice for all.

▶**Three Means of Collecting.**   Unheard of a generation ago, it is now essential to determine at the time of arrival how the guest expects to settle the account at the time of departure. The question is standard on every registration card (see Exhibit 8–5, for example). Each of the three options, cash, checks, and credit cards, has different credit implications, just as each has different accounting procedures.

Cash.   Even cash settlement are not trouble-free. Counterfeiting (see Chapter 11), short-change artists, and light-fingered cashiers add to the woes. Checks and credit-card slips are not nearly as negotiable and not nearly as appealing as cash to a guest or employee set on theft.

Cash adds additional problems to the mechanics of guest service. Guests who have no credit pay in advance on arrival. Paid-in-advance guests are not permitted credit sales anywhere in the house. No credit in the dining room, no telephone calls, no in-room films are allowed. Strange as it seems, hotels prefer credit cards with their inherent fees to cash with its inherent problems.

Checks.   Guests often assume that permission to settle with cash means permission to settle with personal check. Then guests, who are hurrying to depart, become greatly distressed when check outs are delayed because of the special check verification procedures (see Chapter 11) used by the credit managers. Not surprisingly, honest guests give an antiservice interpretation to the whole process.

If settlement is to be by check, the credit manager needs lead time during business hours to confirm the details. Appropriate telephone expenses are charged to the guest. Except in unusual cases, the approval is limited to the amount of the folio; no cash-back is authorized.

Risk is reduced if the check writer offers a bank-guarantee card. The issuing bank guarantees the check below a given dollar ceiling—say, $250. Even then, the hotel must watch the expiration date of the card, verify the card number against the number on the guest's check, and match signatures. The cards are not much help for an industry that draws its clientele from outside the local area. That might change with the coming of interstate banking and smart cards.

Charging a fee of $1 to $5 for accepting a check would not be unreasonable. The larger the check, the less costly the percentage fee would be. Guests already pay a 1% fee for traveler's checks. Hotels do not charge for check cashing because it is a financial service that they do not wish to offer. Usually, hotels only cash checks for guests, and even then there is a $50 or $100 ceiling limit.

Other options for handling checks are the check verification systems, trademarked under names such as Telecheck or Telecredit. Hotels pay a fee to the check-guarantee companies, which insure each check cashed. If a bank is involved, there is an annual fee plus a per use fee. Otherwise, only a larger per use fee is paid to the telecheck companies, which verify the checks through a computer interface system. By telephone or point-of-sale device (see Exhibit 12–1), front-desk personnel enter the guest's identification. The answer returns in less than a minute. Verification is by exception. The check is approved unless information on file triggers a negative response. An approved check is given a guarantee number—the hotel's claim number—which is written on the check's face.

Credit Cards.   Credit cards are the most desirable means of guest identification and payment. In Chapter 8 we treated the handling of credit cards during registration. Although the procedure is the same for all cards, in this chapter we have highlighted the differences in fees, the range of verification options, and the list of additional costs associated with credit-card use. Certainly, the advantages of credit cards must be tempered by their substantial costs. Similarly, credit managers must use care in comparing the known costs of credit cards to the unseen but equally certain costs of settling by cash or check.

Credit cards are verified through credit-authorization procedures that now use electronics almost exclusively. The approval verifies that there is such a card, that the line of credit is sufficient to cover the charges, and that the card has not been reported missing. Whether the person presenting the card is the true cardholder is another matter. Some banks put the user's photograph on the card to address this issue. It's costly, made more so by frequent turnover among cardholders.

Fraud and mishandled credit cards are costly for merchants and hotels but especially for the credit-card companies. Credit-card users are sheltered, because their responsibility is capped by law at $50. So antifraud efforts are concentrated in the credit-card companies with some help from the merchants.

Eliminating paper records was the start of the defensive battle. Discarded credit-card carbons had been used to match names and credit-card numbers as the first step in their fraudulent use. Embossing the credit-card number on both sides has also helped because it requires counterfeiters to make two alterations.

Long-term solutions lie in credit-card technology. Holograms that produce three-dimensional images, which display motion when moved from side to side, are widely used now. Unfortunately, the cost of reproducing these has dissuaded credit-card companies as well as illicit users.

Managing Three Specifics

Credit is an issue for every operating department, but the heaviest burden falls on the front desk. As with all that happens at the front desk, the guest and the staff stand face-to-face, increasing the tension and hardening the positions. Credit issues must be resolved firmly and yet with courtesy even though the pressure of time often demands instantaneous decisions. Poorly conceived and poorly implemented credit policies undermine even the best guest-service programs.

One new difficulty has just crossed the horizon, early departure fees. A guest who leaves before the departure date shown on the reservations is subject to hefty charges, ranging up to $50. Try explaining that to an early check out with a large, yet-to-be-paid folio. Besides, some questions are still unresolved. For example, will the charge be levied if the guest reduces the expected stay from, say, the four days of the reservation to only two days if the intent is made known at check in? And what will be the reaction of the credit-card company to the guest who refuses payment despite the hotel's demands? Answers are apt to revolve around the degree of clarity that structures the arrangement. Was the room guaranteed with a credit card? Are travel agents familiar with the procedure? Was the guest advised of the policy during the telephone call to the reservation office, and was it repeated on the written confirmation, and at check-in time?

At first, notice of early check-out fees might be considered another disclaimer for the registration card. On second thought, certainly not. The issue will disappear when occupancy slips and will die altogether when competition sharpens. It's similar to overbooking; the problem comes and goes as occupancy rises and falls. A more permanent credit question that warrants continued attention is that of chargebacks.

➤*Minimizing Chargebacks.*   Hotels work very hard to find customers and to service those customers after their arrival. Large costs are incurred in marketing and employee training. In light of those efforts and costs, the hotel's failure to collect the bill, never to collect the bill, is beyond understanding. But that is just what happens with an estimated 50% of all chargebacks. Chargebacks are credit-card charges disallowed by the card company because (1) the guest refuses to pay, or (2) a procedural error makes the charge unacceptable to the card company.

By federal law, credit-card companies allow hotels 30 days to respond to and submit evidence about chargebacks. Hotel credit offices simply fail to answer. Reservation no-shows are the most common chargebacks. Guests guarantee the reservation using a credit card and then refuse to pay the first night when they don't show. With the credit-card number and no record of a cancellation number, the hotel has a strong argument, especially if the card company advertises its guarantee of this type of reservation. However, there can be no collection if the credit office fails to complete the inquiry. Of course, not pushing for payment may be more about guest relations than about credit. If that's the case, early check-out fees have no footing at all.

Procedural chargebacks are more the responsibility of the cashiers than of the credit or accounting offices. Procedural chargebacks can be reduced with a well-devised training program that concentrates on the do's and don'ts of taking cards and processing charges.

1. Be aware that every business is assigned a floor limit, which is the maximum dollar volume allowed on a single credit card without additional authorization.
2. Insist that employees know that limit, for, once exceeded, all charges, including those below the floor, are voided.
3. Do not split charges on two or more vouchers to avoid the floor limits.
4. Never give a cash refund if an unused advance deposit was made through a credit-card charge (or travel agency voucher, for that matter).
5. Bill credit-card companies promptly.
6. Refuse to post fictitious items in order to give cash against the credit card.
7. Watch for altered cards, rearranged numbers, or replaced digits that will make a hot card usable. Clues are glue on the card, blurred holograms, color variations, or misaligned numbers. Compare numbers on the back and front sides. Watch for altered signature panels, which are made tamper-evident by repetitive designs on the panels.
8. Adhere to the recommendations of the credit-card companies: Do not place telephone numbers on credit-card slips.
9. Question credit-card signatures made with a felt-tip pen that could be used to cover an original signature.
10. Compare the signature on the departmental voucher with the signature on the credit card. If uncertain still, compare with the registration card signature.
11. Make certain the card imprints completely on all copies of the voucher; check the clarity of the signature.
12. Use the proper voucher form if a manual system is still in place. Each company has its own and may not accept its competitors.
13. Anticipate employee misuse—changed figures or additional charges that permit the employee to pocket some cash.
14. Answer promptly chargeback inquiries from the card companies.
15. Instruct employees not to apprehend anyone suspected of using an invalid card, nor to exercise any force in retrieving a card. Since the card remains the property of the credit-card company, cardholders agree to surrender it on request. Agents of the hotel should not destroy the card nor publicly humiliate the guests.
16. Carry insurance against false arrest based on incorrect information furnished by the credit-card company.
17. Refuse credit cards whose expiration date has passed the last day of the month specified. Watch on some cards for "from" dates; charges before that time will be rejected.
18. Compare the credit card and driver's license signatures when suspicious of the individual or the card. (Many states are treating their driver's licenses with a chemical process that disintegrates, changing the graphics if the data on the card have been tampered with.)
19. Teach cashiers that MasterCard uses numbers that begin with 5; VISA numbers begin with 4; American Express numbers begin with 3; and Discover numbers begin with 6.
20. Maximize recovery by retaining original documents such as signed outlet or room service vouchers.

►*Monitoring Credit.* For most guests, credit is checked only twice: first on arrival and then on departure. A small number of guests is tracked more closely to make certain that the credit policies of the card company and of the hotel are being followed. There are two restrictions placed on hotel credit-card use. Every hotel has a credit limit or floor limit for the premises. The floor limit is the maximum credit that the hotel can extend to any one guest without getting prior approval from the credit-card company. Obviously, the initial floor limit should be as high as the hotel can negotiate. Just as obvious, that limit is a function of the hotel's average daily rate. If the card is approved at registration, the credit-card company guarantees payment up to that floor—actually, a ceiling. In case of default, credit-card charges above that ceiling void the entire guarantee even the amount below the ceiling if prior approval wasn't obtained.

Hotels also need to monitor the ceiling of the guest's own credit line. Each credit-card holder has a personal maximum. Therefore, a freeze is put on the guest's card for the amount that he or she is apt to spend. If less is spent, and usually it is, the hotel is supposed to release the difference at check out. This allows the guest to make other purchases elsewhere. Few hotels bother, which restricts the guest because the personal ceiling is reached before the expenditure has actually been made. New York was the first state to outlaw this practice.

Losses can be substantial if floor limits are breached without prior clearance. But it is a problem with only a small number of guests, and only if those guests fail to pay. Only then does the hotel turn to the credit-card company for reimbursement. The danger is minimized if folio balances are constantly monitored. The job is usually assigned to the swing or graveyard shifts to make certain that an examination takes place at least once daily. In a manual system, the clerk flips through the bucket scrutinizing each folio by noting the daily charges and the cumulative balance of each account receivable. With a computer, an overlimit report, which is an exception report (see Chapter 13), can be screened quickly several times during the day. Whether done manually or electronically, the monitor must project the rate of spending as the folio nears the floor thresholds.

Questionable folios, and even some picked at random, are examined in detail. Is there a credit card for the room? Are the numbers legible? Is the expiration date still valid? Is the balance below the floor? Is an approval number on file? The total charges are examined, but especially the pattern of charges. Suspicious accounts are listed by the night clerk in a report, which the credit manager examines first thing in the morning.

Several situations mandate immediate action. The most serious is the credit-card company's refusal to increase the floor limit on a suspect folio. Paid-in-advance guests who exceed the deposit limit and guests with preapproved direct billing who exceed the agreed limit are additional examples. Actions that portend a skipper are probably the most immediate problem.

If discovered during the day, or as a result of the night clerk's report, the credit manager acts immediately to collect. If unable to collect, the credit manager may take the guest's luggage, lock the guest out of the room, or call the police in case of fraud. (State laws make skipping and bad-check passing prima facie cases of fraud.)

If the credit alert is discovered during the wee hours of the morning, common sense dictates waiting until a more reasonable hour. (Courts have ruled against hotels that lock out guests at unreasonable hours.) Wait too long, however, and the hotel might have a skip.

Credit Alert and Skippers. Intentional skippers can be identified by the pattern of things they do. Indeed, the credit manager should develop a standard description much like airlines have done for the typical hijacker. The average skipper is male, 30 to 35 years old, a late walk-in with light baggage and vague identification. He is a heavy tipper and a quick new friend of the bartender. The skipper makes no telephone calls that can be used to trace him. His address is usually a well-known one in a large city, but it proves to be false. He writes his name and address poorly and offers no business identification.

Skipper alerts begin with light or worthless luggage. Guests become doubly suspect when they charge their folios with small items, which one normally pays for in cash. Skippers compound the hotel's costs by passing bad checks or using stolen credit cards. Bad-check passers concentrate on weekends or holidays when commercial hotels are understaffed and banks are closed. With ATM machines readily available, fewer and fewer hotels are cashing checks. Those that do should maintain a check-cashing record to alert other shifts of ongoing activities. Then a check-cashing report becomes part of the night audit activities.

Skippers and bad-check passers frequently work one area before moving on. A telephone or fax network among local hotels does much to identify the culprit even before his or her arrival. Photographs of suspects and identifying information, perhaps from the police, will undoubtedly be displayed someday on computer terminals.

Something needs to be done because crime has moved from the street into the hotel. Frustrating the criminal takes the combined efforts of all employees. Clerks, bellpersons, house police, cashiers, housekeepers, engineers, and room service waiters, too, must watch for and report the telltale signs. Large quantities of blank checks or money orders, firearms and burglary tools, keys from other hotels, unusual amounts of cash or gems, or just heavy traffic or loitering about a room indicate serious trouble is brewing.

▶*Collecting Receivables.*   Accounts receivable are what the city ledger is all about. Some receivables enter the city ledger directly, credit-card charges in the food and beverage outlets, for example. Most receivables come to the back office from the front office as transfers from the guest ledger to the city ledger. Here is accumulated every category of debt: master accounts, travel agency coupons, wholesaler settlements, skippers, credit cards, direct billings, convention and association activities, due bills, delinquent accounts, executive accounts, and banquet charges. How these debts are collected and by whom reflects on the hotel's cash flow and its profit picture. Having gone to the trouble of marketing, servicing, and charging the account, the hotel can be no less diligent in collecting what's due.

Billing and Chasing.   Like many other retailers, hotels bill receivables monthly. If the guest charges services early in the 30-day cycle and the hotel allows an additional 30 days before payment, 60 plus days elapse before the hotel realizes that there is a possible collection problem. Switching to a 15-day billing cycle improves collections because the longer a bill is unpaid, the less likely it is ever to be paid (see Exhibit 12–6). Similarly, convention and banquet billing must be speeded up to three to five days after the function, direct company billing and express check outs to one to three days after departure. To meet these recommendations, management needs to allocate adequate resources to the credit/accounting department.

Second notices should follow soon after the first billing, usually at the end of the month. Routine notices twice during the next 30 days and telephone calls thereafter should inquire whether the statement has come, whether it is accurate, and when payment can be expected. Each notice should point up the additional interest charges that late payments accrue.

Time Allowed for Account to Remain Unpaid	Percentage Collectible Expected
Due date	99
3 months	90
4 months	86
5 months	81
6 months	63
12 months	42
24 months	26
36 months	17
60 months	Less than 1

Source: Composite of hotel and other industries.

Exhibit 12–6   Accounting offices must bill promptly and pursue unpaid accounts aggressively because the likelihood of accounts receivable becoming bad debts increases over time as a smaller and smaller percentage of unpaid balances are collected.

Chasing unpaid debts should not be a random effort—it must be in someone's job description. Otherwise, customers get the impression that the hotel has forgotten. Nor should the collector be apologetic—the late payer is the wrongdoer. Payment arrangements should be specific in both amounts and dates. Partial payments may be accepted, even encouraged, provided that details (when and how much) are fixed and enforced. Small payments should be avoided since they are costly to administer and tend to be overlooked as insignificant when payments are missed.

What Next?   No matter how carefully credit requests are screened, some bad debts materialize. Faced with a delinquent account, the manager responsible for credit has two main courses of action. Either the hotel can continue its own internal efforts at collection or it can employ a third party, an attorney or a collection agency, that specializes in bad-debt collections. Either way, there are substantial collection costs that must be reckoned with.

Hotels that choose the internal option must be prepared to invest in the process. In addition to outright fees, there are many hidden administrative costs. Credit collection is not a sometimes affair. To be effective, collection must be systematic and thorough, not a passing effort. It takes a flow of information and a stack of records, manual or computerized, to track debtors. Yet the job is one more task added to the office of controller when there is no full-time credit manager. Knowledge of federal and state legislation is another hurdle. If the in-house staff is insensitive to the rights of the debtor (and they have many legally protected rights), the process might best be left to a third party that has the legal expertise.

The worst of the bad debts end up with collection agencies. Oddly enough, their basic technique is writing letters, much like the hotel does. More than 90% of their collections are generated by simple dunning letters. Still, collections are light, especially for small accounts, which have the lowest priority with the collection agencies. Less than 25% of accounts turned over are collected. If no collection is made, there is no fee, but the fee takes 30 to 40% of what is collected.

What success collection agencies have is probably due to psychological effects on the debtor as much as to techniques employed by the agency. For a start, the customer realizes that the matter has grown more serious, more intense, seeing the agency as a more relentless and threatening force than the hotel. Whatever softening existed through the customer–client relationship has dissolved with the appearance of this third party. The debtor is aware that the agency knows more about his entire credit record than the hotel knew. Credit ratings may suddenly be in jeopardy. Sometimes the debtor simply tires of the battle and willingly makes arrangements. *Arrangements* is a good word for any collector to use because it says that some kind of settlement can be negotiated and worked out. That is, after all, the intent of the collection effort.

➤ MECHANICS OF THE ENTRY

Some guests, but very few, settle their front-office folios with cash. They are not accounts receivable. Some guests, a somewhat larger number, settle their food and beverage purchases with cash. Neither are they accounts receivable. With those two exceptions, all hotel customers are accounts receivable. Hotels bill and collect these receivables through the city ledger.

Two methods are used to get the information to the city ledger in the first place. Under one system, the one used for registered guests, charges are accumulated on the front-office folio and transferred to the city ledger. In Chapter 10 many pages are assigned to this procedure. The second source of city-ledger transactions are purchases by credit card or open credit. The front-office folio is not involved, charges are made from the outlets directly to the city ledger. There are no ledger-to-ledger transfers with credit-card purchases. This happens when guests, registered or not, use credit cards or open credit to pay for services throughout the hotel. Obviously, registered guests can use either option when buying food and beverage services. They can charge the folio or they can use a credit card and have it charged directly. Nonregistered customers, who do not pay with cash, have charges posted to the credit card because they have no front-office folio.

Transfers from Guest Folios

Transfers *from* the guest folio *to* the city ledger increase the city-ledger receivable and decrease the guest-ledger folio (see Exhibit 10–1, final line).

Increases in assets, including *accounts receivable* and cash, are made with debits.

Decreases in assets, including *accounts receivable* and cash, are made with credits.

Daily and cumulatively, the total of the transfer debits to the city ledger must equal the total of the transfers from the guest ledger. Once the transfer is made, billing takes place from the city ledger.

When settlement is received (from an individual, company, organization, or credit-card issuer), the check is deposited and the city-ledger account (the debt to the hotel) is reduced.

Increases in assets, including accounts receivable and *cash,* are made with debits.

Decreases in assets, including *accounts receivable* and cash, are made with credits.

For some receivables (the convention group's master account, the bridal shower, etc.), the city-ledger record is closed. Other receivables (credit card) are continuing records with new payments and new charges continually flowing in and out. This basic procedure is followed for every city account originating in the front office with a guest folio: credit cards, late charges, and others. However, two of these—travel agency and frequent-guest programs—require special attention.

➤***Travel-Agency Records.*** A good share of the antipathy that exists between hotels and travel agencies can be ascribed to poor recordkeeping on both sides. Accounting for the travel agency commission starts with the reservation. Commissionable reservations are flagged, and that identification is carried onto the registration card and the folio. Computer systems capture and track the travel agency guest more efficiently than manual systems. Whichever system is used, commissionable folios are segregated from noncommissionable folios, and immediate attention given to DNAs (did not arrive). A notice of nonarrival, frequently a postcard, is mailed to the travel agency. This forestalls a claim and the endless correspondence that follows.

How It Is Supposed to Work. There are so many hotels and so many travel agents in the world that there is no way for each to know another. Therefore, the best working relationship is a prepaid reservation. The agency confirms its reservation with a check or company credit card for the full amount less commission. Accompanying the payment is a reservation form similar to Exhibit 12–7. By returning one

Step 1. Agency types out as much of form as it can.
Step 2. Agency mails Parts 2 and 3 to hotel or completes form by phone.
Step 3. If Step 2 was done by mail, hotel fills out balance of form on both parts and returns Part 3 to agency. If Step 2 was completed by phone, agency throws away Part 2.
Step 4. When form has been all filled out, remittance is attached to Part 4 and mailed to hotel.
Step 5. Part 3 is filed in client's folder and Part 1 is mailed or delivered to client.
Step 6. Part 5 is filed in date tickler for commission collection and/or is thrown out when commission has been collected.

AGENCY REQUEST FOR HOTEL/MOTEL ACCOMMODATIONS

Date______ ☐ INITIAL REQUEST ☐ CANCELLATION ☐ CHANGE

CONFIRM TO AGENCY VIA ☐ RETURN MAIL ☐ AIR MAIL ☐ TELE-PHONE ☐ WIRE

CATEGORY ☐ MINIMUM ☐ MODERATE ☐ DELUXE

CLIENT

AGT.

HOTEL/MOTEL

TEL. NO.

AGENCY LIABILITY SUBJECT TO CONDITIONS ON REVERSE SIDE HEREOF

CONFIRMED RESERVATIONS FOR:

____ ROOMS ____ PERSONS ____ NIGHTS

	HOUR	DAY	DATE	VIA	FROM
ARRIVE					
DEPART					

____ SINGLE ____ TWIN ____ DOUBLE ____ STUDIO ____ SUITE ____ SEE BELOW

☐ NO FACILITIES ☐ PRIVATE TOILET ☐ PRIVATE SHOWER AND TOILET ☐ PRVATE BATH AND TOILET

☐ NO MEALS(EP) ☐ CONTINENTAL BREAKFAST ☐ AMERICAN BREAKFAST

☐ DEMI PENSION (MAP) ☐ FULL PENSION(AP)

CONFIRMED FOR HOTEL BY ______ DATE ______

ROOM RATE $ ______

NO. OF NIGHTS ______

WHEN VALIDATED THIS VOUCHER HAS A VALUE OF
$
EXCLUDING TAXES AND CHARGES FOR SERVICE AND PERSONAL INCIDENTALS

PLEASE REPLY BELOW AND RETURN GREEN COPY TO TRAVEL AGENCY

☐ Quote rates in U.S. Dollars or specify currency exchange rate ______
☐ Advise cancellation date without penalty ______
☐ State if reservations are guaranteed ____ YES ____ NO
☐ May agency deduct commission if fully prepaid ____ YES ____ NO

COMM. $ ______

DEPOSIT ______

HOTEL/MOTEL TO COLLECT FROM CLIENT $ ______

Reply by Hotel/Motel:

THIS BOX FOR AGENCY USE ONLY
CK. NO. DATE SENT

By ______ Date ______

Courtesy: Willow Press, Inc., Syosset, NY.

Exhibit 12–7 Travel agencies confirm room bookings for their customers by providing information about the client and including a deposit check. The system fails when an advanced deposit is not received and the agency is unknown to the hotel. Efforts to standardize the form have not been successful, although the American Society of Travel Agents (ASTA) and the Hospitality Sales and Marketing Association International (HSMAI) have made serious attempts to do so. *Courtesy of Willow Press, Syosset, New York.*

copy of the form, the hotel confirms the reservation and awaits the guest. The travel agency's check, which arrives before the guest, is deposited. Now the hotel owes the travel agency pending the guest's arrival.

Increases in assets, including accounts receivable and *cash*, are made with debits.

Increases in liabilities, including *taxes* and *accounts payable,* are made with credits.

The cash received is less than the room reservation because the agency has kept its commission. The difference in value between the two is a debit to rooms commission, an expense of operation.

The arriving guest presents his or her copy of the same reservation form, now called a *coupon* or *travel agency voucher.*[4] Full credit is given against the guest's voucher, although the actual cash received was less. Net result: The room charges are prepaid, the hotel has its money, the guest is welcomed, the travel agency has its commission. Most important, the guest is accommodated even if the travel agency is unknown to the hotel or is on the other side of the world.

At check out, the coupon-carrying guest pays for incidentals as any other guest would do using cash, allowances, or transfers. An additional commission check is mailed to the agency if the guest stays longer than anticipated; a rebate, less commission adjustments, if the guest leaves sooner than anticipated. The value of the room charge, the original reservation voucher, is transferred to the city ledger, and the guest's folio is zeroed:

Decreases in assets, including *accounts receivable* and cash, are made with credits.

The amount transferred to the city ledger need not be billed, because the hotel is holding the prepayment made by the travel agency. The transfer of the transient guest's folio is balanced against the hotel's liability to the travel agency:

Decreases in liabilities, including *taxes* and *accounts payable,* are made with debits.

Although at first it appears to be poor money management, some hotels hold the undeposited check at the front desk. This isn't done if the sum is large or if the reputation of the specific travel agency is bad. Clerical savings can be significant if the check is held. There is no need to maintain and post agency accounts in the back office. Cancellations are easily handled by returning the original check. And a good deal of record verification is reduced because the check and the coupon are processed together.

Why It Doesn't Always Work.   Rarely does the agency reservation work as well in practice as it does in theory. First of all, the agency may not send the check. There may not be time if the reservation was made by telephone. Even if there were time, the agency may not have the check to send. A corporate account, for example, is customarily settled after the trip, not before. So rather than being prepaid, the guest tenders an IOU (the agency's coupon), naively expecting hotel credit for payment that has not yet been made to the agency, let alone to the hotel.

Unless a good credit relationship has been established with the travel agency, this arrangement is not to the hotel's liking. The hotel finds itself in the position of servicing the guest while attempting to collect from a third party. Quite naturally, the agency's voucher is refused unless a credit relationship exists beforehand. To accommodate the guest, the room clerk takes the guest's personal credit card and resolves the voucher issue later.

A full house presents special problems even if the credit relationship is well established. Without a prepaid reservation, the guest finds himself without a room and without a refund. The deposit, if any, is still with the travel agency. Similarly, a guest who stays fewer days than the reservation stated gets no refund even if the room was prepaid; the excess is rebated to the agency.

Situations grow more intense when the guest is carrying a coupon from an overseas agency. International tourists present foreign vouchers that front-office staffers are often unprepared to deal with. Help is available from the International Hotel Association (IHA), which publishes the *World Directory of Travel Agencies*. The IHA also circulates a list of problematic and late-pay agencies. Members who rely on the IHA's material can recover some debt through the association if an agency proves unwilling to pay.

Foreign-exchange companies such as Deak-Perera have clearinghouses that facilitate international exchanges. For a fee (in addition to the foreign funds exchange fee), they will handle the conversion of foreign agency deposits into U.S. funds and commissions paid with U.S. currency into foreign funds. A few international reps (representatives) and even some airlines will also assist with foreign-currency conversions.

Helping to Make It Work.   The clash between agencies and hotels is about up-front money. If the agency prepays the reservation, the system works as designed. If the reservation is not prepaid, everything depends on whether or not the hotel accepts the agency's coupon (voucher). That involves two issues. First, does the guest-service agent recognize the voucher? They are not standardized, even within the United States. Unfamiliar forms, formats, colors, designs, and languages raise questions, which a busy desk finds easier to reject than to answer. Attempts at standardization, even by companies as big as Hilton and Holiday, have floundered on the second issue: the creditworthiness of the travel agency. Credit is simply not granted willy-nilly to the unknown customer of every unknown travel agency.

VISA and CitiCorp, among others, have interposed their financial credibility between hotels and travel agencies, just as they have done with credit cards between hotels and guests. Agencies that are unknown to the hotel can substitute the recognizable logos and accepted financial security of VISA, CitiCorp, and others when making reservations. The hotel is paid by credit-card voucher (VISA) or by check (CitiCorp). Payment is in U.S. funds (local currency elsewhere) on a standardized and recognizable reservation form. Questions about the travel agent's finances are handed off to the intermediary, for a fee.

These reservation vouchers are numbered so travel agencies can guarantee the reservation by telephone using an identifiable number. Individual guests do the very same thing when they guarantee personal reservations with credit-card numbers. In both cases, the interposing companies guarantee collection. Of course, each transaction involves fees. No surprise, that's why the companies are in business. But transferring accounts to the city ledger and cutting commission checks to the travel agents also involve costs to the hotel.

Until now, international travelers have elected to use vouchers in preference to credit cards. To accommodate the cultural differences and to capture the international tourist in the United States, several chains have sold their own vouchers abroad. Foreign guests buy them in packages of 25, perhaps, at a substantial discount. Besides the bargain, the guest feels secure. The chain also gets a bargain by capturing the business since the vouchers can be used only at company properties. Moreover, the chain has an interest-free loan from the prepayment and the possibility of some breakage if all the vouchers are not used. The individual hotel accepts the prepaid voucher, returning it to the chain for remittance as it does with frequent-guest programs.

➤*Frequent-Guest Programs.* The rationale for frequent-guest programs (FGPs) has been discussed several times throughout the book. The mechanics of the programs are equally clear. Guests earn points toward free room nights and sometimes airline points as well. Each stay is validated electronically or, rarely now, manually. Points are earned in every type and class of hotel within the chain, but are usually cashed in at resort destinations. The resort accepts payment with a FGP coupon and looks to the parent company for reimbursement.

Split folios are used to process the award coupons that frequent guests tender. Onto the B folio are posted all the incidental charges. The guest is responsible for these and pays them at check out. The A folio, which contains the room charge, is transferred at check out to the FGP account, a receivable in the city ledger. The chain is billed either for the full rack rate or at a reduced rate agreed to in the FGP contract. Only rarely does the hotel get reimbursement at the rack rate. Rooms have a high profit margin and the parent company knows that. Besides, sales from guest purchases of food and beverage are additional incomes since they are not covered by the voucher. A rooms allowance reduces the amount between the rack rate charged against the guest's award coupon and the rate reimbursed by the parent company. That allowance can be made when the bill is sent to the chain or when payment is received.

FGPs are marketing programs, so every hotel of the chain contributes on a per room basis towards the costs. From the fund come payments for rooms used as well as the sales and administrative expenses. Reimbursement for bad checks is one such expense. FGPs offer check-cashing privileges. Should the check bounce, the hotel transfers the unpaid amount to the chain's city ledger account and bills along with the reimbursable room charge.

Under some FGPs, the monthly amount due the hotel from the chain is offset against the monthly amount due the chain from the hotel: FGP fees and franchise fees. Others keep the several accounts separate, collecting from the FGP on the normal 30-day cycle of city-ledger billing.

Transfers to Guest Folios

Occasionally, though not often, guests with unpaid city-ledger accounts return to the hotel. The balance owed is then transferred *from* the city ledger *to* the guest ledger at the front desk. Shifting accounts in that direction is the opposite of all the other ledger-to-ledger transfers that have been discussed. When this guest checks out, the total debt (that incurred during the current stay and that transferred *to* from the previous stay) is due. Settlement may simply mean another transfer: that of the new total in the usual manner from the guest ledger back to the city ledger. The most frequent use of these *from*-city ledger *to*-guest ledger transfers are advanced deposits.

➤*Advanced Deposits.* Advanced deposits are not city-ledger receivables in the strictest sense. When the guest prepays the reservation, the hotel owes the guest for services that have not yet been delivered. The hotel is the guest's account receivable. With the usual city accounts, the guest is the hotel's receivable. Nevertheless, advanced deposits are frequently handled as city accounts (that is, receivables) rather than hotel debt (that is, payables). It is a contrary receivable, however, so the advanced deposit is a contra (or opposite) receivable. Even when advanced deposits are carried among the receivables in the city ledger, they appear as liabilities (accounts payable) on the balance sheet.

Advanced deposit procedures are simple. The guest or travel agent sends a deposit check, usually one night's lodging plus tax (see Exhibit 10–9, line 1) to confirm the reservation. The hotel deposits the check in its bank account:

Increases in assets, including accounts receivable and *cash*, are made with debits.

Increases in liabilities, including *contra accounts receivable*, are made with credits.

There the advanced deposit remains until the guest arrives some time later. At check in, the advanced deposit is moved *from* the city-ledger's contra account *to* the newly opened guest folio in the front-office ledger (see Exhibit 10–9, line 1):

Decreases in liabilities, including *contra accounts receivable*, are made with debits.

Decreases in assets, including *accounts receivable* and cash, are made with credits.

The opening credit balance of Exhibit 10–9 starts the relationship with the receivable reduced below zero, that is, a contra receivable where the hotel owes the guest! The hotel will continue to owe the guest until the charges offset the advanced deposit (see Exhibit 10–9, line 4).

Reservations guaranteed by credit cards are not advanced deposits! No cash has been received, and no city-ledger account is opened when the reservation is made. The credit card is charged after the fact, if at all; only if the reservation proves to be a no-show. If the guest arrives, the guarantee has met its purpose, and the folio is handled in the usual manner.

City-Ledger Postings without Transfers

Many guests, whether registered or not, use credit cards to pay for food and beverage services. These credit-card charges become part of the departmental cashiers' daily turn-in (see Chapter 11). As such, they go directly to the accounting office, bypassing the front office and bypassing the ledger-to-ledger transfers that have been discussed. How the accounting office processes these credit-card charges depends on the type of credit-card system in place. Most hotels have replaced the manual slips with electronic capture.

➤ *Manual Charge Slips.* If the hotel still uses the manual credit-card form (see Exhibit 12–8), departmental cashiers process each on an imprinter, get the guest's signature, and include the signed slips as part of the turn-in. These signed slips are separated by type (MasterCard, VISA, etc.) in the accounting office. Then they are batched and bundled, usually in groups of 100 vouchers. As a total, the bundle is posted to the credit-card company's account receivable and forwarded with a transmittal form (see Exhibit 12–8). The accounting entry charges the credit-card company and records the income from the departmental outlet:

Increases in assets, including *accounts receivable* and cash, are made with debits.

Increases in *incomes* (sales of rooms, food, beverage, etc.) are made with credits.

Periodically, the T&E companies reimburse the hotel less fees. With bank cards, the slips are deposited the next day—no need to mail them off—so the funds are available sooner. In both cases the hotel's bank account increases from converting the charge slips into cash less discount fees:

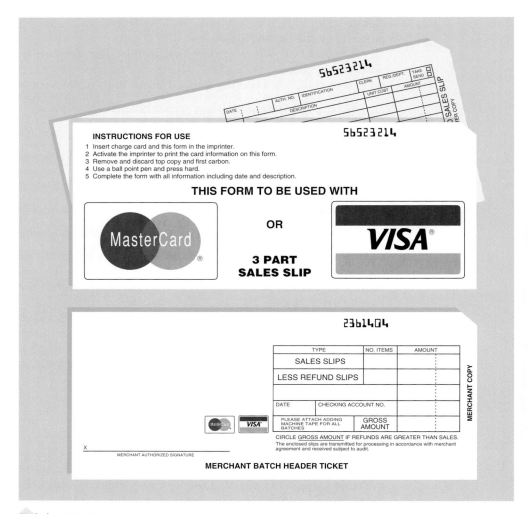

Exhibit 12–8   Manual charge slips for credit cards are still in use. The top slip is signed by the guest, who takes away one copy. The merchant/hotel retains one slip and bundles the third copy in packages, which are shipped to the credit-card company accompanied by *batch header tickets* (bottom form).

Increases in assets, including accounts receivable and *cash*, are made with debits.

Increases in expenses, including *discount fees*, are made with debits.

Decreases in assets, including *accounts receivable* and cash, are made with credits.

Accounting offices usually separate credit-card chargebacks from the original receivables in the packet of vouchers. The chargeback is transferred from the old city account to a new one:

Increases in assets, including *accounts receivable* and cash, are made with debits.

Decreases in assets, including *accounts receivable* and cash, are made with credits.

Identifying them separately helps focus attention on the need for special collection efforts. If the hotel fails to act within 30 days, and even if it does, the new account often becomes a bad debt.

➤*Electronic Draft Capture.*   The communication highway has brought significant changes in the handling of credit-card charges. Guests encounter manual charge slips less and less. Instead, the electronic verification of the card's authenticity (swiping the card through the reader) is followed by an electronic printout of the charges. A slip of paper (see Exhibit 12–9), looking much like the tape of an old-fashioned adding machine, is presented for signature. One copy goes to the guest; the second copy remains with the hotel or merchant as part of the cashier's departmental turn-in.

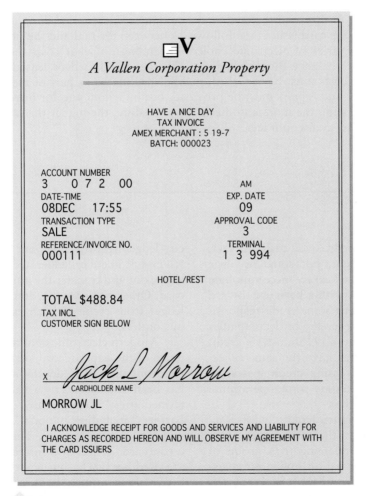

Exhibit 12–9   Pencil-and-paper forms for credit cards (see Exhibit 12–8) have been replaced almost entirely by electronic terminals (see Exhibit 12–1) and connections that verify the card and process the charge quickly and individually (no batch packaging), even across the globe. Although the charge is transmitted electronically, both the hotel and the guest carry away a receipt that looks like an old-fashioned adding machine tape.

What happens with the charge slips is more visible but less important than how it happens. The charge is captured electronically (EDT, electronic draft capture) by the credit-card company. EDT eliminates postage, paper sales drafts, and the batch handling and sorting that accompanies manual city-ledger posting. Communicating with the financial institution through an electronic process also means quicker access to the funds. Besides, credit-card companies reduce the interchange rate (merchant discount fees) for electronic transactions.

Speedy electronic data, much of it by laser imaging, represents additional float for the credit-card company. The earlier that the charge appears on the customer's monthly statement, the sooner the credit-card company gets paid. All credit cards have electronic capture by one of several means.

Dial and touch-tone terminals can be used for credit-card authorization. EFT-POS on-line processing is the other end of the technology. Swiping the card through the terminal obtains the authorization at registration and interfaces the hotel's computer (PMS) with the credit-card computer. Electronic billing and ultimate collection from the card issuer then follows. In between the dial and the on-line interface options are a series of electronic choices depending on what costs the hotel can absorb or counterbalance through savings. Whether purchased or leased, equipment and software costs must be absorbed, perhaps negotiated as part of the discount fee. Maintenance and repairs must be provided, but by whom and for how much is also at issue. In general, the more automatic the procedure, the higher the costs but the greater the savings in discount fees.

➤ SUMMARY

Today's travelers prefer credit over cash. In fact, they see credit as their right, not some privilege granted by the seller. Hotelkeepers accommodate this business fact of life but with a keen eye toward credit management. Assigning some credit responsibilities to third parties, the credit-card companies chiefly, reduces some of the hotel industry's credit woes. Credit-card companies have the same objectives (increasing sales, decreasing credit losses) as the lodging industry, and despite some operational irritations, work closely with it.

Hotels track and bill their credit guests (accounts receivable) through the city ledger. *City ledger* is an easy way of referring to a group of records that contains information about nonregistered persons who owe the hotel for services. Hotels provide rooms, food, beverages, and other services to a variety of city-ledger identities. Among them are banquet and convention groups, travel agents, companies, individuals, including the hotel's own executives, and frequent-guest participants. Most

city-ledger records start out as front-office folios, which become city-ledger accounts when the guests check out and transfer the amounts owed to a credit card. Other city accounts come directly into the city ledger from credit-card charges in the hotel's various outlets.

Modern electronic communication has replaced much of the paper record keeping that once plagued the front desk. The development of this capability has been undertaken by a variety of third-party intermediaries. Lodging now has numerous credit partners, including national credit-card companies and banking institutions. They issue two classes of credit card. Travel and entertainment cards (T&Es) are used heavily by businesses and individuals with better credit ratings. Bank cards are in more widespread use. The two types continue to borrow ideas from one another, so their differences are blurring. Credit cards have become essential and inseparable in the hotel's management of its credit.

➤ QUESTIONS AND PROBLEMS

1. Write two dialogues for a training manual that is to be used by guest-service agents at the front desk. Include the questions posed by a room clerk seeking additional credit information and the responses made by a guest. What disposition does the room clerk make when (a) a walk-in guest arrives with no baggage?; (b) a same-day reservation arrives, but no information has been provided previously?

2. Explain how the following transfers should be handled. Be specific, citing the location of the entry, the ledger or ledgers involved, and the debit or credit requirements.

   (a) A transient guest checks out using a national credit card.

   (b) The president and treasurer of a small company check in for a business meeting. The hotel has been carrying the unpaid balance of a charge generated by these officers at their last business meeting about three months ago.

   (c) A couple departs and requests that the balance of the folio be charged to the couple's parents, who are registered in another room. The parents concur.

   (d) An association completes its meeting and the association executive, after reviewing the balance due, requests billing to the group's headquarters.

3. In terms of the front office and of the city ledger, explain the quick check-out system used by numerous hotels.

4. Many older hotels in the area in which your resort is located have suffered for years from a seasonal influx of skippers and room burglary gangs operating with stolen keys. (Few of these old properties have modern locks.) The local hotel association has asked you to draft a plan for a security network that could be implemented before the next season. Prepare the plan, providing details of the procedure by explaining the roles of the individuals or groups involved.

5. In terms of the front office and of the city ledger, explain how a reservation request from a travel agent is processed if (a) the agency has a good credit relationship with the hotel and the guest pays the agency; (b) the agency has no credit rating with the hotel, and the guest pays the agency; and (c) the guest makes no payment to the agency.

6. A noticeable squeeze on profits had brought the management team to a brainstorming session. One idea is put forth by the controller. Noting the large amount of credit-card business that the hotel is doing, the controller suggests that each tip charged to a credit card be reduced by 4.77% when paid to the employee. (That amount is the average discount fee the hotel is paying to all the credit-card companies.) The controller further suggests that an additional 1.1% be subtracted, representing the percentage of credit-card charges that prove uncollectible. What comments would the food and beverage manager be apt to make? The rooms manager?

➤ NOTES

1. Trademark names are used throughout the chapter.

2. Although not as well known, there are off-line debit cards that have a two- to three-day lag time.

3. With 80% of its market in group/convention business, the Opryland Hotel (Nashville, TN) processes between 80 and 90 group master accounts daily! "Leaping

Over the Paper Chase," *CKC Report,* July–August 1993, p. 7.

4. Travel agency coupons (or vouchers) are different from marketing coupons (distributed as promotional discounts) and tour group coupons (used as tickets for admission and meals).

Rooms Management Technology

Converting hotels from a labor-intensive industry to an electronic-intensive industry has just begun. Rooms management technology is very young relative to the age and maturity of the lodging industry. Moreover, the pace of technological advances is just beginning to accelerate. New devices are constantly being introduced and older ones are being refined. Early innovations such as automated elevators and telephones and electronic room keys were the forerunners of new products that will change the method of managing hotels. Success in the electronic processing of data, which did not come easily to the hotel industry, is now the base for an expanded use of electronics in other, nonclerical areas of operations.

The industry's first need and its earliest efforts at technology, the property management system (PMS), was directed toward the front desk. Paperwork inundated the desk, where labor-intensive tasks led to errors of omission and commission. Early property management systems borrowed from applications in other industries, but failed to do the job. High hopes became reality when suppliers recognized the size of the market and began to invest research dollars for special, hotel systems. The efforts eventually produced reliable and inexpensive programs that reduced paperwork, increased accuracy, and improved reporting. Although not at first, there were also labor savings eventually. Today, costs have fallen low enough for practically every hotel of any size, class, type, or plan to have some sort of PMS.

In the first chapter of this final section we explain the PMS in terms of the night audit. At the same time, we offer a glimpse of the old pencil-and-paper audit in an effort to explain not only the procedure but also the purpose of the audit. Including both systems continues the approach set down in Chapter 10, where guest billing was discussed using both hand-prepared and electronically prepared folios. Whichever the method, the night audit audits what has taken place at the desk during the preceding day. Both systems uncover and correct errors in guest billing and prepare reports for management's use the following day. The PMS does the job faster, with less labor, and with greater accuracy.

On the horizon is the next application of the PMS: improved guest services through more complete information. All industries strive to know more about their customers. Information gathering, storage, and retrieval systems will put guest information at the fingertips of management. We've already seen the beginning of it in frequent-guest programs. We've already discussed it in the smart cards that are gradually being introduced. Technology will graduate from the routine posting and auditing of room rates and taxes (Chapter 13) to a powerful aid for helping managers run an ever-increasing complex, the modern hotel.

Chapter 14 looks at some of the first results of this emerging technology. Among them are call-accounting systems, in-room television, on-demand films, safe-deposit accessibility, in-room vending, and telecommunications. Guests who once selected hotels on the basis of swimming pools and bath amenities are starting to choose on the basis of sophisticated television-based entertainment, and in-room business centers. There soon will be other criteria that we cannot even foresee at this time. And the speed of change will be, indeed, as rapid as it is always forecasted to be. Just a brief few years ago, the centralized business center was the ultimate for commercial hotels; today, the equipment is in the guest's own room, and the center is no more.

The Night Audit

Outline

The hotel's day ends with the night audit, often referred to simply as the audit. The night-auditing crew—in a small hotel, no more than a single person—works the desk's final shift and closes the records of the day. The audit reconciles the accounting activities of the past day and provides information for the issues of the upcoming day. What night auditors do and how they do it have changed dramatically since the introduction of electronic data processing (EDP) to the front desk. EDP has altered the focus and changed the procedure. Prior to the introduction of computers, the audit concentrated on uncovering errors. There are fewer errors with the PMS, and finding them is easier, so management reporting has become the new emphasis.

➤ THE AUDITOR AND THE AUDIT

As all previous discussions have stressed, keeping records for the front office and meeting guests' expectations demand attention to the smallest details. Doing so with a pencil-and-paper system is a tedious task made more difficult as the hotel's size increases. The introduction of property management systems in the last quarter of the 20th Century had the same results as the introduction of structural steel during the last half of the 19th Century. In Chapter 1 we pointed out that structural steel enabled hoteliers to build upward on expensive urban land, moving the industry from a few dozen rooms to a few hundred rooms. Electronic data processing has facilitated the move from hundreds of rooms to thousands of rooms. PMSs ensure the integrity of the front-office record system no matter how large the property.

The Night Auditor

Despite the title, the night auditor is rarely a trained accountant and is an auditor only by the broadest definition. In general terms, an *auditor* is an appraiser–reporter of the accuracy and integrity of records and financial statements. One type of auditing, internal auditing, involves procedural control and an accounting review of operations and records. Internal auditing also reports on the activities of other employees. It is this final definition that best explains the role of the hotel night auditor.

No special knowledge of accounting or even of bookkeeping's debits and credits is required of the night auditor. Having this knowledge is helpful and desirable, but it is sufficient for the auditor to have good arithmetic skills, self-discipline, and a penchant for detailed work. Auditors must be careful, accurate, and reliable. The latter trait is an especially redeeming one because the unattractive working hours make replacements difficult to recruit and almost impossible to find on short notice.

➤**Work Shift.** At large hotels, the audit crew arrives sometime between 11 PM and midnight and finishes about 7 or 8 the next morning. That is, of course, the traditional graveyard shift. Since the work they do in the late-night/early-morning hours is the basis of the front-office work on the following day, night auditors must remain until the audit job is completed, regardless of the hour.

The graveyard shift at the small hotel is the very same hours, except the night auditor of the small hotel also relieves the swing watch (approximately 4 PM to midnight) at the front desk. In turn, the auditor is relieved the following morning by the arrival of the day shift (approximately 8 AM to 4 PM).

➤**General Duties.** The audit staff of a large hotel consists of a senior auditor and assistants. A separate night crew handles the usual duties of the desk, freeing the auditors to perform their functions without interruption. In a small hotel, a single auditor relieves the entire desk, filling the jobs of reservationist, room clerk, cashier, telephone operator, and auditor. Whether or not auditors assume these front-office tasks, they must be conversant with them. It is those very duties that the night audit audits.

When the actual tasks are taken on, the night auditor is likely to be the only responsible employee on duty. The auditor assumes the position of night manager whether the title is there or not. The same range of problems faced by the day manager is involved, but to a lesser degree. Emergencies, credit, mechanical breakdowns, accidents, and deaths are some of the situations encountered by the night manager.

Security and incident reports must be filed by either the night auditor/manager alone or cooperatively with the security staff. Without a security contingent, the auditor may be the one who walks security rounds and fire watch.

Few hotels of less than 150 rooms employ a night engineer. Yet management has generally been lax in preparing the night auditor/manager for the problems that arise in this area of responsibility. Fire, plumbing problems, power failures, elevator mishaps, and boiler troubles are matters that take the auditor's time.

Equally time consuming are guest relations: a noisy party going into the early hours of the morning; the victorious football team shouting in the lobby; a sick guest; visiting conventioneers in the 11th-floor suite; paid reservations yet to arrive and the hotel 100% occupied. Such are the nonaccounting matters for which the night auditor might be responsible.

Mature judgment and experience are needed to carry out these nonaudit functions. The combination of audit skills, working hours, and responsibility merit a higher salary for the night auditor than for the average guest–service agent, but the spread is not noticeably larger.

The Audit

The night audit is an audit of accounts receivable. Cash sales made in the food, beverage, and other outlets of the hotel are not included in the night audit. During the audit, the accounting activities of the previous day are reconciled, balanced, and closed. The audit verifies the balances of the accounts receivable, summarizes the revenue data from sales to accounts receivable, monitors the balances of individual folios, and creates managerial and operational reports.

▶ *Reconciling Accounts Receivable.*   Every business that extends credit to customers reconciles accounts receivable periodically. Whereas other retail establishments close and balance their accounts monthly, hotels do the job nightly. The accuracy and completeness of each guest folio is verified during the night audit.

Hotel auditors lack the luxury of time because hotel keeping is a very transient business. Arrivals and departures keep coming and going without notice at all hours of the day and night. Each new day brings more charges and more credits whether or not the previous day has been reconciled. There is no holding a departing guest until the folio is ready. The night audit must make certain that it always is ready.

The pressure of immediacy is missing with city-ledger guests. City-ledger guests are not registered, so their billing cycle is more like the accounts receivable of other businesses. Depending on the nature of the original charge, city receivables are billed for the first time three days—sometimes 10 days—after the charge is incurred.

Both city and transient guests are receivables and, therefore, part of the night audit, which deals only with receivables. Cash sales are not posted to folios, as earlier chapters have explained. Cash sales are verified by the income auditor, sometimes called the day auditor, in conjunction with the general cashier. Receivable sales pass through the night audit to the same income audit. Both types of sales (cash and credit) are combined in the income audit and recorded ultimately in the sales journal.

The income (or revenue) auditor completes the income audit as early as possible each morning. Among the auditor's final tasks is a daily report to the manager. This report replaces a similar report prepared by the night auditor the previous evening. Except, the night auditor's report, which is described in the final pages of this chapter, reflects charge sales only, not total revenues.

➤ *The Closeout Hour.*   The night audit reviews the records of a single day. Since hotels never close, management selects an arbitrary hour, the *closeout hour* (also called the *close of the day*), to officially end one day and start the next. The actual time selected depends on the operating hours of the lounges, restaurants, and room service of the particular hotel. Each new charge changes the folio, so the audit is prepared when changes are infrequent—in the early morning hours when guests are abed. Departmental charges before the closeout hour are included in today's records. Departmental charges after the closeout hour are posted to the folio on the following date after the night audit has been completed.

A late closeout hour captures the last of the day's charges, but it puts pressure on the auditing staff, which needs to finish the job before the early departures begin leaving. On the other hand, too early a closeout hour throws all the charges of the late evening into the following day, in effect, delaying their audit for 24 hours. Standardized stationery forms list midnight as the closeout hour (see Exhibit 10–6), but the actual time is set by management.

➤ *Posting Room Charges Manually.*   Posting (recording) room charges is one of the night auditor's major tasks. Before the advent of the PMS, room charges were posted manually. That required each folio to be removed one by one from the cashier's well (see Exhibit 10–3). The room charge and the room tax were recorded in pencil, the column totaled, and the folio returned to the well in room number sequence. Exhibit 13–1 illustrates the results on a manual folio: $60 recorded on the horizontal line labeled "rooms" and $3 for the tax. The $78 and $6.24 posted in Exhibit 10–2 offers a second illustration.

Once the room charge and tax are posted, the night auditor adds the column, which includes the previous day's total. (The second columns of Exhibits 13–1 and 10–2 illustrate the addition.) The new balance is carried forward from the bottom of the column to the top of the column of the following day. In this manner a cumulative balance is maintained, and the manual folio is ready at any time for the departing guest.

Included in the cumulative total are departmental charges other than room. These are posted throughout the day by the front-office staff as the charges arrive at the front desk from the operating departments. Exhibit 13–1 shows these as food, bar, and garage. Garage is a cash paid-out made by the hotel to the garage for the guest.

Manual System Errors.   In a manual system, figures are recorded with pencil and paper again and again. The dollar amount, the room number, and the guest's name are written on the voucher and the control sheet by the outlet cashier and on the folio by the front-office cashier. And that is not the end. The night auditor records the room rate by hand, totals the folios, and copies them onto the audit sheet (the transcript). Writing, rewriting, and adding each figure creates numerous human errors that a property management system avoids when it is on-line with point-of-sale terminals.

					#8001	

THE CITY HOTEL
ANYWHERE, U.S.A.

NAME _____ B. M. Oncampus _____

ADDRESS _____ 1 Campus Rd., University City _____

ROOM NUMBER _____ 1406 _____ RATE _____ 60 _____

NUMBER IN THE PARTY _____ 1 _____ CLERK _____ ABC _____

DATE OF ARRIVAL _____ 10/5 _____ DATE OF DEPARTURE _____ 10/7 _____

CHANGES: ROOM NO. _____ TO ROOM NO. _____ NEW RATE _____

DATE	10/5	10/6	10/7			
BAL.FWD		(19)	70			
ROOMS	60	60				
TAX	3	3				
FOOD	10	12				
BAR		6				
TELEPH						
LAUNDRY						
CASH DISBR GARAGE	8	8				
TRANSFERS						
TOT CHRG	81	70				
CASH						
ALLOWANCES						
TRANSFERS	100					
TOT CRDS	100					
BAL DUE	(19)	70				

Exhibit 13–1 Pencil-and-paper folios are still in use despite the falling cost and the user friendliness of property management systems. Writing and rewriting dollar-and-cent values, which pencil-and-paper folios require, lead to numerous human errors that become the main focus of the manual audit. Charges are separated daily by dated, vertical columns, which are copied onto the transcript each night (trace Exhibit 13–1 on to 13–4 line 1). (Note the credit balance on October 6.)

Additional errors are inherent in the manual system. Poor handwriting is the most obvious one. When handwritten, figures 1 and 7, 4 and 9, and 3 and 8 are often confused. Recopying also causes slides and transpositions. Slides are misplaced units, which may involve decimals. Saying 53 21 mentally or aloud may result in either 53.21 or 5,321 being recorded. Transpositions are similar errors, but the digits are reordered—53.21 may become 35.21.

Even simple addition causes problems. The auditor may create errors by incorrectly totaling the folios, the control sheet, or the packets of vouchers. Adding machines help, but there is no guarantee that the figures are accurately entered. Hand audits still require adding-machine tapes to allow comparison between the actual figures and those entered into the calculator.

Subtracting one total from another highlights the error. Errors of addition usually appear as differences of 1 in the unit columns. If the difference in the totals is 1 cent, 10 cents, $1, $10, and so on, the culprit is likely to be an error of addition. If not an error of addition, it might be a slide or transposition. Slides and transpositions are flagged when the difference in the total is evenly divisible by 9. For example, the difference between 53.21 and 35.21 is 18, evenly divisible by 9. Searching for mistakes begins by looking for errors of addition or transpositions and slides.

▶*Posting Room Charges Electronically.*   Posting room charges electronically is faster and easier than posting manually. There are no folios and there is no bucket. Time is saved in not removing and not replacing 100 or 300, or 1,000 folios from the well. Room charges with the appropriate tax have been programmed into the computer. Memory knows how much each room is to be billed, and the proper tax is automatically computed: No math errors here. Individual postings and folio totaling are not required. Activating the audit program brings all the accounts receivable up-to-date in memory, although most hotels will also get a nightly printout, a hard copy, for emergency backup (see Exhibit 13–2).

Folio totals accumulate as they do with the manual system. Included in the cumulative total are departmental charges other than room. Unlike the manual system, these are not posted throughout the day by the front-office staff. With a POS (see Exhibit 13–3), the departmental charges (vouchers) do not come to the front desk. Postings are done electronically by the departmental cashier into computer memory. With a PMS, folios are not even visible. Everything is maintained in computer mem-

---

THE CITY HOTEL, ANYWHERE, U.S.A.   Page 1
03/16   Guest Ledger Summary Report

Room #	Name	Folio #	Open Bal	Charges	Credits	Close Bal
3004	Huent	0457	–0–	81.30	.00	81.30
3005	Wanake	0398	65.72	91.44	.00	157.16
3008	Lee	0431	132.00	101.01	.00	233.01
3110	Langden	0420	–0–	99.87	100.00	0.13–
3111	Nelston	0408	233.65	145.61	.00	379.26
3117	O'Harra	0461	789.75	121.10	.00	910.85
6121	Chiu	0444	32.60–	99.87	.00	67.27
6133	Valex	0335	–0–	165.30	.00	165.30
7003	Roberts	0428	336.66	109.55	.00	446.21
7009	Haittenberg	0454	19.45	87.43	.00	106.88
Totals			44,651.07	18,632.98	950.00	62,334.05

Exhibit 13–2   A hard (printed) copy of closing folio totals is prepared nightly as part of the PMS audit to be used if the property management system fails during the following day. Each column has a corresponding column on the hand-prepared transcript.

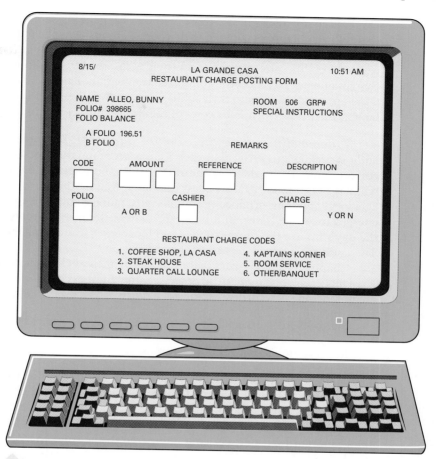

Exhibit 13–3   A display mask on the POS screen guides the departmental cashier through the posting sequence. Without a POS, posting is done at the front desk from pencil-and-paper vouchers sent there by the departmental cashiers.

ory. Guests can view the data from their in-room television sets; staff can view the data from their front-office screens. Copies can always be printed, of course.

Room Charges Not Posted by the Auditor.   Normally, room charges are posted by the night auditor. Infrequently, and then only because of three special circumstances, room and tax are posted by the day crew, not by the night auditor. In two of the instances, the auditor is simply not there at the time the charge is to be posted. The first of these involves guests who arrive and depart the same day, called *day rate, use rate,* or *part day rate guests.* These guests arrive during the day after the previous night's audit has been finished. They depart before the night audit of the following day. Since the folio is opened and closed without any intervening audit, the room charge, which is often less than a full night's rate, must be posted by the day watch.

Extra room charges for late check outs are the second special case. Brief extensions to the check-out hour are usually accommodated without charge when space allows. Extraordinary delays, or even brief occupancy when demand is high, incur late-departure charges, occasionally as much as a full night's rate. Here again, the guest leaves before the arrival of the graveyard shift, so the front-office cashier posts the charges and collects the total folio at check out.

Paid-in-advance guests, those without baggage or satisfactory credit, pay room charges even before occupying their rooms. Hotels receipt the payment with copies of the folio showing the room charge plus tax and the balancing payment. The cashier who collects the prepayment and provides the receipted folio needs to post the room charges in order to reflect the completed transaction. Paid-in-advance guests are not permitted to make charges to their folios and usually leave the following day without stopping at the desk. The hotel's copy of the transaction is available to the night auditor.

► *Reconciling Revenues before Property Management Systems.* The audit is designed to prove that each folio is accurate, that guests have been charged the correct amounts. By the time the audit begins, hundreds or even thousands of charges will have been made against guest accounts. Among them are charges for food; beverage; local and long-distance telephone calls; laundry and valet; cash advances; in-room charges for films, safes, and bars; greens fees; saunas; ski-tows; and more. Added to the day's list are the room charges and local taxes just completed by the night auditor. The audit must prove the accuracy of all.

Chapter 10 emphasized that every departmental charge has equal debits and credits. Thus each time a guest buys service, the guest account is charged and the departmental income is recorded:

Increases in assets, including *accounts receivable* and cash, are made with debits.

Increases in *incomes* (sales of rooms, food, beverage, etc.) are made with credits.

The mathematical rule that the total is equal to the sum of its parts has application here. The audit proves that the total of all the income earned by the department, say room service, equals the total of all the individual charges made on guest folios for room service. After the closeout hour, the audit reconciles the two totals. The total sales reported by room service is compared to the total charges made on guest folios. It's done easily with a property management system, less so with a pencil-and-paper system.

With a property management system, separating and totaling departmental charges are not difficult tasks—the computer does them. Charges are posted to the individual folio from the point-of-sale terminal and, simultaneously, accumulated by department: food, beverage, telephone, and so on. With one entry at the POS, the hotel charges the guest and tracks the sales of each department. As required, the computer spits out the information: the individual folio, the income of the single department, the total of all folio balances, and the total of all departmental incomes.

Manual folio systems are more demanding than property management systems. Each departmental posting (bar, restaurant, and paid-outs, for example) is recorded on the folio (see Exhibit 13–1), but there is no electronic total. Therefore, the night auditor must obtain that total by adding up the departmental postings made to the individual folios. What is done instantaneously by the electronic PMS is a long and tedious task when done by hand on a transcript sheet.

The Hand Transcript. The transcript is used to separate the charges that appear as accounts receivable on the many folios into separate incomes by individual departments. The PMS does that electronically. The transcript does it manually. Once separated—broken apart by department charges—it is a simple task to compare the sales totals of each department to the total sum recorded on the folios. "Once separated" is the operative phrase.

Let's review the sequence of the manual audit. The night auditor comes on duty, posts all the vouchers that arrive before the closeout hour, posts the room charges and tax, adds the folios, and carries the balances forward (see Exhibit 13–1). The transcript is the next step.

In room number sequence, each folio is copied onto a large spreadsheet (see Exhibit 13–4). Lines that appear horizontally on the folio (see Exhibit 13–1) are vertical columns on the transcript. Follow the October 6 column of Exhibit 13–1 onto the first horizontal line of Exhibit 13–4.) Thus, there is a transcript column for each department—rooms, taxes, food, and so on—just as there is a horizontal line for these

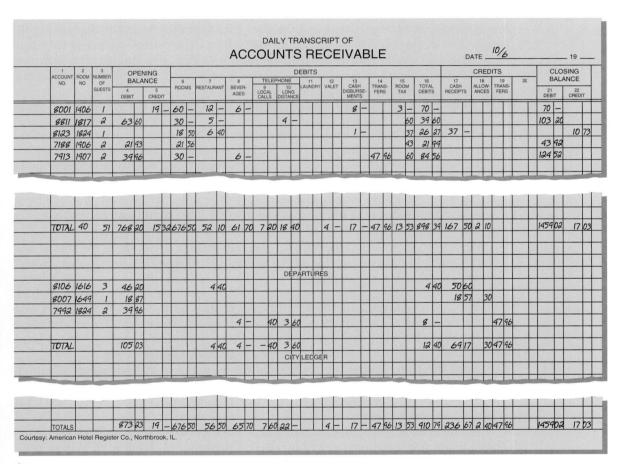

Exhibit 13–4 The transcript sheet is prepared by the night auditor, who copies the vertical column of each folio (see Exhibit 13–1, October 6) onto a horizontal line (see line 1) of the transcript. This separates departmental incomes by columns, allowing the totals to be verified against the income reported on the departmental control sheet. Two methods of transcribing the transcript are mixed here for instructional purposes. Only one would be used at any one time. Line 1 (the folio of Exhibit 13–1) includes the opening balance (columns 4 and 5) in the total of column 16. The rest of the exhibit illustrates the second approach, in which column 16 represents only the debits of the day (columns 6–15), without the opening balance. The closing balance (columns 21 minus 22) is the same with both methods. [The values used in the exhibit are unrealistically small in order to improve the clarity of the presentation.]

departments on the folio. As each folio is copied across the sheet, the departmental charges are separated by the vertical columns.

When all the folios, including the day's departures, are copied onto the transcript—and that may take several transcript sheets—the night audit is back to the basic premise: Do the totals of the columns, which are the sum of the postings to the individual folios, agree to the charges originating in the departments, as shown on the control sheets?

Although the form of the control sheet differs somewhat in the several departments (in some instances, only the cash register tape is available), the method of proving departmental charges is identical department to department.

Vouchers from the various departments arrive at the desk all during the day. After being posted, each voucher is marked to lessen the chance of duplicating the charge. Next, the checks (vouchers) are sorted by departments—a job made easier with different colors for each department—and filed into pigeonholes. There they remain for the night auditor, who totals them on an adding machine. The adding machine tape is then attached to the pile of vouchers.

Three different totals are available to the auditor for each department:

1. The total derived from the departmental control sheet. Each time a guest charges a departmental service to the folio, the departmental cashier makes an entry on the control sheet. At the end of the day, this sheet is totaled and forwarded to the night auditor.
2. The total on the adding machine tape of the individual vouchers, which have arrived at the desk one at a time. These are the communicative devices between the departmental cashier and the front-office billing clerk.
3. The total posted to the folio for that department. This total is the sum of the postings made to the folios. The auditor gets that value from the departmental column of the transcript.

If the system is working, the departmental control sheet (which records the event) has a total equal to the vouchers (which communicate the event) and to the folios (which are the ultimate record of the event). If the system isn't working, one or more of the totals will be out of balance. Then the night auditor goes to work.

If the three totals agree, the auditor moves on to the next department. When one of the figures fails to reconcile, the audit begins in earnest as the auditor searches for errors. If two of the three totals agree, the search is concentrated on the unequal total, among several likely causes.

Mistakes in mathematics account for a large portion of the errors. The major ones—slides, transpositions, and additions—were explained earlier in this chapter.

When the control sheet figure is larger than the other two balances, the auditor searches for a lost check. If the check was posted and then lost, the check (voucher) total will be the smallest of the three totals.

Too small a transcript figure for several columns suggests a folio was left off the transcript, so its missing values are having an impact on all the departments. Simple oversights like this seem less simple in the early morning hours. Then, a check omitted from the departmental control sheet or a voucher filed before it was posted means long minutes of searching by the weary auditor.

Vouchers posted to the correct department but to the wrong guest account will not be evident to the auditor. All three totals will agree even though the wrong guest account is charged. This is not so with the reverse situation—when the charge is made to the proper folio but to the wrong department. Then the audit total will be out of balance with the voucher total and the total of that particular departmental control sheet. Of course, the other department—the one that received the extra posting—will be out of balance by the same amount, providing a clue to the error.

One error, special to the pencil-and-paper folio, is particularly difficult to find. It occurs when a departmental posting is recorded in the column of a previous day. The posting clerk inadvertently posts a current charge to a previous day. Having been posted to a folio column that has already been balanced, the charge doesn't even appear on the transcript, which is a copy of the current day's folio column. Transcript totals that are smaller than voucher and control sheet totals highlight this error. Finding it requires the auditor to sort the departmental vouchers by room number sequence and search down the transcript column, which is also in room number sequence. Matching the vouchers against the transcript entries uncovers the error.

It is sometimes easy to forget that reconciling the three balances is not the purpose of the audit. Reconciling balances is only a means to the end. As each error is uncovered, the record must be corrected. Either the folio is changed or departmental sales are restated, or both. Making the corrections ensures the guest of an accurate billing and determines the exact revenues of each department. As errors are uncovered, corrections are made and the audit moves to the next department.

Proving Room Charges with the Hand Audit.   Unlike the charges in other departments, room charges originate at the desk. Since no interdepartmental communication is needed, there is no control sheet and no package of vouchers. Instead, the rooms column (that is, the room sales column) of the transcript, which is the sum of the folios, is tested against the room rack. The information on both the room rack and the folio originates with the same source, the registration cards. Therefore, the information on each is identical. Summarizing the individual folios on the transcript should produce the same total as summarizing the information from the room rack.

The *room count sheet,* also called a *daily rooms report* or a *night clerk's report,* is prepared from the room rack (see Exhibit 13–5). It is a permanent record of room occupancy at the close of the day. Three informational items are taken from the rack: the number of rooms occupied, the number of persons in each occupied room, and the rate paid for each room. Identical information is copied from the folios onto the transcript: the number of rooms occupied (see column 2 of Exhibit 13–4), the number of persons in each room (column 3 of Exhibit 13–4), and the rate paid for each room (column 6). When the columns are added, the totals must agree with the corresponding totals on the room count sheet. When they do not agree, the auditor searches for and corrects the underlying error.

The Housekeeper's Report.   Further verification of room status comes from the housekeeper's report. Housekeeping forwards the report to the desk once or twice each day. Using a generally accepted set of abbreviations, housekeeping reports the status of guest rooms to the desk. Occupied rooms are indicated by checkmarks or lines (see Exhibit 13–6). *Sleep-outs,* rooms with baggage but no occupants, are flagged with a *B.* Occupied rooms with no baggage or light baggage are shown with an × mark. Other codes (see Exhibit 13–7) mix handwritten symbols with alphanumeric symbols, which have been adopted from property management systems.

Discrepancies between the housekeeper's report and room status at the desk are investigated by the front office or the housekeeping staff. Sometimes a bellperson (the last) is dispatched to look at the room and report back. The credit manager is espe-

| OCCUPANCY AND ROOM REVENUE REPORT | **Hotel Gary** | DAY _Monday_ | DATE _9-18-_ |

EAST WING

ROOM	No Guests	RATE	ROOM	No Guests	RATE		ROOM	No Guests	RATE		ROOM	No Guests	RATE	ROOM	No Guests	RATE	ROOM	No Guests	RATE
3101			3319				3615				3910			4206			4501		
3102			3320				3616				3912			4207			4502		
3103			S3322	4	80		3617				3914			4208			4503		
3104			3401				3618				3915			4210			4504		
3105			3402	2	66		3619				3916			4212			4505		
3106			3403	2	66		3620				3917			4214			4506		
3107			3404				S3622				3918			4215			4507		
3108			3405	2	68		3701				3919			4216			4508		
3110			3406				3702				3920			4217			4510		
3112			3407				3703				S3922			4218			4512		
3114			3408	1	58	—	3704				4001			4219			4514		
3115			3410				3705				4002			4220			4515		
3116			3412	3	72		3706				4003			S4222			4516		
3117			3414	1	59	50	3707				4004			4301			4517		
3118			3415	3	66	—	3708				4005			4302			4518		

ROOM	No Guests	RATE	ROOM	No Guests	RATE		ROOM	No Guests	RATE		ROOM	No Guests	RATE	ROOM	No Guests	RATE	ROOM	No Guests	RATE
3312			3606	2	66		3903				S4122			4418			4712		
3314			3607	2	66		3904				4201			4419			4714		
3315			3608	3	71		3905				4202			4420			4715		
3316			3610	1	66		3906				4203			S4422			4716		
3317			3612				3907				4204						4717		
3318			3614				3908				4205						4718		
TOTAL			TOTAL	57	3,731	00	TOTAL				TOTAL			TOTAL			TOTAL		

Exhibit 13–5   The manual room count sheet reports the status of the house (number of occupied rooms by how many persons paying what rate) at the closeout hour of each day. A similar report is prepared during the electronic audit.

HOUSEKEEPER'S DAILY REPORT

Kayco Form No. 1209   DATE _10-6_   19 __

ROOM NO.	OCCUPIED	VACANT	BAGGAGE	BED USED	ROOM NO.	OCCUPIED	VACANT	BAGGAGE	BED USED	ROOM NO.	OCCUPIED	VACANT	BAGGAGE	BED USED
2529	/				3517	/				4211	⁵⁄₀			
2530	/				3518	/				4212	⁵⁄₀			
2531		⁽ᶜ⁄₀			3519	/				4213		/		
2532		/			3520	/				4214	P			
2533			B		3521	/				4215			/	
2534		/			3522		⁽ᶜ⁄₀			4216		/		
2535		/												

Exhibit 13–6   Using symbols (see Exhibit 13–7) to indicate the status of rooms, housekeeping summarizes the floor reports of the individual maids (see Exhibit 13–8) and sends the Housekeeper's Daily Report to the front desk for comparison to the rack. *Courtesy of Kayco Systems, Lake Elsinore, California.*

Exhibit 13–7
Widely accepted alphabetic and numeric symbols are used by the front desk and the housekeeper to communicate the status of rooms.

Baggage: no occupant (sleep-out)	B
Check out: room on change	c/o
Cot	C
Do not disturb	DND
Double-locked room	DL
Early arrival	EA
No service wanted (Do not disturb)	NS
Occupied	✓
Occupied, but dirty	OD
Occupied, with light baggage or no baggage	X
OK	ok
Out of order	O (also OOO)
Out of inventory	OOI
Permanent guest	P
Ready for sale	/
Refused service	RS
Stayover	s/o
Stayover, no service	SNS
Vacant	V (also no symbol at all)
Vacant and dirty (on change)	VD

cially interested in reports of light luggage, in discrepancies in the number of occupants, and in potential skippers—x-marked rooms.

The second report of the day, the afternoon report, is the chief means of uncovering sleepers, skippers, and whos. *Sleepers* are guests who have checked out, but are still being carried as if the room were occupied. *Skippers* are guests who have left without checking out, without paying. *Whos* are unknown guests—someone is occupying a room but the desk doesn't know who it is.

These additional situations keep the housekeeper's report in use even if room status is being maintained electronically with a PMS. Internal control is difficult in a small hotel, where the desk is staffed by one person who sells the room, collects the money, and posts the record. The housekeeper's report was originally furnished to the income auditor. Having a second party compare the room status at the front office to the independently prepared housekeeper's report established a degree of internal control. It is still important for the small hotel! As front offices grow larger and departmentalize, the internal control function of the housekeeper's report diminishes.

Property management systems have helped eliminate the old and irritating way of verifying occupancy by banging on the guest-room door. Indeed, the PMS has actually reversed the flow of the housekeeper's report. The room occupancy status report is prepared by the night audit for housekeeping, which gets its copy early in the morning. This preworkday report on the status of rooms speeds the work of the housekeeper. Room attendants are assigned early in the day, so they begin work immediately. With early knowledge of the room count, the housekeeper refines the work schedule, calling in extras or scheduling days off for full-time staff. This reverse housekeeper's report also communicates guest complaints, ensuring that they get attention early in the day.

The housekeeper's report alerts the desk to special circumstances. Among these are double-locked rooms (DL) and do not disturb rooms (DND) that remain unchanged between the morning and afternoon reports. Floor attendants mark these rooms NS, not serviced, or RS, guest refused service (see Exhibit 13–8). Wise hotel managers telephone such rooms before the day has passed to verify the condition of the occupant. If no one answers the call, the room is entered in the company of security or housekeeping.

Balancing the Mathematics of the Transcript. Property management systems monitor their own mathematics, but a manual, pencil-and-paper transcript requires a mathematical check of additions and subtractions. *Crossfooting,* which is adding horizontally across the transcript totals, ensures the mathematical accuracy of all lines of the transcript. A review of the several steps in the manual audit will explain why crossfooting works.

Step 1: The night auditor posts room charges and taxes to the folios.

Step 2: The folios are totaled and the balances carried forward to the next day.

Step 3: Folios are copied onto the transcript. Within the figures are errors created by steps 1 and 2 and errors made during the day by the desk cashiers. Among the mathematical errors will be slides and transpositions, inaccurate figures,

Exhibit 13–8   The desk manages the inventory of rooms using room status information that is gathered in part by the floor housekeepers, who visit the rooms before reporting room status.

Floor Report

Floor # 16

01	V	28	RS
02	V	29	✓
03	✓	30	✓
04	✓	31	OOO
05	B	32	V
06	✓	33	X
07	✓	34	C
08	V	35	✓
09	V	36	✓
10	DND	37	✓
27	✓	54	✓

Code:
V = Vacant   RS = Refuse Service
B = Baggage   DND = Do Not Disturb
X = No Baggage   C   = Cot
✓= Occupied   EA = Early Arrival

oversights, duplications, and mistakes in addition and subtraction. The audit is designed to uncover all these errors.

Step 4: The total of each transcript column is proved against other documents, as explained earlier, chiefly control sheets, vouchers, cash sheets, and the room count sheet. Corrections are made on the transcript and on the folio as errors are uncovered. This verification ensures the mathematical accuracy of all the departmental columns, which are vertical columns 6 through 19, except column 16 (see Exhibit 13–4).

Step 5: The opening balance columns, vertical columns 4 and 5, are now verified. Unlike columns 6 to 15, columns 4 and 5 are not income columns, so there are neither control sheets nor vouchers. The opening balance of each folio is the guest's cumulative debt, carried forward from yesterday. Therefore, the opening balances of today (columns 4 and 5, debit and credit) are compared to the closing balances of yesterday, *yesterday's* transcript columns 21 and 22. The guest goes to bed the previous night owing columns 21 and 22 of yesterday's transcript and awakens the following morning owing the same exact amounts, now reflected in columns 4 and 5 of the new day. If today's opening balance does not agree with yesterday's closing balance—perhaps a folio has been left off today's transcript—a search begins for the discrepancy.

Step 6: Crossfoot (horizontally add) the totals of columns 6 to 15 to obtain a value. If the transcript is in balance, that value will equal the total of vertical column 16. This can be understood by doing the very same thing on any one horizontal line. Columns 6 to 15 on any horizontal line should equal column 16 of that line. Therefore, crossfooting the grand totals of columns 6 to 15 should equal the sum obtained by vertically adding column 16. (The total should equal the sum of its parts.) If the sum of all the columns does not equal the total of column 16, there is an error on one of the horizontal lines, which is, of course, someone's folio. [That folio was added by the night auditor (step 2) and copied onto the transcript (step 3). Obviously, it was added or copied incorrectly.] Each horizontal line must be crossfooted until the mathematical error that contributed to the total error is uncovered. Once uncovered, column 16 of that line will be changed, and since that line represents a folio—the line of figures was copied from the folio—the folio itself must also be corrected.

Step 7: Verify the three credits. Previous discussions have stressed the three methods of settling folios: cash, allowances, and transfers. Credit column 17 is the cash settlement and that transcript total is compared to the receipts reported on the cashiers' front-office cash sheets. (Similarly, disbursements on those sheets must agree to the cash disbursement column, column 13 of Exhibit 13–4.) Column 18, allowances, is compared to the sum of the allowance vouchers granted at the desk that day. The final and most common credit is column 19, transfers to the city ledger. It will be tested by comparison to the total debit transfers of column 14, since every transfer must have equal debits and credits. On some transcripts, column 20, which is blank in the illustration, is a total of columns 17, 18, and 19. As such it represents the sum of the day's credits, as column 16 represents the sum of the day's debits.

Step 8: Crossfoot and balance the transcript. Begin with the opening balance (the net of column 4, debit, minus column 5, credit), add the day's charges (column 16), and subtract the day's credits (the sum of columns 17, 18, and 19) to arrive at the closing balance. That closing balance should be the same as the closing balance obtained when closing balance credits (column 22) are subtracted from closing balance debits (column 21). Once mathematically verified, the net of column 22 minus column 21 will be the basis for verifying *tomorrow's* opening transcript total (column 4 minus column 5). If step 8 fails to check, the auditor follows the same routine used to prove column 16 when it didn't check, but this time, each horizontal line is added only from columns 16 to 22. That's possible because columns 6 to 15 have already been proven in the total of column 16.

The transcript is a summary of accounts receivable, a summary of folios. The closing balance represents the total amount that all accounts receivable owe the hotel at the close of the day. It's possible for the hotel to owe one or more guests temporarily, so some lines (folios) will have credit balances, probably as a result of advanced deposits. For two different examples, see column 2 of Exhibit 13–1 and the third horizontal line of Exhibit 13–4, column 22.

Step 9: Vertical addition is easier to visualize than horizontal crossfooting. It's just a more traditional way to do the mathematics. Then the proof, or the formula as it is sometimes called, looks like this (see Exhibit 13–4, line 2):

> Opening balance, column 4 minus 5 (debit minus credit)
> + Charges and services used by guests, column 16 (debits)
> − Payments made by guests, columns 17 to 19 (credits)
> = Closing balance, column 21 minus 22 (debit minus credit)

The closing balance is the cumulative balance of guests' debt to the hotel and is a debit balance.

The math can also be done by having column 16 represent the running total (see Exhibit 13–4, line 1). Then the formula would look different:

> Opening balance, column 4 minus 5 (debit minus credit)
> + Charges and services used by guests, columns 6 to 15 (debits)
> = Total, column 16 (cumulative debit balance before payments of the day)
> − Payments made by guests, columns 17 to 19 (credits)
> = Closing balance, column 21 minus 22 (debit minus credit)

The result of the two approaches is the same. The difference is the handling of column 16. Some auditors use column 16 to reflect only the day's debits, as the top formula illustrates. Other auditors use column 16 to reflect the cumulative balance, including the balances of yesterday, the bottom illustration.

► THE PROPERTY MANAGEMENT SYSTEM

The night audit provides the most spectacular demonstration of the property management system in action. Only those who have machine-posted (old NCR system) hundreds of folios or hand-copied pages of transcripts can appreciate the savings in time and annoyance. In less than one hour—10 to 15 minutes for a small hotel—the tedious tasks of posting room rates and taxes, balancing the folios, and totaling the charges are finished. That's a job that once took several persons an entire night to complete. Labor savings, the oft-touted but rarely delivered advantage of computer installations, is certainly evident in the night audit. Since a minimum crew is always needed, the greatest labor savings are in the largest hotels.

The computer has altered the mechanics of the audit, its purpose, and its scope. Traditionally, the night audit concentrated on finding and correcting errors—except the errors were caused by the system. Initial errors, transmittal errors, posting errors, and errors of addition are inherent in the hand audit. The entire thrust of the hand audit is discovery and repair. The computer audit has no such problems. The information that is input with the departmental POS appears everywhere, and everywhere it appears the same. Of course, there are errors of input, and these shall be discussed shortly.

There are also problems with the PMS—computer bugs. When the situation becomes very serious, the bug is upgraded to a virus. Viruses or glitches (misplaced decimals is a very simple example) are errors of installation, not errors of audit. Increases in the number of such incidents can usually be traced to additional interfaces, linkages between equipment pieces of various manufacturers. The interface is a third system used to link two unrelated systems. Hotels have as many as eight or 10 such linkages. Common links to the property management system are POS terminals and call accounting systems (see Chapter 14).

Interface problems are created when systems differently designed by different manufacturers are purchased to be used with an already existing PMS. In addition to POS and call accounting (CA), there might be interfaces for in-room minibars, in-room films, reservation programs, housekeeping room status, and others. Recent efforts by the American Hotel & Motel Association have focused on developing integration standards.[1] These will ensure the compatibility of different products by different manufacturers and not require the special interface programs that bring grief to many hotel systems.

A second wave of integration is being driven by the large franchise companies. To increase seamless communications, particularly reservations between the parent and the franchisee, several large franchisors are now insisting on a single PMS for each franchisee.[2] Once in place, last-room availability (see Chapter 4) will be accessible across a wide range of channels, including the Web. Consolidation, so apparent in the hotel business, is a likely outcome of technology standardization. The number of technology vendors should certainly decline from the 100 plus that compete currently.

The PMS Equivalent of the Transcript

The property management system is updated daily in a process akin to the manual night audit with its room postings and transcript spreadsheet. Although the PMS update could be done at any time—so could the transcript, for that matter—the quiet hours of the early morning are favored for both. Like the manual system, the PMS has a closeout hour. During this time, departmental point-of-sale terminals cannot interface with the PMS. They must wait until the conclusion of the audit.

➤*Closing Routine.*   Updating the PMS requires the night auditor to monitor what is happening rather than to make it happen. Room charges and room taxes are posted automatically. It is an internal function that the auditor doesn't see until the job is completed with a hard-copy printout. The printout is not intrinsic to the job, but it is desirable. With a PMS hard-copy equivalent of the transcript, the hotel is able to settle guest accounts in the event of a computer crash. At least the folio balances that started the day are available on hard copy (see Exhibit 13–2).

Departmental reconciliations similar to the hand transcript's departmental control sheet balances are also made with a PMS. Rare discrepancies are corrected by comparing the PMS audit figures (essentially, the daily report data) to the receivable debits (register readings and vouchers) and credits (cash receipts and credit slips).

POS terminals are not used by every hotel. Even those that have them may operate some departments manually. If so, the manual system of vouchers, control sheets, and folios may be partially in place. Even if this is so, the night audit is simplified tremendously with the PMS. The property management system creates the folios and the spreadsheet electronically and ensures the accuracy of the mathematics.

The night auditor finishes the PMS audit with an end-of-the-day routine much like that of the hand audit. A trial balance of debits and credits is made. Debits are charges to the receivable folios; credits are earnings in the several departments. The day and date are closed and the next day opened. The POS terminals are put back on-line. Monthly and annual totals are accumulated as part of the reporting process that follows next. The sequence varies at each hotel. At some properties, the routine is pre-programmed; at others, the update proceeds by prompts from the system to which the auditor responds.

Folios of guests who are departing the following day may be printed as part of the audit procedure. Preprinting folios speeds the check outs. Copies are filed by room number sequence in the cashier's well and produced without delay when the departing guest appears at the desk. If subsequent charges—breakfast, for example—alter the previous night's balance, the old folio is merely discarded and a new one printed.

A copy of the preprinted folio might be left under the guest-room door for use in express check outs. This wouldn't be necessary if the hotel provides express checkout by means of the TV set.

➤*Express Check Out.*   Express check out is one of computerization's exciting stories because standing in departure lines is the bane of hotel guests. One of the first PMS innovations to focus on the problem was flexible terminals able to quickly shift from registration to departure status, or vice versa. This increased the number of front-office stations when demand was greatest. Lines were shortened, but not enough.

Because early output printers were slow, many operations began printing the folios of expected departures during the previous night's audit. From printing them to delivering them to the room wasn't a large conceptual jump, but it created *zip-out check out,* also called *speedy check out, no-wait check out,* or *VIP check out.*

Zip-out check out is only for guests using direct billing or credit cards—but that is almost everyone. At first, guests who wanted the service completed a request card. Later, every departure using a credit card had a folio under the door. If the folio was accurate, the guests left after completing one additional step: They either telephoned an extension to give notice, or they dropped a form with the key in a lobby box (see Exhibit 13–9). The final folio was mailed to the guest within a day or two, and the charges were processed through the credit-card company.

Express check-out leaped ahead with the interface of Spectradyne's TV pay-movie system into the hotel's PMS. Delivering folios to the room was necessary no longer. The folio appeared on the TV set any time the guest wanted it. From then on, the procedure was the same. With a click of the remote control, the guest signaled departure. As with zip-out check out, the folio followed in the mail, and the credit-card charges

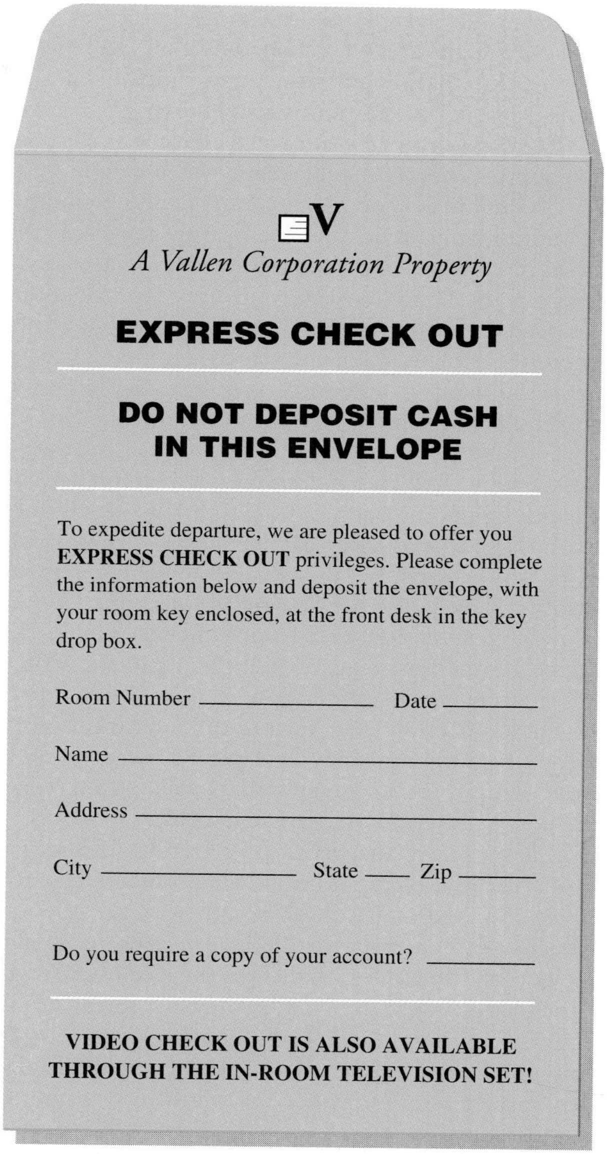

Exhibit 13–9 Express check out provides quality service to harried guests who zip out using either room TV sets or express envelopes to give notice of their departure.

□V

A Vallen Corporation Property

EXPRESS CHECK OUT

DO NOT DEPOSIT CASH
IN THIS ENVELOPE

To expedite departure, we are pleased to offer you **EXPRESS CHECK OUT** privileges. Please complete the information below and deposit the envelope, with your room key enclosed, at the front desk in the key drop box.

Room Number _____ Date _____

Name _____

Address _____

City _____ State ____ Zip _____

Do you require a copy of your account? _____

**VIDEO CHECK OUT IS ALSO AVAILABLE
THROUGH THE IN-ROOM TELEVISION SET!**

were processed. An integrated PMS transfers the charges, which have been accumulated in the front-office folio, to the city ledger module.

Another great leap forward was taken when self-check-in/check-out terminals were interfaced with the ever-expanding PMS. At freestanding locations within the lobby, self-check-out terminals present guests with their folios and accept their credit cards to speed them on their way. This completes the PMS cycle, which was started when the guest registered at the same terminal (see Exhibit 8–10). It is another step closer to the fully electronic hotel.

➤*PMS Posting Errors.*   The PMS does not guarantee error-free operations. Employees make mistakes whether the system is manual or electronic. Striking the wrong POS key means an overcharge—or undercharge—is posted. The PMS provides consistent figures throughout the system, but they will be the wrong value if the wrong key was struck. Charges are sometimes overlooked altogether—not posted at all. At other times, charges are posted twice. Human errors range all over the place— for example, cashiers may record credit-card charges as cash sales and cash payments as credit-card receipts. Property management systems do not create error-free environments, but they do minimize system-caused errors and facilitate error discovery.

The night auditor prints a detailed list of transactions as the first step in pinpointing errors. The hard copy itemizes transactions by register keys or by reference codes. Reference codes are illustrated on the folio figures throughout Chapter 10. Departmental cashiers need authority to post charges to someone's folio. A source document, such as a signed departmental voucher, provides that authority. Since most source documents are maintained in numerical sequence, the voucher number becomes the reference code. The POS program doesn't post until the cashier inputs that reference number or code.

A different code is used to validate the identity of the guest who is making the charge. The cashier inputs the guest's room number, which the guest provides, and on prompt, enters the first several letters of the guest's surname, which the guest also provides. The charge is processed, but not before the system matches the POS information with the registration data in the file of the PMS. Exhibit 13–3 illustrates the computer screen that a dining room cashier uses to post a charge.

Matching the guest-room keycard (with its magnetic strip) to the PMS's registration data file is another means of verifying the guest's identity. The guest inserts the keycard into a POS and the system verifies the identification. Implementation of this system has already begun, but it may be replaced before it even goes into general use. The smart cards of Chapter 12 suggest that one's own credit card may become the keycard for the next generation of electronic locks.

The POS reduces receivable losses by rejecting invalid postings. The guest may have checked out already; be a paid-in-advance customer with no charges permitted; or have exceeded the credit-card floor or other credit ceiling set by the hotel. Late charges are reduced dramatically when POS terminals are in place.

Departing guests sometimes challenge the accuracy of departmental postings. Denying that the charges were ever made, they ask for offsetting allowances from the front desk. Obtaining a copy of the check (voucher) signed by the guest to show its accuracy is a slow process with a pencil-and-paper system. So time consuming is it that the front-office cashier simply grants the allowance without further investigation. Until recently, the results were the same with a PMS. Now disputed charges are being met with proof in a test program introduced at the Boca Raton Resort and Beach Club. The PMS is able to display the protested voucher despite the range of operating departments at the Boca: 84 revenue sources, 23 different voucher forms, and 13 different sizes of paper![3]

Reports from the Night Auditor

Once information is captured, and it need be captured but once, an unlimited number of reports can be generated. The proper programs must be in place, of course, but they generally are with the turnkey systems that will be discussed very shortly. With programs in place, the same data can be arranged and reordered in a variety of ways. The single registration is a good example. The guest's geographic origin, source of reservation, membership in a convention, credit limits, and length of stay provide data for five different reports.

The ease of obtaining reports undoubtedly contributed to the vast numbers that were demanded when property management systems were first introduced. Much of that has shaken out. Management took control and pared the numbers by emphasizing exception reports. One no longer sees piles of reports prepared by the night auditor trashed, unread by the recipient the next day.

Still, the night audit produces a wide range of reports for all departments of the front office. Many of these are day-end summaries, since unit managers use (through display terminals or hard-copy print) the same data several times throughout the day. Some reports are traditional from the days of the pencil-and-paper audit: the balancing of accounts receivable, credit alerts, and statistical reports to the manager.

▶ *Turnkey Systems.*   With rare exceptions, every hotel uses the same kinds of reports. Although the formats differ with each supplier, with some more user friendly than others, the purpose and content vary very little. It's difficult to say whether a uniform need caused the turnkey system, or whether mass production created similar needs property to property.

In a turnkey installation, the buyer merely "turns the key" to activate the system. Everything has been done in advance by the vendor. Nothing is ever quite that easy, but it is unlikely that the hotel industry would be so far along if the burden of development had remained with the individual hotel, which was the norm in the early stages of computer use by the lodging industry.

Prior to the turnkey concept, each hotel shopped among manufacturers for its own hardware. Then it developed its own software by employing computer specialists, who at that time knew nothing about the business of keeping a hotel. The large data processing departments that appeared as a result of in-house programming disappeared quickly with the introduction of the turnkey package.

Now systems are purchased off-the-shelf, shopping among suppliers for an existing system that is close to what the hotel needs. And systems are close to what is needed. Generic programs are much alike because hotels are much alike. What differences there are in off-the-shelf products diminish as third- and fourth-generation programs are developed. Each generation improves flow and screening, new or missing functions being added to remain competitive. Most recently, the push has been toward a Windows/Intel environment.

Turnkey companies now dominate the field. Single suppliers furnish both the hardware and the software. If the supplier specializes in one segment, other vendors supply the missing parts. Responsibility remains with the primary vendor, who puts together the package, gets it up and running, trains the staff, and services the installation—not without some major grief for the hotel, of course. Vendors who adopt the Hospitality Information Technology Integration Standards (HITIS) that the AH&MA is encouraging will offer systems that interface with all others who comply with HITIS. Hotels that specify HITIS in their bid solicitations will enjoy reduced risks, lower costs, and savings in installation time. Access to the World Wide Web will also change the hotel's PMS from one with dedicated hardware to one that uses Web technology. As that happens, the front-office workstation will become a general-purpose rather than a specific-purpose screen.

Currently, vendors are modifying their off-the-shelf systems to meet special needs. Just as often, however, hotels modify their special needs to conform to the standardized product. As a result, programs are almost identical among hotels with the same vendor and very similar among hotels with different vendors. Nowhere is this more apparent than in the range of reports prepared nightly by the PMS.

➤ *Kinds of Reports.*   Reports from the night audit fall into several categories: reservation reports; rooms management reports, including reports of room status; accounting reports; and reports to the manager. Unless management remains selective, an excessive number of reports involving expensive machine time, labor, storage, and paper costs is spewed out nightly. Since a good deal of the information keeps changing, viewing it on screens is just as effective and far more economical. Reporting by exception is another approach to the issue.

Exception Reports.   Exception reports highlight situations that digress from the norm. Reporting everything that is as it should be serves no purpose. Reports by exception alert the reader to problem areas without requiring the time-consuming inspection of normal data. A report on credit limits is a good example. Listing the folio balance of every guest against the credit ceiling is unnecessary. It is unduly long and requires a tedious search to find the important information. An exception report lists only those folios that are at, above, or close to the hotel's limit. The size of the report is reduced and the important data is emphasized.

Some common exception reports are listed here:

Allowance Report: identifies who authorized each allowance, who received the allowance, the amount, and the reasons.

Cashier's Overage and Shortage Report: pinpoints by stations overages and shortages that exceed predetermined norms.

Comps Report: similar to an Allowance Report; identifies who authorized each comp, who received the comp, the amount, and the reasons.

No Luggage Report: lists occupied rooms in which there is no luggage (see Exhibit 13–8); a credit report.

Room Rate Variance Report: compares actual rates to standard rate schedule and identifies the authority for granting the variance (not meaningful if the hotel is discounting frequently and deeply).

Skipper Report: provides room identification, dollar amount, and purported name and address.

Write-off Report: lists daily write-offs, usually late charges, whose account balances are less than a specified amount.

Downtime Reports.   Downtime reports, for use when the computer crashes, provide insurance against disaster. Like a great deal of insurance, the reports usually go unused because emergencies rarely materialize. Downtime reports are dumped 24 hours later when the contingency has passed and the backup reports of the following day have been printed.

Basic downtime reports include the following:

Folio Balance Report: itemizes in room number sequence the balances due from receivables; comparable to columns 21 and 22 of a manual transcript (see Exhibit 13–4).

Guest-List Report: alphabetizes registered guests with their room numbers; computer version of a manual information rack.

Room Status Report: identifies vacant, out-of-order, on change, and occupied rooms at the beginning of the new day; a computerized room count sheet (see Exhibit 13–5).

Disk Backup: not a report, but part of the closing sequence of the auditor's shift; data is replicated onto another disk to be retrieved if a malfunction erases the working disk.

Credit Reports.   The night auditor is the credit manager's first line of defense. In that capacity, the night auditor handles both routine matters and special credit situations.

Mention has already been made of the auditor's responsibility to preprint the folios of expected check outs. Although not nearly as numerous, folios must also be prepared for guests who remain longer than one week. On the guest's seventh night, the auditor prints the folio (or prepares a new folio if the system is manual) for delivery to the guest the next day.

The night auditor also makes an analysis of guest account balances. With a manual system, the auditor scans the last column of the transcript (see Exhibit 13–4, column 21) and itemizes those rooms with balances at or near the hotel's limit. The computer makes the same list.

If the audit team has time, additional credit duties may be assigned. There are occasional guests, especially walk-ins, that concern the credit manager. The night auditor might be asked to verify the guest's identity by getting a telephone number for that person or the person's business affiliation at the address given. Although the absence of a number is inconclusive, it is another bit of information for the credit department in making its evaluation.

All credit reports are sensitive and may be viewed as exception reports:

Credit Alert: list of rooms whose folio charges exceed a given amount in a single day. That amount varies with the class of hotel.

Cumulative Charges Report: similar to the credit alert except a cumulative figure for the guest's entire stay.

Floor Report: list of guests whose folio balances approach the maximum allowed the hotel by the credit-card company, or the maximum the credit-card allows on the guest's own card.

Three-Day Report: weekly statements that remain unpaid three days after billing.

Reservation Reports.   Computerizing the reservation function added an entirely new dimension to the process. It introduced new reservation techniques, the 1-800-WATS number; it globalized the reservation network through the ultraswitch and the Web; and it facilitated instant confirmation for dates months away in hotels thousands of miles apart. No less important, computerized reservations produced reams of information.

Information is the power to decide. Reservation managers must know the number of rooms sold and the number available, by type, rate, and accommodations. They must know the number of arrivals, departures, stayovers, cancellations, out of orders, and walk-ins, for a start. This information comes to the reservation department in a variety of reports.

Supplemental information flows from the same database. Which rooms are most popular and at which rates? Do no-show factors vary with the season and the day of the week? If so, by how much? How many rooms in which categories are turnaways?

How many reservations were walked? How many in-WATS calls were there? How many were initiated by travel agents? Questions of this type illustrate again the dual management–operations capability of the computer.

An alphabetical list of arrivals is an example of the computer in operations. It reduces the number of lost reservations and facilitates the recognition of VIPs. It helps the bellcaptain schedule a crew. It identifies group affiliation, which improves reservation and billing procedures.

Reservation data can be displayed on a monitor or preserved on hard copy for slower digestion and evaluation. A permanent copy turns the data into a report. Then it serves more as a management tool than an operational one. Although different vendors format reports differently, there is a common grouping for the reservation department, which includes the following:

Arrivals Report: alphabetical list of the day's expected arrivals, individually and by groups.

Cancellation and Change Report: list of reservation cancellations for the day or reservation changes and cancellations for a later date.

Central Reservations Report: analysis of reservations made through the central reservations system, including numbers, kinds, rates, and fees paid.

Convention (Group) Delegates Report: compilation of group (and tour) room blocks; the number of rooms booked, and the number still available by rate category and name of group. Also called a **Group Pickup Report.**

Daily Analysis Report: one or more reports on the number and percentage of reservations, arrivals, no-shows, walk-ins, and so on, by source (travel agent, housing bureau, etc.) and by type of guest (full rack, corporate rate, etc.).

Deposit Report: reservations by deposit status—deposits requested and received, deposits requested and not received, deposits not requested. Could be treated as an exception report.

Forecast Report: one of a variety of names (**Extended Arrival Report, Future Availability Report**) for projecting reservation data forward over short or long durations (see Exhibit 6–6).

Occupancy Report: projection within the computer's horizon of expected occupancy by category of room.

Overbooking (Walk) Report: list of reservations walked, including their identification; the number of walk-ins denied; and the number farmed out to other properties.

Regrets Report: report on the number of room requests denied.

Rooms Management Reports.   Computerization has brought major procedural changes to the front office but not to the functions that need doing. Comparisons of the old and the new are best illustrated through the room rack. Unlike manual room racks, which one can see and physically manipulate, computerized racks are in computer memory, viewable only on the monitor screen (see Exhibits 13–10 and 13–11). Whether the clerk turns to one rack type or the other, the information is the same: room rates, location, connecting and adjoining rooms, bed types and room status.

The computer restructures the data. It separates into different windows what is visible with one glance to the user of the manual rack. Separate menus (see Exhibit 13–11) are needed to view what the manual rack identifies as one class of information. With a glance at the manual rack, one sees the rooms vacant and occupied, the

Exhibit 13–10
The screen displays an electronic room rack, including room availability by type, rate, location, and status. The clerk's selection, lower left, must agree with previous input of room type requested. If satisfactory, the guest-service agent exits with Y (yes), lower right. Compare with the manual rack, Exhibit 13–13.

SELECT ROOM AVAILABILITY

HOTEL ALIONETTE   10:23AM AUG 4, 9–

ROOM NO	TYPE	$	LOC	CONN WITH	ADJN WITH	STATUS	COMMENTS
1101	K	A	N		1103	OCC	NEAR ELEV
1102	K	A	N		1104	OCC	
1103	T	B	N		1105	OOO	UNTIL 8.6
1104	T	B	N	1106		OK	
1105	T	B	NW	1107		OK	
1106	P	P	W	1108		OK	
1107	Q	C	SW	1109		OK	
1108	S	D	S		1110	OCC	EARLY ARR
1109	DD	E	S		1111	OK	
1110	DD	E	S		1112	OCC	
1111	Q	C	S		1113	OCC	
1112	Q	C	S		1114	OCC	

SELECTION   RETURN TO SELECT _____
   ROOM TYPE   ACCEPT (Y)   _____
   ROOM NUMBER

Exhibit 13–11
Each function performed by a guest-service agent requires a different screen, which is called up from this main menu onto a second or third mask that is used to complete the task.

3/3/   2:29 PM

HOTEL UNIVERS
FRONT OF THE HOUSE MENU

1. RESERVATIONS   5. CREDIT
2. REGISTRATION   6. POSTING
3. GUEST NAME INQUIRY   7. TELEPHONE
4. ROOM STATUS   8. REPORTS

INPUT NUMBER [ ]

USER CODE ID [ ]

rooms out of order and on change, the names of the guests and their city of residence, the number in the party and their company or group affiliation, the rate on the room, and the anticipated check-out date. It doesn't work that way with an electronic system, where separate programs are needed for each function. Room identification (see Exhibit 13–10) is different from guest identification (see Exhibit 13–12).

Far more information is available from the computer rack than from the manual rack (see Exhibit 13–13), but the information has to be manipulated to provide the data. For example, the computerized rack can display all the vacant rooms on a given floor. All the king rooms in the tower or all the connecting rooms in the lanai building can be listed. Facts that would take many minutes to ascertain, if at all, from the manual rack are flashed onto the screen in seconds.

Information is more complete and can be processed more rapidly with the computerized rack than with the manual one. This is true for the whole, although a greater amount of time may be required for the computer to process a single fact. In a contest to identify a guest whose name begins with either "Mac" or "Mc," for example, the manual user may be able to beat out the computer user.

Exhibit 13–12   Input code 3 of Exhibit 13–11, guest name inquiry, would eventually lead to the identification of this individual guest. Compare the display information to that of the room rack slip of Mr. and Mrs. O. Strable, rooms 905/907, in the manual room rack, Exhibit 13–13.

Exhibit 13–13 The manual room rack indicates with one glance which rooms are vacant and which occupied; who the occupants are; their home cities; rates being paid; and arrival and departure dates. Additional facts can be communicated by using a range of colors and symbols.

Computer reports for the rooms function include the following:

Change Report: identification of room changes, rate changes, and the number in the party.

Convention Use Report: summary of the room use by different convention groups in order to justify the number of complimentary rooms.

Expected to Depart Report: list of anticipated departures. The converse would be a Stayover Report.

Flag Report: list of rooms flagged for special attention by the desk.

House Use Report: list of rooms occupied by hotel personnel.

Out-of-Order Report: list of rooms that are out of order or out of inventory with reasons.

Pickup Report: names and room numbers picked up by members of a specific group against its block.

Rate Analysis Report: display of distribution of rates by sources—reservations, walk-ins, travel-agency made, res system, hotel sales department, packages, company-made.

Room Productivity Report: evaluation of housekeeping's productivity in total and by individual room attendant.

VIP Report: list of distinguished guests and very important persons, including casino high rollers.

Rooms Status Reports.   Rooms status offers what is probably the best example of an old function with a new face. Whether the hotel uses a manual rack or a computer, room status (on change, vacant and ready, out-of-order, or occupied rooms) must be communicated between the desk and housekeeping. Clerks need to know which rooms are ready for sale, and housekeeping needs to know which rooms require attention. A room status display on the monitor is called up innumerable times throughout the day by both ends of the communication link.

The communication procedure hasn't changed with the computer. The cashier still puts the room on change as the guest checks out. (This is done electronically if the guest uses the speedy check-out option.) That's how the room clerk learns that a given room will be available soon. On-change status tells housekeeping that the room needs attention. When the room is clean, the housekeeper updates the system, switching the on-change room to ready. Immediately, the desk clerk has the information. The room is sold and the cycle begins anew. The faster the process goes around, the quicker the new guest is settled and the room sale consummated.

Prior to the computer, the cashier–desk–housekeeping link was direct conversation person to person; by means of paper notations; by telephone calls; and, frequently, not at all. The chambermaid on the floor wasn't included in the communication loop. Although the critical link, she couldn't be reached at all. Today, the chambermaid communicates by telephone, not by conversation, but as an electronic input device to the computer. Either the chambermaid taps in through the telephone or by means of a terminal located in the linen closet on each floor. Personal PCs are being introduced into guest rooms to upgrade guest service, but they also provide the chambermaid with still another terminal.

With access to the computer, the housekeeper's office tracks room attendants as they dial in and out of the system (see Exhibit 13–14). Daily job assignments can also be computer designed. At the start of the shift, each employee gets a hard-copy list of rooms that each is to do. The printout also includes special assignments such as mirrors in the corridors, attention to sick guests, or messages from management to the staff.

		MAID-ROOM SCHEDULE								01:53 PM NOV 11			
NAME						NUMBER		DUTY H		MESSAGE SIGNAL OFF			
	NUMBER OF ROOMS ASSIGNED						0			BEGINNING ROOM NUMBER			
ROOM	U-R	IN	OUT	SL	HK	CO		ROOM	U-R	IN	OUT	SL	HK	CO
1200	A	9:35A	9:49A	SG	OK	SO		1209	A			SD	D	SO
1201	A	9:50A	10:14A	SS	OK	SO		1210	A	8:44A	9:02A	SD	OK	SO
1202	A	11:50A	12:12P	SS	OK	SO		1211	A	1:13P	1:48P	OK	I	OK
1203	A	9:20A	9:35A	SS	OK	SO		1212	A	9:03A	9:19A	SG	OK	SO
1204	A	10:54A	11:17A	SM	OK	SO		1213	A	1:48		OK	57	DO
1205	A	11:17A	11:50A	SD	OK	SO		1214	A			OK	D	DO
1206	A	10:31A	10:54A	SS	OK	SO		1215	A			OK	D	DO
1207	A	10:14A	10:31A	SS	OK	SO								
1208	A	12:12P	1:13P	OK	OK	OK								

END DISPLAY

Exhibit 13–14   The PMS can be used to track each room attendant, allowing management to monitor productivity and to locate the employee if communication is required.

In addition to the reports that housekeeping uses to manage the department, room status includes the following:

Out-of-Order Report: special focus on out-of-order or out of inventory rooms containing dates the rooms went down, expected ready dates, and the causes of each OOO or OOI room.

Permanent Guest Report: list of permanent guests by room number and name.

Room Status List: room-by-room identification of occupied and vacant rooms, made-up and not-ready rooms, out-of-order rooms, and on-change rooms. (This report is also included among the downtime reports.)

Sick Guest Report: list of sick guests by room number and name.

Accounts-Receivable Reports. The PMS prepares electronically the same records that are hand-prepared by the manual audit. What is the very function of the manual night audit becomes a series of reports by the computerized night audit. Both the manual and the electronic audit deal with the day's accounts receivable. A cumulative inventory of accounts receivable is the essence of the audit. The opening balance of receivables, the amount owed to the hotel, is increased by new charges and decreased by payments made that day. The new balance is thus obtained; it becomes the opening balance of the following day's audit.

The computerized audit reflects this emphasis on receivables through a group of related reports:

Alpha List: alphabetically lists the entire guest (account receivable) population. Other alpha lists include arrivals and departures.

City-Ledger Transfers: itemizes all the accounts transferred to city ledger that day; a city-ledger journal.

Credit-Card Report: reports amounts and identities of credit-card charges by both registered and nonregistered guests.

Daily Revenue Report: analyzes revenue totals from all sources by outlet and means of payment. Comparable to the old machine audit D report (and sometimes called a D report).

Departmental Sales Journal: shows the individual transactions of each department (comparable to the vertical columns of a hand transcript).

Guest Ledger Summary: displays the daily activity for both the A and B folios of individual guest accounts—opening balance, charges and credits, and closing balance (comparable to the horizontal lines of a hand transcript).

Late-Charge Report: identifies late charges that were transferred to city ledger that day.

Posting Report: displays posting activity by individual POS terminal (comparable to a departmental control sheet).

Room Revenue (Posting) Report: displays room, rate, and tax posted at the day's close. Room revenue can be obtained floor by floor (comparable to a room count sheet).

▶**Report to the Manager.** Information furnished by the night auditor helps the income auditor, sometimes called the day auditor, to complete a Daily Report to the Manager. The income audit, which deals in part with cash flows, casts a wider net than the night audit, which is limited to accounts receivable. The income auditor is delayed at times until midday, just as the night auditor sometimes has problems in reconciling by the close of the shift. To offset that wait, the night auditor leaves a preliminary report for the manager. This report is abbreviated because only account receivable data is included. Still, most hotel sales are account receivable sales. After all, room income, the hotel's largest source of revenue, is sold only on account; there are no cash sales in the rooms department.

Exhibit 13–15 illustrates an electronically prepared Night Auditor's Report to the Manager. Three items are reported: charge sales in the several departments, a cumulative balance of account receivable debt, and room statistics. One or all of the values may change with the income audit. Corrections to income that are uncovered by the day audit may affect income, accounts receivable, and/or room statistics. But then again, there may be no changes at all.

THE CITY HOTEL, ANYWHERE, U.S.A.   Page 1
03/16   Night Auditor's Report

SALES		ROOM STATISTICS	
Rooms	$12,900.00	Total Rooms	320
Coffee Shop	1,524.80	House Use	–0–
Steak House	CLOSED	Out of Order	–0–
Cap'tn Bar	896.00	Complimentary	–0–
Telephone	990.76	Permanent	2
Laundry	100.51	Room Count	180
Total Sales	$16,412.07	Vacant	140
		House Count	210

Other Charges:	
Cash Advance	987.76
Taxes Payable	540.00
Transfers	693.15
	$18,632.98

ACCOUNTS RECEIVABLE		ROOM RATIOS	
Opening Balance	$44,651.07	% Occupancy	56.3
Charges	18,632.98	% Double Occupancy	16.7
		Average Daily Rate	$71.67
Total	$63,284.05	RevPar	$40.31
Credits	950.00		
Closing Balance	$62,334.05		

Exhibit 13–15   An abbreviated report to the manager is prepared by the night auditor whether a manual or electronic system is used. Basic information includes charge sales, but not cash sales, and room statistics. To date figures are not provided except for the running balance of receivables.

The three segments are familiar to users of this book. Accounts-receivable sales, the upper left portion of the report, are identical to columns 6 to 16 of the hand transcript illustrated in Exhibit 13–4. Room statistics and ratios, on the right side of the page, were introduced in Chapter 1. The recap of accounts receivable is the same formula developed during the discussion of the hand transcript several pages back. Then it was displayed as:

> Opening balance, column 4 minus 5 (debit minus credit)
> + Charges and services used by guests, columns 6 to 15 (debits)
> = Total, column 16 (cumulative debit balance before payments of the day)
> – Payments made by guests, columns 17 to 19 (credits)
> = Closing balance, column 21 minus 22 (debit minus credit)

Room Count, House Count, and Room Income.   Room count, the number of rooms sold (occupied), house count, the number of guests (persons) registered, and room income (room sales) are computed during the night audit. The three values can be verified by a second calculation, the same kind that results in the cumulative balance of any continuing inventory, including that of accounts receivable, above. Opening balance plus additions minus withdrawals equals the closing balance. That formula holds true whether one is counting sheets in housekeeping, bottles of scotch at the bar, or room count, house count, and room income.

As with any running balance computation, the closing balance of one day is the opening balance of the next. Consider the scotch at the bar. When the bar closes at 2 AM, there are six bottles of scotch. Twelve hours later, when the bar is reopened, the same six bottles are there. In other words, the closing balance of one day is the opening balance of the next. The rule is the same for room statistics. The number of rooms, guests, and dollar income from yesterday's close is increased with today's arrivals and decreased with today's departures to arrive at the new day's values.

Occasional changes that do not involve arrivals or departures are also added in or subtracted out. These might be room count changes (guest shifts from a three-room suite to a single room), house count changes (a spouse departs from a two-person occupancy with a single folio), or rate changes (previous rate was in error and subsequent nights are charged less). The simple mathematics is illustrated so:

	Room Count	House Count	Room Income
Opening balance	840	1,062	$174,200
+ Arrivals	316	391	80,100
= Total	1,156	1,453	$254,300
– Departures	88	122	16,400
= Total	1,068	1,331	$237,900
± Changes	+6	–2	+1,730
= Closing balance	1,074	1,329	$239,630

Room Statistics.   Both the Night Auditor's Report to the Manager and the income auditor's Daily Report to the Manager contain statistics. Statistics are merely special ways of grouping data in an orderly and usable manner. Statistics are the facts expressed in dollars, cents, or numbers. For example, instead of itemizing:

Guest A	Room 597	$50.25
Guest B	Room 643	$48.75
Guest C	Room 842	$59.25

and so on, one might say there are 220 guests in 189 rooms paying a total of $9,158. A great deal of information has been grouped, classified, and presented to become a statistic.

Taking the next step, these room figures are expressed in ratios, which are more meaningful than the simple statistic. So the 189 rooms sold is expressed in relation to the number of rooms available for sale, 270. The result is a percentage of occupancy, a mathematical expression of how many rooms were sold in relation to how many could have been sold. The occupancy percent is a widely quoted figure and one discussed as early as Chapter 1. Using the illustration, the percentage of occupancy is

$$\frac{\text{number of rooms sold (room count)}}{\text{number of rooms available for sale}} = \frac{189}{270} = 70\%$$

A frequent companion to the percentage of occupancy computation is the average daily rate (ADR). Both ratios appear in the night auditor's report to the manager. Sales per occupied room, as this figure is sometimes called, is the income from room sales divided by the number of rooms sold.

$$\frac{\text{room income}}{\text{number of rooms sold (room count)}} = \frac{\$9,158}{189} = \$48.46$$

A similar computation, RevPar, once called *sales per available room,* is derived by dividing room income by the number of rooms available for sale rather than by the actual number of rooms sold.

$$\frac{\text{room income}}{\text{number of rooms available for sale}} = \frac{\$9,158}{270} = \$33.92$$

The fourth most frequently cited ratio in the manager's daily report is the percentage of double occupancy. Double occupancy is the relationship of rooms occupied by more than one guest to the total number of rooms occupied. That is what the following ratio expresses:

$$\frac{\text{number of guests} - \text{number of rooms sold}}{\text{number of rooms sold}} = \frac{220 - 189}{189} = 16.4\%$$

Having finished the audit with the preparation of the night auditor's report to the manager, the night auditor lays aside the pencils and erasers—or more likely, rubs some stiff shoulders from working at the keyboard—and, at the end of the shift, goes home to bed.

➤ SUMMARY

Hotels balance their accounts receivable nightly. During this procedure, known as the night audit, the amounts owed by individual accounts receivable (guests) are verified. Each receivable (folio) grows larger or smaller as the guest buys services or pays down debt throughout the day. Since every accounting transaction has equal debits and credits, each purchase of service or each payment of debt has an offsetting record. The offset is an equal and opposite entry in a record other than the folio. Therefore, an audit that proves the accuracy of the folio can also be used to prove the offsetting entries. The night audit does just that. It proves the incomes earned by sales to accounts receivable, and it proves the payments (cash, credit card, allowances) made by accounts receivable as they settle their debts.

The night audit proves the balances of accounts receivable. Since cash sales in the various outlets (restaurants, lounges, gift shops, etc.) do not affect accounts receivable, cash sales are not part of the night audit. They are left, rather, to the income or day audit, which is completed every morning following the night audit. The income audit examines all incomes, so it retests the work of the night audit's charge sales. Both audits prepare reports for the manager. The night audit's report is preliminary and may be changed by the permanent report filed by the income auditor.

The mechanics of the night audit have changed as the industry has gained computer capability. Manual pencil-and-paper systems are gone for the most part replaced by computerized property management systems (PMS). The objective has remained unchanged, however; accuracy is still the goal. The audit proves the individual folios, the departmental sales, and the changes taking place in total accounts receivable. That total amount changes almost by the minute as purchases and payments by each guest affect the total. The audit reports this total at the close of each night. The figure is captured like a snapshot after the closeout hour and presented in the daily report.

Tracking total receivables, which are nothing more than a running inventory, is a simple computation. It is the same calculation used for any inventory: linen, wine, steaks, and so on. The opening balance of receivables (the cumulative amount owed from previous days) is increased by charges purchased by guests and decreased by payments made by guests. The new closing balance become the start of the next day's computation. Thus, a rolling balance of accounts receivable: some days larger, some days smaller. The calculation is more apparent on the manual spreadsheet (the transcript) than in the bowels of the computer, where the result is visible but not the process.

The PMS has simplified the work of the night audit, especially the posting of room rates and taxes. The PMS was introduced to the hotel industry to help manage information technology. It has done that job so well that additional services have been added to the PMS to improve the overall capability of the hotel. In Chapter 14 we enlarge on the PMS's capacity and hints of robotics yet to come. New technological linkups to the PMS will become easier and less costly as the industry adopts and implements the Hospitality Information Technology Integration Standards (HITIS). These standards are being developed to facilitate the interface of different products from different vendors. A variety of configurations now cost the industry time, expense, and possible malfunctions.

➤ QUESTIONS AND PROBLEMS

1. Explain how the three backup reports discussed in the section "Downtime Reports" would be used in the event of a computer malfunction.

2. A guest checks in at 4:30 AM on Tuesday, January 8. Under hotel policy, the guest is to be charged for the room-night of Monday, January 7. The closeout hour of Mon-

day, January 7, was 12:30 AM, January 8, and the room charge postings were handled automatically by the PMS at approximately 3 AM on that morning. The room rate is $72 and the tax is 5%; no other charges were incurred. Sketch a computer-prepared folio as it would appear when the guest departs on Wednesday, January 9, at 10 AM. Identify each posting by day and hour and briefly explain who made which posting.

3. **Given**

Rooms occupied	440
Rooms vacant	160
Total rooms sales	$32,330
House count	500

Required

The percentage of occupancy	_____
The percentage of double occupancy	_____
ADR	_____
RevPar	_____

4. Use Exhibits 13–2 and 13–4, and identify your answers by room numbers.

   (a) Which guests, if any, arrived today?

   (b) Which guests, if any, had advanced deposits?

   (c) Which guests, if any, checked out today?

   (d) Which guests, if any, used credit cards at departure?

   (e) Which guests, if any, had amounts due from the hotel?

5. The discussion on reservation reports cites a central reservation report that includes fees. Explain who pays what fees and to whom. About how much might those fees be? (Refer to earlier chapters if necessary.)

6. Is the transcript in balance? If not, what error or errors might account for the discrepancy? What percentage of sales tax is being charged in this community?

Allowances	$ 100.00
Telephone	670.70
Transfers to	395.05
Rooms	9,072.00
Cash advance	444.25
Debit transfer	395.50
Beverage	1,920.00
Credit-card charges	14,482.07
Cash	10,071.22
Closing balance	3,670.41
Opening balance	48,341.50
Rooms tax	725.76
Food	3,000.10
Closing balance	43,007.33
Opening balance	185.00
Total charges	$64,384.81

▶ NOTES

1. The AH&MA is developing integration standards in cooperation with several large chains, notably Holiday (Bass) and Microsoft. Vendors who adopt the Hospitality Information Technology Integration Standards (HITIS) will offer systems that interface with all others who comply with HITIS. Hotels that specify HITIS in their bid solicitations will enjoy reduced risks, lower costs, and savings in installation time. The first set of standards is the interface between POS and PMS.

2. Cendant Corporation is installing chain-mandated property management systems free of charge in all franchise properties because it believes that 60% of hotels at the midtier or lower levels operate with only racks, cigar boxes, and cash registers. *Lodging Hospitality*, June 1998, pp. 26, 28. (Because the authors concur, this edition of *Check-In, Check-Out* continues to include sections on the hand-prepared folio and audit.)

3. *CKC Report*, May 1988, p. 14.

CHAPTER 14

Property Management System Interfaces

Outline

➤ INTEGRATED CALL ACCOUNTING SYSTEMS

Since in-room telephones were the first automated system to be introduced in hotels, it makes sense that the telephone was also the first system to be successfully interfaced to a property management system (PMS). Telephones have been used in hotel rooms since the first ones were installed in New York City's Netherland Hotel in 1894.[1] Today's more sophisticated telephone systems are generally referred to as call accounting systems (CASs).

In addition to being the oldest property management system interface, telephone systems are also the most common PMS interface. Due to the number of telephone posting transactions and the front desk's need to activate in-room telephones, the call accounting system is often interfaced to the PMS even in small (or unsophisticated) properties where no other system interfaces are present. Therefore, the CAS provides an excellent introduction to electronic interface technology.

Communications Architecture

The property management system (PMS) serves as more than just a mechanism to check guests in and out. It also serves as the electronic clearinghouse and interface center for a number of auxiliary electronic systems in the hotel. The energy management system (EMS), call accounting system (CAS), and electronic locking system (ELS) are three of the more common interfaces that operate in connection with the PMS. In-room movies or entertainment, self-check-in and self-check-out systems, in-room safes, and in-room minibar or beverage units are additional examples of PMS interfaces.

In most cases, each of these interfaced systems stands alone with its own processing capabilities. The interface or connection between the stand-alone system (for example, the EMS) and the PMS provides an uninterrupted flow of guest information. An energy management system interface, for example, allows the front-desk property management system to monitor room activity; shut-off heating systems and nonessential lighting in unoccupied rooms; and adjust water temperatures as a function of occupancy. Although the EMS is a complete system with its own input, output, and processing, it functions better with a communication interface to the PMS.

➤*Uniform Connectivity.*   The history of interface connectivity is one of hit and miss, trial and error. In the 1970s, there were close to 100 vendors of property management systems and numerous manufacturers of point-of-sale systems (POS), call accounting systems, back-office accounting systems, and guest history databases.

An unsophisticated hotel operator could easily purchase a PMS, POS, and CAS from three separate vendors. Of course, each salesperson promised his or her system would interface with the other systems. Yet months later, the frustrated hotel operator could find no company willing to take responsibility for the interface. The POS vendor blamed the PMS vendor who blamed the CAS vendor, and so on.

There are plenty of horror stories about hotel operators who spent thousands of dollars on software programming to get one system to electronically interface with another. Many times, however, the hotel was left with a dysfunctional system. Downtime would be common, the interface would slow the processing speed of each system, and valuable data would be lost between the source system and the PMS. This last problem was the worst of all, because hotel revenue (say, from a CAS) was forever lost between systems!

The problem of incompatible interfaces is gradually being eradicated with today's state-of-the-art technologies. Practically every PMS has the capacity to interface with almost every auxiliary system. Indeed, if a property has a stand-alone system that has never been previously interfaced to any brand of PMS, the PMS vendor will often provide free interface software programming. This is a marketing approach many PMS vendors use to enable them to add another system to their list of compatible products. This has been so successful that there are few PMS system–auxiliary system incompatibilities anymore.

New properties have the best of all worlds. Technology managers can choose various interface systems (CAS, EMS, etc.) based on the beneficial synergy each may offer (price, support, guest history, or some other operational feature) without being overly concerned with the interface compatibility between systems.

Standardization.   In 1994, a consortium of hospitality vendors began establishing a standard platform against which all hardware, software, databases, and communication formats must conform. Although conformity will be voluntary, such standardization platforms have performed well in other industries.

Unfortunately, the lodging industry, with its myriad of competitors, has had less success bringing standardization to market than other industries. The problem is that standardization is only as strong as the number of vendors who comply voluntarily. Few hospitality vendors, it seems, are willing to risk their competitive edge for the good of the industry. Until compliance and cooperation increase among competitive vendors, the introduction of standardization may be a long time coming. In fact, since 1994, three separate attempts have been made to bring standardization to the lodging industry. In 1994, the Integrating Technology Consortium (ITC) was created. In 1996, Microsoft started the Windows Hospitality Interface Standards (WHIS) initiative. And in 1997, the AH&MA convened the Hospitality Industry Technology Interface Standards (HITIS) committee.

Once HITIS is fully introduced, it will become the standard for industry purchases of technological hardware and software. By joining the voluntary consortium, vendors will be entitled to promote their products as complying with industry standards. That's a powerful message because hoteliers who purchase noncomplying products would be at risk.

Data Browsing.   Standardization may reach the industry from an unusual direction; it may be market driven. The increasing consolidation of major chains, which we noted in Chapter 1, has accelerated the standardization of property management systems. How long this trend will continue is hard to know, but the results are already evident. In terms of technological capacity, the hospitality industry is quite mature. Hundreds of millions of dollars have been invested year after year to ensure that individual and chain properties are wired. They have successfully automated every stage from check in to check out. That's the problem—too much "data" but not enough "information."

The successful competitor of the future will be the chain that strategically utilizes guest history information (generated by the PMS and its interfaces) and turns it into worthwhile and marketable information. To that end, a standardization of PMS systems makes good sense. Chains have an easier time browsing warehoused data (corporate data browsers are usually Internet-based) when each property in the organization stores information in a like manner—standardization.

As we highlighted earlier, Cendant, the world's largest franchising organization (Days Inn, Howard Johnson, Knights Inn, Ramada, Super 8, Travelodge, Villager

Lodge, and Wingate Inns), announced a huge $75 million plan to implement a standardized PMS across all properties beginning in 1998. The new standardized property management system—at no charge to the individual franchisees—will replace over 60 different PMS systems currently in use chainwide.

Once the standardized systems are installed, the parent organization will uniformly be able to:

➤ Ensure that all revenues are reported accurately
➤ Browse data at the property, regional, national, and international levels
➤ Display like rooms inventory screens and last-room availability information to central reservationists
➤ Create central databases for warehousing such programs as guest history, frequent-guest and frequent-flyer programs, corporate and group activity, and travel agent accounts

History of Hotel Telephone Service

In 1944, the Federal Communications Commission (FCC) approved a proposal that was to structure the economic relationship between the hotel industry and the telephone industry for almost four decades. The ruling required telephone companies to pay hotels a 15% commission for all long-distance calls originating in hotel rooms. As expected, this rule expedited the general introduction of telephones into American hotels. Despite the success, the two industries battled about the size of the commission almost from the start. Hotels argued that the fee was too low to offset costs and earn a fair profit. AT&T countered by arguing that the department shouldn't be a profit center.

The year 1981 was another critical date. Once again, the federal government acted to restructure the system. Within a short time, three traumas rocked the telephone industry. First, the large, integrated Bell system was dissolved, its long-distance service separated from its local operations. Second, competition from other manufacturers and service companies was invited in, weakening the monopoly still further. And third, hotels were permitted once again to levy their own fees on calls originating from their premises. The 1944 commission schedule had been rescinded.

On June 1, 1981, the FCC ruled that hotels could make their own surcharges on interstate calls, just as they had done prior to 1944. A stroke of the pen undid a 37-year experiment. Before the year was out, the Bell system had an announcement of its own: Commissions (estimated in 1981 at $230 million annually) would no longer be paid. Bell's decision was not mandated by the FCC. It was a business decision, and it was a gutsy one at that, since the new federal policy encouraged competition against the Bell system.

A series of court pronouncements destroyed once and for all the concept of the telephone as a utility. Competition was encouraged, and it appeared on the scene with some appealing deals. By an earlier court decision, the Carterfone Case allowed non-Bell equipment to be interconnected with Bell equipment.[2]

Motivated by a great deal of uncertainty and an equal lack of information, the AH&MA negotiated a year's delay with the Bell system. The 15% commission, which had caused such strident arguments earlier, looked awfully good in the face of uncertainty. Commissions were paid until December 31, 1982, while the hotel industry shopped for alternatives.

➤*Historical Billing Procedures.* Before automation, the guest's telephone request was completed by the hotel's operator, who dialed the local call. Long-distance numbers were passed on to the telephone company operator, who dialed that connection. The front office posted to the guest folio from a voucher forwarded by the hotel's telephone operator. Local calls were billed at a fixed amount per state regulations. Long-distance charges were called in by the telephone company after the call was completed.

Because of the telephone industry's sophisticated technology, automated billing came to the hotel's telephone department years before property management systems were installed. Each step that will now be reviewed might not seem significant today, but each one brought an incremental improvement in speed and accuracy to the billing cycle.

Long-Distance Billing. Semiautomation came first to long-distance (LD) billing. The first development allowed guests to bypass the hotel operator and dial the telephone company's long-distance operator directly. This system also allowed the telephone company to send room charges directly to the hotel by way of teletype.

The next development allowed the guest to dial directly into the telephone company equipment (HOBIC; see the next section). Except for billing, the guest now bypassed even the telephone company's operator. The equipment completed the call, and the charge was again teletyped to the front desk for posting. The next step, and we are there now, eliminated the teletypewriter. Instead, the telephone computer posts the charge directly to the property management system computer. The guest's bill is updated automatically. Moreover, if the guest challenges the charge, the telephone number called can be displayed on the front-desk computer screen or printed on the folio.

HOBIC. HOBIC (Hotel Outward Bound Information Center) is an acronym for the telephone company's long-distance network. Even today, HOBIC is the system that guests encounter when they use AT&T's traditional service. HOBIC, the workhorse of the precomputerized system, is still an option for certain hotels (see Exhibit 14–1).

With HOBIC, the guest direct-dials long-distance calls from the room telephone. The first digit dialed, 8, tells the system that long distance is going through. Digit 1, or digit 0 to get the operator, follows; then comes the number to be called. Zero-digit operator intercepts are for person-to-person calls, third-party calls, credit-card calls, and collect calls. The distinction between digit 1 and digit 0 is critical. It dictated the strategy of AT&T following deregulation. The pursuit of that strategy accounted in large measure for the appearance of the alternative operator services (AOS).

Hotel Options following Deregulation

Following deregulation of the telephone industry in 1981, hoteliers settled down to the task of choosing among several alternatives. That choice sums up the intent of deregulation. Alternatives could be pursued, new telephone companies could be tried, special equipment could be tested, and profits could be made.

With AT&T out of the commission business, the scramble for a viable replacement began. The one-year delay negotiated with the telephone company passed quickly as one plan after the other was suggested. Three options faced the hotel industry.

➤*First Option: Status Quo.* A very workable option, but one that was initially ignored, was to maintain the status quo. Keeping the HOBIC system of AT&T,

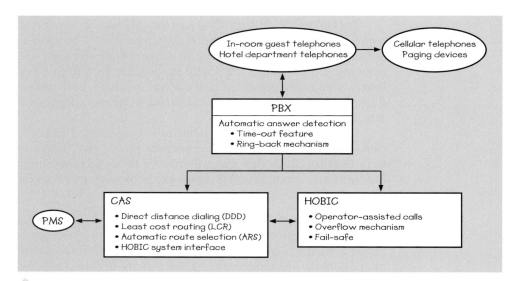

Exhibit 14–1   Graphical representation of the call accounting system. The automatic answer detection function offers two possibilities. The time-out feature (found in older systems) cannot detect when the placed call connects, and automatically begins charging after a standard grace period (usually 1 minute), even if the placed call is still ringing. In more sophisticated systems, the ring-back mechanism begins charging only after the placed call has actually been answered.

which was in place and working very well, would cost nothing. No heavy investment in capital equipment, no new training for front-office personnel, and no change in guest habits would be required. The equipment and procedures were still Bell's, so the infrastructure and support of the telephone company were still there.

This plan required the hotel to levy its own commission. Guest telephone charges increased, because the hotel continued to pay the telephone company the operator-assisted rates, and the hotel's fee was added on. Some price resistance did appear among the guests. Compared to what happened elsewhere, and compared to what happened later on with alternative operator services, the price increases were moderate.

The do-nothing decision proved a wise one for the small hotel. It provided the luxury of time to examine what was happening elsewhere. After the fact, many larger hotels wished they, too, had waited. Some decisions proved disastrous.

➤ *Second Option: Install a Call Accounting System.*   The same technology that AT&T was using—HOBIC—was available for hotel use in the form of a microprocessor called AIOD. AIOD, *automatic identification of outward dialing*, enabled the hotel to identify the calling guest's room number without an operator intercept from the telephone company. Charges went through at direct-distance dialing (DDD) rates rather than operator-assisted rates. AIOD was installed on hotel switchboards, but not without difficulty.

Through a number of trunk lines, the PBX (private branch exchange) connects the numerous internal lines to various outside telephone systems. But PBX switchboards are not all created equal; some are smart and others are dumb.

With smart switches in place, additional equipment, such as automatic identification of outward dialing (AIOD) or least cost routers (LCR), could be installed with little cost and difficulty (see Exhibit 14–1). Smart switches allowed the newest PBXs to function with AIOD and LCR as integral parts of the equipment. Additional property management capability could also be handled through the smart boards.

After committing to AIOD, however, many hoteliers learned that they had dumb switchboards. Because dumb switches cannot handle sophisticated functions such as AIOD and LCR, managers now faced a whole series of new decisions about which boards to acquire, from which company, with what options, and with whose money. It also opened the floodgates for unqualified third-party intermediaries to gain access to the unwary hotel industry.

▶ *Third Option: Shop the Competition.* Some hotels elected to move beyond call accounting by shopping among other common carriers (OCCs, such as MCI and GTE (Sprint), as well as AT&T, for the least expensive long-distance lines (see Exhibit 14–2). To do this, more technology was needed—least cost routing (LCR) equipment. Here the emphasis is on the cost of the call rather than the resale price. With reduced costs, small surcharges, which maintain the hotel's competitiveness, could produce substantial profit gains.

The smart switches of the LCR equipment work in tandem with the smart switches of the call accounting equipment to evaluate each call and to route it over the most economical trunk line. Eventually, the charge finds its way to the folio (see Exhibit 14–3). The cost of calls has come down, and gross income has gone up. The

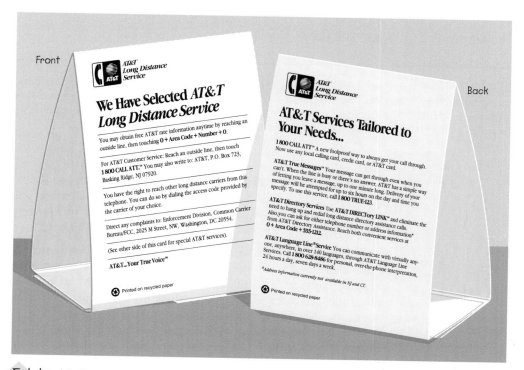

Exhibit 14–2 AT&T promotional tent designed to stand near each guestroom telephone. This document tells guests which common carrier (AT&T) the hotel has selected. Notice that the tent reads "You have the right to reach other long distance carriers from this telephone." *Courtesy of AT&T, Basking Ridge, New Jersey.*

	ROOM	PLACE CALLED		NUMBER	TIME	MIN	TYP	CLASS	RATE
A 2-22	103	LOS ANGELES	CA	213 555-7784	2245	6	1	S	1.51
A 2-22	104	HUNTITNBCH	CA	714 555-7711	1317	3	1	K	1.36
A 2-22	107	WICHITA	KS	316 555-5020	0747	2	1	B	.43
A 2-22	107	VAN NUYS	CA	213 555-7487	0916	2	1	K	.97
A 2-22	107	LEWISTON	ME	207 555-6141	1628	12	1	K	6.13
A 2-22	107	CHICAGO	IL	312 555-5134	1832	7	1	S	1.96
A 2-22	107	CANOGAPARK	CA	213 555-4815	1935	14	1	S	3.39
A 2-22	108	PHOENIX	AZ	602 555-4958	0810	2	1	K	.97
A 2-22	111	ROOPVILLE	GA	404 555-4422	0806	3	1	K	1.52
A 2-22	111	NO HOLLYWD	CA	213 555-9540	0908	1	1	K	.58
A 2-22	114	GREELEY	CO	303 555-5876	1750	38	1	S	9.91
A 2-22	117	STPETERSBG	FL	813 555-1411	1620	4	1	K	2.21
A 2-22	118	OCILLA	GA	912 555-7464	1238	1	1	K	.64
A 2-22	118	HUNTITNBCH	CA	714 555-7243	1801	5	1	S	1.28
A 2-22	125	CANOGAPARK	CA	213 555-4815	1114	8	1	K	3.31
A 2-22	125	CODY	WY	307 555-2245	1131	5	1	K	2.34
A 2-22	202	DRAPER	UT	801 555-5093	1745	3	1	S	.85
A 2-22	203	BOULDER	CO	303 555-1181	0902	7	1	K	3.20
A 2-22	203	LONG BEACH	CA	213 555-8832	1747	8	1	S	1.98
A 2-22	206	BAMMEL	TX	713 555-7580	0811	7	1	K	3.28
A 2-22	206	GREELEY	CO	303 555-7067	1723	10	1	S	2.69
A 2-22	209	FORD CITY	PA	412 555-9600	1656	12	1	K	4.56
A 2-22	210	LITTLETON	CO	303 555-9999	1331	2	1	K	1.05

* * * N24 * * *

Exhibit 14–3   Printout of long-distance charges generated by the call accounting system. Although this printout was produced in numerical room order, it could just as easily have been printed in chronological order beginning with the first call of the day. The 555 exchange is used to mask actual telephone numbers—you've probably heard it used in television and movies. *Courtesy of Centel, Las Vegas, Nevada.*

counterbalance has been the cost of the investment, of the consultants, and of the technology. Large commercial hotels, whose clients are heavy users of telephones, are able to amortize the costs more rapidly. They have a greater economic justification for their entry into the telephone business than do smaller hotels.

➤**WATS.**   Like the entire telecommunications industry, wide area telephone (also sometimes transmission) service (WATS) has changed since its introduction. The original concept of one flat monthly fee, for which the user could talk indefinitely at any time, has been modified. Charges are now based on increments of time. Rates vary according to the time of the day and the day of the week.

Hundreds of companies have gone into the resale of WATS lines. They buy long-distance lines from AT&T and other OCCs at quantity discounts and resell to customers at a lower charge than that of the common carriers.

In-WATS (incoming toll-free 1-800 or -888 numbers) have a critical role in the development of central reservation offices, as explained in Chapter 4. It has become quite fashionable to substitute catchy phrases for traditional telephone numbers in an attempt to retain the number in the user's memory (see Exhibit 14–4).

Company Name	Phone 1-800-
Clarion Hotels	Clarion
Club Med	Club Med
Colonial Williamsburg	History
Embassy Suites	Embassy
Harrah's (Atlantic City)	2 Harrah
Hilton Hotels	Hiltons
Marriott Hotels & Resorts	USA WKND
National Car Rental	Car Rent
Nikko Hotels International	Nikko US
Omni Hotels	The Omni
Ramada Hotels	2 Ramada
Renaissance Hotels	Hotels 1
Southwest Airlines	I Fly SWA

Exhibit 14–4   Some of the more creative 1-800 numbers used by the hospitality industry. Replacing telephone numbers with catchy words and phrases makes the chains' phone numbers more memorable and hopefully creates a higher level of repeat business.

Out-WATS have a critical role in call accounting system profitability. Hotels that route guest long-distance calls over WATS lines may save substantially over normal long-distance costs. These savings may be returned to the guest or are more likely converted into additional hotel profit.

More Recent Developments

The deregulation of the telephone industry is still not fully resolved. The latest and most wide-reaching step occurred in 1996 with passage of the Telecommunications Act. This latest tale in the deregulation saga supposedly removed all remaining barriers to competition, freeing long-distance carriers, local telephone companies, and cable companies to compete head-on with one another. For the hospitality industry, the implications of this act are still unclear. However, in recent years, other issues have developed about which hotel managers should be aware.

▶ *Alternative Operator Services.*   One important issue deals with the rise in alternative operator services (AOSs) in the late 1980s. The rise in AOSs came as a direct result of the first stage of deregulation in 1981. As hotels found themselves free to levy higher fees to their guests for telephone use, the guests themselves turned toward services for which the hotel did not charge—0-digit dialing. And though AT&T offered hotels a commission for all 0-digit calls originating from their rooms, a new third-party, the alternative operator service, paid far higher commissions.

High commissions from AOSs meant that guests were paying high fees to get the service. That is the negative side of AOS. Although high rates can be explained, hotels didn't bother to do so. Guests were shocked when the charges arrived by way of their monthly business or residential bill. That sometimes took weeks, because the charges for 0-digit calls were run through the local or regional telephone companies. And the fees were high—as much as 10 times the prevailing AT&T rate!

Ticking off the reasons for the high rates does little to appease guests. Here they are, anyway. Hotels want their commission, the bigger the better. AOS companies have their own expenses and profits. The cost of the call still has to be paid, even with discounted lines that may be greater than AT&T rates. The call needs to go to the operator center of the AOS. That's the first charge. The call is then forwarded to the AOS connection center, which might actually be in the direction opposite to the direction in which the call is headed, ("back-hauling"). Tack on another charge. When the call is completed through AT&T or an OCC, another cost is added. Finally, there is a fee to get the local telephone companies to include the charge and collect the billing.

AOS Regulations.   The biggest and loudest complaints came from guests who were unaware of how the system worked and how much it cost. Hotels never told their guests things like: "If there is no answer in 10 rings (or 45 seconds), you will be charged nevertheless;" "If you use our convenient in-room AOS, the charge might be 10 times the AT&T operator-assisted rate;" "If you prefer to 'splash off' the AOS and use AT&T, here's how to do it".

Companies such as Hampton Inns heard the complaints and eliminated all 8–0 service charges. Others didn't hear and left the listening to the FCC and various states. On April 27, 1989, the FCC followed the lead of several states (Exhibit 14–2) and required that notice be posted. Moreover, it required that *call blocking,* which prevents a caller from reaching a competitive carrier, be halted.

▶*Emergency 9-1-1 Calls.*   Another telephone-related issue is the risk caused the hotel from in-house emergency 9-1-1 (E 9-1-1) calls. Many E 9-1-1 calls that pass through the hotel's PBX systems are routed over normal telephone trunk lines to the Public Safety Answering Point assigned to that jurisdiction. If the caller is unable to talk to the PSAP operator, or cannot remember the room number from which he or she is calling, valuable time is lost in the emergency response. That's because the PSAP will only see the name and physical address of the hotel, not the number of the room from which the call is being made. Upon arrival, there may be hundreds of rooms to choose from. Indeed, even if the front desk is able to look up which room made the E 9-1-1 call, chances are the hotel will not be aware of the emergency until the vehicles are pulling up out front. Again, valuable time will be lost.

In this age of increasing technological sophistication, only those hotels boasting a PBX system equipped with enhanced 9-1-1 capabilities are safe from potential litigation. With enhanced 9-1-1 capabilities, not only will the PSAP be given the guest's room number, but the hotel front office and/or security staff will also be alerted to the emergency (see Exhibit 14–5). In many cases, faster hotel staff response time can make a significant difference in the guest's well-being.

Although legislation mandating enhanced 9-1-1 information for PBX-generated calls has been proposed at the federal level, no regulations have yet been established. At the state level, however, PBX E 9-1-1 enhancements have been passed in such states as Colorado, Illinois, Mississippi, Texas, and Washington.

▶*Mandatory and Voluntary System Upgrades.*   The hotel industry has begun providing increasing varieties of telephone services to appeal to guests. Sometimes the law mandates such telephone services (as with volume-control features). In other cases, it is as much a marketing decision as anything else. For example, dual lines to data ports may serve corporate hotel guests' needs, but they may represent an unnecessary investment for leisure guests.

Exhibit 14–5   Feature phones, such as this one from Teledex Corporation, offer safety, convenience, and revenue-generating options to the hotel. Safety because they clearly display the emergency button (especially attractive to hotels with large international markets); convenience because common guest services are available at the touch of a button; revenue-generating because some hotels lease telephone buttons to local merchants (proximate restaurants, exercise clubs, and dry cleaning, for example). *Courtesy of Teledex Corporation, San Jose, California.*

Volume Controls.   The Federal Communications Commission passed a ruling that volume control features on guest-room telephones are required for all new telephones installed after January 1, 2000. Although the ruling applies only to new telephones, it affects existing hotels planning to renovate rooms and replace existing phones. Because guest-room telephones are replaced often in the course of regular room renovations and enhancements, it won't be long before the majority of all hotel rooms are equipped with volume-control features.

This ruling is an attempt by the FCC to make the hotel industry friendlier to guests who are hearing-impaired. Although it falls under a different implementation schedule, the FCC has also required the installation of hearing-aid-compatible telephones in hotel guest rooms.

Recognition of Area Codes.   Surprising as it may sound, not all PBX systems recognize all possible area codes. This issue was first brought to light in 1995, when a number of new area codes were introduced to supplement the 144 existing codes. Prior to 1995, all 144 area codes used either the numbers 1 or 0 as the middle digit.

As the increasing surge in various technologies (for example, fax machines, pagers, cell phones, and modems) created a need for new area codes, Bellcore's North American Numbering Plan Administrative Group found it necessary to begin introducing the numbers 2 through 9 in the middle digit of new area codes. Introducing these new digits caused a number of difficulties with older hotel PBX systems. Guests would often receive a fast busy signal or a recording stating that the number dialed is not working.

The problem was fixed just in time for the new 888 and 877 toll-free area codes. Many hotel phone systems were not programmed to recognize these new toll-free numbers. As such, for the first several months following their introduction, guests were being charged exorbitant long-distance charges because the PBX system recognized the new numbers as toll calls rather than toll-free calls.

Increased Capacity.   The average guest-room telephone call used to be 2 to 5 minutes in duration. Today, with Internet access, e-mail, modem transmissions, and the like, the average corporate phone call lasts 45 to 90 minutes. And with Marriott estimating that 76% of all their corporate guests carry laptop computers, the problem will only worsen.

The result of this new lifestyle is a growing need for increased hotel telephone capacity. Where one phone line per room was the norm 10 years ago, the trend is to two or even three lines for each guest room (hotels that offer in-room fax machines often provide three separate lines for each room). That is an expensive enhancement. It is especially expensive when you realize that the bulk of these calls are being placed to toll-free 800 numbers for which the hotel may receive no revenue!

The cost grows again as hotels introduce other features for which corporate guests clamor. The demand for speaker phones has been growing according to a number of corporate guest surveys (see Exhibit 14–5). A second telephone by the bedside or desk has also become the standard for corporate excellence.

The solution to the rising costs of increased telephone equipment is to increase revenues as well. New venues for generating telecommunications revenues are gaining popularity. Certainly hotels profit from incoming and outgoing fax services, but other options should be considered as well. For example, there is a growing expectation that hotels be able to provide corporate guests with cellular phones for use during their visit. In addition, wireless pagers are also an option. In fact, a number of hotels now provide integrated service from guest room to cellular telephone—after the guest room phone rings for the guest a predetermined number of times, the caller is provided the option of leaving a message or ringing through to the guest's cellular line. Now that's first-class service!

▶**Other Telephone Considerations.**   Aside from the preceding discussion of call accounting systems, there are numerous additional telephone-related issues for hotel management to consider. Among the most profitable may be the pay phone.

Profitable Pay Phones.   First it was call accounting, then AOS, and now pay phones. Of course, the scope is far greater than the hotel business. Whereas call accounting affected chiefly aggregators—hotels, hospitals, and dormitories—the deregulation of pay telephones touches the gas station, the convenience store, the shopping mall, the airport, and many more locations.

Anyone can own a telephone. That means that anyone can own a pay phone. In the airport, the owner could be the airport authority. In the convenience store, it might be the 7-Eleven chain. And in the lobby, it is the hotel. Anyone who has done a modicum of travel has seen the variety of telephones in the national airports: phones for each company, one phone for all companies, phones that operate on credit-card magnetic strips, phones that operate with cash, phones in calling centers. The race is on.

Into the marketplace have come all the players that we have seen before: the OCCs and the AOSs. And their roles and motivations are pretty much the same as they were with call accounting and 0+ calling: fees and commissions. It all came to a head on January 1, 1990, when pay phone locations (hotels, for example) were ordered to select a long-distance carrier. (Remember, interstate calls are controlled at the federal level.)

Hotels see profits as they did with call accounting. Instead of a paltry $30 per month from a 15% commission on an AT&T pay phone, they can get four times that much from a vending–machine–company partnership, and even more from outright ownership. Furthermore, if they own their own telephones nothing can stop them from running local calls through their own switchboard, long-distance calls through their call accounting system, and 0+ calls through their AOS. And the revenues are staggering. The typical gas station pay phone generates $350 to $400 per month. Hotel lobby pay phones often experience substantially higher revenues.

In 1997, hotel lobby pay phones received another nudge toward increased profitability: The entire pay phone industry was detariffed by the FCC. Detariffing essentially eliminated any ceilings on local call rates. Within months of the deregulation, most pay phones nationwide increased rates from $0.25 to $0.35 or more. If lobby pay phones were profitable at $0.25 per local call, imagine how much more profitable the hotel's lobby pay phone could be at $0.35 per call or higher.

1-900 Premium Priced Calls (PPCs).   Guests contact 1-900 numbers for a wide range of activities, including sports scores, horoscopes, trivia contests, opinion polls, stock quotes, and pornographic sex hotlines. Generally, PPCs charge guests for each minute they are on-line with the 1-900 number. Charges may range from under $1 per minute to as high as a $100 flat fee per call. However, no matter what the purpose or cost of the call, the hotel rarely shares in the revenue.

Here's how it works. The call accounting system only charges the guest's folio for the toll charge of the call. In some cases, this is a local call with perhaps a $0.50 charge attached. In other cases, it may post as a long-distance call generating, say, $0.25 per minute. In any event, the guest is long gone when the 1-900 service charge shows up on the hotel's monthly telephone billing statement. Before the problem was recognized, many hoteliers were hit for thousands of dollars in uncollectible PPCs in a single month.

Although most telephone companies will forgo the charges for one month if the hotel complains, that is merely a short-term solution. More permanent solutions include the following:

> ➤ Block all 1-900 telephone calls from the source. Sophisticated CASs can differentiate 1-900 prefix calls and prevent connection from occurring.
> ➤ If the call accounting system cannot block the calls, possibly the local telephone company can. There may be a charge for this 1-900 prefix block, but it is probably money well spent.
> ➤ If neither of the above-mentioned electronic solutions will work, good old-fashioned manual labor certainly will. During the night audit shift each day, have an employee search the printed CAS revenue report line by line. This report prints every single phone number dialed throughout the entire day from each hotel room. Check the report for phone numbers beginning with a 1-900

prefix. When found, charge the guest's folio some exorbitant fee—such as $100 for each call.

Feature Phones.   Today's in-room guest telephones have the capacity to perform a multitude of functions not generally associated with telephones. These feature phones have met with outstanding approval from hotel guests. Feature phones offer one-button speed dialing to in-house departments or local merchants (who pay for the convenience of a captive audience). In addition, they usually offer a hold button and call-waiting function. Such phones are commonly found with a built-in speakerphone, alarm clock, and even an AM/FM radio (see Exhibit 14–5).

Telephones of a higher (and more expensive) class are commonly referred to as *hard-wired multipurpose phones.* These phones may cost the property $500 or more per unit but are easily justified from an energy-savings standpoint. Hard-wired telephones are available that can regulate temperature levels in the room; control as many as six remote lighting fixtures; turn the television set on, change the channels, and adjust the volume; open and close the curtains; and even change the room status to "do not disturb."

Many hard-wired telephones require the guest to activate the room by inserting a keycard in a specially designed slot. When the room is unoccupied, the system automatically disengages most lights, the television, and even heating and air conditioning units.

➤ **Supplemental Guest Services.**   Some of the most exciting new innovations come in the form of supplemental guest services. Supplemental or *auxiliary* guest services are clearly designed with the guest in mind. They have a positive impact on the perception of quality service by providing the guest with some of the comforts of home or office. Examples of supplemental guest services—commonly viewed as additions to the call accounting system—include electronic voice messaging and automated wake-up systems.

Electronic Voice Messaging.   Guest telephone messages have historically been a cumbersome affair. Some callers wish to leave lengthy messages, operator-transcribed return telephone numbers are often incorrect, and the growing number of international travelers adds a non-English-speaking component to many of the calls. Today's hotels have answered most of these issues with the introduction of electronic voice messaging.

Electronic voice messaging or voice mailboxes are quite similar to the standard answering machine found in a person's home. However, rather than servicing one incoming telephone line, electronic mailbox systems may be capable of handling thousands of extensions. Mailboxes are usually designed to handle hotel executive office extensions as well as guest-room telephone lines.

Many systems allow newly arrived hotel guests a chance to record their own personalized messages. This is an especially powerful feature in an international market. Guests can leave customized messages in whichever language they speak, and the hotel does not need to translate their incoming messages.

Furthermore, these systems also allow various hotel departments to prerecord messages. An interested guest can call the main dining room mailbox and learn the special entrée of the night or the hours of operation. Another mailbox might be reserved for use by the concierge staff to promote certain activities in the hotel or across town. The possibilities from such a service are endless.

Automated Attendant Services. Automated attendant services actually relieve the PBX department from answering the telephone at all. Instead, the caller is asked to select from a series of choices and to press the corresponding telephone digit accordingly.

Automated attendant systems are gaining popularity across the world. Most high-volume telephone centers sport some form of this service. In the hospitality industry, however, there are some guest-service purists who believe automated attendant systems are too impersonal and mechanical to find a home in such a customer-oriented business. Although they raise a good point, let's remember that practically every national central reservation office currently operates some type of automated attendant system.

Automated Wake-up Systems. Automated wake-up systems are consistent with other auxiliary guest services because they both save labor and provide higher levels of customer service. Not only do automated wake-up systems remove the front-desk department from the repetitive early morning task of phoning each guest room and waking the occupant, they also offer a number of unique features.

Although some automated wake-up systems still require the front-desk employee to enter the room number and time of the wake-up call, most systems allow guests to directly input the wake-up time themselves. In addition, most systems produce reports identifying which rooms were called, the time of the calls, and the guest's wake-up status. Wake-up status—call was answered, call was not answered the first time but was eventually answered during one of the routine system callbacks, or phone was never answered—is an important tool for addressing potential guest complaints.

Automated wake-up systems also serve as a unique marketing medium because the groggy guest makes for a wonderful captive audience. In this regard, hotels not only inform guests about the day's weather conditions, they also describe the breakfast specials in the dining room. Some automated wake-up systems even provide an option for guests to self-design their own personalized wake-up calls!

➤ GUEST-ROOM LOCKING SYSTEMS

All guests demand safety and security in the guest room. Certain guest markets (for example, corporate female travelers) place hotel security near the very top of their list when selecting a chain or independent property. And guests are not alone in their quest for enhanced security.

Hotel employees, managers, and owners are equally concerned with providing high levels of guest security. In the wake of numerous lawsuits charging hotels with inadequate standards of security, a heightened awareness has ensued. This awareness has not been lost on the insurance companies, either. Most insurers of lodging properties offer deep discounts for modern electronic security improvements such as electronic locking systems, property surveillance systems, and fire-system monitoring devices.

Major chains have taken guest security to heart in recent years. A number of chains recommend, and some (such as Hilton Hotels, with its 100% electronic locking system compliance in all hotels) require, that electronic security devices be installed in all new construction. Indeed, even AAA includes guest security protection as part of its property rating system!

Although security involves surveillance, intrusion detection, fire prevention, employee screening, and numerous other concerns, initial efforts have been directed toward lock and key security. It's here that some of the electronic smart switches hold the greatest promise.

The Room Key Revolution

In recent years, the historical tasks of maintaining key security, tracking lost guest-room keys, managing the distribution of master keys, rekeying locks, and inventorying several keys for each of hundreds of rooms have given way to a simple electronic interface. You see, with smart switches, there are no keys to track. The key is disposable or renewable, and each guest gets a new key and a new key combination. With traditional keys, the types that are still used in homes, key loss is staggering. Estimates put the number at one key per room each month. Many hotels have four or five lost keys per day. Before smart switches, lock replacement for Holiday Inns, for example, was pegged at $1 million annually.

Not so many years ago, there was a strong black market for stolen hotel keys (up to $1,000 for a master key), and many hotel employees knew about it. Forced entry into guest rooms was almost unknown, because access through stolen, duplicated, or master key blanks was so easy. One group of blitzers (6- to 10-person units) "did" nearly 200 rooms in Anaheim, California, in one morning. And *Los Angeles Magazine* reported the capture of a person who had master keys for 17 hotels.

Those kinds of statistics, and the potential liability they represented, made hoteliers quickly convert to the smart switch electronic locking system (ELS) technology.

➤ *Levels of Access.*   Control of keys begins with an understanding of the type and number of keys available. Most key systems are comprised of four or five levels of access. Although modern electronic locking systems have changed the format of that access, the terminology and the service performed by each level remain roughly the same as the traditional locking systems of yesteryear.

For the most part, each level of the hierarchy exceeds the level below. The guest-room key level (and the fail-safe level) can access only one room. The next level, the maid or housekeeping level, can access an entire wing of rooms. The third level, the general manager or master level, can access the entire hotel property. And the final level, the emergency or E-key level, can access the entire property even when the guest-room deadbolt has been activated.

Although the levels of hierarchy are much the same with both ELS and standard hardware locking systems, electronic locking systems add a new dimension of security. The electronic keycard is designed to override and invalidate previous keycard combination codes.

For example, Daniel Adams checks into room 1111 on Monday evening. On Tuesday morning, Adams checks out of the hotel. Because the ELS keycard is disposable, he keeps the card as a souvenir for his daughter. Later in the morning, Adams realizes that he has left his wallet hidden in the room. Retrieving the keycard from his pocket, Adams is able to enter the room and find his wallet. That's because the hotel front desk has not yet rented room 1111 to a new guest.

Later in the morning, a maid inserts her housekeeping keycard and enters room 1111. Although she accessed the room after Adams, inserting a housekeeping card in the lock does not invalidate the guest's (Adams's) card. That's because the maid's card is on a separate level of the hierarchy. At this point, Adams could still access the room. Still later in the day, room 1111 is rented to Elizabeth Brown. Her insertion of the new guest-level keycard into the lock electronically invalidates Adams's card. In fact, Brown's card is designed to invalidate all guest-level keycards with lower code sequences than her own. Similarly, Brown's card can only be overridden with a higher-coded card inserted by the next new guest to check in to room 1111.

This scenario is true for most electronic locking systems in use today, those commonly referred to as micro-fitted ELS. However, some hotels have a more expensive hard-wired electronic locking system in place. A hard-wired ELS literally connects each room doorlock to the front-desk computer system. Therefore, with a hard-wired system, Adams's key would have been invalidated at the time he checked out. The difference is that in the previous Adams example, a new keycard must physically be inserted in the doorlock to invalidate the previous code.

The Guest-Room Key.   The single guest key, which fits a standard lock and deadbolt (see Exhibit 14–6), an electronic lock (see Exhibit 14–7), or a nonelectronic lock (see Exhibit 14–8), gives the guest access to the room. In some hotels, the same key that fits the guest-room door may also unlock connecting doors between rooms (when such access is warranted), open spa or health club facilities, and even open lobby entrance doors. With electronic locking systems, a single keycard can be programmed to open an almost unlimited variety of doors. A meeting planner who wishes to leave a welcoming gift in the rooms of arriving guests, for example, would probably be given one key programmed to access all arriving rooms. The key would have an expiration time on it, so the meeting planner could leave gifts between, say 2 and 4 PM, but it would become invalid as guests began arriving after 4 PM.

Once inside the room, virtually all types of hotel locks (traditional, electronic, or nonelectronic) provide guests with deadbolts for added security. However, locking the door from inside sometimes trips a signal, which tells the room attendant the room is occupied. In this age of enhanced security and concern for potential litigation, such signal devices may be outdated. You see, signal systems of all types—Do Not Disturb signs, lock signals, light systems, room service trays left in the corridor, signals on latches, and message notes on the door—tell the thief as well as the room attendant whether the room is occupied.

Exhibit 14–6   Even traditional mechanical locks have improved with technology. This one can easily be rekeyed. Using a special control key, the interchangeable core is quickly removed and replaced with a new one. *Courtesy of Schlage Lock Company, San Francisco, California.*

Exhibit 14–7   Some guests prefer traditional-looking room keys (possibly, they feel more secure than with a simple plastic keycard). Those shown here have a reprogrammable magnetic strip embedded in them. They are really just a variation of the keycard. Other, more creative variations, are displayed in Exhibit 14–12. *Courtesy of ILCO Unican, Inc., Montreal, Quebec, Canada.*

Burglars have been known to enter a room marked by the guest to be made up, change the sign to Do Not Disturb, and finish their business in peace. Thieves will also enter when they hear the shower running or when the guest is asleep. Burglars have an edge when they know where their victims are. Estimates suggest that one in every three guests fails to double-lock the door.

The Fail-Safe Key.   The second level in the key distribution hierarchy is only found with electronic locking systems. The fail-safe level provides a preestablished option for use during computer downtime. Most hotels create at least two fail-safe keys

Exhibit 14–8 A nonelectronic locking system utilizes mechanical hardware. As a result, they are less costly than ELSs and require no batteries, electrical connections, or dedicated computers (see Exhibit 14–11). Yet the code of nonelectronic locks can still be changed with each new guest key. *Courtesy of CORKEY Control Systems, Hayward, California.*

for each guest room. Once created, fail-safe keys are secured by management until they are needed.

When the host ELS computer is down (inoperative), either due to a power outage or a hardware/software operations problem, the hotel resorts to the use of fail-safe keys. Just like a new guest keycard, fail-safe keys invalidate previous guest-level key-cards. Yet fail-safe keys do not alter the normal sequence of guest-level key codes.

They temporarily interrupt the stream of codes, but once the ELS computer is operational again, the new guest-level keycard will invalidate the fail-safe key and everything will be back to normal.

Hotels create two fail-safe keys to gain plenty of time. Two fail-safe keys are good for two new sequences. That's at least two days of fail-safe operation. Once the ELS computer comes back on-line, front-office management will create new back-up fail-safe keys, always keeping at least two such keys in storage for another down period.

The Maid or Pass Key.   The next-highest level in the key hierarchy is the maid level, also known as the housekeeping level, the pass key level, the submaster level, the section level, or even the area key level. Each maid-level key controls the room attendant's section of the floor, usually 12 to 18 rooms. Since the pass key fits no other subset, both the hotel and the individual room attendant are protected. Well-trained employees of every department refuse guests' requests to be admitted to rooms. Pass keys are used for this purpose only after proper authorization is obtained from the desk.

Room attendants must not permit guests without identification—that is, a room key—to enter open rooms where they are working. Similarly, rooms must not be left unlocked if the room attendant is called away before the room is completed. Obviously, then, the room attendant's own keys should not be hung on the cart or left in the door. That's why a plastic ELS keycard hung around the room attendant's neck proves both secure and convenient.

The Master Key.   The master or general manager level may be next in the key hierarchy. However, depending on the design of the hotel, there are a number of key hierarchy possibilities between the maid level and the master level. For example, some properties may wish to create an inspector- or floor-level key. This level would exceed the maid's key (which opens something like 12 to 18 rooms) by opening all rooms on a given floor or section (probably 60 to 100 rooms).

Another possibility is an executive housekeeping–level key that would probably open every room in the hotel. The difference between the executive housekeeping level and the general manager or master level is that the executive housekeeper is restricted from access to certain high-security areas. While the general manager level will access all locks in the hotel, the executive housekeeper may be denied access to such areas as the accounting office, the food and beverage department, and other administrative offices.

The Emergency Key.   The highest level in the hierarchy is the emergency or E-key (sometimes called the grand master). Like the general manager-level key, the E-key can access every lock in the hotel. The difference is that the emergency key can access all rooms regardless of lock status. In other words, even when the guest has activated the deadbolt from inside the room, the E-key can still gain access. During periods of extreme emergency—for example, a guest has taken ill and cannot answer the door, or the fire department needs to enter a guest room—the E-key can literally be the difference between life or death!

►*Enhanced ELS Security.*   The loss of guests' personal belongings from their rooms can be traced to three causes: outsiders (intruders), insiders (employees), and the guests themselves. The smart-switch locks of modern technology have affected primarily the outsiders. However, there have been important spin-offs protecting the hotel from insiders and even from guests. Careless guests lose, misplace, forget, and accuse. Dishonest guests manipulate their hotel stays to bring claims against the property or against their own insurance companies.

The director of research and security for the AH&MA maintains that 30% of employees are honest; 30% are dishonest; and 40% must be protected from themselves—as opportunists, they will take advantage of weaknesses in the system.

ELS Identification Database.   Electronic locking systems provide the best line of defense against unethical guests, employees, and even outsiders. That is because the ELS is a smart switch capable of communicating critical information to management.

Many a manager has dealt with an upset guest accusing a hotel employee of theft. In some cases, guests are correct about the employee who has wronged them; in other instances, guests are incorrect. Maybe the "stolen" wristwatch was merely misplaced, lost, or never packed in their luggage in the first place.

Answers to such questions and accusations are ready and waiting inside the microprocessor of the ELS. Hotel management need merely download the information to a handheld computer (or, in the case of a hard-wired ELS, the front-desk computer can access the information) to learn which keycards have accessed the guest's room during the period in question. Most systems hold at least the last dozen keycard entries—other systems hold substantially more. In many cases, the ELS keycard–access database provides enough information to solve the "crime."

Distribution Control.   Control must be established over the numbers of employees who have legitimate access to keys. That includes all the front-office and uniformed services personnel, the housekeeping staff, and the maintenance crews—well over half of all the employees in the hotel. Control must be established on the distribution of keys to the vast number of guests who make legitimate demands for access to their rooms.

An earlier discussion pointed out what the room attendants and the housekeeping department must and must not do with keys on the guest-room floors. Good key security invariably focuses back on the front desk. Clerks must never issue keys without verifying the guest's identity, a procedure that takes but seconds. Still, in the pressure of the rush hours, many keys are issued with abandon. Almost anyone can request a key and get it (see Exhibit 14–9).

Well-publicized lawsuits with huge settlements have pounded security into the minds of every hotel manager. Security is a serious matter. That's the attitude that must be instilled in the staff, who may otherwise treat the subject rather nonchalantly.

Other Hardware Considerations.   If the reported and unreported losses from guest rooms truly equal the $5,000 per room per year figure that is sometimes quoted, there is strong economic incentive for buying the very best of locks.

Among the simple pieces of hardware being introduced are peepholes (observation ports), a code requirement in some jurisdictions, and chain latches. Latch guards are either of the chain-and-slide-variety or a simple cable chain looped from the door stud over the knob. Even though these devices (or others, such as Charlie bars on sliding doors) are provided, some guests opt not to use them. Reminders attached to the insides of doors, notices on the rooming slips, and bureau cards try to convince the guest to participate in his or her own security.

Doors, along with their frames, hinges, and pins, must be heavy and solid, especially those on motel units that open onto a parking lot. Too much space between the door frame (or doorjamb) and the wall stud allows the frame to be spread, disengaging the lock.

Exhibit 14–9   This photo says it all. Protection from litigation aside, electronic locking systems are so much simpler than managing the inventory of thousands of keys required with a traditional locking approach.

All security devices should be cleared first with the fire marshall. Most fire codes, for example, require the deadbolt and the doorknob to be operated as one from inside the room. If the guest panics because of an emergency, the deadbolt is released with the turn of the knob.

Categories of Locking Systems

There are three categories of guest-room doorlocks available in the marketplace. The most basic of these locks is the standard mechanical keyed doorlock found in older lodging properties and personal residences. Next in line in terms of sophistication is the nonelectronic locking system doorlock. Nonelectronic locking systems offer many of the positive attributes found in ELS locks but cost substantially less. Electronic locking systems are the third type of doorlock available. ELSs come in both microfitted and hard-wired systems.

➤ *Traditional Mechanical Locks.*   Although the handwriting is on the wall, mechanical locks are still widely used. They are more appropriate for the small property, which can track the history of the individual room lock. Rekeying mechanical locks can be done only by going from door to door and only by keeping good records. That's not feasible with large hotels, which favor the smart switches and their remote rekeying capability.

Changing Mechanical Locks.   Changing locks originally meant just that: moving the entire lock from one room to another. With new technology, the method of rotating mechanical locks has changed.

One system uses a removable lock core. With a twist, a control key removes the whole pin–tumbler combination, allowing it to be used in some other housing. The key core is replaced with a different core requiring a different room key. The lock housing remains intact. It is a rapid and effective means of rotating locks for either emergency situations or periodic replacements.

The other innovation, changeable tumblers, is even simpler. The change is made in the tumblers without removing the core. It is the key, not the tumbler, that is replaced (see Exhibit 14–10). Initially, a new cylinder is put into the current mortise hardware. Thereafter, rekeying is done at the door without removing the tumblers, the core, or the hardware.

Rekeying time is less than one minute for both the guest key and the master key, according to the manufacturer. Keys are not discarded; they are reused. A removable, colored room number disk snaps in and out of the key, which permits the key to be used in other rooms. Changing disk colors distinguishes previously used keys from the combination currently in use.

▶*Nonelectronic Locking Systems.*   Nonelectronic locking systems are really just sophisticated mechanical locks. However, because a card is used instead of a key, there is often confusion between electronic and nonelectronic locking systems. Nonelectronic locks use a snap-off card with holes in the plastic (see Exhibit 14–8). According to one manufacturer, 4 billion combinations are possible. Both sides of the card have the same configuration. The door opens when the configuration of holes on the guest card, inserted from the corridor, coincides with the configuration on the control card, which is inserted from the room side.

One variation employs a separate cylinder lock for access by employees and management. Changes can be made in the cylinder lock for the maid, master, and E-keys without altering the guest card entry. In another variation, each change in the guest card is made without adjusting the cylinder access.

The recodeable cylinder is like the changeable tumblers just described. The whole system is like all the other mechanical systems. Someone needs to come to the door and change the card. The change could be done by the bellperson each and every time

Exhibit 14–10   Different than Exhibit 14–6, rekeying this deadbolt lock is done externally by changing the key, not the tumbler core. Making the change requires a master key and the old and new guest-room keys. *Courtesy of Winfield Locks, Inc., Costa Mesa, California.*

a new guest is roomed. The bellperson, who gains access through the cylinder lock, breaks off the card parts and completes the rekeying. Rekeying need not be done with each guest, provided the previous guest returned the key(s) at check out.

Benefits of Nonelectronic Locking Systems.   There are several reasons a hotel might select a nonelectronic locking system. First, when compared to standard mechanical locks, nonelectronic locking systems are superior. Their rapid rekeying feature is foremost on the list of advantages over the traditional keyed lock.

In addition, nonelectronic locking systems offer many of the security advantages associated with electronic locking systems. Similar to an ELS, a new guest keycard inserted in the lock will invalidate the previous guest's card. Indeed, hotel managers who select nonelectronic locking systems can provide a strong defense in court that their hotels are providing reasonable care and proper levels of guest security. However, the biggest reason newly constructed properties choose nonelectronic locking systems is cost—they are significantly less expensive than even the least costly electronic locking systems.

➤*Electronic Locking Systems.*   Although electronic locking systems are the best of all guest-room door-locking systems, they are expensive. Average costs range in the neighborhood of $150 to $350 per door plus the cost of the dedicated computer processor, one or more key-writing terminals, an audit trail interrogator, a printer, software, and programming. Yet most newly constructed properties have electronic locking systems. Over the past 10 to 15 years, it is estimated that the lodging industry has spent well over $200 million on electronic locking systems. The price only seems high until you analyze the alternatives.

Electronic locks save direct expenses in two ways: labor and key cost. They also provide less direct monetary savings in terms of lower insurance premiums, reduced liability risk, happier guests, and less property theft. In terms of direct expenses, let's look at the experience of the San Diego Marriott Hotel and Marina.

This property was originally constructed with a standard mechanical locking system in all 682 rooms. Today, this property has retrofitted an electronic locking system in its original rooms, and here's why. Guests were constantly losing or misplacing room keys. According to the property's chief engineer, it was not uncommon for the Marriott to rekey up to 40 rooms per day! Each lost room key required the maintenance person to rekey the lock, make four copies of the key, and log in each one. Key blanks cost $2 each (compared to electronic keycards, which cost only about $0.10 each). But the real expense was not key blanks; it was labor. The maintenance department spent upwards of 30 hours per week rekeying doorlocks. Today, that same property spends less than three hours per week maintaining its electronic locks.

Power Sources.   The system is energized either by a hard-wire hookup using utility power or by a battery power pack on the door. The hard-wire installations have more capability, but they are far more costly. Each door must be cabled to the console at the front desk (there are also systems that use radio waves, paging, and infrared technology to communicate with the front desk). This proves too expensive for retrofits, which tend toward the microfitted electronic systems.

Hard-wire installations need to provide for power failures, which make the locks inoperative. One seldom-used option is a battery pack on each door. The batteries have a life of one to three years. Small, portable computers with auxiliary power packs can be carried door to door. However, that's not much of an option if the entire system goes down. Large, centralized power packs are generally used, unless the hotel has emergency generators that back up the entire hotel during power failures.

The Control Center.   The control center is at the front desk, where the key is issued as part of the registration process (see Exhibit 14–11). What happens there depends on whether the system is hard-wired or microfitted.

If the system is hard-wired, then the code in the card that is processed at the time of registration is forwarded over the wires (or radio waves) to the lock in the door. Hard-wiring makes the door code and the console code at the desk one and the same. A self-correcting feature verifies the accuracy of the keycard, saving the guest from a duplicate trip to the desk because the card doesn't work.

As previously discussed, microfitted electronic locking systems communicate with the desk by way of the keycard. Physically inserting the keycard in the lock updates

Exhibit 14–11   Combinations for individual room keycards are processed at the console in the front office. Each guest receives a disposable keycard (other options are displayed in Exhibits 14–7 and 14–12). The combination is changed between occupants. *Courtesy of ILCO Unican, Inc., Montreal, Quebec, Canada.*

the code sequence in the doorlock with the code sequence maintained at the front-desk control center (see Exhibit 14–11). If the two code sequences (the front-desk computer and the guest-room doorlock) become out of sync with each other, the doorlock may fail to accept the guest's keycard.

Assume that an arriving guest on the way to the room changes his mind. He returns to the desk, changes rooms, or leaves (DNS). The desk issued a key, which used the next sequence on the console. The key was not used, so the sequence in the lock was not advanced. Each time such an event occurs, the codes in the lock and the console become farther apart. Eventually, the door won't open. Several other causes account for a misplaced sequence, but the problem isn't frequent, so it isn't a serious one.

On-line Locking Systems. Although other automated applications (CAS, EMS, POS) are usually interfaced with the property management system, electronic locking systems often perform as stand-alone (off-line) systems. Off-line systems are easier to use, require no interface software, have dedicated computer hardware (see Exhibit 14–11), and still provide a high level of guest security. With off-line systems, the front-office clerk merely adds one extra step (cutting a keycard) in the check-in process. Off-line systems work extremely well and are the most common form of ELS in use today, but they are not the leading-edge technology of the new millenium.

The trend in the coming years will be toward increased integration between the ELS and the PMS, in other words, towards on-line locking systems. As technology im-

Exhibit 14–12   Electronic locking systems are flexible in terms of where (or on what) the magnetic strip is attached. Creative companies have left the keycard behind as they seek new innovations. Shown here are TESA's new programmable watches, which eliminate the need to carry a keycard. Another company (Sphinx Dialock) has introduced programmable clips, which conveniently hook to the guest's pocket or belt. Another variation requires carrying nothing at all; the guest simply enters a custom-designed pin number to access the guest room (see also Exhibit 14–7). *Courtesy of TESA Entry Systems, Norcross, Georgia.*

proves and prices drop, on-line ELSs will become more widely used. Any hard-wired (or those using infrared, radio waves, or pager technology) ELS can be converted to an on-line system (see Exhibit 14–12). For many properties, the enhanced capabilities of an on-line ELS more than compensate for the added cost.

Probably the most valuable enhancement in terms of the hotel's bottom line lies with energy management. Tying energy management systems (EMSs) to the guest-room door lock allows the system to monitor when the guest is in the room. Certainly when the room is occupied, all air conditioning, lighting, television, and related functions must be operational. But the moment the guest leaves the room, many systems can be shut down or reset to an unoccupied energy-savings status. Integrating the EMS through the ELS to the PMS saves the average hotel $10,000 per month or better. A more thorough discussion of the integration of the EMS is provided later in this chapter.

Other benefits of on-line systems include increased guest-related information. For example, every time a guest enters a certain area (say, the health club), the door-lock card reader automatically sends a record of who accessed the area, the time, and date. This log can provide management valuable information about the movement of guests in and around the hotel. On-line systems also aid housekeeping efficiencies by alerting room attendants when guests depart their rooms. Hotel security is enhanced as well, because the system can warn management when a guest-room door has been left open or if there has been forced entry. Management can also track the minute-by-minute whereabouts of all employees who use an electronic keycard to access guest-room and other secured locks.

► OTHER COMMON INTERFACES

As the hotel industry continues its trek and investment toward fully automated and fully integrated properties, a number of decisions face management. Depending on the size, type, age, and market of the property, certain applications and potential interfaces become more or less necessary. Whenever management seeks to enhance its current system, it must ask itself a series of questions.

Prior to the Interface

Although the questions below are designed around the concept of interfaced systems, they are appropriate for any hotel investment—management should ask the questions and analyze the answers before making investments.

►*Degradation.*   Management should first ask: Will the interfaced system degrade my existing PMS? Interfaced applications have a dedicated central processing unit that "polls," that is, communicates, with the host PMS. Still, interfaces act as "phantom" users, and there are limits to the numbers and types of interfaces appropriate for each property management system. When degradation occurs, the speed of the host PMS slows down. This slower operating time may affect service levels as well as guest and employee satisfaction.

It is critical to assess the degree of degradation that will occur prior to performing the interface. If the PMS is appreciably slowed, significant new hardware and software investment may be necessary. Management should apprise itself of this additional potential cost well in advance of performing the interface.

➤*Synergy.*   Another question management should ask itself is: What is the synergistic value from the interface? Most interfaces provide added value (synergy) to the existing property management system. For example, rather than manually turning on guest-room telephones and tracking, pricing, and posting calls, the electronic interface between the CAS and the PMS performs those functions automatically. However, if there is little or no synergy to be gained, management would be wise to forgo the interface.

➤*Cost–Benefit Relationship.*   Another question that must be addressed asks: Is there a positive cost–benefit relationship? Management needs to clearly understand the purpose for the interface, the value added from this new application, and the cost of installing the system. If long-term employee and/or guest benefits are something less than the investment required, management might reconsider the venture.

There is currently a trend to automate everything in sight. Rather than analyzing the cost–benefit relationship, many properties merely follow the industry trend. Yet the reasons for interfacing applications are different for each property. If management cannot answer the cost–benefit question, it should not make the investment.

➤*Compatiblity.*   Finally, management might ask: Is this interface possible with my existing PMS? Although less a problem with today's modern systems, some applications are simply not compatible (refer to the section earlier in this chapter on uniform connectivity). Management should be wary of interfacing two distinct vendors if no other property has successfully performed this feat. Unless the software companies are willing to perform the job with specific guarantees, stay away.

Other PMS Interfaces

Aside from the call accounting and electronic locking systems already discussed, there are several other common PMS interfaces. A fully integrated property might also boast a point-of-sale system (POS), an energy management system (EMS), and additional phone services.

➤*Point-of-Sale.*   Point-of-sale (POS) systems provide true synergy to the hotel operation in terms of labor savings, lower transcription error rates, and reduced late charges. That is because the POS communicates directly with the host PMS. No matter how distant from the front desk, a computer located at the point of sale (for example, restaurants, lounges, gift shops, and health club centers) is electronically linked to the front-office PMS.

A point-of-sale system removes the hotel from the labor-intensive, error-ridden, manually posted room charge process of yesteryear. The interface poses electronically the same questions the nonautomated system asked manually. Before accepting the room charge, the system polls the front-desk PMS and asks: Is the guest registered under that name and in that room? Is the amount of this charge acceptable to the guest's current credit status? After the PMS validates the guest's ability to charge, the POS accepts the transaction and transmits the data directly to the guest folio. At the POS, the cashier merely inputs the guest name, guest-room number, amount of transaction, and check voucher or reference code number (see Exhibit 13–3).

There are no late charges because a cashier forgot to bring the check to the front desk. There are no errors of fact from posting the wrong amount to the wrong room. And labor is minimal because the POS interfaces directly with the PMS.

▶**Energy Management Systems.**   Energy management is another common interface to the property management system. By effectively controlling energy (for example, heating, airconditioning, lights, and power to run equipment), the hotel can provide a full level of services and comfort to the guest while effectively minimizing utility-related costs. An energy management system (EMS) conserves electricity, gas, and water by electronically monitoring the property's mechanical equipment.

An energy management system saves money in three ways. First, it conserves overall energy utilization by turning down or shutting off nonessential equipment. It also prevents premium charges on utility bills by shedding energy loads during otherwise peak demand periods. And it enhances the useful life of equipment by duty-cycling machines on and off.

Guest-Room Consumption.   Although some 19% of the energy used in full-service properties is used in guest rooms (see Exhibit 14–13), guest-room consumption increases to as much as 80% for limited service properties. An EMS/PMS interface can provide substantial savings in terms of guest-room energy utilization. As discussed earlier in this chapter, such interfaces often function around hard-wired electronic locking systems. That's because the hotel already has a physical (hard-wired) connec-

Exhibit 14–13
Breakdown of energy consumption in a full-service, 300-room hotel. A small effort in reducing HVAC in guest-room use can realize significant annual savings, especially in limited service hotels.

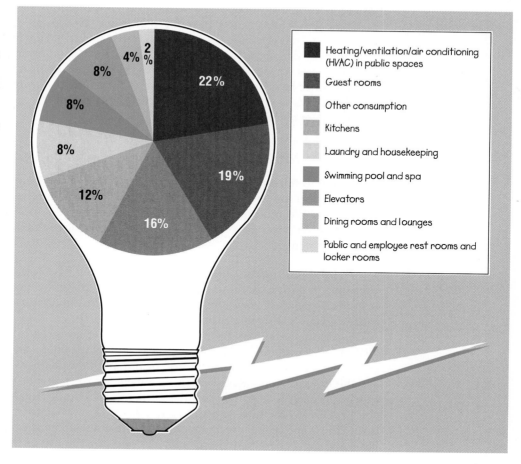

tion between every guest room and the front desk; the EMS simply adds a new dimension to electronic equipment already functioning.

Through an EMS, the property management system reduces energy consumption in unoccupied rooms. Depending on the time of day, the temperature, and forecasted room demand, the EMS may decide to curtail heating and cooling by a few degrees, or it may substantially reduce energy consumption by closing everything down.

Through the use of computer algorithms, the EMS may actually control the property management system by determining which rooms should be sold and which rooms should remain unoccupied. A guest checking into a 60% occupied house may be routed (through the room availability screen of the PMS) to a well-occupied floor. This would leave other floors or wings of the hotel totally empty. In such cases, the computer could then shut down hallway ventilation systems, turn off every other ceiling light in the hallway, and reduce the temperature at the remote water heater site.

An EMS interface might also incorporate in-room occupancy sensors. Tied to the electronic locking system, these sensors use either infrared heat-sensing technology or ultrasonic motion detection equipment to register occupancy in the guest room. A door that has been opened from the inside (without using a keycard to gain access) probably indicates the occupant has left the guest room. This information is validated against the occupancy sensor technology, and if the room is truly unoccupied, the EMS reduces or turns off nonessential energy consumption.

Some less-sophisticated in-room occupancy sensors are not connected to the doorlock and merely sense body heat (infrared detection) or body movement (ultrasonic motion detection) without verification. Such equipment works fine except in those instances where a heavy sleeper pulls the blankets up over his head. In these situations, neither heat nor movement registers the room as occupied. The guest may be surprised to wake up and find the TV set turned off and the room temperature somewhat less than comfortable.

Guest-Operated Interfaces

In addition to the interfaces described in the preceding section, today's PMSs also provide a number of guest-operated interfaces. The following section provides a brief overview of the more popular guest-operated interfaces. Included here are in-room safes, in-room beverage or minibar systems, fire-safety systems, and in-room entertainment systems.

▶ *In-room Safes.*   In-room safes (see Exhibit 14–14) may be either manual or electronic in nature. Both manual and electronic safes allow guests the opportunity to custom-design their own combination codes. Few modern safes use the traditional lock and key—guests lose them too easily.

Electronic safes may be hard-wired to an interfaced central processing unit. If the PMS is interfaced, daily charges are posted automatically to the electronic folio. Manual systems charge guests for the use of the safe in a number of creative ways. Some ask the housekeeping attendant to document whether or not the safe was used. Another approach is to simply ask the guest at check in or check out. Other properties charge a fee for the safe—usually $1 to $3 per day—whether it was used or not (obviously, this approach causes a few guest complaints at check out). And a recent growing trend is to charge all guests a small "fee" for the use of the guest-room safe, in-room coffee, and free local phone calls.

Exhibit 14–14   In-room safes reduce guest losses as well as guest demands on front-desk personnel. Although in-room safes are sometimes provided as a complimentary amenity, some hotels charge between $1 and $3 per day. Guests create their own personal code. *Courtesy of Elsafe of Nevada and Elsafe International, Vanvikan, Norway.*

Of course, the hotel can provide the safe without charge, as it does other amenities. Charging came about because vendors developed quick payback schemes by which management could justify installing in-room safes.

Other than direct cost recovery, there are economic arguments for not charging. The safes reduce the number of thefts, and that should reduce the cost of insurance. Traffic at safe deposit boxes falls dramatically, reducing front-office labor costs. Fewer claims means even larger savings in security and management time. Investigations, guest relations, reports, police inquiries, and correspondence may represent days of lost work. Legal fees, court costs, settlements, and more management time must be factored in if the case goes to trial. Thus, a safe reduces losses, which reduces costs.

Evidence suggests that safes do reduce theft. Electronic door locks do battle with external theft and in-room safes with internal theft. Experts say that internal theft by employees is usually an impulsive act caused by temptation (laptop computers are proving to be one of the most tempting items of all). The safe reduces employee opportunity. It also undermines guest moves to defraud the hotel or the insurance company.

▶*In-room Minibars.*   In-room beverage, minibar, or vending systems may be automatically interfaced to the property management system, semiautomatically interfaced (with a hand-held microprocessor), or fully manual in design (see Exhibit 14–15). Both manual and semiautomated minibars rely on a guest honor system. At the time of check out, front-desk clerks ask departing guests if they had occasion to

Exhibit 14–15   Electronic in-room minibar systems can easily support 75 to 100 items. By design, some sections remain at room temperature (nuts and candy) while other sections (soda and champagne) are refrigerated. A new trend offers healthier snacks and personal toiletries in addition to the obligatory liquor and soda. *Courtesy of Minibar North America, Inc., Bethesda, Maryland.*

utilize the minibar in the last 24 hours. Although some departing guests will invariably fleece the hotel, minibar profits are significant enough to cover a sizable number of losses.

Minibars are extremely convenient—that's their attraction. And guests are often willing to pay a premium for the convenience of having snacks and drinks available in the room. As a result, some hotels have realized rapid payback (sometimes in less than 12 months) from their in-room minibar systems.

With semiautomated minibars, changes in inventory are recorded on a hand-held microprocessor by the room attendant or minibar employee. The microprocessor is capable of storing inventory information from a number of guest rooms before being downloaded via the telephone directly into the property management system interface (see Exhibit 14–16).

Some delay in installing honor bars was caused by jurisdictions such as New York State. Without control of consumption by minors, liquor was not permitted in the rooms. Automatically interfaced minibars have changed that: The system can be turned off at certain hours or whenever children are registered.

Interfaced minibars brought additional benefits: eliminating the frequent late charge of the honor system, for one. Automatically interfaced minibars utilize fiber-

ROBOBAR COMMUNICATION SCHEMATIC

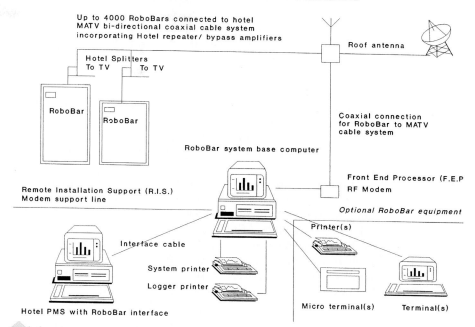

Exhibit 14–16 Advanced systems, such as this one from Robobar's, deliver in-room amenities with maximum efficiency. Several notable features: Purchases are posted to the folio electronically as the guest removes the product; bars can be locked remotely to comply with local liquor laws; and restocking reports are prepared automatically, no need for a physical count. *Courtesy of Minibar North America, Inc., Bethesda, Maryland.*

optic sensors to identify when a product has been removed for consumption. These sensors are often programmed with a slight delay to allow for those guests who wish to handle, look at, and then possibly return the product to the refrigerator. Once the product has been removed for a period of time, the sensor alerts the interface, which then charges the guest folio for the minibar item. Not only does this minimize cheating and late charges, it also produces a restocking report that simplifies the job of the minibar employee. There is no longer any reason for the minibar employee to enter and check every guest room—only those from which an item was removed.

Aside from the recent technological advances in minibars, there has been a revolution of purpose as well. Gone are the days when minibars were stocked exclusively with liquor and stale snacks. The new purpose has minibars stocking a multitude of items ranging from healthier snacks and beverages to indispensable products such as toiletry items. Imagine the relief of the guest who doesn't discover until morning that he has forgotten his razor, and finds one conveniently located in the minibar (that's far better than walking downstairs in pajamas).

Even the pricing of minibar products has become somewhat more user friendly in recent years. A grand opening special at the Nikko Hotel in Hanoi included the entire original content of the in-room minibar free of charge. Who knows, the future may see more hotel minibar promotions and creative uses (even complimentary continental breakfast) in years to come.

➤*In-room Entertainment Systems.* In-room movie or entertainment systems hold a great deal of promise for the years to come. However, the TV set remains the entertainment center above all else, at least for now. The availability of in-room movies, for which most hotels charge (using the electronic folio), is an upgrade from the standard set (see Exhibit 14–17). Videocassette viewing is another upgrade. Some hotels charge, and some don't; some rent films via electronic vending machines, and some supply them gratis on the concierge floors.

Although not exactly entertainment, the proceedings taking place in the conference area of the hotel can be viewed on the TV screen in some hotels. Other TV channels offer airline schedules; news, sports, and stock market reports; local restaurant guides; the guest folio; weather reports; advertising; and personal messages left for the guest.

When some of the capabilities of the telephone and personal computer are added in, television broadens its service offerings. Express check out and room status are two common functions. A room-service menu can be viewed (changes are easier to make and less costly than printed menus) and orders placed. Other orders can also be placed: a morning wake-up call; a reservation in a dining room that hasn't opened; goods from shops in the hotel (or mall merchants, if the hotel is so located). Even airline tickets can be ordered. With a remote printer at the desk—eventually, perhaps, in the guest room—the tickets can also be picked up.

Exhibit 14–17 SpectraVision is one of the big three lodging pay-per-view and in-room technology companies (along with LodgeNet Entertainment and On Command Video). The top photo promotes many of the services available in a fully integrated system. The bottom photos show how simple it is for the guest to read messages, review the folio, and check out from the room. *Courtesy of SpectraVision, Richardson, Texas.*

The trend by the big three lodging pay-per-view companies—SpectraVision, LodgeNet Entertainment, and On Command Video—has changed in recent years. Where a signed pay-per-view contract once guaranteed the hotel a free TV set in every room, today's contracts provide more information technology without the free sets. Less sophisticated hotels can still get the free TV sets, but more advanced properties are opting to buy the sets themselves in order to get the pay-per-view company to include a wider range of differentiated services in the contract.

➤ *Fire-Safety Systems.*   Although fire-safety systems are not truly guest-operated devices, they do monitor and detect activities occurring in the guest room. Like most interfaced functions, fire-safety systems began as stand-alone devices. An example is a single smoke detector in the corridor. Change came quickly after several widely publicized fires occurred. In quick response, many municipalities passed retrofit legislation. The emphasis was toward interfacing fire technology and the PMS, using the hard wires of the call accounting or locking systems, or through wireless broadcasting. Some jurisdictions mandated hard-wiring—integrating the control panels and the room communication systems.

Hard-wire systems tie each room sensor to a fire-control panel on the premises. In-room smoke detectors and sprinkler-head sensors can also be included to provide an early-warning network. An annunciator on the panel pinpoints the source of the smoke or fire. The interfaced system then does several things automatically:

➤ It releases the magnetic locks that hold open the fire doors.

➤ It adjusts the ventilation and air-handling (HVAC) systems to minimize the spread of fire and externally vent smoke as necessary.

➤ It automatically notifies guests in their rooms through the activation of horns or speakers, it may dial each guest-room telephone and play a prerecorded message, and it notifies the local fire department. On arrival at the scene, the fire department takes control of the speakers and announces specific instructions.

➤ It automatically overrides all affected elevators and returns them to the ground floor.

Codes require evacuation routes in corridors and rooms to be clearly marked. In-room signage now identifies that route and the closest exit. Lighted, phosphorescent signs in the corridors at crawling height have gained popularity since their introduction in the Far East over a decade ago.

Instead of ignoring the reality of the danger, which had been the stance for a long time, hotel companies have begun communicating their concerns. Written booklets and evacuation instructions have been prepared. With electronic systems, audio instructions are also being offered. Other emergency systems use the music channels or the television speakers. The voice comes through even if the switch is off. Special hard-wired systems and in-room sprinklers are legislated in several places that have experienced especially deadly fires, such as Las Vegas and San Juan.

A message that is recorded tends to be more calming and informative than a live one made during the excitement of the emergency. Several hotels have gotten the local fire marshal to tape the message.

➤ *The Electronic Concierge.*   In an effort to provide guests with additional information while easing the strain on the concierge desk (or eliminating the position altogether), hotels have heartily embraced electronic concierge technology. Through either the guest-room television, a dedicated kiosk or a computer terminal in the lobby, or even a phone-based system (where guests interact by pushing the appropriate phone buttons), guests receive answers to questions about local attractions, restaurants, museums, shows, and so on. Some of the more sophisticated systems even provide maps (which can be printed at the front desk or concierge desk if warranted) and recommended routes.

Hotels are not the only venue that supports electronic concierge systems. They are also commonly found at bus depots, airline terminals, city halls, and other public or quasipublic buildings. Hotels, however, benefit tremendously from this new technology, which is usually installed free of charge. Whether the electronic service replaces or merely supplements a live concierge desk, the guest saves time and gains an overview of community attractions from the information available through the electronic concierge.

However, the guest is not always provided a full and accurate picture. You see, electronic concierge services are provided by businesses that profit from advertising included at the site. Large communication companies (Bell Atlantic and U.S. West are two such examples) often fund the investment necessary to start such services. To be listed at the site, local merchants pay rates ranging from $100 to $1,000 per month. Not all merchants choose to participate, and that's where the picture gets muddled. Asking the concierge desk where the nearest Italian restaurant is located may point you to a lovely place right next door. The electronic concierge, however, will highlight only those Italian restaurants that pay the monthly fee. As such, the guest may drive miles out of the way seeking the closest Italian restaurant, having been provided something less than full disclosure.

► SUMMARY

The lodging industry lagged behind most other businesses in terms of adopting computer automation in the 1970s. As a result, most hotel operations avoided the first generations of computer development, choosing instead to wait for the faster, cheaper, more perfected systems that were soon to follow. The waiting is over, and hospitality computer applications have gained acceptance at a dizzying rate. Today, technology prevails across all spectrums of the lodging industry.

Few properties operate without a computerized call accounting system (CAS). The CAS performs many tasks that historically belonged to the hotel telephone operator: It identifies when a guest call is made, the originating room, the duration, the destination, and the cost of the call. Once the long-distance carrier cost of the call is determined, most properties add a profit margin to help defray CAS equipment costs and to make a reasonable return on investment for the hotel. Some chains, however,

choose to make no profit on either long-distance or local guest phone calls. Functioning in concert with the CAS are sophisticated guest-room telephones. These feature telephones are actually capable of serving as a remote control for a number of in-room services. Pressing a few buttons on the phone may close the drapes, dim the lights, adjust the temperature, or lower the television volume.

Another common technological interface found in hotels is the electronic locking system (ELS). Few newly constructed hotels are built without some form of locking system technology. This technology may include nonelectronic locking systems that utilize specially encoded keys, but more often than not it will be an electronic locking system. The ELS may be microfitted (that is, battery-operated) or hardwired. Though more expensive, the hard-wired systems are capable of a number of enhancements. Since each hard-wired lock is actually wired directly to the front desk, the hotel can integrate fire safety, occupancy sensors, and energy management components directly through the door lock.

In addition to the CAS and ELS, a number of guest-room or guest-service interfaces are also available in full-service, technologically sophisticated properties. Common guest-service interfaces include point-of-sale and energy management systems. In the guest room, there may be electronic-safe, mini-bar, entertainment, and fire-safety system interfaces.

➤ QUESTIONS AND PROBLEMS

1. The relationship of the telephone and hotel industries has changed significantly since the 1960s. List three major pieces of legislation, court rulings, findings by the FCC, or decisions by members of either industry that caused or contributed to the changes. How did each alter the way in which the hotel's telephone department operates?

2. Undoubtedly, some PMS vendors will comply with the new HITIS standards and others will not. What are the benefits and disadvantages to a hotel manager who purchases software from a vendor in compliance?

3. Most hotel operations charge a premium for the convenience of placing long-distance phone calls directly from the room. This premium may range from 10 to 25% above the cost of the call. Other properties charge as much as 10 or more times the cost of the call. Assuming that the hotel announces its surcharge with a notice similar to the one shown in Exhibit 14–2, discuss the fairness of charging the guest such a premium. Is it ethical to charge a small premium (say, 10 to 25%)? Is it ethical to charge a large premium (say, 10 times the cost)? At what point does the hotel overstep the limits of "fairness"?

4. Using professional terminology correctly is important to understanding and being understood. Identify the following acronyms and briefly discuss what they represent:
   (a) HOBIC   (i) PBX
   (b) AOS   (j) AIOD
   (c) WATS   (k) POS
   (d) PMS   (l) CAS
   (e) FCC   (m) AH&MA
   (f) ELS   (n) LCR
   (g) OCC   (o) PPC
   (h) AT&T

5. Identify by name the levels of keys that comprise the locking systems of most hotels. Explain who has access to which keys and what purpose is served by each level. How does the system work if the mechanical lock and key are replaced by the computer and the computer keycard?

6. Be creative and imagine the hotel room of the future. Describe several guest-operated interfaces or devices that might be available in your fictitious hotel room of tomorrow.

➤ NOTES

1. Donald E. Lundberg, *Inside Innkeeping* (Dubuque, IA: William C. Brown Company, Publishers, 1956), p. 91.

2. Another landmark case was decided in 1968, when the FCC ruled in favor of Carterfone. In this case, the FCC reversed AT&T's policy which prevented the interconnection of private telephones to AT&T equipment. This opened the door to a new industry of equipment sales as opposed to the lease-only policy that AT&T was trying to protect.

Bibliography

● ● ●

Abbot, P. *Front Office: Procedures, Special Skills and Management.* Oxford: Butterworth-Heinemann, 1991.

The ABCs of Travel. New York: Public Transportation and Travel Division, Ziff-Davis Publishing Co., 1972.

Anolik, Alexander. *Travel, Tourism and Hospitality Law.* Elmsford, NY: National Publishers of the Black Hills, Inc., 1988.

Arthur, Roland, and Gladwell, Derek. *The Hotel Assistant Manager,* 3rd ed. London: Barrie & Rockliff, 1975.

Astroff, Milton, and Abbey, James. *Convention Sales and Services,* 5th ed. Cranbury, NJ: Waterbury Press, 1998.

Axler, Bruce. *Room Care for Hotels and Motels.* Indianapolis, IN: ITT Educational Publishing, 1974.

———. *Focus on . . . Security for Hotels, Motels, and Restaurants.* Indianapolis, IN: ITT Educational Publishing, 1974.

Baird, C., and Carla, L. *Front Office Assignment.* London: Pitman Publishing Ltd., 1988.

Baker, Sue, Bradley, Pam, and Huyton, Jeremy. *Principles of Hotel Front Office Operations,* 2nd ed. London: Cassell PLC, 1996.

Barba, Stephen. "Operating the Traditional American Plan Resort," in *The Practices of Hospitality Management,* editors Pizam, Lewis, and Manning. Westport, CT: AVI Publishing Co., Inc., 1982.

Bardi, James A. *Hotel Front Office Management,* 2nd ed. New York: John Wiley & Sons, Inc., 1996.

Beavis, J. R. S., and Medlik, S. *A Manual of Hotel Reception,* 3rd ed. London: William Heinemann Ltd., 1981.

Berman, Shelley. *A Hotel Is a Place. . . .* Los Angeles: Price/Stern/Sloan Publishers, Inc., 1972.

Boomer, Lucius. *Hotel Management.* New York: Harper & Row, 1938.

Borsenik, Frank. *The Management of Maintenance and Engineering Systems in the Hospitality Industry,* 4th ed. New York: John Wiley & Sons, Inc., 1997.

Braham, Bruce. *Computer Systems in the Hotel and Catering Industry.* London: Cassell Educational Ltd., 1988.

———. *Hotel Front Office,* 2nd ed. Gloucestershire, England: Stanley Thornes, 1993.

Browning, Marjorie. *Night Audit Procedure.* Columbus, OH: The Christopher Inn, March 1, 1969.

Bryson, McDowell, and Ziminski, Adele. *The Concierge: Key to Hospitality.* New York: John Wiley & Sons, Inc., 1992.

Bucher, A. F. *101 Tips on Check Cashing.* New York: Ahrens Publishing Co., Inc., circa 1930.

Burstein, Harvey. *Hotel Security Management.* New York: Praeger Publishers, Inc., 1975.

Buzby, Walter J. *Hotel and Motel Security Management.* Los Angeles: Security World Publishing Co., 1976.

Chandler, Raymond. *Trouble Is My Business.* New York: Ballantine Books, Inc., 1972.

Check and Credit-Card Fraud Prevention Manual. New York: The Atlantic Institute, Atcom Publishing, 1984.

Collins, Galen, and Malik, Tarun. *Hospitality Information Technology: Learning How to Use It,* 3rd ed. Dubuque, IA: Kendall/Hunt Publishing Company, 1997.

Convention Liaison Council Manual, 6th ed. Washington, DC: Convention Liaison Council, 1994.

The Credit Card Industry. National Education Program of Discover Card. Riverwoods, IL: Novus Network Services, 1996.

Dahl, J. O. *Bellman and Elevator Operator.* Revised by Crete Dahl. Stamford, CT: The Dahls, 1993.

———. *Room Clerk's Manual.* Revised by Crete Dahl. Stamford, CT: The Dahls, 1993.

Dervaes, C. *The Travel Dictionary.* Tampa, FL: Solitaire Publishing, 1992.

Deveau, Jack, and Penraat, Jaap. *The Efficient Room Clerk.* New York: Learning Information, Inc., 1968.

DeVeau, Linsley, and DeVeau, Patricia. *Front Office Management and Operations.* Upper Saddle River, NJ: Prentice Hall, 1996.

Directory of Hotel and Motel Companies, 66th ed. Waldorf, MD: American Hotel & Motel Association 1997.

Dix, Colin, and Baird, Chris. *Front Office Operations,* 3rd ed. London: Pitman Publishing Ltd., 1988.

Drury, Tony, and Ferrier, Charles. *Credit Cards.* London: Butterworth, 1984.

Dukas, Peter. *Hotel Front Office Management and Operations,* 3rd ed. Dubuque, IA: William C. Brown Company, Publishers, 1970.

Dunn, David. "Front Office Accounting Machines in Hotels," unpublished master's thesis, Cornell University, Ithaca, NY, June 1965.

Dunseath, M., and Ransom, J. *The Hotel Bookkeeper Receptionist.* London: Barrie & Rockliff, 1967.

Ellis, Raymond. *Hotel/Motel Security Management.* East Lansing, MI: Educational Institute, 1986.

Fidel, John. *Hotel Data Systems,* rev. ed. Albuquerque, NM: September 1972.

Foster, Dennis. *Rooms at the Inn: Front Office Operations and Administration.* Peoria, IL: Glencoe Publishing Co., 1992.

———. *The Business of Hospitality: Back Office Operations and Administration.* Peoria, IL: Glencoe Publishing Co., 1992.

Front Office and Reservations. Burlingame, CA: Hyatt Corporation, 1978.

Front Office Courtesy Pays. Small Business Administration. Washington, DC: U.S. Government Printing Office, 1956.

Front Office Manual. New York: New Yorker Hotel, 1931.

Front Office Manual: Franchise Division. Sheraton Hotels & Inns, Worldwide [no date].

Front Office Operations Manual (of the) Hotel McCurdy, Evansville, Indiana. Research Bureau of the American Hotel Association, April 1923.

Front Office Selling. East Lansing, MI: Educational Institute of the American Hotel & Motel Association [no date].

Front Office Selling "Tips." New York: Hotel Sales Management Association, 1960.

Gatiss, Gordon. *Total Quality Management.* London: Cassell PLC, 1996.

Giroux, Sharon. *Hosting the Disabled: Crossing the Communication Barrier.* Albany, NY: Delmar Publishers, 1994 (video).

Godowski, S. *Microcomputers in the Hotel and Catering Industry.* London: William Heinemann Ltd., 1988.

Gomes, Albert. *Hospitality in Transition.* Houston, TX: Pannell Kerr Foster, 1985.

Goodwin, John, and Gaston, Jolie. *Hotel, Hospitality and Tourism Law,* 5th ed. Scottsdale, AZ: Gorsuch Scarisbrick, Publishers, 1997.

Gray, William S., and Liguore, Salvatore C. *Hotel and Motel Management and Operations,* 3rd ed. Upper Saddle River, NJ: Prentice Hall, 1994.

Guest Relations Training for Front Office Cashiers. Boston: Sheraton Corporation of America, 1961.

A Guide to Terminology in the Leisure Time Industries. Philadelphia: Laventhol & Horwath, [no date].

Hall, Orrin, *Motel–Hotel Front Office Procedures.* Hollywood Beach, FL: circa 1971.

Hall, S. S. J. *Quality Assurance in the Hospitality Industry.* Milwaukee, WI: ASQC Quality Press, 1990.

Hamilton, Francis. *Hotel Front Office Management.* Miami, FL: 1947.

Haszonics, Joseph. *Front Office Operation.* New York: ITT Educational Services, Inc., 1971.

Heldenbrand, H. V. *Front Office Psychology.* Evanston, IL: John Wiley & Sons, Inc., 1944. Republished by American Hotel Register Company, Chicago, circa 1982.

Hilton, Conrad. *Be My Guest.* Englewood Cliffs, NJ: Prentice Hall, 1957.

Hitz, Ralph. *Standard Practice Manuals for Hotel Operation, I, Front Service Division.,* 2nd ed. New York: Harper & Row, 1936.

The Hotelman Looks at the Business of Meetings. St. Paul, MN: 3M Business Press, 1968.

Hubbart, Roy. *The Hubbart Formula for Evaluating Rate Structures of Hotel Rooms.* New York: American Hotel & Motel Association, 1952.

Hyatt Travel Futures Project Report on Business Travelers. New York: prepared for Hyatt Hotels and Resorts by Research & Forecasts, Inc., December 1988.

Implications of Microcomputers in Small and Medium Hotel and Catering Firms. Prepared for the Hotel and Catering Industry Training Board by the Department of Hotel, Catering, and Tourism Management, University of Surrey, Guildford, Surrey, England, November 1980.

Iverson, Kathleen M. *Introduction to Hospitality Management.* New York: Van Nostrand Reinhold, 1989.

Jones, Christine, and Paul, Val. *Accommodations Management.* London: Botsford Academic and Education, 1985.

Kasavana, Michael, and Brooks, Richard. *Managing Front Office Operations,* 5th ed. East Lansing, MI: Educational Institute, 1998.

———, and Cahill, John. *Hospitality Industry Computer Systems,* 3rd ed. East Lansing, MI: Educational Institute, 1997.

Lawrence, Janet. *Room Sales and Reception Management.* Boston: The Innkeeping Institute of America, 1970.

Lefler, Janet, and Calanese, Salvatore. *The Correct Cashier.* New York: Ahrens Publishing Co., Inc., 1960.

Link Hospitality Consultants, Ltd. *Canadian Job Strategy: Hotel Front Office Specialist.* Calgary, Alberta, Canada: Southern Alberta Institute of Technology, 1986.

Lundberg, Donald. *Front Office Human Relations.* Distributed by NU:PAK, San Marcos, CA, 1970.

Martin, Robert, and Jones, Tom. *Professional Management of Housekeeping Operations,* 3rd ed. New York: John Wiley & Sons, Inc., 1998.

MasterCard International Frequent Business Traveler Study. Presented at the American Hotel & Motel Association Annual Meeting, November 14, 1983.

Medlik, S. *The Business of Hotels.* London: William Heinemann Ltd., 1980.

———. *Dictionary of Travel.* Oxford: Butterworth-Heinemann, 1993.

———. *Profile of the Hotel and Catering Industry,* 2nd ed. London: William Heinemann Ltd., 1978.

Meek, Howard B. *A Theory of Room Rates.* Ithaca, NY: Cornell University, Department of Hotel Administration, June 1938.

A Meeting Planner's Guide to Master Account Billing. Developed by the Insurance Conference Planners, and published by The Educational Institute of the American Hotel & Motel Association, May 1980.

Metelka, Charles J. *The Dictionary of Hospitality, Travel and Tourism,* 3rd ed. Albany, NY: Delmar Publishers, Inc., 1989.

Ministry of Tourism. *The Front Desk Business.* Toronto, Ontario, Canada: Ontario Ministry of Tourism, 1978.

Moreo, Patrick, Sammons, Gail, and Dougan, James. *Front Office Operations and Night Audit Work Book,* 4th ed. Upper Saddle River, NJ: Prentice Hall, 1996.

O'Connor, Peter. *Using Computers in Hospitality and Tourism.* London: Cassell PLC, 1995.

Ogilvie, A. W. T. *Lecture Outline in Front Office.* American Hotel Association, 1923.

Paananen, Donna. *Selling Out: A How-to Manual on Reservations Management.* East Lansing, MI: Educational Institute, 1985.

Paige, Grace, and Paige, Jane. *The Hotel Receptionist,* 3rd ed. London: Holt, Rinehart and Winston, 1988.

———. *Hotel Front Desk Personnel,* rev. ed. New York: Van Nostrand Reinhold Co., Inc., 1988.

Pfeiffer, W., Voegele, M., and Wolley, G. *The Correct Service Department for Hotels, Motor Hotels, Motels and Resorts.* New York: Ahrens Publishing Co., Inc., 1962.

Picot, Derek. *Hotel Reservations.* Jersey City, NJ: Parkwest Publications, 1997.

Poynter, James. *Foreign Independent Tours.* Albany, NY: Delmar Publishers, 1989.

Property Management and Point of Sale Systems: Guide to Selection. New York: American Hotel & Motel Association.

Relieving Reservation Headaches. East Lansing, MI: Educational Institute of the American Hotel & Motel Association, 1979.

Renner, Peter. *Basic Hotel Front Office Procedures,* 3rd ed. New York: Van Nostrand Reinhold Co., Inc., 1993.

"Resale in the Lodging Industry: A Bell System Perspective." American Hotel & Motel Association, Mid-year Meeting, Nashville, TN, April 1982.

"Room Clerk, The Man Up Front." *Motel/Motor Inn Journal,* 1977.

Rosenzweig, Stan. *Hotel/Motel Telephone Systems: Opportunities through Deregulation.* East Lansing, MI: Educational Institute of the American Hotel & Motel Association, 1982.

Ross, Bruce. "Hotel Reservation Systems Present and Future." Unpublished master's monograph, Cornell University, Ithaca, NY, May 1977.

Rushmore, Stephen. *Hotel Investments: A Guide for Lenders and Owners.* New York: Warren, Gorham & Lamont, Inc., 1990.

Saunders, K. C. *Head Hall Porter.* London: Catering Education Research Institute, 1980.

———, and Pullen, R. *An Occupational Study of Room Maids in Hotels.* Middlesex, England: Middlesex Polytechnic, 1987.

Scatchard, Bill. *Upsetting the Applecart: A Common Sense Approach to Successful Hotel Operations for the '90s.* Box 19156, Tampa, FL 33686; 1994.

Schneider, Madelin, and Georgina Tucker. *The Professional Housekeeper.* New York: Van Nostrand Reinhold Co., Inc., 1989.

Self, Robert. *Long Distance for Less.* New York: Telecom Library, Inc., 1982.

Sherry, John. *How to Exclude and Eject Undesirable Guests.* Stamford, CT: The Dahls, 1943.

Sicherman, Irving. *The Investment in the Lodging Business.* Scranton, PA: Sicherman, 1977.

Starting and Managing a Small Motel. Small Business Administration. Washington, DC: U.S. Government Printing Office, 1963.

The State of Technology in the Lodging Industry. New York: American Hotel & Motel Association, 1980.

Stiel, Holly. *Ultimate Service: The Complete Handbook to the World of the Concierge.* Upper Saddle River, NJ: Prentice Hall, 1994.

Stutts, Alan, and Borsenik, Frank. *Maintenance Handbook for Hotels, Motels and Resorts,* 4th ed. New York: John Wiley & Sons, Inc., 1997.

Successful Credit and Collection Techniques. East Lansing, MI: Educational Institute of the American Hotel & Motel Association, 1981.

Tarbet, J. R. *A Handbook of Hotel Front Office Procedure.* Pullman, WA: Student Book Corporation, circa 1955.

Taylor, Derek, and Thomason, Richard. *Profitable Hotel Reception.* Elmsford, NY: Pergamon Press, Inc., 1982.

Trends in the Hotel-Motel Business. New York: Pannell Kerr Forster & Co., various years.

Uniform-Service Training. Boston: Sheraton Corporation of America, 1960.

Uniform System of Accounts for the Lodging Industry, 9th ed. New York: Hotel Association of New York City, 1996.

Vallen, Jerome, and Abbey, James. *The Art and Science of Hospitality Management.* East Lansing, MI: Educational Institute, 1987.

Van Hoof, H., McDonald, M., Yu, L., and Vallen, G. *A Host of Opportunities: An Introduction to Hospitality Management.* Chicago: Richard D. Irwin, Inc., 1996.

VanStrien, Kimberly, et al. *Front Office Management and Operations.* Upper Saddle River, NJ: Prentice Hall, 1998.

Weissinger, Suzanne S. *Hotel/Motel Operations.* Cincinnati, OH: South-Western Publishing Co., 1989.

White, Paul, and Beckley, Helen. *Hotel Reception,* 4th ed. London: Edward Arnold (Publishers) Ltd., 1982.

Wingenter, Tom, et al. *The Relationship of Lodging Prices to Occupancy: A Study of Accommodations in Northern Wisconsin.* Madison, WI: University of Wisconsin Cooperative Extension Service, 1982–83.

Wittemann, Ad. *Hotel Room Clerk.* Las Vegas, NV: Camelot Consultants, 1986.

Yellowstone Park Company Cashier Training Program. Yellowstone: Yellowstone Park Co., 1978.

Woods, Robert, and King, Judith. *Managing for Quality in the Hospitality Industry.* East Lansing, MI: Educational Institute, 1996.

Woods, Robert, Heck, William, and Sciarini, Michael. *Turnover and Diversity in the Lodging Industry.* New York: American Hotel Foundation, 1998.

Yeoman, Ian, and Ingold, Anthony. *Yield Management.* London: Cassell PLC, 1997.

Glossary

Words in *italic* in each definition are themselves defined elsewhere in the Glossary. (Words not listed might be found in the Index.) cf. means "compare."

A card   A form once used with the *NCR front-office posting machines* to reconcile and report cash at the close of the first shift and alternate shifts thereafter; see also *B card.*

account balance   The difference between the *debit* and *credit* values of the *guest bill.*

account card   See *guest bill.*

account receivable   A company, organization, or individual, *registered* or not, who has an outstanding bill with the hotel.

accounts receivable ledger   The aggregate of individual *account receivable* records.

acknowledgment   Notice of a *confirmed reservation* usually by letter, postcard, or preprinted form.

ADA   See *Americans with Disabilities Act.*

adds   Last minute *reservations* added to the reservation list on the day of arrival.

ADR   See *average daily rate.*

adjoining rooms   Rooms that abut along the corridor but do not connect through private doors; cf. *connecting rooms.*

advance deposit   A deposit furnished by the guest on a room *reservation* that the hotel is holding.

advances   See *cash paid-outs.*

affiliated hotel   One of a chain, *franchise,* or *referral* system, the membership of which provides special advantages, particularly a national reservation system.

after departure (AD)   A *late charge.*

afternoon tea   A light snack comprising delicate sandwiches and small sweets served with tea, or even sherry.

agency ledger   A division of the *city ledger* dealing with *travel agent* (agency) accounts.

agent   Representative of an individual or business; term that is a popular substitute for clerk, as in guest-service agent rather than room clerk.

AIOD   Telephone equipment that provides *Automatic Identification of Outward Dialing* for billing purposes.

allowance   A reduction to the *folio,* as an adjustment either for unsatisfactory service or for a posting error. Also called a *rebate.*

amenities   Literally any extra product or service found in the hotel. A swimming pool, concierge desk, health spa, and so on, are all technically known as amenities. However, this term has primarily come to be used for in-room guest products. Such complimentary in-room items as soap, shampoo, suntan lotion, mouthwash, and the like are most commonly considered amenities.

amenity creep   The proliferation of all guest products and services when hotels compete by offering more extensive amenities; originally referred to in-room amenities or toiletries only.

American Hotel & Motel Association (AH&MA)   A federation of regional and state associations that are composed of individual hotel and motel properties throughout the Americas.

American plan (AP)   A method of quoting room *rates* where the charge includes room and three meals.

American Society of Association Executives (ASAE)   An organization of the professional executives who head numerous associations in the United States.

American Society of Travel Agents (ASTA)   A professional association of retail *travel agents* and wholesale tour operators.

Americans with Disabilities Act (ADA)   Established in 1990, the ADA prohibits discrimination against any guest or employee because of his or her disability.

arrival, departure, and change sheet   A pencil-and-paper form to record guest *check ins, check outs,* and *changes* under a hand audit system; sometimes three separate forms.

arrival time   The hour which the guest specifies as the time that he or she will arrive to claim the *reservation.*

authorization code   (1) Response from a credit-card issuer that approves the credit-card transaction and provides a numbered code referral if problems arise; (2) a code for entry to a computer program.

available   The room is ready.

available basis only   (1) Convention *reservations* that have no claim against the *block* of convention rooms (see *blanket reservation*) because the request arrived after the *cutoff date;* (2) no reservations permitted because the rate being granted is too low to guarantee space, employee *reservations,* for example.

available rooms   The number of guest rooms the hotel has for sale—either the total in the hotel or the number unoccupied on a given day.

average daily rate (ADR)   The average daily *rate* paid by guests; computed by dividing room revenue by the number of rooms occupied. More recently called *sales per occupied room.*

back to back   (1) A sequence of consecutive *group* departures and arrivals usually arranged by tour operators so that rooms are never vacant; (2) a floor plan design that brings the piping of adjacent baths into a common shaft.

bank   Coins and small bills given to the cashier for making change.

bank cards   Credit cards issued by banks, usually for a smaller fee than that charged by *travel and entertainment cards.*

batch processing   A computer procedure that collects and codes data, entering it into memory in batches; cf. *on-line computer.*

B card   A form once used with the *NCR's front-office posting machines* to reconcile and report cash at the close of the second shift and alternative shifts thereafter; see also *A card.*

bed and board   Another term for the *American plan.*

bed and breakfast (B&B)   Lodging and breakfast offered in a domestic setting by families in their own homes; less frequently, the *Continental plan.*

bed board   A board placed under the mattress to make a firmer sleeping surface.

bed night   See *guest day (night).*

bed occupancy　A ratio relating the number of beds sold to the number of beds available for sale; *occupancy* measured in available beds rather than in *available rooms*.

bellcaptain　(1) The supervisor of the bellpersons and other uniformed service personnel; (2) a proprietary in-room vending machine.

bellcaptain's log　See *callbook*.

bellstand　The bellperson's desk located in the lobby close to and visible from the front desk.

Bermuda plan　A method of quoting room *rates*, where the charge includes a full breakfast as well as the room.

best available　A *reservation* requesting (or a confirmation promising) the best room available or the best room to open prior to arrival; cf. *available basis only*.

B folio　The second *folio* (the individual's folio) used with a *master account*.

blanket reservation　A *block* of rooms held for a particular *group*, with individual members requesting assignments from that block.

block　(1) A restriction placed in a *pocket* of the *room rack* to limit the clerk's discretion in assigning the room; (2) a number of rooms reserved for one *group*.

book　To sell hotel space, either to a person or to a *group* needing a *block* of rooms.

bottom line　The final line of a profit-and-loss statement: either net profit or net loss.

box　Reservation term that allows no *reservations* from either side of the boxed dates to spill through; cf. *sell through*.

breakage　The gain that accrues to the hotel or tour operator when meals or other services included in a *package* are not used by the guest.

brunch　A meal served after breakfast but before lunch and taking the place of both.

bucket　See *cashier's well*.

budget motel　See *limited service*.

building cost rate formula　A rule-of-thumb formula stating that the average room rate should equal $1 for every $1,000 of construction cost; see also *rule-of-thumb rate*.

cabana　A room on the beach (or by the pool) separated from the main *house* and sometimes furnished as a sleeping room.

café complet　Coffee snack at midmorning or midafternoon.

California length　An extra-long bed, about 80 to 85 inches instead of the usual 75 inches. Same as *Hollywood length*.

call accounting system (CAS)　Computerized program that prices and records telephone calls on the guest's electronic *folio* through a *property management system (PMS) interface*.

callbook　The bellperson's record of calls and activities.

call sheet　The form used by the telephone operator to record the room and hour of the *morning call*.

cancellation　A guest's request to the hotel to void a *reservation* previously made.

cancellation number　Coded number provided by the hotel or *central reservations office* to a guest who cancels a *reservation*.

cash advance　See *cash paid-outs*.

cash disbursement　See *cash paid-outs*.

cashier's drop　A depository located in the front-desk area where others can witness cashiers depositing their *turn-ins*.

cashier's report　The cash *turn-in* form completed by a departmental cashier at the close of the *watch*.

cashier's well　The file that holds the guest *folios*, often recessed in the countertop; also known as *tub*, *bucket*, or *pit*.

cash paid-outs　Monies disbursed for guests, either advances or loans, and charged to their accounts like other departmental services.

cash sheet　The *departmental control sheet* maintained by the front-office cashier.

casualty factor　The number of *reservations* of a *group* (cancellations plus *no-shows*) that fail to appear.

cathode ray tube (CRT)　A television screen that displays information put out by the computer; also called a VDT, *video display terminal*.

central processing unit (CPU)　The *hardware/software* nucleus of the computer that performs and monitors the essential functions.

central reservations office (CRO)　A private or chain-operated office that accepts and processes *reservations* on behalf of its membership.

central reservations system (CRS)　The sophisticated *hardware* and *software* used by a *central reservations office* to accurately track and manage *reservations* requests for member properties.

change　Moving a party from one guest room to another; any change in room, *rate*, or number of occupants.

chargeback　Credit-card charges refused by the credit-card company for one reason or another.

check in　All the procedures involved in receiving the guest and completing the *registration* sequence.

check out　All the procedures involved in the departure of the guest and the settlement of the *account*.

check-out hour　That time by which guests must vacate rooms or be charged an additional day.

city ledger　An *accounts receivable ledger* of nonregistered guests.

city-ledger journal　The form used to record transactions that affect the *city ledger*.

class　The quality of hotel, with *average daily rate* the usual criterion.

closeout hour　Also called *close of the day*.

close of the day　An arbitrary hour that management designates to separate the records of one day from those of the next.

closet bed　See *Murphy bed*.

colored transparency　A colored celluloid strip placed in the *room rack pocket* as a *flag* or indicator of room status.

commercial hotel　A *transient hotel* catering to a business clientele.

commerical rate　A reduced room *rate* given to businesspersons to promote occupancy.

commissionable　An indication that the hotel will pay *travel agents* the standard fee for business placed.

comp Short for "complimentary" accommodations—and occasionally food and beverage—furnished without charge.

company-made (reservation) A *reservation* guaranteed by the arriving guest's company.

concession A hotel tenant (concessionaire) whose facilities and services are indistinguishable from those owned and operated by the hotel.

concierge (1) A European position, increasingly found in U.S. hotels, responsible for handling guests' needs, particularly those relating to out-of-hotel services; (2) designation of the sleeping floor where these services are offered.

condominium A multiunit dwelling wherein each owner maintains separate title to the unit while sharing ownership rights and responsibilities for the public space.

conference center A property that caters to small business meetings, corporate retreats, and conferences. Generally considered smaller in size and more personable in nature than a convention property.

confirmed reservation The hotel's *acknowledgment*, usually in writing, to the guest's *reservation* request.

connecting rooms *Adjoining rooms* with direct, private access, making use of the corridor unnecessary.

continental breakfast A small meal including some combination of the following: bread, rolls, sweet rolls, juice, or coffee. Often set up in bulk by the innkeeper or host; continental breakfasts are usually self-service.

Continental plan A method of quoting room *rates* where the charge includes a *continental breakfast* as well as the room rate.

convention rate See *run-of-the-house rate.*

convertible bed See *sofa bed.*

corner (room) An *outside room* on a corner of the building having *two exposures.*

correction sheet A form once used with *NCR front-office machines* to record posting errors for later reconciliation by the *night auditor.*

cot See *rollaway bed.*

coupon (1) A checklike form issued by *travel agents* to their clients and used by the clients to settle their hotel accounts; (2) a ticket issued by tour groups for the purchase of meals and other services to be charged against the *master account.* Also called a *voucher.*

credit An accounting term that indicates a decrease in the *account receivable*; the opposite of *debit.*

cutoff date The date on which unsold rooms from within a convention's *block* of reserved rooms are released for sale.

cutoff hour That time at which the day's unclaimed *reservations* are released for sale to the general public.

daily rooms report See *room count sheet.*

day rate A reduced charge for occupancy of less than overnight; used when the *party* arrives and departs the same day. Also *part day rate* or *use rate.*

D card A form once used with the *NCR front-office posting machines* as the machine equivalent of the *transcript*; the term is still used for the daily revenue report prepared now by the *property management system.*

dead room change A physical change of rooms made by the hotel in the guest's absence so no tip is earned by the *last* bellperson.

debit An accounting term that indicates an increase in the *account receivable*; the opposite of *credit.*

deluxe A non-U.S. designation implying the best accommodations; unreliable unless part of an official rating system.

demi-pension (DP) A non-U.S. method of quoting room *rates* similar to the *modified American plan (MAP)* but allowing the guest to select either luncheon or dinner along with breakfast and room; also called *half pension.*

density board (chart) A noncomputerized *reservation* system where the number of rooms committed is controlled by type: *single, twin, queen*, etc.

departmental control sheet A form maintained by each *operating department* for recording data from departmental *vouchers* before forwarding them to the front desk for *posting.*

departure *Check out.*

deposit reservation See *advance deposit.*

destination hotel The objective of—and often the sole purpose for—the guest's trip; cf. *transient hotel.*

did not stay (DNS) Means the guest left almost immediately after *registering.*

difference returnable See *exchange.*

dine-around plan A method of quoting *AP* or *MAP* room rates that allows guests to dine at any of several independent but cooperating hotels.

display room See *sample room.*

D.I.T. Domestic independent tour or domestic inclusive tour; cf. *F.I.T.*

double (1) A bed approximately 54 by 75 inches; (2) the *rate* charged for two persons occupying one room; (3) a room with a double bed.

double–double See *twin–double.*

double occupancy (1) Room occupancy by two persons; (2) a ratio relating the number of rooms double occupied to the number of rooms sold.

double-occupancy rate A *rate* used for tours where the per person charge is based on two to a room.

double-up A designation of *double occupancy* by unrelated parties necessitating two *room rack* identifications or two *folios.*

downgrade Move a *reservation* or registered guest to a lesser accommodation or *class* of service; cf. *upgrade.*

downtime That time span during which the computer is inoperative because of malfunction or preemptive operations.

ducat See *stock card.*

due back See *exchange.*

due bank See *exchange.*

due bill See *trade advertising contract.*

dump To *check out* early; with reference to *groups.*

duplex A two-story *suite* with a connecting stairwell.

early arrival A guest who arrives a day or two earlier than the *reservation* calls for.

EBITDA   See *house profit.*

economy class   See *tourist class.*

efficiency   Accommodations that include kitchen facilities.

electronic data processing   A data handling system that relies on electronic (computer) equipment.

ell   A wing of a building usually at right angles to the main structure.

emergency key (E-key)   One key that opens all guest rooms, including those locked from within, even those with the room key still in the lock; also called the great *grandmaster.*

English breakfast   A hearty breakfast of fruit, cereal, meat, eggs, toast, and beverage generally served in the United Kingdom and Ireland, but less often of late.

en pension   See *full pension.*

European plan (EP)   A method of quoting room *rates* where the charge includes room accommodations only.

exchange   The excess of cash *turn-in* over *net receipts;* the difference is returnable (due back) to the front-office cashier; also called *due back, due bank,* or *difference returnable.*

executive floor   See *concierge* (floor).

executive room   See *studio.*

exposure   The direction (north, south, east, or west) or view (ocean, mountain) that the guest room faces.

express check out   Mechanical or electronic methods of *checkout* that expedite *departure* and eliminate the need to stop at the desk; also called *zip-out.*

extra meals   An *American plan* charge made for dining room service over and above that to which the guest is entitled.

family plan   A special room *rate* that allows children to occupy their parent's room at no additional charge.

family room   See *twin–double.*

fam trip   Familiarization trip taken by *travel agents* at little or no cost to acquaint themselves with *properties* and destinations.

farm out   Assignment of guests to other *properties* when a *full house* precludes their accommodation.

fenced rates   One of several tools used by the reservations department to maximize room revenues under *yield management* systems, including nonrefundable, prepaid *reservations* and *reservations* not subject to change.

first class   A non-U.S. designation for medium-priced accommodations with corresponding facilities and services.

F.I.T.   Foreign independent tour, but has come to mean free independent tour, a traveler who is not *group* affiliated; by extension, frequent independent traveler, or full inclusive tour.

flag   A device for calling the room clerk's attention to a particular room in the *room rack.*

flat rate   (1) See *run-of-the-house rate;* (2) same price for *single* or *double occupancy.*

float   The free use of outstanding funds during the period that checks and credit-card charges are in transition for payment.

floor key   See *master key.*

floor (release) limit   The maximum amount of charges permitted a credit-card user at a given *property* without clearance; the limit is established for the property, not for the user.

folio   See *guest bill;* a folio is also called an *account card.*

forecast   A future projection of estimated business volume.

forecast scheduling   Work schedules established on the basis of sales projections.

forfeited deposit   A *deposit reservation* kept by the hotel when a *no-show* fails to cancel the reservation; also called a lost deposit.

franchise   (1) An independently owned hotel or motel that appears to be part of a chain and pays a fee for that right and for the right to participate in the chain's advertising and reservation systems; (2) the chain's right (its franchise) to sell such permission; or the permission itself, or both.

franchisee   One who buys a *franchise.*

franchisor   One who sells a *franchise.*

free sale   Occurs when a *travel agent,* airline, or other agency commits hotel space without specific prior confirmation with the *property.* See also *sell and report.*

from bill number . . . to bill number   A cross-reference of *account* numbers when the bill of a guest who remains beyond one week is transferred to a new *folio.*

front   The next bellperson eligible for a *rooming* assignment or other errand apt to produce a *gratuity;* cf. *last.*

front office   A broad term that includes the physical front desk as well as the duties and functions involved in the sale and service of guest rooms.

front of the house   (1) The area of the hotel visible to guests in contrast to the back-of-the-house, which is not in the public view; (2) all of the functions that are part of the *front office.*

full day   The measure of a chargeable day for accounting purposes; three meals for an *AP* hotel, overnight for an *EP.*

full house   Means 100% *occupancy,* all guest rooms sold.

full pension   A European term for the *American plan.*

full service   Means a complete line of services and departments are provided, in contrast to a *limited-service* hotel or motel.

futon   A Japanese sleeping arrangement made of many layers of cotton-quilted batting that is rolled up when not in use.

garni   A non-U.S. designation for hotels without restaurant service except for *continental breakfast.*

general cashier   The chief cashier with whom deposits are made and from whom *banks* are drawn.

general manager (GM)   The hotel's chief executive.

global distribution system (GDS)   The *hardware, software,* and computer lines over which *travel agents,* airlines, on-line subscription networks, and others access *central reservations systems* and individual *property management systems.*

grande dame   French for an aristocratic lady; hence, an elegant, grand hotel.

grandmaster   One key that opens all guest rooms except those locked from within; see also *emergency key.*

gratuity   A tip given to an employee by a guest, sometimes willingly and sometimes automatically added to the charges; see also *plus, plus.*

graveyard   A work shift beginning about midnight.

greens fee   A charge for the use of the golf course.

group A number of persons with whom the hotel deals (reservation, billing, etc.) as if they were one party.

guaranteed rate The assurance of a fixed *rate* regardless of *occupancy*, often given in consideration of a large number of *room-nights* per year pledged by a company.

guaranteed reservation Payment for the room is promised even if the occupant fails to arrive.

guest account See *guest bill.*

guest bill An accounting statement used to record and display the charges and payments made by registered guests *(accounts receivable)* during their hotel stay. Different formats are used for hand-prepared bills and bills prepared by *property management systems;* also known as *folio* or *account card.*

guest check The bill presented to patrons of the dining rooms and bars and, when signed, often used as the departmental *voucher.*

guest day (night) The stay of one guest for one day (night); also called *room-night* or *bed-night.*

guest elevators Lobby elevators for guest use exclusively; employees are permitted only during guest service, as bellpersons *rooming (a guest);* cf. *service elevators.*

guest history A record of the guest's visits including rooms assigned, *rates* paid, special needs, credit rating and personal information; used to provide better guest service and better marketing approaches.

guest ledger All the *guest bills* owed by registered guests *(accounts receivable)* and maintained in the *front office,* in contrast to the group of *city-ledger* bills (nonregistered guests) maintained in the accounting or back office.

guest night See *guest day.*

guest occupancy See *bed occupancy.*

guest-service area See *front office.*

half-board See *modified American plan.*

half-pension See *demi-pension.*

handicap(ped) room A guest room furnished with devices and built large enough to accommodate guests with physical handicaps.

hard copy Computer term for material that has been printed rather than merely displayed.

hardware The physical equipment (electronic and mechanical) of a computer installation and its peripheral components; cf. *software.*

HFTP Hospitality Financial and Technology Professionals, an association specializing in hotel accounting, finance, and technology; formerly the IAHA, International Association of Hospitality Accountants.

hide-a-bed See *sofa bed.*

high season See *in-season rate.*

high tea A fairly substantial later afternoon or early evening meal.

HITIS An acronym for Hospitality Industry Technology Integration Standards, which are computer *interface* standards developed to facilitate the *interface* of computer systems from various vendors onto the hotel's *property management system.*

HOBIC An acronym for Hotel Outward Bound Information Center, the telephone company's long-distance hotel network.

holdover See *overstay.*

Hollywood bed *Twin* beds joined by a common headboard.

Hollywood length An extra-long bed of 80 to 85 inches instead of the usual 75 inches. Same as *California length.*

Hospitality Sales and Marketing Association International An international association of hotel sales and marketing managers.

hospitality suite (room) A facility used for entertaining, usually at conventions, trade shows, and similar meetings.

hostel An inexpensive but supervised facility with limited services catering to young travelers on foot or bicycle.

hotelier Innkeeper or hotelkeeper, originally from the French.

hotel manager Hotel executive responsible for the front of the house, including *front office,* housekeeping, and uniformed services; sometimes called rooms manager or house manager.

hotel rep See *rep(resentative).*

hot list A list of lost or stolen credit cards furnished to hotels and other retailers by the credit-card companies.

house A synonym for hotel, as in *house bank, house count, house laundry;* see also *property.*

house bank See *bank.*

house call Telephone call made to the outside of the hotel by a member of the staff doing company business; not subject to a *posting* charge as guest calls are.

house count The number of registered guests; cf. *room count.*

housekeeper's report A report on the status of guest rooms, prepared by the *linen room* and used by the front desk to verify the accuracy of the *room rack.*

house laundry A hotel-operated facility, usually on premises, in contrast to an *outside laundry* that contracts with the hotel to handle *house* and/or guest laundry.

house profit Net profit before income taxes from all *operating departments* except *store rentals* and before provision for rent, interest, taxes, depreciation, and amortization; renamed as "earnings before interest, taxes, depreciation, and amortization (EBITDA)" by the 1977 edition and subsequent editions of the *Uniform System of Accounts;* see also *bottom line.*

house rooms Guest rooms set aside for hotel use and excluded, therefore, from *available rooms.*

housing bureau A citywide reservation office, usually run by the convention bureau, for assigning *reservation* requests to participating hotels during a citywide convention.

Hubbart room rate formula A basis for determining room *rates* developed by Roy Hubbart and distributed by the *American Hotel & Motel Association.*

ideal average room rate This formula assumes a hotel sells an equal number of rooms from both the least expensive upward and from the most expensive downward. The resulting average rate is a theoretical benchmark against which to compare actual operating results.

imprest petty cash A technique for controlling petty cash disbursements by which a special, small cash fund is used for minor cash payments and periodically reimbursed.

incentive (group, guest, tour, or trip) Persons who have won a hotel stay (usually with transportation included) as a reward for meeting and excelling their sales quotas or other company-established standards.

inclusive terms (1) Phrase that is sometimes used in Europe to designate the *American plan*; (2) indicates that a price *quote* includes tax and gratuity.

independent A *property* with no chain or *franchise* affiliation, although one proprietor might own several such properties.

information rack An alphabetic listing of registered guests with a room number cross-reference.

in-house On the premises, such as an in-house laundry; cf. *off premises*.

in-season rate A *resort's* maximum rate, charged when the demand is heaviest, as it is during the middle of the summer or winter; cf. *off-season rate* or *low season*.

inside call A telephone call that enters the switchboard from inside the hotel; a telephone call that remains within the hotel; cf. *outside call*.

inside room A guest room that faces an inner courtyard or light court enclosed by three or four sides of the building.

inspector Supervisory position in the housekeeping department responsible for releasing *on change* rooms to ready status.

interface Computer term designating the ability of one computer to communicate with another; see *HITIS*.

International Association of Travel Agents (IATA) A professional affiliation which both lobbies on behalf of the travel industry and identifies/verifies legitimate *travel agents* to other vendors.

interstate call A long-distance call that crosses state lines.

intrastate call A long-distance telephone call that originates and terminates within the same state.

in-WATS See *wide area telephone service*.

IT number The code assigned to an inclusive tour for identification and *booking*.

joiner A guest who joins another guest or *party* already *registered*.

junior suite One large room, sometimes with a half partition, furnished as both a *parlor* and a bedroom.

king An extra-long, extra-wide *double* bed at least 78 by 82 inches.

lanai A Hawaiian term for "veranda"; a room with a porch or balcony usually overlooking gardens or water.

last The designation for the bellperson who most recently completed a *front*.

last-room availability A sophisticated reservations system that provides real-time access between the chain's *central reservations system* and the hotel's *in-house property management system*.

late arrival A guest with a *reservation* who expects to arrive after the *cutoff hour* and so notifies the hotel.

late charge A departmental charge that arrives at the front desk for billing after the guest has *checked out*.

late check out A departing guest who remains beyond the *check-out hour* with permission of the desk and thus without charge.

least cost router (LCR) Telephone equipment that routes the call over the least expensive lines available. Also called automatic route selector (ARS).

light baggage Insufficient luggage in quantity or quality on which to extend credit; the guest pays in advance.

limited service A hotel or motel that provides little or no services other than the room; a *budget hotel (motel)*; cf. *full service*.

linen closet A storage closet for linens and other housekeeping supplies usually located conveniently along the corridor for the use of the housekeeping staff.

linen room The housekeeper's office and the center of operations for that department, including the storage of linens and uniforms.

lockout (1) Denying the guest access to the room, usually because of an unpaid bill; (2) a key of that name.

log A record of activities maintained by several *operating departments*.

lost and found An area, usually under the housekeeper's jurisdiction, for the control and storage of lost-and-found items.

low season See *off-season rate*.

maid's report A status-of-rooms report prepared by individual room attendants and consolidated with other reports by the *linen room* into the *housekeeper's report*.

mail and key rack An antiquated piece of *front-office* equipment where both guest mail and room keys were stored by room number.

maitre d' The shortened form of maitre d'hotel, the headwaiter.

market mix The variety and percentage distribution of hotel guests—conventioneer, tourist, businessperson, and so on.

master account One *folio* prepared for a *group* (convention, company, tour) on which all group charges are accumulated.

master key One key controlling several *pass keys* and opening all the guests rooms on one floor; also called a *floor key*.

menu An array of function choices displayed to the computer user who selects the appropriate function.

message lamp A light on the telephone, used to notify an occupant that the telephone system has a message to relay.

minisuite See *junior suite*.

minor departments The less important *operating departments* (excluding room, food, and beverage) such as valet, laundry, and gift shop.

miscellaneous charge order (MCO) Airline *voucher* authorizing the sale of services to the guest named on the form, with payment due from the airline.

modified American plan (MAP) A method of quoting room *rates* in which the charge includes breakfast and dinner as well as the room.

mom-and-pop A small, family-owned business with limited capitalization in which the family, rather than paid employees, furnishes the bulk of the labor.

moment of truth A popular term describing the interaction between a guest and a member of the staff, when all of the advertising and representations made by the hotel come down to the quality of the service delivered at that moment.

morning call   A *wake-up call* made by the telephone operator or automatically by the *property management system* at the guest's request.

move-in date   The date that a group, convention, or trade show arrives to begin preparing for their meeting or exhibit; cf. *move-out date.*

move-out date   The date that a group, convention, or trade show vacates the *property* after a meeting or exhibit; cf. *move-in date.*

Ms   An abbreviation used to indicate a female guest without consideration for any marital status.

Murphy bed   A standard bed that folds or swings into a wall or cabinet in a closet-like fashion, trademarked.

NCR front-office posting machine   A mechanical device used to post folios and automatically accumulate *account receivable* and revenue balances; two popular models, the NCR (National Cash Register Company) 2000 and the NCR 42(00), neither of which are manufactured today, were replaced by electronic *property management systems.*

NCR paper   No carbon required; paper is specially treated to produce copies without carbon.

net rate   A room *rate quote* that indicates no additional commissions or fees are to be paid to *travel agents* or other third parties.

net receipts   The difference between cash taken in and *cash paid-outs.*

night audit   A daily reconciliation, which is completed during the *graveyard* shift, of both *accounts receivable* and incomes from the *operating departments.*

night auditor   The person or persons responsible for the *night audit.*

night auditor's report   An interim report of *accounts receivable,* room statistics, and incomes earned; prepared by the *night auditor* for the *general manager.*

night clerk's report   Another name for the *room count sheet.*

no reservation (NR)   See *walk-in.*

no-show   A *reservation* that fails to arrive.

occupancy (percentage of occupancy, occupancy percentage)   A ratio relating the number of rooms sold *(room count)* to the number of *rooms available* for sale.

occupied   (1) A room that is sold or taken and is not available for sale; (2) someone is physically in the room at this time.

ocean front   A front room with an *exposure* facing directly on the ocean; cf. *ocean view.*

ocean view   Other than a front room, but with some view of the ocean; cf. *ocean front.*

off line   See *batch processing.*

off premises   Not on the *property;* cf. *in-house.*

off-season rate   A reduced room *rate* charged by *resort hotels* when demand is lowest; cf. *in-season rate.*

off the shelf   Standardized, not customized, computer software.

off the street (OS)   See *walk-in.*

on change   The status of a room recently vacated but not yet available for new occupants.

one- (two-) pull dialing   One (two)-digit telephone dialing (or Touch-Tone) that connects the caller to hotel services such as room service and bellstand.

on-line (computer)   Computer facilities hooked directly to input and output devices for instantaneous communication; cf. *batch processing.*

operating departments   Those divisions of the hotel directly involved with the service of the guest, in contrast to support divisions such as personnel and accounting.

out of inventory (OOI)   A significant problem has removed this room from availability. Although *out of order (OOO)* rooms are usually available in only a matter of hours, OOI rooms may be unavailable for days or weeks.

out of order (OOO)   The room is not available for sale because of some planned or unexpected temporary shutdown of facilities.

outside call   A telephone call that enters the switchboard from outside the hotel; a call that terminates outside the hotel; cf. *inside call.*

outside laundry (valet)   A nonhotel laundry or valet service contracted by the hotel in order to offer a full line of services; cf. *house laundry.*

outside room   A room on the perimeter of the building facing outward with an *exposure* more desirable than that of an *inside* room.

out-WATS   See *wide area telephone service.*

over or short   A discrepancy between the cash on hand and the amount that should be on hand.

overbooking   Committing more rooms to possible guest occupancy than are actually available.

override   (1) Extra commission above standard percentage to encourage or reward quantity bookings; (2) process by which the operator bypasses certain limits built into the computer program.

overstay   A guest who remains beyond the expiration of the anticipated stay.

package   A number of services (transportation, room, food, entertainment) normally purchased separately but put together and marketed at a reduced price made possible by volume and *breakage.*

paid in advance   A room charge that is collected prior to occupancy, which is the usual procedure when a guest has *light baggage;* with some motels, it is standard procedure for every guest.

paid-outs   See *cash paid-outs.*

parlor   The living room portion of a *suite.*

part day rate (guest)   See *day rate.*

party   *Front-office* term that references either the individual guest ("Who's the party in room 100?") or several members of the group ("When will your party arrive?").

pass key   (1) A sub *master key* capable of opening all the locks within a limited, single set of 12 to 18 rooms, but no other; (2) guest key for access to public space (spa, pool).

PBX   See *private branch exchange.*

penthouse   Accommodations, most always *suites,* located on the top floor of the hotel, theoretically on the roof.

percentage of occupancy   See *occupancy.*

permanent guest   A resident of long-term duration whose stay may or may not be formalized with a lease.

petite suite   See *junior suite.*

petty cash   See *imprest petty cash.*

pickup   (1) The procedure used with *NCR front-office posting machines* to accumulate the *folio* balance by entering the previous balance into the machine before posting the new charges; (2) the figure so entered.

pit   See *cashier's well.*

plan   The basis on which room *rate* charges are made; see *American plan* and *European plan.*

plus, plus   Shorthand for the addition of tax and tip to the check or price per cover.

pocket   A portion of a manual *room rack* made to accept the *room rack slips* and provide a permanent record of accommodations and *rates.*

point-of-sale (POS) terminal   An electronic "cash register" providing *on-line* communications to the *property management system* from a remote sales location, in contrast to an input device at the *front office.*

porte–cochere   The covered entryway that provides shelter for those entering and leaving a hotel; French: coach gate [port-ko-shâr].

porterage   (1) Arrangements made to handle luggage; (2) the charge for luggage handling.

posting   The process of recording items in an accounting record, such as a *folio.*

preassign   *Reservations* are assigned to specific rooms that are *blocked* before the guests arrive; cf. *prereg(istration).*

prereg(istration)   Registration is done by the hotel before the guest arrives, although the actual *(reg)istration card* is not completed; used with groups and tours to reduce *front-office* congestion, since individual guests need not then approach the desk; cf. *preassign.*

private branch exchange (PBX)   A telephone switchboard.

projection   See *forecast scheduling.*

property   Another way to reference a hotel, includes physical facilities and personnel.

property management system (PMS)   A hotel's, that is a *property's,* basic computer installation designed for a variety of functions in both the back office and *front office.*

published rate   The full *rack rate* quoted or published for public information; the rate quoted without discounts.

quad   Accommodations for four persons; see also *twin–double.*

quality assurance   A managerial and operational approach that enlists employee support in delivering a consistently high level of service.

quality circle   A group of persons from different but related departments who meet on a regular basis for dialogue and problem resolutions as part of a *quality assurance* program.

quality management   See *total quality management* and *quality assurance.*

quality of the reservation   Differentiates *reservations* on how likely they are to be honored by the guest: *paid-in advance reservation* vs. *guaranteed reservation* vs. *6 PM cutoff hour,* etc.

queen   An extra-long, extra-wide *double* bed, about 80 to 85 inches long by 60 inches wide; see *California length;* see *king.*

queuing theory   The management of lines (queues of persons waiting their turn) in order to maximize the flow and minimize the inconvenience, but doing so with attention to operating costs. Also called *waiting-line theory.*

quote   To state the cost of an item, room *rates* in particular.

rack   See *room rack.*

rack rate   The full *rate,* without discounts, that one *quotes* as a room charge; so called because the *room rack* is the source of the information.

rate   The charge made by a hotel for its rooms.

rate cutting   A reduction in *rate* that attracts business away from competitors rather than creating new customers or new markets.

real estate investment trust (REIT)   A form of real estate ownership (public corporation) that became popular during the real estate recovery of the mid-1990s because of its income tax advantages.

rebate   See *allowance.*

recap   A summary or recap(itulation) of several *transcript* sheets in order to obtain the day's grand totals.

referral   A *central reservation system* operated by *independent* properties in contrast to that operated by chains and *franchisors* for their *affiliated hotels.*

registered, not assigned (RNA)   The guest has *registered,* but is awaiting assignment to a specific room until space becomes available; see *on change.*

register (ing), registration   (1) Indication (completing and signing the *registration card*) by a new arrival of intent to become a guest; (2) register: the name for a book that served at one time as the registration record.

(reg)istration card   A form completed during *registration* to provide the hotel with information about the guest, including name and address, and to provide the guest with information about the hotel, including legal issues.

REIT   See *real estate investment trust.*

reminder clock   A special alarm clock that can be set at 5-minute intervals across a 24-hour day; used by the *front office* chiefly for *wake-up calls.*

rep(resentative)   Short for *hotel representative:* An agent under contract, rather than an employee under salary, who represents the hotel in distant cities or for special activities, chiefly marketing activities, but sometimes gaming related.

reservation   A mutual agreement between the guest and the hotel, the former to take accommodations on a given date for a given period of time, and the latter to furnish the same.

reservation rack   A piece of *front-office* equipment, largely replaced by the *property management system,* providing an alphabetic list of anticipated arrivals with a summary of their needs, filed chronologically by anticipated date of arrival.

residential hotel   A hotel catering to long-stay guests who have made the *property* their home and residence; see also *permanent guest.*

resident manager   See *hotel manager.*

resort hotel A hotel that caters to vacationing guests by providing recreational and entertainment facilities; usually a *destination hotel*.

revpar Short for revenue per available room, a ratio of room revenue to the number of *available rooms*.

road warrior Slang for a frequent traveler battling the hardships and indignities of being on the road, that is, of traveling, for long periods of time.

rollaway bed A portable utility bed approximately 30 by 72 inches; also called a *cot*.

room charge sheet See *room count sheet*.

room count The number of occupied rooms; cf. *house count*.

room count sheet A permanent record of the *room rack* prepared nightly and used to verify the accuracy of room statistics; also called a *night clerk's report*.

rooming (a guest) The entire procedure during which the desk greets, *registers*, and assigns new arrivals, and the bell staff accompanies them to their rooms (rooms them).

rooming slip A form issued by the desk during the *rooming* procedure to the bellperson for guest identification, and left by the bellperson with the guest to give the guest an opportunity to verify name, *rate*, and room number.

room inspection report A checklist of the condition of the guest room prepared by the *inspector* when the room attendant has finished cleaning.

room-night See *guest day (night)*.

room rack A piece of *front-office* equipment, largely replaced by the *property management system*, in which each guest room is represented by a metal *pocket* with colors and symbols to aid the room clerk in identifying the accommodations.

room rack slip (card) A form prepared from the *registration card* identifying the occupant of each room and filed in the *pocket* of the *room rack* assigned to that guest.

rooms available See *available rooms*.

room service Food and beverage service provided in the privacy of the guest room by a designated (room service) waiter or waitress.

rooms ledger See *guest ledger*.

rule-of-thumb rate A guideline for setting room rates with the hotel charging $1 in rate for each $1,000 per room construction costs; see also *building cost rate formula*.

run-of-the-house rate A special *group* rate generally the midpoint of the *rack rate* with a single, flat price applying to any room, *suites* excepted, on a *best available* basis.

ryokan A traditional Japanese inn.

safe deposit boxes Individual sections of the vault where guests store valuables and cashiers keep house *banks*.

sales per occupied room See *average daily rate*.

sales rack A piece of *front-office* equipment, now replaced by the *property management system*, used for the storage and control of *stock cards* (*ducats* or *sales tickets*).

sales ticket See *stock card*.

salon The European designation for *parlor*.

sample room A guest room used to merchandise and display goods, usually in combination with sleeping accommodations.

seamless connectivity The next step beyond *last room availability*. *Travel agents*, airlines, on-line subscription networks, and others can access a *property*'s room availability right down to the last room.

season rate See *in-season rate*.

segmentation The proliferation of many hotel types as the lodging industry attempts to target its facilities to smaller and smaller market niches (segments).

sell and report *Wholesalers*, tour operators, *reps*, airlines, and *central reservation systems free sell* rooms, periodically reporting the sale to the hotel; also called status control.

sell through Denoting days for which no *reservation* arrivals are accepted; reservations for previous days will be accepted and allowed to stay through the date; cf. *box* date.

sell up Convince the arriving guest to take a higher priced room than was planned or reserved.

service charge A percentage (usually from 10 to 20%) added to the bill for distribution to service employees in lieu of direct tipping; see also *plus, plus*.

service elevators Back elevators for use by employees (room service, housekeeping, maintenance, etc.) on hotel business and not readily visible to the guests; cf. *guest elevator*.

share More than one person occupying the guest room.

shoulder Marketing term designating the period between peaks and valleys; the time on either side of the *in-season rate* or the leveling off between two peaks.

Siberia Jargon for a very undesirable room, one sold only after the *house* fills and then only after the guest has been alerted to its location or condition.

single (1) A bed approximately 36 by 75 inches; (2) a room with accommodations for one; (3) occupancy by one person; (4) the *rate* charged for one person.

single supplement An extra charge over the tour *package* price assessed for *single* occupancy when the total price was based on a *double-occupancy rate*.

sitting room See *parlor*.

size The capacity of the hotel as measured by the number of guest rooms.

skip See *skipper*.

skipper A guest who departs surreptitiously, leaving an unpaid bill.

sleeper A departed guest whose record remains active giving the appearance of an *occupied* room.

sleeper occupancy See *bed occupancy*.

sleep out A room that is taken, *occupied*, and paid for but not slept in.

slide The transcription error caused by a misplaced decimal, as when 36.20 is written 3.62.

smart card A credit card or other card containing a microprocessor capable of interfacing with the *PMS* or other computer configurations.

sofa bed A sofa with fixed back and arms that unfolds into a standard *single* or *double bed*; also called a *hide-a-bed*.

software The programs and routines that give instructions to the computer; cf. *hardware*.

special attention (SPATT)   A label assigned to important guests designated for special treatment; see *very important person.*

split rate   Division of the total room *rate* charge among the room's several occupants; see *share.*

split shift   A work pattern divided into two working periods with an unusually long period (more than a rest or mealtime) between.

spread rate   Assignment of *group* members or conventioneers using the standard *rate* distribution, although prices might be less than *rack rates;* cf. *run-of-the-house rate.*

star rating   An unreliable ranking (except for some well-known exceptions) of hotel facilities both in the United States and abroad.

star reservation   Indicates the arrival of a *very important person.*

stay   See *stayover.*

stayover   (1) Any guest who remains overnight; (2) an anticipated check out who fails to depart; also called *holdover* or *overstay.*

stock card   Once used with a *sales rack* to represent the content of the *room rack pocket* when the room rack was distant and therefore inaccessible to the room clerk; also called a *ducat.*

store rentals   Income earned from shop leases; cf. *concession.*

studio   (1) A bed approximately 36 inches wide by 75 inches long without headboard or footboard that serves as a sofa during the day; (2) the room containing such a bed; cf. *sofa bed.*

suite   A series of *connecting rooms* with one or more bedrooms and a *parlor;* very large suites occasionally include additional rooms such as dining rooms; see *hospitality suite.*

summary transcript sheet   See *recap.*

supper   (1) A late-night meal; (2) the evening meal when midday service is designated as dinner.

swing   The work shift between the day *watch* and the *graveyard* shift; usually starts between 3 and 4 PM.

take down   Cancel *reservations* without an *advance deposit* after the *cutoff hour.*

tally sheet   See *density board.*

TelAutograph   A proprietary piece of communication equipment that transcribes written messages.

timeshare   (1) A method of acquiring vacation accommodations by which each occupant purchases the right to use the facility (room or apartment) for a specified period; partial ownership of the real estate, which was not possible initially, has broadened the market; (2) term for users who share computer facilities.

time stamp   A clock mechanism that prints date and time when activated.

to-date   Designates a cumulative amount; the sum of all figures in the current period (usually monthly or annually) including the day or date in question.

total quality management (TQM)   A way to continuously improve performance at every level of operation, in every functional area of an organization, using all available human and capital resources. See also *quality assurance.*

tour group   See *package.*

tourist class   A non-U.S. designation for *limited-service* hotels whose accommodations frequently lack private baths; also called *economy class.*

trade advertising contract   An agreement by which hotel accommodations are swapped for advertising space or broadcast time; also called a *due bill.*

traffic sheet   A *departmental control sheet* used by the telephone department before *call accounting systems.*

transcript   A form used by the *night auditor* to accumulate and separate the day's charges by departments and guests.

transcript ruler   The headings of a transcript sheet attached to a straightedge and used as a column guide at the bottom of the long *transcript* sheet.

transfer   (1) An accounting technique used to move a figure from one form to another, usually between *folios;* (2) the movement of guests and/or luggage from one point to another (e.g., from the airline terminal to the hotel); see *porterage.*

transfer folio   A special unnumbered *folio* used to carry non-computerized guest accounts beyond the first week when the original folio was numbered and cross referenced to the *registration card.*

transfer from   The *debit* portion of a *transfer* between accounts or ledgers.

transfer journal   A *front-office* form used to record *transfer* entries between different accounts or different ledgers.

transfer to   The *credit* portion of a *transfer* between accounts or ledgers.

transient guest   A short-term guest; see *transient hotel.*

transient hotel   A hotel catering to short-stay guests who sometimes stop en route to other destinations; cf. *destination hotel.*

transient ledger   See *guest ledger.*

transmittal form   The form provided by national credit-card companies for recording and remitting nonelectronic credit-card charges accumulated by the hotel.

transposition   A transcription error caused by reordering the sequence of digits, as when 389 is written as 398.

travel agent (TA)   An entrepreneur who *books* space and facilities for clients in hotels and public carriers and receives a commission for placing the business; hotels usually pay 10 percent.

travel and entertainment card (T&E)   A credit card issued by a proprietary company other than a retailer for which the user pays an annual fee; cf. *bank card.*

Travel Industry Association of America (TIA)   A nonprofit association of many travel-related agencies and private businesses working to develop travel and tourism in the United States.

tray service   The fee charged *American plan* guests for *room service.*

tub   See *cashier's well.*

turn-away   (1) To refuse *walk-in* business because rooms are unavailable; (2) the guest so refused.

turn-downs   An evening service rendered by the housekeeping department, which replaces soiled bathroom linen and prepares the bed for use.

turn-in   The sum deposited with the *general cashier* by the departmental cashier at the close of each shift.

turnkey   A facility (computer, *franchise,* entire hotel) so complete that it is ready for use at the turn of a key.

twin   (1) A bed approximately 39 inches wide by 75 inches long to sleep a single occupant; (2) a room with two such beds, *twins.*

twin–double (1) Two double beds; (2) a room with two such beds capable of accommodating 4 persons; see *quad.*

twins Two *twin* beds.

type The kind of market toward which the hotel is directed, traditionally: *commercial, residential,* and *resort.*

understay A guest who leaves before the expiration of the anticipated stay.

Uniform System of Accounts for the Lodging Industry A manual and dictionary of accounting terms, primarily incomes and expenses, to ensure industry-wide uniformity in terminology and use.

United States Travel and Tourism Administration (USTTA) A division of the Department of Commerce responsible for promoting travel to the United States; successor to the U.S. Travel Service (USTS).

unoccupied (1) An unsold room; (2) a room that is *occupied,* but is temporarily vacant, the guest is out.

u-owe-me See *exchange.*

upgrade Move a *reservation* or a currently registered guest to a better accommodation or class of service; cf. *downgrade.*

use rate See *day rate.*

user-friendly Computer design, application, or implementation that minimizes the user's fears, encouraging purchase and use of the equipment.

vacancy The hotel is not fully *occupied,* so there are rooms available for sale.

very important person (VIP) A reservation or guest who warrants *special attention* and handling.

video display terminal (VDT) See *cathode ray tube.*

voucher (1) The form used by the *operating departments* to notify the front desk of charges incurred by a particular guest; (2) form furnished by a *travel agent* as a receipt for a client's advance *reservation* payment; see *coupon.*

waiting-line theory See *queuing theory.*

wake-up call See *morning call.*

walk (a guest) To turn away guests holding confirmed *reservations* due to a lack of available rooms.

walk-in A guest without a *reservation* who requests and receives accommodations.

walk-through A thorough examination of the *property* by a hotel executive, *franchise* inspector, prospective buyer, etc.

watch Another term for the work shift.

WATS See *wide area telephone service.*

who An unidentified guest in a room that appears vacant in the *room rack.*

wholesaler An entrepreneur who conceives, finances, and services *group* and *package* tours that he or she promotes (often through *travel agents*) to the general public.

wide area telephone service (WATS) Long-distance telephone lines provided at special rates—even wholesaled—to large users; separate charges are levied for incoming and outgoing WATS lines.

worldwide travel vouchers (WTVs) Form of payments drawn against a well-known financial institution (usually a major credit-card company).

xenodogheionology The study of the history, lore, and stories associated with inns, hotels, and motels (zeno-dog-hi-on-ology).

yield The product of *occupancy* times *average daily rate.*

yield management (1) Controlling room *rates* and restricting occupancy in order to maximize gross revenue *(yield)* from all sources; (2) a computerized program using artificial intelligence.

youth hostel See *hostel.*

zero out To balance the *guest bill* as the guest *checks out* and makes settlement.

zip-out See *express check out.*

Index

• • •

B

C

D

E

530 Index

Index

Y

Z